Frank Graham Finlayson

Street Work Laws of the State of California

Frank Graham Finlayson

Street Work Laws of the State of California

ISBN/EAN: 9783337187538

Printed in Europe, USA, Canada, Australia, Japan

Cover: Foto ©ninafisch / pixelio.de

More available books at **www.hansebooks.com**

STREET WORK LAWS

OF THE

STATE OF CALIFORNIA

ANNOTATED

By FRANK G. FINLAYSON, LL B.

Of the Los Angeles Bar

Published by

CHAS. W. PALM CO.

Los Angeles, Cal.

1893.

6 / 3 / 0

PREFACE.

The street laws peculiar to the state of California are those statutory enactments which provide for improvements upon existing streets—streets opened or dedicated to public use; also, those enactments which provide for the opening, widening, extending or closing up of streets, in whole or in part. To many these street laws are *terra incognita*. They, are *sui generis*, covering a special territory by themselves quite outside of the common and ordinary domain of the general and usual practice. Heretofore these laws have constituted a branch of the practice so specialized that it has been explored by but few members of the profession; nevertheless, it is one of the most important branches in the whole wide range of jurisprudence. Municipal corporations are little more than public improvement corporations on a large scale; and, as the present tendency seems to be in the direction of a still further centralization of power in the municipalities of the country, with the investiture of still greater powers over public improvement in the municipal authorities, confiding to their care the conduct of many enterprises which have heretofore usually been in the hands of private individuals, it follows that any branch of the law which deals with the exercise of these powers is of great and growing importance, both to the profession and the laity. Cities and towns are rapidly springing up in this empire commonwealth, and streets are as rapidly being opened up and improved. Hence the necessity for some book which shall facilitate the researches of those whose business it is to study these street laws and assist in their administration. With this end in view the author has prepared this book for publication, and will feel himself amply repaid for his labors if he has succeeded in bringing together between the covers of one book such material upon the subject of the street laws of this state as will serve to simplify the subject and render a comprehensive knowledge thereof easy of attainment.

One reason why the realm covered by this special department has hitherto remained unfamiliar to many, is that the statutes themselves upon the subject of street work, and the many amendatory acts, have been scattered through numer-

ous volumes of our statute books. Prior to the adoption of
the new constitution, these statutory provisions consisted of
a heterogeneous mass scattered through the charters of the
various municipalities of the state, and found in special and
local laws. Therefore any general systemization of the subject of street laws under the old constitution was practically
impossible, since each city had a special and separate system of its own. Under the new constitution, however, general laws upon the subject have been passed, operative
throughout the length and breadth of the state, and superseding all special laws in conflict therewith. It is therefore
possible now to reduce these general laws to some system,
and present them as they exist at the present time, i. e., as
amended up to date. The mere presentation, therefore, of
the naked statutes in force to-day, will serve to remove
much doubt that would otherwise harass the mind of the
busy practitioner, who, after exploring the statute books for
hours or even days, might still doubt whether he had found
all the statutory enactments upon the subject, or whether
some amendment had escaped his search or not. The
author has therefore set forth in full all the general street
laws of the state now in force in every municipality, as the
same have been amended up to date, and has also referred
to each and every amendment which has been made to
each section of the acts from the time of the original enactment. Thus, any person seeking to know what the statute
provisions are at present, will find them set forth in full.
Should he desire to know what the statute provisions have
been at any time intermediate, between the time of the
original enactment and the present date, he has but to turn
to the book and page of the statutes containing the original
enactment, or any subsequent and intermediate amendatory act.

Another, and perhaps still less surmountable obstacle
lying in the path leading to a comprehensive knowledge of
these street laws is the fact that, even when the practitioner
has unearthed from the statute books all the enactments in
force upon the subject of street work or street improvement, and has carefully studied their provisions, he must
still, in the absence of an authoritative construction by the
Supreme Court, remain in doubt as to the correct interpretation of many of the provisions; or he may even entertain a
fixed, but mistaken, opinion as to the true meaning or scope
of a provision, without being aware of his mistake. A careful study of the decisions which have been rendered by our
Supreme Court in cases calling for a construction of these,
and of similar prior street work laws, will undoubtedly do

PREFACE V

much to illumine the doubtful provisions of these enactments, and dissipate the mists that obscure their true
meaning.

Therefore, by publishing in book form the statutes now
in force, relative to street work, and annotating the sections
with notes and excerpts from the decisions of our Supreme
Court construing these or similar provisions, the reader,
in a comparatively short time, may so far master this
whole subject as to equip himself with a comprehensive
knowledge of these laws.

The aim and object of this book is, therefore, to present
together in one book all the general statutory enactments
upon the subject of street work, together with such annotations and citations from the decisions of our Supreme
Court as will serve to interpret the true meaning of these
statutes, and in doing so the author has endeavored
to cite every case upon this subject that has ever been
decided by the Supreme Court of this state.

It is not the purpose of this book to consider *general principles*, either of street law in general or of street
assessments. These general principles may readily
be found in works upon streets, roads and highways, and
in works upon assessments and taxation. The sole aim of
the author is to present to the profession, and to those
interested therein, the street law of California as the same
is found in the general statutory enactments of this state
upon the subject of street work and street improvement,
and to exemplify the meaning of these statutory provisions
by cases cited from the decisions of our own courts. The
questions arising out of these statutes are principally questions of interpretation and construction, and it would be
idle, therefore, to cite the decisions of the courts of other
states whose statutory provisions are unlike our own.
Nevertheless, wherever the author has thought there might
be any question as to the constitutionality of any of these
statutes or of any of the provisions thereof, that has not
been directly settled by the decisions of our own Supreme
Court, he has stated the questions that have thus
suggested themselves to his mind, and has in this connection, cited some few decisions by the highest courts of
other states. However, as the questions which these statutes give rise to are, in the main, questions of interpretation or construction, it is impossible to foresee, how many
of the questions arising out of these street laws, will ultimately be settled by the Supreme Court. Nevertheless, the
author has everywhere endeavored to reach a correct interpretation, and to extract from the cases a statement of gen-

eral doctrines which shall aid in the solution of future questions, and has not hesitated to express his own views and opinions, but such speculations and arguments are always plainly indicated and represented in their real character, so that the reader need never confound them with the results of actual judicial decision, and be thus led to accept as settled law what is only a personal conviction or suggestion of the author.

Los Angeles, Cal., December 1, 1893.

FRANK G. FINLAYSON.

TABLE OF CONTENTS.

INTRODUCTION XXI.

x STREET WORK LAW—CONTENTS

PLANT AND SHADE TREE ACT. 236-240

STREET OPENING ACT OF MARCH 6, 1889. 241-271.

STREET OPENING ACT OF MARCH 23, 1893.
272–294.

SANITARY DISTRICT ACT. 295–307

Municipal Indebtedness Act.   308–312

TABLE OF CASES CITED.

INTRODUCTION.

CLASSIFICATION OF THE STREET LAWS.

The object of this book is to bring together in one volume all the statutes of this state now in force bearing upon the subject of street work, and, by a system of annotations, taken from the decisions of our Supreme Court upon these and prior acts, illustrate, in so far as possible, the workings of the acts and the questions which their operation has given rise to from time to time.

The term "street work" is a phrase of common usage and has a well-defined signification. The words mean exactly what they indicate upon their face, namely, work upon a street—work in repairing or improving an existing street, or in making a street. [Electric Light and Power Co. *v*. City of San Bernardino, No. 19,282, decided Nov. 25, 1893.]

The street laws of this state naturally divide themselves into what may be called the "street improvement acts" and the "street opening or street widening acts." The street opening acts do not make any provision for nor authorize any improvement upon streets. They merely authorize the creation or partial creation of or the widening or closing of streets. The street improvement acts make provision for *improvements* upon *existing* streets. In fact, this is their sole aim and object. The street opening and closing acts provide for the closing of streets or for the taking of property to open, widen or extend streets, and the assessment of the costs and expenses thereof upon the property benefited thereby. Beyond the acquisition of the right of way for the street, or perhaps its fee in the land, if the council deem that necessary, and clearing the surface of such obstructions as exist on the surface of the earth and interfere with the " opening," " extending," or " widening" of the street, they do not provide for any artificial improvement upon the street, such as grading or paving. The term " opening " does not include the improving of a street by grading, paving, etc. It refers to throwing open to the public what before was appropriated to private use. Such street improve-

ments as grading, paving, sewering, etc., are provided
for by the street improvement acts. Hitherto it has been
the policy of the legislature to provide for improvements
upon existing streets by acts entirely distinct from the acts
providing for opening, extending, widening and closing
streets.

The "street improvement acts" include those acts which
provide for improvements upon existing streets—streets
opened or dedicated to public use, and include specifically:
(1.) The Vrooman Act of March 18, 1885—" An act to provide for work upon streets, lanes, alleys, courts, places and
sidewalks, and for the construction of sewers within municipalities"—together with various amendments thereto. Said
amendments include the amendments whereby sections 38
to 53, inclusive, were added to the act. These added sections contain provisions for changing the grade of streets in
all cases where the official grade has once been established.
(2.) The Bond Act of February 27, 1893—an act to provide
a system of street improvement bonds. This act is in the
nature of a supplementary act to the Vrooman act of March
18, 1885, and is appropriately classified as a "street improvement act." (3.) The Tree Planting or Shade Tree Act of
March 11, 1893—an act to provide for the planting, maintenance and care of shade trees upon streets, etc. This act may
also be classified with the "street improvement acts." (4.)
The Sanitary District Act of March 31, 1891—an act to provide for the formation, government, operation and dissolution of sanitary districts in any part of the state; for the
construction of sewers, etc. The foregoing acts, four in
number, constitute the existing distinctively "street improvement acts" of this state.

The second class of acts—the "street opening" or "street
widening" acts—includes the street opening and widening
act of March 6, 1889, and the act of March 23, 1893.

Lastly, the Municipal Indebtedness Act of March 19,
1889—an act authorizing the incurring of indebtedness by
cities, towns, etc. This act, since it affords means for paying the expenses of the work, either of improving streets
already opened or dedicated, or of opening or widening
streets, may be said to be common to both of the above clas-
sifications. It, in effect, supplements the provisions of each
of the foregoing acts.

The street improvement and street opening acts, with
annotations consisting of such decisions by the Supreme
Court of this state as relate to the provisions of these acts,

or to similar provisions of former street work acts, constitute the subject matter of this book.

No adequate knowledge of the provisions of the street work acts now in force throughout the state can be had without a study of the decisions construing similar provisions of prior acts. And for this reason some knowledge of these prior acts and of their history is necessary. The history of the street work acts of this state naturally divides itself into two periods. First, there are those acts which existed prior to the adoption of the new constitution—the constitution of 1879, which went into effect on the 1st day of January, 1880. And, secondly, there are those acts which have existed since the adoption of the new constitution. Prior to the new constitution special and local legislation was permissible and constitutional. Consequently, under the old constitution the great body of statutes relating to street improvements was to be found in the charters of the several municipalities of the state and in the acts amendatory thereof. Each municipality performed its street work, not under some general statute operating uniformly all over the state, in every municipality of the state, but under those provisions of its own charter which related to street work, or under statutes amendatory thereof, or under special and local statutes applicable only to that particular municipality. But the new constitution prohibits the passage of any special or local legislation authorizing the laying out, opening, altering, maintaining, or vacating highways, streets or alleys, or in fact, any special or local legislation whatever, where a general law can be made applicable. [Const. Art. IV section 25.] And it has been held, under the new constitution, that street work laws, such, for example, as the Vrooman act of March 18, 1885—which apply to all the municipalities of the state—are "general laws" within the meaning of that term as used in section 6 of article XI of the constitution; that such general street work laws control the provisions of municipal charters granted by the legislature prior to the adoption of the new constitution—the charter of the city and county of San Francisco, for example—and that in such municipalities public improvements upon streets and highways must be performed under such general street laws, and not under the charters of such municipalities or special laws amendatory thereof. [Thomason v. Ashworth, 73 Cal. 73; People v. Henshaw, 76 Cal. 436; Ex parte Ah You, 82 Cal. 339.] And, it has likewise been held that such general laws control and supersede the provisions of charters framed or adopted since the new constitution went into effect—"freeholders charters." [Davies v. City of Los Angeles, 86 Cal. 37.] In Thomason v. Ashworth, 73 Cal. 78, Mr. Justice Thornton said: "It is argued that, according to the views herein expressed, a city may have its charter totally changed without its consent. This is a proper deduction from the ruling herein, but this cannot be done by a special or local law applicable only to a particular charter. The result can only be reached by a general law affecting all municipal corporations, or it may be all of a class, and we can see no probability that a city can be injured by general legislation."

Whatever may be said about the destruction of local self-government and of municipal autonomy in purely municipal affairs, which these decisions may be supposed to lead to, at least one advantage of considerable importance is derivable from these rulings, viz: Where each city operated under special charter provisions or special or local laws authorizing work to be done upon the streets of such city, a decision construing a provision in the charter of any particular city, or construing a provision in some special or local law, was of little use as a precedent in cases arising under the charters of other cities, and hence, because of the heterogeneity of the street laws of the state, there could be but little certainty, no matter how numerous the decisions might be. Whereas, under the ruling that the provisions of a general street work law —such as the Vrooman act of March 18, 1885, or the street opening act of March 6, 1889—are applicable to municipalities all over the state, every decision construing any particular provision of the law tends to clear away all uncertainties, and is as helpful in determining the nature and extent of the powers and duties of the municipal authorities of any city of the state, as it is helpful in determining such powers in the particular municipality in which the case arose. It is a guide to future action in every municipality of the state; and, as certainty in a bad law is often more desirable than a good law without certainty, it follows that advantages which may flow from holding these general street work laws to control and supersede all inconsistent charter provisions, by reason of the greater certainty in the law which may be attained thereby, may outweigh all those advantages which might possibly accrue to each municipality if its own charter provisions controlled in the matter.

History of Street Improvement Acts in San Francisco Prior to the New Constitution. As stated *supra*, no adequate knowledge of the present general street improvement act—

the Vrooman act of March 18, 1885—is attainable without
some knowledge of the history of prior street improvement
acts. But as these prior street improvement acts consisted
of a mass of charter provisions or of special and local statutory enactments, it is neither convenient nor necessary to
set them forth here, but the history of the statutory provisions made specially applicable to the city and county of
San Francisco will suffice as an illustration of all the others.
And, as the principal distinguishing characteristic, which
distinguished the successive San Francisco street work
acts, related to the principle of assessment—i. e., the principle according to which the costs and expenses of the work
were apportioned among the property owners—only the
date of each act will be given and the principle of assessment by which it was characterized. Thus the various
acts of the legislature appertaining to and regulating street
work in the city and county of San Francisco, including
the charters of that municipality, may be used to illustrate
the history or growth of the street law in all of our municipalities prior to the new constitution, though many of the
charters of the other cities, and the various special and
local acts of the legislature applicable to them, may exhibit
many features or characteristics differing widely from the
charters of San Francisco and from the special laws applicable to public improvements in this particular municipality. But, if it be remembered that all of the charters of
the several municipalities of the state, together with the
special acts of the legislature amendatory thereof, or acts
which in any manner provided for work upon the streets,
sewers, etc., in the several cities, passed through many
similar stages in the progress of their evolution from the
establishment of the municipal governments in these cities
up to the present date, it will be obvious that, for the purpose of illustrating this growth of the street laws of this
state prior to the adoption of the new constitution, it will
be sufficient to briefly sketch the history of the charters of
the city of San Francisco, and the special acts amendatory
thereof, prior to the adoption of our present constitution.
In this way the history of the street laws applicable to one
city may be made to serve as a sufficient illustration of the
growth of similar laws in all the cities of the state, notwithstanding the fact that the charters of the different
cities and these special amendatory acts differed materially.

The history of the street improvement acts applicable to
the city of San Francisco, prior to the new constitution, is
as follows:

April 15th, 1850, the first legislature of the state of

California passed an act entitled "An act to incorporate
the city of San Francisco." This was the first charter of
the city of San Francisco and by it the municipality known
as the "city of San Francisco" was established and incorporated. [Statutes of 1850, page 223].

Under this first charter of San Francisco, one-third of the
expense of doing the work was paid out of the city treasury,
and two-thirds "paid in equal proportions by the land on both
sides of the street," etc., but the principle of apportionment,—whether according to the value of the property
fronting the street, or the benefits accruing to such property,
or according to the number of front feet,—was not indicated by this charter.

April 15, 1851, the legislature passed an act entitled
"An act to re-incorporate the city of San Francisco."
This is known as the charter of 1851. By this charter the
expenses were apportioned according to the *benefits* received
or "advantages respectively derived from such improvement"—at least two-thirds of the expenses to be borne by
and assessed upon the adjacent property. [See statutes of
1851, page 365.]

By the charter of 1855,—created or granted by an act
approved May 5, 1855, entitled "An act to re-incorporate
the city of San Francisco,"—it was provided that the "cost
and expenses of all such works shall be assessed upon the
property particularly benefited thereby, in proportion to
the benefit received from such work by said property,
exclusive of the general benefit shared by said property, in
common with the rest of the city." [See statutes of 1855,
page 264.]

The act known as the "consolidation act" was approved
April 19, 1856. It is entitled "an act to repeal the several
charters of the city of San Francisco, to establish the
boundaries of the city and county of San Francisco, and to
consolidate the government thereof." By this act the corporation known and existing as the city of San Francisco
was expressly continued as a body politic under the name
of the "city and county of San Francisco," and all the
property and effects of both the city of San Francisco and
the county of San Francisco were transferred to the corporation known as the "city and county of San Francisco,"
which municipality, was, by the "consolidation act," formed
by the union or consolidation of both the city and county.
[Wood *v.* Election Commissioners, 58 Cal. 561.] Article IV
of this consolidation act contains the provisions of the
charter of the municipal corporation known as the "city
and county of San Francisco," which apply to street work.

[Statutes of 1856, pages 156-162.] This charter adopted the "front-foot" principle of apportionment, and provided that "the total amount of the expense * * * * shall be assessed upon and borne with absolute equality by all the lands fronting thereon and in proportion to the frontage, at a rate per front foot sufficient to cover such total expense of the work."

In 1859 the legislature passed an act amendatory of the consolidation act. By this amendment the mode of apportionment of expense was changed from the front-foot principle to the *ad valorem* principle. This amendatory act provided that the expenses "shall be assessed upon * * * the adjacent lots and land on each side of the street. Each lot or portion of a lot, being assessed in proportion to the assessed *value* of the same according to the assessment roll last completed."

In 1861 an act was passed by the legislature amendatory of the "consolidation act" and also of the amendatory act of 1859. By this act of 1861, the legislature returned to the front-foot mode of apportionment of expense,—this mode having been found to be the most just and equitable and satisfactory in its operations. It is the same mode that is now in force under the existing general street improvement act,—the Vrooman act of March 18, 1885. [See *infra* page 1 *et seq.*] This amendatory act of 1861, provided that the expense shall be assessed upon each lot fronting on the street "according to its proportion of frontage."

An amendatory act of 1862 amended article IV of the "consolidation act," relating to street work. This act, while making many changes in the mode of procedure, and elaborating the provisions relating to the various steps to be taken by the city to acquire jurisdiction to do the work, etc., did not change the mode of apportionment,—it continued the front-foot principle of assessment.

Mr. Justice Sawyer, in the case of Emery *v.* S. F. Gas Co., 28 Cal. 373-4, speaking of the different principles of apportionment, said, in the course of his opinion, and in respect to these charters of San Francisco, and acts amendatory thereof: "Possibly it might tend to promote equality and justice to leave to the local communities, which have the supervision of this class of improvements, the discretion to adopt that principle of apportionment which the exigencies of each particular district designated for improvement may require. In this state, particularly with reference to the city of San Francisco, nearly, if not quite all the various modes of apportionment have been tried, and among them the *ad valorem* principle was for several years pursued. Each was in turn attacked as unjust, and abandoned. Under the first charter of San Francisco, (act of 1850) one-third of the expense was paid out of the city treasury, and two-thirds 'paid in equal proportions by the land on both sides of the street,' etc., but the principle of apportionment is not indicated. Under the charters of 1851 and 1855 the apportionment was according to benefits. The great reform charter,—the consolidation act of 1856—adopted the front-foot principle, and this continued in force till 1859, when it was amended, and an *ad valorem* apportionment adopted. After trying this system two years, and after having given each principle a fair trial, in 1861 the legislature again returned to the front-foot principle, which had been in force from 1856 to 1859 the only instance of a return to a principle once tried and abandoned. And finally in 1862, —after twelve years experience—the present principle of assessing upon the front-foot was continued."

By the amendatory acts of 1866 [statutes of 1865-6, page 549], 1868 [statutes of 1867-8, page 358] and 1870, [statutes of 1869-70, page 890], article four of the "consolidation act" and the intermediate amendatory acts were amended in various particulars. These amendments made many changes in the mode of procedure, but the principle of assessment remained unchanged, that is, the expenses were apportioned and assessed according to the front-foot principle.

In 1872, by an act approved April 1, 1872, [statutes of 1871-2, page 804] the legislature passed an act repealing article four of the "consolidation act," and all acts amendatory thereof, and "substituting this act [act of 1872] for said article four." This act of 1872 amplified many of the provisions contained in the original article four of the consolidation act and in the acts amendatory thereof, but continued in force the front-foot principle of assessment.

The general street improvement act now in force—the Vrooman act of March 18, 1885,—is so similar to the said act of April 1, 1872, amending the charter of the city and county of San Francisco, that it seems but reasonable to conclude that this act of April 1, 1872, furnished the model upon which the said general act now in force was patterned.

In addition to these charters of the city of San Francisco, and the acts above mentioned which are amendatory of said charters, there were many special acts passed, prior to the present constitution, which related to or provided for work upon certain particular streets or localities of the city. Thus, for example, the legislature of 1875-6 passed an act

entitled "An act to provide for the opening and extending
of Leidesdorff street, in the city and county of San Francisco." [Statutes of 1875–6, page 563.] Similar special
acts were passed by almost, if not every legislature, prior to
the new constitution, relative to particular streets and localities in other cities of the state. The charters of each city
and the acts amendatory thereof were general in their operation within the boundaries of each particular city, but
these last mentioned special acts applied specially to some
particular street or locality within the city.

*History of the Street Improvement Acts passed since the
Adoption of the New Constitution.* Under the old constitution it was permissible to pass special and local laws, such
as those described *supra*, relative to street work in the city
and county of San Francisco. Such special and local laws
might consist of acts providing charters for municipalities
of the state, or acts amendatory of such charters, or might
consist of acts making provision for the opening of, or
improvement upon, some particular street of some city.
But, under the new constitution—the constitution of 1879—
the provisions of which are expressly declared to be man
datory and prohibitory [section 22, article I], the legislature may not pass local or special laws authorizing the laying out, opening, altering, maintaining or vacating highways, streets, or alleys, or in any case where a general law
can be made applicable [section 25, article IV], and all laws
of a general nature must have a uniform operation. [Sec-
tion 11, article I.] Since the adoption of the new constitution general laws have been passed by our legislature,
which, in so far as public improvements upon streets, etc.,
are concerned, have superseded those provisions of the
charters of the several cities of the state which relate to
street work, as well as all acts of special or local legislation
theretofore made applicable to these public municipal
improvements. The history of these general laws passed
since the adoption of the new constitution relative to
improvements upon public streets is as follows:

The first attempt to pass a general law, (after the new
constitution went into effect) in relation to municipalities,
was what is commonly known as the " McClure Charter."
This was an act approved April 24, 1880, and entitled "An
act to provide for the organization, incorporation, and government of merged and consolidated cities and counties of
more than one hundred thousand population, pursuant to
the provisions of section seven, of article eleven, of the constitution of this state." This act came before the Supreme
Court in the case of Desmond *v.* Dunn, 55 Cal. 242. The

act in question attempted or purported to provide a charter
or complete organic law for all consolidated cities and
counties of more than one hundred thousand population—
although there was but one municipal corporation in the
state at the date of the passage of the act to which it could
by its terms apply, that is, the city and county of San Francisco. The court held the act to be unconstitutional. It
was held, *First:* That the act, even if constitutional, could
not take effect as to the corporation known as the city and
county of San Francisco, because the constitution, impliedly
at least, provides that cities incorporated previously to the
adoption of the constitution, shall continue to exist under
their existing acts of incorporation, until a majority of the
electors determine to be organized under general laws, or
frame a charter for their own government, as provided by
sections 6 and 8, article XI of the constitution. Until
superseded or supplanted by a charter framed and adopted
in accordance with either of these provisions of the constitution, all present charters remain in full force and effect, except as to such parts as may come in conflict with the constitution. *Second:* In the second place it was held that this act
known as the "McClure Charter," was unconstitutional
because sections 6 and 7 of article XI of the constitution contemplate the enactment of general laws which shall provide
for *all* municipal corporations regardless of population or the
character of the municipal government, and not for *some*
only; and such laws must be as general as the subject to
which they relate; such general laws may themselves classify municipal corporations according to population, and
make provision for each class, but each law must be general
enough to cover *all* municipal corporations, of whatever
class. *Held,* therefore, that this act is unconstitutional
because, *1st.* It excludes from its operation all municipal
corporations, except "consolidated city and county governments;" and *2nd,* because it is limited to municipal corporations having more than 100,000 inhabitants, and makes
no provision for those having less than that population.

In 1883 by an act approved March 13, 1883, the legislature
passed an act entitled "An act to provide for the organization,
incorporation and government of municipal corporations."
[Statutes 1883, page 93.] This act of March 13, 1883, commonly
called the "Municipal Incorporation Act," "is in harmony
with, and passed in obedience to the provisions of section
6, article XI, of the constitution." [*Ex parte* Campbell, 74
Cal. 26.] By this act, and the municipal classification act
of March 2, 1883, [statutes 1883, page 24], the municipalities of the state were divided into six classes according to

population, and a complete charter provided for cities of each class, electing to be incorporated thereunder, that is to say, a charter for cities of the first class (cities having a population of more than 100,000), a charter for cities of the second class (cities having a population of more than 30,000 and not exceeding 100,000), etc.

This municipal incorporation act of March 13, 1883, provides that "any portion of a county containing not less than five hundred inhabitants, and not incorporated as a municipal corporation, may become incorporated under the provisions of this act, and *when* so incorporated, shall have the powers conferred, or that may hereafter be conferred by law upon municipal corporations of the class to which the same may belong." Such territory is incorporated as a municipal corporation of the class to which it belongs when a majority of the votes cast at the election held for that purpose are for incorporation. The same act also provides that "any city and county, city or town, organized or incorporated prior to the first day of January, eighteen hundred and eighty, at twelve oclock meridian" may become re-organized and re-incorporated under the provisions of said act, upon the proper steps being taken therefor. This is in accordance with that provision of the constitution [section 6, article XI] which provides that "cities and towns heretofore organized or incorporated may become organized under such general laws [that is general laws providing for the incorporation, organization and classification of cities and towns] whenever a majority of the electors voting at a general election shall so determine." This is one of the modes pointed out by Justice Myrick in his concurring opinion in the case of Desmond *v.* Dunn, 55 Cal. 253, whereby cities and towns may be incorporated. But, until the people of a city or town, incorporated prior to the 1st day of January, 1880, or the people of any portion of a county, determine to become organized under a general municipal incorporation law, such as the municipal incorporation act of March 13, 1883, and until a majority of the electors vote therefor, the provisions of such general municipal incorporation act do not apply to such city or town, or territorial portion of a county. Therefore there are but few cities or towns in this state to which the provisions of the municipal incorporation act, approved March 13, 1883, apply. [See *In re* Guerrero, 69 Cal. 100.] Consequently the provisions of that act need not be regarded save in those few cities or towns, which being incorporated prior to January 1st, 1880, have elected to re-incorporate under that act, or those cities

and towns, which, coming into existence since the new
constitution took effect, have been organized under said
act of March 13, 1883; and even as to such cities and towns,
the provisions of the general street improvement and street
opening acts, passed since the passage of said municipal
incorporation act of March 13, 1883, are controlling where
inconsistent with the provisions of the said municipal
incorporation   act,   but   when   not   inconsistent   the
provisions of the latter act,—the municipal incorporation act,—even in respect to street work may
be applicable in those cities and towns which
have incorporated thereunder. Thus in Capron *v.* Hitchcock, decided June 3, 1893, 33 Pac. Rep. 431, it was held
that no valid assessment can be made for street work done
under the general street improvement act—the Vrooman act
of March 18, 1885,—if the contract therefore is void under
section 628 of the municipal incorporation act of March 13,
1883, providing that no officer of a city of the fourth class,
organized under said act, shall be interested in a contract
to which the city is a party, and that any contract contrary
to the provisions thereof shall be void: *held*, further, that
the said municipal incorporation act of March 13, 1883—
section 628—forbidding any officer of a city of the fourth
class to be interested in a contract with the city, is not
impliedly repealed by section 5 of the general street
improvement act—the Vrooman act of March 18, 1885—
providing that under certain circumstances a street contract shall be awarded to the owners of a majority of the
frontage on the street to be improved.

In this case, the action was brought by plaintiff
to enforce the lien of an assessment on the lot of
defendant in the city of San Diego, for street work
alleged to have been done by plaintiff under a contract awarded to him by the city council of San Diego,
and executed on the part of the city by the superintendent
of streets. At all the times mentioned in plaintiff's complaint the city of San Diego was a municipal corporation
of the fourth class organized and existing under said general municipal incorporation act of March 13, 1883, and
plaintiff, to whom said contract to do said street work was
awarded as aforesaid, was a school trustee of said city of
San Diego, duly elected, qualified and acting as such
school trustee for the third ward of said city of San Diego,
held, that, for the reasons given above,—*i. e.* because of the
letting of the contract to plaintiff, was violative of said provision of section 628 of the municipal corporation act, under

which the municipality was incorporated,—the contract was void, and plaintiff could not recover.

Cities and towns incorporated under the general municipal incorporation act of March 13, 1883, have for their charter the provisions of such act applicable to the particular class of cities or towns to which such cities and towns belong. If any provisions of this general act, applicable to street improvements and not inconsistent with the provisions of the general street improvement act—the Vrooman act of March 18, 1885,— be in force in cities and towns incorporated under said municipal incorporation act, and if such provisions may be applied in street improvement proceedings,—provisions relative to the qualifications of the contractor, for example— then it is difficult to perceive why similar provisions in the charters of other cities and towns, freeholders charters for example, should not in like manner be applied to and govern in street improvement proceedings. The Vrooman act of March 18, 1885, may have entirely superseded all provisions in the general municipal incorporation act bearing *directly* upon the subject of street improvements, and may in like manner have superseded *all* charter provisions bearing *directly* upon the subject of street improvements, and yet other provisions of said general municipal incorporation act or of such charters, not directly relating to the subject of street improvements, but which, nevertheless, may be applicable in street improvement proceedings,— provisions prescribing the qualifications of contractors, for example, as that no officer of the city shall be interested in any contract with the city—may perhaps be properly applied to and govern in all proceedings relating to street improvements. This conclusion seems warranted by the decision in Capron *v.* Hitchcock, *supra.* In other words, if Capron *v.* Hitchcock is authority for the proposition that any part of the general municipal incorporation act is controlling in street work proceedings, in cities incorporated under said act, then, by a parity of reasoning, it must likewise be authority for the proposition that similar provisions in the charters of cities, incorporated under special or free-holders charters, are in like manner applicable to street work proceedings.

It is provided by section 6, article XI of the constitution that "cities or towns *heretofore* or *hereafter* organized, and all charters thereof framed or adopted by authority of this constitution, shall be subject to and controlled by general laws." Mr. Justice McKinstry, in his dissenting opinion in the case of Thomason *v.* Ashworth, 73 Cal. 85, says: "On the 13th of March, 1883, (seven days after the approval of the act 'to provide for the improvement of streets, etc., within municipalities') an act was approved entitled 'An act to provide for the organization, incorporation and government of municipal corporations.' [That is to say, the first Vrooman act, approved March 6th, 1883, was approved seven days before the approval of the " municipal incorporation act," which was approved March 13th, 1883.] The last act [that is, the municipal incorporation act of March 13, 1883] is a general statute, providing for the incorporation, organization, classification and government of cities and towns, and was unquestionably intended to be a compliance with the mandate of the first clause of section 6, article XI of the constitution. It provides for the election of a superintendent of streets, and prescribes his duties, which are such as the title of his office would imply. Amongst the powers of the municipal council is enumerated the power of opening, altering, constructing, repairing, etc., streets, highways, etc., and in subsequent sections is supplied an entire scheme for 'street work.' If both these statutes [that is, the municipal incorporation act, approved March 13, 1883, and the Vrooman act, approved March 6, 1883] were valid, the provisions of the act of March 13 were substituted for those of the act of March 6, 1883—at least so far as street work done in cities and towns organized under the act of March 13 is concerned. * * * But the act of 1835 [*i. e.*, the Vrooman act, approved March 18, 1885—statutes of 1884-5, page 147] *was an amendment of the act of March 13, 1883*, [the "municipal incorporation act"] *or an entire revision and consequent repeal of those provisions of that act relating to 'work upon streets, alleys,' etc., within municipalities formed under the general law.* * * * It was a substitution of one system of street work for another system. If operative at all, it made an end of the provisions of the general law of 1883 relating to street work." [That is to say, if operative at all, it made an end of those provisions of the "municipal incorporation act" which related to and regulated street work.]

However, these observations of the learned justice from whose opinion they are quoted, are not entirely compatible with the subsequent decision of the Supreme Court in said case of Capron *v.* Hitchcock, cited *supra*, although it may be said of the decision in this latter case, that it was not held that any part of the general municipal incorporation act, relating directly to street work, was in force, but that a very salutary provision, limiting the powers of officers of the municipality to enter into contracts generally to which the city is a party, was not inconsistent with any provision

of the general street improvement act—the Vrooman act of
March 18, 1885—and was in full force in cities incorporated
under said municipal incorporation act, notwithstanding
any of the provisions of said general street improvement act
of March 18, 1885.

See, also in this connection, the language of Mr. Commissioner Belcher, in Anderson v. De Urioste, 96 Cal. 405,
when the learned commissioner said: "The act of March
18, 1885, was a general street law, and was in force in the
city and county of San Francisco from the date of its passage. [Thomason v. Ashworth, 73 Cal. 74.] *It therefore,
as to all matters provided for, superseded the consolidation act
and became the governing law of the city.*" While, however,
it is quite probable, as stated by Mr. Commissioner Belcher,
that this general street law of March 18, 1885, superseded
all charter provisions providing for street work, in cities
having "freeholders' charters," or charters granted by
special enactment prior to the new constitution,—the consolidation act of San Francisco, for example,—still, it is
also quite probable that in these cities, as in municipalities
incorporated under the general municipal corporation act,
such charter provisions as do not *directly* relate to or provide for street work, but which, nevertheless, are, in the
nature of things, capable of being applied to street work
proceedings, will be so applied, when not inconsistent with
any provision of the said general street improvement act,
—such general charter provision, for example, as prescribe
generally the qualifications of persons entering into contracts with the city. But, as to all provisions of these
charters, relating directly to and making express provisions
for street work, it is undoubtedly correct to conclude that
all of these charter provisions have been superseded by
the general street improvement act of March 18, 1885,—
the Vrooman act.

The act known as the "Vrooman act of 1883" was
approved March 6, 1883—seven days prior to the municipal
incorporation act. This act, approved March 6, 1883, commonly known as the "Vrooman act of 1883," is entitled,
"An act to provide for the improvement of streets, lanes,
alleys, courts, places and sidewalks, and the construction of
sewers within municipalities." [Statutes of 1883, page 32.]
It takes its name from its putative author, Senator Vrooman of Alameda county, by whom the bill was introduced
in the senate at the session of the legislature held in 1883.
The same senator, at the session of the legislature held in
1885, likewise introduced the bill which subsequently
became the general street improvement act of March 18,

1885, the general street improvement act now in force in the municipalities of the state, the provisions of which are to be found *post*, pages 1–216. These two acts may be designated respectively as the first and second Vrooman acts, or, as the "Vrooman act of 1883," and the "Vrooman act of 1885." The latter act, the "Vrooman act of 1885," expressly repealed the former act—the "Vrooman act of 1883."

The act of March 6, 1883, known as the first Vrooman act, or Vrooman act of 1883, constituted a complete system of street work. At the date of the passage and approval of this act, the constitution [section 19, article XI] provided that "no public work or improvement of any description whatsoever shall be done or made, in any city, in, upon, or about the streets thereof, or otherwise, the cost and expense of which is made chargeable, or may be assessed upon, private property by special assessment, unless an estimate of such cost and expense shall be made, and an assessment *in proportion to benefits*, on the property to be affected or bene-fited, shall be levied, collected and paid into the city treas-ury *before* such work or improvement shall be commenced, or any contract for letting or doing the same authorized or performed." To meet the requirements of this provision of the constitution, the said act of March 6, 1883—the Vroo-man act of 1883—provided that an assessment should be levied according to benefits, and that the city council should proceed to award the contract for the work and improve-ment, after receiving notice from the city treasurer that sufficient money has been received by the treasurer, on account of any such assessment, to pay the estimated costs and expenses of such work and improvement, for the pay-ment of which such assessment was levied and collected. The act of April 1, 1872 [statutes 1871–2, p. 804] providing for work upon streets in the city and county of San Fran-cisco, was very similar, in its general aspects, to the present general street improvement act—the Vrooman act of March 18, 1885, *post*, pp. 1–216. Like the present general street improvement act, the said San Francisco street improvement act of April 1, 1872, adopted the "front foot" principle of assessment, and provided that the assessments should be levied *after* the execution of the contract, and after the work had been fulfilled to the satisfaction of the superintendent of streets. [Section 9 of act of April 1, 1872, stats. 1871–2, p. 813.] In McDonald *v.* Patterson, 54 Cal. 245, it was held that the provisions of section 19 of article XI of the consti-tution, as originally adopted, the provisions of which are quoted *supra*, providing that an estimate of the cost and

expense shall be made, and an assessment levied and collected *before* the letting of the contract, is not a provision
which requires legislation to enforce it; and that the provisions of said act of April 1, 1872, relating to street improvements in San Francisco, which authorize the superintendent of streets to execute contracts for such improvements—
in advance of the levy and collection of the assessment—are
inconsistent with said section of the constitution, as it then
stood, and ceased to be operative on the 1st day of January,
1880. In other words, as said by Mr. Justice McKinstry in
his dissenting opinion in People *v.* Henshaw, 76 Cal. 453,
when the constitution of 1879 went into effect the vital parts
of the San Francisco street work act of April 1, 1872, were
"struck dead," and some act such as the first Vrooman act
—the Vrooman act of March 6, 1883—was necessary to
enable the municipalities of the state, whose charter provisions had thus been "struck dead," to proceed with their
street improvements until the constitution could be amended
by the repeal of said provisions of section 19 of article
XI. Accordingly the said Vrooman act of March 6, 1883,
was drawn conformably to said requirements of section 19
of article XI of the constitution, and was passed by the legislature at its session in 1883. The decision in McDonald
v. Patterson, *supra*, was rendered by the court in department. It was subsequently re-affirmed, however, by the
court in bank in Donahue *v.* Graham, 61 Cal. 276, Justices
McKinstry and Sharpstein dissenting. At the same session
in which it passed the said Vrooman act of March 6, 1883,
the legislature proposed an amendment to the constitution
abrogating the requirement of the constitution above quoted,
viz., the first sentence of section 19, article XI. By said
proposed amendment, said first sentence of section 19, article XI, referring to public work, was entirely omitted and
dropped from the constitution. [See statutes of 1883, page
2.] This proposed amendment was adopted by the people
at the general election in 1884, and, if the amendment was
properly proposed by the legislature, the constitution was
duly amended in this particular, and the constitution, after
the adoption by the people of said proposed amendment, no
longer required the assessment to be in proportion to "benefits," or to be levied and collected *prior* to the commencement of the work, or the awarding of the contract.

In 1885 the legislature passed the second Vrooman act,
—the Vrooman act of March 18, 1885,—entitled "An act
to provide for work upon streets, lanes, alleys, courts,
places and sidewalks, and for the construction of sewers
within municipalities." This act was approved March

18, 1885. It expres°ly repealed the first Vrooman act,—
the Vrooman act of March 6, 1883, —and like the latter
it contains within itself a complete system for street work.
It differs mainly from the Vrooman act of 1883 in this that
it provides for the levy and collection of the assessment
after the letting of the contract and the completion of the
work, and adopts the "front-foot" principle of assessment
instead of apportioning the expenses according to the "benefits," [statutes of 1885 page 147,] and, if the said proposed constitutional amendment, abrogating said requirements of
section 19 of article XI of the constitution, was properly
submitted to the people, and adopted by them at the general election in 1884, as aforesaid, then said Vrooman act
of March 18, 1885, repealed the first Vrooman act,—the act
of March 6, 1883,—and from the time of its passage has
been the street improvement act in force in the municipalities of this state.

These two acts,—the Vrooman act of 1883 and the Vrooman act of 1885,—came before the Supreme Court in the
case of Thomason v. Ruggles, 69 Cal. 465. Four of the
justices, viz., JJ. Myrick, Ross, Morrison and McKee,
held that the act of April 1, 1872, relating to street
improvements in the city and county of San Francisco,
in so far as it authorized the doing of street work before a
levy and collection of an assessment, was repealed by section 19 of article XI of the constitution. Three of said four
justices, viz., JJ. Myrick, Ross, and Morrison, held: *1st.* That
the amendment to the constitution adopted by the people November 4, 1884, dispensing with the necessity of such previous levy and collection of assessment, was constitutionally
adopted. [Two of the justices—McKee and Thornton—held
that the failure to enter the proposed amendment at large
in the journals of the senate and assembly during its progress through the legislature, was in violation of section 1
of article 18 of the constitution, and that therefore the
proposed amendment never took effect—see opinion of
McKee, J., in this case and his concurring opinion in Oakland Paving Co. v. Hilton, 69 Cal. 479, also opinion of
Thornton, J., in said last mentioned case.] *2nd.* That said
act of April 1, 1872, repealed by said section 19, article XI of
the constitution, as originally adopted, was not revived by
said amendment dispensing with the said requirements of said
section 19 of article XI. *3rd.* That the second Vrooman
act,—the act of March 18, 1885,—providing for street work
in municipalities, and repealing the act of March 6, 1883,
[the first Vrooman act] was a general law within the meaning of the constitution; was conformable to the constitution

as amended by said amendment of November 4, 1884, and
as a general law was in force in all the municipalities of
the state. [See also Oakland Paving Co. v. Hilton, 69 Cal. 479
and People v. Henshaw, 76 Cal. 436.]

In Oakland   Paving   Co.   v.   Tompkins,   72   Cal.
5,   it   was   decided   by   the   court   in   bank,   Mr.
Justice   Thornton   alone   dissenting,   that   section   1
of article XVIII of the constitution, providing that proposed
amendments to the constitution shall be entered in the
journals of the senate and assembly, does not require a
proposed amendment to be copied at large in the journals,
a reference to it by title and number being sufficient; and
that therefore said amendment to section 19 of article XI,
adopted by the people November 4, 1884, dispensing with
the necessity of previous levy and collection of assessment,
was constitutionally adopted.   In this case the point was
squarely presented, was plainly and unequivocally decided,
and was completely removed from the realm of doubt.

Finally, in the case of Thomason v. Ashworth, 73 Cal. 73,
all question as to what law was in force, relative to street
improvement work, was put an end to.   Mr. Justice Thornton delivered the opinion of the court.   The *opinion*, as
well as the judgment was concurred in by three of the
other justices, making the constitutional number, four,—
requisite to the pronouncing of a judgment in bank.

It was held in that case:

1st.   That the act of April 1, 1872, in so far as it conflicted with the provisions of section 19 of article XI of the
constitution, as that section of the constitution originally
stood, was repealed by said section 19 of article XI.

2nd.   That afterwards said act of April 1, 1872, was
entirely repealed by the act of March 6, 1883,—the first
Vrooman act,—providing for the improvement of streets,
lanes, etc.

3rd.   That said section 19 of article XI of the constitution of 1879, providing that no street work should be made
until after the assessment had been levied and collected,
was repealed by the amendment adopted by the people at
the general election in 1884.

4th.   That the act of March 18, 1885,—the second Vrooman act, or Vrooman act of 1885,—repealed the Vrooman
act of 1883 on the same subject.

5th.   That these acts of March 6, 1883, and March 18,
1885, are general laws, within the meaning of section 6 of
article XI of the constitution, affecting all municipal corporations in the state, and were within the powers of the legislature to enact, and that the provisions of such general

laws are paramount to the provisions of the charter of any city in the state upon the same subject matter.

The prevailing opinion of the court concludes as follows: "It follows from the above, (*1*.) That the act of 1872 was entirely done away with by the constitution; (*2*.) That the act of 1883 was constitutional when passed, and repealed all portions of the act of 1872 in conflict with it; (*3*.) That the act of 1885 is a constitutional act under the constitution as amended; that the act of 1885 repealed the act of 1883, *and has been and is now in force since its passage on the eighteenth day of March, 1885.*" Mr. Justice Thornton, in giving the opinion of the court, said, page 78: "It is argued that, according to the views herein expressed, a city may have its charter totally changed without its consent. This is a proper deduction from the ruling herein, but this cannot be done by a special or local law applicable alone to a particular charter. The result can only be reached by a general law affecting all municipal corporations, or may be all of a class, and we can see no probability that a city can be injured by general legislation." [See also Davies *v.* City of Los Angeles, 86 Cal. 37.]

Therefore, unless the act of March 18, 1885, has been repealed or amended, it is in full force and effect throughout the length and breadth of the state, and all street work provided for by the provisions of said act must be done under and pursuant to its provisions in every municipality of the state. Has it been repealed or amended? It has been amended by the legislature at each of its sessions since 1885.

Since its original passage and approval, March 18, 1885, the Vrooman act of 1885 has been amended as follows:

1887: By an act approved March 15, 1887, [statutes 1887, page 148] section 32 was amended.

1889: By an act approved March 14, 1889, [statutes 1889, page 157] sections 2, 3, 4, 5, 7, 8, 9, 12, 13, 19, 24, 26, 34 and 37 were amended, and a new section, called section 12½, relating to payment for work in installments, was added thereto. This act of March 14, 1889, likewise purported to amend section 35, though no mention was made of it in the title to the act. Some of the sections amended by this act of March 14, 1889, have been amended by subsequent acts.

1891: *(a.)* By an act approved March 17, 1891, [statutes 1891, page 116] it was amended or attempted to be amended, by adding thereto, an additional part, numbered part IV, and consisting of seven new sections, numbered respectively, 38, 39, 40, 41, 42, 43 and 44, relative to a system of street improvement bonds. This act of March

17, 1891, was repealed by the bond act of February 27, 1893.

(b.) By an act approved March 31, 1891, [statutes 1891, page 196] sections 2, 3, 4, 5, 7, 9, 24, 26, 34, 35 and 37 were amended.

(c.) By an act approved March 31, 1891, [statutes 1891, page 461] sixteen new and additional sections numbered, respectively, sections 38, 39, 40, 41, 42, 43, 44, 45, 46, 47, 48, 49, 50, 51, 52 and 53 were added. These sixteen new sections thus added to the Vrooman act by said amendatory act of March 31, 1891, purport to empower the city councils to change the grade of any street, the official grade of which has been already established, and provide the machinery for accomplishing this purpose. These sixteen new and added sections should be read in connection with section 2 of the act as amended in 1893. Since said section 2 as amended in 1893, [act of March 11, 1893, statutes 1893, page 172] provides that "whenever the grade of a street, avenue, etc., shall hereafter be changed, the petition of the owners of a majority of the feet fronting thereon, asking for grading the same to the new grade, shall be a condition precedent to the ordering of such grading to be done."

1893: (a.) By an act approved February 27, 1893, [statutes 1893, page 33] commonly known as the street improvement bond act, provision was made for the issuance of serial bonds representing the cost of any work or improvement provided for by the Vrooman act of 1885. This bond act of February 27, 1893, repeals the said act of March 17, 1891, by which a new part, numbered part IV, and including seven new sections, sections 38 to 44, inclusive, was added to the Vrooman act of 1885. Said act of March 17, 1891, by which said part IV was added, or attempted to be added, to the Vrooman act of 1885, was likewise an act to provide a system of street improvement bonds. It did not stand alone, but purported to amend the Vrooman act of 1885, "by adding thereto an additional part numbered four, consisting of sections 38, 39, etc., relative to a system of street improvement bonds." Whereas the said bond act of February 27, 1893, by which the bond act of March 17, 1891, was superseded and repealed, does not purport in terms to amend the Vrooman act of 1885. In form it stands alone, but, in effect, it is at least supplementary to the Vrooman act of March 18, 1885, and it is a question whether it does not, also, in effect and for the accomplishment of its own purposes, amend the Vrooman act of 1885.

(b.) By an act approved March 9, 1893, [statutes 1893,

page 89] the legislature passed an act entitled "An act to amend sections 38 to 53, inclusive, of an act approved March 31, 1891, adding those sections to 'an act to provide for work upon streets, alleys, lanes, courts, places and sidewalks, and for the construction of sewers within municipalities' approved March 18, 1885."

(c.) By an act approved March 11, 1893, [statutes 1893 page 172] sections 2, 24 and 37 of the Vrooman act of 1885 were amended.

The act, therefore, under which improvements upon opened or dedicated public streets, lanes, alleys, courts or places, is to be performed, in the municipalities of this state, and under which sidewalks and sewers are to be constructed, is the Vrooman act of March 18, 1885, as the same has been amended by the said amendatory acts of 1887, 1889, 1891 and 1893. This act of March 18, 1885, as thus amended, is in force in all the cities, towns, cities and counties, and municipalites of the state; and the work and improvement therein provided for must, in every municipality of the state, be done and performed by and under the authority of said act, and pursuant to its terms and provisions. It contains within itself a complete system for street improvements, and sewer construction, upon streets already opened or dedicated, or which may be hereafter opened or dedicated.

THE VROOMAN ACT OF MARCH 18, 1885.

The Vrooman act of March 18, 1885, as amended by subsequent amendatory and supplementary acts, is the act now in force by which streets which have been opened or dedicated to public use, may be graded or regraded, planked or replanked, paved or repaved, sewered or sidewalked by the city council, or otherwise improved as provided by the act. Section 2 of the act declares what improvements may be made under the act upon such streets. These improvements may be done by private contract in the municipalities of this state, by any private person or contractor on behalf of and contracting directly with the owners of the property fronting upon the street, as well as by the municipal authorities themselves.

But, when a private contract is thus entered into between the property owners and a contractor to improve a street by grading, etc., the property owners, before the work is done, must first obtain permission so to do from the council as provided for by subdivision 10 of section 7 of the act. [See post, page 65.] Such private contracts have no connection with the provisions of these street improvement acts. The object of this street improvement act, and of all other street work acts, is to empower the municipal authorities to do the work therein provided for, and assess the cost thereof upon the property made liable therefor, e. g., the property which fronts upon the street improved, or the property which is declared to be benefited by the improvement.

Where the improvement is done by the municipal authorities under and pursuant to the provisions of the said general street improvement act, the property owners, in that case, are not parties to the contract whatever. Their property is assessed under the taxing power to pay for the improvement, but the only parties to the contract are the municipality and the contractor. The city government and the contractor are the only parties to the proceeding, so far as making the improvement is concerned; that being done, the city government acts alone in its political capacity in apportioning and levying the tax upon the property of the property owner or taxpayer; but when the time arrives for the collection of the tax, the city government steps out of the triangular relation existing between the contractor, the city government and the property owner or taxpayer, and the contractor steps in the place of the city government and is made her agent for the purpose of collecting the tax, i. e. where the assessment is collected by suit, and not by summary sale of the property as for taxes due and unpaid, as provided by some of the acts. "Independent of the statute, the tax would be due from the taxpayer to the city, and the city would have to demand and sue for it, if necessary; but the statute provides that the city shall not be responsible for the collection of the tax, or subject to the risk, trouble and annoyance, but shall virtually assign her right of action for the tax to the contractor, in full payment for his work and labor under her contract with him, and authorize him to sue in his own name to recover it, if necessary. This being done, his relation of contractor is at an end. * * * The thing sued for is not the contract price, or a part of it, but the tax specified in the assessment or warrant, for which he sues, not as a contractor but as assignee of the city." [Hendrick v. Crowley 31 Cal. 472.]

When, however, the property owners do the work themselves, and enter into a *private* contract therefor, such contract is controlled by the general law of contracts, and not by the provisions of these street work acts. And where such private contract is entered into by the property owners, the contractor, or person who does the work, may have a lien under the Code of Civil Procedure to secure payment for his work and labor done or material furnished. [§§ 1183–1203 C. C. P.—particularly § 1191.]

Where the improvement is made under any such private contract, the property owner is a party to the contract. It is his will that the contract should be made, and the improvement contracted for be done, and questions arising out of any such contract, between the parties thereto, are to be determined by the general law of contracts, and in some respects at least, by the law relating to the "Liens of mechanics and others"—C. C. P. chapter II, title IV, part III. The municipal authorities of the municipalities of this state are authorized to make certain contracts for the performance of certain improvements upon the streets of the municipality, under and by virtue of certain general laws of the state, and as it is the general street work laws of this state, now in force, that constitute the subject matter of this book, such private contracts as are above referred to need no further consideration. The general street improvement act now in force all over the state, under which most of the improvements upon public urban highways are made, is the said act of March 18, 1885, commonly known as the Vrooman act of 1885.

Where an improvement is made by the municipal authorities, under a contract executed pursuant to the provisions of this general street improvement act, the Vrooman act of March 18, 1885, the property owners are not parties to the contract; the proceedings as to them are *in invitum*; their liability is, in a sense, that of taxpayers, [see *post.* pp. 70–72, for a definition of the terms "assessment" and "taxation"], and the proceedings to be valid, so as to entitle the contractor to recover the amount of the tax or assessment assessed against the property of the lot owner or taxpayer, must be strictly in accord with the requirements of the statute; the mode in such cases constitutes the measure of the power of the municipal authorities. To entitle the contractor to recover against the property assessed, there must be a valid contract under which the work must be performed; this must be followed by a valid assessment; and, to vest a right of action in the contractor, certain other acts must be performed after the issuance of the assessment.

Outline of the Provisions of the Vrooman Act of March 18, 1885, as amended. The statute provides that the contract shall be executed by the superintendent of streets. To empower him to execute a valid contract, so as to bind the property of the lot owner or taxpayer, there are at least ten essential prerequisites, viz: *(1.)* Passage of a resolution of intention; *(2.)* posting and publication of the resolution; *(3.)* posting and publication of notices of passage of the resolution; *(4.)* passage of an order for the work to be done, or resolution of construction; *(5.)* publication of the order for the work to be done. [These five prerequisites are provided for by section 3 of the act.] *(6.)* posting and publication of notices inviting sealed proposals; *(7.)* opening and considering the bids by council; *(8.)* award of the contract to the lowest bidder; *(9.)* posting and publishing notice of award of contract; and *(10.)* execution of the written contract by the superintendent of streets. [These last five prerequisties are provided for by section 5 of the act.] There are seven more prerequisites to a valid right of action in the contractor to sue and recover from the lot owner the amount of his assessment, viz: *(1.)* Making an assessment roll as provided for by section 8 of the act; *(2.)* attaching to the assessment a diagram as provided for by said section 8; *(3.)* making, signing and countersigning a warrant for the collection of the assessment and attaching the same to the assessment roll as provided by section 9 of the act; *(4.)* recording said warrant, assessment and diagram, together with the certificate of the city engineer, as provided by said section 9; *(5.)* demand upon the lot owner assessed or his agent, or upon the premises, as provided by section 10 of the act; *(6.)* return of the warrant, with a return endorsed thereon, signed and verified, as provided by said section 10; and *(7.)* recording the said return endorsed on the warrant, and also recording the original contract, if not already recorded, as provided by said section 10. The foregoing seventeen essential requirements of the act are jurisdictional, and constitute the important and indispensable requirements to the existence of a valid right in the contractor to enforce payment by the taxpayer whose property has been assessed.

Section 1 of the act declares what streets and highways are within the purview of the act, viz: All streets, lanes, alleys, places or courts in the municipality opened or dedicated to public use. Section 2 of the act declares when and what kinds of work the city council may order to be done upon said streets and highways. Sections 3, 4, 5 and 6, prescribe the jurisdictional prerequisites to a valid contract. Section 7 declares the rules of assessment under and according to which the lots and lands of the property owners are to be assessed. Section 8 provides when and how the assessment roll shall be made, and its form. Section 9 prescribes two essentials to the existence of a valid assessment lien, viz: (*1.*) Issuance of the warrant; and (*2.*) recordation of the warrant, assessment, diagram and certificate of the city engineer. Section 10 provides three more acts necessary to the existence of a valid right of action in the contractor, viz: (*1.*) Demand upon the persons assessed, or their agents, or upon the premises; (*2.*) return of the warrant, with a return endorsed thereon, signed and verified; and (*3.*) recordation of the return endorsed upon the warrant, and also the original contract if not already recorded. In addition to the foregoing prerequisites a petition for grading must be presented to the council, as provided for by section 2, whenever grading is to be done upon a street the official grade of which shall have been changed since the amendment of section 2 by the act of March 11, 1893. [See sections 38–52 for the procedure for changing or modifying the grade lines of any street the official grade of which has once been established.]

Section 11 provides a remedy to an "aggrieved" property owner, dissatisfied with any act of the superintendent of streets, by an appeal to the council. Section 12 prescribes the rules of procedure in an action to enforce the lien of the assessment. Sections 13, 14 and 15 relate to "repairs" and "reconstructions" upon streets that are out of repair or need reconstruction, and are in a condition to endanger persons or property passing thereon, or in condition to interfere with the public convenience in the use thereof. Sections 16 to 26, inclusive, contain miscellaneous provisions of various kinds. Part II of the act, embracing sections 27 to 33, inclusive, relates to sewer construction, and contains certain provisions for paying the costs of constructing sewers. Part III, embracing sections 34 to 37, inclusive, contains definitions and other miscellaneous provisions. Sections 38 to 53, added to the original act of March 18, 1885, by an act approved March 31, 1891, [statutes 1891, p. 461] and amended by the act of March 9, 1893, [statutes 1893, p. 89,] prescribe the procedure for changing or modifying the grade of any street after the official grade has once been established, and for paying the damages resulting from such change of grade to any property owner whose property is damaged by reason thereof.

The foregoing constitutes a brief outline of the provisions of the general street improvement act of March 18, 1885,— the Vrooman act—the principle act relating to improvements upon open, public or dedicated streets.

THE STREET IMPROVEMENT BOND ACT OF FEBRUARY 27, 1893.

The bond act of February 27, 1893, [statutes 1893, p. 33] may be classified as a "street improvement act." Although, it does not, in terms, purport to be amendatory of, or supplementary to, the general street improvement act,—the Vrooman act of March 18, 1885,—yet, in effect, it is supplementary to said general street improvement act. As stated in its title, its object is "to provide a system of street improvement bonds;" and it authorizes the city council, whenever it shall find, upon estimates of the city engineer, that the cost of any proposed work or improvement, authorized by said Vrooman act of March 18, 1885, will be greater than one dollar per front foot along each line of the street so proposed to be improved, to determine, in its discretion, that serial bonds shall be issued to represent the cost of said work or improvement.

By an act approved March 17, 1891, [statutes 1891, p. 116] the legislature passed an act amending the Vrooman act of March 18, 1885, by adding thereto an additional part numbered part IV, consisting of seven new sections numbered 38 to 44, inclusive. This act of March 17, 1891, was very similar in its provisions to the bond act of February 27, 1893, except that, while the former added its provisions to the Vrooman act of 1885. the latter act,—the bond act of February 27, 1893—in a measure, stands by itself, and only by *reference* incorporates within itself any of the provisions of the general street improvement act,—the Vrooman act of March 18, 1885. Section 8 of the bond act of February 27, 1893, expressly repeals the said act of March 17, 1891, except as to proceedings theretofore commenced thereunder, and the bond act of February 27, 1893, is the act now in force,—if constitutional—authorizing the issuance of serial bonds representing the cost of any work or improvement done or performed under the general street improvement act,—the Vrooman act of March 18, 1885.

THE TREE PLANTING OR SHADE TREE ACT OF MARCH 11, 1893.

The tree planting, or shade tree act of March 11, 1893, [statutes 1893, p. 153] entitled "An act to provide for the planting, maintenance, and care of shade trees upon streets, lanes, alleys, courts, and places within municipalities, and of hedges upon the lines thereof; also, for the eradication of certain weeds within the city limits," may also be included in the classification of street improvement acts. This shade tree act is the first general law of the kind ever passed in this state.

THE SANITARY DISTRICT ACT OF MARCH 31, 1891.

The sanitary district act of March 31, 1891 [statutes 1891, p. 223], authorizes the formation of a sanitary district within any county of the state, after an election therefor, ordered by the board of supervisors of the county, upon the presentation of a petition therefor to the board, signed by twenty-five persons in the county. Such sanitary district, it seems, may be wholly without or wholly within any incorporated city or town in the county, or may be partly within and partly without such incorporated city or town. The sanitary district thus created is a *quasi* municipal corporation, and has power to construct and maintain and keep clean such sewers and drains as in the judgment of the sanitary board shall be necessary or proper.

The Vrooman act of March 18, 1885,—the general street improvement act in force in the cities, towns, and cities and counties of the state—authorizes the city council of any city, town, or city and county, to construct and maintain and keep clean sewers and drains. This sanitary district act provides for the creation of a sanitary district, or *quasi* municipal corporation, and within the limits of such district a board of directors, called the sanitary board, exercises powers similar, in many respects, to the powers exercised by the city council of an incorporated city or town, in the construction and maintenance of sewers or drains, and in keeping the same clean. It will be seen, therefore, that this sanitary district act may be embraced within the catagory of "street improvement acts."

By an act approved March 9, 1893 [statutes 1893, p. 88], section 15 of the sanitary district act was amended.

THE STREET OPENING ACT OF MARCH 6, 1889.

Thus far the history and evolution of the street *improvement* acts, *i. e.*, acts providing for work and improvements upon *existing* streets, or streets already opened or dedicated, have been briefly traced. It remains now to trace, in the briefest possible manner, the history of the street opening acts, *i. e.*, acts providing for the opening, widening, closing, etc., of streets. These street opening acts do not make any provision for nor authorize any improvement upon streets. They merely authorize the creation or partial creation or widening of streets and the closing of streets. Heretofore it has been the policy of the legislature to provide for improvements upon existing streets by acts entirely distinct from acts providing for opening, extending and widening streets. [City and County of San Francisco v. Kiernan, 33 Pac. Rep. 723.] Acts providing for improvements upon existing streets, and acts providing for opening, extending, widening or closing streets belong to two entirely distinct classes. Nevertheless, the history of the street improvement acts, given *supra* [page XXIII *et seq.*] and what is said in connection therewith, will also serve as an illustration of the growth and history of the acts providing for opening, extending, widening and closing streets prior to the adoption of the new constitution.

History of Street Opening, Widening and Closing Acts prior to the New Constitution. Like the acts passed under the old constitution providing for improvements upon existing streets, the acts passed during the existence of said constitution, relative to the opening, closing, widening and extending of streets, were in almost all, if not in every case, special and local laws, found in the charters of the various municipalities, or in the acts amendatory thereof, or else were acts providing especially for the opening, widening, extending or closing of some particular street designated by name. The San Francisco consolidation act, the act providing for the consolidation of the city of San Francisco and the county of San Francisco, into the municipal corporation known as the city and county of San Francisco [statutes 1856, p. 145], provided for the opening of streets, and may serve as an illustration of charter provisions relative to the subject matter of this class of acts. Thus, it is provided in section 34 of the said consolidation act, [statutes 1856, p. 156], "that the board of supervisors shall have power to lay out and open new streets within the former corporate limits of the city of San Francisco, * * * * but shall have no power' to subject the city and county to any expense therefor, exceeding the sum of one thousand dollars."

The act of April 25, 1863 [statutes 1863, p. 560], entitled "An act to confer further power upon the board of supervisors of the city and county of San Francisco,"—empowering the said board of supervisors "to provide, by order, for laying out, opening, extending, widening, straightening or closing up, in whole or in part, any street, square, lane or alley, within the bounds of said city"—was, in effect, an act amendatory of the consolidation act, and affords an illustration of the special and local laws amendatory of existing city charters, passed prior to the new constitution, relative to the subject matter of acts providing for the opening and closing of streets, etc. [See also the act of April 4, 1864, statutes 1863-64, p. 347.]

STREET WORK LAW—INTRODUCTION

Acts illustrative of those special and local laws passed under the old constitution, and which provided especially for the opening, widening, extending or closing of some particular street in a city, may be found in the following acts: (*1.*) An act entitled "An act to open and establish a public street in the city and county of San Francisco, to be called 'Montgomery avenue,' and to take private lands therefor," approved April 1, 1872. [Statutes 1871–2, p. 911.] This "Montgomery avenue" act was considered by the Supreme Court in Mulligan *v.* Smith, 59 Cal. 206, and Kahn *v.* Board of Supervisors, 79 Cal. 388. (*2.*) An act entitled "An act to authorize the widening of Dupont street, in the city of San Francisco," approved March 23, 1876. [Statutes 1875–76, p. 433.] This "Dupont street" act came before the Supreme Court in Lent *v.* Tillson, 72 Cal. 404, when its constitutionality was upheld in a very learned opinion by Mr. Justice Temple.

History of Street Opening, Widening and Closing Acts since the Adoption of the New Constitution. Under the new constitution—the present organic law of the state—the legislature may not pass any local or special law "authorizing the laying out, opening, altering, maintaining, or vacating roads, highways, streets, alleys, town plats, parks, cemeteries, grave yards, or public grounds not owned by the state," nor "in all other cases where a general law can be made applicable." [Constitution, article IV, section 25, subdivisions 7 and 33.] Accordingly general laws, operative in every municipality of the state, have been passed, empowering the city council of any municipality, "to order the opening, extending, straightening, or closing up in whole or in part, of any street, square, lane, alley, court, or place within the bounds of such city and to condemn and acquire any and all land and property necessary or convenient for that purpose." The first act of the kind passed since the adoption of the new constitution was the act of March 6, 1889, [statutes 1889, page 70.] This act is still in force in every city, town, or city and county in the state having a population of less than forty thousand inhabitants. The act itself does not confine its provisions to municipalities of less than forty thousand inhabitants; on the contrary, it purports to be uniform in its operation in every municipal corporation throughout the state. But, by an act approved March 23, 1893, [statutes 1893, page 220] the legislature has attempted to limit the provisions of the said street opening act of March 6, 1889, to cities and cities and counties having a population of less than forty thousand inhabitants, and, if the said act of March 23, 1893, is constitutional, the provi-

sions of the street opening act of March 6, 1889, are thus
limited and circumscribed. [See *post* pp. 272-287.]

The street opening act of March 6, 1889, came before the
Supreme Court in Davies *v.* City of Los Angeles, 86 Cal. 37,
and was held to be constitutional and operative in all the
municipalities of the state, including cities having "freeholders' charters," framed since the adoption of the new
constitution under the provisions of section 8 of article XI,
as well as in municipalities organized and incorporated
under the old constitution. Justices Fox and Beatty dissented. The act subsequently came before the Supreme
Court in Dehail *v.* Morford, 95 Cal. 457; City and County of
San Francisco *v.* Kiernan, 33 Pac. Rep. 721; and in City of
Santa Ana *v.* Harlin, No. 19,030, decided Sept. 13, 1893.

THE STREET OPENING ACT OF MARCH 23, 1893.

The street opening, widening, extending and closing act
of March 23, 1893, is very similar, in its essential provisions,
to the street opening act of March 6, 1889. Only whereas
the street opening act of March 6, 1889, is, in terms, uniform
in its operation throughout all the municipalities of the state,
regardless of size or population, the act of March 23, 1893,
on the other hand, is, in terms, limited in its operation to
cities and cities and counties having a population of forty
thousand inhabitants or over. It is entitled "an act to
provide for laying out, opening, extending, widening,
straightening, diverging, curving, contracting, or closing
up, in whole or in part, any street, square, lane, alley,
court or place, within municipalities, or cities, and cities
and counties, of forty thousand inhabitants or over, and to
condemn and acquire any and all land and property necessary or convenient for that purpose." This title expresses
the general subject of the act. Section 23 of the act provides as follows: "The act approved March sixth, eighteen
hundred and eighty-nine, entitled 'an act for opening,
widening, and extending streets,' etc., after the passage of
this act, shall not apply to any city, or city and county having a population of forty thousand inhabitants or over, but
as to any city or city and county having a population of
forty thousand inhabitants or over said act shall not apply;
but said cities and cities and counties shall be subject only
to the provisions of this act in all matters embraced within
the perview of this act."

It is a serious question as to whether this street opening
act of March 23, 1893, is constitutional. If it is not constitutional, then the street opening act of March 6, 1889, is the
act which is in force and effect in all the municipal corpora-

tions of the state, regardless of size or population. [For a consideration of its constitutionality see *post* pp. 272–286.]

THE MUNICIPAL INDEBTEDNESS ACT OF MARCH 19, 1889.

The municipal indebtedness act now in force in all the municipalities of the state is the act approved March 19, 1889, [Statutes 1889, page 399] as amended by subsequent amendatory acts. It is a general act. Its subject and purpose is sufficiently shown by its title. It is entitled "An act authorizing the incurring of indebtedness by cities, towns and municipal corporations, incorporated under the laws of this state, for the construction of water-works, sewers, and all necessary public improvements, or for any purpose whatever, and to repeal the act approved March 9, 1885, entitled an act to authorize municipal corporations of the fifth class, containing more than three thousand and less than ten thousand inhabitants, to obtain water-works; also to repeal an act approved March 15, 1887, entitled an act authorizing the incurring of indebtedness by cities, towns, and municipal corporations, incorporated under the laws of this state."

This general municipal indebtedness act is common to both of the classes of acts which constitute the street laws of this state, *i. e.*, acts providing for improvements upon *existing* streets, and acts providing for the creation or partial creation or closing up of streets. For, under this municipal indebtedness act, the city council is authorized to "incur an indebtedness to pay the cost of *any* municipal improvement, or for *any purpose whatever*, requiring an expenditure greater than the amount allowed for such improvement by the annual tax levy." And, while the street opening and closing acts have been distinguished in this book from the acts which have been designated as "street improvement acts," because the latter provide for improvements to be made in or upon existing streets, still the word "improvement" in its broadest sense, includes the opening, closing, widening, extending and straightening of streets. Thus in section 23 of the street opening act of March 6, 1889, and in section 21 of the street opening act of March 23, 1893, it is provided that "the words 'work' and 'improvement,' as used in this act, shall include all work mentioned in section one of this act."

The history of these municipal indebtedness acts since the new constitution went into effect, is as follows:

1. In 1885, by an act approved March 9, 1885, [statutes 1885, page 42] the legislature passed an act entitled "An act to authorize municipal corporations of the fifth class, containing more than three thousand and less than ten thousand inhabitants, to obtain water-works." This act of March 9, 1885, was repealed by the general municipal indebtedness act now in force—the act of March 19, 1889.

2. In 1887, by an act approved March 15, 1887 [statutes 1887, page 120], the legislature passed an act entitled "An act authorizing the incurring of indebtedness by cities, towns or municipal corporations, incorporated under the laws of this state." This was the first general municipal indebtedness act, operative in all the municipalities of the state, passed since the adoption of the new constitution. It was repealed by the general municipal indebtedness act of March 19, 1889.

3. In 1889, by an act approved February 16, 1889,[statutes 1889, page 14] the legislature passed an act amending section four of said act of March 15, 1887.

4. In 1889, the legislature passed the said general municipal indebtedness act of March 19, 1889,—the general municipal indebtedness act now in force. [Statutes 1889, p. 399.] By this act each of said prior acts relative to municipal indebtedness, viz., the act approved March 9, 1885, and the act approved March 15, 1887, were expressly repealed, and likewise "all general acts, or special acts, or parts of acts," conflicting with said act of March 19, 1889.

5. In 1891, by an act approved March 11, 1891, [statutes 1891, p. 94] the legislature passed an act amending section 2 of the general municipal indebtedness act of March 19, 1889.

6. In 1891, by an act approved March 11, 1891, [statutes 1891, p. 84] the legislature passed an act amending section 5 of the general municipal indebtedness act of March 19, 1889.

7. In 1891, by an act approved March 19, 1891, [statutes 1891, p. 132.] the legislature passed an act amending sections 9 and 10 of the general municipal indebtedness act of March 19, 1889.

8. In 1893, by an act approved March 1, 1893, [statutes 1893, p. 61] the legislature passed an act amending sections 6 and 8 of said general municipal indebtedness act of March 19, 1889. By these amendments to sections 6 and 8, it was provided that the bonds issued under the act should run for forty years instead of twenty, and that one-fortieth part, instead of one-twentieth part, of the whole amount of indebtedness shall be paid each and every year. These amendments to sections 6 and 8, were made pursuant to the amendment to the constitution adopted at the general election held in 1892, by which section 18 of article XI was amended so as to permit the issuance of forty year bonds.

The foregoing pages attempt to give, in as brief a manner as possible, a succinct statement of the history and growth of the street laws of this state, and a brief statement of the acts now in force relative to improvements in and upon existing streets, as well as those relating to street opening, extending, widening and closing. In the following pages these several acts, now in force, as amended up to date, are set forth in full, and with such notes thereto—consisting, for the most part, of decisions by our Supreme Court construing the provisions of these and similar acts—as will serve to illustrate the meaning of their provisions and such points as have arisen in their operation from time to time since their enactment or such as may hereafter arise.

In the appendix, the Vrooman act of March 18, 1885, the street bond act of February 27, 1893, and the street opening act of March 6, 1889, are again set forth in full, and as amended up to date. It was thought best to duplicate these last mentioned acts, as, by setting them forth separately, unincumbered with the annotations, the busy practitioner will be the more easily enabled to find any particular provision which he may be looking for, and in this way an examination of the provisions of these acts will be facilitated without having to run over a great number of pages devoted to the annotations.

In the appendix will also be found some of the forms most commonly in use in proceedings under these acts.

Street Work Act of March 18th, 1885

AS AMENDED BY

SUBSEQUENT AMENDATORY AND SUPPLEMENTARY ACTS UP
TO AND INCLUDING ACTS OF 1893.

---

*An Act to provide for work upon streets, lanes, alleys, courts,
places and sidewalks, and for the construction of sewers
within municipalities.*

[Approved March 18, 1885.]

PART I.

SECTION 1. All streets, lanes, alleys, places, or courts, in the municipalities of this state now open or dedicated, or which may hereafter
be opened or dedicated to public use, shall be deemed and held to be open
public streets, lanes, alleys, places, or courts, for the purposes of this act,
and the city council of each municipality is hereby empowered to establish
and change the grades of said streets, lanes, alleys, places, or courts, and
fix the width thereof, and is hereby invested with jurisdiction to order to
be done thereon any of the work mentioned in section two of this act,
under the proceedings hereinafter described. [*Statutes 1885, page 147.*]

[Section 1 of the act of March 18, 1885, has never been altered or
amended.]

1. Scope of Section 1. The municipal government of a
city, in causing street improvements to be made, acts under
the authority conferred upon it by the legislature, and is
subject to all the constitutional limitations and retraints
imposed on the legislature, and has no other or greater
power than is, and lawfully may be, conferred on it by the
legislative act. [Creighton *v.* Manson, 27 Cal. 613.]

Section one of the act declares what streets and urban
highways are within the purview of the act, and empowers
the city council of each municipality to establish and
change the grade of such streets and urban highways; and
fix the width thereof, and invests such city council with
jurisdiction to order to be done on such streets, lanes, etc.,
any of the work mentioned in section two of the act, under
the proceedings in the act thereafter described and provided for.

Section two of the act declares when and what kinds of
work the city councils may order to be done upon said
streets and other urban highways.

Subsequent sections of the act describe the proceedings necessary to cloth the council with jurisdiction to order such street work to be done, the mode and manner of letting the contracts, principles of assessment to pay the expenses, mode of making the assessment, proceedings necessary to acquire a lien for the amounts assessed, proceedings necessary to enforce the lien, etc.

The urban highways subject to the jurisdiction of the act are, "all streets, lanes, alleys, places, or courts, in the municipalities of this state, now open or dedicated, or which may hereafter be opened or dedicated to public use."

Streets, lanes, alleys, etc., open or dedicated to public use are public highways. The term "highway" is generic. It is the name for all kinds of public ways, including county and township roads, streets and alleys, turnpikes and plank roads, railroads and tramways, bridges and ferries, canals and navigable rivers. In short, every public thoroughfare is a highway, but every highway need not be a thoroughfare, as it is now well settled that a *cul de sac* may be a highway. [Elliott on Roads and Streets, page 1.]

. The term "highways" includes "rural highways," usually denominated "roads," and "urban highways," or the public ways of a town or city, usually called "streets." But the term "highways" is a very comprehensive one, embracing in its wide sweep more ways than urban streets or suburban roads.

2. Meaning of the Word "Street." A street is a road or public way in a city, town or village. [Elliott on Roads and Streets, page 12.] In its ordinary acceptation the term "street" is a generic term and includes all urban ways which can, and are, generally used for the ordinary purposes of travel. A narrow way, less in size than a street, is generally called an alley. [*Id.*] " 'Street' means more than the surface; it means the whole surface and so much of the depth as is or can be used, not unfairly, for the ordinary purpose of a street. It comprises a depth which authorizes the urban authority to do that which is done in every street, namely, to raise the street, and lay down sewers —for, at the present day, there can be no street in a town without sewers—and also for the purpose of laying down gas and water pipes. 'Street,' therefore, includes the surface and so much of the depth as may not unfairly be used as streets are used." [Coverdale *v.* Charlton, 4 L. R. Q. B. Div. 104.]

In its ordinary legal signification the term "street" includes all parts of the urban highway, namely, the roadway, the gutters, the curbs and the sidewalks. [Elliott on

MEANING OF WORD "STREET" Sec. 1, Act of Mar. 18, 1885. 3

Roads and Streets, page 17; Bonnet v. San Francisco, 65 Cal. 230; Marini v. Graham, 67 Cal. 130.] But, while the term is ordinarily used as designating the whole of the urban way it does not invariably receive this meaning. Whether the term "street," as used in a statute, means simply the roadway between the curbs or sidewalks, or whether it includes the curbs and sidewalks, as well as the roadway, depends upon the context, and it may be used in either or both senses in the same statute. Thus, there is no doubt that in section 1, of the act of March 18, 1885, the word "street" is used in its broader sense, and includes sidewalks as well as the roadway, while in the very next section, section 2, it is used in its limited sense, i. e., it means simply the roadway and does not include the curbs or sidewalks. For, as section 1 of the act declares that the counsel is invested with jurisdiction, under the proceedings thereinafter described, to order to be done upon all streets, lanes, alleys, places or courts, now open or dedicated, or which may hereafter be opened or dedicated to public use, any of the street work mentioned in section 2 of the act, and as section 2 enumerates the construction of sidewalks and curbs as part of the work authorized by the act to be done, and as section 1 says nothing about sidewalks, it follows that, since the construction of sidewalks and curbs upon open or dedicated streets is part of the work authorized by section 2 to be done, that the word "street," as used in section 1 of the act, includes all parts of the highway, the roadway, gutters, curbs, and the sidewalks. But, as used in section 2 of the act the word "street" is limited to the roadway, i. e., the part intended especially for the use of horsemen and vehicles, lying between the sidewalks. Section 2 authorizes the council to order the whole or any portion, either in length or width of the streets, etc., to be graded, paved, macadamized, etc. and likewise especially authorizes the council to order sidewalks, curbing, etc., to be constructed therein. This section mentions the work authorized to be done upon streets, lanes, alleys, etc., i. e., grading, paving, planking, macadamizing, etc., and likewise mentions, as separate, and distinct work, the construction of sidewalks and curbs. The work authorized to be done upon streets, lanes, etc., and the construction of sidewalks and curbs are mentioned as different and distinct kinds of street work, which circumstance shows that in the sense in which the terms "street" and "sidewalk" are used in section 2, the former does not include the latter. [See Baudry v. Valdez, 32 Cal. 269; Himmelmann v. Satterlee, 50 Cal. 69.] In the latter case the resolution of intention and the resolution directing the improvement to be made in terms provided for "macadamizing the street." The contract for the improvement, and the assessment, both called for macadamizing the street and the sidewalk. It is a well established principle that the contract must be for the work authorized by the resolution of intention and no more. If more is called for by the contract the contract is void as to the excess, and if that which is authorized to be done cannot be segregated from the unauthorized excess, and the assessment is for the whole, the assessment is *void in toto* so that, if the term "street" in a resolution authorizing a "street" to be macadamized, does not include the term "sidewalk," so as to authorize the macadamizing of the sidewalk, it follows that a resolution directing a "street" to be macadamized is not authority for macadamizing a "sidewalk," and a decision holding that a resolution directing a street to be macadamized is not authority for macadamizing the sidewalk, must necessarily include the corollary that the term "street" does not include the sidewalks. Such was the decision in Himmelmann *v.* Satterlee, *supra.* In Baudry *v.* Valdez, 32 Cal. 276, it was said: "The question whether the term 'macadamizing' also includes 'curbing' is settled by the statute under which the parties having the matter in charge were working. The second section prescribes what street improvements the city council shall have power to cause to be made. Each kind is separately named and described. 'Macadamizing' is named as one, and 'curbing' as another. Hence, whether the former might or might not, under other circumstances, include the latter, is not the question. Does it, within the meaning of the statute under which the parties were working is the question, and it is clear that it does not, for they are there mentioned as different and distinct kinds of street work, which circumstance shows that in the sense in which the former term is used in the statute, it does not include the latter."

We conclude therefore, that, while the term "street," in ordinary legal signification, includes all parts of the way— the roadway, the gutters, curbing and sidewalks—still in statutes and municipal ordinances, directing the grading and paving and improvement of urban ways, the word "street" is often, and, indeed, generally understood to mean the roadway only, that is, the part of the way intended especially for the use of horsemen and vehicles, lying between the curbs and sidewalks. [See Elliott on Roads and Streets, page 17.] In any event, whether the terms "street," as used in a statute, is used in its ordinary

signification as including the sidewalks as well as the roadway, or whether it is used in its limited sense, meaning
the roadway only, is a question which must be decided in
each case in the light of the context.

As stated above the term "alley" is used to designate a
narrow way, less in size than a street, but it is obvious
that whether the way is or is not to be called an alley
depends upon the relation it bears to other ways in the same
city or town; for in some cities or towns the way would be
deemed so narrow as to be merely an alley and not a street,
while in others it would be comparatively of such a considerable width as to take rank as a street.

3. Dedication. As stated in section 1, the street, alley,
lane, etc., must be open or dedicated, but no formal acceptance of the same by the legislative body of the city is
necessary. The mere dedication of land by the owner to
public use, as public streets, lanes, alleys or other public
places, converts it into a public street, lane, alley, or other
public place, for the purposes of said act, without any
formal acceptance of the same as such by the legislative
body of the city, who may thereafter improve them in the
manner provided by law. [Stone *v.* Brooks, 35 Cal. 490.]
Held, therefore, that where the owner of a lot fronting on
Perry street, a *cul de sac,* sells the same, and at the sale
represents the lot as fronting on an extension of the *cul de
sac* so extended as to terminate at and open upon a public
street running at right angles that this is a dedication to
public use as a street of that portion of the lot represented
on the map as an extension of Perry street, and as such
was thereafter subject to the jurisdiction of the board for
all purposes of its improvement, which, when made,
operates as a complete acceptance of the dedication, and
perfects the right of the public to its use as a public highway for all purposes. [*Id.*] [See Spaulding *v.* Bradley, 79
Cal. 450.]

SECTION 2. Whenever the public interest or convenience may require, the
city council is hereby authorized and empowered to order the whole, or any
portion, either in length or width, of the streets, avenues, lanes, alleys, courts,
or places of any such city graded or re-graded to the official grade, planked
or re-planked, paved or re-paved, macadamized or re-macadamized, graveled, or re-graveled, piled or re-piled, capped or re-capped, sewered or
re-sewered, and to order sidewalks, manholes, culverts, cesspools, gutters,
tunnels, curbing, and cross-walks to be constructed therein, or to order break-
waters, levees, or walls of rock, or other material to protect the same from
overflow or injury, and to order any other work to be done which shall be
necessary to complete the whole or any portion of said streets, avenues,
sidewalks, lanes, alleys, courts, or places, and it may order any of the said
work to be improved; and also to order a sewer or sewers, with outlets, for

drainage or sanitary purposes, in, over or through any right of way granted
or obtained for such purpose; *provided*, that whenever the grade of a street,
avenue, lane, alley, court, or place shall hereafter be changed, the petition
of the owners of a majority of the feet fronting thereon, asking for grading
the same to the new grade, shall be a condition precedent to the ordering
of such grading to be done. [*Amendment, approved March 11, 1893, Statutes 1893, page 172.*]

[Section 2 was amended 1889, by act of March 14, 1889, statutes 1889,
page 157; again in 1891, by act of March 31, 1891, statutes 1891, page 196;
and again in 1893, by act of March 11, 1893, statutes1893, page 172.]

1. Scope of Section 2. Section two of the act declares
what kinds of street work may be done upon the streets,
lanes, alleys, etc., which section one declares to be subject
to the provisions of the act. Section one designates the
kinds of highways subject to the provisions of the act, and
section two designates the kinds of work which may be
done upon these highways.

The section allows work to be ordered for less than the
width of the roadway or street, and for any defined part of a
block in length. There is no limit to the length of the proposed work, except that it must be confined to *streets, lanes,*
etc.,—that is, it must not include any extension, like the discharge of a sewer, over private property, unless, for sewers,
the right of way has been obtained. The jurisdiction
of the council is limited to streets, lanes, alleys, etc., opened
or dedicated.

Under the San Francisco Street Work Act of 1863,
authorizing the city council to order "*the whole or any portion*
of the streets" to be improved, the council has power to let
the work of improving separate portions of a street by one
proceeding and in one contract therefor. [Macadamizing
Co. v. Williams, 70 Cal. 534.]

The work authorized by section two of the act may be
separated into three kinds, viz: *(1)* Work upon the roadway only, viz., grading and re-grading, planking and
replanking, paving and repaving, etc. "Re-grading" is
when a street, degraded by use, is brought back again to
the *same* grade. But if the grade of the street has been
officially changed meanwhile by ordinance "re-grading" is
not the proper word. The work will then be, as in the
first instance, grading to the official grade. In McVary v.
Boyd, 89 Cal. 305, it was held, that, whenever the condition of a street is such as, in the estimation of the legislative authorities of the city, it is proper that the burden of
"re-grading" should be borne by the entire block, the
improvement may be ordered even though a similar
expense had been previously borne by the property owners
for the original grading. (What is said about re-grading

applies also to re-planking, re-paving, etc.) *(2.)* The second class of work provided for by section two is such as is not necessarily confined to the roadway, or street in its limited sense, viz., sidewalks, manholes, culverts, cesspools, gutters, tunnels, curbing, etc. *(3.)* The third class of work provided for by section two is the improvement of any of the other work mentioned in the section. The word "improved" is here used in its most technical sense, *i. e.*, the restoration, or enlargement, or completion of work once done on the same grade. In common speech, and frequently throughout the act [See subd. 2 of sec. 34] the word is applied also to work in the first instance. But wherever work is to be ordered, after the first instance, and on the previous grade, and adds certain things to complete the street, the proceedings should designate the work to be done "to *improve* * * * street, by" etc.

2. Grading. Section 2 of the act provides that "the city council is hereby authorized and empowered to order * * * the streets * * * graded or re-graded *to the official grade.*" Consequently the council only has power to grade a street to the official grade, and therefore, whether the grade was officially established or not before proceedings were begun to grade it, is a material issue in an action upon a street assessment, and must be proved by the plaintiff if denied by defendant.

"The power to lay out, open and grade streets carries with it, by necessary implication, the power to establish the grade of such streets, unless the power be expressly reserved or granted to another body or officer." [Himmelmann *v.* Hoadley, 44 Cal. 224.] As to what is evidence of the establishment of the official grade of a street, see Gafney *v.* San Francisco, 72 Cal. 146; Dorland *v.* Bergson, 78 Cal. 637; City of Napa *v.* Easterby, 61 Cal. 510; Chambers *v.* Satterlee, 40 Cal. 497; Himmelmann *v.* Hoadley, 44 Cal. 213.

As the city council can only grade a street to its *official grade*, it is not necessary that the resolution of intention to do the work should state that the street is to be graded to the *official grade;* a statement that it is to be *"graded"* is sufficient. For, in view of the fact that the street can only be graded to its official grade, "a resolution that a street be *graded* is equivalent to a resolution that it be graded to the *official grade.*" [Emery *v.* S. F. Gas. Co., 28 Cal. 376–7.]

Grading must necessarily precede macadamizing but where the statute does not expressly provide that no contract for macadamizing shall be made until the street is graded, the city authorities may authorize a contract for macadamizing after a contract for grading has been entered into, but before the grading has been done. [Dyer v. Hudson, 65 Cal. 374.] The board may order a street to be *planked* before it is graded, and it seems before a contract for grading has been entered into, provided the grade and width has been officially established. [Knowles v. Seale, 64 Cal. 377—under a San Francisco street act.]

Under section two as amended in 1893 (Sts. '93, p. 172–3) where the grade of a street, avenue, lane, alley, etc., has been changed, the street, avenue, lane, etc., can not be graded to the new grade, except upon petition of the owners of a majority of the frontage, asking for grading the same to the new grade. Without such petition proceedings to grade such street, avenue, lane, etc., to the new grade, would be void. [See Turrill v. Grattan, 52 Cal. 97; Dyer v. Miller, 58 Cal. 585; Gately v. Leviston, 63 Cal. 365.]

SECTION 3. Before ordering any work done or improvement made, which is authorized by section two of this act, the city council shall pass a resolution of intention so to do, and describing the work, which shall be posted conspicuously for two days on or near the chamber door of said council, and published by two insertions in one or more daily, semi-weekly, or weekly newpapers published and circulated in said city, and designated by said council for that purpose. The street superintendent shall thereupon cause to be conspicuously posted along the line of said contemplated work or improvement, at not more than one hundred feet in distance apart, but not less than three in all, or when the work to be done is only upon an entire crossing or any part thereof, in front of each quarter block and irregular block liable to be assessed, notices of the passage of said resolution. Said notice shall be headed "Notice of Street Work," in letters of not less than one inch in length, and shall, in legible characters, state the fact of the passage of the resolution, its date, and briefly the work or improvement proposed, and refer to the resolution for further particulars. He shall also cause a notice, similar in substance, to be published for six days, in one or more daily newspapers published and circulated in said city, and designated by said city council, or in cities where there is no daily newspaper, by one insertion in a semi-weekly or weekly newspaper so published, circulated, and designated. In case there is no such paper published in said city, said notice shall be posted for six days on or near the chamber door of said council and in two other conspicuous places in said city, as hereinafter provided. The owners of a majority of the frontage of the property fronting on said proposed work or improvement, where the same is for one block, or more, may make a written objection to the same within ten days after the expiration of the time of the publication and posting of said notice, which objection shall be delivered to the clerk of the city council, who shall indorse thereon the date of its reception by him, and such objections so delivered and indorsed shall be a bar for six months to any further proceedings in relation to the doing of said work, or making said improvements unless the owners of the one-half or more of the frontage, as aforesaid, shall meanwhile petition for the same to be done. At any time before the issuance of the assessment roll, all owners of lots or lands liable to assessment therein, who, after the first publication of said resolution of intention, may feel aggrieved, or who may have objections to any of the subsequent proceedings of said council in relation to the performance of the work mentioned in said notice of intention, shall file with the clerk a petition of remonstrance, wherein they shall state in what respect they feel aggrieved, or the proceedings to which they object; such petition or remonstrance shall be passed upon by the said city council, and its decision therein shall be final and conclusive. But when the work or improvement proposed to be done is the construction of sewers, man-holes, culverts, or cesspools, cross-walks or sidewalks, and curbs, and the objection thereto is signed by the owners of a majority of the frontage liable to be assessed for the expense of said work, as aforesaid, the said city council shall, at its next meeting, fix a time for hearing said objections, not less than one week thereafter. The city clerk shall thereupon notify the persons making such objections, by depositing a notice thereof in the postoffice of said city, postage prepaid, addressed to each objector, or his agent, when he appears for such objector. At the time specified said city council shall hear the objections urged, and pass upon the same, and its decisions shall be final and conclusive, and the said bar for six months to any further proceedings shall not be applicable thereto. And when not more than two blocks, including street crossings, remain ungraded to the official grade, or otherwise unimproved, in whole or in part, and a block or more on each side upon said street has been so graded or otherwise improved, or when not more than two blocks at the end of a street remain so ungraded or otherwise unimproved, said city council may order any of the work mentioned in this act to be done upon said intervening, ungraded, or unimproved part of said street, or at the end of a street, and said work upon said intervening part, or at the end of a street, shall not be stayed or prevented by any written or other objection, unless such council shall deem proper. And if one-half or more in width or in length, or as to grading one-half or more of the grading work of any street lying and being between two successive main street crossings, or if a crossing has been already partially graded or improved, as aforesaid, said council may order the remainder improved, graded, or otherwise, notwithstanding such objections of property owners. At the expiration of twenty days after the expiration of the time of said publication by said street superintendent, and at the expiration of twenty-five days after the advertising and posting, as aforesaid, of any resolution of intention, if no written objection to the work therein described has been delivered, as aforesaid, by the owners of a major frontage of the property fronting on said proposed work or improvement, or if any written objection purporting to be signed by the owners of a major frontage is disallowed by said council, as not of itself barring said work for six months, because, in its judgment, said objection has not been legally signed by the owners of a majority of said frontage, the city council shall be deemed to have acquired jurisdiction to order any of the work to be done, or improvement to be made, which is authorized by this act; which order, when made, shall be published for two days, the same as provided for the publication of the resolution of intention. Before passing any resolution for the construction of said improvements, plans and specifications and careful estimates of the costs and expenses thereof shall be furnished to said city council, if required by it, by the city engineer of said city; and for the work of constructing sewers, specifications shall always be furnished by him. Whenever the contemplated work of improvement, in the opinion of the city council, is of more than local or ordinary public benefit, or whenever, according to estimate to be furnished by the city engineer, the total estimated costs and expenses thereof would exceed one-half the total assessed value of the lots and lands assessed, if assessed upon the lots or land fronting upon said proposed work or improvement, according to the valuation fixed by the last assessment roll whereon it was assessed for taxes for municipal purposes, and allowing a reasonable depth from such frontage for lots or lands assessed in bulk, the city council may make the expense of such work or improvement chargeable upon a district, which the said city council shall in its resolution of intention declare to be the district benefited by said work or improvement, and to be assessed to pay the costs and expenses thereof. Objections to the extent of the district of lands to be affected or benefited by said work or improvement, and to be assessed to pay the costs and expenses thereof, may be made by interested parties, in writing, within ten days after the expiration of the time of the publication of the notice of the passage of the resolution of intention. The city clerk shall lay said objections before the city council, which shall, at its next meeting, fix a time for hearing said objections, not less than one week thereafter. The city clerk shall thereupon notify the persons making such objections by depositing a notice thereof in the postoffice of said city, postage prepaid, addressed to each objector. At the time specified the city council shall hear the objections urged, and pass upon the same, and its decision shall be final and conclusive. If the objections are sustained, all proceedings shall be stopped; but proceedings may be immediately again commenced by giving the notice of intention to do the said work or make said improvements. If the objections are overruled by the city council, the proceedings shall continue the same as if such objections had not been made. [*Amendment, approved March 31, 1891. Statutes 1891, page 192.*]

[Section 3 was amended in 1889 by act of March 14, 1889, Sta. '89, p. 158; and again in 1891,.by act of March 31, 1891, Sta. '91, p. 196.]

1. Jurisdiction. Street work under the act is inaugurated by a resolution of intention, followed by certain notices and advertised proposals, ending in a written contract. The superintendent of streets is required to approve the work, when satisfactorily performed, and to issue to the contractor, in payment for the work, an assessment upon the adjoining lots, or lots liable to assessment. Here the concern of the city ends. The contractor assumes control of all further proceedings, and the issuance of the assessment discharges the city from all further liability to him. Under this system the lot owner can set up to defeat the action, not only jurisdictional defects in the proceedings before the contract was let, but also jurisdictional defects in the assessment, which assessment, except as provided in section 12½ of the act, can only be made after the superintendent of streets has determined that the contract has been fully performed. The contractor cannot control the action of the superintendent, except by appeal to the council, and he is liable to lose the entire reward of his labor through an oversight of this officer. The proceedings having been held to be *in invitum*, a strict compliance with the statute is exacted, and very frequently great hardship results without fault on the part of the contractor. Before the contractor can acquire any rights under his contract, the city council must have acquired jurisdiction—that is power—to award the contract, and the superintendent of streets must have acquired jurisdiction or power to enter into and formally execute the written contract. The contract is in fact complete when the contractor's bid is accepted. There is then a contract between the council and the contractor. This contract made by the council is formally reduced to writing by the superintendent of streets, and executed by him on behalf of the city authorities. [Opinion of Temple, J., in Chambers *v.* Satterlee, 40 Cal. 526.] Notwithstanding the fact, however, that there may be a meeting of minds between the city authorities and the contractor, and therefore, theoretically at least, an agreement, just as soon as the contractor's bid is accepted, still "a written contract duly authorized under the act, and executed according to its requirements is indispensable to the validity of any assessment upon property to pay for street improvements." [Dougherty *v.* Hitchcock, 35 Cal. 512.] There are certain things required by the statute which are essential to the acquisition of jurisdiction or power to enter into and execute a valid contract, and for the purpose of acquiring this jurisdiction every one of these essentials must be complied with in the manner and mode required by the statute. "After the jurisdiction has once been acquired, subsequent proceedings can be attacked for only such irregularities as affect substantial rights, *but for the purpose of acquiring jurisdiction every requirement must be regarded as of equal necessity.*" [Dehail *v.* Morford, 95 Cal. 460.]

The resolution of intention, in due form and properly adopted, is the foundation of the proceedings to acquire jurisdiction, but it alone is not sufficient to clothe the city authorities with jurisdiction or power to enter into and execute a valid contract. To authorize a valid contract all the essentials leading up to its execution must be complied with in the manner provided and required by the statute. And to authorize a recovery by the contractor after the due performance of the work by him or his assignee, under a valid contract, all the essentials of a valid assessment must be complied with. As said by Mr. Justice Temple in Chambers *v.* Satterlee, 40 Cal. 525, "There is no magic in the fact that, after notice of intention, the board acquire jurisdiction, which will excuse to any extent, a compliance with the requirements of the statute. The word jurisdiction, of course, means power, for there is nothing of a judicial nature in that portion of the proceedings which relates to ordering the work and letting the contract. There is nothing peculiar in this statute in this respect. It is generally, if not always the case, in statutes conferring the power to divest vested rights that notice is given to the parties, whose rights are affected, as a condition precedent to the exercise of the power. The statutes in regard to laying out or changing highways provide for notice, which must be given before the board has jurisdiction to act; *but I never heard the proposition advanced that this dispensed with a full compliance with the statute, in the exercise of the power, after the jurisdiction had been acquired.*" [See also Hewes v. Reis, 40 Cal. 255.]

Thus, after the proper adoption of a resolution of intention, due posting and publication of the same, and likewise due posting and publication of a proper notice of the passage of such resolution, the council, after the lapse of a certain length of time, if the work is not barred by a sufficient objection in writing by the property owners, acquires jurisdiction or power to pass an order, ordering the work to be done. But this is not sufficient to authorize the execution of a valid contract by the superintendent of streets. There are other essentials to be done leading up to the execution of the written contract with the contractor. After the council has passed the order, ordering the work to be done, the order must be published; then a notice inviting sealed proposals must be posted and published; after this the bids must be considered; then the contract must be awarded to the lowest bidder; after this notice of the awarding of the contract must be posted and published, and within a certain time thereafter—if nothing intervenes to prevent, such, for example, as an election by the property owners themselves to take the work and enter into a contract to do the same—the superintendent acquires the power to execute the written contract with the contractor. But all these things are essentials to a valid contract. Thus the contract is not valid unless there be a valid award, and the contract must follow the award. Any substantial variance between the contract and the award is fatal. Thus in Dougherty v. Hitchcock, 35 Cal. 512, the board of supervisors of San Francisco adopted a resolution of intention to grade Clay street from Taylor to Jones, and from Jones to Leavenworth streets, and the crossings of

Clay and Jones streets, and, after ordering the work to be done, and after notice to bidders, awarded a contract for the *whole* work. The contract executed by the superintendent of streets was for the grading of one block only— that from Jones to Leavenworth. *Held,* that the award constituted the sole authority to the superintendent, who acted ministerially only in making a contract under it, and that the contract by reason of variance between its terms and the award, was unauthorized and void; also that a written contract duly authorized under the act, and executed according to its requirements, is indispensable to the validity of any assessment upon property to pay for street improvements. [See also Brock *v.* Luning, 89 Cal. 316; Perine *v.* Forbush, 97 Cal. 305.] "The resolution of intention and its publication confer upon the council jurisdiction to *proceed in the prescribed mode* to order the proposed work to be done," [Dougherty *v.* Hitchcock, 35 Cal. 523] that is, jurisdiction to take all the steps necessary to the execution of a valid contract eventuating in a valid assessment, but in thus proceeding to do the work proposed to be done, the city authorities must proceed by doing or causing to be done all those essentials pointed out by the statute. As stated by Mr. Justice Sanderson in Nicolson Pavement Co. *v.* Painter, 35 Cal. 705, "In the matter of street improvements the board of supervisors have whatever power the statutes upon that subject have conferred upon them, and no other; and that the power which they possess must be exercised in the mode prescribed by the statute, and in no other; *'the mode in such cases constitutes the measure of the power.'* "

When the jurisdiction of the council depends upon the existence of some fact, as to the existence of which the statute has expressly said that the council shall have the power to adjudicate upon, after a hearing to those affected thereby, the decision of the council upon such fact is conclusive. Thus, for example, the San Francisco Street Law Act of 1871–72 provided that, to start proceedings for grading, a petition therefor by the owners of a majority of the frontage should be necessary, and expressly authorized the board of supervisors to adjudicate upon the fact as to whether or not the owners of a majority of the frontage had joined in such petition, providing also that the adjudication of such jurisdictional fact by the the board should be final and conclusive after a hearing to the parties affected; and it was held in Spaulding *v.* Homestead Association, 87 Cal. 40, that judgment of the council upon this jurisdictional fact, after due opportunity for hearing, was final and conclusive.

In the matter of Grove Street, 61 Cal. 453–4, Mr. Justice McKinstry said: "An inferior board may determine *conclusively* its own jurisdiction or power by adjudicating the existence of *facts*, upon the existence of which its jurisdiction or power depends. Where, however, the power depends not upon the existence or non-existence of matters *in pais*, to be established by evidence, but upon allegations in a petition, a portion of the record, the question is not the same." That is to say, while the council, for example, might conclusively determine, by its decision thereon, that the owners of a majority of the frontage had actually joined in signing the petition for the work, provided an opportunity to be heard is given to those interested, still its decision upon the sufficiency of the petition would not be conclusive, where, for any reason, it appears upon its face to be insufficient, as where, for example, the statute requires the petition to state that "in the opinion of the petitioners the public interests require that the improvement should be made," and the petition merely states that "in the opinion of the petitioners the improvement asked for should be made."

Not only does the passage of the resolution of intention and its publication confer upon the council jurisdiction or power to proceed in the mode prescribed by the statute to take the steps necessary to bring about the due performance of the work under a valid contract therefor, eventuating in a valid assessment and lien against the property of the lot owners, but in the language of Chief Justice Sawyer in Dougherty *v.* Miller, 36 Cal. 87, after the expiration of the notice of intention, the council acquires "jurisdiction of the subject matter of the improvement." Whatever the phrase "subject matter of the improvement" may mean, it was used there as including the lots fronting on the street; so that it was held in that case that, if, after the expiration of the notice of intention to improve, a lot owner should divide his lot by conveying to a third party a narrow strip along the whole line of the improvement, thereby cutting off the whole of the remainder from a frontage on the street, the owner thus separating the remainder from a frontage upon the street, could not in this manner prevent the assessment attaching to the whole lot as it existed at the time when the notice of intention was given. Mr. Justice Sawyer, speaking for the court, said: "The board of supervisors acquired jurisdiction of the subject matter of the improvement after the expiration

of the notice of intention.   *   *   *   *   *   The jurisdiction when it once attached [that is attached to
the subject matter of the improvement] extended
through all subsequent proceedings *regularly* had, till
the assessment was made and collected. That jurisdiction could not be ousted by the act of a lot owner.
*   *   *   *   *   The whole lot as it existed when the
jurisdiction of the board of supervisors attached, is liable
to be assessed upon the completion of the work, no
matter who owns it, or what subdivisions, fraudulent,
fanciful or otherwise, may subsequently have been made
by the owner."

But while jurisdiction of the subject matter of the
improvement in the sense used by the court in this case of
Dougherty *v.* Miller, may attach to the subject matter of
the improvement, upon the due passage and publication of
the resolution of intention, nevertheless jurisdiction or
power to execute a valid contract and make a valid assessment, so that the contractor shall have a valid lien upon
the property of the lot owner, does not exist unless the contract and assessment are preceded by a due performance of
all of the jurisdictional prerequisites, which include the due
performance of a large number of necessary acts. Thus,
as held in Dougherty *v.* Hitchcock, 35 Cal. 512, and many
other cases, the superintendent of streets has no jurisdiction or power to execute a valid contract unless the council
has previously made an award of the contract, and the
formal written contract must correspond with the award.

It is often difficult to draw the line of demarkation
between the necessary jurisdictional prerequisites to a valid
contract or a valid assessment, and those mere irregularities which do not effect substantial rights. This question
frequently arises where the question is: Was the irregularity complained of waived by a failure to appeal to the
council? Section eleven authorizes the property owner to
appeal to the council, and by section three he is authorized to file a petition of remonstrance at any time before the
issuance of the assessment roll, wherein he can specify his
grievances and "such petition or remonstrance shall be passed
upon by the city council, and its decision therein shall be final
and conclusive." The San Francisco street law act of 1862,
[Statutes 1862, page 392] contained similar provisions, and
it was said in Emery *v.* Bradford, 29 Cal. 86, that "this
conclusive determination on appeal doubtless refers to
those matters upon which the superintendent is required
in the discharge of his duties to exercise his judgment—
those matters in which his errors are to be revised and

corrected. There are acts to be performed of a jurisdictional character essential to the validity of any assessment. It is not to be supposed that the conclusiveness of the decision of the board of supervisors is to extend to that class of acts. The provisions in section twelve [Section 11 of the Vrooman Act] indicate the kind of errors upon which the decisions of the board are to be final. It is that 'all the decisions and determinations of said board, upon notice and hearing aforesaid, shall be final and conclusive upon all persons entitled to an appeal under the provisions of this section, as to all errors and irregularities which said board could have avoided.' "

The last clause of section eleven of the Vrooman act (*post*) seems to make, or attempt to make, all proceedings of the council, subsequent to the passage and publication of the notice of intention, unimpeachable, unless an appeal has been taken to the council as provided in that section. It seems, however, from recent decisions of our Supreme Court that a failure to appeal to the council is not a waiver, under this act, of the right to attack the proceedings in court, for failure to comply with those jurisdictional requirements which are to be performed subsequently to the publication of the notice of intention. In Perine *v.* Forbush, 97 Cal. 305, the proceedings were had and the work done under the act of March 18, 1885. There was no objection made to the resolution of intention or to the regularity of its publication. It was held that the contract was void because not entered into within fifteen days after the first posting of the notice of award, as required by section 5 of the act. It was claimed, however, by the plaintiff that, even if the contract were void for this reason, the property owner could not complain and the assessment could not be held invalid, because the property owner had failed to appeal to the city council from the action of the superintendent in entering into the contract after the expiration of fifteen days from the posting of the notice of award. *Held*, that the property owner is not required to appeal to the council when the assessment is based upon an invalid contract. The same ruling was made in McBean *v.* Redick, 96 Cal. 191, where the proceedings were had and work done under the act of March 18, 1885.

In Manning *v.* Den, 90 Cal. 610, the question was directly considered. In that case the proceedings and work were performed under the act of March 18, 1885. It was held that the contract executed by the superintendent of streets was void because it was entered into prior to the expiration of ten days after the first posting of notice of the award; held, also, that the property owner, notwithstanding the provisions of section 11 of the act, does not waive his right to object to the proceedings by reason of his failure to appeal to the council. The court, quoting from Dougherty *v.* Hitchcock, 35 Cal. 524, said: "A contract authorized and executed in the mode prescribed by the act is indispensable to the validity of the assessment. This defect is not cured by the failure of the lot holders to appeal to the board, because, had an appeal been taken, the defect could not have been remedied by the board. The premature action of the superintendent was one which affected his *power or jurisdiction.* His action was void, *and that which was void does not become valid by reason of a failure to appeal.* The property owners were not '*aggrieved*', and the failure of the contractor to appeal did not operate, *(1.)* To create a *grievance* on the part of defendants [property owners], and, *(2.)* To *estop* them from complaining of it."

In Capron *v.* Hitchcock, decided June 3, 1893, the Supreme Court said: "The provision authorizing a petition of remonstrance against the acts and proceedings of the city council was intended to be applicable only to acts and proceedings *within the power* of the council."

In Dougherty *v.* Hitchcock, 35 Cal. 520, counsel for appellant said: "These provisions [that is provisions for appeal] cannot be regarded as furnishing an exclusive remedy in respect to proceedings invalid for want of jurisdiction. Such a construction would place the board on a higher footing than any other tribunal in the state, and enable it to act independent of the law from which it derives its power. Its proceedings could never be collaterally assailed, and whatever it chose to do the courts would be compelled to accept as valid and binding. The objection we make is, not that the board proceeded irregularly, but that it acted without jurisdiction."

(See this same subject of appeal considered in notes to section eleven of the act, *post.*)

From the foregoing it appears:

1. That an assessment is not valid unless all the jurisdictional prerequisites or jurisdictional acts are performed by the proper persons, *i. e.,* all the acts required by the statute to be done, and which affect substantial rights, must be done, and if any one of them is omitted or is not done as required by the act the omission is fatal.

2. That if any one of the necessary jurisdictional acts is not done as required, the property owner may defeat an action upon the assessment, or what purports to be the assessment, even though he has not appealed to the council. He is not a party "aggrieved" within the meaning of the act, and therefore need not appeal, and he may thus, without appealing to the council, defeat an action upon the assessment, where one of the jurisdictional prerequisites has been omitted, notwithstanding the fact that a resolution of intention in due form has been passed and published in the manner required by the statute.

II. *Jurisdictional Prerequisites.* There are ten things required by the act to be done before there is a valid contract, each one of which is jurisdictional and without any one of them there is no valid contract under which the contractor may proceed. An omission of any one of these jurisdictional prerequisites to a valid contract is fatal. (There are likewise certain jurisdictional prerequisites to a valid assessment, to be done after the written contract has been entered into, and after the completion of the work under the same by the contractor. These jurisdictional acts subsequent to the execution of the contract are considered in the notes to sections eight, nine and ten (*post*).

The ten jurisdictional prerequisites to a valid contract are: *(1.)* Resolution of intention, passed by the council. *(2.)* Posting and publication of the resolution of intention. *(3.)* Posting and publication of notices of the passage of the resolution of intention. *(4.)* Order for the work to be done, or resolution for construction passed by council. *(5.)* Publication of order for work to be done. *(6.)* Publication and posting of notices inviting sealed proposals. *(7.)* Consideration of bids. *(8.)* Award of contract to lowest responsible bidder. *(9.)* Publication and posting of notices of award. *(10.)* Execution of written contract by the superintendent of streets.

The first five of these ten jurisdictional prerequisites—one to five inclusive—are provided for by the above section of the act (section 3) and will therefore be considered in these notes to that section. The last five of these ten jurisdictional acts—six to ten inclusive—are provided for by section 5 of the act, and will therefore be considered in the notes to that section.

In addition to the said ten jurisdictional prerequisites to a valid contract, it is also required by section 2 of the act, as amended in 1893, that "whenever the grade of a street, avenue, etc., shall hereafter be changed, the petition of the owners of a majority of the feet fronting thereon, asking for grading the same to the new grade, shall be a condition precedent to the ordering of such grading to be done."

The above division of the jurisdictional prerequisites, precedent to the existence of a valid contract, into ten in number—or eleven, where the work to be done is grading and the grade has been changed since the amendment of 1893 to section 2—is not to be deemed as inclusive of all the acts which circumstances might make necessary to the existence of a valid contract. Thus, for example, a petition of remonstrance might, under section 3 of the act, be filed by the property owners. In such case the council must hear and pass upon such petition of remonstrance before it can proceed further. Again, some of the said ten jurisdictional acts might be generic and include one or more other acts. Thus, for example, the second jurisdictional act given above is the publication and posting of the resolution of intention. But this includes also, and as a part thereof, the passage or adoption of an order or resolution by the council, directing the resolution of intention to be posted and published. Therefore, the above division of the necessary jurisdictional acts into ten in number, might be thought to be more or less arbitrary. But it is adopted because it includes all these generic acts, which are necessary, in any event, to the existence of a valid contract. Circumstances may or may not, in the course of the proceedings, develop a necessity for other acts.

1. Resolution of Intention. By subdivision 11 of section 7 of the act it is expressly provided that "the council may include in one resolution and order any of the different kinds of work mentioned in this act, and it may except therefrom any of said work already done upon the street to the official grade."

The power to include different kinds of work in one resolution has frequently been upheld under this and other acts. [See Emery v. S. F. Gas Co., 28 Cal. 346; Dyer v. Hudson, 65 Cal. 374.]

The resolution, to give the council jurisdiction, must describe the work to be done. [Brady v. King. 53 Cal. 44.] It sufficiently describes the work to be done if it declares that the street will be graded and macadamized from one designated point to another. [Emery v. S. F. Gas Co., 28 Cal. 346.] It must specify the work to be done. It is not sufficient to declare the council's intention to cause certain repairs to be made "where necessary." [Randolph v. Gawley, 47 Cal. 458; Himmelman v. McCreery, 51 Cal. 562; Richardson v. Heydenfeldt, 46 Cal. 68.] Publication of the resolution of intention, describing the property affected, is in the nature of constructive service by publication of summons in an ordinary action at law, and as some such constructive service is necessary to give the council jurisdiction over the property to be affected, it follows that the resolution must describe the property, otherwise the property owners will have no notice. [See Boorman v. Santa Barbara, 65 Cal. 313.] It need not, however, contain a complete plan and specifications of the proposed improvement. It need not describe the work with any more exactness than it is described in the law itself. [Harney v. Heller, 47 Cal. 15.] When the district assessment plan is adopted the exterior boundaries of the proposed district should be accurately described in the resolution. It is not sufficient to describe the land in the district, as all lots fronting on a certain street. [Dehail v. Morford, 95 Cal. 457; Boorman v. Santa Barbara, 65 Cal. 313.]

A resolution excepting that part of a street which a railroad company is required by law to keep in order, is not void for uncertainty of description. As every citizen is conclusively presumed to know this provision of the law he is presumed to know the portions excepted. [Whiting v. Townsend, 57 Cal. 515.] A resolution providing that a particular crossing be planked and that the angular corners be reconstructed sufficiently describes the work. The meaning of such a resolution is that the angular corners formed by the crossing of the two streets are to be reconstructed in accordance with plans and specifications to be prepared by the superintendent of streets. [Deady v. Townsend, 57 Cal. 298.]

The resolution of the council need not be signed by the mayor unless there is some special provision of the statute requiring the mayor's signature. [Taylor v. Palmer, 31 Cal. 241; Baudry v. Valdez, 32 Cal. 269.] Under the act of March 18, 1885, the resolution need not be presented to or approved by the mayor, provided it be approved by a three-fourths vote of the council. If it receives less than a three-fourths vote of the council it must then be approved by the mayor. [McDonald v. Dodge, 97 Cal. 112.]

The signature of the clerk, where required, may be printed. [Williams v. McDonald, 58 Cal. 527.]

2. Posting and Publishing Resolution of Intention.

(a.) Posting. Prior to the amendment of 1891 [Statutes 1891, page 196] it was held that the act of March 18, 1885, as amended by the act of 1889 [Statutes 1889, page 157] did not require the resolution to be posted, where there was a paper in which publication could be made, and that if there is no such paper, then, and only then, must the notice be "posted" as provided in section 34 of the act. [Washburn v. Lyons, 97 Cal. 314.] But section 3 of the act as it now reads,

i. e., as amended by the act of 1891 [Statutes 1891; page 196] expressly provides that, in addition to publication, the resolution shall likewise "be posted conspicuously for two days on or near the chamber door of said council."

(b.) Publication. In addition to such posting the resolution must be "published by two insertions in one or more daily, semi-weekly, or weekly newpapers published and circulated in said city and *designated by said council for that purpose.*"

Under this express provision of the statute the council must "designate" the paper in which the resolution is to be published. In addition to "designating" the newspaper, the council, it seems, should, either in the resolution itself, or by a separate order, order that particular resolution to be published for the length of time prescribed by law, in some newspaper designated by the resolution or by such separate order. The usual method is for the resolution itself to direct its own publication in a designated newspaper.

It is often customary for the council or board of supervisors, by an ordinance or resolution passed at the commencement of the calendar year, to designate some newspaper as the official newspaper for all municipal advertisements during that year. And it has often happened in such case that the resolution has been published by the clerk in such official newspaper without any special order therefor, and without any designation by the council of that particular newspaper for that particular case, and the question has frequently arisen as to whether such publication was sufficient. It would seem from the plain letter of the statute, as amended in 1891, that publication is not sufficient unless the council in each instance especially orders the resolution to be published, and for that purpose designates the particular newspaper for that particular purpose. The statute says that the resolution must be published in a newspaper "designated by said council *for that purpose,*" *i. e.*, for the purpose of that particular resolution, and if the council must in each case *"designate"* the newspaper in which the resolution is to be published, it would seem that it must likewise, in each case *"order"* the resolution to be published. For designating the newspaper and ordering the publication are so intimately blended that it would seem difficult to "designate" the newspaper without also ordering the publication to be made.

The San Francisco street law act of 1863, authorized the board to order the work to be done "after notice of their intention so to do, in the form of a resolution describing the work, and signed by the clerk of said board, has been

published for a period of ten days." In Chambers v. Satterlee, 40 Cal. 497, Mr. Justice Wallace held that the publication need not be ordered by the board, while Justice Temple, page 521, said: "The statute says the board may order
the work to be done after notice of their intention so to do
(signed by the clerk) has been published for ten days. As
I understand this statute, it requires notice to be given by
the board itself. At that time there were no parties to the
proceedings, and consequently the notice can be given by
no one but the board itself. The power to grade streets is
in them, but the very first step in the exercise of that power
is to give the notice, or rather this is a condition precedent
to their exercising the power at all. The requirement that
the resolution shall be signed by the clerk is directed to the
board and not to the clerk. He is the mere servant of the
board and has no power except as their servant. The
provision only directs the mode of attestation by the board.
The manner of giving notice is by publishing the resolution; and it seems to me it must inevitably follow that the
publication must be made by the board. * * No one is
authorized to contract for the city and county save the
board of supervisors, and I think the publication required
by the statute can only be made by their authority," that
is the board must order the publication to be made.
[Pages 521–522.] See Dyer v. North, 44 Cal. 160, for
explanation of Chambers v. Satterlee on this point. In
Shepard v. Colton, 44 Cal. 628, it was held that the notice
of award of the contract was not sufficient because the
board never passed any resolution directing a notice of the
resolution of award to be published in any manner.

In the case of Chambers v. Satterlee, Judge Temple says
that "the publication must be made by the board." In the
same statute it was provided, in the part relating to sealed
proposals for doing the work, that the board, before giving
out contracts for street work shall "cause notice to be
* * * posted * * * and also published * * *
inviting sealed proposals," etc. [Statutes 1862, p. 393.]
In the case of Meuser v. Risdon, 36 Cal. 239, it was held,
under the same statute that was considered in Chambers v.
Satterlee, that where a contractor fails to perform his
work, and it becomes necessary to relet the contract,
the same course must be pursued in reletting; which
is prescribed in the first instance; that the clerk has no
authority in the first instance, independent of an order
of the board therefor, to give the notice inviting sealed
proposals, and that, therefore, in case of such reletting, he has no such power, independent of such order;

also, held that each proceeding to improve a street is a 'separate and independent proceeding, and must stand or fall by itself, and that, therefore, authority can not be conferred upon the clerk to post notices by a general resolution directing him in all cases where the contractors fail to perform to re-advertise for bids. If, therefore, as held by Mr. Justice Temple in Chambers v. Satterlee, the council must make the publication of the resolution of intention, or cause it to be made, it must follow, under the decision in Meuser v. Risdon, that it can only do so by ordering the posting and publication of the resolution in each particular case, and designate, in each particular case, the newspaper in which the publication is to be made. [See Donnelly v. Tillman, 47 Cal. 40; Donnelly v. Marks, 47 Cal. 187.]

However the statute as it now reads seems to settle all doubts which formerly existed relative to the necessity for a direction or order by the council that the resolution be published as required by law in a newspaper designated "for that purpose" by the council.

It must appear that the newspaper is both published and circulated in the city—either alone is insufficient. [Haskell v. Bartlett, 34 Cal. 281.]

The act says the resolution must be "published by two insertions," but does not expressly except Sundays or other non-judicial days, and the question arises: Would the publication be sufficient if one of the days fell on Sunday? It was held in S. F. v. McCain, 50 Cal. 210 and People v. McCain, 51 Cal. 360, that under the act of April 4, 1870, the resolution must be published five days exclusive of Sunday, and that the proceedings were void if the fifth day fell on a Sunday. But in that case the statute required the publication to be made for five days, "Sundays and non-judicial days excepted," whereas the present act does not thus expressly except Sundays and non-judicial days. In Taylor v. Palmer, 31 Cal. 241, it was held that the publication was sufficient if published for a period of ten days only, even though a Sunday should have intervened between the first and the last insertion. But in that case the statute only required the resolution to be published for a *period* of ten days, without making any exception of Sundays. Consequently the publication was sufficient if it covered the period of ten days; i. e. if published every day, except Sundays, for a *period* of ten days—not for ten days. These cases do not, on account of the difference in the reading of the statutes, throw much light upon the question arising under the act of March 18, 1885, as amended. In the case of S. & L. Society v. Thompson, 32 Cal. 347, it was held that constructive service of summons by publication is sufficient even if some of the publications, including the last, were made on Sunday. It is a mere ministerial act and may be performed upon a *dies non juridicus.* There does not seem to be any reason why a resolution of intention may not likewise be published on a Sunday, or rather there does not seem to be any reason why the fact that one of the publications falls on a Sunday, should vitiate the constructive notice to property owners of the passage of a resolution of intention, any more than that fact should vitiate the constructive service of a summons—in the absence of a statute expressly excepting Sundays.

Furthermore, it would seem from the express language of the act that part of the publication may be made on Sunday, that is, that a publication of the resolution of intention on Saturday and the following Sunday, for example, if made in a daily newspaper published on Sundays, would be sufficient. For section 34, subdivision 4, expressly provides that all notices, resolutions, orders, etc., when published in a newspaper shall be published "as often as the same is issued."

A newspaper which is published six days in each week is a "daily" newspaper, [Richardson *v.* Tobin, 45 Cal. 30] and where the statute does not specify a particular language in which it must be published, a publication in a German newspaper, but in the English language, is sufficient. [*Id.*]

If the resolution is not published for the length of time required by law the whole proceedings are void. [Brady *v.* Burke, 90 Cal. 1.]

3. Posting and Publication of Notices of the Passage of the Resolution. The superintendent of streets is required by section 3 of the act to cause to be conspicuously posted along the line of the contemplated work, at not more than 100 feet in distance apart, etc., notices of the passage of the resolution. Also to cause a notice, similar in substance, to be published for six days in one or more daily newspapers, designated by the city council, or in cities where there is no daily newspaper, by one insertion in a semi-weekly or weekly newspaper, so published, circulated and designated. Or, "in case there is no such paper published in said city, said notice shall be posted for six days on or near the chamber door of the council, and in two other conspicuous places in said city," as provided in sections 3 and 34 of the act.

(a.) Posting. The act requires the notices to be posted along the line of the contemplated work, *or*, "when the work to be done is *only* upon an entire crossing, or any part thereof, in front of each quarter block, or irregular block,

liable to assessment." [See section 7, subdivisions 3, 4, 5
and 6, for mode of assessing for work done on street crossings.]

In Miller *v.* Mayo, 88 Cal. 568, it was held that where the
contemplated work is work along a street for two or more
blocks so as to include one or more crossings made by the
intersections of other streets with the street along which the
work is to be done, it is sufficient if the notices required to
be posted along the line of the contemplated improvement
are posted without posting any notices in front of the quarter blocks adjoining and cornering upon the crossings, or
quarter blocks liable to assessment. The reason is that the
proviso in section 3 of the act of 1885, " or when the work
to be done is the improvement of an entire crossing, in front
of each quarter block liable to be assessed," is in the dis-
junctive, and is a separate mandate from that with which it
is connected. This is still more clearly the case under the
act as amended in 1891. For, as it now reads, the notices
are to be posted in front of the quarter blocks cornering
upon a crossing, "when the work to be done *is only* upon an
entire crossing or any part thereof." Accordingly, when
the proposed work is along a street, causing notices to be
posted along the line of the contemplated work, *i. e.* along
the street at not more than 100 feet in distance apart, but
not less than three in all, is sufficient even if one or more
crossings are included. But when the work to be done is
only upon an entire crossing, or any part thereof, the notices
must be posted in front of each quarter or irregular block
adjoining and cornering upon the crossings, or quarter
blocks liable to be assessed.

(*b.*) *Publishing.* The act likewise requires the superintendent of streets to cause to be published a notice of the
passage of the resolution, similar in substance to the notices
to be posted. It need not be exactly identical in all respects,
provided it be "similar in substance." It must be published for six days, if there be a daily, semi-weekly or
weekly newspaper printed and circulated in the city. If
there is no such paper, it must be posted for six days on or
near the chamber door of the council and in two other
conspicuous places.

A notice published by the superintendent of streets, containing the whole of the resolution of intention, and stating
the date and fact of its passage, is sufficient, and is not rendered defective because of an omission to refer to the resolution for further particulars. [Schmidt *v.* Market St. R.
R. Co., 90 Cal. 37.]

4. Order for the Work to be Done. A certain length of
time after the posting and publication of the notices of the
passage of the resolution of intention is allowed the property
owners within which to file written objections to the doing
of the proposed work. In some kinds of work, the filing of
such written objections by the owners of a majority of the
frontage operates as a bar to further proceedings for six
months. In other classes of work, e. g., sewers, man-holes,
etc., the council, after the filing of such written objections,
and notices to the objectors, may determine to go on with
the work notwithstanding the objections. Nor will a protest against the proposed work by the owners of a majority
of the frontage bar further proceedings when the proposed
work is to be done in a block lying between blocks which
have already been graded or otherwise improved. And in
such case the work shall not be stayed, unless the council
deem proper. Accordingly, when such objections have been
filed, and the judgment of the trial court is nevertheless in
favor of the assessment for work done upon a block, it will be
presumed on appeal, unless the contrary appear in the
record, that the block in question was between graded blocks.
[McDonald *v.* Dodge, 97 Cal. 112.]

At the expiration of twenty days after the expiration of the
time of the publication of the notices of the passage of the
resolution, and at the expiration of twenty-five days after the
advertising and posting of the resolution of intention, if
further proceedings have not been barred or ceased by reason
of the filing of written objections, the council has "jurisdiction to order any of the work to be done or improvement to
be made."

The council, when it has thus acquired jurisdiction to
order the proposed work to be done, should then make and
pass such an order.

The order that the proposed work be done is not an
"ordinance," and need not follow the for mof ordinances.
[City of Napa *v.* Easterby, 76 Cal. 222.] An order for street
work, made after the council has acquired jurisdiction, is
in the nature of a judgment. The subsequent proceedings
are ministerial in their character, and are taken for the
purpose of carrying the order into execution, and for this
reason, if the contractor fails to enter upon the performance
of his work within the time fixed in his contract the council may re-advertise for bids and relet the contract without
taking steps to acquire jurisdiction as in the first instance.
[Dougherty *v.* Foley, 32 Cal. 402.]

In Burnett *v.* Sacramento, 12 Cal. 76, it was held that an
ordinance for the improvement of streets, passed by the

council before the expiration of the time for the presentation of the protest, was not thereby, under the then charter
of Sacramento, invalid. It is doubtful if an order for work
passed before the time for protest had expired, would be
valid under the present general law—the act of March
18, 1885. This act says that "at the expiration
of twenty days after the expiration of the time
of said publication by said street superintendent,"
etc., the city council shall be deemed to have acquired jurisdiction to order the work to be done. And upon the principle of *expressio unius etc.*, it would seem that the council
has no jurisdiction to make such an order until after the
expiration of the time for the presentation of the protest.

Parties who do not remonstrate against a proposed street
improvement, can not claim the benefit of a remonstrance
filed by others. [Handy v. Heller, 47 Cal. 15.]

5. Publication of Order to do Work. Section 3 of the
act provides that the order to do the work when made or
passed by the council "shall be published for two days, the
same as provided for the publication of the resolution of
intention." The same section provides that the resolution
shall be published as follows: It shall be "published by
two insertions in one or more daily, semi-weekly or weekly
newspapers published and circulated in said city, *and
designated by said council for that purpose."* By sub-division
4 of section 34 of the act, it is provided that "the notices,
resolutions, *orders,* or other matter required to be published
by the provisions of this act, * * * * shall be published in a daily newspaper, in cities where such there is,
and where there is no daily newspaper, in a semi-weekly or
weekly newspaper, to be designated by the council of such
city, as often as the same is issued." From which it follows (*1*) that, if there be a daily newspaper, the order
should be published in a daily newspaper, and in a semi-
weekly or weekly newspaper only when there is no daily
newspaper published and circulated in the city; (*2*) that
the council should either in the order for work itself, or in
a separate order or resolution, designate the paper in which
it is to be published, and (*3*) that it should be published
as often as the paper is issued, *i. e.* if published in a daily
newspaper, for example, it should be published two days in
immediate succession, without any intervening day of
non-publication, provided the paper is issued on such intervening day.

The order may perhaps refer to certain maps on file in
the street superintendent's office, and while by a fiction of
law, such maps by such reference, become constructively

and for certain purposes, a part of the order, still it seems they need not be published as a part of the order. [City of Napa v. Easterby, 76 Cal. 222.]

III. *"Petition of Remonstrance" and "Written Objections."* The first five steps to be taken in the proceedings to acquire jurisdiction to enter into and execute a valid contract, viz: (*1*) Passage of resolution of intention; (*2*) posting and publishing the resolution; (*3*) posting and publishing notices of the passage of the resolution; (*4*) passage of order for the work to be done, and (*5*) publication of the order to do the work, have been described above in the notes to this section. The remaining five steps necessary to the execution of a valid contract are described in the notes to section five, *infra.* There are certain other requirements of this section, (section 3), which must be complied with if occasion gives rise to them, *e. g.*, if written objections to sewer work be filed notices must be mailed to each objector by the clerk, etc. These other requirements will be considered under the heading "Written Objections," and "Petition of Remonstrance."

1. *Petition of Remonstrance.* The "Written Objections" must not be confounded with the "Petition of Remonstrance." The object of the former is to enable a certain proportion of the property owners, by filing written objections, to bar all further proceedings for six months—as respects some classes of work—or, as respects other classes of work, to call forth the decision of the council as to whether or not the proceedings shall be continued. The object of the "Petition of Remonstrance" is to enable any property owner, who may feel aggrieved because the proceedings have not been regularly conducted, or because of some inequity, to appeal to the council, and there have his grievance passed upon. The written objections must be filed with the clerk within a certain time after notice to the property owners of the council's intention to do the work, viz., within ten days after the expiration of the time of the publication and posting of the notices of the passage of the resolution, if the front foot-plan of assessment is adopted, and must, in that case, in order to effect a six months' bar of the proceedings, be signed by the owners of a majority of the frontage. The delivery of such written objections to the clerk within said time operates *ipso facto* to bar any further proceedings for six months, except in certain specially excepted cases, such as sewers, man-holes, etc. The provision for the filing of "written objections," signed by the owners of a majority of the frontage, is intended to enable the owners of a majority of the frontage to determine for themselves, in

some cases, whether the proposed work shall be done, or, in the excepted cases, such as sewers, etc., to call forth the decision of the council as to the wisdom or desirability of further continuance of the proceedings. It has no necessary connection with the question as to whether the proceedings, assessments, etc., are regular or just and equitable in their nature. But, if any of the property owners, even *less than a majority* of the frontage, deem the work inadvisable, or that it would work a hardship or inequalities, or if there has been any inequality or irregularity in the proceedings of the council in relation to the performance of the work, a "petition of remonstrance" may be filed. Unlike the "written objections," the "petition of remonstrance" may be filed "*at any time before the issuance of the assessment roll,*" and by *any* owner or "owners of lots or lands liable to assessment thereon, who, after the first publication of said notice of intention, may feel aggrieved, or who may have objections to *any of the subsequent proceedings* of said council in relation to the performance of the work mentioned in said notice of intention * * * such petition or remonstrance shall be passed upon by the said city council, and the decision therein *shall be final and conclusive.*" The object of this petition of remonstrance is, not to stop or bar the work or proceedings, as in the case of written objections; but to enable any owner or owners of land liable to assessment to point out wherein the proceedings are unjust or inequitable, or irregular. The council may pass upon the petition or remonstrance, and in doing so it exercises *quasi* judicial functions, and it may correct the alleged abuse or not, or may find that there is no substantial irregularity, and if there be none—that is, no irregularity of a jurisdictional nature—its decision is final and conclusive. Whereas, when the written objection is delivered to the clerk, signed by the owners of a majority in frontage, the council exercises no judicial function whatever except in the especially excepted cases of sewers, man-holes, etc., and except that it may determine whether the petition has been signed by a majority of the frontage or not, in which respect, it seems, its decision would be final and conclusive. [Spaulding *v.* Homestead Ass'n, 87 Cal. 40; *In re* Grove Street, 61 Cal. 453–4.] It has no discretion in the matter, (except when the proposed work is the construction of sewers, man-holes, etc.) but must, *nolens volens*, stop all proceedings for six months. The object of the "petition of remonstrance" is to secure to each individual his constitutional right which guarantees that he shall not be deprived of his property without "due process of law." Compliance with this con

stitutional safeguard requires that the act should provide
for due notice to the property owner, and afford him an
opportunity to be heard. The posting and publication of
the resolution of intention and the posting and publication
of the notices of the passage of the resolution of intention
constitute such "due notice," when read in conjunction with
all the provisions of the act, as they should be; and the
provision for the filing of the " petition of remonstrance "
would seem to afford sufficient opportunity for a hearing.
" When a hearing is given by the act, as to the apportionment among the land owners, which furnishes to them an
opportunity to raise all pertinent and available questions,
and to dispute their liability, or its amount and extent, such
hearing is sufficient, and the act is, in this respect, constitutional." [See Spencer v. Merchant, 125 U. S. 345; Wal-
ston v. Nevin, 128 U. S. 578; Davidson v. New Orleans, 96
U. S. 97; Hagar v. Reclamation District, 111 U. S. 701;
Palmer v. McMahon, 10 Supreme Court Rep. 324; Lent v.
Tillson, 72 Cal. 404.]

If a petition of remonstrance is filed with the council, and
is referred to a committee, and the council, before the committee reports, and without acting directly on the petition
or remonstrance, directs the work to be done, it is practically and in effect a passing upon and a decision against the
petition or remonstrance. [Harney v. Heller, 47 Cal. 15.]

This part of section 3 of the Vrooman act, providing for
a petition of remonstrance, in reality provides for an appeal
to the council, and should be read in connection with section 11 of the act (*post*) which section provides for appeals
to the council and the procedure therein. For a further
consideration of this subject—" petition of remonstrance "
and " appeal to council "—see notes under section 11 *infra.*

2. "Written Objections." The effect of filing the written
objections, the time of filing the same, and the number of
property owners who must sign, depend upon the class of
work to be done, and whether the front-foot or district
assessment plan is adopted. For the purpose of determining the effect of filing the objections, etc., the work which
the act authorizes the council to do, is divisible into three
classes, viz:

(*a.*) *First Class.* The first class includes any work authorized by section 2 of the act, excepting that mentioned in the
next class below [see second class, *infra*, p. 32] *i. e.* all work
other than sewers, man-holes, etc., provided the proposed
work is for one block or more, and it is proposed to follow the
front-foot plan of assessment. In this class the owners of a
majority of the frontage may make a written objection within

ten days after the expiration of the time of the publication and posting by the superintendent of streets of the notices of the passage of the resolution of intention. The objection must be delivered to the clerk, who shall endorse thereon the date of its reception by him, and such objections so delivered and indorsed shall be a bar for six months to any further proceedings, unless the owners of one-half or more of the frontage shall meanwhile petition for the same to be done. In this class of work the filing of the written objections by a majority of the frontage works a bar of six months *ipso facto*, and the bar continues for six months, "unless the owners of the one-half or more of the frontage, as aforesaid, shall meanwhile petition for the same to be done."

In Dougherty *v.* Harrison, 54 Cal. 428, it was held that where the work has been barred for six months by the filing of sufficient objections, and, before the expiration of the six months, proceedings are resumed, the burden of proof is upon those asserting the validity of the proceedings to prove that the bar effected by the objections has been removed by the filing of a petition, pending the bar, by one-half or more of the frontage, petitioning for the work to be done, and in the absence of such proof, it will not be presumed *prima facie* even that the bar was removed. The court said: "The protest or written objections of the property owners introduced in evidence displaced the *prima facie* proof of regularity made by the warrant, assessment and diagram introduced by plaintiff, and throw upon him (plaintiff) the burden of showing that the bar effected by the objections on file had been removed. The bar existing, the proceedings subsequent thereto were irregular and void."

The statute, inferentially at least, authorizes the council to decide whether the written objection has been legally signed by the owners of a majority of the frontage. It provides that "at the expiration of twenty days after the expiration of the time of said publication by said superintendent [of notice of the passage of the resolution of intention] * * * if any written objection *purporting* to be signed by the owners of a major frontage is disallowed by said council, as not of itself barring said work for six months, *because in its judgment, said objection has not been legally signed by the owners of a majority of said frontage,* the city council shall be deemed to have acquired jurisdiction," etc. And it would seem from the ruling in Spaulding *v.* Homestead Ass'n, 87 Cal. 40, that the judgment of the council upon the question as to whether or not the owners of a majority of the frontage have legally signed the petition or not is final and conclusive, although the act does not expressly say so. To give the ruling of the council the effect of a conclusive determination, it must be an adjudication upon the existence of *facts*, or matters *in pais*, to be established by evidence *dehors* the petition itself. [*In re* Grove Street, 61 Cal. 453–4.]

As to who are, for the purposes of the act, deemed to be "owners," see section 16 of the act, *infra*.

(b.) Second Class. The second class of work or improvement includes "the construction of sewers, man-holes, culverts, or cesspools, crosswalks, or sidewalks, and curbs; also any work or improvement upon the intervening ungraded or unimproved part of a street, where not more than two blocks, including street crossings, remain ungraded to the official grade, or otherwise unimproved, in whole or in part, and a block or more on each side upon said street has been so graded or improved, so that the two blocks or less, ungraded or unimproved, lie between blocks which have been already graded or improved. [See McDonald *v.* Dodge, 97 Cal. 112.] The second class also includes work upon not more than two blocks at the end of a street remaining so ungraded or otherwise unimproved; also work or improvement upon the unimproved or ungraded portion of a street lying and being between two successive main street crossings, where one-half or more in width or in length of such street has been already partially graded or improved, also work upon a crossing that has been already partially graded or improved.

The filing of written objections does not *ipso facto* bar proceedings under this second class, but the council may proceed with the work, notwithstanding the filing of written objections, if they deem proper. Provision is also made by the act for a hearing upon the objections filed, after notice served by the clerk upon the objectors through the mails, where the proposed work is the construction of sewers, man-holes, culverts, or cesspools, crosswalks or sidewalks, and curbs. At the hearing the council hears and passes upon the objections urged, and its decision is final and conclusive, and the bar for six months does not apply.

Section 24 of the act likewise provides that none of the work or improvements described in said section 24, namely, work upon sewers, gutters, man-holes, culverts, cesspools, crosswalks and sidewalks, shall be stayed or prevented by any written or any other remonstrance or objection, unless the council deems proper.

(c.) Third Class. The third class of work includes any of the work or improvement authorized by section 2 of the act, where the council, deeming the work to be of more

than local or ordinary public benefit, or that the total estimated costs and expenses will exceed one-half the total assessed value of the lots and lands assessed—if the front-foot plan should be adopted—determines to make the expense of the work or improvement chargeable upon a district. In other words, the third class includes all work done under the district assessment plan. Where the district assessment plan is adopted, the council must in its resolution of intention describe the district [Dehail *v.* Morford, 95 Cal. 457; Boorman *v.* Santa Barbara, 65 Cal. 313; Lent *v.* Tillson, 72 Cal. 404–416] and declare it to be the district to be benefited by said work or improvement, and to be assessed to pay the costs and expenses thereof. Objections in writing to the extent of the district may be filed within ten days after the expiration of the time of the publication of the notice of the passage of the resolution of intention. The clerk serves notices upon the objectors, through the mail, of the time and place set for hearing. At the hearing the council passes upon the objections, and its decision is final and conclusive. If the objections are sustained, all proceedings are stopped; if overruled, the proceedings continue as if no objections had been made.

IV. *District Assessments.* Section 3 of the Vrooman act, as amended in 1891 [Statutes 1891 p. 198] provides that the council, instead of following the front-foot plan of assessment provided for by the act, *may* make the expense of the work chargeable upon a district in two cases, viz: *1st.* Whenever the contemplated work or improvement, in the opinion of the council, is of more than local or ordinary public benefit; or *2nd.* Whenever, according to estimates to be furnished by the city engineer, the total estimated cost and expenses would exceed one-half of the total assessed value of the lots and lands assessed, if assessed upon the lots and lands fronting upon said proposed work or improvement, etc.

It was held in Kreling *v.* Muller, 86 Cal. 465, that under the act of March 18, 1885, the Vrooman act, a lot can not be charged in a greater sum than one-half of its value upon the preceding assessment roll. Therefore, under the act of 1885, prior to the amendments of 1889 and 1891, if the contemplated work or improvement would, according to the estimate furnished by the city engineer, cost more than one-half of the assessed value of the lots to be assessed, or any of them, under the front-foot plan of assessment, the council had no option but either to adopt the district assessment plan, and declare in its resolution the district to be assessed, or else pay all over one-half of such assessed value of any lot or lots out of the city funds. The decision in this case is based upon the provisions of sections 3 and 7 (sub. 1 of section 7) of the act of 1885, as those sections stood prior to the amendments of 1889 and 1891. Section 3 of the act of 1885, prior to these amendments, provided that whenever the expense exceeded one-half of the assessed value of any lot, the amount exceeding such one-half *"shall"* be paid out of the city treasury, unless the owner shall, in writing, consent that the whole expense may be made a charge against the lot. Section 7, subdivision 1, provided, in substance, that such excess *"shall"* not be assessed upon the lot, but shall be assessed to the city and be payable out of the city treasury. These mandatory provisions of the statute, in express terms forbidding a lot to be charged with more than one-half of its assessed value, were swept away by the amendments of 1889, [Statutes 1889, pp. 159, 160, 163] and likewise by the amendments of 1891, [Statutes 1891, pp. 198, 201] the amendments of 1891 being in this respect similar to the amendments of 1889, and the act as it now reads simply provides that whenever, according to the estimates to be furnished by the city engineer, the total estimated costs and expenses would exceed one-half the total assessed value of the lots and lands assessed, if assessed upon the front-foot plan, etc., the city council *"may"* make the expense chargeable upon a district. There does not, therefore, seem to be any reason why, under the act of 1885, as it now reads, that is, as amended by the amendatory act of 1891, the whole lot may not be taken to pay for the improvement. The legislature has no power to authorize a personal judgment against the person whose property is assessed, [Taylor v. Palmer, 31 Cal. 241] but the whole of the lot itself may be taken to pay for the improvement, if there be no contrary provision in the statute and if the lot may be fairly deemed to be benefited by the improvement. It seems, therefore, that under the act, as it now reads, the council may adopt the district assessment plan, in those cases where, under the front-foot plan, more than half of the assessed value of the lot will have to be taken to pay the expenses of the improvement or, it seems, it may follow the front-foot plan even to the extent of taking all the lots fronting upon the proposed improvement.

A district assessment is void unless every lot within the district, liable to assessment, is included. [People v. Lynch, 51 Cal. 19; Diggins v. Brown, 76 Cal. 318; Davies v. Los Angeles, 86 Cal. 37; Moulton v. Parks, 64 Cal. 181; Dyer v. Harrison, 63 Cal. 447.]

V. *Sewer Construction and District Assessments.* It has recently been held by Judge Wade of the Superior Court of Los Angeles county in the case of White *v.* Harris, on demurrer to complaint, that the front-foot plan of assessment cannot be adopted when the work to be done is sewer construction, but that the mode of payment for sewer construction is that prescribed by section 27 of the act, and must be either by *district assessment* or out of the street contingent fund. In this connection the learned judge says:

"Defendant claims that the mode of payment for sewer construction is that prescribed by section 27, and must be either by *district assessment* or out of the street contingent fund, while plaintiff contends that the council may resort to either of these methods or to that prescribed by section 7, subdivision 1. Assessment 'in proportion to the frontage, at a rate per front foot sufficient to cover the total expense of the work.' The language of section 27 is as follows:

"'Whenever the city council deem it necessary to construct a sewer, then the said council may in its discretion determine to construct said sewer and assess the cost and expenses thereof upon the property to be affected or benefited thereby, in such manner and within such assessment district as it shall prescribe, and the lien therefor upon said property shall be the same as is provided in section nine of this act; or said council may determine to construct said sewer and pay therefor out of the street contingent fund.'

"Plaintiff's contention hinges upon the words 'in its discretion.' If this section stood alone, so far as any reference to sewers is concerned, there could be no doubt whatever that the discretionary authority of the council was limited to the two methods of payment therein mentioned. There are, however, several other references to sewers. Section two mentions sewers, and they are not expressly excepted from the provisions of section seven, as to assessments by frontage. The exceptions are (*1.*) of repairs, etc., on railroad streets; (*2.*) work done and assessments made in districts, and (*3.*) street crossings and street junctions, set out in section seven, subdivisions two to seven, inclusive. It does not seem reasonable that the mention of street work at crossings, or where one street terminates in another street, 'main' streets and 'small or subdivision' streets (whatever those terms may mean) were intended to have reference to the making of sewers. But mention is also made of assessment by districts, in several other places than in section twenty-seven. It is a method of payment not strictly confined to sewer construction.

And yet it is peculiarly adapted to this sort of work. Assessment by frontage would seem to be notably inapt for the purpose of paying the expense of constructing a sewer. The rule would seem to be almost universal that one would have ingress and egress to and from his lot by means of the street in front thereof. The rule is not nearly so uniform that one would discharge his sewage through a conduit laid on the street upon which he fronted. The topography of the ground and many other circumstances might include a particular lot in an assessment district for a sewer laid upon another street, for the reason that the lot 'would be benefited thereby.' The probabilities of such being the case were fully discussed when the demurrer in this case was argued. Taking all the different sections of this difficult statute into consideration, it seems that the correct interpretation of section *twenty-seven* is that the discretion with which the council is there clothed is to choose which of the two methods of securing payment therein mentioned it will adopt. Had it been intended to include the method of assessment by frontage, it would have been so easy for the legislature to have so expressed itself, while the subject of sewers was before it as the chief subject of consideration, that the omission seems significant. The assessment in this case was clearly not made by districts nor was there any district established so far as the pleadings show."

The learned judge says in effect that if it had been the intention of the legislature to include assessments for sewer construction in the method of assessing by frontage, the legislature would have so expressed itself while treating of the subject of sewers in part II of the act. But the act does provide as follows: "The expenses incurred for *any work* authorized by this act   *   *   [Sec. 2 of the act specifies the work which the act authorizes to be done, and includes sewer construction] shall be assessed upon the lots and lands fronting thereon, except as hereinafter *specifically provided*; each lot or portion of a lot being separately assessed, in proportion to the frontage, at a rate per front foot sufficient to cover the total expense of the work." [Section 7, subdivision 1.] And section three of the act expressly recognizes the application to sewer work of the front foot method of assessment. Section three provides that "when the work or improvement proposed to be done is the construction of *sewers*, man-holes, culverts, or cesspools, crosswalks or sidewalks, and curbs, and the objection thereto is signed by the owners of a majority of the *frontage* liable to be assessed for the expense of said work, as aforesaid, the said city council shall, at its next meeting, fix a time for hearing said objections," etc.

The last sentence of subdivision 8 of section 7 likewise recognizes the applicability of the front-foot method of assessment to work of this kind. It provides that "when sewering or resewering is ordered to be done under the sidewalk on only one side of a street for any length thereof, the assessment for its expenses shall be made only upon the lots and lands fronting nearest upon that side," etc.

Part II of the act, which includes section 27, was inserted in the act as it was originally passed, i. e., before the adoption or passage of any subsequent amendatory acts. At that time, section 3 of the act did not, as it does now, give the council authority to adopt the district assessment plan, whenever, in its opinion, the contemplated work or improvement is of more than local or ordinary public benefit, and therefore section 27 was necessary as a specially enabling provision to enable the council to adopt the district assessment plan whenever a sewer was to be constructed. And, as sewer construction is very often a work or improvement of more than local or ordinary public benefit, it follows that some such specially enabling provision was wise and just. See notes to section 27 of the act for a further consideration of this subject.

Section 4. The owners of a majority in frontage of lots and lands fronting on any street, avenue, lane, alley, place or court, or of lots or lands liable to be assessed for the expense of the work petitioned to be done, or their duly authorized agents, may petition the city council to order any of the work mentioned in this act to be done, and the city council may order the work mentioned in said petition to be done, after notice of its intention so to do has been posted and published as provided in section 3 of this act. [*Amendment approved March 31, 1891, statutes 1891, page 199.*]

[Section 4 was amended in 1889 by act of March 14, 1889, statutes '89, p. 160; and again in 1891 by act of March 31, 1891, statutes '91, p. 199.]

Except where the work to be done is the grading of a street, avenue, lane, etc., to a new grade—the old grade having been changed since the amendment of March 11, 1893, to section 2 of the act—the council may, under section 3 of the act, on its own motion, or on petition of *less* than a majority of the frontage, inaugurate proceedings to do any of the work which the act authorizes to be done—the council in that case taking the chances of the proceedings being barred for six months by the filing of "written objections" signed by a majority of the frontage, as provided for by section 3. By section 4 it is provided that the owners of a majority of the frontage, or their duly authorized agents, may inaugurate the pro-

ceedings by filing a petition petitioning the council to order
to be done any of the work mentioned in the act, in which
case the council, if it deems it proper to do so, may order
the work mentioned in such petition to be done. In either
case the object of the law is to make the wishes of the owners of a majority of the frontage, as to certain classes of
work, controlling in the matter. If the proceedings are begun
under section 3 of the act, the owners of a majority of the
frontage may, as to certain classes of work, stop all proceedings by filing written objections. If the proceedings are
begun under section 4 of the act, i. e., inaugurated by a petition signed by a majority of the frontage, the will of the
majority thus expressed is controlling upon the minority if
the council sees fit to order the work to be done. But the
law aims to collect the wishes of the majority once and only
once. Whenever a majority appears either way, there is no
need to collect further the votes of the owners. Therefore,
section 3 provides for written objections when there has
been no sufficient petition, and section 4 provides for .such
a petition without providing for any objections to be filed.
If such objections are filed they are of no avail, and cannot
bar the work. If, after filing the petition provided for by
section 4, some of the owners change their minds, this will
not avail to stop the proceedings.

Judge Shaw, of the Superior Court of Los Angeles county,
in an opinion delivered in the case of Charnock *v.* City of
Los Angeles, passing upon a motion for an injunction, com-
pares these provisions of sections 3 and 4 of the act, and, in
this connection, says: " The proceedings were instituted
under what is known as the Vrooman act, which provides
[here section 4 is quoted in full.] In this proceeding the
initiatory step was a petition to the council signed by a
majority of the owners. Afterwards, and within the time
limited after the passage of the resolution of intention, a
protest, also signed by the owners of a majority of the frontage, was duly delivered to the clerk of the council. This
was signed by some of the persons who had previously
signed the petition, and without their names would not
have had a majority of the frontage.

"It is contended by the defendant that the provisions of
section 3 of the act concerning the protest of a majority of the frontage against the work, and the consequent stay of proceedings for six months, have no application to a proceeding begun by petition under section 4.

"I am of the opinion that this is the correct interpretation
of the act.

EFFECT OF PETITION UNDER SECTION FOUR Sec. 4 as amended
Mar. 31. 1891. 39

"Section 1 of the act invests the city council with jurisdiction to order to be done on the streets any of the work mentioned in section 3 under the proceedings thereinafter prescribed.

"Section 2 gives the council power, of their own motion and without request or petition from any person, to begin the proceedings whenever in their opinion the public interest or convenience may require the work.

"Section 3 outlines the method of procedure in detail. It provides that they shall first pass a resolution of intention to do the work and describe the work therein. Then certain notices are to be given by the street superintendent. At this stage of the case an objection in writing by the owners of one-half or more of the frontage stops the proceedings for six months unless within that time the owners of one-half or more of the frontage shall petition for the same to be done. Each of these may be by one-half only, which is not a majority. This objection is the only means by which the owners of the property can interfere with the proceedings when they are instituted by the council of its own motion. It seems to me that the provision was inserted for the sole purpose of giving the owners of the frontage the power to check the council to the extent of a six months' stay. Without this they would be entirely powerless and the council would have full control. There was, therefore, a good reason for inserting this provision and making it apply to a proceeding begun by the council without petition. *But there is no good reason for making this provision apply to a case begun upon the voluntary petition of the owners of a majority of the frontage asking for the doing of the very work in question.*

"It would appear silly to allow the owners to stop work which is ordered upon their own petition. Such a construction of the act ought not to be made unless the language clearly requires it either expressly or by implication. This it does not do.

"Section 4 prescribes the method of proceeding when the work is ordered on the petition of the owners. In the first place it requires the petition of more than one-half the frontage. *It implies that the petition must describe the work desired to be done,* and the council have no authority under this section to order any other work done. The language is: 'The city council may order the work mentioned in said petition to be done.' Therefore this section gives no authority for other work. In my opinion it calls for the application of the rule: '*Expressio unius est exclusio alterious.*' It declares that the council may order the work to be done "after notice of its intention so to do has been posted as required in section 3 of this act.' *This is the only reference to section 3 and it is the only prerequisite to the ordering of the work. It follows from the application of the rule that the other restrictions of section 3 do not apply.*

"Again, it must be admitted that the legislature in enacting section 4 had some object in view.

"If, however, the theory of the plaintiff is correct, and after the petition under section 4 is filed, all the proceedings mentioned in section 3 are necessary or allowable, then there is no use for section 4. It would be without any force whatever. For the owners have the right of petition without section 4. Now, if, under section 4, the council must pass a resolution of intention, which they could do without the petition, then of what use is the petition? And the council might refuse to pass the resolution. If it did refuse, the petitioners could not force its passage.

"*It is my opinion that the petition mentioned in section 4 is intended to take the place of the resolution of intention required by section 3, and that when the proceeding is begun by the proper petition no resolution of intention is necessary, but the notice of intention must be the intention to do the work mentioned in the petition, and the provisions of section 3 as to stay of proceedings or objections in writing do not apply to proceedings by petition under section 4.*

"This, however, leads to another consideration which is fatal to the proceedings. When the proceeding is by petition the work ordered to be done must correspond in all respects to the work described in the petition. The council in such a proceeding can order to be done only 'the work mentioned in said petition.' [Sec. 4.]"

The foregoing opinion of Judge Shaw shows clearly the relation of sections 3 and 4 of the Vrooman act to each other and to the question of jurisdiction by the council to order the work to be done—a question to which these sections (3 and 4) are mutually related. The opinion also clearly shows the mode which, in the opinion of the learned judge, is provided for by each of said sections for the attainment of such jurisdiction, in the cases to which said sections respectively relate.

The judge is doubtless correct in his conclusion that where the proceeding is inaugurated under the provision of section 4 of the act, by the filing of a petition, it can not be barred by the filing of written objections as provided for by section 3 of the act, even if some of the owners have meanwhile changed their minds so that a majority of the frontage appears on the written objections. But the opinion also declares "the petition mentioned in section 4 is intended to take the place of the resolution of intention required by section 3, and when the proceeding is begun by the proper petition no resolution of intention is necessary, but the notice of intention must be the intention to do the work mentioned in the petition." In so far as the opinion holds that the petition takes the place of a resolution of intention, the learned judge seems to be in error. The mere filing of a petition signed by the owners of a majority of the frontage, while it might be sufficient to cut off all possibility of barring the proceedings by written objections filed thereafter, is not sufficient as notice to the possible minority who have not signed the petition. Every owner whose property is liable to be assessed is entitled to notice of some kind, and if the act does not contain provisions for such notice it is unconstitutional, or if notice is not given to the lot owners in some proper manner his constitutional rights are violated and the proceedings are void. [Lent v. Tillson, 72 Cal. 404; Boorman v. Santa Barbara, 65 Cal. 313.] Judge Shaw's opinion seems to contemplate some sort of notice. But if the act has provided what kind of notice shall be given, when the proceedings are inaugurated under section 4 by the filing of a petition—and if the notice thus provided for by the act includes the passage of a resolution of intention—then a resolution of intention to order to be done the work mentioned in the petition, must be filed, notwithstanding the filing of the petition. The act provides [Sec. 4] that upon filing the petition, the council "may order the work mentioned in said petition to be done, after notice of its intention so to do has been posted and published as provided in section 3 of this act." Section 3 of the act provides that notice of the council's intention to order the work to be done shall be given by two postings and two publications, viz.: *1.* By posting the resolution of intention, and by posting notices of the passage of the resolution of intention, (which notices of passage of the resolution, after stating the fact of the passage of the resolution, and the work proposed, must "refer to the resolution for further particulars;") *2.* By publishing the resolution of intention and by publishing said notices of the passage of the resolution. So that, in order to post and publish notice of its intention to order to be done the work mentioned in the petition, in the manner provided by section 3 of the act, the council must pass a resolution of intention to order said work to be done.

The words "notice of its [the council's] intention so to do" have in all the acts, when used, meant "notice of its

intention só to do, *in the form of a resolution,* describing
the work, and published or posted for a certain time."
Thus the act of 1862, amending San Francisco's consolida-
tion.act, provided that "the board of supervisors may order
any work * * * to be done, after notice of their intention so to do, *in the form of a resolution,* describing the
work, * * * has been published for a period of ten
days." [Statutes 1862 p. 392.] So that it would seem from
the meaning heretofore placed upon the phrase, "notice of
its intention," as well as the context in which it appears in
section 4 of the act, that the true meaning of this section
(section 4) is that "the council may order the work mentioned in said petition to be done, after notice of its intention so to do, *(in the form of a resolution)* has been posted
and published as provided in section 3 of this act."

SECTION 5. Before the awarding of any contract by the city council for
doing any work authorized by this act, the city council shall cause notice,
with specifications, to be posted conspicuously for five days on or near the
council chamber door of said council, inviting sealed proposals or bids for
doing the work ordered, and shall also cause notice of said work inviting
said proposals, and referring to the specifications posted or on file, to be
published for two days in a daily, semi-weekly ,or weekly newspaper published and circulated in said city, designated by the council for that
purpose, and in case there is no newspaper published in said city, then it
shall only be posted as hereinbefore provided. All proposals or bids
offered shall be accompanied by a check payable to the order of the mayor of
the city, certified by a responsible bank, for an amount which shall not be
less than ten per cent. of the aggregate of the proposal, or by a bond for the
said amount and so payable, signed by the bidder and by two sureties,
who shall justify, before any officer competent to administer an oath, in
double the said amount, and over and above all statutory exemptions.
Said proposals or bids shall be delivered to the clerk of the said city
council, and said council shall, in open session, examine and publicly
declare the same; *provided, however,* that no proposal or bid shall be considered unless accompanied by said check or bond satisfactory to the
council. The city council may reject any and all proposals or bids should
it deem this for the public good, and also the bid of any party who has
been delinquent and unfaithful in any former contract with the municipality, and shall reject all proposals or bids other than the lowest regular
proposal or bid of any responsible bidder, and may award the contract for
said work or improvement to the lowest responsible bidder at the prices
named in his bid, which award shall be approved by the mayor, or a three-
fourths vote of the city council. If not approved by him, or a three-fourths
vote of the city council, without further proceedings, the city council may
readvertise for proposals or bids for the performance of the work as in the
first instance, and thereafter proceed in the manner in this section provided, and shall thereupon return to the proper parties the respective
checks snd bonds corresponding to the bid so rejected. But the checks
accompanying such accepted proposals or bids shall be held by the city

clerk of said city until the contract for doing said work, as hereinafter provided, has been entered into, either by said lowest bidder or by the owners of three-fourths part of the frontage, whereupon said certified check shall be returned to said bidder. But if said bidder fails, neglects, or refuses to enter into the contract to perform said work or improvement, as hereinafter provided, then the certified check accompanying his bid and the amount therein mentioned, shall be declared to be forfeited to said city, and shall be collected by it, and paid into its fund for repairs of streets; and any bond forfeited may be prosecuted, and the amount due thereon collected and paid into said fund. Notice of such awards of contract shall be posted for five days, in the same manner as hereinbefore provided for the posting of proposals for said work, and shall be published for two days in a daily newspaper published and circulated in said city, and designated by said city council, or in cities where there is no daily newspaper, by one insertion in a semi-weekly or weekly newspaper so published, circulated and designated; *provided, however*, that in case there is no newspaper printed or published in any such city, then such notice of award shall only be kept posted as hereinbefore provided. The owners of three-fourths of the frontage of lots and lands upon the street whereon said work is to be done, or their agents, and who shall make oath that they are such owners or agents, shall not be required to present sealed proposals or bids, but may, within ten days after the first posting and publication of said notice of said award, elect to take said work and enter into a written contract to do the whole work at the price at which the same has been awarded. Should the said owners fail to elect to take said work, and to enter into a written contract therefor within ten days, or to commence the work within fifteen days after the first posting and publication of said award, and to prosecute the same with diligence to completion, it shall be the duty of the superintendent of streets to enter into a contract with the original bidder to whom the contract was awarded, and at the prices specified in his bid. But if such original bidder neglects, fails or refuses, for fifteen days after the first posting and publication of the notice of award, to enter into the contract, then the city council, without further proceedings, shall again advertise for proposals or bids as in the first instance, and award the contract for the said work to the then lowest regular bidder. The bids of all persons and the election of all owners as aforesaid, who have failed to enter into the contract as herein provided, shall be rejected in any bidding or election subsequent to the first for the same work. If the owner or contractor who may have taken any contract, do not complete the same within the time limited in the contract, or within such further time as the city council may give them, the superintendent of streets shall report such delinquency to the city council, which may relet the unfinished portion of said work, after pursuing the formalities prescribed hereinbefore for the letting of the whole in the first instance. All contractors, contracting owners included, shall, at the time of executing any contract for street work, execute a bond to the satisfaction and approval of the superintendent of streets of said city, with two or more sureties and payable to such city, in such sums as the mayor shall deem adequate, conditioned for the faithful performance of the contract; and the sureties shall justify before any person competent to administer an oath, in double the amount mentioned in said bond, over and above all statutory exemptions. Before being entitled to a contract, the bidder to whom the award was made, or the owners who have elected to take the contract, must advance to the superintendent of streets, for payment by him, the cost of publication of the notices, resolutions, orders, or other incidental expenses and matters required under the proceedings prescribed in this act, and such other notices as may be deemed requisite by the city council. And in case the work is abandoned by the city before the letting of the contract, the incidental expenses incurred previous to such abandonment shall be paid out of the city treasury. [*Amendment approved March 31, 1891, statutes 1891, page 199.*]

[Section 5 was amended in 1889, by act of March 14, 1889, statutes 1889, p. 160, and again in 1891 by act of March 31, 1891, statutes, 1891, p. 199.]

As stated in the notes to section three, there are, ordinarily, at least ten things essential to the acquisition of jurisdiction or power to execute a valid contract under which the property of the lot owner will be liable, including the execution of the contract itself. [*Pages 18–19, supra.*] Five of these jurisdictional prerequisites, viz: (*1.*) Passage of resolution of intention; (*2.*) posting and publication of resolution; (*3.*) posting and publication of notices of passage of the resolution; (*4.*) passage of order for the work to be done, and (*5.*) publication of order for the work to be done or resolution of construction—are considered in the notes under section 3, *supra.* The remaining five jurisdictional prerequisites to the existence of a valid contract are provided for by section 5 of the act. They are: (*1.*) Posting and publication of notices inviting sealed proposals; (*2.*) consideration of bids; (*3.*) award of contract; (*4.*) posting and publication of notice of award of contracts, and (*5.*) execution of written contract by superintendent of streets.

1. Posting and Publication of Notices Inviting Sealed Proposals. Notices inviting sealed proposals must be both posted and published.

(a.) Posting Notices Inviting Proposals. The act provides [Sec. 5] that notices inviting sealed proposals for doing the work ordered to be done shall be posted conspicuously for five days on or near the council chamber door; that the *city council shall cause* such notices to be posted, and that the *"specifications"* shall be posted along with such posted notices. The section provides that the *council shall cause* the notices to be posted. From which it would seem that the posting is not sufficient unless the council passes an order or resolution directing the notices inviting sealed proposals to be posted by the clerk or by the superintendent of streets, or by some one under their authority. This direction may be contained in a separate and independent order or in the resolution of construction or order for the

work to be done. Thus, in Shepard v. Colton, 44 Cal. 628, the resolution of construction, or order for the work to be done, after resolving that the work be done, contained a provision, as follows: "And the clerk is hereby authorized to advertise for proposals to do the above work." *Held*, that the resolution directing or authorizing the clerk to "advertise" for proposals was sufficient authority to the clerk to advertise for proposals in the mode provided by law—that it authorized him to post the notice as well as to publish it. This case holds that the use of the word "advertise" was sufficient authority to the clerk to both post and publish the notice. At the same time it seems to be assumed that the posting or publishing by the clerk would not be sufficient unless there was some kind of order or direction to him from the council to do so. [See also opinion of Temple J. in Chambers v. Satterlee, 40 Cal. 521–522; Hewes v. Reis, 40 Cal. 255.]

In Meuser v. Risdon, 36 Cal. 239, it was held that where the contractor fails to perform the work, and it becomes necessary to relet the contract the same course must be pursued in reletting which is prescribed in the first instance after the order to do the work is made and published; *that in the first instance the clerk has no authority independent of an order of the board therefor to give the notice inviting sealed proposals;* and, therefore, in case of such reletting, he has no such power independent of such order, and if there be no such order the second contract made after such attempted reletting is void; also that each proceeding to improve a street is a separate and independent proceeding and must stand or fall by itself, and that, therefore, authority cannot be conferred upon the clerk to post notices by a general resolution directing him in all cases where the contractors fail to perform to re-advertise for proposals. [See also Donnelly v. Tillman, 47 Cal. 40; Donnelly v. Marks, 47 Cal. 187.]

The posting of the notice inviting sealed proposals in the manner required by the law is one of the necessary, indispensable jurisdictional prerequisites, and if not posted for the time required by law, the contract and all subsequent proceedings are void. [Hewes v. Reis, 40 Cal. 255.]

The order of the council authorizing the clerk to advertise for proposals to do street work is sufficient, although it does not mention *"sealed"* proposals, nor specify the time or place of giving notice. [Himmelman v. Byrne, 41 Cal. 500.]

When the statute directs a notice to be posted in the office of any official, as, for example, in the office of the superintendent of streets, for a certain number of days, it must be posted in such office and kept posted for each one of such days during the whole time during which the office is by law to be kept open. That is, in such case the days during which the notice is to be posted are "official" days. Thus, in Himmelmann v. Cahn, 49 Cal. 285, the law required the notice inviting sealed proposals to be posted in the office of the superintendent of streets for five days, and it was held that it must be posted before the commencement of the first official day, that is, before 9 o'clock A. M., when by statute the office was to be opened, and remain posted during the whole of the first, second, third, fourth and until 4 o'clock of the fifth day, at which hour the statute authorized the office to be closed. [Brooks v. Satterlee, 49 Cal. 289.]

If a resolution to "grade" a street is properly passed, posted and published, and the notice inviting sealed proposals is "for grading" the street, and refers to the resolution, it will not vitiate the notice, if, as explanatory, it also informs bidders that the street is to be "regraded." [Brady v. Feisel, 53 Cal. 49.]

The act provides that "specifications" must be posted along with the posted notice, and also that the published notice shall refer to "the specifications posted or on file." If the city engineer has previously prepared specifications, but has done so without authority or order from the council directing them to be made, the subsequent passage of a resolution directing the clerk to post and publish the notices inviting proposals, to be done "in accordance with the plans and specifications now on file in the office of the city clerk," is tantamount to a prior direction to the city engineer to make the specifications, and will be sufficient. [Stockton v. Skinner, 53 Cal. 85.]

(b.) Publishing Notices Inviting Proposals. The act provides [Sec. 5] not only for posting the notice inviting sealed proposals, but that the council "shall also cause notice of said work, inviting said proposals, and referring to the specifications posted or on file, to be published for two days in a daily, semi-weekly or weekly newspaper published and circulated in said city, designated by the council for that purpose, and in case there is no newspaper published in said city, then it shall only be posted as hereinbefore provided."

Many of the notes and citations relative to the publication of the resolution of intention, of notice of the passage of the same, publication of the order to do the work, and likewise the notes and citations relative to posting the notices inviting sealed proposals, are applicable here. For example, the citations relative to the questions:—"What is a 'daily' newspaper?"—"Must there be an order directing the publication?" etc. And, therefore, these notes and citations should be read in this connection.

If the published notice inviting sealed proposals does not refer to the specifications posted or on file, the proceedings are invalid. [Stockton v. Clark, 53 Cal. 82.]

The act requires the notices inviting proposals to perform the work to be posted for five days and published for two days. Judge Shaw of the Superior Court of Los Angeles county recently held, in the case of May v. Lyons, that the publication and the posting of the notices must be contemporaneous in point of commencement. The act provides that the published notice shall refer to the specifications on file or to the copy posted along with the posted notice, and, therefore, when the notice is published there must be a notice posted with specifications, to which the published notice may refer. The opinion of the learned judge in that case upon this point is in substance as follows:

"One objection to the validity of the lien was that the publication of the notice calling for proposals to perform the work was not made at the proper time. In this case the notice, with specifications, was posted on the 19th day of August, 1889, and kept standing until the 23rd of the same month, both days included, and the notice of such posting was published on the 24th and 25th of August. The defendant insisted that the notice of posting should be contemporaneous with the posting itself, while the plaintiff contended that the notice must be of a posting that is complete, and that, therefore, the publication of the notice must not begin until after the specifications have been posted five days.

"The object of the proceedings required by the statute was evidently to publish as widely as possible the fact that bids for the proposed work were to be received, and that the specifications could be seen on file and also posted at the council chamber door. The specifications were to be posted so as to make them easy of access, and at the same time the original copy was to be seen on file. It was a necessary implication that there were to be two copies. It was intended that those who read the published notice might have time afterward to consult the specifications on file or those posted, as might be most convenient. It followed that a publication of the notice after the posting was completed and the specifications removed was not a compliance with the statute. In a case construing a statute similar to this it had been held that any failure to make the publication as required rendered all subsequent proceedings void, including the assessment. It follows, therefore, that the assessment which the plaintiff sought to foreclose was void."

2. Consideration by Council of Proposals or Bids. The seventh jurisdictional prerequisite, according to the division adopted in the notes to section 3 [page 18 *supra*], is the consideration by the council of the proposals or bids put in by the bidders in response to the posted and published notices inviting proposals.

All proposals or bids must be accompanied by a certified check for not less than ten per cent. of the aggregate of the proposal, or by a bond therefor. After all the proposals or bids are delivered to the clerk within the time provided by the notices inviting the same, the council, in open session, examines and publicly declares the same. The council may reject any and all bids, and advertise for bids over again, and must reject all but the lowest regular proposal or bid of any responsible bidder. If it is satisfied to accept the lowest regular responsible bid, it may thereupon award the contract to such lowest responsible bidder at the prices named in his bid, returning to the other bidders their checks or bonds as provided by the act.

3. Award of Contract. The eighth jurisdictional prerequisite is the awarding of the contract. The council must award the contract for the proposed work or improvement to the lowest regular and responsible bidder at the prices named in his bid. This it may do by an order or resolution to that effect. See Dougherty *v.* Hitchcock, 35 Cal. 517, for form of a "resolution of award." The resolution, order or ordinance of award is the authority of the superintendent of streets to enter into and execute the contract. [Dougherty *v.* Hitchcock, *supra.*] The award, if made by less than a three-fourths vote of the city council—as, if made by a bare majority of a quorum, for example—must be approved by the mayor, if made by a three-fourths vote of the whole council, it need not receive the mayor's approval. [McDonald *v.* Dodge, 97 Cal. 112.]

4. Posting and Publishing Notice of Award. The ninth jurisdictional prerequisite to the existence of a valid contract is the posting and publishing of a notice that the contract has been awarded. Notice of the award of the contract must be posted for five days and published for two days.

(a.) Posting Notice of Award. Notice of the award of the contract to the lowest regular and responsible bidder

must be posted for five days in the same manner as notices inviting proposals are directed to be posted, viz., conspicuously for five days on or near the council chamber door of the city council.

(b.) Publishing Notice of Award. Notice of award must likewise be published for two days in a daily newspaper published and circulated in said city and *designated* by the city council, or in cities where there is no daily newspaper, by one insertion in a semi-weekly or weekly newspaper so published, circulated and *designated.* If there is no such daily, semi-weekly or weekly newspaper, then the notice need not be published, but must be posted and kept posted as above provided.

The council must pass a resolution or order directing notice of the resolution of award to be posted and published, or else all proceedings, subsequent to the resolution of award, will be void.

In Donnelly *v.* Tillman, 47 Cal. 40, the court held that the board of supervisors of the city and county of San Francisco must make an order that the notice of the award of the contract for improving a street be published. A publication of the notice without such order is void. The court in that case said: "The plaintiff claims that this duty [publication of notice of award] is incumbent on the superintendent of streets, and the defendant claims that it devolves on the board of supervisors. The power to improve the streets is granted to the board, and authority is given to it to institute and conduct the proceedings in the cases where the law requires a contract for the doing of the work. The board makes all orders up to and including the award of the contract to the successful bidder, and in most respects it has control or supervision of all subsequent proceedings. The statute declares that at a certain stage in the proceedings the board shall be deemed to have acquired jurisdiction to order the proposed work to be done. These provisions lead to the conclusion that it is the intention of the statute that the board should have all authority in respect to the improvement of streets, which is granted by the statute, but which is not conferred *expressly or by necessary implication* upon some of the officers mentioned in the statute, and not as contended by plaintiff, that the statute grants such residuary authority to the superintendent of streets." [See also Donnelly *v.* Marks, 47 Cal. 187; Shepard *v.* Colton, 44 Cal. 628; Himmelmann *v.* Townsend, 49 Cal. 150; Himmelmann *v.* Satterlee, 49 Cal. 387; Reis *v.* Graff, 51 Cal. 86.]

5. Execution of the Contract by the Superintendent of Streets. The tenth and last act necessary to the existence of a valid contract, under which the contractor may proceed to do the work, is the execution of the formal written contract by the superintendent of streets.

For some purposes, and in some respects, the contract is complete when the council accepts the contractor's bid and awards the contract, although it is subject to the right of the property owners to come in and elect to take the work and enter into a contract therefor themselves. The drawing up of a formal written contract, specific in its terms, executed by the superintendent on behalf of the city, is a formal reduction to writing of the contract made by the acceptance of the contractor's proposals. In Chambers v. Satterlee, 40 Cal. 526, Judge Temple said: "The agreement is complete when the bid is accepted, and it is the contract made by the board [council] which the superintendent is required to reduce to writing." [See also Argentia v. San Francisco, 16 Cal. 256, 280.] Nevertheless, in order to make the property of the lot owners liable under an assessment to pay for the work, a formal written contract duly authorized by the act, and executed according to its requirements, is indispensable. In other words, the agreement called into existence by the acceptance of the contractor's proposals, or bid, must be formally reduced to writing and signed by the superintendent of streets before the property of the lot owners can be held liable. [Dougherty v. Hitchcock, 35 Cal. 512.]

Under the act the owners of three-fourths of the frontage have ten days after the first posting and publication of the notice of award, within which to elect to take the work themselves, at the price at which the same has been awarded, and enter into a written contract therefor. If the said owners fail to elect to take said work, or, if after entering into a contract to do so, they fail to commence the work within fifteen days after the first posting and publishing of notice of the award, and to prosecute the same with diligence, it becomes the duty of the superintendent of streets to enter into and execute a contract with the original bidder to whom the contract was awarded and at the prices specified in his bid.

Section 6 of the act (*post*) specifically authorizes the superintendent of streets to make all written contracts, and provides that the contract shall contain certain provisions, viz: (*1.*) The contract shall fix the time for the commencement of the work, which shall not be less than fifteen days from the date of the contract, and for the completion. (*2.*) A proviso to the effect that the work must be done under the direction and to the satisfaction of the superintendent of streets. *(3.)* Likewise that the materials shall comply with the specifications and be to the satisfaction of the superintendent of streets, and *(4.)* Express notice that in no case, except where it is otherwise provided by said act, will the city, or any officer thereof, be liable for any portion of the expense, nor for any delinquency of persons or property assessed.

The resolution of award, or order awarding the contract, is the letter of authority to the superintendent, and the contract executed by him must be such as is authorized by the resolution of award and no other. [Dougherty *v.* Hitchcock, 35 Cal. 512; Brock *v.* Luning, 89 Cal. 316.]

The act [Section 5], in addition to the execution of the formal written contract by the superintendent of streets, provides that all contractors, including contracting owners, shall, at the time of executing any contract for street work, execute a bond to the satisfaction and approval of the superintendent of streets, conditioned for the faithful performance of the contract. But while the due execution of the formal written contract is jurisdictional, it seems that the execution of such accompanying bond is not. In Miller *v.* Mayo, 88 Cal. 568, it was held that "a failure to execute a bond that should be satisfactory to the superintendent of streets might be a sufficient reason for the superintendent to refuse to enter into the contract with the contractor but after the work has been completed to the satisfaction of the superintendent of streets the property owner can not object to the correctness of the assessment by reason of the omission on the part of the superintendent to approve the bond of the contractor."

The superintendent has no power or jurisdiction to enter into a contract at any time prior to the expiration of the time within which the property owners may take the contract, *i. e.,* within ten days after the first posting and publication of the notice of award, and if the superintendent does execute the contract within that time, it, and all proceedings following, are void, and do not become valid by reason of a failure to appeal. [Burke *v.* Turney, 54 Cal. 486; Manning *v.* Den, 90 Cal. 610.] Not only is a contract entered into prematurely, *i. e.,* prior to the expiration of ten days after the first posting and publishing of the notice of award, void, but likewise, a contract is void which is not entered into within the time prescribed by the statute, which, according to the express provision of the act, is fifteen days after the first posting and publication of the notice of award, and a failure to appeal does not cure the defect. [Perine v. Forbush, 97 Cal. 305.]

The successful bidder may by power of attorney, authorize another person to enter into the contract with the superintendent. [McVerry v. Boyd, 89 Cal. 304.]

Contents of Contract. The contract must contain a provision fixing the time for the commencement of the work, which shall not be less than fifteen days from the date of the contract, and also for its completion. [Section 6 of the act.] If the contract does not contain such a provision it is void. [Libby v. Ellsworth, 97 Cal. 316; Washburn v. Lyons, 97 Cal. 314.] The same result would follow if either of the other three things required by section 6 of the act were omitted from the contract, that is to say, the contract must, in addition to a provision fixing the time for the commencement of the work, and for the completion, likewise contain the following provisions, viz.: *(1.)* A provision to the effect that the work shall be done under the direction and to the satisfaction of the superintendent of streets; *(2.)* that the materials used shall comply with the specifications and be to the satisfaction of the superintendent of streets, and *(3.)* that in no case except where it is otherwise provided by the act, will the city or any officer thereof, be liable for any portion of the expense, nor for any delinquency of persons or property assessed. If the contract does not contain these provisions, it, and all subsequent proceedings, are void.

If specifications made by the superintendent of streets are annexed to the contract, and the contract refers to the specifications so as to make them a part thereof, and the specifications state what kind of material shall be used—in this case "Goat island rock," for macadamizing purposes—this is a sufficient compliance with the requirement that the contract shall contain a provision to the effect that the materials used shall "be to the satisfaction of the superintendent of streets," etc. [Emery v. S. F. Gas Co., 28 Cal. 346, 347, 377; Taylor v. Palmer, 31 Cal. 240.] In this latter case the court said: "It is next claimed that the contract in suit * * is invalid, because it does not contain the condition—*made essential by the statute*—that 'the materials used shall be such as are required by the superintendent of streets.' The objection is without substantial foundation. The contract may not follow the precise language of the statute. It is not necessary that it should. If it can be held to contain the condition in question by a fair and reasonable construction, the call of the statute is fully answered."

If the council, in the advertisement for proposals or bids, calls for a patented article for doing the street work in question—as, to pave a street with Nicolson pavement, for example—and awards a contract therefor to one who owned the exclusive right to put down such pavement in the city, the award, and the written contract made in pursuance thereof, are void. The reason is that the council has no power, in making street improvements, to do any kind of work which for any reason cannot be let or contracted for in the mode prescribed in the statute, or which the owners of the frontage are legally prohibited from performing. In such a case there could be no letting to the "lowest bidder," since there could be but one bidder who would enjoy a monopoly. All persons, other than the owner of the patent, would be precluded from bidding. [Nicolson Pavement Co. v. Painter, 35 Cal. 699; Nicolson Pavement Co. v. Fay, 35 Cal. 695.]

Where, however, the advertisement for proposals, the award and the contract, are all silent as to the use of patented materials—neither requiring nor prohibiting the use of the same—and the contractor, in performing his contract, uses patented materials, the mere use of such materials by the contractor will not vitiate the assessment, where the superintendent of streets certifies that the work was properly done. [Dunne v. Altschul, 57 Cal. 472. See subdivision 6 of section 34 of the act.]

The council has jurisdiction or power to contract only for such street work as is named in the resolution of intention, and the contract should be for the exact work named in the resolution of intention—no more and no less. However, if the contract includes *more* work than is mentioned in the resolution of intention, the result may be different from what it would be if the contract were for *less* work than that mentioned in the resolution.

In the former case, *i. e.*, where the contract includes *more* work than is named in the resolution, the right of the contractor to recover depends upon whether the contract is severable or not.

If the contract includes work not named in the resolution the right of the contractor to recover, in that case, depends upon whether the work named in the resolution and in the contract therefor, can be separated from the work included in the contract but not named in the resolution. Thus, if the resolution of intention declares only an intention to macadamize a street, and the contract should include curbing as well as macadamizing, the contractor may, nevertheless, recover for the macadamizing, if it can be separated from the curbing so that the cost of macadamizing, according to the contract price of the same, can

be separated from the cost of the curbing. The only
remedy of the property owner is by appeal to the council.
[Baudry v. Valdez, 32 Cal. 269; Dyer v. Scalmanini, 69 Cal.
637.]

So, also, if the resolution of intention includes two or
more kinds of work, and the contract follows the resolution
in this respect, and as to one of the kinds of work ordered
the council never acquired jurisdiction, the contract is still
valid as to the work properly included in the resolution of
intention. Thus under the act of 1872, a petition was
necessary to empower the board of supervisors to order
grading, but was not necessary to empower the board to
order macadamizing; nevertheless, if both be ordered in one
resolution of intention, without any petition being filed, the
contract for macadamizing is valid, though void as to the
grading. [Gafney v. San Francisco, 72 Cal. 146, 151.]

The assessment and demand, however, must be for the
amount recoverable. [Dorland v. Bergson, 78 Cal. 637;
Chambers v. Satterlee, 40 Cal. 497; Dyer v. Chase, 52 Cal.
440; Donnelly v. Howard, 60 Cal. 291.] On the other hand
the contractor cannot recover at all if the work named in
the resolution of intention, and the cost thereof cannot
be separated from that which is not mentioned in the resolution. The contract is void as to the work not mentioned
in the resolution, because as to this work the council never
acquired jurisdiction to order it to be done, and if the contract is not severable, the whole must fall. [Himmelmann
v. Satterlee, 50 Cal. 68; Nicolson Pavement Co. v. Fay, 35
Cal. 695; Dorland v. Bergson, 78 Cal. 637; City of Stockton
v. Creanor, 45 Cal. 643; Partridge v. Lucas, decided Sept.
11, 1893.]

While the contractor may recover, notwithstanding the
fact that the contract calls for *more* work than the resolution of intention authorizes, provided the contract be severable, the converse of the proposition is not true. That is
to say, if the contract calls for *less* work than that
named in the resolution of intention, it is void and there
can be no recovery under it. [City of Stockton v. Whit-
more, 50 Cal. 554; McBean v. Redick, 96 Cal. 191; Dougherty v. Hitchcock, 35 Cal. 512.]

The written contract must follow the award, and if it
grants more time for the completion of the work than is
specified in the award, it is not the contract the superintendent is authorized to execute, and is, therefore, void.
[Brock v. Luning, 89 Cal. 316.]

The contract will not be invalidated if it contain a
provision to the effect that there shall be no assessment on

the adjoining property for improving that part of the street occupied by a street railway company, but that the company shall pay therefor. [Perine v. Forbush, 97 Cal. 305.]

A clause in a contract to the effect that the contractor shall keep the street in repair for five years imposes an additional burden on the property owner, not authorized by the statute, and the contract and assessment under it are void. It matters not that the testimony of the contractor shows that this clause did not enhance the amount of his bid, as others might have bid a less amount if the contract had not contained such requirement. [Brown v. Jenks, decided by our Supreme Court, March 27, 1893, 32 Pac. Rep. 701.]

Fraud on the Part of the Contractor in Entering into the Contract. If the contractor, before the contract is awarded, combines and confederates with a portion of the property owners, and, for the purpose of inducing those with whom he thus combines to sign a petition asking the council to do the work, he enters into a private side agreement with these property owners, agreeing to charge them less for their portion of the cost of the work than the other property owners, this side agreement is a fraud upon the property owners not confederating with the contractor. It was held in Nolan v. Reese, 32 Cal. 484, that, notwithstanding the fact that this side agreement was a fraud in law, the defrauded property owners could not set it up as a defense to an action by the contractor upon the assessment, because the act then in existence—the act of 1862, statutes 1862, page 391 *et seq.*—did not admit such a defense, and that the property owner's only remedy was by appeal to the council. [Chambers v. Satterlee, 40 Cal. 520; Himmelmann v. Hoadley, 44 Cal. 213.]

In the case of Brady v. Bartlett, 56 Cal. 350, however, it was held that under the 13th section of the act of 1872 [Statutes 1871-2, p. 817], this defense could be set up by the property owner, and in that case it was held that such fraudulent side agreement invalidated the contract with the city, and also the assessment made thereunder. This act of 1872 expressly provided that "fraud in the assessment or in any of the acts or proceedings prior thereto" might be set up in defense to the action. [Statutes 1871-2, p. 817.] Section 12 of the Vrooman act is the section which corresponds to section 13 of this act of 1872. [See section 12 of the Act, *post.*] Section 12 of the Vrooman act does not expressly provide for such a defense, and it is probable, unless there be some provision overlooked by the author, that the doctrine of Nolan *v.* Reese, 32 Cal. 484, will be followed by the courts in actions arising under the Vrooman act, if such a defense is interposed to an action upon an assessment for work done under the Vrooman act. By section 11 of the Act it is provided that "no assessment shall be held invalid, except upon appeal to the city council, as provided by this section, for any error, informality or other defect in any of the proceedings prior to the assessment, or in the assessment itself, when notice of the intention of the council to order the work to be done, for which the assessment is made, has been actually published in any designated newspaper of said city for the length of time prescribed by law, before the passage of the resolution ordering the work to be done." This language is, in itself, broad enough to shut out all inquiry (except upon appeal to the council) into the performance of the jurisdictional prerequisites to be performed subsequent to the publication of notice of intention to order the work to be done. But, as held in Manning *v.* Den, 90 Cal. 610, the property owner does not, by failing to appeal to the council, waive the right to resist payment of an assessment when there has been a failure to perform any one of the jurisdictional prerequisites in the manner provided for by the statute, as, for example, where the superintendent of streets and the contractor have executed the contract prematurely or have neglected to enter into and execute the written contract within the time required by the statute. But this ruling does not prevent a failure to appeal from operating as a waiver of the right to collaterally attack the contract or assessment because of some error, informality or other defect in the proceedings, not amounting to a failure to perform a jurisdictional prerequisite, and it appears from the decision in Nolan *v.* Reese that a fraudulent side agreement is an informality or defect which does not effect the jurisdiction or power of the city authorities.

The ten necessary jurisdictional prerequisites to the existence of a valid contract, under which the contractor may recover upon assessments for work performed, have now been considered in the notes to the above section of the act [Sec. 5] and in the notes to section 3. They are: (*1.*) Passage of resolution of intention; (*2.*) posting and publication of resolution of intention; (*3.*) posting and publication of notices of passage of the resolution of intention; (*4.*) passage of resolution of construction or order that the work be done; (*5.*) publication of order to do the work (these five jurisdictional prerequisites are provided for by section 3 of the act); (*6.*) publication and posting

of notices inviting sealed proposals; (*7.*) consideration of
the bids by the council; (*8.*) award of the contract; (*9.*)
publication and posting of notices of award of contract;
(*10.*) execution of written contract by the superintendent
of streets. [See *supra*, pp. 18–19.]

6. *Other requirements of Section 5.* Section 5 of the act likewise provides for certain other requirements, some of
which must be complied with if occasion gives rise to
them, *e. g.*, the re-advertisement for bids, etc., while
others are a part of the procedure attending the regular
performance of the jurisdictional requirements. These
requirements are:

(*1.*) Proposals must be accompanied by a certified check
or bond, and "no proposal or bid shall be considered unless
accompanied by said check or bond satisfactory to the
council."

(*2.*) *Re-advertisement for Proposals or Bids.* There are three
cases in which it might become necessary to re-advertise for
bids, viz:

(*a.*) The council may reject any and all proposals, should
it deem this for the public good, and also the bid of any
party who has been delinquent and unfaithful in any former
contract with the municipality. Should the council thus
reject all proposals or bids, it may re-advertise for bids.

(*b.*) A majority of the council, less than three-fourths,
may vote to award the contract to a bidder, but the mayor
may not approve the award; in such case, the award not
being approved by the mayor or a three-fourths vote of the
council, the council, without further proceedings, may re-advertise for proposals or bids, as in the first instance.

(*c.*) If an original bidder to whom the contract was duly
awarded in the first instance neglects, fails or refuses, for
fifteen days after the first posting and publication of the
notice of award, to enter into the contract, the council, without further proceedings, may again advertise for proposals
or bids, as in the first instance, and award the contract to
the lowest bidder.

The contractor, or the owners who have themselves taken
the contract, might not complete the same within the time limited in the contract, or within such further time as the city
council may have given them. In such case, after the
superintendent of streets has reported such delinquency to
the council, the council " may relet the unfinished portion
of such work, after pursuing the formalities prescribed
hereinbefore for the letting of the whole in the first
instance." In such case, *i. e.*, where the contractor by failing
to complete his contract within the proper time has left a

portion of the work unfinished, the council does not re-advertise for bids, or relet the contract, as in the three cases
above enumerated, but commences original proceedings, *de
novo*, and relets such unfinished portion only "after pursuing the formalities prescribed hereinbefore for the letting
of the whole in the first instance." The portion thus left
unfinished is not the same work as that described in the
original resolution of intention and the notices subsequent
thereto. It is a smaller part of the work originally proposed
to be done, and therefore, as such unfinished work is not
the same work originally described in the resolution of
intention, it would seem but reasonable to require entirely
new proceedings, *de capo*, to be begun.

Furthermore, the portion of the work thus left unfinished
is not the work which the council, in the first instance,
ordered to be done. It is true that if, after the council has ordered certain work to be done, no valid
contract therefor is let, or, if being let, the contract
is not performed at all, the council may proceed to
re-advertise for bids and relet the contract without taking steps to acquire jurisdiction as in the first instance.
The order to do the work is in the nature of a judgment
[Dougherty *v.* Foley, 32 Cal. 403], and the subsequent proceedings are ministerial in their character and for the purpose of carrying this order or *quasi* judgment into effect.
In such case there is a valid subsisting order for the work
which may be made the foundation for a subsequent contract to do the work described in the order and ordered to
be done. But where a contract has been duly let and the
work partly performed and left unfinished, there is then no
order for doing that particular work which constitutes such
unfinished portion, and to bring into existence a valid
order upon which a contract for doing this unfinished portion may be based, it seems to be necessary for the council
to commence entirely new proceedings *de capo* so as to
acquire jurisdiction to make an order to do such unfinished
portion, in order that the contract may follow the order and
be a contract for the performance of the particular work
thus ordered to be done.

Procedure on Re-advertising and Reletting Contract. If,
after the contract has been let and entered into, but before
any portion of the work has been done, the contractor fails
to enter upon the performance of the work within the
time fixed in his contract to perform, the council may
re-advertise for bids and relet the contract without taking
steps to acquire jurisdiction as in the first instance. And
this, even though there should be no express provision of

the statute authorizing re-advertising and reletting in such case. [Dougherty *v.* Foley, 32 Cal. 403.] In this case the court, per Shafter, J., said: "The board having acquired jurisdiction in the manner pointed out in the fourth section of the act of 1862 [statutes 1862, p. 392], ordered the work to be done. This order was in the nature of a judgment. The subsequent steps were ministerial in their character. They were taken for the purpose of carrying the order into execution. The failure of the contractor to perform his contract could not on any known principle affect the validity nor impair the efficiency of the order. If the contract had been kept, the order would have been *functus officio*; but as it was not kept the requirement that the 'work should be done' stood unexecuted, and as mandatory as ever. * * * The work having been ordered, the process of doing it was by contract. When the contract failed by the bad faith of the man who made it, *the case stood as it would if no contract had ever been made*, and the statute process could be repeated upon the unexecuted order." [See also Himmelmann *v.* Oliver, 34 Cal. 246.]

If the contractor, or the owners who take the contract, fail to perform any part of it, and the council re-advertises for proposals, and relets the contract, or if in any case where it is proper, proposals are re-advertised for, the same course must be pursued which is prescribed in the first instance for letting the contract, in so far as the proceedings subsequent to the order for doing the work are concerned. Therefore, as in the first instance, it is necessary that the council should pass a resolution or order directing the clerk to post and publish the notices inviting proposals, it follows that if, in re-advertising for sealed proposals, the clerk posts and publishes such notices without a resolution or order by the council therefor, the posting and publishing are insufficient and the proceedings are therefore void. [Meuser *v.* Risdon, 36 Cal. 239.]

(3.) Lot Owners Taking Contract. The owners of three-fourths of the frontage, or their agents, who shall make oath that they are such owners or agents, may, without presenting sealed proposals or bids, and within ten days after the first posting and publication of the notice of the award of the contract to the successful bidder, elect to take the work and enter into a contract to do it at the same price at which it was awarded.

(4.) Bond Accompanying Contract. All contractors, contracting owners included are, by the act, required to give a bond, at the time of executing the contract, conditioned for

the faithful performance of the contract, the bond to be to the satisfaction and approval of the superintendent of streets.

It was held in Miller *v.* Mayo, 88 Cal. 568, that the property owner, in an action to foreclose a lien for street assessment can not object to the correctness of the assessment by reason of the omission of the superintendent of streets to approve the bond of the contractor.

7. *Assignment of Contract.* A contract to perform street work may be assigned, and the contract may be fulfilled by the assignee, who can enforce the same. [Taylor *v.* Palmer, 31 Cal. 241.] These street work contracts do not belong to that class of contracts which the party who is to perform the stipulated work is not permitted to assign by reason of the trust and confidence reposed in his skill and ability by the other contracting party. [*Id.*]

Where a contract is thus assigned and the assignee does the work, the warrant running to the original contractor, his agents or assigns, may be issued and delivered to the original contractor, and the demand for payment may be made by him. In such case the original contractor acts as the agent of his assignee. [*Id.*]

If a lot owner takes the contract and then assigns it to some one else, who performs the contract, the assignee may sue his assignor—the lot owner and original contractor—for the assessment against his lot, and it cannot be objected that the lot owner, as contractor, cannot sue himself as lot owner upon a contract made with himself, and that therefore his assignee cannot sue him. The reason is that the contractor or his assignee does not sue upon the contract, but takes the place of the city in suing to recover the tax levied or assessed upon the lots to pay for the improvement. A triangular relation exists between the city, the contractor and the lot owner. The city government and the contractor are the only parties to the proceeding so far as making the improvement is concerned. The adjoining property holders are not parties to the contract. The improvement being done, the city government acts alone in its political capacity in apportioning and levying the tax; but when provision is made for the collection of the tax the city government steps out of the triangle, and the contractor is thrust into her place and made her agent for the collection of the tax. [Hendrick *v.* Crowley, 31 Cal. 472.] In case of an assignment of the contract, a debt due to a property owner from the contractor agreed to be set off by the latter, cannot be set off against the contractor's assignee by whom the whole work was done without notice of the agreement. [Himmelmann v. Reay, 38 Cal. 163.] In this case the contractor agreed with one of the property owners whose property was assessed to pay for the improvement, and to whom the contractor was indebted, that the contractor's debt to the property owner might be credited by the amount of the property owner's assessment. Before any work was done by the contractor he assigned his contract to another who did the work. The assignee of the contractor after doing the work, assigned his claim to the plaintiff. Neither the plaintiff nor his assignor who did the work—the assignee of the contractor—had any notice of the agreement between the property owner and the contractor. In an action by plaintiff against defendant, the property owner, for the amount of his assessment, it was held that the indebtedness from the contractor to the defendant furnished no ground for a counter claim.

If certain of the property owners take the contract, and after they have done the work and the assessment is made, assign all their right and title in the contract and in the assessment, warrant and diagram, and all the moneys due and to grow due thereon, they are estopped to deny the validity of the contract and of the assessment. [Callender v. Patterson, 66 Cal. 356.]

SECTION 6. The superintendent of streets is hereby authorized, in his official capacity, to make all written contracts, and receive all bonds authorized by this act, and to do any other act, either express or implied, that pertains to the street department under this act; and he shall fix the time for the commencement, which shall not be more than fifteen days from the date of the contract, and for the completion of the work under all contracts entered into by him, which work shall be prosecuted with diligence from day to day thereafter to completion, and he may extend the time so fixed from time to time, under the direction of the city council. The work provided for in section 2 of this act, must, in all cases, be done under the direction and to the satisfaction of the superintendent of streets, and the materials used shall comply with the specifications and be to the satisfaction of said superintendent of streets, and all contracts made therefor must contain a provision to that effect, and also express notice, that, in no case, except where it is otherwise provided in this act, will the city, or any officer thereof, be liable for any portion of the expense, nor for any delinquency of persons or property assessed. The city council may, by ordinance, prescribe general rules directing the superintendent of streets and the contractor as to the materials to be used, and the mode of executing the work, under all contracts thereafter made. The assessment and apportionment of the expenses of all such work or improvement shall be made by the superintendent of streets in the mode herein provided. [*Statutes 1885, p. 151.*]

[Section 6 of the act of March 18, 1885, never has been amended.]

Section 6 of the act expressly directs the superintendent to insert four certain provisions in the written contract, viz: (*1.*) A provision fixing the time for the commencement and completion of the work; (*2.*) a provision that the work shall be done under his direction and to his satisfaction; (*3.*) that the materials used shall comply with the specifications and be to the satisfaction of the superintendent of streets, and (*4.*) that, in no case, except where it is otherwise provided in the act, will the city or any officer thereof be liable for any portion of the expense, nor for any delinquency of persons or property assessed. These four provisions must be inserted in the contract or else it will be void. [*Supra*, page 52; Libby *v.* Ellsworth, 97 Cal. 316; Washburn *v.* Lyons, 97 Cal. 314.] But the contract need not follow the precise language of the statute, the call of the statute will be satisfied if the contract "can be held to contain the condition in question by a fair and reasonable construction." [Taylor *v.* Palmer, 31 Cal. 240; Emery *v.* S. F. Gas Co., 28 Cal. 346, 377.]

Section 6 likewise empowers the superintendent of streets as follows:

1. To make all written contracts and receive all bonds, and to do any other act, either express or implied, that pertains to the street department. The clause, authorizing the superintendent of streets "to do any other act, either express or implied, that pertains to the street department," received a construction in Donnelly *v.* Tillman, 47 Cal. 40, where it was held that it is the intention of the statute that the *council* should have all the authority in respect to the improvement of streets, which is granted by the statute, but which is not conferred expressly or by necessary implication upon some of the officers mentioned in the statute, and that the statute only grants to the superintendent of streets power over such acts as relate to the business of the street department.

2. Section 6 likewise authorizes the superintendent of streets to extend the time fixed for the completion of the work, from time to time, "*under the direction of the city council.*" The superintendent has no authority to grant an extension of time except "under the direction of the city council," *i. e.*, pursuant to an order or resolution of the council granting an extension, and the extension, if granted, must be granted during the life of the contract, *i. e.*, before the time for completion has run out. If not granted during the life of the contract the assessment is void. [Dougherty *v.* Coffin, 69 Cal. 454; Fanning *v.* Schammel, 68 Cal. 428; Beveridge *v.* Livingstone, 54 Cal.

54; Mappa *v.* Los Angeles, 61 Cal. 309; Turney *v.* Dougherty, 53 Cal. 619.] The fact that the extension was made with knowledge that the work had not been finished, and that upon the faith thereof the contractor expended money in good faith to complete the contract, cannot cure the invalidity of the extension. [Raisch *v.* San Francisco, 80 Cal. 1; Dougherty *v.* Nevada Bank, 81 Cal. 162.] The extension must be granted by the council during the life of the contract, and if, during this time, the council grants the extension, the extension will be valid even if the ministerial acts which the statute requires of the superintendent to be done in this connection, be not done. McVary *v.* Boyd, 89 Cal. 304, where it was held that a failure of the superintendent of streets to endorse upon the original contract any extension of time properly granted by the board of supervisors—under the act of 1872—or to cause the resolution of extension to be recorded until after the period fixed by the contract, does not render the extension ineffectual. [See Ede *v.* Knight, 93 Cal. 159; Brock *v.* Luning, 89 Cal. 316.] The extension will be sufficient if, by an application of the maxim *id certum est quod certum reddi potest* it can be sufficiently seen that the resolution of extension points to the particular contract in question. Thus, if the resolution of extension refer to the contract by number and specify the streets and the work to be done as described in the contract, it will not be invalidated because of an error in naming the contractor. [Anderson *v.* De Urioste, 96 Cal. 404.] If the work is not completed within the time mentioned in the contract, or within the time provided for by regular extension, granted during the life of the contract, the assessment will be void and the fact that the city failed to furnish a steam roller as provided in the specifications, and that therefore the contractor could not complete the work in time, will not prevent the assessment from being void. [Heft *v.* Payne, 97 Cal. 108.]

3. Section 6 likewise empowers the superintendent of streets to make the assessment and apportion the expense in the mode provided by the act.

The next section (section 7 of the act) provides the rules in accordance with which the assessments are to be made, and section 8 prescribes the form of the assessment. [*Vide* sections 7 and 8 and the notes thereto.]

SECTION 7. *Subdivision One*—The expenses incurred for any work authorized by this act (which expense shall not include the cost of any work done in such portion of any street as is required by law to be kept in order or repair by any person or company having railroad tracks thereon, nor include work which shall have been declared in the resolution of intention to be assessed on a district benefited) shall be assessed upon the lots and lands fronting thereon, except as hereinafter specifically provided; each lot or portion of a lot being separately assessed, ir. proportion to the frontage, at a rate per front foot sufficient to cover the total expense of 'the work.

Subdivision Two—The expense of all improvements, except such as are done by contractors under the provisions of section thirteen of this act, until the streets, avenues, street crossings, lanes, alleys, places, or courts are finally accepted, as provided in section twenty of this act, shall be assessed upon the lots and lands as provided in this section, according to the nature and character of the work; and after such acceptance the expense of all the work thereafter done thereon shall be paid by said city out of the street department fund.

Subdivision Three—The expense of the work done on main street crossings shall be assessed at a uniform rate per front foot of the quarter blocks and irregular blocks adjoining and cornering upon the crossings, and separately upon the whole of each lot or portion of a lot having any frontage in the said blocks fronting on said main streets, half way to the next main street crossing, and all the way on said blocks to a boundary line of the city where no such crossing intervenes, but only according to its frontage in said quarter blocks and irregular blocks.

Subdivision Four—Where a main street terminates in another main street, the expenses of the work done on one-half of the width of the street opposite the termination shall be assessed upon the lots in each of the two quarter blocks adjoining and cornering on the same, according to the frontage of such lots on said main streets, and the expense of the other half of the width of said street upon the lot or lots fronting on the latter half of the street at such termination.

Subdivision Five—Where any alley or subdivision street crosses a main street, the expense of all work done on said crossing shall be assessed on all lots or portions of lots half way on said alley or subdivision street to the next crossing or intersection, or to the end of such alley or subdivision street if it does not meet another.

Subdivision Six—The expense of work done on alley or subdivision street crossings shall be assessed upon the lots fronting upon such alley or subdivision streets on each side thereof, in all directions, half way to the next street, place, or court, on either side, respectively, or to the end of such alley or subdivision street, if it does not meet another.

Subdivision Seven—Where a subdivision street, avenue, lane, alley, place, or court terminates in another street, avenue, lane, alley, place, or court, the expense of the work done on one-half of the width of the subdivision street, avenue, lane, alley, place, or court opposite the termination, shall be assessed upon the lot or lots fronting on such subdivision street, or avenue, lane, alley, place or court so terminating, according to its frontage thereon, half way on each side, respectively, to the next street, avenue, lane, alley, court or place, or to the end of such street, avenue, lane, alley, place or court, if it does not meet another, and the other one-half of the width upon the lots fronting such termination.

Subdivision Eight—Where any work mentioned in this act (man-holes, cesspools, culverts, crosswalks, piling and capping excepted) is done on either or both sides of the center line of any street for one block or less, and further work opposite to the work of the same class already done is ordered to be done to complete the unimproved portion of said street, the assessment to cover the total expenses of said work so ordered shall be made upon the lots or portions of the lots only fronting the portions of the work so ordered. And when sewering or resewering is ordered to be done under the sidewalk on only one side of a street for any length thereof, the assessment for its expenses shall be made only upon the lots and lands fronting nearest upon that side, and for intervening intersections only upon the two quarter blocks adjoining and cornering upon that side.

Subdivision Nine—Section one of chapter three hundred and twenty-five of the laws of this state entitled "An act amendatory of and supplementary to 'An act to provide revenue for the support of the government of this state,' approved April twenty-ninth, eighteen hundred and fifty-seven," approved April nineteenth, eighteen hundred and fifty-nine, shall not be applicable to the provisions of this section; but the property herein mentioned shall be subject to the provisions of this act, and be assessed for work done under the provisions of this section.

Subdivision Ten—It shall be lawful for the owner or owners of lots or lands fronting upon any street, the width and grade of which have been established by the city council, to perform at his or their own expense (after obtaining permission from the council so to do, but before said council has passed its resolution of intention to order grading inclusive of this) any grading upon said street, to its full width, or to the center line thereof, and to its grade as then established, and thereupon to procure, at his or their own expense, a certificate from the city engineer, setting forth the number of cubic yards of cutting and filling made by him or them in said grading, and the proportions performed by each owner, and that the the same is done to the established width and grade of said street, or to tne center line thereof, and thereafter to file said certificate with the superintendent of streets, which certificate the superintendent shall record in a book kept for that purpose in his office, properly indexed. Whenever thereafter the city council orders the grading of said street, or any portion thereof, on which any grading certified as aforesaid has been done, the bids and the contract must express the price by the cubic yard for cutting and filling in grading; and the said owner or owners, and his or their successors in interest, shall be entitled to credit on the assessment upon his or their lots and lands fronting on said street for the grading thereof, to the amount of the cubic yards of cutting and filling set forth in his or their said certificate, at the prices named in the contract for said cutting and filling; or, if the grade meanwhile has been duly altered, only for so much of said certified work as would be required for grading to the altered grade; *provided, however,* that such owner or owners shall not be entitled to such credit as may be in excess of the assessments for grading upon the lots and lands owned by him or them, and proportionately assessed for the whole of said grading; and the superintendent of streets shall include in the assessment for the whole of said grading upon the same grade the number of cubic yards of cutting and filling set forth in any and all certificates so recorded in his office, or for the whole of said grading to the duly altered grade so much of said certified work as would be required for grading thereto, and shall enter corresponding credits, deducting the same as payments upon the amounts assessed against the lots and lands owned, respectively, by said certified owners and their successors in interest; *provided, however*, that he shall not so include any grading quantities or credit any sums in excess of the proportionate assessments for the whole of the grading which are made upon any lots and lands fronting upon said street and belonging to any such certified owners or their successors in interest. Whenever any owner or owners of any lots and lands fronting on any street shall have heretofore done, or shall hereafter do, any work (except grading) on such street, in front of any block, at his or their own expense, and the city council shall subsequently order any work to be done of the same class in front of the same block, said work so done at the expense of such owner or owners shall be excepted from the order ordering work to be done, as provided in subdivision eleven of this section of this act; *provided*, that the work so done at the expense of such owner or owners shall be upon the official grade, and in condition satisfactory to the street superintendent at the time said order is passed.

Subdivision Eleven—The city council may include in one resolution of intention and order any of the different kinds of work mentioned in this act, and it may except therefrom any of said work already done upon the street to the official grade. The lots and portions of lots fronting upon said excepted work already done shall not be included in the frontage assessment for the class of work from which the exception is made; *provided*, that this shall not be construed so as to affect the special provisions as to grading contained in subdivision ten of this section.

Subdivision Twelve—Whenever the resolution of intention declares that the costs and expenses of the work and improvement are to be assessed upon a district, the city council shall direct the city engineer to make a diagram of the property affected or benefited by the proposed work or improvement, as described in the resolution of intention, and to be assessed to pay the expenses thereof. Such diagram shall show each separate lot, piece, or parcel of land, the area in square feet of each of such lots, pieces, or parcels of land, and the relative location of the same to the work proposed to be done, all within the limits of the assessment district; and when said diagram shall have been approved by the city council, the clerk shall, at the time of such approval, certify the fact and date thereof. Immediately thereafter the said diagram shall be delivered to the superintendent of streets of said city, who shall, after the contractor of any street work has fulfilled his contract to the satisfaction of said superintendent of streets, or city council, on appeal, proceed to estimate upon the lands, lots or portions of lots within said assessment district, as shown by said diagram, the benefits arising from such work, and to be received by each such lot, portion of such lot, piece, or subdivision of land, and shall thereupon assess upon and against said lands in said assessment district the total amount of the costs and expenses of such proposed work, and in so doing shall assess said total sum upon the several pieces, parcels, lots, or portions of lots, and subdivisions of land in said district benefited thereby, to wit: Upon each, respectively, in proportion to the estimated benefits to be received by each of said several lots, portions of lots, or subdivisions of land. In other respects the assessment shall be as provided in the next section, and the provisions of subdivisions three, four, five, six, seven and eight of this section shall not be applicable to the work or improvement provided for in this subdivision. [*Amendment approved March 31, 1891, Statutes 1891, p. 201.*]

[Section 7 was amended in 1889, by act of March 14, 1889, statutes '89, p. 163; and again in 1891, by act of March 31, 1891. statutes '91, p. 201.]

SUBDIVISION 1 OF SECTION SEVEN.

Subdivision 1. Subdivision 1 of section 7 provides: (*1.*) That the expense incurred for any work authorized by the act shall not include the cost of any work done in such portion of any street as is required by law to be kept in order or repair by any person or company having railroad tracks thereon, nor shall such expense include work which shall have been declared in the resolution of intention to be assessed on a district benefited; (*2.*) that the expense incurred for any work authorized by the act shall be assessed upon the lots and lands fronting thereon, except as in this act otherwise specially provided; and (*3.*) that each lot or portion of a lot shall be separately assessed in proportion to the frontage, at a rate per front foot sufficient to cover the total expense of the work.

I. *Cost of Work Upon Such Portion of a Street as is Required by Law to be Kept in Order or Repair by Owners of Street Railways.* The law—not the act under consideration providing for work upon streets, alleys, lanes etc., but section 498 of the Civil Code—requires the city authorities to impose upon street railway companies, as a condition to grants of their franchises, an obligation or agreement "to plank, pave, or macadamize the entire length of the street used by their track, between the rails, and for two feet on each side thereof, and between the tracks, if there be more than one, and to keep the same constantly in repair, flush with the street and with good crossings." [Civil Code section 498.] Section 511 of the Civil Code makes the above provisions of section 498, applicable to street railroads constructed, owned and operated by natural persons, as well as corporations. The act providing for work upon streets, lanes, alleys, etc., *i. e.* the act of March 18, 1885, and the several acts amendatory thereof,—prior to the act of February 27, 1893—do not include any mode for collecting from the owners of street railways any portion of the expense of improving a street. [Schmidt *v.* Market St. R. R. Co., 90 Cal. 39.] The above section of the act—*i. e.* section 7 of the

act of March 18, 1885, as amended—exempts from the
expense assessable against the lots of the property owners,
all the expense of any work done in such portion of any
street as is required by law to be kept in order or repair by
any person or company having railroad tracks thereon,
and section 6 of the act of February 27, 1893, [statutes
1893, pages 36–38] provides that whenever any railroad
track or tracks exist upon any street or streets on which
street or streets the city council has ordered work to be
done or improvements made, the council may, at any time
thereafter; order the person or company having such tracks
to perform upon the portion required by law to be kept in
order or repair by such person or company, the work or
improvements, similar in all respects to that already ordered
to be performed upon the main part of the street, under the
same specifications and superintendence, with the same
materials, within the same time, and to the like satisfaction
and acceptance by the superintendent of streets.
The section then proceeds to provide how the work
shall be ordered done and how done, in case the
person or company having the railroad tracks refuses to
obey the order, and how the cost thereof shall be paid, etc.

Prior to the passage of this act of February 27, 1893,
there was no machinery provided by law for collecting
from a street railway company, whose road occupies a portion of the street, any portion of the expense of improving the street. [Schmidt v. Market St. R. R. Co. supra.]

If section 6 of the act of February, 27, 1893,
be considered as providing such machinery, it
is a provision injected into an act, which, as expressed
in its title, is "An act to provide a system of street improvement bonds to represent certain assessments
for the cost of street work and improvements
within municipalities, and also for the payment of
such bonds." It is essentially and primarily an act to provide for the issuance of bonds as a means of paying the cost
of street work. The title of the act says nothing about providing the machinery for imposing upon the owners of
street railways, whose tracks occupy a portion of the street,
the cost of the improvements which the law [section 498 C.
C.] requires to be done by such owners. The act is constructed upon the assumption or theory that other acts,
which it collectively designates as the "Street Work Act,"
provide all the machinery for acquiring jurisdiction to
order street work to be done, for levying assessments to pay
for the same, etc. Its primary object is to provide for a system of serial bonds, each bond representing the amount which

has been assessed against each lot or parcel of land under the provisions of the acts collectively designated as the "Street Work Act." And, *quaere*, if the title of the act did state that one of its objects was to provide the machinery for collecting from the owners of street railways the portion of the expense which the law [Sec. 498 C. C.] imposes upon them as a condition of the grant of their franchises, would not the act be repugnant to the provisions of article IV, section 24 of the constitution? "Every act shall embrace but one subject, which subject shall be expressed in its title." And, as the title of the act states, its subject is "a system of street improvement bonds."

If section 6 of the act of Feby. 27, 1893—in so far as it purports to provide a mode for collecting from street railway owners the cost of the work which the law [section 498 C. C.] requires such owners to do—be repugnant to article IV of section 24 of the constitution, then, the statement by Mr. Justice Harrison in Schmidt *v.* Market St. R. R. Co., 90 Cal. 39—"no mode is provided in the act for collecting from a street-railroad corporation, whose road occupies a portion of the street, any portion of the expense of improving the street"—is as true now as it was prior to the said act of Feb. 27, 1893.

In said case of Schmidt *v.* Market St. R. R. Co., it was held that the amount of the assessment might be recovered by the contractor upon an *implied contract* on the part of the railroad company, arising out of its acceptance of its franchise under a grant containing a condition that the company should be held for the payment of its proportion of the cost of the improvement, and that the amount of the assessment might be collected in the manner provided by law for the collection of other street assessments. But, *quaere*, in the absence of such a condition in the ordinance granting the franchise, how shall a street car company, or persons owning and operating street cars, be compelled to pay the cost of improving the street between the rails, etc.? [See notes to section 6 of the act of Feby. 27, 1893, *post.*]

II. *Front-Foot Mode of Assessment is the Mode Provided by the Act.* Subdivision 1 of section 7 of the act lays down the general rule which is to govern in levying assessments to pay the expense incurred for any work authorized by the act. That general rule is that such expense shall be assessed upon the lots and lands fronting upon the work. That is, the act adopts the front-foot mode of assessment, and the only exceptions thereto are such as are *specially* provided by the act.

The last part of subdivision 1 of the section defines this front-foot mode and general rule of assessment as follows: Each lot or portion of a lot fronting on the work shall be separately assessed, in proportion to the frontage, at a rate per front foot sufficient to cover the total expense of the work. That is, the total expense of the work—including the incidentals, as printing, etc.,—is divided by the total number of front feet fronting on the whole work or improvement, and the quotient is the rate of assessment per front foot, and there is assessed against each lot or portion of a lot fronting on the work an amount equal to this quotient, or rate of assessment per front foot, multiplied by the number of front feet in such lot or portion of a lot.

In People v. Lynch, 51 Cal. 22–23, Mr. Justice McKinstry said: " It has been repeatedly held that an attempt by the legislature to compel each lot upon a street to pay the whole expense of grading and paving along its front can not be maintained, because, while there is an apparent uniformity, the measure of equality required by the constitution is entirely wanting"—citing 9 Dana 513; 8 Mich. 274. That is to say, a law which should attempt to make each lot liable for the whole cost of doing that particular part of the improvement which lies in front of each lot, would be unconstitutional. But the front-foot mode of assessment, as defined by subdivision 1 of section 7 of the act is constitutional, because it apportions to each lot its share of the total expense according to the amount of frontage of each lot, and the amount assessed against each lot is increased or diminished by the assessment upon the adjacent lots. [See Cooley's Constitutional Limitations, page 508, 3rd Ed.]

III.   *Front-Foot Mode of Assessment is Constitutional.*

The front foot mode of assessment is constitutional. [Emery v. S. F. Gas Co., 28 Cal. 346; Emery v. Bradford 29 Cal. 82; Taylor v. Palmer 31 Cal. 241; Whiting v. Quackenbush, 54 Cal. 306; Whiting v. Townsend, 57 Cal. 515; Lent v. Tillson, 72 Cal. 426; Jennings v. Le Breton, 80 Cal. 8, 15–16.]

The power of assessment is a part of the general power of taxation. The word "assessment," however, while it represents in part the general power of taxation vested in the government, is used to designate a particular branch of that power specifically different in its purpose and mode of working from that intended by the more general and comprehensive term of "taxation." By the latter the power of imposing taxes upon the property of the citizens generally, for the support of the government, is intended. By the former i. e., "assessment," is meant the power of imposing for the purpose of improving the streets of cities and incorporated villages, a tax upon the property bordering upon or in the vicinity of the improvement. In Emery v. S. F. Gas Co. *supra*, page 357, Judge Sawyer said: "The term 'taxation,' both in common parlance and in the laws of the several states, has been ordinarily used, not to express the idea of the sovereign power which is exercised, but the exercise of that power for a particular purpose, viz., to raise a revenue for the *general and ordinary* expenses of the government, whether it be the state, county, town or city government. But there is another class of expenses, also of a public nature, necessary to be provided for, peculiar to the local governments of counties, cites, towns and even smaller subdivisions, such as opening, grading, improving in various ways, and repairing, highways and streets, and constructing sewers in cities, and canals and ditches for the purpose of drainage in the country. These burdens have always, in every state, from its first settlement, been charged upon the localities benefited, and have been apportioned upon various principles; but whatever principle of apportionment has been adopted they have been known, both in the legislation and ordinary speech of the country, by the name of assessments"

It was held in the case of Burnett v. Mayor, etc., of Sacrament 12 Cal. 76, that the provision of the constitution requiring "taxation" to be equal and uniform, was not applicable to assessments for street purposes, and in Emery v. S. F. Gas. Co., *supra*, it was held that the further provision of the constitution that "all property in this state shall be taxed in proportion to its value" is equally inapplicable to "assessments." In this latter case, the court, Sawyer justice, after quoting from the opinion in Burnett v. Mayor etc., of Sacramento, said: "The question was [in the case of Burnett vs. Mayor etc. of Sacramento] whether the term 'taxation,' as used in that section [section 13, article XI, constitution of 1863], is applicable to assessments for street improvements. If the term 'taxation' in the first clause,—'taxation shall be equal and uniform,'—is inapplicable to a street assessment, of course the term, as used in the second clause of the same section,—'all property in this state shall be taxed in proportion to its value,'—must also be inapplicable." [28 Cal. 361.] Accordingly, it was held in this latter case, Emery v. S. F. Gas. Co., that there is no restriction in the constitution upon the power of the legislature to impose assessments to defray the expenses of public improvements in the nature of grading, planking and improving streets upon the property supposed to be benefited thereby. And that it is authorized to apportion the amount to be raised according to value, according to the benefits received, in proportion to frontage or the superficial contents, or to adopt *any principle of apportionment* that can be referred to the general sovereign rights of taxation. [28 Cal. pp. 372–3.] While the term "assessment" though referable to the general power of taxation, is not synonomous with the term "taxation" as used in common parlance and in the restrictions of the constitution upon the exercise of the power of taxation for purposes of raising revenue for the general and ordinary expenses of the government, still an assessment is a *tax*. And although it is such a tax as is not prohibited by that clause of the constitution which provides that "all property shall be taxed in proportion to its value," it is of the very essence of all taxation, *in every form*, that it be levied with equality and uniformity, and therefore there must be some system of apportionment. The express written inhibitions of the constitution relative to "taxation" may not be applicable to "assessments," because of the difference between these two branches of the general power of taxation, as pointed out *supra*, nevertheless, aside from the provisions of all written constitutions, in every free country an approximation toward equality and uniformity in the exercise of the sovereign power of taxation is inherently necessary, and, as an "assessment" is made by the exercise of that power, it follows that, to approximate equality and uniformity, the assessment must be levied pursuant to some general system of apportionment. The legislature may adopt any principle of apportionment that can be referred to the general sovereign power of taxation, but there must be some system of apportionment which will approximate equality and uniformity. For, whatever the standard of apportionment, or the basis of taxation, the requirement that it shall be uniform is universal, the difference being only in the character of the uniformity. [People *v.* Lynch, 51 Cal. 15; Whiting *v.* Quackenbush, 54 Cal. 306.] In People *v.* Lynch, *supra*, Mr. Justice McKinstry said: "The terms 'tax' and 'assessment' both include the idea of some ratio or rule of apportionment; so that, of the whole sum to be raised the part paid by one piece of property shall have some known relation to or be affected by that paid by another."

An assessment for local improvements, as improvements upon streets, etc., is not required to be equal and uniform because a section of the constitution dealing with the general subject of revenue may say that "taxation shall be

equal and uniform" [Burnett *v.* Mayor, etc., of Sacramento
12 Cal. 83; Emery *v.* S. F. Gas. Co., 28 Cal. 361-2,] but
every assessment is required to approximate equality and
uniformity and therefore to be levied under a system which
apportions it with reference to some standard which will
approximate equality and uniformity, because it is a tax.
And all taxes, in free countries, should be levied upon principles that approximate uniformity and equality whether
their constitutions expressly require it or not. Therefore,
it is held that, in levying an assessment, if a lot of land,
within the district declared to be benefited, be not assessed,
there is no equality or uniformity in the assessment, and the assessment is, therefore, void. The
omission of the lot from the assessment disturbs the
equality and uniformity of the levy, and renders the
assessment void. [People *v.* Lynch, 51 Cal. 15;
Whiting *v.* Quackenbush, 54 Cal. 310; Moulton *v.* Parks, 64
Cal. 181; Dyer *v.* Harrison, 63 Cal. 447; Diggins *v.* Brown,
76 Cal. 318; Davies *v.* Los Angeles, 86 Cal. 49.] In Whiting
v. Quackenbush, *supra,* the court said: "Every tax must be
levied with equality and uniformity under some system of
apportionment; an assessment for improving a street in a
city is a tax; therefore, every assessment must be levied
with equality and uniformity. But if it be so levied, under
a system which apportions it with reference to *the number
of feet fronting on the improvement,* or to any other standard
which will approximate equality and uniformity, it is not
void for want of equality and uniformity." While, as held
in the cases last above cited, the assessment is at least irregular if any lot liable to assessment is omitted from the
assessment roll, still section 11 of the act provides that an
appeal may be taken to the council by any owner raising
any objection to the legality or correctness of the assessment;
that on such appeal the council may correct the assessment;
that its decision shall be final, and that no assessment
shall be held invalid, *except upon appeal to the city council,*
for any error, informality or defect in the assessment. And
in the very recent case of Dowling *v.* Altschul, decided
June 13, 1893, 33 Pac. Rep. 495, it was held that, under the
act of March 18, 1885, an appeal on the ground that an
assessment for paving a *cul-de-sac* failed to assess the land
at the end of the same, presented a question which the
city council had power to determine on appeal, and that,
therefore, its decision was conclusive. This case does not
hold that an assessment is valid if a lot, liable to assessment, be omitted from the assessment roll; but, as the
statute now in force—section 11 of act of March 18, 1885,—

provides a tribunal for the litigation of this question,—namely the city council—and as the statute expressly states that the decision of such tribunal upon such a question, shall be final and conclusive, it is therefore held that an appeal is the only remedy of a lot owner dissatisfied because a lot, liable to assessment, has been omitted, and that the decision of the council upon such question is final and conclusive. An error in the assessment roll is an error capable of correction by the council on appeal if the work has been properly done under a valid contract therefor. And it seems that, if the error or irregularity complained of is capable of correction by the council on appeal, the appeal to the council is the only remedy. [See opinion of Temple J., in Chambers *v.* Satterlee 40 Cal. 524. See *post* section 11 of the act, and the notes thereto.]

IV. *General Principles of Street Assessments.*

(*a.*) *Legislature can not Directly Exercise Power of Assessment.* The legislature can not directly exercise the power of assessment within an incorporated city, but may empower the municipal authorities to do so. In cities the power of assessment can only be exercised through the medium of the corporate authorities. [People *v.* Lynch, 51 Cal. 15; Taylor *v.* Palmer, 31 Cal. 240; Brady *v.* King, 53 Cal. 44; Schumacker *v.* Toberman, 56 Cal. 508.]

(*b.*) *Owner not Personally Liable.* The owner of the land, bordering upon an improved street, can not be made liable for the cost of the improvement beyond the value of his land. The legislature can not impose a personal liability upon the owners of the property assessed, and any statute purporting to impose such personal liability is, in this respect, unconstitutional and void. [Taylor *v.* Palmer, 31 Cal. 240; Guerin *v.* Reese, 33 Cal. 296; Coniff *v.* Hastings, 36 Cal. 292; Gaffney *v.* Donohue, 36 Cal. 104; Himmelmann *v.* Steiner, 38 Cal. 175, 178; Randolph *v.* Bayue, 44 Cal. 366; Gillis *v.* Cleveland, 87 Cal. 214; Manning *v.* Den, 90 Cal. 610.] Nor can the property owner be held liable upon the ground of a contract. [Dyer *v.* Barstow, 50 Cal. 652.]

(*c.*) *Not an Exercise of Power of Eminent Domain.* Street assessments do not take private property for public use. [Emery *v.* S. F. Gas Co., 28 Cal. 346; Chambers *v.* Satterlee, 40 Cal. 497.]

(*d.*) *Contract Not Affected by Subsequent Changes in the Law.* Improvement begun under a law, after execution of the contract, makes that law a part of the contract as to mode of assessment, which subsequent amendment of the law does not affect. [Houston *v.* McKenna, 22 Cal. 550.] The same is true as to changes in the constitution made

after the contract is made. If, after the contract is made,
the constitution is changed so as to provide a new method
of assessment, it will not affect the contract, and the granting of an extension of time for the completion of the work
will not constitute a new contract. The provisions of the
law under which a contract is made enter into and become a
part of the contract, including all provisions for extensions
of time, and a valid contract can not be abrogated by the
adoption of a new constitution, any more than it can
by the enactment of a new law by the legislature. If
it did it would impair the obligation of the contract
and thus controvene the provision of section 10, article I
of the federal constitution, providing that no state shall
pass any law impairing the obligation of contracts. [Oak-
land Pvg. Co. v. Barstow, 79 Cal. 45; Ede v. Cogswell, 79
Cal. 278; Ede v. Knight, 93 Cal. 159.]

The contractor is entitled to have the improvement
opposite a lot assessed to the whole lot without regard to
subsequent sales of portions. The lien attaches to the
whole lot in the hands of a subsequent purchaser. After
the expiration of the notice of intention—that is posting
and publication of the resolution of intention and of notice
of its passage—the council acquires jurisdiction of the subject matter of the improvement, and the contractor acquires
a right, under his contract, to have the assessment made
upon the lots fronting the improvement as they existed at
the time the jurisdiction of the council over the subject
matter attached under the statute, and the owner of a lot
cannot defeat this right by subsequently conveying a portion of the lot. The whole lot, as it existed when the jurisdiction of the council over the subject matter of the improvements attached, is liable to be assessed upon completion
of the work, no matter who owns it, or what subdivisions
may subsequently have been made by the owner. [Dough-
erty v. Miller, 36 Cal. 83.]

*(e.) The Property Owner Cannot set up a Counter Claim
for Damages.* An assessment for the improvement of
streets is a municipal tax, levied by the corporation upon
the property adjacent to the street, to defray the expenses of
the improvement, and therefore the property owner in a
suit to recover the amount assessed against his lot cannot
set up a counter claim for damages to his land. "The
origin, obligatory force and whole nature of a tax, is such
that it is impossible to conceive of a demand that might be
set off against it, unless expressly so authorized by statute."
[Himmelmann v. Spanagel, 39 Cal. 389.]

(f.) Sale for Taxes Extinguishes Assessment Lien. A valid

tax deed extinguishes the prior lien of a street assessment.
For, as a general rule, a sale and conveyance in due form
for taxes extinguishes all prior liens, whether for taxes or
otherwise, and therefore where, pending an action to enforce
the collection of a street assessment, a third party procures
a valid tax deed, the tax deed extinguishes the lien of the
assessment. [Dougherty v. Henarie, 47 Cal. 10; Chand-
ler v. Dunn, 50 Cal. 15.]

(g.) Public Property Exempt from Street Assessment.
Public property is exempt from street assessments and such
property may be exempted from the assessment although
situated within an assessment district declared to be benefited by the improvement; and such exemption will not render the assessment violative of the principle that all assessments must be equal and uniform. [Doyle v. Austin, 47
Cal. 353.]

(h.) Assessment need not be Presented to Administrator.
An assessment made after the death of a property owner
need not be presented to his estate for allowance. It is a
municipal tax, and the rule is that taxes assessed against
the property of an estate, pending administration, are not
claims against the estate which must be presented to the
administrator for allowance. [Hancock v. Whittemore, 50
Cal. 522; People v. Olvera, 43 Cal. 492.]

(i.) Can Only be Made Pursuant to Terms of a Statute.
An assessment can only be made according to the terms of
the statute, and where the statute does not provide for an
assessment for doing a particular kind of work, or does not
provide for an assessment for work done upon some particular place, the assessment is void. [Bassett v. Enwright, 19
Cal. 636; Kelly v. Luning, 76 Cal. 311.]

*(j.) A Void Assessment Cannot be Validated by Ratifi-
cation.* The doctrine of ratification has no application to
street assessments, and, so far as the lot owner is concerned,
the city cannot, by any act on its part, ratify proceedings
taken to improve a street and impose an assessment on the
lot for the same, so as to make the same valid, when they
were invalid in the first instance. So far as the lot owner
is concerned, these proceedings are but steps taken for the
purpose of imposing upon him a tax for a specific purpose,
and to such proceedings the doctrine of ratification has no
application. The power of ratification, if it exits at all, is in
the legislature. [Meuser v. Risdon, 36 Cal. 239.] And the
power of the legislature to ratify the proceedings, if it exists at
all in the case of assessments for municipal improvements,
is limited to dispensing with those things which it might
have dispensed with in the first place. That is to say, if the

thing wanting, or which failed to be done, and which constitutes the defect in the proceedings, is something the necessity of which the legislature might not have dispensed with by prior statute, then it is beyond the power of the legislature to dispense with it by subsequent statute. [People *v.* Lynch, 51 Cal. 15.] In this case of People *v.* Lynch, the "thing wanting" in the original proceeding was "uniformity" in the assessment. If the assessment is void the legislature cannot validate it, nor can it make an assessment within an incorporated city. [Brady *v.* King, 53 Cal. 44; Schumacker *v.* Toberman, 56 Cal. 508, 511; Kelly *v.* Luning, 76 Cal. 309.]

In San Francisco *v.* Certain Real Estate, 42 Cal. 513, it was said that it is competent for the legislature, by subsequent enactment, to cure defects in the original proceeding. But in People *v.* Lynch, *supra,* Mr. Justice McKinstry seems to be of the opinion that since, according to the decision in Taylor *v.* Palmer, 31 Cal. 242, the legislature cannot exercise the power of assessment directly within municipalities, that therefore it cannot, in any case, ratify an assessment proceeding.

In Reis *v.* Graff, 51 Cal. 86, the court, through Mr. Justice Rhodes, stated that validating a void assessment is equivalent to making an assessment in the first instance. In that case Judge Rhodes said: "Assuming that the legislature may itself make the assessment, or, *what amounts to the same thing, validate a void assessment,* does the act have the effect to make the assessment valid, by relation, as of the date of the invalid assessment," etc. If, therefore, validating an assessment amounts to making an assessment, and if the legislature may not make an assessment within a municipality, it would seem to follow, necessarily, that the legislature cannot in any case validate an assessment within municipalities. In this case of Reis *v.* Graff it was held that even if the legislature may validate a void assessment within municipalities, the assessment can only become valid at the date when the curative act takes effect, and the curative act can not, by relation, make the assessment valid as of the date when it was levied. [See also People *v.* McCain, 51 Cal. 360.]

In Fanning *v.* Schammel, 68 Cal. 428, the work was not completed within the time limited by the contract. Subsequently the board of supervisors extended the time, but as it had no jurisdiction to extend the time after the life of the contract, (see notes to sec.6 of the act, pages 62-63 *supra*) the order of extension was unauthorized and void. Nearly a year after this void order of extension, the legislature passed

an act purporting to validate, ratify and confirm "all orders
and resolutions heretofore from time to time passed by said
board of supervisors * * * in relation to street work," etc.,
and it was contended that this act cured said defect in the
proceedings, and validated said order of extension, but the
court said: "So far as the statute attempts to vitalize a dead
contract and validate a void assessment for street work, it is
unconstitutional and void."

The validity of an assessment does not depend upon the
validity of the remedy for its enforcement. [Appeal of N. B.
and M. R. R. Co., 32 Cal. 520.]   An assessment to pay for
prior work under an abortive contract is invalid.   [In the
Matter of Market Street, 49 Cal. 546.]

*(k) Severable Assessments Severed and Recovery had on
Valid Part.*   If an assessment be severable, and part be void
and part valid, the total assessment may be severed and
recovery had upon the valid part, provided there be a proper
demand for the part that is valid.   That is to say, where
there are two assessments—one void and the other valid—
as, for example, where several assessments are made to pay
the expenses of different kinds of work contracted to be
done pursuant to a resolution of intention and order, ordering several kinds of work to be done, these assessments may
be severed and separate demands made, and in such case
the contractor is entitled to recover the amount of the valid
assessment.   [Parker v. Reay, 76 Cal. 103;   Ede v. Knight,
93 Cal. 159, 165.]

In Frick v. Morford, 87 Cal. 576, an excess of work was
done outside of the limits fixed by the resolution of intention.   That is, the plans and specifications required eight
feet more of sewer to be laid, than was authorized by the
resolution of intention.   These faulty plans and specifications were a part of the contract, and the contractor laid
this extra eight feet of sewer, being an excess of eight feet
outside of the limits fixed by the resolution of intention.
Held: *(1.)* That the work done outside of the limits fixed by
the resolution was unauthorized, and the contractor was not
entitled to an assessment for the work in excess.   *(2.)* That
if the lot assessed wholly fronts upon the work done in
excess of authority, it cannot be held liable for any assessment.   *(3.)* That if it fronts in whole or in part upon the
work authorized by the resolution of intention, the assessment against it will not necessarily be rendered void by the
fact that the entire assessment purports to make a charge
upon lots not within the limits fixed by the resolution of
intention.   *(4.)* That if it is in part within the excess, the
contractor is not entitled to an assessment against that part

of the lot not fronting upon the work authorized by the resolution. *(5.)* That an excess of work done outside the limits fixed by the resolution of intention, will not invalidate an assessment against lots within those limits for that part of the work which was authorized by the resolution, if the cost of the work was estimated by the linear foot, so that the cost of excess can be easily segregated from the cost of the remainder, since in that case the assessment being severable the void part may be segregated from the valid part. *(6.)* That if the lot was wholly within the excess beyond the limits authorized by the resolution of intention, the owner was not a party "aggrieved," since in such case his lot could not be made liable, and therefore he was not required to appeal to the council. *(7.)* If his lot was partly within such excess, and he felt aggrieved because the assessment included the expense of laying the sewer in the eight feet outside of the limits fixed by the resolution of intention, his only remedy was by appeal to the council. [See Blair *v.* Luning, 76 Cal. 134; Dyer *v.* Scalmanini, 69 Cal. 637; Himmelmann *v.* Hoadley, 44 Cal. 276; Baudry *v.* Valdez, 32 Cal. 269.]

(l.) *When the Assessment is not Severable, if Part is Void it Vitiates the Whole.* When an assessment is made in gross for the work of curbing and macadamizing a street, and the assessment is invalid as to the macadamizing, and the amount due for curbing cannot be segregated from the total amount assessed against the lot, the invalidity of the assessment as to the macadamizing vitiates it as to the curbing, and the whole is void. [Dorland *v.* Bergson, 78 Cal. 637. Partridge *v.* Lucas, decided Sept. 11, 1893; See also Perine *v.* Forbush, 97 Cal, 305].

(m.) *Each Lot is Independently Liable.* Each lot, or portion of a lot, is separately liable for its proportion of the cost of the improvement, and the liability of each is independent of any other, and constitutes a separate liability, upon which a separate cause of action may be based. And therefore a recovery of the amount assessed against one lot is not a bar to an action to recover the amount assessed against another lot, although between the same parties. The expense of the improvement is a charge upon the property benefited, or supposed to be benefited, and is not a charge against the owner personally, and in furtherance of this end, the identity of the lot assessed, and not the person who may be the owner, is made the essential requirement of the statute; the first must be specifically described, while the latter may be designated as "unknown." [Gillis *v.* Cleveland, 87 Cal. 214.]

SUBDIVISION 2 OF SECTION SEVEN.

Subdivision 2. As stated *supra* in the notes to sub-division 1 of this section, the front-foot mode of assess-ment is the general rule, and the only exceptions thereto are such as are *"specifically"* provided in other parts of the act. Subdivision 2 provides that as to all improve-ments—except the work of repairing and reconstructing provided for by section thirteen of the act—the expense shall be assessed as provided in this section—section seven —according to the nature and character of the work, until acceptance of the streets, alleys, lanes, etc., by the council. So that—except as to the work of repairing and reconstruct-ing provided for by section thirteen of the act—section seven is the section, and the only section, which can be looked to for the purpose of ascertaining what property is liable to be assessed to pay for the expenses. That is, the expenses incurred for any work authorized by the act— except the work of repairing and reconstructing provided for by section thirteen of the act—shall be assessed upon the lots and lands fronting on the work, each lot or portion of a lot being separately assessed in proportion to the front-age, at a rate per front foot sufficient to cover the total expense of the work, as provided in sub-division 1—except where a different mode is specifically provided in this same section of the act—section seven. Section seven provides a different mode of assessment where the resolution of in-tention declares that the costs and expenses of the work and improvement are to be assessed upon a district. [See sub-division 12 of section 7] subdivision 1 of the section de-clares the *general* rule of assessment to be the *"front-foot plan,"* But, where the resolution of intention declare that the costs and expenses shall be assessed upon a district, the assessments are made according to the *"benefits"* received. Subdivision 1 of section 7 lays down the general rule, and subdivision 2 states that the exceptions to this general rule must be found in this same section—section 7—and not elsewhere, except as to work of repairing and reconstruct-ing done pursuant to the provisions of section 13 of the act. The work provided for by section 13 of the act is the work of repairing and reconstructing any portion of any *improved* street, lane, etc., out of repair or needing recon-struction, and in condition to endanger persons or property passing thereon, or in a condition to interfere with the public convenience in the use thereof. For example, if a street has been paved with asphaltum and subsequently a portion of the pavement in front of some lot becomes loose, and a hole is made, so as to leave this portion in a condition to interfere with the public convenience in the use of the street, in such case the street does not need repaving, but this particular spot needs to be filled up with asphaltum and repaired, and section 13 purports to impose the duty of doing this, and of paying the expense thereof, upon the owner of the lot fronting on this portion of the street. [See *infra* notes to section 13.]

SUBDIVISION 3 OF SECTION SEVEN.

Subdivision 3. [See sec. 34, subdivisions 7 and 12 for definitions of the words "street," "main street," " blocks" and "quarter block."]

In Parker *v.* Reay, 76 Cal. 103, it was held that under the act of 1872, where an assessment is made for work done on a main street crossing, if a lot is partly within and partly without one of the quarter blocks cornering upon the crossing, only such portion of the lot must be assessed as lies within the quarter block. Subdivision 3 of section eight of the act of 1872, corresponds with subdivision 3 of section seven *supra.* The language of subdivision 3 section 7 of the present street work act, seems to be capable of the same construction as that placed upon the corresponding provision of the act of 1872 by the Supreme Court in Parker *v.* Reay, *supra.*

Subdivision 3 of section seven of the act is divisible into two parts. The first part declares what the rate per front foot shall be and how it shall be obtained. The second part declares what property shall be subjected to the assessment lien. (*1.*) The first part or clause of subdivision 3 of section seven, provides that the expense of the work done on street crossings, "shall be assessed at a uniform rate per front foot of the quarter and irregular blocks adjoining and cornering upon the crossings." That is, the property made subject to the lien of the assessment, whatever it is, shall be assessed at a certain rate per front foot. This rate is to be found by dividing the total amount of the expense by the number of front feet in the four quarter or irregular blocks cornering upon the crossing, and the quotient thus obtained is the rate of assessment per front foot to be assessed upon the property made subject to the lien of the assessment by the second clause of this subdivision according to the frontage of such property. The first part or first clause of subdivision 3 provides the mode for measuring the amount per front foot which is to be assessed upon the land made subject to the lien of the assessment. (*2.*) The sec-

82   STREET WORK LAW—STREET IMPROVEMENT ACT

ond part or second clause of subdivision 3 of section 7,declares what property shall bear the lien of the assessment, and that it shall be assessed according to its frontage in said quarter blocks and irregular blocks. The property upon which this part of the section declares the assessment shall be made, is the following, viz.: "The whole of each lot or portion of a lot, having any frontage in the said (quarter or irregular) blocks fronting on said main (intersecting) streets, *half way to the next main street crossing*, and all the way on said blocks to a boundary line of the city where no such crossing intervenes." If, therefore, the property upon which the assessment is to be made,— where there is such a next main street crossing,—is the property which consists of each lot or portion of a lot to a point "half way to the next main street crossing," it would seem to follow that the property beyond this point, is not subject to the lien of the assessment, and therefore, as held in Parker *v.* Reay, *supra*, where there is a lot in the middle of a block, portion of which is on one side of this halfway point and portion on the other side, only that portion of the lot is liable to the assessment which lies on that side of the point nearest the crossing upon which the improvement was made.

SUBDIVISION 4 OF SECTION SEVEN.

Subdivision 4. The meaning of subdivision 4 can be most clearly explained by means of a diagram as follows:

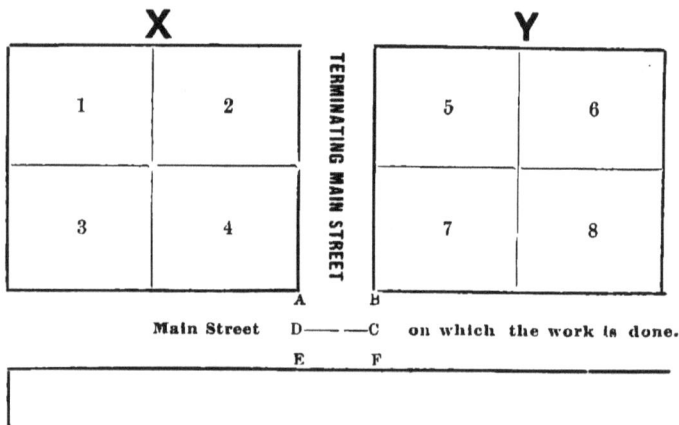

The quarter blocks of block X are 1, 2, 3 and 4; and 5, 6, 7 and 8 are the quarter blocks of block Y. E F is the line of termination and has frontage on the main street of the work at such termination. A B C D is one-half of the width of the main street on which the work is done, and is the half "opposite" the termination. The expense of the work done on this half must be assessed upon the lots in each of the two quarter blocks adjoining and cornering upon this half of the street, namely, the lots in the quarter blocks 4 and 7, according to the frontage of such lots in each of the two main streets. C D E F is the other half of the width of the main street upon which the work is done, and the expense of improving this half is assessed upon the lot or lots fronting on this half of the street at said termination, namely, the lot or lots of which the line E F forms part or all of the frontage.

The word "termination" as used in this part of the act in connection with street work does not seem to have any well defined meaning of its own independent of its context. It seems from its context in this part of the act that the word is used to mean the line E F in the diagram. But in the act of March 18, 1861, (Statutes of 1861, page 545,) amendatory of the San Francisco Consolidation Act, it is evident from the context that the word "termination" is used to designate the line A B in the diagram. In section 3 of this act of March 18, 1861, it is provided that "where a main street terminates at right angles in another main street the expense of the construction of one-half of the width of the street, *at the termination*, shall be assessed upon the lots *in each of the two quarter blocks* adjoining and cornering on the same, according to the frontage of such lots on said main streets, and the other half upon the lots fronting on the street opposite such termination."

SUBDIVISION 8 OF SECTION SEVEN.

Subdivision 8. Subdivision 10 of section 8 of the San Francisco street work act of 1872 is the subdivision which corresponds with subdivision 8 of section 7, *supra*, although the two are not identical in language. In Diggins v. Brown, 76 Cal. 318, this subdivision of section 8 of the act of 1872 was construed, and it was held that it did not provide that each lot should pay for the work done in front of it, but that the cost of the work done on one side of a street should be apportioned to all the lots on that side fronting on the work; that, therefore, when the board of supervisors order "that plank sidewalks be constructed on Olive avenue, between Laguna and Buchanan streets, where not already constructed, and that the roadway be macadamized where not already done," the lots to be assessed are all the lots on each side of the street in the block between Laguna and Buchanan streets, and the cost of the work on one side of the street must be distributed against all of the lots on that side of the street in said block, even though no work be done in front of some one or more of them, and if any lot be omitted because no work was done in front of it, the assessment is void. However, the language of subdivision 8 of section seven of the present street work act differs so much from the language of subdivision 10 of section 8 of the act of 1872, that Diggins v. Brown can hardly be regarded as an authority in the construction of the present act. Still, if the legislature did, by subdivision 8 of section seven of the present act, intend to impose upon each lot the whole cost of doing the particular portion of the work upon which each lot fronts, then as stated in Diggins v. Brown, "the method of assessing each lot for the work done in front of it has been condemned by high authority," and consequently, such an intention is not to be imputed to the legislature, if the subdivision is capable of a construction consonant with the requirements of the constitution.

SUBDIVISION 9 OF SECTION SEVEN.

Subdivision 9. Why this provision was inserted in the act is inexplicable, save upon the theory that the act was, in a great measure, copied from former San Francisco street work acts, and copyists sometimes blindly copy without any other reason than that the provision is in the statute from which the copy is taken. The legislature of 1857 passed a general revenue act, entitled "An act to provide revenue for the support of the government of this state," [Statutes of 1857, page 325,] and the legislature of 1859 passed an act to amend this general revenue act, entitled "An act amendatory of and supplementary to an act to provide revenue for the support of the government of this state, approved April twenty-ninth, eighteen hundred and fifty-seven." [Statutes 1859, page 343.] The provisions of this latter act are expressly confined to the city and county of San Francisco. Subdivision 12 of the San Francisco street work act of 1863 [Statutes 1863, pages 396–7,] is the same as subdivision 9 of section 7 of the present general street work act, and it seems to have been needlessly copied into the present street work act.

SECTION 8. After the contractor of any street work has fulfilled his contract to the satisfaction of the street superintendent of said city, or city council on appeal, the street superintendent shall make an assessment to cover the sum due for the work performed and specified in said contract (including any incidental expenses), in conformity with the provisions of the preceding section according to the character of the work done; or, if any direction and decision be given by said council on appeal, then in conformity with such direction and decision, which assessment shall briefly refer to the contract, the work contracted for and performed, and shall show the amount to be paid therefor, together with any incidental expenses, the rate per front foot assessed, if the assessment be made per front foot, the amount of each assessment, the name of the owner of each lot, or portion of a lot (if known to the street superintendent); if unknown the word "unknown" shall be written opposite the number of the lot, and the amount assessed thereon, the number of each lot or portion or portions of a lot assessed, and shall have attached thereto a diagram exhibiting each street or street crossing, lane, alley, place, or court, on which any work has been done, and showing the relative location of each district, lot or portion of lot to the work done, numbered to correspond with the numbers in the assessments, and showing the number of feet fronting, or number of lots assessed, for said work contracted for and performed. [*Amendment approved March 14, 1889. Statutes 1889, p. 166.*]

[Section 8 was amended in 1889 by act of March 14, 1889, statutes 1889, p. 166.]

Section 8 of the act prescribes the *form* of the assessment. This section provides: *(1.)* That the assessment shall be made by the superintendent of streets only after the contractor has fulfilled his contract to the satisfaction of the street superintendent. *(2.)* That it shall be made in conformity with the provisions of the preceding section [Sec. 7] according to the character of the work done, *i.e.* the assessment shall be made against the particular property which is made liable by section 7 of the act, and it shall be made by the street superintendent alone, unless any direction or decision be given by the council on appeal, in which case the street superintendent shall make the assessment in conformity with such direction and decision, and *(3.)* That the assessment shall contain eight provisions, viz, *(a.)* a brief reference to the contract; *(b.)* a brief reference to the work contracted for and performed; *(c.)* it shall show the amount to be paid for the work, together with any incidental expenses; *(d.)* the rate per front foot assessed—if the assessment be made per front foot; *(e.)* the amount of each assessment; *(f.)* the name of the owner of each lot, or portion of lot—if known to the street superintendent—or, if unknown, the word "unknown" shall be written opposite the number of the lot; *(g.)* the amount assessed upon each such lot or portion of a lot, and *(h.)* the number of each lot or portion or portions of a lot assessed. *(4.)* The section likewise provides for a diagram to be attached to the assessment. This diagram shall show *(a.)* each street or street crossing, lane, alley, place, or court, on which any work has been done; *(b.)* the relative location of each district, lot or portion of lot to the work done; *(c.)* the lots and portions of lots shall be numbered on the diagram to correspond with the numbers in the assessment; (d.) the diagram shall show the number of feet fronting, or number of lots assessed, for the work contracted for and performed.

The section provides that "the assessment shall cover the sum due for the work performed and specified in said contract (including any incidental expenses)." See subdivision 3 of section 34 and section 35 for a definition or enumeration of the things embraced by the term "incidental expenses."

I.   *Contract Fulfilled to Satisfaction of Superintendent.* The superintendent of streets is only authorized to make an assessment after the contractor has fulfilled his contract "to the satisfaction of the street superintendent," so that when the superintendent makes an assessment he, in so doing, necessarily determines that the contract has been performed to his satisfaction. His determination in this respect is final and conclusive, except upon an appeal to the council. An error by the superintendent in determining whether the contractor has properly fulfilled his contract is not a jurisdictional defect, and therefore, the only remedy of a lot owner, dissatisfied with the decision of the superintendent of streets that the contractor has fulfilled his contract, is an appeal from such decision to the council, as provided for by section 11 of the act. [Emery *v.* Bradford, 29 Cal. 75; Shepard *v.* McNeil, 38 Cal. 72; Fanning *v.* Leviston, 93 Cal. 186; Jennings *v.* LeBreton, 80 Cal. 8, 11.]

"The law does not prescribe any particular mode or form in which the superintendent shall manifest his approval or acceptance of the work done under a street contract, nor does it require the approval to be expressed in writing. As the assessment and warrant attached thereto are not to be made or given until 'after the contractor of any street work has fulfilled his contract to the satisfaction of the superintendent,' the assessment and warrant in due form are certainly *prima facie* evidence that the work was completed to the satisfaction of the superintendent, and that he approved and accepted the same." [Jenning *v.* LeBreton, 80 Cal. 8.]

The superintendent may approve the work without personal inspection, and proof of lack of personal inspection by him does not overcome the proof of acceptance from certificates showing that the work was completed according to contract, taken in connection with the personal making and signing of the assessment diagram and warrant by the superintendent. [Jennings *v.* Le Breton, *supra.* See Brady *v.* Bartlett, 56 Cal. 350.]

II. *Assessment Made after Fulfillment of Contract.* Section 19 of article 11 of the new constitution, as originally adopted, provided that no contract should be let for doing any street work *until after* an assessment, in proportion to the benefits on the property to be affected or benefited, should have been levied, collected and paid into the city treasury. Prior to this constitutional provision, most of the street work acts provided, as does 'the present street work act,—section 8, *supra*,—that the assessment should be made by the superintendent of streets after the contract had been fulfilled to his satisfaction. Thus the act of 1872, providing for street improvements in San Francisco, authorized the superintendent of streets to execute contracts for such improvements in advance of the levy and collection of the assessment, instead of afterwards, as required by section 19 of acticle 11 of the new constitution, prior to its amendment in 1884, just as section 8 of the present street work act,—act of March 18, 1885,—requires the contract to be let and the work to be done in advance of the levy and collection of the assessment.

In McDonald *v.* Patterson, 54 Cal. 245, it was held that section 19 of acticle 11 of the new constitution, as it then stood, was not a provision which required legislation to enforce it, and that the provisions of the act of April 1, 1872, relating to street improvements in San Francisco, which authorize the superintendent of streets to execute contracts for such improvements—in advance of the levy and collection of the assessment—were inconsistent with said section of the constitution, and ceased to be operative on the 1st day of January, 1880, when the new constitution went into effect. This ruling was followed in Donahue *v.* Graham, 61 Cal. 276.

The legislature, at its regular session in 1883, proposed an amendment to said section 19 of article 11 of the constitution, wiping out all of that portion of the section relating to assessments to pay for street improvements. This amendment was ratified by the people at the general election in 1884, so that, if this amendment of 1884 to section 19 of article 11 of the constitution was properly submitted, and ratified by the people, street work acts, since then, may provide for assessments *after* the letting of the contract and the performance of the work, or in advance thereof.

The legislature, at its regular session in 1883, for the purpose of enacting a statute which should conform to the provisions of said section 19 of article 11 of the constitution, as it then stood, passed the act known as the Vrooman act, entitled "An act to provide for the improvement of streets, lanes, alleys, courts, places and sidewalks, and the construction of sewers within municipalities,"—approved March 6, 1883. [Statutes. 1883, p. 32.] This act provided for the levy and collection of the assessment before the letting of any contract.

In 1885, the legislature at its regular session in that year, passed the general street work act—the act of March 18, 1885—which, with the subsequent amendatory acts, is the statute now in force. This act was passed after the adoption and ratification of the said amendment to the constitution, eliminating said restriction upon the right of assessment.

In People v. Strother, 67 Cal. 624, it was held that the said amendment of 1884 to said section 19 of article 11 of the constitution was properly adopted. Subsequently, in the case of Oakland Paving Company v. Hilton, 69 Cal. 479, an opinion was rendered by Mr. Justice Thornton, concurred in by Mr. Justice McKee, holding that the said proposed constitutional amendment was never properly submitted to the people for ratification and adoption, because it was not entered at large in the journals of the two houses of the legislature, and that therefore the provision of section 1 of article 18 of the constitution, prescribing the mode by which the constitution shall be amended, was not complied with.

In Oakland Paving Company v. Tompkins, 72 Cal. 5, it was held,—Mr. Justice Thornton only dissenting—that the said proposed amendment to the constitution was properly entered in the journals of the two houses of the legislature and that the amendment to the constitution was properly adopted.

In Thomason v. Ashworth, 73 Cal. 73, the ruling of the court in Oakland Paving Company v. Tompkins, was affirmed.

It has, therefore, now become a settled proposition that under the constitution as it now stands, the superintendent of streets may make an assessment after the contract has been fulfilled to his satisfaction. In the case of Thomason v. Ashworth, supra, it was likewise held, (1.) That the act of 1872, providing for the improvement of streets in San Francisco, in so far as it authorized a contract to be entered into in advance of the assessment and collection of the money to be paid for the work done under it, was repealed by said section 19 of acticle XI of the constitution of 1879; (2.) that it was afterwards entirely repealed by the said act of March 6, 1883, and (3.) that this latter act was repealed by the act of March 18, 1885—the act now in force.

III. *Street Superintendent to Make Assessment in Conformity with the Provisions of Section 7.*   Section 8 of the act provides

that the assessment shall be made in conformity with the
provisions of the preceding section—section 7—according
to the character of the work done, unless any direction or
decision be given by the council on appeal, in which case
the street superintendent shall make the assessment in conformity with such direction and decision.

Therefore the assessment, is, in the first instance, to be
made by the superintendent acting upon his own judgment,
and, unless the council, in its resolution of intention, has
declared that the costs and expenses of the work are to be
assessed upon a district, the superintendent shall make
the assessment upon the lots and lands according to
the front-foot plan of assessing, the expense being
assessed at a uniform rate per front-foot, as provided in
section seven. If the resolution of intention declares that
the cost and expenses are to be assessed upon a district, the
superintendent of streets, after the contractor has fulfilled
his contract to the satisfaction of the superintendent or of
the council on appeal, must proceed to estimate upon the
lands, lots, or portions of lots within the assessment district,
the benefits arising from the work, and must assess upon
all pieces, parcels, lots or portions of lots in said district,
the total amount of the cost and expense—assessing upon
each piece, parcel, lot or portion of a lot, such proportion
of the total amount of the expenses and cost as is proportionate to the estimated benefits received by it.

In either of the above cases, that is, whether the front-
foot plan or the district assessment plan be the mode adopted, the assessment must, in the first instance, be made by
the street superintendent acting upon his own judgment.
In the one case he determines the rate of assessment per
front foot to be assessed upon the lots according to the front-
foot plan, in the other case he estimates the benefits to be
received by the lots and parcels of land within the assessment district, and assesses against each lot and parcel of
land such an amount of the total cost and expenses as is
proportionate to the benefit received by it. In either case
his decision is final and conclusive, except upon appeal to
the council. If a property owner appeal to the council, as
provided for by section 11 of the act, the council may
change the assessment, and in such case the street superintendent must make the assessment in conformity with the
council's direction and decision. For example, a property
owner may deem the benefit actually received by his land,
when the district assessment plan has been adopted by the

council in its resolution of intention, to be less than the amount estimated by the street superintendent. In such case the owner may appeal to the council, and the council may, if it agree with the property owner's contention, decide that the benefit received by the lot is less than that estimated by the superintendent of streets. In such case the superintendent must make the assessment in conformity with the direction and decision of the council.

IV. *Form of Assessment Roll and How Made.* Section 8 requires the assessment to contain eight provisions, enumerated, *supra*, page 85, and likewise a diagram showing four things. Some, at least, of these requirements, *i. e.* the things which the assessment and diagram must show, affect substantial rights, and, therefore, must be complied with as required by the act; [Smith *v.* Cofran, 34 Cal. 316.] For example, the requirement that the assessment shall show the name of the owner, if known to the superintendent, or, if unknown, the word "unknown" written opposite the number of the lot. And, as the property owner has a constitutional right to receive notice that his property has been assessed, and as the assessment may be made against him by the words "owner unknown," it follows also that the assessment should contain a description of the property sufficient to impart notice to the owner. [See Blackwell on Tax Titles, section 223, *et seq.;* Desty on Taxation, Vol. II, page 1329; Sharpe *v.* Johnson, 4 Hill, 92.] "The identity of the lot assessed, and not the person who may be the owner, is made the essential requirement of the statute, the first must be *specifically* described, while the latter may be designated as 'unknown.' " [Gillis *v.* Cleveland, 87 Cal. 217.]

(a.) *Name of Owner if Known, if not to Owner Unknown.* The assessment must be made against the true owner either by name or by the designation of "unknown," as provided in the statute. If not made against the true owner by name or by the designation "unknown," it creates no liability against the land or against the true owner or against the person in whose name it is erroneously made. The assessment must be made against the true owner, if known to the superintendent of streets, and if not known the word "unknown" must be written opposite the number of the lot and the amount of the assessment. Therefore, if the assessment be against a deceased person, it is void. [Smith *v* Davis, 30 Cal. 537; see Taylor *v.* Donner, 31 Cal. 481; Mayo *v.* Ah Loy, 32 Cal. 477.] And no person can be made to pay an assessment, even if he is the owner of a lot in the assessment district, unless the assessment has been

against him by name or by the designation "unknown."
[Blatner v. Davis, 32 Cal. 328.] It is the duty of the
superintendent of streets, if, upon reasonable inquiry, he
entertains doubts about the ownership of property to
be affected by the assessment, to assess it to "owners
unknown" [Himmelmann v. Steiner, 38 Cal. 175], and an
assessment to "unknown owners," made by the superintendent of streets, amounts to an official certificate by the
proper officer, that the owner of the particular lot designated was unknown to him. The certificate is conclusive
of the truth of the fact certified, and cannot be called in
question in an action brought upon the assessment.
[Chambers v. Satterlee, 40 Cal. 498, 518.] Section 8 of the
act prescribes what an assessment shall show, and, among
other things, that it "shall show * * * the name of the
owner of each lot, or portion of a lot (if known to the
street superintendent); if unknown the word 'unknown'
shall be written opposite the number of the lot," etc. And
in Smith v. Cofran, 34 Cal. 316–317, it was said: "There is no
authority for making an assessment that does not embrace
these essentials. There is no authority to make an assessment
strictly *in rem* without reference to owners, either known or
unknown, or an assessment that shall effect the interest of any
party, unless designated in the assessment by name, or, if
unknown, it be so expressly stated." In Himmelmann v.
Steiner, *supra*, it was held that the assessment by the
superintendent of streets to the defendant as an "owner
unknown" was conclusive of the fact that the owner was
unknown to the superintendent, even though the premises
stood of record in the name of the defendant all the time,
and was substantially enclosed, with a dwelling house
thereon, occupied by defendant. [See also Hewes v. Reis,
40 Cal. 255.]

In Himmelmann v. Hoadley, 44 Cal. 227, it was said:
"According to the repeated constructions of the statute, the
superintendent, unless he is satisfied *beyond all doubt* as to
the ownership of a lot, may assess it to 'unknown' owner;
and it is almost, if not quite, impossible to show that he
did not know the owner." Consequently the safest course is
to assess all lots to owners "unknown." For, if assessed to
the owner in his name, it must be assessed to the true
owner, and as this is almost always a matter of doubt the
only safe course is for the superintendent to avail himself
of the alternative allowed by the statute and assess to
"owner unknown."

It will be a great advantage to the contractor if the
assessment is in every case assessed to unknown owners,

since, in that case, under the provisions of section 10 of the act, the "demand" need not be made upon the owner in person or his agent, but may be made upon the premises.

An assessment to "Shubal Dunham and unknown" is void, likewise an assessment to "S. Dunham or unknown." [City of Stockton v. Dunham, 59 Cal. 608; Same v. Same, 59 Cal. 609.] The assessment must be against the owner in his true name alone, or against him simply as an "owner unknown."

If the property belongs to tenants in common, it should be assessed to them jointly. [Blatner v. Davis, 32 Cal. 331.]

(b.) The assessment may be made upon a gold basis and collected in gold coin. [Baudry v. Valdez, 32 Cal. 270.]

(c.) Attestation of Assessment. The assessment when made must be attested by the official signature of the street superintendent. Without such signature it is not an official document, and this, even though the statute does not expressly require the assessment to be thus attested, and it cannot be helped out by the signature to the warrant and diagram. [Dougherty v. Hitchcock, 35 Cal. 512.]

(d.) Time Within which to make Assessment and Re-assessment. No time is limited within which the assessment must be made, although it is the duty of the street superintendent to make it immediately after the fulfilment of the of the contract to his satisfaction. Nor is the fact that a void assessment has been already made, any excuse for not making a valid one and he may be compelled by *mandamus* to do so. [Himmelmann v. Cofran, 36 Cal. 411.] And if the first assessment is invalid for failure to authenticate his record by his official signature, it is his duty afterward to make a valid assessment. [Shepard v. McNeil, 38 Cal. 73.] See also section 9 of the act, *infra*, where provision is expressly made for a second assessment in case the first be adjudged invalid. But if the first assessment is valid the contractor cannot compel a second one to be made. [Frick v. Morford, 87 Cal. 576.] Where, in an action to recover the amount of the assessment, the property owners set up that the assessment is void and it is not, but the court erroneously holds that it is, the property owners are estopped to deny the authority of the street superintendent to make a second assessment. [Dyer v. Scalmanini, 69 Cal. 637.]

(e.) Description of Property. An assessment giving the number and frontage of lots, and referring to the diagram for further description, sufficiently describes the property to be assessed. [Hewes v. Reis, 40 Cal. 255; Ede v. Knight, 93 Cal. 159, 163.]

But the assessment and diagram when taken together
must intelligibly describe the property. And, if the diagram is referred to for a description, it must contain
such a description or such references as will enable the
description of the premises to be understood. If the
description is confined to the diagram, it will be insufficient
if there be nothing on the diagram to show the points of
the compass and locality of the streets. [Himmelmann v.
Cahn, 49 Cal. 285; San Francisco v. Quackenbush, 53 Cal.
52.] However, it is not necessary that the letters N and S,
to indicate the points of the compass, north and south
respectively, should be used. If an arrow is used, its barb
alone is competent without the letter N to denote north on
the diagram, and the point of a scroll is as competent as the
barb of an arrow to denote north on a map or diagram.
[Whiting v. Quackenbush, 54 Cal. 306; Williams v. McDonald, 58 Cal. 527.] The assessment is void if it does not
show the dimensions of the lot. [Himmelmann v. Bateman,
50 Cal. 11.]

But it will be sufficient if the dimensions of two of the
side lines only are shown, if the map show that the figure is
a rectangle, so that the dimensions of the lot may be
ascertained from a knowledge of the dimensions of the two
side lines. [Whiting v. Quackenbush, supra.] The assessment is insufficient if it fail to show on what side of the
street the lot is. [San Francisco v. Quackenbush, 53 Cal.
52.]

If the assessment describe the lot by metes and bounds, it
will be sufficient even if the diagram does not indicate the
course of the streets by an arrow or a scroll, as the courts
will take judicial notice of the streets and of their relation
to each other, and of the directions in which they run.
[Brady v. Page, 59 Cal. 52, 301; Williams v. Savings &
L. Soc., 97 Cal. 122.]

The venue in the caption of the assessment is sufficient
to show that the property sought to be charged is within
the city within which the improvement was made, and that
the street superintendent of such city has jurisdiction to
make the assessment. [Whiting v. Quackenbush, supra.]

If the assessment number a small street running at right
angles to the street upon which the work was done and
terminating therein, also designating such small, terminating street by its name, referring to it as a lot having a
frontage upon the main street equal to its width, and
charging it with a certain amount as its proportion of the
cost of the work, this will not invalidate the assessment.
It will be considered merely as a mode of distributing the

cost of the work as between the lots liable therefor. [Dyer
v. Martinovich, 63 Cal. 353.

The assessment and diagram, *as recorded*, must contain a
sufficient description of the lot, and must not vary
materially from the diagram attached to the original assessment. [Norton v. Courtney, 53 Cal. 691.]

    V. *Remedy for Irregularities in Assessment.*

    (a.) Appeal by Lot Owner. According to the require-
ments of section 8 of the act, the assessment must show and
contain certain things. It might be difficult to draw the
line of demarkation in particular cases so as to clearly
determine when a failure of the assessment roll to show
these things, or an irregularity in showing them, operates to
render the assessment wholly void, and when it is merely
an irregularity to be corrected on appeal. One of the questions in each particular case is: Does the alleged irregularity affect substantial rights? If substantial rights
are not affected, then such appeal is probably the only
remedy of the aggrieved property owner. In Dehail v.
Morford, 95 Cal. 460, Mr. Justice Harrison said: "After the
jurisdiction has once been acquired, subsequent proceedings
can be attacked for only such irregularities as affect *substantial* rights." It has been decided that a failure
to make the assessment against the true owner, either
by his name or by the designation "unknown," is a failure
in respect to a "substantial right," and that therefore the
owner need not appeal to the council, but may attack the
assessment in an action against him. Or rather, it has been
decided that in such case the owner is not a party to the
assessment at all, and one not a party to the assessment in
one of the modes designated by the statute, *i. e.* either as
owner in his true name, or by the designation, "unknown,"
is not affected by it; he is a stranger to it and not "aggrieved," and those only can be concluded by the decision of the
council, on appeal, who have been made parties to the
assessment in one of said modes. [Smith v. Cofran, 34 Cal.
316; opinion of Mr. Justice Sawyer on petition for rehearing.]
The same result might also follow where the assessment
is to "owner unknown," and fails to describe the
land so as to give sufficient notice to the owner
that his lot had been assessed. [See authorities *supra*
on "description of property."] A description sufficient to give notice to the taxpayer that his
land is assessed is an essential which the legislature cannot
dispense with, nor work a cure upon any proceedings defective in that regard. [Blackwell on Tax Titles, section 223

et seq.; Desty on Taxation, Vol. II, p. 1329; Sharpe *v.* Johnson, 4 Hill 92.]

We have said that one of the questions in each particular case is: Does the alleged irregularity affect substantial rights? But this we believe is not decisive of the question as to whether the irregularity is one which may be corrected on appeal or not. For, while it is probable that if substantial rights are not affected by the alleged irregularity, an appeal to the council is the only remedy of the aggrieved property owner, [See language of Mr. Justice Harrison in Dehail *v.* Morford, quoted *supra*,] it does not therefore follow that an appeal to the council is not the sole remedy, if substantial rights are affected by irregularities in the assessment. Thus, if a lot, liable to assessment, be omitted from the assessment roll, the substantial rights of those whose property is assessed, are certainly affected thereby. [People *v.* Lynch, 51 Cal. 19; Diggins *v.* Brown, 76 Cal. 318; Davies *v.* Los Angeles, 86 Cal. 47; Moulton *v.* Parks, 64 Cal. 181; Dyer *v.* Harrison, 63 Cal. 447.] Nevertheless, it seems that, if the error or irregularity complained of is capable of correction by the council on appeal, an appeal to the council is the only remedy. [See opinion of Temple J. in Chambers *v.* Satterlee, 40 Cal. 524. On page 526, Mr. Justice Temple said: "I have no doubt but that this right [right to appeal] is exclusive of any other remedy as to all matters which can be revised and corrected on such appeal." See also notes to section 11 *post.*] Accordingly it was held in Dowling *v.* Altschul, 33 Pac. Rep. 495, that, where an assessment for paving a *cul-de-sac* failed to assess the land at the end of the same, a question is presented which the city council has power to determine on appeal under the provisions of section 11 of the act of March 18, 1885—the Vrooman act—and that, therefore, its decision is conclusive, although Mr. Justice Harrison, in his concurring opinion in this case, hesitates to affirm that the act of the board of supervisors of San Francisco confirming an assessment which is made in manifest violation of the provisions of the statute, concludes the owner from making such defense in an action to enforce the assessment. If, however, the prevailing opinion in this case of Dowling *v.* Altschul be correct, then it seems that, to enable a property owner to successfully attack the assessment in an action to enforce it, not only must some "substantial right" of the property owner be affected by the alleged error or irregularity, but the error or irregularity complained of must be one which cannot be corrected by the council on appeal—the mischief must be past remedy. Now it is difficult to conceive of an

error or irregularity in the assessment itself which is past
remedy, where the work has been properly done under a
valid contract for the same, since, under the decisions cited
supra, no time is limited within which an assessment may
be made, and, if the first assessment be invalid for any
reason, the superintendent of streets may make another.
(*supra* page 92.)

However, if the prevailing opinion in Dowling v. Altschul
be correct, then it seems that, to determine whether or not
an appeal to the council was the property owner's exclusive
remedy for an omission of, or irregularity in, any one of the
things which section 8 of the act requires to be shown by
or contained in the assessment, two questions are involved,
viz: (*1.*) Does the alleged omission or irregularity affect
any substantial right of the property owner? and (*2*) If it
does affect a substantial right of the property owner, can
the error complained of be corrected by the council on
appeal, so as to restore or preserve the substantial rights of
the "aggrieved" property owner?—*i. e.*, is the error or irregularity complained of past remedy or not?

But, even if the error complained of might have
been corrected by the council on appeal, the property owner is not an "aggrieved" party, and therefore is not concluded by a failure to appeal,—
or by the decision of the council on appeal, if one be taken,—
unless he is a party to the assessment. [Smith *v.* Cofran, 34
Cal. 316, opinion of Mr. Justice Sawyer on petition for
rehearing.] And he is not a party to the assessment unless
he is assessed in his true name, or by the designation,
"unknown." [Smith v. Cofran, *supra*.] The same reasoning would seem likewise to be applicable where neither the
assessment nor the diagram contains a sufficient description
of the land. For, since "the identity of the lot assessed, and
not the person who may be the owner, is made the essential
requirement of the statute," [Gillis v. Cleveland, 87 Cal. 217]
it would seem to follow that, if the lot be not sufficiently
described, the lot owner is not a party to the assessment,
and therefore not a party "aggrieved," and need not appeal
to the council—especially if the assessment be not made
against him in his true name. [See authorities cited *supra*
page 93, under the caption, "Description of Property."]
So also, where a lot is not liable to be assessed at all, the
owner is not a party directly interested in the contract,
work or assessment; he is not a party to the assessment,
and therefore need not appeal. [Bassett v. Enwright, 19
Cal. 636.] See also Frick v. Morford, 87 Cal. 576, where it
was held that if the lot assessed is wholly outside of the

limits of the work as fixed by the resolution of intention, it cannot be held liable for any assessment, or if only part is within the limits as fixed by the resolution, the contractor is not entitled to an assessment against that part of the lot not fronting upon the work authorized by the resolution, and if the lot is wholly outside of the limits as fixed by the resolution of intention, the owner is not a party "aggrieved," since in such case his lot could not be held liable at all, and therefore he is not required to appeal to the city council.

Therefore, where all the proceedings leading up to the execution of the contract have been regular and proper, and the contract is valid and the work done thereunder has been properly performed and within the proper time, and the only irregularity complained of is one inhering in and directly appertaining to the assessment itself, then it seems that, for the purpose of ascertaining whether an appeal to the council is the property owner's only remedy, the following rules are determinative:

1. Was the property owner alleging the irregularity a party to the assessment? If he was not a party to the assessment he is not a party "aggrieved" and therefore need not appeal to the council. If the assessment is not made against him in his true name or under the designation "unknown," he is not a party to the assessment. And it seems that if the lot be not sufficiently described, or if the lot is not liable to be assessed at all, he is not a party to the assessment.

2. If the property owner complaining of the irregularity was a party to the assessment, did the alleged omission or irregularity in making the assessment affect any of his substantial rights? If it did not, then it seems that an appeal was his only remedy.

3. If the property owner complaining of the irregularity or omission, was a party to the assessment, and if the irregularity or omission complained of did affect a substantial right, was the mischief past remedy, or was it possible for the council on appeal to have corrected the assessment so as to have restored or preserved all the substantial rights of the aggrieved property owner? If the council might so have corrected the assessment, then it seems that an appeal to the council was the only remedy of the complaining property owner. [See notes to section 11 of the act.]

The rule that "after the jurisdiction has once been acquired, subsequent proceedings can be attacked for only such irregularities as affect substantial rights," is plain and simple, but to apply the rule, *hoc opus est.*

(b.) Appeal by Contractor. The contractor, under section 11 of the act, has the right to appeal to the council, as well

as a lot owner. If there be some irregularity in the assessment, which, however, does not render it void,—does not affect a substantial right of the property owner,—the contractor, if the property owner fails to have the irregularity corrected by appealing to the council, will doubtless lose nothing by himself failing to appeal, but if the irregularity in the assessment be one which renders it nugatory, the contractor's only remedy is by appeal to the council where the irregularity may be corrected. [Smith *v.* Cofran, 34 Cal. 310; Frick *v.* Morford, 87 Cal. 576, 580; See notes to section 11 of the act.]

VI. *Diagram.* Section 8 likewise requires a "diagram" to be attached to the assessment. This diagram is required to exhibit "each street or street crossing, lane, alley, place, or court on which any work has been done, and showing the relative location of each district, lot, or portion of lot to the work done, numbered to correspond with the numbers in the assessment, and showing the number of feet fronting, or number of lots assessed, for said work contracted for and performed;" and in McDonald *v.* Conniff, No. 15,085, decided Aug. 30, 1893, the Supreme Court, per Harrison, J., said: "There is no requirement in the statute that the 'work' shall be shown or even designated upon the diagram; but if it [the objection] be construed as an objection that the diagram does not show upon what portion of Tenth street the work was done, it may also be said that the statute does not make this requirement. * * * The diagram is only auxiliary to the assessment, and is intended to be merely a map *exhibiting* 'each street' upon which the work was done. The requirement that it shall show 'the relative location of each lot assessed to the work done,' is satisfied if it shows their location in relation to the 'exhibited' street upon which the work was done. Taken in connection with the description of the work for which the assessment was made, it can then be seen from an inspection whether any of the lots assessed are so located as to be liable for any part of the expense of the work, and if for any reason a particular lot ought not to have been assessed for that work, the error can be corrected upon application to the proper tribunal. The diagram is not intrinsically invalid unless the lots shown thereon are so located that they could not under any circumstances be made liable for a portion of the expense of the work. It is not essential to the validity of an assessment that the lots assessed should front upon the entire portion of the street exhibited upon the diagram. In the case of an assessment for work done upon main street crossings, or at the termination of one street in another, the street crossing or the termination is required to be exhibited on the diagram, while the lots to be assessed front upon portions of the streets on which none of the work was done, and the diagram is to show their relative location to the work done by showing that they are within the quarter blocks or territory liable to be assessed. The diagram in the present case sufficiently complies with the statute. It exhibits Tenth street as the street upon which the work was done, and it also delineates the several lots assessed and shows that each of the lots assessed fronts upon Tenth street, and that its location is within the territory liable to be assessed for work done upon Tenth street."

Section 9. To said assessment shall be attached a warrant, which shall be signed by the superintendent of streets, and countersigned by the mayor of said city. The said warrant shall be substantially in the following form:

FORM OF THE WARRANT.

By virtue hereof, I (name of the superintendent of streets), of the city of ——, county of —— (or city and county of ——), and state of California, by virtue of the authority vested in me as said superintendent of streets, do authorize and empower (name of contractor), (his or their) agents or assigns, to demand and receive the several assessments upon the assessment and diagram hereto attached, and this shall be (his or their) warrant for the same.

(Date.) ——(name of superintendent of streets).

Countersigned by (name of mayor).

Said warrant, assessment and diagram, together with the certificate of the city engineer, shall be recorded in the office of said superintendent of streets. When so recorded the several amounts assessed shall be a lien upon the lands, lots, or portions of lots assessed, respectively, for the period of two years from the date of said recording, unless sooner discharged; and from and after the date of said recording of any warrant, assessment, diagram and certificate, all persons mentioned in section eleven of this act shall be deemed to have notice of the contents of the record thereof. After said warrant, assessment, diagram and certificate are recorded the same shall be delivered to the contractor, or his agent or assigns, on demand, but not until after the payment to the said superintendent of streets of the incidental expenses not previously paid by the contractor, or his assigns; and by virtue of said warrant said contractor, or his agent or assigns, shall be authorized to demand and receive the amount of the several assessments made to cover the sum due for the work specified in such contracts and assessments. Whenever it shall appear by any final judgment of any court of this state that any suit brought to foreclose the lien of any sum of money assessed to cover the expense of said street work done under the provisions of this act has been defeated by reason of any defect, error, informality, omission, irregularity or illegality in any assessment hereafter to be made and issued, or in the recording thereof, or in the return thereof made to or recorded by said superintendent of streets, any person interested therein may, at any time within three months after the entry of said final judgment, apply to said superintendent of streets who issued the same, or to any superintendent of streets in office at the time of said application, for another assessment to be issued in conformity to law; and said superintendent shall, within fifteen days after the date of said application, make and deliver to said applicant a new assessment, diagram and warrant in accordance with law; and the acting mayor shall countersign the same as now provided by law, which assessment shall be a lien for the period of two years from the date of said assessment, and be enforced as provided in section seven of this act. [*Amendment approved March 31, 1891, statutes 1891, page 205.*]

[Section 9 was amended in 1889, by act of March 14, 1889, statutes 1889, page 167; and again in 1891 by act of March 31, 1891, statutes 1891, page 205.]

The proceedings necessary to the existence of a valid lien terminate with the recording of the warrant, assessment and diagram, together with the certificate of the city engineer, as provided for by section 9 of the act. Hitherto the lien has been inchoate, commencing with the first acquisition and exercise of jurisdiction by the council, which was operative only so far as to prevent owners from affecting the assessment by changing the area and boundaries of the land as it stood when jurisdiction over the subject matter first attached. The Supreme Court has held that the sale of a thin frontage for the purpose of confining the assessment to this comparatively valueless strip is unavailing. [Dougherty *v.* Miller, 36 Cal. 87.] But, under the provisions of section 9 of the act, the lien, for the first time, becomes perfected by the recordation of the warrant, assessment, diagram, etc, unless upon appeal to the council, as provided for by section 11, the assessment shall be amended, or set aside and a new one issued. In such case the lien is perfected according to and by the final recordation.

There are, therefore, at least fourteen acts necessary to the existence of a valid lien and, where the proceedings are inaugurated by a petition as provided for by section 4 of the act, or where grading is to be done after a change of grade, and the petition required by section 2 of the act, as amended in 1893, is filed, there are, including such petition, fifteen necessary acts to the existence of a valid lien. In other cases, the fourteen necessary acts to the existence of a valid lien are: (*1.*) Passage of resolution of intention; (*2.*) posting and publication of resolution; (*3.*) posting and publication of notices of passage of resolution; (*4.*) passage of order for the work to be done; (*5.*) publication of order for the work to be done; (these first five requisites are provided for by section 3 of the act,) (*6.*) posting and publication of notices inviting sealed proposals; (*7.*) consideration of bids; (*8.*) award of contract; (*9.*) posting and publication of notice of award of contract; (*10.*) execution of written contract by superintendent of streets; (these requisites—from

Sec. 9 as amended
March 31, 1891. 101

6 to 10 inclusive—are provided for by section 5 of the act,)
(*11.*) making an assessment, as provided by section 8 of the
act; (*12.*) attaching to the assessment a diagram as provided
by said section 8; (*13.*) making, signing and countersigning
a warrant for the collection of the assessment and attaching
the same to the assessment as provided by section 9 of the
act; and (*14.*) recording said warrant, assessment and diagram, together with the certificate of the city engineer, as
provided by said section 9 of the act.

When these fourteen acts, terminating with the recordation of the warrant, assessment and diagram, together with
the certificate of the city engineer, have been performed as
required by the statute, "the several amounts assessed shall
be a lien upon the lands, lots or portions of lots assessed,
respectively, for the period of two years from the date of
said recording, unless sooner discharged."

Section 9 provides for: (*1.*) A warrant for the collection of the assessment, the form of which is given, to be
signed by the superintendent of streets and countersigned
by the mayor. (*2.*) Recordation of the warrant, assessment
and diagram, together with the certificate of the city engineer.
(*3.*) Effect of such recordation. (*4.*) Delivery of warrant,
assessment, diagram and certificate to the contractor, his
agents or assigns, and effect of such delivery. (*5.*) Re-assessment in case the original assessment be adjudged invalid
by reason of any defect, error, informality, omission or
irregularity, or illegality in the original assessment itself.

I. *Warrant, Signing and Counter-signing.* The form of
the warrant is given in the act (Sec. 9) and, as a part of that
form, provision is made for filling in the date of the warrant.
Therefore it is a part of the statutory requirement that the
warrant be dated. It was accordingly held in Shipman *v.*
Forbes, 97 Cal. 572 that if the warrant be not dated
so as to show the day of the month and year, it can
not serve as the foundation of proceedings for the
collection of the assessment. The court by Mr. Justice
Harrison, said: "The form prescribed by the statute,
makes the date as much a part of the warrant as it
does the signature of the officer, and in matters of this
character, in which the property of a citizen is to be taken
in invitum, it cannot be said that any requirement of the
statute is to be disregarded. Every requisite having the
semblance of benefit to the owner must be complied with;
and when the form of a statutory proceeding is prescribed, its
observance becomes essential to the validity of the proceedings."

The fact that the mayor, before his election, had become

the assignee of a contract for the improvement of a street, as security for a debt due him by the contractor, does not affect the validity of the contract or the assessment for the work, nor incapacitate him from countersigning the warrant for the collection of the assessment. [Baudry v. Valdez, 32 Cal. 269.] The act of the mayor in countersigning the warrant, is purely ministerial, and if there were any irregularity in countersigning the warrant under such circumstances, such irregularity is waived by a failure to appeal to the council as provided for by section 11 of the act. [Id.]

The mayor's function in countersigning the warrant, is limited merely to approval, and whatever is essential to the issuance and validity of the warrant, must be done before it reaches the mayor; and no act of his can supply any defect, or cure any irregularity in the prior proceedings. [Shipman v. Forbes, supra.]

While the warrant must be countersigned by the mayor, it has been held, nevertheless, that an omission of his name and the designation of his office from the recorded warrant, as recorded in the record book of the street superintendent, does not render the recording ineffectual. [Gillis v. Cleveland, 87 Cal. 215; see also S. F. v. Certain Real Estate, 50 Cal. 188.]

II. *Recording Warrant, Assessment, etc.* The warrant, as we have seen, must be substantially in the form provided by the act, without the omission of anything prescribed by that form, and must be signed by the superintendent and countersigned by the mayor, and attached to the assessment, as provided by section 9 of the act. After this, and as an essential to the existence of a valid assessment lien, "*said*" warrant, that is, the warrant in the form prescribed and signed and countersigned as required by the act, together with the assessment, diagram and certificate of the city engineer, must be recorded in the office of the superintendent of streets. These documents must be recorded by the street superintendent at full length, in a book to be kept for that purpose in his office. Section 10 provides that, after the contractor has made return of the warrant, "the superintendent of streets shall record the return so made, *in the margin of the record of the warrant and assessment*, and also the original contract referred to therein, if it has not already been recorded, at full length *in a book to be kept for that purpose in his office*, and shall sign the record." From which it appears that the warrant, assessment, diagram and certificates of the city engineer are to be recorded in a book kept for that purpose in the office of the superintendent. Section 21 provides that the superintendent shall keep "such records as may be required by the provision of this act." And by section 18 it is provided that such record "shall have the same force and effect as other public records, and copies therefrom, duly certified, may be used in evidence with the same effect as the originals." The certificate of the city engineer must be recorded together with the warrant, assessment and diagram. Its character is described in the first subdivision of section 34 of the act. [See Jennings *v.* LeBreton, 80 Cal. 8, 14, for remarks upon a provision in the act of 1872 similar to sections 18 and 34 of present street work act.]

Until the assessment, diagram, warrant and certificate of the city engineer are *"recorded"* in the record-book kept in the office of the street superintendent, the contractor does not acquire a lien for the work done. The warrant must be so recorded before it is delivered to the contractor or his assigns. [Himmelman *v.* Danos, 35 Cal. 441; Gillis *v.* Cleveland, 87 Cal. 214, 219.]

What constitutes a *"record"*? This question was considered in Himmelman *v.* Danos, *supra,* in Dougherty *v.* Hitchcock, 35 Cal. 512, and in Himmelmann *v.* Hoadley, 44 Cal. 213, and the conclusion to be deduced from these decisions is: There is no "record" until the official character of the entry or copy of the warrant, assessment, diagram and certificate in the record book has been made to appear upon its face by adding a certificate *signed* by the superintendent of streets or by a deputy in his name. In Himmelman *v.* Danos, *supra,* 35 Cal. 451, it is said, "The making of the record is an official act, and its official character must be made to appear upon its face, *which can be done only by adding a certificate signed by the officer authorized to make the record.* Until certified and signed by the proper officer, it is but waste paper, of which no one need take notice. To become a record, it must be the official act of the officer authorized to make it; to become his act it must have his signature. Until signed it is the act of no one, and is as valueless for any purpose as an unsigned deed or sheriff's return. The only difference between that which is record and that which is not, is the official stamp or authenticity which the former bears upon its face. The former proves itself; the latter does not. The former proves itself because it bears the stamp of an officer of the law, acting under the solemnities of an oath, or at least of official duty, and it is the official stamp, and nothing else, which makes it record." In Dougherty *v.* Hitchcock, 35 Cal. 521–2, it was said, "In Himmelman *v.* Danos, it is held that the copies of the assessment, warrant, and diagram found in the superintendent's book could not be considered as a record until signed by the superintendent, because the making of the record was an official act, and its official character must be made to appear on its face."

In Himmelmann v. Hoadley, 44 Cal. 225, it was said: "In Himmelman v. Danos, 35 Cal. 441, the question whether the record of the assessment should be separately signed was reserved. The usual, and, in our opinion, proper mode for the authentication of such a record, is by appending the official certificate of the officer whose duty it is to make the record. He need not specify in his certificate the pages of the record upon which the assessment, etc., are copied; but when he does certify in that form, the certificate will be limited to the pages specified, unless the record itself shows that the reference to the pages is a clerical error."

Therefore, while in the case of Himmelman v. Danos, the question, whether the record of the assessment should be separately signed, was reserved, it is established that copies of the assessment, warrant, diagram and certificate, found in the record book in the superintendent's office, can not be be considered as "*recorded*" until there is added to it a certificate signed by the superintendent himself, or by a duly authorized deputy in his name, or at least there must be added the signature of the superintendent or his deputy, even if no certificate is added; and, while, according to the provisions of section 10 of the act, it is expressly required that the record, when *completed*, by the addition of the contract and the return, shall be signed by the superintendent, nevertheless, it seems to be imperatively necessary that the copy of the warrant, assessment, diagram and certificate in the record-book, should be followed by the signature of the superintendent or his deputy, and that the same be done prior to the entry of the contract and return, or, at least, prior to the return, and likewise prior to the demand by the contractor. For the contractor is not authorized to make a demand until there is a lien, a charge against the land, and there is no lien, according to the express provisions of the act, until the warrant, assessment, etc., are recorded, and, according to the decisions cited above, the warrant, assessment, etc., are not recorded until they are copied into the record-book kept in the superintendent's office, and signed by him or his deputy in his name. A separate certificate and signature of the officer need not follow each of the documents recorded, *i. e.* need not follow, separately, the warrant, and the assessment, and the diagram and the certificate of the city engineer, but one certificate signed by the authorized officer, appended to the copy of the warrant, assessment, diagram and certificate of the city engineer is sufficient. [Himmelmann v. Hoadley, 44 Cal. 213.]

III. *Effect of Recording Warrant, Assessment, etc.*

The effects of recording the warrant, assessment, diagram etc., are: (*1.*) To create a lien for the several amounts assessed upon the lands, lots or portions of lots assessed, for the period of two years from the date of recording, unless sooner discharged. This lien, by virtue of the provisions of section 10 of the act, is liable to be lost if the contractor does not make due return of the warrant within thirty days after its date. Section 10 provides, that "if any contractor shall fail to return his warrant within the time and in the form provided in this section he shall thenceforth have no lien upon the property assessed." If an action upon the assessment lien is commenced within two years from the recording of the warrant, assessment, etc., the lien will not lapse, though judgment is rendered after the two years expire. [Dougherty v. Henaire, 47 Cal. 9; Randolph v. Bayue, 44 Cal. 366.] A street assessment lein is a creature of the statute, and if it is allowed to expire by lapse of time, it cannot be enforced upon any grounds of equitable consideration. [Brady v. Burke, 90 Cal. 2.] (*2.*) From and after the date of said recording of any warrant, assessment, diagram and certificate, all persons mentioned in section 11 of the act shall be deemed to have notice of the contents of the record thereof. Said persons, by virtue of the provisions of said section 11, have thirty days after the date of the warrant within which to appeal to the city council.

The contractor, if he finds the assessment to be incorrect or illegal in a particular which may be remedied by the council on appeal, should appeal to the council within thirty days from the date of the warrant, and have the assessment corrected and made legal. [See Smith v. Cofran, 34 Cal. 315; Frick v. Morford, 87 Cal 580.]

IV. *Delivery of Warrant, Assessment, etc., to the Contractor.*

After the warrant, assessment, diagram and certificate have been recorded, i. e., copied into the record-book, and authenticated by the signature of the superintendent or his deputy, they must be delivered to the contractor, or his agent or assigns, on demand, after the payment to the superintendent of all incidental expenses, not previously paid by the contractor or his assigns. By virtue of said warrant, the contractor, his agent or assigns are authorized to demand and receive the amount of the several assessments made to cover the sum due for the work specified in the contract and assessment.

If the original contractor has assigned his contract, the warrant may, nevertheless, be delivered to him as the agent of his assignee, and, as agent of his assignee, he may make the demand, Taylor *v.* Palmer, 31 Cal. 241, where it is said, page 249, "The form of the warrant is the same in all cases, [*i. e.* it is always issued running to the original contractor, his agent or assignees] and in the absence of any notice of an assignment of the contract, and perhaps in any event, the superintendent delivers it, as a matter of course, to the original contractor if applied for by him; if not, to any other person authorized by him to receive it either as agent or assignee. Likewise the demand for payment may be made by the original contractor, his authorized agent or assignee. When an assignment has been made, and the demand is by the original contractor, he acts as the agent of his assignee. The property owner may safely pay to anyone who, on the face of the warrant is entitled to receive the money, especially in the absence of any notice to the contrary." [See also Foley *v.* Bullard, No. 15,305, decided September 11, 1893.]

V. Re-assessment after Judgment adjudging an Assessment Illegal. The re-assessment provided for by section 9 of the act must be made after a *"final"* judgment of a court of this state. The judgment must be *final.* And it must appear from such final judgment that the suit in which it was rendered has been defeated by reason of some "defect, error, informality, omission, irregularity, or illegality" in *(1.)* the assessment itself, or *(2.)* in the recording thereof, or *(3.)* in the return thereof made to the superintendent of streets, as provided for by section 10, or *(4.)* in the return recorded by the street superintendent, as provided for by said section 10.

This merciful provision of the act only applies to errors, etc., in the assessment itself, or in its record, or in the contractor's return, or in the record thereof. It is not applicable to errors in the council's proceedings, or in the contract. But independently of this provision of the statute, if the council has properly acquired jurisdiction to order the work to be done, and a contract therefor has been properly made, and fulfilled to the satisfaction of the street superintendent, and all the proceedings up to this point have been regular, it seems that, under the decision in Himmelmann *v.* Cofran, 36 Cal. 411, and Wood *v.* Strother, 76 Cal. 545, the superintendent may make a new assessment, and proceedings subsequent thereto, where the first assessment is void by reason of any defect, error, informality, omission, irregularity or illegality. And if, independently of any statutory provision therefor, the superintendent may make a new assessment when the first one is void by reason of some error or omission in making it, it does not appear why, for the same reason he may not issue a new warrant, for example, when for any reason the first warrant is void. [See Elliott on Roads and Streets, pp. 435–6.]

In Wood *v.* Strother, 76 Cal. 545, it was held that if an assessment has been adjudged to be void for causes affecting the assessment itself, and not the proceedings upon which it rests, a new assessment may be made within a reasonable time, and that what is a reasonable time is to be determined upon a consideration of all the circumstances, also that the fact that some of the owners have paid what was charged against their property by the void assessment, is not of itself a reason why a valid assessment should not be made and that a court of equity will treat the payments made as payments in advance, and compel the contractor to credit them on the second assessment; also that *mandamus* will lie to compel the auditor to countersign the warrant on the second assessment, notwithstanding that the act requiring him to countersign the warrant [San Francisco street work act of 1872] provided that "before countersigning it, [he] shall examine the contract, the steps taken previous thereto, and the record of assessments, *and must be satisfied that the proceedings have been legal and fair.*"

SECTION 10. The contractor, or his assigns, or some person in his or their behalf, shall call upon the persons assessed, or their agents, if they can conveniently be found, and demand payment of the amount assessed to each. If any payment be made the contractor, his assigns, or some person in his or their behalf, shall receipt the same upon the assessment in presence of the person making such payment, and shall also give a separate receipt if demanded. Whenever the person so assessed or their agents, cannot conveniently be found, or whenever the name of the owner of the lot is stated as "unknown" on the assessment, then the said contractor, or his assigns, or some person in his or their behalf, shall publicly demand payment on the premises assessed. The warrant shall be returned to the superintendent of streets within thirty days after its date, with a return indorsed thereon, signed by the contractor, or his assigns, or some person in his or their behalf, verified upon oath, stating the nature and character of the demand, and whether any of the assessments remain unpaid, in whole or in part, and the amount thereof. Thereupon the superintendent of streets shall record the return so made, in the margin of the record of the warrant and assessment, and also the original contract referred to therein, if it has not already been recorded at full length in a book to be kept for that purpose in his office, and shall sign the record. The said superintendent of streets is authorized at any time to receive the amount due upon any assessment list and warrant issued by him, and give a good and sufficient discharge therefor; *provided*, that no such payment so made after suit has been

commenced, without the consent of the plaintiff in the action, shall operate
as a complete discharge of the lien until the costs in the action shall be
refunded to the plaintiff; and he may release any assessment upon the
books of his office, on the payment to him of the amount of the assessment
against any lot with interest, or on the production to him of the receipt of
the party or his assigns to whom the assessment and warrant were issued;
and if any contractor shall fail to return his warrant within the time and in
the form provided in this section, he shall thenceforth have no lien upon the
property assessed; *provided*, however, that in case any warrant is lost, upon
proof of such loss a duplicate can be issued, upon which a return may be
made, with the same effect as if the original had been so returned. After
the return of the assessment and warrant as aforesaid, all amounts remaining due thereon shall draw interest at the rate of ten per cent. per annum
until paid. [*Statutes 1885, p. 155*].

Section 10 of the act of March 18, 1885, never has been amended.

In the notes to section 9 it is stated that the proceedings
necessary to the existence of a valid lien terminate with the
recording of the warrant, assessment, diagram and certificate
of the city engineer, as provided for by said section 9, and
that there are at least fourteen acts necessary to the existence of a valid lien commencing with the passage of the
resolution of intention. Section 10 provides for three more
acts necessary to the existence of the right to successfully
maintain a suit against the lot owners, as provided for by
section 12 of the act. The three things required by section
10 as necessary prerequisites to the right to successfully
maintain a suit against the lot owners, are: (*1.*) Demand
upon the persons assessed or their agents, or on the premises
assessed. (*2.*) Return of warrant, with a return indorsed
thereon, signed and verified, and (*3.*) Recording of the return
and also the original contract referred to in the warrant and
assessment, if it has not already been recorded. These three
things, therefore, required by section 10 as necessary prerequisites to the existence of a valid right of action, together
with the other fourteen acts mentioned in the notes to section 9 of the act, as necessary to the existence of a valid
assessment lien, making in all seventeen necessary acts, are
the seventeen prerequisites to the existence of a valid right
of action in any case; and in some cases there may be more,
as when it is necessary to inaugurate proceedings to grade
by a petition, as provided for by section 2 of the act, for
example. Section 10 likewise provides for interest upon
the amounts due on the assessment.

I. *Demand.* There are three modes provided by the
statute (section 10) in which demand may be made by the
contractor for street assessments, to wit: (*1.*) of the person
assessed; (*2.*) of his agents; and (*3.*) a demand, publicly
made, on the premises assessed. And there are three per-

sons or classes of persons, by whom the demand may be made, to wit: (*1.*) The contractor himself; (*2.*) the assignee of the contractor, or (*3.*) some person on behalf of the contractor or his assignee.

(*a.*) *Demand upon the Persons Assessed or their Agents.* The section provides that the contractor or person making the demand "shall call upon the persons assessed or their agents, *if they can conveniently be found,* and demand payment of the amount assessed to each." The section likewise provides that the demand "*shall*" be made on the premises in two cases, viz: (*1.*) whenever the persons assessed, or their agents, cannot conveniently be found, or (*2.*) whenever the name of the owner of the lot is stated as "unknown" on the assessment. When, therefore, the assessment is made against the owner by name, demand *must* be made upon him or his agent, with but one exception, viz., where "*they cannot conveniently be found.*" But it is not sufficient to excuse personal demand—when the assessment is against the owner by name—that the persons assessed, or their agents, cannot conveniently be found by the contractor or his agent. The fact that the contractor, or his agent or assignee, cannot conveniently find the persons assessed or their agents, does not excuse personal demand. Guerin *v.* Reese, 33 Cal. 293, where it was held that the legal purpose of the demand is to give to the owner, as far as practicable, actual notice of the existence of the lien created by the assessment and resting upon his property, so as to enable him to take the proper steps for its discharge. Also, that the warrant is a process in the hands of the contractor, which he is required to serve, and he will be held to the same measure of diligence in its service as is an officer holding legal process for service; that, in making the service, it is the duty of the contractor (*1.*) to make a reasonable effort to find and serve the person assessed; (*2.*) failing in this, it is next his duty to make a like effort to find and serve the agent of the person assessed, and (*3.*) only when such first and second efforts have failed, is he authorized to make service by a public demand for the assessments upon the premises assessed. Also, that the contractor's return should show a personal demand upon the person assessed, or a satisfactory reason why it was not done, before resorting to the other modes of making the demand, *i. e.,* if the demand was not made upon the person assessed because he could not conveniently be found, the returns should show why he could not conveniently be found, as, that he is a non-resident of the city or state, or is temporarily absent, or has absconded or else should state that "he cannot be found."

To the same effect is the decision in McBean v. Martin, 96 Cal. 188, where the work was done, and the proceedings had, under the present street work act. The court followed the ruling in Guerin v. Reese.

In Himmelmann v. Townsend, 49 Cal. 151, Mr. Justice McKinstry gave it as his opinion that if the owner cannot conveniently be found, and the assessment is made against him by name, if there is a tenant occupying the premises, demand ·should be made of such occupant personally. In such case the requirements of the statute would not be satisfied by a demand made by the contractor standing upon one corner of the lot and speaking in a tone of voice ,which, while it might be said to be audible, would not be audible to a person upon the opposite corner of the lot, or within a dwelling house on the lot.

(b.) *Demand on the Premises.* According to repeated decisions of the Supreme Court, the superintendent may assess the lot to "unknown" owners, and his assessment to an unknown owner is conclusive evidence, in all collateral proceedings—suits upon the assessment for example—that the name of the true owner was unknown to him; and, when the assessment is made to an unknown owner, the contractor is only required to "publicly demand payment on the premises assessed"—in fact where the assessment is made to an unknown owner the demand must be made publicly upon the premises assessed; a personal demand upon the owner made elsewhere will not suffice. And, as it is a simple matter to publicly make a demand upon the premises assessed, and as it might frequently be inconvenient to the contractor to find the true owner, without its being a fact that the true owner "can not conveniently be found,"—within the meaning of that phrase as construed by the Supreme Court in said case of Guerin v. Reese, 33 Cal. 293—it follows that it is greatly to the advantage of the contractor to, in all cases, make the assessments to owners "unknown." Besides which when the assessment is attempted to be made to the true owner by name the superintendent takes the risk of being mistaken in his supposition as to who the true owner is—and in a new country where titles are unsettled it is seldom that any one can know who the true owner is without a laborious search of the records and not always even then. And, as has been frequently held since the case of Smith v. Davis, 30 Cal. 536, if the assessment purports to be made to the owner by name it is void unless the name given is the name of the true owner. Therefore, by making all assessments to unknown owners, the superintendent avoids the risk of assessing the property to a person not in fact the true owner, and likewise enables the contractor to make simply a demand on the premises, thus saving him the trouble of ascertaining whether the owner can conveniently be found or not.

In Himmelmann v. Hoadley, 44 Cal. 214, it was held that the superintendent, unless he is satisfied beyond all doubt as to the ownership of a lot, may assess it to "unknown owner," and when the assessment is made to "unknown owner," payment may be demanded publicly upon the premises.

In Whiting v. Townsend, 57 Cal. 515, it was held that where the property is assessed to unknown owners no personal demand is required. And in Macadamizing Co. v Williams, 70 Cal. 534, it was held that where the assessment is made to "unknown owners," the demand *must* be made upon the premises. Mr. Commissioner Searls, in that case, page 541, said: "The statute provides but one mode of making a demand in cases where, as in the present case, the property is assessed to 'unknown owners,' and that is by a demand upon the premises. It matters not that other methods may be as efficacious as the one provided. The lawmakers have prescribed a method, and the courts are not at liberty to adopt a substitute therefor." In this case a personal demand was made, and also a demand by a person standing on the sidewalk in front of and close to the fence bordering the lots, but was not actually made upon them (unless such lots extended to the middle of the street). The person making the demand stood on the sidewalk and there made a demand in an audible voice. The point was raised that under section 831 of the Civil Code the lots must be presumed to extend to the middle of the street, and that, therefore, a demand made by a person standing on the sidewalk was a demand "on the premises," but as the complaint described the land assessed as bounded by the side line of the adjoining street, this presumption was not permissible, under the allegations of the complaint. It was held that the statute requires the demand to be made on the premises, and that this requirement was not met by a demand made by a person standing on the sidewalk — the lot being held to be bounded by a side line of the street and not its center line— even though the voice of the person making the demand could be heard on the lot. Mr. Commissioner Searls, page 543, said: "The land is charged with the payment of the assessment, and where the owner is designated as 'unknown,' the statute is imperative in requiring the demand to be made *publicly on the premises*; and a demand made near to, in the neighborhood of or within hearing of the premises does not satisfy the requirements of the statute." The court must determine whether the demand was made in a sufficiently audible tone of voice, and upon this the decision of the trial court is necessarily conclusive. [Himmelman v. Booth, 53 Cal. 50.]

(c.) By Whom Demand to be Made. When more than one person, either by the original contract or by assignment from the contractor, is interested in a contract for improving a street, the demand is sufficient if made by one alone of the parties interested in the contract. Thus in Gaffney v. Donohue, 36 Cal. 104, Gaffney, the contractor, assigned one-half interest in the contract to Donohue. *Held*, Gaffney, after the assignment, could make a legal demand. He, as contractor, is one of the persons designated by the statute to make the demand. In Himmelmann v. Woolrich, 45 Cal. 249, it was objected that the demand was made by one who was the agent of the assignee and not the agent of the contractor, but it was held that the agent of the assignee might make the demand and return as well as an agent of the contractor. The statute (section 10) now expressly provides that the demand might be made by "the contractor, or his assigns, or some person in his or *their* behalf." And in Foley v. Bullard, No. 15,305, decided Sept. 11, 1893. it was held that the demand was made on behalf of the assignees of the original contract, and was in all respects sufficient, although the person making the demand was shown to be the agent of persons to whom the assignees had assigned the contract as security. This case arose under the street work act now in force—the Vrooman act—and the court cited, with approval, the case of Godfrey v. Donohue, *supra.*

(d.) Amount of Demand. The demand must be made for the exact amount lawfully chargeable against each lot, or, at any rate, it must not be for an amount greater than is lawfully chargeable against each lot. A demand for the aggregate sum due on two lots is insufficient. The demand should be on each lot for the amount assessed thereon. [Schirmer v. Hoyt, 54 Cal. 280.]

If the resolution of intention calls for the macadamizing of a street and curbing the same, and the contract is let for macadamizing the sidewalks as well as the roadway, then, as held in Himmelman v. Satterlee, 50 Cal. 68, and Baudry v. Valdez, 32 Cal. 269, the resolution does not include work on the sidewalks, but is limited to that done on the roadway, as the word "street," as used in section 2 of the act, in connection with macadamizing, is limited to the roadway, and the assessment for work done on the sidewalks in such case is void. And if the demand made by the contractor, in such case, is for the whole assessment, and not for the portion thereof which would be chargeable for the work on the roadway, the contractor cannot recover, even though the court should find the cost of the work on the roadway and that on the sidewalk separately, and even though, as held in Baudry v. Valdez, 32 Cal. 269, the contractor may recover if the whole assessment is severable so as to permit of a segregation of the valid part from the invalid part. The demand must be for the amount legally due and chargeable against the lot. [Dyer v. Chase, 52 Cal. 440; Donnelly v. Howard, 60 Cal. 291; Dorland v. Bergson, 78 Cal. 637; see Partridge v. Lucase, 33 Pac. Rep. 1082.]

If, however, the assessment is severable and demand is duly made for the amount properly due and chargeable against the land, or, if separate assessments have been made for different portions of the work, and separate demands are made for the payment of each assessment, the invalidity of one of the assessments does not render the other invalid, and the contract may recover the amount of the valid assessment. [Parker v. Reay, 76 Cal. 103; Ede v. Knight, 93 Cal. 160.] In Parker v. Reay, the work consisted in constructing basalt block gutter-ways, in macadamizing the roadway, and in laying granite crosswalks. The assessment for gutter-ways and macadam were levied separately from the assessment for the crossings. The assessment against defendant's lot for crossings was void because not made against that part only of the lot contained in the quarter block subject to assessments for crossings. The court said: "This portion of the assessment, [i. e., assessment for crossings] was void, and the demand therefor was invalid; but the assessment for macadam and gutter-ways having been made separately, and for the proper amount, and the proper demand having been made, as shown by the return, the motion for a non-suit was properly denied, notwithstanding the invalidity of the assessment for work on the crossing."

II. *Contractor's Return.* Section 10 provides that "the warrant shall be returned to the superintendent of streets within 30 days after its date, with a return endorsed thereon, signed by the contractor or his assigns, or some person in his or their behalf, verified upon oath, stating the nature and character of the demand and whether any of the assessments remain unpaid, in whole or in part, and the amount thereof." It is absolutely essential that such return should be made within thirty days after the date of the warrant and also in the form prescribed by the statute, as the section (section 10) likewise provides that "if any contractor shall fail to return his warrant within the time *and in the form* provided in this section he shall thenceforth have no lien upon the property assessed."

III. *Return as Evidence of Demand.* The affidavit of demand, indorsed upon the warrant, is *prima facie* evidence of such demand. In Dyer *v.* Brogan, 57 Cal. 234, it was held that such affidavit is *prima facie* evidence of demand under section 11 of the act of 1872 [Statutes 1871-2, pages 814, 815,] and as section 11 of the act of 1872 is substantially identical with section 10 of the act of March 18, 1885, except with respect to the time within which the return is to be made and the rate of interest, it follows that if that decision be correct the return is, under the present street law, *prima facie* evidence of demand likewise. [See also Himmelmann *v.* Hoadley, 44 Cal. 214.] In Deady *v.* Townsend, 57 Cal. 298, it was held that the affidavit of demand, indorsed on the return, is *prima facie* evidence of such demand, though made by an agent of the contractor. In Whiting *v.* Townsend, 57 Cal. 515, it was held that the statement by affiant in his affidavit that he was the agent of the contractor is *prima facie* evidence that he was such agent. [See Himmelmann *v.* Woolrich, 45 Cal. 249.] In Ede *v.* Knight, 93 Cal. 160, it was held that the verified return of the contractor, stating that he went upon each of the lots exhibited in the diagram, and publicly demanded on each lot payment of the sum assessed to each is *prima facie* evidence of the facts stated, and, if not disputed, shows a proper demand. See section 12 of the act, where it is said: "The said warrant, assessment, certificate and diagram, with the affidavit of demand and non-payment, shall be held *prima facie* evidence of the regularity and correctness of the assessment, etc., * * * and *like evidence of the right of the plaintiff to recover in the action.*"

IV. *Recording the Return.* The last act necessary to the existence of a valid right in the contractor to successfully maintain suit against the lot owner to recover the amount of the assessment lien, is the recordation of the return, and also of the original contract, if it has not already been recorded. The act (section 10) provides, that, upon return of the warrant being made to the superintendent of streets, he "shall record the return so made, in the margin of the record of the warrant and assessment, and also the original contract referred to therein, if it has not already been recorded, at full length in a book to be kept for that purpose in his office, and shall sign the record."

In the notes to section 9, it is stated that it is essential to the existence of a valid assessment lien that the warrant, assessment, diagram and certificate of the engineer should, before delivery to the contractor or his assigns, be recorded by the superintendent in a book kept by him for that purpose in his office, and also that it is essential to the recording of these documents that they should not only be copied in full into the record book, but that such copy should be authenticated by the signature of the superintendent or of a duly authorized deputy, as, without such signature, authenticating such copy, there is no record. Section 10 of the act provides for a completion of this record by the recording of the contractor's *"return"* in the margin of the record of the warrant and assessment, and likewise the original contract, if not already recorded. The proper recording of the warrant, assessment, diagram and certificate of the city engineer, as provided for by section 9, is necessary to the existence of a valid lien, and the recording of the return and the original contract, after the contractor has returned the warrant to the superintendent of streets, with a return endorsed thereon, is essential to the existence of a right to maintain a suit on the lien.

When the sworn return and the original contract are recorded in the office of the street superintendent, a certificate of their recording should be attached to the same, signed by the superintendent or an authorized deputy. Without such authentication they cannot be deemed to be recorded. [Himmelman *v.* Danos, 35 Cal. 441; Himmelmann *v.* Hoadley, 44 Cal. 213; Shepard *v.* McNeil, 38 Cal. 73. See *supra*, pages 102–105.]

The statute does not prescribe any time within which the return or affidavit of demand shall be recorded by the street superintendent, and if it is not recorded until two months after the return is made, it will not vitiate the proceedings. [Himmelmann *v.* Reay, 38 Cal. 163.]

V. *Interest.* Section 10 likewise provides that "after the return of the assessment and warrant as aforesaid, all amounts remaining due thereon shall draw interest at the rate of ten per cent. per annum until paid."

In the absence of a provision in the statute allowing interest on street assessments, the city council can not impose interest as a penalty for non-payment. [Weber *v.* City of S. F., 1 Cal. 455; see also Bucknall *v.* Story, 36 Cal. 67.] Although a judgment for street assessments may draw interest from the time of its rendition. [Sec. 1920 Civil

Code; Himmelman *v.* Oliver, 34 Cal. 246; Randolph *v.* Bayue, 44 Cal. 366.] If street work is done under an act which does not make any provision for interest upon the assessments, and subsequently an act is passed providing that after the return of the assessment and warrant, all amounts remaining due thereon shall draw interest at a certain rate, and the assessment for such work is made after the passage of this latter act, the contractor will be entitled to interest upon the assessment as provided by such latter act. The reason for this rule is that there is no contract between the contractor and the property owners, and therefore no obligation of any contract is impaired. The property owner has the opportunity, and it is his duty to pay before the return of the warrant, and if he does not do so the legislature may enact that if he neglects this duty, the amount due shall thereafter bear interest. [Dougherty *v.* Henaire, 47 Cal. 9.] Section 12 of the act expressly provides that in any suit upon the assessment the contractor may "recover the amount of any assessment remaining unpaid, *with interest thereon at the rate of ten per cent. per annum until paid.*"

SECTION 11. The owners, whether named in the assessment or not, the contractor, or his assigns, and all other persons directly interested in any work provided for in this act, or in the assessment, feeling aggrieved by any act or determination of the superintendent of streets in relation thereto, or who claim that the work has not been performed according to the contract in a good and substantial manner, or having or making any objection to the correctness or legality of the assessment or other act determination, or proceedings of the superintendent of streets, shall, within thirty days after the date of the warrant, appeal to the city council, as provided in this section, by briefly stating their objections in writing, and filing the same with the clerk of said city council. Notice of the time and place of the hearing, briefly referring to the work contracted to be done, or other subject of appeal, and to the acts, determinations, or proceedings objected to or complained of, shall be published for five days. Upon such appeal, the said city council may remedy and correct any error or informality in the proceedings, and revise and correct any of the acts or determinations of the superintendent of streets relative to said work; may confirm, amend, set aside, alter, modify, or correct the assessment in such manner as to them shall seem just, and require the work to be completed according to the directions of the city council; and may instruct and direct the superintendent of streets to correct the warrant, assessment, or diagram in any particular, or to make and issue a new warrant, assessment and diagram, to conform to the decisions of said city council in relation thereto, at their option. All the decisions and determinations of said city council, upon notice and hearing as aforesaid, shall be final and conclusive upon all persons entitled to appeal under the provisions of this section, as to all errors, informalities, and irregularities which said city council might have remedied and avoided; and no assessment shall be held invalid, except upon appeal to the city council, as provided in this section, for any error, informality, or other defect in any of the proceedings prior to the assessment, or in the assessment itself, where notice of the intention of the city council to order the work to be done, for which the assessment is made, has been actually published in any designated newspaper of said city for the length of time prescribed by law, before the passage of the resolution ordering the work to be done. [*Statutes 1885, p. 156.*]

[Section 11 of the act of March 18, 1885, never has been amended.]

I. *Differences Between the "Appeal" Provided for by Section Eleven and the "Petition of Remonstrance" Provided for by Section Three.* Section 11 of the act provides for an appeal to the city council, and as there is no other remedy when an appeal lies [Dorland *v.* McGlynn, 47 Cal. 48, 51], it follows that it is very important to ascertain when an appeal should be taken. The section provides that an appeal may be taken by three classes of persons, viz: (*1.*) the owners, whether named in the assessment or not; (*2.*) the contractor or his assigns, and (*3.*) all other persons directly interested in any work provided for in the act, or in the assessment.

The "petition of remonstrance," provided for in section 3 of the act, differs in at least three important respects from the "appeal" provided for by section 11, viz: *(1.)* as to the classes of persons by whom they may be taken or prosecuted; *(2.)* as to the time within which they must be taken or prosecuted; and *(3.)* as to the persons whose acts may be complained of.

(*a.*) *Classes of persons by whom a remonstrance may be filed or an appeal be taken.* An appeal under section 11 may be taken by *(1.)* the owners, whether named in the assessment or not; *(2.)* the contractor or his assigns, or, *(3.)* all other persons directly interested in any work or in the assessment; whereas, section 3 only makes provision for a petition of remonstrance by owners whose lots are liable to assessment.

(*b.*) *Time within which an appeal may be taken or a remonstrance filed.* Section 11 provides that an appeal may be taken at any time within thirty days *after the date of the warrant.* Section 3 provides that "*at any time before the issuance of the assessment roll,* all owners of lots or lands liable to assessment therein who * * * * may feel aggrieved * * * shall file with the clerk a petition of remonstrance."

(*c.*) *Persons whose acts may be complained of on appeal and on petition of remonstrance.* Section 11 provides that the persons entitled to appeal under that section, "feeling aggrieved by an act or determination of the *superintendent of streets* in relation thereto, or who may claim that the work has not been performed according to the contract in a good and substantial manner, or having or making any objection to the correctness or legality of the assessment, or other act, determination or proceedings of the *superintendent of streets*, shall * * * appeal;" etc. Section 3 provides that "all owners of lots or lands liable to assessment, * * * who, after the first publication of said resolution of intention, may feel aggrieved, or who may have objections to any of the subsequent proceedings of said *council*, * * * shall file with the clerk a petition of remonstrance," etc. Section 11 allows objections to be presented to any act or determination of the *superintendent of streets*, or to the failure of the *contractor* to execute his contract faithfully. Section 3 confines the objections which may be made on petition of remonstrance to the proceedings of the *council*.

It was in view of these distinguishing characteristics between the "petition of remonstrance," provided for by section 3 of the act, and the "appeal," provided for by section 11, that Mr. Justice Shafter used the following language in Nolan *v.* Reese, 32 Cal. 487, in determining whether a fraudulent side agreement was fatal to the assessment or whether an appeal to the council was the only remedy. [See such fraudulent side agreements considered *supra*, page 55.] Said the learned justice in Nolan *v.* Reese, page 487: "Should the fraud with which the contractor was charged be considered as affecting the 'award of the work' to him by the board of supervisors [Section 6 of the act of 1862; section 5 of the act of the Vrooman act], then, under the fourth section of the act [Section 3 of the Vrooman act], it should have been brought to the notice of the board of supervisors by a remonstrance coming from one or more of the lot owners. If, on the other hand, the fraud is considered as affecting the 'legality' of the assessment,' then any person having objections to make should have appealed to the board of supervisors within thirty-five days subsequent to the date of the assessment. [Section 12 of the act of 1862; section 11 of the Vrooman act.] Such are the methods pointed out by the act for reviewing the decisions of the board and the acts of the superintendent, and they exclude all others by positive provision."

II. *Other Provisions of Section Eleven.* Section 11 also provides: (*1.*) How the appeal shall be taken; (*2.*) the powers of the council upon the appeal and that its decision shall be final and conclusive, and (*3.*) the effect of not appealing. Under the third head, the section provides that "no assessment shall be held invalid except upon appeal to the city council, as provided in this section, for any error, informality or other defect in any of the proceedings prior to the assessment, or in the assessment itself, where notice of the intention of the city council to order the work to be done for which the assessment is made, has been actually published in any designated newspaper of said city for the length of time prescribed by law, before the passage of the resolution ordering the work to be done." According to the letter of this part of the section, no error, informality or defect, even though jurisdictional in its character, and of vital importance to the property owners, can operate to defeat an assessment,—provided notice of intention has been published as provided in the act,—unless upon appeal to the council. This provision is not found in the prior acts. But, according to recent authorities, construing this part of the act, and cited *infra*, such a literal interpretation of the section is not the correct construction. [See *supra*, pages 16–17, under the caption *"Jurisdiction."*] If, subsequent to the publication of the notice of intention, *i. e.*, if, after a resolution of intention in due form has been passed, posted and published and notice thereof posted and published as provided for by section 3 of the act, there is any jurisdictional error, which is past correction by the council upon appeal, —*e. g.*, if the contract be void because let for less work than is described in the resolution and order, and the assessment is, therefore, illegal,—the owner is not required to appeal; and, notwithstanding such failure to appeal, he may defeat all actions upon such illegal assessment. The important question, therefore, is, *in what cases is an appeal the exclusive remedy?*

III. *Principles Governing Appeal Under Prior Street Improvement Acts.* In Emery v. Bradford, 29 Cal. 75, the court held that, under the San Francisco street work act of 1862, if an owner is dissatisfied with the decision of the superintendent of streets that the contractor has fulfilled his contract, his only remedy is an appeal from such decision to the board of supervisors of the city and county of San Francisco. And on page 86, the court, per Sawyer, J., said: "An error of the superintendent in the respect complained of can be corrected on appeal. * * * This conclusive determination on appeal doubtless refers to those matters upon which the superintendent is required in the discharge of his duties to exercise his judgment—those matters in which his errors are to be revised and corrected. There are acts to be performed of a jurisdictional character essential to the validity of any assessment. It is not to be supposed that the conclusiveness of the decision of the board of supervisors is to extend to that class of acts. The provisions in section twelve [section 12 of the act of 1862 is the section corresponding with section 11 of the present street work act] indicate the kind of errors upon which the decisions of the board are to be final. It is that 'all the decisions and determinations of said board, upon notice and hearing aforesaid, shall be final and conclusive upon all persons entitled to an appeal under the provisions of this section, as to all errors and irregularities which said board could have avoided.' Now, this would not include jurisdictional acts, which it would be too late to remedy after the time for appeal had arrived." The court further, considering the question immediately before it, said: "But an error in determining whether the contract has been in all respects performed, is not one of the jurisdictional defects that could not be remedied. The power to direct the improvement of streets, and to make or authorize the making of contracts therefore, is properly vested in the board of supervisors, and it would seem to follow necessarily, that the authority to ultimately determine whether or not the contract has been fulfilled, should be vested in the same body that has the power to order and make the contracts."

In Dougherty v. Hitchcock, 35 Cal. 512, the contract was for less work than that described in the resolution of intention and order for the work to be done. It was, therefore, unauthorized and void, [see *supra* pages 53–54] and it was held that in such case under the act of 1862,—the act under which the proceedings were had,— this defect was not cured by a failure to appeal. On page 524 Mr. Justice Rhodes said: "A contract authorized and executed in the mode prescribed by the act is indispensable to the validity of the assessment. This defect is not cured by the failure of the lot holders to appeal to the board, because had an appeal been taken, the defect could not have been remedied by the board." And on page 526, Sawyer, J., said: "The contract sued on was, therefore, unauthorized. The defect is not one that could be cured by appeal, *for when the time for appeal came the work was done and the mischief past remedy.* The contract made, did not pursue the authority, and was, therefore, wholly unauthorized. By the course pursued, the property holders were deprived of an opportunity to avail themselves of important rights, which the statute secures to them as a condition precedent to the levy of a valid assessment upon their property."

In Burke *v.* Turney, 54 Cal. 486, the superintendent entered into the contract prematurely, and the contract was therefore void. [See *supra* page 51.]   Upon this part of the case, the court, per McKinstry, J., said: "The superintendent had no *power* to enter into the contract until after the expiration of the five days."   Plaintiff urged, however, that the defendant's failure to appeal cut off this defense.   On this branch of the case, Mr. Justice McKinstry said: "The premature action of the superintendent was one which affected his *power* or *jurisdiction.* His action was *void,* and that which was void does not become valid by reason of a failure to appeal.   The property owners were not *aggrieved,* and the failure of the contractor to appeal did not operate, *1st,* to *create* a grievance on the part of the defendants, and *2nd,* to *estop* them from complaining of it."

In Chambers *v.* Satterlee, 40 Cal. 497, Mr. Justice Wallace, page 520, said: "We think that while the statute intended to leave open for judicial inquiry all questions which can be said to be of a jurisdictional character, its purpose was to submit all other questions to the decision of the board itself."   And on page 524, Mr. Justice Temple said, in reference to the decision in Dougherty *v.* Hitchcock, 35 Cal. 512:   "In that case it is said, in reference to an objection somewhat similar, that when the appeal came, the work was done and the mischief past remedy.   *It is, however, impliedly admitted that if the mischief could have been remedied, the answer to the objection would have been good."*   And on page 526, the same justice said: "I have no doubt but that this right [the right of appeal] is exclusive of any other remedy *as to all matters which can be revised and corrected on such an appeal."*

The foregoing cases were decided under statutes similar in many respects to the present street work act; and the principles which seem to be deducible from these cases, by which to determine whether an appeal is the exclusive remedy or not, are as follows:

1.   The right of appeal refers to those matters upon which the *superintendent of streets* is required in the discharge of his duties to exercise his judgment—as, for example, whether the work has been properly done or not—and all matters not of a jurisdictional character.

2.   The right of appeal does not refer to those matters of a *jurisdictional* character essential to the validity of the contract, which it would be too late to remedy after the time for appeal had arrived—as, for example, the requirement that the contract shall be authorized by the resolution of intention and order of award.

If the irregularity or omission affect the *power* or *jurisdiction* of the superintendent, so that his act is void, and the mischief past remedy, it cannot be waived by a failure to appeal.

3. The failure to appeal cannot operate as a waiver of the right to object to an assessment when the omission or irregularity is one affecting the substantial rights of the property owners, if the omission, error or irregularity occurs at such a stage of the proceedings that it could not be remedied after the time for appeal had arrived. As, for example, if the contract should be for less work than that described in the resolution of intention and order awarding the contract. In such case the contract would be void; the work would be done under a void contract, and when the time for appeal had arrived—within thirty days after the date of the warrant—the work would be done and the mischief past remedy.

4. If, however, the error or irregularity complained of has occurred in such a stage of the proceedings that it might have been remedied or avoided by the city council on appeal, then it seems that an appeal to the city council is the exclusive remedy of the "aggrieved" property owner, even though the alleged error or irregularity be one which might be considered as affecting his substantial rights. As, for example, if all the jurisdictional prerequisites to the existence of a valid contract have been regularly complied with, and the work has been properly done within the time allowed by law and the contract, but the assessment is irregular by reason of some omission or defect therein, provided the property assessed is liable to assessment, is sufficiently described and the owner thereof is assessed in his true name or under the designation "unknown." [See *supra*, pp. 94–97.]

In short, the question as to whether or not an appeal to the council is the exclusive remedy in any case, involves and includes two other subordinate questions, viz.: (*1.*) Is the error or irregularity complained of *jurisdictional, i. e.,* does it affect the *power* of the council to award the contract, or of the superintendent to make an assessment? and (*2.*) is the error or irregularity complained of past remedy? If the error or irregularity complained of is jurisdictional, and if it would be too late to remedy it, after the time for appeal has arrived, then a failure to appeal is not a waiver of the right of the property owner to resist payment of the alleged assessment.

In Dehail *v.* Morford, 95 Cal. 460, Mr. Justice Harrison
said: "For the purpose of acquiring jurisdiction every
requirement [of the statute] must be regarded as of equal
necessity." This language was used in connection with
the street opening act of March 6, 1889. [Statutes 1889, page
70.] But in so far as it serves to show what are the necessary jurisdictional requirements it is as applicable to the
Vrooman, or street improvement act,—the act of March 18,
1885,—as to the street opening act. In Nicolson Pavement Co. *v.* Painter, 35 Cal. 705, Mr. Justice Sanderson
said: "In the matter of street improvements the board of
supervisors have whatever power the statutes upon that subject have conferred upon them, and no other; the power
which they possess must be exercised in the mode prescribed by the statute, and in no other; *the mode in such
cases constitutes the measure of power.*" And in Shipman *v.*
Forbes, 97 Cal. 572, Mr. Justice Harrison says: "In matters
of this character in which the property of a citizen is to be
taken *in invitum* it cannot be said that any requirement of
the statute is to be disregarded. Every requisite having
the semblance of benefit to the owner must be complied
with; and when the form of a statutory proceeding is prescribed, its observance becomes essential to the validity of
the proceedings."

As stated above, the question whether or   not an
appeal to the council is the exclusive remedy in   any
case, involves two subordinate questions, viz: (*1.*) Is the
error, omission or irregularity complained of jurisdictional?
and   (*2.*) Is it past remedy?   And these quotations
from Dehail *v.* Morford, Nicolson Pavement Co. *v.* Painter,
and Shipman *v.* Forbes, have been given for the purpose of
showing what requirements are jurisdictional.   According
to the language of Mr. Justice Harrison in Shipman *v.*
Forbes, "every requisite having the semblance of benefit
to the owner" is jurisdictional.

But, though every requirement of the statute having the
semblance of benefit to the owner may be jurisdictional,
and of equal necessity,—as stated by Mr. Justice Harrison
in Dehail *v.* Morford and Shipman *v.* Forbes—still it does
not necessarily follow therefrom that such irregularity may
not be waived by a failure to appeal. Since it seems
that a failure to appeal is a waiver of the irregularity,
if it was possible for the council to have remedied and corrected it when the time for appeal arrived, so as to restore
or preserve to the property owner all the rights or benefits secured to him by the statute. The council on appeal
is, it seems, the proper and exclusive tribunal for the liti-

gation of all such questions, and the correction of all such errors as occur at such a stage of the proceedings that they are capable of correction by the council on appeal when the time for appeal arrives. When the mischief is past remedy, and the error or irregularity complained of affects substantial rights, or consists in the omission of some requirement of the act which has the semblance of benefit to the owner, then and only then is the error, irregularity or omission fatal, and not waived by a failure on the part of the property owner to appeal to the council.

It would seem, therefore, that if any of the requirements necessary to the existence of *a valid contract* has been omitted, the property owner may defeat an action upon the assessment, even though he has taken no appeal to the council, since in such case the mischief, it would seem, would be past all possibility of remedy. [See *supra* pages 18, 19 and 44, for an enumeration of the jurisdictional prerequisites to a valid contract.] In fact, section 11 of the present street improvement act seems to contemplate an "appeal" only where the act or omission complained of is the "act, determination or proceedings of the superintendent of streets," and, prior to the execution of the written contract, all proceedings are done by or under the direction of the city council—not the superintendent of streets.

In Emery *v.* Bradford, 29 Cal. 75, Mr. Justice Sawyer, on page 86, said: "An error of the *superintendent* in the respect complained of can be corrected on appeal. * * * This conclusive determination on appeal doubtless refers to those matters upon which *the superintendent* is required in the discharge of his duties to exercise his judgment—those matters in which *his* errors are to be revised and corrected."

Property owners who may have objections to any of the proceedings of the *council* between the first publication of the resolution of intention and the issuance of the assessment roll, may file with the clerk the "petition of remonstrance," provided for by section 3 of the act. Such objections are reached by a "petition of remonstrance," and not by "appeal." [See *supra* pp. 117–118.]

On the other hand, if all the requirements leading up to the execution of a valid contract have been properly complied with, if the council had jurisdiction to award the contract, and if after due publication, etc., the superintendent has executed a valid contract following the award, and if the work has been properly done under the contract, an appeal would seem to be the sole remedy for an omission of any of the requirements provided for by section 8 of the act as essentials to the existence of a valid assessment, provided the omission might have been remedied or corrected by the council when the time to appeal arrived, and provided, also, that the property owner was a party to the assessment. [See the subject of "Appeal by Lot Owners" for irregularities in the assessment, pages 94–97, in the notes to section 8 of the act.]

On page 123 *supra*, the language of Mr. Justice Harrison in the case of Shipman v. Forbes, 97 Cal. 572, is quoted for the purpose of showing what requirements are deemed to be jurisdictional. As the decision in that case might seem to conflict with the statement made above, to the effect that even some jurisdictional requirements, *i. e.*, requirements having the semblance of benefit to the owner, may be waived by the property owner's failure to appeal, if it was possible for the omission, error or irregularity complained of to be remedied cr corrected by the council on appeal, when the time for appeal arrived, so as to restore or preserve to the property owner every requirement of the statute having the semblance of benefit to him,—it is deemed proper, in this connection, to give a little further consideration to this case of Shipman v. Forbes. In that case the work had been done under a contract made pursuant to the provisions of the San Francisco street improvement act of 1872. [Statutes 1872, p. 804.] A warrant had been issued by the superintendent of streets after the assessment roll had been made up. This warrant was not dated. It was held that if the warrant be not dated so as to show the day of the month and the year, it cannot serve as the foundation of proceedings for the collection of the assessment. Mr. Justice Harrison, rendering the opinion for the court, held that the omission of such date from the warrant was a jurisdictional defect. Still, if the deductions from the opinions given in the decisions cited *supra*, upon the various street improvement acts, be correct, even the omission of a jurisdictional requirement is not fatal, if the property owner was a party to the assessment and the mischief might have been remedied by the council on appeal. And, while a failure to date the warrant may be a jurisdictional defect, as held by Mr. Justice Harrison, still the case of Shipman v. Forbes does not seem to be determinative of the question as to whether, under the present street improvement act,—the Vrooman act of March 18, 1885,—an appeal to the council is the property owner's exclusive remedy for any jurisdictional defect in the warrant. Because, (*1.*) the decision in that case was under a different act,—the San Francisco street improvement act of April 1,

1872; and (*2.*) the question as to whether or not an appeal to the council was the exclusive remedy does not seem to have been raised in Shipman *v.* Forbes, or, if it was, it was not considered by the court in its opinion.

The present street work .act, in section 11, expressly authorizes the council, on appeal, to "instruct and direct the superintendent of streets to correct the warrant, * * in any particular, or to make and issue a new warrant." The act of April 1, 1872, under which Shipman *v.* Forbes was decided, did not contain such express provisions in relation to the correction of the warrant or the issuance of a new one, although it did authorize the council on appeal to "make any order or decision * * * in relation to any of the acts of * * * the said superintendent of public streets," etc. [Sec. 12 of act of April 1, 1872, statutes 1872, p. 815.] This clause of the act of 1872 seems to be broad enough to include any correction in the warrant. However, under the said act of 1872, the appeal had to be taken "within fifteen days after the issuance of said assessment." It is possible that under that act the warrant need not have been issued until more than fifteen days after the issuance of the assessment, and, if the act be capable of such a construction, then the provisions for an appeal would not seem to contemplate jurisdictional defects in the warrant, since such defects might occur after the time to appeal had expired; and if such construction of the act be correct, the decision in Shipman *v.* Forbes must have remained unchanged even if the question had been raised as to whether or not an appeal to the board of supervisors was the property owner's exclusive remedy for a failure to date the warrant.

But, under the present street improvement act,—the Vrooman act of March 18, 1885,—the appeal need not be taken until "within thirty days after the date of the warrant," and on such appeal the council "may instruct and direct the superintendent of streets to correct the warrant, * * * in any particular, or to make and issue a new warrant." And therefore it is possible that, as to *some* defects in the warrant, an appeal to the council is the property owners' exclusive remedy, even though the defect be of a jurisdictional character, *i. e.*, even though the defect complained of consists in the omission of some requirement of the statute having the semblance of benefit to the property owner. But it is probable that an appeal is the exclusive remedy only as to "*some*" jurisdictional defects of the warrant, because there is one jurisdictional defect, at least, which even under the present street improvement act, would not be waived by a failure to appeal, and that is the very defect which existed in Shipman *v.* Forbes, viz., an omission to date the warrant. Because, under the present street improvement act, the right of appeal does not spring into existence until the warrant is dated. The appeal may be taken at any time "within thirty days after the *date* of the warrant," and, therefore, until the warrant is dated no appeal need be taken. The expression "*date* of an instrument," as commonly used, does not mean the time when the instrument was actually executed, but the time of its execution as given or stated in the instrument itself. [Bement *v.* Trenton L. & M. Co., 32 N. J., L. 515.]

The conclusion deducible from the above is, therefore, that as to some defects in the warrant an appeal is the exclusive remedy, even though they be jurisdictional, *i. e.*, consist in the omission of some requirement of the statute having the semblance of benefit to the property owner, provided the property owner was a party to the assessment, and the error or irregularity complained of is capable of correction upon appeal so as to restore or preserve to the property owner all benefits secured to him by the statute. But these remediable defects do not include a failure to date the warrant, as the right to appeal does not spring into being until the warrant is dated, and Shipman *v.* Forbes does not, in any respect, militate against those cases cited *supra*, which hold that an appeal is the exclusive remedy where the error or irregularity complained of is capable of correction on appeal, and it will be seen *infra*, under the caption: "Cases in which it has been held that an appeal is the only remedy," that the Supreme Court in the later case of Dowling *v.* Altschul, 33 Pac. Rep. 495, has fully sustained the proposition that an appeal is the exclusive remedy in all such cases. [See *supra*, pages 94–97, "Appeal by lot owners for errors in the assessment."]

The term "jurisdictional requirements," as used in the statement of the foregoing conclusions, is used synonymously with the expression "requirements of the statute having the semblance of benefit to the owner." As thus used there can be no doubt that there are some jurisdictional requirements, the omission of which is waived, if an appeal to the council be not taken by the property owner. In other words, an appeal to the council is the exclusive remedy for some of said defects, and the test in each case seems to be: Was the property owner a party to the assessment? and, if he was, was the omission or irregularity complained of capable of correction by the council on appeal so as to preserve or restore to the property owner all the rights and benefits secured to him by the statute? As to those jurisdictional defects which occur prior to the award of the contract, an appeal does not seem to afford any remedy; the property owner is, therefore, not a party "aggrieved," and may avail himself of such defects to defeat an action upon the assessment. Nor would a "petition of remonstrance" afford a remedy in such case. The provision authoriizng "a petition of remonstrance" against the acts and proceedings of the city council was intended to be applicable only to acts and proceedings *within the power* of the council. [Capron *v.* Hitchcock 33 Pac. Rep. 431.] As to what constitutes a property owner a stranger to the assessment roll, so as to exempt him from the provisions relative to "appeal," see *supra* pp. 94–97.

The decisions cited above were cited for the purpose of exemplifying the principles which were held to govern the right of appeal, and the extent of the remedy thereby afforded, under street improvement acts passed prior to the passage of the present street improvement act,—the Vrooman act of March 18, 1885. Those statutes were, in most respects, similar to the present street improvement act, except that the last clause of the present act adds a provision to the effect that if notice of intention has been duly published,—"no assessment shall be held invalid, except upon appeal," etc. However, the recent decisions under the present act do not seem to have altered the principles declared in the decisions under the former street improvement acts, and these principles remain the same now as under the former acts. [See *supra* pp. 16–17.]

IV. *Principles Governing Appeal under Present Street Improvement Act.*

In Manning *v.* Den, 90 Cal. 610, the contract was void, because entered into by the superintendent prematurely. The proceedings were had, and the work done, under the present street work act—act of March 18, 1885. It was held that a failure to appeal did not cure the defect, nor would the owner be estopped if he had taken an appeal, and the appeal had been decided by the council against him. The court, per Harrison J., pages 615-616, said: "Any objections to the correctness of the proceedings by reason of the foregoing defects were not waived by the defendant by his failure to appeal to the city council. Section 11 of the statute in question provides for an appeal to the city council by those who feel aggrieved or have any objection to any act, determination, or proceeding of the superintendent of streets, and after authorizing the city council to remedy and correct any error or informality in the proceedings, declares that the decisions and determinations of said city council upon such appeal shall be final and conclusive, 'as to all errors, informalities and irregularities which said city council might have remedied and avoided.' It is evident, however, that the foregoing defects in the proceedings could not have been remedied or avoided by the city council upon any appeal from the assessment. At that time the work had been done, and there was no occasion for any contract to be entered into, and any direction from the city council to the superintendent of streets to enter into a contract would have been nugatory as to anything that had taken place prior thereto. A contract entered into by the superintendent at that date would not validate an assessment for work that had been done prior thereto. Unless the superintendent had entered into a contract in pursuance of the award at a time when by the provisions of the statute, he was authorized to do so, there was no foundation for any of the subsequent proceedings, and the person who did the work acquired no rights thereby against the owner. 'A contract authorized and executed in the mode prescribed by the act is indispensable to the validity of the assessment. This defect is not cured by the failure of the lot holders to appeal to the board, because, had an appeal been taken, the defect could not have been remedied by the board.' [Dougherty v. Hitchcock, 35 Cal. 524.] 'The premature action of the superintendent was one which affected his *power* or *jurisdiction*. His action was *void*, and that which was void does not become valid by reason of a failure to appeal. The property owners were not *aggrieved*, and the failure of the contractor to appeal did not operate, (*1.*) To create a *grievance* on the part of defendants, and (*2.*) to *estop* them from complaining of it.' [Burke v. Turney, 54 Cal. 487.] The provision, in the latter part of section 11, that 'no assessment shall be held invalid except upon appeal to the city council,' etc., has no application to a case in which an appeal is not authorized, or in which, even if taken, the city council could not have remedied the defect. The legislature did not intend to declare that the owner should be deprived of his defense to any claim upon an assessment, where the assessment was void by reason of incurable defects, because he had failed to invoke the aid of a tribunal which was powerless to grant him any relief. Nor would the owner be estopped from presenting any such defects because he had appealed to the city council, and that body had denied him relief. Their denial of relief may have been based upon the express ground that the matter appealed from was not such as they could remedy, and therefore they would decline to take any action." [See also Dowling v. Altschul, 33 Pac. Rep. 495; Perine v. Forbush, 97 Cal. 305; also McBean v. Redick, 96 Cal. 191; Frick v. Morford, 87 Cal. 576.]

As stated *supra*, the provisions of section 3 relative to a "petition of remonstrance" are applicable only to the acts and decisions of the *council*, while the provisions of section 11 relative to "appeal" seem to contemplate only the acts and decisions of the *superintendent of streets*, and we have seen from the above that an appeal is not the exclusive remedy where the assessment is void and incurable by reason of some act of the superintendent of streets in excess of his powers. The same principle seems to be applicable to the provisions relative to the petition of remonstrance. In Capron v. Hitchcock, 33 Pac. Rep. 431, the court, per Vanclief, commissioner, said: "The provision authorizing 'a petition of remonstrance' against the acts and proceedings of the city council was intended to be applicable only to acts and proceedings *within the power* of the council."

V.   *Cases in which it has been Held that an Appeal is the only Remedy.*

1.   If a property owner feels aggrieved by the action of the superintendent of streets in extending the time for completion of the work, his only remedy is by appeal. [Conlin v. Seaman, 22 Cal. 546.]

2.   If a property owner is dissatisfied with the decision of the superintendent that the contract has been properly fulfilled, his only remedy is by appeal. [Emery v. Bradford, 29 Cal. 75; Cochran v. Collins, 29 Cal. 130; Shepard v. McNeil, 38 Cal. 72; Jennings v. Le Breton, 80 Cal. 8; Fanning v. Leviston, 93 Cal. 186.]

3.   If the assessment is made to one of several joint owners instead of to all, the only remedy of the single joint owner to whom it is made is by appeal. [Taylor v. Palmer, 31 Cal. 242.] In this case, page 257, Mr. Justice Sanderson said: "If, for the reason suggested, the assessment was not properly made, the appellant's remedy was by appeal to the board of supervisors, as provided in the twelfth section of the act. [Act of 1862.] He is named in the assessment, and was therefore put upon his appeal, if he had any fault to find. If he owned in common with others, or if he owned only a part of the premises, he could have appealed to the board of supervisors, and had the assessment corrected to suit the facts. Not having done so, he cannot now question the validity of the assessment upon the ground suggested."

4.   The fact that the mayor of Oakland, before his

election, had become the assignee of a contract, as security
for a debt due him by the contractor, does not affect the
validity of the assessment under the Oakland street law of
April 4, 1864; and if a property owner is dissatisfied with
the act of the mayor in countersigning the warrant under
these circumstances, his only remedy is by appeal. [Bau-
dry v. Valdez, 32 Cal. 270.]

5. If there be a fraudulent side agreement between
the contractor and some of the lot owners, whereby the
contractor, for the purpose of inducing some of the lot
owners to sign a petition for the work, agrees with them to
do the work at a specified rate in lieu of and less than the
rate to be awarded in the contract,—while this side agreement is a fraud upon the other owners, and impregnates
the assessment with the fraud,—nevertheless an appeal to
the council is the only remedy of the defrauded property
owners, unless the statute expressly allows the fraud to be
set up in defense of an action brought upon the assessment.
Thus in Nolan v. Reese, 32 Cal. 486, the work was done and
the proceedings had, under the San Francisco street work
act of 1862. In that case it was held that "if the person
who contracts with the street superintendent to improve a
street, before the contract is made makes a private contract
with a part of the owners of the lots liable to be assessed
for the improvement, to do their work for less than the price
allowed by the contract, this private contract is in fraud of
the law under which the streets are improved; but the fraud
is no defense in an action by the contractor to recover
the assessment, and must be taken advantage of by a
remonstrance to or appeal to the board of supervisors."
[Statutes of 1862, page 391, §§ 6, 12.] Mr. Justice Shafter,
delivering the opinion of the court, says, page 487:
"Should the fraud with which the contractor was charged
be considered as affecting the 'award of the work' to him by
the board of supervisors [section 6 of act of 1862; section
5 of the act of March 18, 1885], then under the fourth
section of the act [section 3 of the act of March 18, 1885],
it should have been brought to the notice of the board of
supervisors by a remonstrance coming from one or more of
the lot owners. If, on the other hand, the fraud is considered as affecting the 'legality of the assessment,' then
any person having objections to make should have appealed
to the board of supervisors within thirty-five days subsequent to the date of the assessment. [Section 12 of the
act of 1862; section 11 of the act of 1885.] Such are the
methods pointed out by the act for reviewing the decisions
of the board and the acts of the superintendent, and they

exclude all others by positive provision. The reason for
this narrowness in the remedies provided for by the act is
found in the fact that the legislature, in framing it, was
providing for a matter of public concern through an exercise of the sovereign power of taxation. The meagerness
averted to has its origin in the necessities of the power."
To the same effect is the decision in Himmelmann *v.*
Hoadley, 44 Cal. 214, 227, decided under the same statute.
In Brady *v.* Bartlett, 56 Cal. 350, however, it was held that
where there had been such a fraudulent side contract, the
fraud could be set up in defense to an action upon the
assessment, and that if proven it would defeat all recovery
by the contractor. But this was because the act under
which the work was done expressly allowed such a defense.
In this case the work was done and the proceedings had
under the San Francisco street work act of 1872, by the
the 13th section of which such defense was expressly
allowed. That section provided that "in suits brought to
recover street assessments * * * no defense shall be
interposed except * * * . *Third.* Fraud in the assessment, or in any of the acts or proceedings prior thereto."
Unless there be some equivalent provision in the present
street work act it is altogether probable that in any future
case arising out of proceedings had under the present act,
the Supreme Court will follow the rule laid down in Nolan
v. Reese, and Himmelmann *v.* Hoadley, and hold
that where there is such a fraudulent side agreement the property owner's only remedy is by appeal to the
council,—there to make a direct attack upon the proceedings. If there is any provision in the present street work
act similar to or the equivalent of the provision of the 13th
section of the act of 1872, relied upon in Brady *v.*
Bartlett, *supra*, it has escaped the author's notice.

In Chambers *v.* Satterlee, 40 Cal. 520, it is said: "While
the statute intended to leave open for judicial inquiry all
questions which can be said to be of a *jurisdictional* character,
its purpose was to submit *all other* questions to the decision
of the board itself." [See also Emery *v.* Bradford, 29 Cal.
page 86, cited *supra* p. 119.] Therefore, if the line which divides those matters, over which the decision of the council on
appeal is final and conclusive, from those matters over
which its decision is not thus final and conclusive,—matters as to which the provisions for appeal are not referable
—be that line which likewise divides matters of a jurisdictional character from matters of a non-jurisdictional character,—and this seems to be the rule deducible from the
authorities, provided the defect be both jurisdictional, and

past remedy or appeal,—it follows that in answer to the question in any case, Is an appeal the sole remedy of the property owner?—we must first answer the question, Is the matter complained of jurisdictional in character or non-jurisdictional? If jurisdictional it may be availed of in defense to an action upon the assessment, and is not waived even if the property owner has prosecuted an unsuccessful appeal to the council, provided the error or irregularity complained of was past remedy at the time the appeal was taken. That is to say, even if the alleged irregularity or error be jurisdictional in character, in the sense that it is an *essential* requirement, or requirement having the semblance of benefit to the owner, still under the provisions of section 11 of the act, an appeal to the council is the sole and exclusive remedy of the property owner, if the alleged error or irregularity might have been avoided or remedied by the council on appeal. The remedy by appeal is exclusive of any other remedy as to all matters which can be revised and corrected on such appeal. For example, if the error or irregularity complained of be one inhering in and directly appertaining to the assessment only—all the proceedings up to the assessment having been regular and proper—then, if the error be capable of correction on appeal, such appeal is the only remedy of the "aggrieved" property owner. [Dowling *v.* Altschul, 33 Pac. Rep. 495.] If the alleged error or irregularity is non-jurisdictional, an appeal to the council is the only remedy. But those matters are of a jurisdictional character which are *essential* to the validity of the assessment. So that, ultimately, the important question in determining whether the matter complained of is jurisdictional or not, is, Is the matter *essential* to the validity of the assessment or to the right to recover in an action upon the assessment? If it is, then an appeal is not the exclusive remedy, if the error is incapable of correction upon appeal. As to the rules by which to determine what requirements of a statute are *essential* and what are *non-essential,* see the opinion of Mr. Justice Thornton, and authorities cited, in the above case of Brady *v.* Bartlett, 56 Cal. pages 357, 358. But, as is well said by the learned judge, in that case, the rule by which to determine what provisions in a statute are mandatory and what not, —and, therefore, what is essential and what non-essential,— is plain and simple; but to apply them, *"hoc opus est."*

Throughout the notes to this section of the act [Sec. 11] the expression "jurisdictional requirements," has been used synonymously with the expression, "requirements of the statute having the semblance of benefit to the property owner." As thus used it has been stated that, notwithstanding some one of such requirements may be omitted, the omission is nevertheless not necessarily fatal in an action upon the assessment, unless the omission was incapable of correction on an appeal to the council, so as to preserve or restore to the property owner the right or benefit thus omitted. But, the term "jurisdictional requirements" might have been used in a more limited and restricted sense. It might have been restricted to those requirements which not only have the semblance of benefit to the owner, but which are to be performed at such a stage of the proceedings that if any of them be omitted or irregularly performed, the omission or irregularity is incapable of correction on appeal — the mischief is past remedy when the time to appeal has arrived, e. g., all such requirements of the statute as are necessary to give the council jurisdiction to order the work to be done. As thus used every jurisdictional requirement is essential to the validity of the assessment and to a recovery thereon, since if any such requirement be omitted, the mischief is past remedy by the council on appeal,—when the time for appeal has arrived, no correction can possibly be made so as to restore to the property owner the benefit secured to him by the statute. It is therefore important that the reader should bear in mind the meaning which has been placed upon the word "jurisdictional," as used throughout the notes to this section, and remember that it is used in the broader of the two possible significations given above, namely, synonomously with the expression "every requirement of the statute having the semblance of benefit to the owner."

When Mr. Justice Wallace, in Chambers v. Satterlee, 40 Cal. 520, said that, "While the statute intended to leave open for judicial inquiry all questions which can be said to be of a *jurisdictional* character, its purpose was to submit *all other* questions to the decision of the board itself," he undoubtedly used the term "jurisdictional" in the more restricted of the two significations given above. That is, he used the term "jurisdictional" to designate those requirements which not only have the semblance of benefit to the property owners, but which are provided for at such a stage of the proceedings that, if omitted, it is, in the nature of things, too late to remedy the evil when the time for an appeal to the council has arrived; and this is doubtless a more accurate use of the expression; although the term "jurisdictional" does not seem to be appropriate in this con-

nection at all, since it is used, not to express the power of a
judicial body to hear and determine, but rather the power
of certain officials to do certain acts, most of which are of
a ministerial character; and, since the term seems to be
wholly inappropriate in this connection, it really matters
little in what sense it is here used, provided the meaning to be attached to it in this connection be accurately
defined *pro hac vice*.

It is to be regretted that the word "jurisdictional" should
ever have been used at all in this connection, as some other
and more appropriate word would have avoided much confusion of thought and expression. It is not an appropriate word to use in this connection, for, as stated by Mr.
Justice Temple, in Chambers *v.* Satterlee, 40 Cal. 525,
"The word 'jurisdiction' [as here used] means *power*,
for there is nothing of a judicial nature in that portion of
the proceedings which relates to ordering the work and letting the contract." The word is more appropriately used
in connection with judicial proceedings, in which connection it has recently been defined to mean the power to hear
and determine a cause, and to render the particular judgment or order entered in the particular case. But there is
perhaps no word in the English language that has been
more frequently defined than this word "jurisdiction," and
the decisions are still far from being in accord with each
other. [See Am. and Eng. Encyclopædia of Law, Vol. 12,
p. 244, *et seq.*] The term may be appropriately used in
connection with the power of the council to hear and determine the questions presented to it on an appeal by a
property owner, or on a petition of remonstrance. In such
a case the council exercises judicial functions. But it is
not correctly used when employed to express the power or
authority of the superintendent of streets, for example,
to make any particular assessment, or to issue any particular warrant.

However, following what seems to be a general custom,
the expression "jurisdictional requirements" has been used
in the notes to this section as including "every requirement having the semblance of benefit to the property
owner,"—including those things which the statute requires
to be done by the superintendent of streets after the execution of the contract and after the performance of the work
as well as those requirements necessary to give the council
jurisdiction to order the work done. Although it would
doubtless have been more accurate if the expression had
been used to express merely those requirements of the statute which are absolutely essential to any recovery upon

the assessment—those requirements which not only affect substantial rights, but which are incapable of being remedied by the council on appeal.

6. If the street superintendent includes in the assessment any sum which he ought not to have included, an appeal to the council is the only remedy, if there be any part of the assessment which is legal and proper, and if the lots charged with the assessment are lawfully chargeable with some part of the total amount assessed to pay the cost of the work, provided the part which is lawfully assessable against the property, is severable from the part which is not lawfully assessable. Thus in Himmelmann v. Hoadley, 44 Cal. 276, the contract was awarded for macadamizing and curbing California street from Gough street west to Cemetery avenue in San Francisco. Subsequent to the award, the line of Cemetery avenue was extended to the west so that the distance from Gough street to Cemetery avenue was increased about 200 feet. The contractor macadamized and curbed this additional 200 feet, and the superintendent included the cost of the additional work in the assessment. The lots sought to be charged with the lien, lie to the east of the former line of Cemetery avenue, *i. e.*, they lie within the limits of California street included in the award of the contract made by the board, and were properly chargeable with the cost of the work if no additional work had been done. The court, per Rhodes, J., said: "It is very clear that the superintendent had no authority to make an assessment for the work on the additional two hundred feet of the street. * * * The plaintiff maintains, that as the superintendent had jurisdiction to make an assessment for the expense of the work performed on the street, up to the former line of Cemetery avenue, if he included in the assessment any sum which, for any reason, ought not to have been included, then the property holder should have appealed to the board of supervisors. This position is sustained by Emery v. Bradford, 29 Cal. 88; Smith v. Davis, 30 Cal. 536; Nolan v. Reese, 32 Cal. 484; Smith v. Cofran, 34 Cal. 314, and many other cases in this court. The question would be different had the action been brought to enforce a lien upon property fronting on the street lying west of the former line of Cemetery avenue, [*i.e.*, the property not on that part of California street, lying within the lines of intersection described in the award of the contract,] a question of jurisdiction would have been presented. But when the contract is valid, if the superintendent includes in the assessment the expense of work not provided for in the contract, or not performed under it, it is an error on his part, which may be corrected on appeal to the board, as provided for in the statute."

To the same effect are the following cases: Boyle *v.* Hitchcock, 66 Cal. 129, where incidental expenses for engineering and printing were objected to; Frick *v.* Morford, 87 Cal. 577; McVerry *v.* Boyd, 89 Cal. 304, 309; Fanning *v.* Leviston, 93 Cal. 188; Perine *v.* Forbush, 97 Cal. 305. In this latter case the superintendent included in the assessment the cost of certain bulkheads, though they were not provided for in the contract. In this case it was said, per De Haven, J.: "It is true that, as the contract did not provide for constructing these bulkheads, the superintendent of streets ought not to have included their cost in the assessment which he made, but for such erroneous action on his part the only remedy was an appeal to the city council, as provided for in section 11 of the act. * * * Such an objection to the assessment could have been made to the city council, and the defendant waived his right to now make it by not appealing to that body for its correction. When, however, an assessment includes the cost of work not falling within the general description of that which is referred to in the resolution of intention, or when such work bears no relation whatever to that which is described in the contract, this rule would not apply. But this is not such a case. The construction of the bulkheads was not, so far as appears here, an entire departure from the general plan or scope of the improvements described in the resolution of intention, although mention of them is omitted in the plans and specifications attached to the contract. In such a case the determination of the superintendent of streets that their construction was necessary in order to fully complete the work called for by the contract, was only an error of judgment, and his action in making an assessment to cover their cost was only a mere error, which it is too late now to correct, and which does not render the assessment wholly void."

7. If it is objected that the contract was made with a corporation acting through its president, who was not authorized to enter into the contract, the objection must be raised on appeal to the council. [Oakland Pvg. Co., *v.* Rier, 52 Cal. 270.]

8. If there is a purely technical omission in the diagram not amounting to an omission in respect to something made essential by the act, or affecting substantial rights, the only remedy is by appeal. [Dyer *v.* Parrott, 60 Cal. 551.]

9. Appeal is the only remedy where a second contract

is awarded during the existence of a previous contract for the same work. [Spaulding v. Homestead Ass'n, 87 Cal. 41.]

10. Appeal is the only remedy where a lot, properly assessable under section 7 of the act and chargeable with a portion of the expenses is omitted from the assessment. Dowling v. Altschul, decided June 13, 1893, 33 Pac. Rep. 495, decision of department, opinion by Commissioner Vanclief, Mr. Justice Harrison concurring in the judgment but not in the opinion. This is a most important decision, and if in such case an appeal is the only remedy where the front-foot plan of assessment is adopted, there does not seem to be any reason why it should not be the only remedy, where the council has declared an assessment district to be benefited by the work or improvement, as provided for by section 3 of the act, and the superintendent, in assessing the lots within such district,—as provided for by subdivision 12 of section 7—has omitted some lot from assessment. There is an assessment district in the one case just as much as in the other. In the one case the council fixes the boundaries of the district and declares it the district to be benefited, in the other case, *i. e.* where the front-foot plan is adopted, the statute establishes the district. [See Diggins v. Brown, 76 Cal. 318; Davis v. City of Los Angeles, 86 Cal. 49; Dyer v. Harrison, 63 Cal. 448; People v. Lynch, 51 Cal. 15.]

VI. *Cases in which it has been held that Appeal is not a Remedy.*

1. Where a lot is not liable to be assessed at all, the owner is not a party directly interested in the contract, work, or assessment, within the meaning of the act, and is not bound to appeal from the assessment. Although assessed, and in that sense he might be said to be interested in the assessment, the section does not mean that a mere stranger to the locality, and who might have no suspicion that he had been assessed until too late to appeal, should be cut off from his defense. [Bassett v. Enwright, 19 Cal. 636.]

2. If the lot is not assessed to "unknown owner" or to the true owner by his true name, the owner need not appeal. [Smith v. Cofran, 34 Cal. 316.] On page 317 it is said: "Nobody, except the person named as owner, is a party to the assessment at all, unless the owner is stated as unknown, and one not a party to the assessment in one of the modes designated, is in no way affected by it." He is a stranger to the assessment, and a stranger to the assessment need not appeal. "On the other hand, if a lot owner is assessed by name or by designation 'unknown owner,' and is a party to and bound-by the proceedings, he can not attack them for mere error, in a collateral action. In respect to such error, his remedy is by appeal." [Bucknall v. Story, 46 Cal. 589, 601.]

3. If the contract made by the superintendent calls for *less* work than is described in the resolution of intention and the award, the contract is void, and no appeal need be taken. "A contract authorized and executed in the mode prescribed by the act is indispensable to the validity of the assessment. This defect is not cured by the failure of the lot holders to appeal to the board, because had an appeal been taken, the defect could not have been remedied by the board." [Dougherty *v.* Hitchcock, 35 Cal. 512, 524, 526.] In this case the resolution of intention described the work to be done as being work on a certain street—Clay street in San Francisco—for several blocks in length, from Taylor to Leavenworth streets, and the board of supervisors awarded a contract for the *whole* work. The only contract entered into by the superintendent was for the grading of one block only—that from Jones to Leavenworth streets. To the same effect is McBean *v.* Redick, 96 Cal. 191, decided under the present street improvement act.

In Chambers *v.* Satterlee, 40 Cal. 498, the contract made by the street superintendent included *more* work than that called for by the resolution of intention and the award. In that case the board ordered the street to be graded—which of course means to the official grade—but the contract provided that the street should be "graded to the official height and line,"—and then, instead of stopping here, went on to say,—"except the roadway, which is to be graded twelve inches below the official grade—and when completed is to have a crown to the center eighteen inches from the bottom of the gutter-ways." Chambers *v.* Satterlee differs from Dougherty *v.* Hitchcock in this, that while in the latter case the contract made by the superintendent called for less work than the award, in the former case the contract called for more. In Chambers *v.* Satterlee it was held that an appeal to the board of supervisors was the only remedy of a property owner dissatisfied with the contract made by the superintendent, because it called for more work than that described in the resolution of intention, and the concurring opinion of Mr. Justice Crockett seems to present the clearest reasoning on this branch of the case. He says, page 531: "In embracing in the contract additional work, not ordered to be done, the superintendent committed an irregularity which, by the express terms of the statute, could be corrected on an appeal to the board from the assessment."

Whereas, in Dougherty *v.* Hitchcock, the written contract was for *less* work than that called for by the award, the contract was void, and the defect jurisdictional, but where the written contract calls for *more* work than the award, the contract is not void—if the excess can be segregated from that properly called for by the award—and the defect is not jurisdictional. [See also Perine *v.* Forbush, 97 Cal. 305.]

4. Where the written contract executed by the street superintendent gives more time for completion than that allowed by the award, it is void, and no appeal is necessary. [Brock *v.* Luning, 89 Cal. 316.]

5. The demand, required by section 10 of the act to be made by the contractor or his assigns, or some person on his or their behalf, must be for the amount properly chargeable against the lot. If demand is made for more than is properly chargeable, the contractor or his assigns can not recover, and the defense is not affected by the failure of the parties aggrieved to appeal. [Donnelly *v.* Howard, 60 Cal. 292.]

6. If the contract is executed by the superintendent prematurely, it is void, and the defect is not waived by a failure to appeal. [Burke *v.* Turney, 54 Cal. 486; Manning *v.* Den, 90 Cal. 610; Perine *v.* Forbush, 97 Cal. 305.]

VII. *Appeal by Contractor.* An assessment which, for any reason, is void and incurable, does not create any lien upon the land assessed, and the owner thereof is not required to appeal to the city council, because he is not a person "aggrieved," within the meaning of that term as used in the statute. The *contractor,* however, may appeal, and, on appeal, may have curable errors corrected. [Frick *v.* Morford, 87 Cal. 576, 580; Smith *v.* Cofran, 34 Cal. 310.] Under the provisions of the statute, the assessment and warrant, after having been recorded, are put into the hands of the contractor, and he has thirty days from the date of the warrant within which to examine it, and if found in any respect to be incorrect or illegal, to apply to the council by appeal to have it corrected and made legal. In Smith *v.* Cofran, 34 Cal. page 315, Mr. Justice Sawyer said: "All the means open to the superintendent for determining the correctness and legality of the assessment and warrant are equally open to the contractor, and an opportunity is afforded to examine the proceedings and apply for correction if found to be incorrect or illegal. Moreover, as we have said, it is provided that the 'contractor * * * having or making any objection to the correctness or legality of the assessment * * * *shall* * · * * appeal to the board of supervisors,'

etc. Thus, if he has objections of the kind in question, he
not only has an opportunity, but it is made his duty, to
have them obviated in the mode prescribed. If he fails to
avail himself of the means of protection afforded by the
law, the loss in consequence of defects of the kind under
consideration results as much from his own negligence as
from that of the superintendent."

VIII. *Unsuccessful Appeal no Estoppel in Action on Assessment.* If an assessment is, for any reason, illegal, and a property owner takes an appeal to the council and the council
denies him relief, the fact that he has taken this unsuccessful appeal will not estop him from relying upon the defects
in the assessment in any action brought thereon. The
jurisdiction of the council being limited and special, it
may be shown that the facts conferring jurisdiction upon
them did not exist. [Manning v. Den, 90 Cal. 611; Dehail
v. Morford, 95 Cal. 457.]

IX. *Council Cannot Dismiss Appeal.* If an appeal to
the council be taken by a property owner in time
and regularly, the council has no power to dismiss
it; and even if an order is made dismissing it, the
appeal is regarded as still pending, the assessment
does not become a finality, and an action can not be
maintained on it. [People v. O'Neil, 51 Cal. 91.] If,
however, it does not appear that any testimony was offered
by the person taking the appeal, as this fact is consistent
with the fact that the only matter urged on the appeal was
a question of law, the appeal will not be regarded as
still pending, and an action might be maintained on the
assessment. [Mahoney v. Braverman, 54 Cal. 565, 570.]

X. *Practice on Appeal.* On appeal the same strictness
which would be required in a pleading at common law is
not exacted from persons objecting to an assessment in
stating their objections. [Barber v. San Francisco, 42 Cal.
630.]

SECTION 12. At any time after the period of thirty-five days from the
day of the date of the warrants, as herein provided, or if an appeal is
taken to the city council, as provided in section eleven of this act, at any
time after five days from the decision of said council, or after the return
of the warrant or assessment, after the same may have been corrected,
altered or modified, as provided in said section eleven (but not less than
thirty-five days from the date of the warrant), the contractor or his assignee
may sue, in his own name, the owner of the land, lots or portions of lots,
assessed on the day of the date of the recording of the warrant,
assessment and diagram, or any day thereafter during the continuance of the lien of said assessment, and recover the amount of any
assessment remaining unpaid, with interest thereon at the rate of ten per

cent. per annum until paid. And in all cases of recovery under the provisions of this act the plaintiff shall recover the sum of fifteen dollars in addition to the taxable cost, as attorney's fees, but not any percentage upon said recovery. And when suit has been brought, after a personal demand has been made and a refusal to pay such assessment so demanded, the plaintiff shall also be entitled to have and recover said sum of fifteen dollars as attorney's fees in addition to all taxable costs, notwithstanding that the suit may be settled or a tender may be made before a recovery in said action, and he may have judgment therefor. Suit may be brought in the Superior Court within whose jurisdiction the city is in which said work has been done, and in case any of the assessments are made against lots, portions of lots, or lands the owners thereof cannot, with due diligence, be found, the service in each of such actions may be had in such manner as is prescribed in the codes and laws of this state. The said warrant, assessment, certificate and diagram, with the affidavit of demand and non-payment, shall be held prima facie evidence of the regularity and correctness of the assessment and of the prior proceedings and acts of the superintendent of streets and city council upon which said warrant, assessment and diagram are based, and like evidence of the right of the plaintiff to recover in the action. The court in which said suit shall be commenced shall have power to adjudge and decree a lien against the premises assessed, and to order such premises to be sold on execution, as in other cases of the sale of real estate by the process of said courts; and on appeal the appellate courts shall be vested with the same power to adjudge and decree a lien and to order such premises to be sold on execution or decree as is conferred on the court from which an appeal is taken. Such premises, if sold, may be redeemed as in other cases. In all suits now pending, or hereafter brought to recover street assessments, the proceedings therein shall be governed and regulated by the provisions of this act, and also, when not in conflict herwith, by the codes of this state. This act shall be liberally construed to effect the ends of justice. [*Amendment approved March 14, 1889, statutes 1889, page 168.*]

[Section 12 was amended in 1889 by act of March 14, 1889, statutes '89, page 168.]

Section 12 of the act contains the provisions relating to suits to enforce the assessment lien. It provides that at any time after the period of 35 days from the date of the warrant, or at any time after 5 days from the decision of the council on appeal,—if an appeal has been taken as provided in section 11,—or after the return of the warrant or assessment, after the same have been corrected, altered or modified on appeal, as provided in section 11, (but not less than 35 days from the date of the warrant) the contractor or his assignee, may sue in the Superior Court within whose jurisdiction the city is in which the work was done, and recover the amount of any assessment remaining unpaid, with interest thereon at the rate of ten per cent. per annum until paid, etc. The section provides that the proceedings "shall be governed and regulated by the provisions of this act, and also, when not in conflict herewith, by the codes of this state."

I. *Procedure, General Principles.* When the assessment is invalid, but the property owner has, nevertheless, allowed the contractor to proceed with the work to completion without objection so that his property has thereby received the benefit of the improvement, he cannot, by injunction, enjoin the sale of the land for the purpose of avoiding the payment of his assessment. Injunction proceedings, if desired, must be instituted before the work is done. This is upon the principle that he who seeks equity must do equity. If the proceedings are irregular the property owner will be left to his strict legal rights, if he has any; and in an action by the contractor or his assigns to enforce the assessment lien, the property owner may set up the irregularities by way of a defense to the action. But he can not seek the aid of equity unless he is prepared to do equity, and therefore can not, by injunction, prevent a sale of the property, unless he is prepared to pay at least the reasonable value of the improvement to his property or the amount which in equity and good conscience he ought to pay. [Weber *v.* San Francisco, 1 Cal. 455.] The rule is the same whether the acts complained of are mere irregularities or such as render the assessment illegal and void. [Esterbrook *v.* O'Brien, decided July 13, 1893, 33 Pac. Rep. 765.] In this case the court said: "Courts of equity do not review the proceedings of officers entrusted with the assessment of the property. If proceedings taken by them are void, no title will pass by a sale of the real estate, and the party claiming to be injured must litigate his rights in an action at law for the possession of the premises. Of course there are exceptions to the rule, as where it is shown that the lands are not at all subject to taxation, or that there is no law authorizing any proceedings therefor.   *   *   *   So long as the moral obligation to pay any portion of the tax exists, a court of equity will not lend its aid to prevent a cloud upon the title, but will leave the party to his remedy at law." [See also Bucknall *v.* Story, 36 Cal. 67; Lent *v.* Tillson, 72 Cal. 433.]

According to the express provision of the contract, neither the city nor the city authorities are to be held liable in any event. Only the property assessed can be held liable. [See section 6.] Nor can the legislature appropriate money to pay the claim of a contractor who has failed to obtain compensation for the work done by him, by reason of any errors, omissions or irregularities of the municipal officers, which prevented them from having jurisdiction to order the work done, or rendered the contract or assessment invalid, nor can the legislature empower the municipal authorities of a city to appropriate or pay any money for any such purpose. An act of the legislature appropriating public moneys to pay any portion of the claim of a contractor who failed to recover from the property owner, because of irregularities in the proceedings committed by the municipal authorities, or an act to empower the city authorities of a city to pay city moneys to such contractor, under such circumstances, would be a "gift" within the meaning of section 31 of article IV of the constitution, and such legislative act would, therefore, be unconstitutional and void. The contractor must look to the property of the property owners, as provided by section 12 of the act; and, to entitle him to recover against them, the proceedings must be regular and valid or capable of correction by the council on appeal.[Conlin v. Board of Supervisors of San Francisco, decided July 21, 1893, 33 Pac. Rep. 753.]

The statute under which the contract is made becomes a part of the contract, and the provisions of the statute in reference to the enforcement of the assessment lien and the remedies of the contractor are not affected by a subsequent repealing act,—so far as such contract is concerned. [Creighton v. Pragg, 21 Cal. 115; Dyer v. Pixley, 44 Cal. 153; Dyer v. North, 44 Cal. 157–160; Dyer v. Barstow, 53 Cal. 81.]

The action is not upon the contract. If it were, it is probable that the assignee of a contractor could not sue his assignor when the latter is also a property owner, since the assignee would stand in the shoes of his assignor, the contractor, and the contract would create no right in the contractor against himself. The action is in reality an action to collect a tax. The city government and the contractor are the only parties to the proceeding, so far as making the improvement is concerned; that being done, the city government acts alone in its political capacity in apportioning and levying the tax upon the property of the property owner or taxpayer; but when provision is made for the collection of the tax, the city government steps out of the triangular relation existing between the contractor, the city government and the property owner or taxpayer, and the contractor is thrust into her place and made her agent for the purpose of collecting the tax. "Independent of the statute, the tax would be due from the taxpayer to the city, and the city would have to demand and sue for it, if necessary; but the statute provides that the city shall not be responsible for the collection of the tax, or subject to the risk, trouble and annoyance, but shall virtually assign her right of action for the tax to the contractor, in full payment for his work and labor under her contract with him, and authorize him to sue in his own name to recover it, if necessary. This being done, his relation of contractor is at an end. * * * The thing sued for is not the contract price, or a part of it, but the tax specified in the assessment, or warrant, for which he sues, not as contractor, but as assignee of the city, and he is compelled to make the same averments and the same proof which the city would have had to make had she undertaken to collect the tax; in other words, he has to show that the entire proceedings which terminated in imposing upon the property-holder a liability to pay the tax in suit have been in conformity with the provisions of the statute by which the tax was authorized. Without doing this, the city could not have recovered under the more ordinary mode adopted in such case, nor can he." [Hendrick v. Crowley, 31 Cal. 472.]

The title to a lot, if put in issue by the pleadings, may be litigated in an action on the assessment. All the owners of the lot must be made defendants, and if any defendant denies his ownership this is a material issue and may be litigated. [Taylor v. Donner, 31 Cal. 481; Robinson v. Merrill, 87 Cal. 11.]

The relief sought in actions on street assessments is equitable, and the action an action in equity, and consequently must be brought in the Superior Courts, without reference to the amount claimed. [Muhlstadt v. Blanc, 34 Cal. 577.]

The contractor does not lose his lien by the mere lapse of two years before the entry of judgment, provided his action be commenced within that time. [Randolph v. Bayne, 44 Cal. 367; Dougherty v. Henarie, 47 Cal. 9; Himmelmann v. Carpentier, 47 Cal. 42; Dorland v. McGlynn, 47 Cal. 48.]

An action can not be maintained to enforce a lien for a street improvement, unless the lien exists at the time the action is commenced, and therefore, even if it be admitted that the legislature has the constitutional right to validate an assessment for improving a street, the validating act, if of any effect, makes the assessment valid only from the time of its passage. So that pending suits brought to enforce the lien are not affected by the act, and there can be no recovery in such suits by reason of such act. [Reis v. Graff, 51 Cal. 86; People v. O'Neil, 51 Cal. 91; People v. Kinsman, 51 Cal. 92; see People v. Lynch, 51 Cal. 15.]

While there can be no personal judgment against the owner of the property [Taylor v. Palmer, 31 Cal. 241; Manning v. Den, 90 Cal. 610], still the action to enforce the lien is not a suit *in rem* against the real estate only. On the contrary the statute provides that the action must be against the owner to enforce the lien. [City of Santa Barbara *v.* Huse, 51 Cal. 217.]

II. *Parties.*

(a.) Plaintiffs. The act expressly provides that the contractor or his assignee may sue in his own name; likewise, that the proceedings shall be governed and regulated by the codes of this state, when not in conflict with the provisions of the act.

(b.) Defendants. The act provides that the contractor or his assignee may sue the owner of the land, lots or portion of lots assessed, on the day when the amounts assessed became a lien thereon,—viz., on the day when the warrant, assessment, diagram and certificate of the city engineer were recorded—or any day thereafter during the continuance of the lien of the assessment.

All the owners of the property must be made defendants and they must all be served with summons, and if all the owners are not made parties defendant the defendant may set up this fact in his answer, and urge it as a reason why judgment should not be entered against him until all the owners are brought into court. The lien can not be enforced against any of the owners in the absence of another owner who is not joined as a defendant. [Hancock *v.* Bowman, 49 Cal. 413; Clark *v.* Porter, 53 Cal. 409; Diggins *v.* Reay, 54 Cal. 525; Harney *v.* Appelgate, 57 Cal. 205; Robinson *v.* Merrill, 87 Cal. 11.]

See section 16 of the act for a definition, description or enumeration of the persons who are declared by the act "shall be regarded, treated and deemed to be the 'owner' [for the purpose of this law] according to the intent and meaning of that word as used in this act."

It was held in Parker *v.* Bernal, 66 Cal. 113, that, under the San Francisco street work act of 1872, an action on a street assessment may be maintained against the executor of an estate, although the heirs of the decedent are in fact the owners of the land assessed; that the heirs are not necessary parties, and if originally joined as defendants the action may be dismissed as to them and judgment rendered against the executor.

But in Phelan *v.* Dunne, 72 Cal. 229, it was held that where the owner dies prior to the assessment his heirs or devisees are the only necessary parties, and the executors need not be joined.

In this case of Phelan *v.* Dunne the work had been done under the San Francisco street improvement act of April

1, 1872. The defendant was the devisee of James Dunne. The contract was let prior to the death of James Dunne, who was the owner of the land at that time, but the assessment was not made until after his death. It was claimed by defendant that the administration of the estate of James Dunne, deceased, being still open, and no decree of distribution having been made, the executors of the will should be made parties defendant. In this connection the court said: "By an act approved April 1, 1872, and apparently to avoid the necessity of making all parties having an interest in the property defendants in the action, it was provided [section 13] that the action might be brought against the *owner* of the land; and section 17 of the act provides that 'the person owing the fee or the person in the possession of the lands, lots, or portions of lots or buildings under the claim of ownership, or exercising acts of ownership over the same for himself or as the administrator or guardian of the owner, or the person in whom, on the day the action was commenced, appears the legal title to the lands by deeds recorded in the recorder's office in the city and county of San Francisco, shall be regarded, treated and deemed to be the owner [for the purpose of this law], according to the meaning and intent of that word as used in this act.' It may be that under these provisions persons other than the heirs and devisees are *proper* parties to the action; and that their rights cannot be foreclosed unless they are made defendants; but as to that we express no opinion. It is sufficient to say that the defendant is the owner in fee, that he is the only *necessary* party, and that plaintiff is entitled, under this act, to a decree of foreclosure, whatever may be the rights of other parties interested who are not joined as defendants." Section 12 of the Vrooman act is substantially the same as section 13 of the said act of April 1, 1872; and likewise section 16 of the Vrooman act is substantially the same as section 17 of the said act of April 1, 1872, except that the former is a general act, while the provisions of the latter were confined to the city and county of San Francisco, and the former expressly includes "executors" in the same category with administrators and guardians of the owner, so that the present street improvement act (section 16) provides that "the person * * * exercising acts of ownership over [the lands, lots, etc.,] * * * as the executor * * of the owner shall be regarded, treated and deemed to be the 'owner,'" etc. But whether this provision is sufficient to make the executor a *necessary* party may be open to question, since, under the decision in Phelan *v.*

Dunne, *supra*, the fee is vested in the devisee, and if he be made a party defendant the suit is brought against the "owner." And the present street improvement act (section 12) like the said act of April 1, 1872, only requires the action to be brought against the "owner," and not against all persons interested in the land.

In Brady *v.* Burke, 90 Cal. 1, it was held that the statute under which the work was done and proceedings had, in that case, contemplated that the legal owner at the time of the rendition of the judgment should be a party, unless he is a purchaser *pendente lite* affected with notice of the action; and that one who has acquired title to the land, under the foreclosure of a prior street-assessment lien, pending a suit for the foreclosure of later assessment liens, but without notice of such suit, should be made a party thereto before judgment, and he is not bound by the judgment if not so made a party defendant.

It does not appear from the opinion in this case what act it was under which the street work in question was done, so that, when the court says that the act contemplated that the legal owner at the time of the rendition of the judgment should be a party, it cannot be known from the opinion which street improvement act was referred to; but it was one of the San Francisco street improvement acts, and in this respect there does not seem to be any material difference between any one of the former San Francisco street improvement acts and the present street improvement act; so that it is probable that the present street improvement act likewise contemplates that the legal owner at the time of the rendition of the judgment shall be a party. In fact, this conclusion seems to be deducible from the provisions of the present street improvement act itself, from internal evidences, and seems to require no authority to support it.

III. *Pleadings.*

1. *What Statute Governs.* Under the old constitution, it was held that the legislature, in actions to recover upon street assessments, might prescribe the requirements of the complaint, and prescribe for such actions special rules of pleading and practice. [Richardson *v.* Tobin, 45 Cal. 30; Whiting *v.* Townsend, 57 Cal. 515.] But, under the present constitution, the legislature is prohibited from passing any special or local laws regulating the practice of courts of justice. "The legislature shall not pass local or special laws in any of the following enumerated cases, that is to say: * * *Third.* Regulating the practice of courts of justice. * * *Thirty-third.* In all other cases where a general law can be made applicable." [Const. Art. IV, § 25, subdivi-

sions 3 and 33.] The Code of Civil Procedure of this state is a general law, and as such must have a uniform operation. [Const. article I, section 11.] And section 421 of the Code of Civil Procedure provides that "the forms of pleadings in civil actions, and the rules by which the sufficiency of the pleadings is to be determined, are those prescribed in this code." Accordingly, the question presents itself: Can the legislature, without contravening the above quoted provisions of the constitution, make any rules of pleading or of evidence, or of practice generally, whose application shall be limited and confined to cases arising under this street improvement act? And if it can, how far may it proceed in that direction?

In People v. Central Pac. R. R. Co., 83 Cal. 393, it was held that the provisions of the Political Code (section 3665 to 3670) relating to the assessment and collection of taxes levied upon railroads operated in two or more counties, are in conflict with said section 25 of article IV of the constitution. It was held in that case that section 3670 of the Political Code, which purported to provide the form of complaint in suits to recover taxes levied upon railroads operated in two or more counties, was special legislation and therefore unconstitutional; that the sufficiency of the complaint in an action to recover delinquent taxes must be tested by the rules of pleadings in civil actions prescribed by the Code of Civil Procedure, and not by section 3670 of the Political Code; and that thus tested the complaint in that case was insufficient. Mr. Chief Justice Beatty dissented, and in his dissenting opinion said: "In my opinion, the legislation referred to is neither local nor special; it is not local, because it operates throughout the state; and it is not special, because it applies to all railroads of a class created and defined by the constitution itself."

The decision in this case might leave the question as to the power of the legislature to enact rules of practice applicable only to street assessment cases, somewhat in doubt. But a recent decision of the Supreme Court, bearing directly upon street assessment suits [McDonald v. Conniff, No. 15,085, decided Aug. 30, 1893], does much to remove this question from the realm of doubt, and the case seems to be ample authority for the proposition that the legislature may prescribe different rules of procedure, as well of pleading as of evidence, for different classes of action, e. g., for action brought to foreclose street assessment liens. All of such actions constitute a class by themselves. Mr. Justice Harrison, delivering the opinion of the court, said:

"The statute makes the assessment, with the other documents offered by the plaintiff, *prima facie* evidence of the regularity and correctness of the assessment and of the prior proceedings and acts of the superintendent of streets and city council upon which it is based, and it was therefore not necessary to offer any evidence of these prior proceedings as the foundation for introducing these documents. It is competent for the legislature to prescribe rules of evidence for the trial of actions, and statutes which make a document *prima facie* evidence of the regularity of official proceedings in reference thereto, or which cast the burden of proof in an issue upon either party to the action, are within the constitutional power of the legislature. [Cooley Const. Lim., 450.] Neither does this provision of the statute contravene the provision of the constitution prohibiting the legislature from passing special or local laws 'regulating the practice of courts of justice.' It is not necessary that a law shall affect all the people of the state in order that it may be general, or that a statute concerning procedure shall be applicable to every action that may be brought in the courts of the state. A statute which affects all the individuals of a class is a general law, while one which relates to particular persons or things of a class is special. A statute regulating the rights of married women, or which affect all mining corporations, or confers rights upon municipal corporations of a certain class, or places restrictions upon all foreign corporations, is a general law. [City of Pasadena *v.* Stimson, 91 Cal. 238; *In re* Madera Irrigation District, 92 Cal. 316; Wheeler *v.* Philadelphia, 77 Penn. 348; Iowa R. R. Co. *v.* Soper, 39 Iowa, 112; Matter of N. Y. Elevated R. R. Co., 70 N. Y. 350.] The provision under consideration is neither a local nor a special law. It is applicable to all actions for the foreclosure of street assessment liens, and is in force in all parts of the state. That the legislature may prescribe different rules of procedure, as well of *pleading* as of evidence, for different actions, is illustrated by what it has done in defining the form of pleading upon judgments and in other special actions, in requiring the pleadings in forcible entry and detainer to be verified, in denying a divorce upon the mere default of the defendant, in making a tax deed *prima facie* evidence of the regularity of the proceedings prior to its issuance, and in requiring a different form of proof for the execution of a will from that of any other written instrument as well as in numerous other instances."

And in City and County of San Francisco *v.* Kiernan, 33 Pac. 721, decided June 13, 1893, it was held that section 18 of the Street Opening act of March 6, 1889, [statutes

1889, p. 75] providing that "the complaint (in an action to condemn) may aver that it is necessary for the city to take or damage and condemn the said land, * * * without setting forth the proceedings herein provided for," is constitutional.

2. *Complaint, What Must Allege.*

(a.) General Principles. A complaint to recover the amount of an assessment for street improvements should show by general or special averments a compliance by the council and city authorities with all the steps prescribed by law to confer jurisdiction on the council and to vest a right of action in the plaintiff. [Himmelman *v.* Danos, 35 Cal. 441; People *v.* Clark, 47 Cal. 456.] An action to recover the amount of a street assessment is, in reality, an action to recover a *tax*. As stated by Sanderson, J., in Hendrick *v.* Crowley, 31 Cal. 471, "The thing sued for is not the contract price or a part of it, but the *tax* specified in the assessment or warrant, for which he sues, not as contractor or as assignee of somebody else who was the contractor, but as assignee of the city, and he is compelled to make the same averments and the same proof which the city would have had to make had she undertaken to collect the *tax*." And in People *v.* Central Pac. R. R. Co., 83 Cal. 400, it is said: "Tax proceedings are *in invitum*, and, to be valid, must be *stricti juris*. If not valid they constitute no cause of action. It therefore becomes necessary that a complaint in an action for the collection of a tax should show upon its face facts sufficient to make out a *prima facie* case of valid tax, and that it is delinquent."

In Himmelman *v.* Danos, *supra*, 35 Cal. 441, the complaint contained an averment that on a certain day the board of supervisors of San Francisco awarded the contract, under which the street work in question was done, to plaintiff's assignor, but none of the precedent steps which the statute prescribed were generally or specifically alleged. In other words, the facts conferring jurisdiction upon the board were not stated. The complaint was silent as to the notice of intention, and as to all steps which, following the course of the statute, precede the awarding of the contract. The several steps, however, which follow the award were alleged either specifically or generally. It was held that the complaint failed to state a cause of action, and in this connection the court, pages 447–9, per Sanderson, J., said: "If, admitting all the facts stated to be true, the liability of the defendant does not follow as a legal conclusion, the complaint is bad. This is true of every complaint, regardless of the subject matter. The

performance of all conditions which are precedent to the
liability of the defendant, whether founded upon a contract or a statute, must be alleged in some form, either
general or special. * * * In the present case the
liability of the defendant depends upon the performance
of the several steps enumerated in the statute by the
officers of the city government. The complaint must show
by either special or general averments of the character
permitted by our statute that the various provisions of the
statute under which it is sought to charge the defendant
were complied with, for, unless they have been complied
with, the defendant is not liable. According to the mode
of procedure prescribed by the statute, the award of the
contract is not the first step to be taken by the board of
supervisors, yet the complaint is entirely silent as to all
previous steps. In relation to them there is no allegation
either special or general. If they were not taken the
board had no power to award the contract, and hence no
liability was cast by it or the subsequent steps, however
regular they may have been, upon the defendant. In short,
the liability of the defendant cannot be affirmed in view of
the facts stated, and for that reason the complaint is
defective. The alleged sufficiency of the complaint is
grounded, however, by the respondent, upon a provision
found in the thirteenth section of the statute in relation to
street improvements [Statutes 1863, page 531,] which is to
the effect that the assessment, warrant and diagram, with
the affidavit of demand and non-payment, shall be *prima
facie* evidence of defendant's indebtedness, and of the
right of the plaintiff to recover. [Section 12 of the present act—the Vrooman act of March 18, 1885.] Upon that
head it is sufficient to say that the provision in question
does not establish a rule of pleading, but a rule of evidence
only." In this same case it is said, page 448, that in
actions upon contracts a general allegation of performance
of conditions precedent is sufficient under our statute, but
that a general allegation of the performance of conditions
prescribed by a statute is not sufficient. It is likewise
stated that the same rule prevails as to judgments and
determinations of courts, tribunals, boards and officers of
inferior or special jurisdiction, that, in favor of such, the
law intends nothing, and hence, if the liability of the
defendant depends upon them, the facts conferring jurisdiction must be specially alleged *at common law*. But our
Code of Civil Procedure [section 456] changes the common
law rule that, in counting upon the judgment of an
inferior tribunal, it is necessary to state the facts conferring

jurisdiction, and expressly provides that "in pleading a judgment, or other determination of a court, officer, or board, it is not necessary to state the facts conferring jurisdiction, but such judgment or determination may be stated to have been duly given or made. If such allegation be controverted, the party pleading must establish on the trial the facts conferring jurisdiction." Accordingly it was held by the Supreme Court in Pacific Paving Co. v. Bolton, 97 Cal. 8, that an order of the council ordering certain work to be done is the judgment or determination of a court, officer or board, within the meaning of said section 456 of the C. C. P., and that, therefore,—although it is necessary that the council should pass a resolution of intention, and that the superintendent of streets should post and publish the notice required by section 3 of the act before the council has jurisdiction to order the work to be done,— nevertheless, if the complaint alleges that on a certain day the city council, "deeming it necessary, duly gave and made its determination to order the work done," there is a sufficient averment of the action of the council, and the allegation that the order was duly given is under the special provision of said section 456 of the C. C. P., equivalent to the statement that everything necessary to be done to give the order validity had been done, or, rather it is equivalent to the specific allegation of each of the steps necessary to give this order validity.

In Bituminous Lime Rock Pvg. Co. v. Fulton, 33 Pac. Rep. 1117, it was held that in an action to enforce the lien of a street assessment an averment "that all the several acts required to be done by said city council, said superintendent of streets and this plaintiff, have been duly done, made and performed by it and them, in the manner, and at the times and in the form required by law," is sufficient on general demurrer.

Therefore, in an action upon a street assessment, the pleader must (1.) either follow the rule of the common law and allege specifically all the facts necessary to give the council jurisdiction to order the work to be done, allege specifically all the steps preceding the award of the contract, and likewise allege specifically all the steps following the award up to the final step necessary to vest a valid right of action in the contractor or his assigns, or (2.) he may avail himself of the provisions of section 456 of the Code of Civil Procedure, and, as to all judgments or determinations of the council or of an officer, may allege generally that such judgment or determination was duly given or made, and this allegation, as to such judgment or determination, will be equivalent to an allegation of the several facts and steps necessary to confer jurisdiction to give or make the judgment or determination. When the pleader adopts the course permitted by section 456 of the Code of Civil Procedure, he must allege *generally* the facts necessary to confer jurisdiction to give or make such judgment or determination by alleging generally such judgment or determination,—with the allegation that it was duly given or made,—and must also *specifically* allege every other necessary prerequisite to the existence of a valid right of action which does not enter into or become a part of the facts necessary to confer jurisdiction to give or make a judgment or determination. That is to say, while the pleader need not allege specifically the passage of the resolution of intention, its publication, etc., and all the other steps necessary to confer jurisdiction upon the council to order the work to be done, but may allege these facts generally by the equivalent allegation that the order to do the work was duly given or made by the council, still, he must, for example, allege specifically that the superintendent of streets recorded the return in the margin of the record of the warrant and assessment, as this is one of the acts necessary to the existence of a valid right of action, and yet is not an act conferring jurisdiction upon the council or any officer to give or make any judgment or determination. [See notes to section 10 of the act for a statement of the necessary prerequisites to the existence of a valid right of action in the contractor.]

(b.)   Some Special Rules Applicable to Complaints.

1.   It is necessary to the validity of the proceedings that the council should order the notice of the award to be published; a publication without such order is void. [Donnelly v. Tillman, 47 Cal. 40.] Therefore it is necessary that the complaint should show that notice of the award of the contract was published by order of the council. [Himmelmann v. Townsend, 49 Cal. 150; *Contra*, Himmelmann v. Haskell, 46 Cal. 67; Dyer v. North, 44 Cal. 157.]

2.   The complaint must allege that the defendants are owners or have an interest in the land sought to be charged. [San Francisco v. Doe, 48 Cal. 560.]

3.   Two causes of action for enforcing liens for two street assessments, on the same lot, at different times and on different contracts, and for improving the same street, can not be joined in the same suit. In such case the claims of the plaintiff do not "arise out of contracts" within the meaning of section 427 of the Code of Civil Procedure. The contracts there spoken of are contracts to which the person sued was a party, and it is settled that the owners of property adjacent to a street improvement are not in any sense parties to the contract between the contractor and the superintendent of streets. The action is an action to recover the amount of a *tax*. The thing sued for is not the contract price, or a part of it, but the tax specified in the assessment. [Dyer *v.* Barstow, 50 Cal. 652.]

4. The complaint must allege that the assessment was made as prescribed by the statute, and a complaint alleging that the assessment was made "upon the property benefited by said street improvement" is not sufficient, as it does not show a compliance with the statutory provision that the expenses incurred "shall be assessed upon the lots and lands fronting thereon, each lot or portion of a lot being separately assessed in proportion to the frontage." [Miller *v.* Mayo, 88 Cal. 568.]

5. The complaint must show that the contract was made with the plaintiff or his assignor. [Bays *v.* Lapidge, 52 Cal. 481.]

6. The complaint must show that the contract was entered into and executed within the time prescribed by the statute, viz., within 15 days after the posting of the notice of the award, but not earlier than 10 days after the first posting and publication of said notice of award, as provided by section 5 of the act. [Perine *v.* Forbush, 97 Cal. 305; Manning *v.* Den, 90 Cal. 610; Burke *v.* Turney, 54 Cal. 486.]

7. The complaint must show that the contract fixed the time for the commencement and completion of the work as provided by section 6 of the act. [Libbey *v.* Elsworth, 97 Cal. 316; Washburn *v.* Lyons, 97 Cal. 314]

IV. *Answer; Defenses.* Want of jurisdictional facts not curable by the council on appeal may be shown in defense. [Emery *v.* Bradford, 29 Cal. 87.] An allegation in the answer that the council had no authority or jurisdiction to order the work done, is a mere conclusion of law, and a finding responsive to such allegation is insufficient. The facts should be alleged and specifically found. [Spaulding *v.* Wesson, 84 Cal. 141.] But the facts necessary to confer jurisdiction upon the council to order the work to be done, and the facts necessary to the existence of a valid right of action in the plaintiff, must be alleged in the complaint, either generally or specifically, [Himmelman *v.* Danos, 35 Cal. 441, cited *supra.* See *supra,* page 151, *et seq.*] and the defendant may deny any material allegation of the complaint. And the fact that a street improvement act, such as the San Francisco street work act of 1870, prohibits all but certain defenses, does not prevent the defendant from denying any material averment of the complaint. Such provisions of the statute are merely intended to restrict the *affirmative* defenses to those enumerated. [People *v.* Eaton, 46 Cal. 100.]

The lot owner may show and rely on as a defense any substantial error in the proceedings which could not have been remedied by an appeal to the council. [City of Stockton *v.* Creanor, 45 Cal. 644.]

A promise to pay can not be implied from the fact that the defendant, a property owner, saw the work done without objection, and even made suggestions to the workman as to the proper way of doing it. [Nagle *v.* McMurray, 84 Cal. 539.]

One made a party defendant by reason of some claim or interest, and not as owner, must show his claim or interest before he can be heard to defend upon the merits. [Himmelmann *v.* Spanagel, 39 Cal. 389.] And allegations of the complaint are not proof of such interest. [*Id.*] A fraudulent side agreement between the contractor and some of the property owners can not be set up in defense unless the statute, like the San Francisco street work act of 1872, expressly allows fraud to be set up in defense to the action. [Nolan *v.* Reese, 32 Cal. 486; Chambers *v.* Satterlee, 40 Cal. 513; Himmelmann *v.* Hoadley, 44 Cal. 214, 227; Brady *v.* Bartlett, 56 Cal. 350. See notes under section 11, *supra*, page 131 *et seq.*] "That the work was more than half done under a private contract, to which defendant was not a party, before any steps were taken to let a public contract, and that the plaintiff went on and completed the work, and after its completion the party who had taken the public contract, assigned it to plaintiff, does not constitute fraud *per se.*" [Conniff *v.* Kahn, 54 Cal. 284.] If the superintendent enters into the contract before the expiration of the time provided by section 5 of the act, within which the property owners may elect to take the contract, this premature action is one that affects the jurisdiction or power of the superintendent, and the contract is void; and a failure to appeal does not validate it. The defendant may, therefore, rely upon this premature action of the superintendent as a defense, and as the complaint must show that the contract was made in the proper time, this defense is not an affirmative defense of new matter, and consequently could be availed of, even if the statute prohibited all but certain affirmative defenses,—as did the San Francisco street work act of 1870. [Burke *v.* Turney, 54 Cal. 486; see also Perine *v.* Forbush, 97 Cal. 305; Manning *v.* Den, 90 Cal. 610.]

When a complaint is amended by striking out the names of certain defendants, the answer may be amended by averring that such defendants were owners of the lot. [Harney *v.* Appelgate, 57 Cal. 205.] To sustain the action it is sufficient to show that the defendants are owners in fee of the land, without regard to the amount of interest claimed by any defendant in his answer, and if the court finds him to be a part owner of the land, this is sufficient without finding his interest to be such as is alleged by him in his answer. [Whiting *v.* Townsend, 57 Cal. 515.] The defendant may set up in his answer that the assessment included a sum for work not authorized by the resolution of intention, or the award, and that the demand was for the total sum, including the part not legally a charge against the land. [Donnelly *v.* Howard, 60 Cal. 291.] If defendants in their original answer admit their ownership, and afterwards ask leave to amend by denying ownership, it is not an abuse of discretion for the court to deny the motion to amend. [Harney *v.* Corcoran, 60 Cal. 314.] Denial by defendant of his own ownership, for want of information or belief, will raise an issue if no motion is made to strike out. [Harney *v.* McLeran, 66 Cal. 35.] And if plaintiff in such case introduces no evidence in support of his allegation of defendant's ownership, a non-suit should be granted. [*Id.*]

V. *Evidence.* The plaintiff must prove every material averment alleged in the complaint and denied by the answer,—as, that "notice of the award of the contract was published in a newspaper, *pursuant to the order of the board of supervisors.*" [Shepard *v.* Colton, 44 Cal. 628; Donnelly *v.* Tillman, 47 Cal. 40.] Also the fact that "an assessment for the work was made and issued." [People *v.* Eaton, 46 Cal. 100.] Also that "defendant owns the lot." [City of Santa Barbara *v.* Huse, 51 Cal. 217; Harney *v.* McLeran, 66 Cal. 34.]

Section 12 of the act provides that "the said warrant, assessment, certificate and diagram, with the affidavit of demand and non-payment, shall be held *prima facie* evidence of the regularity and correctness of the assessment, and of the prior proceedings and acts of the superintendent of streets and city council, upon which said warrant, assessment and diagram are based, and like evidence of the right of the plaintiff to recover in the action."

Under this provision of the statute, the warrant, assessment, certificate and diagram, with the affidavit of demand and non-payment, are *prima facie* evidence that everything has been done which may be necessary to entitle the plaintiff to recover in the action,—*prima facie* evidence, for example, that a valid contract was entered into for the street improvement for which the assessment was made. But, it is only made *prima facie* evidence, and it is competent for the defendant, if he denies any material allegation of the complaint, to overcome the *prima facie* evidence resulting from the production of said documents. Thus, if the defendant denies the contract, he may overcome the evidence of the contract which the production of said documents affords. Accordingly it was held in Manning v. Den, 90 Cal. 610, that documentary proof from the office of the superintendent of streets, showing that the original contract on file therein was prepared for execution by both parties, and was not signed by the superintendent, and that the bond on file was in blank, without specifying the names of the obligors or the penalty, or any contract for specific work, and without date, is admissible for the defendant, as tending to show that no contract for doing the work had been entered into by the superintendent. While the defendant, if he has denied any of the material allegations of the complaint, may, by the introduction of evidence to the contrary, overcome plaintiff's *prima facie* case resulting from the introduction of the warrant, assessment, diagram, etc., still, if he does not introduce any evidence, the court must find all the facts in plaintiff's favor, if he has introduced the warrant, assessment, diagram, etc., as these documents are made *prima facie* evidence of his right to recover. [Jennings v. Le Roy, 63 Cal. 397.]

If it be a fatal error to include in the assessment any portion of the expense of improving that portion of the street occupied by the tracks of a railroad company, and which is made the duty of the railroad company to improve, the burden of proof is upon the property owner who contests the validity of the assessment to show that the expense of improving such portion of the street was included in the assessment, as the production by the plaintiff of the warrant, assessment, etc., makes out a *prima facie* case. [McVerry v. Boyd, 89 Cal. 305.]

The warrant, assessment, etc., are *prima facie* evidence that the work was done to the satisfaction of the street superintendent. [Jennings v. LeBreton, 80 Cal. 8.] In that case it was held that under the act under which the work in that case was done, the superintendent, without personal inspection might approve the work upon the certificates of the city surveyor or city engineer that the work has been duly performed, and proof of lack of personal inspection by him does not overcome the proof of acceptance from those certificates showing that the work was completed according to contract, taken in connection with the personal making and signing of the assessment, diagram and warrant by the superintendent.

Under the San Francisco street work act of 1872, a block of a street might be graded, without a petition therefore by the property owners, whenever two or more adjacent blocks had been graded on each side of the ungraded block. In Fanning v. Bohme, 76 Cal. 149, the work was done under this act. The grading of a certain block was ordered to be done, upon the determination by the city officials that an adjacent block had been graded about twenty years previously. The defendant set up that such adjacent block never had, in fact, been graded. The evidence showed that the present grade of such adjacent block varied in places from the official grade from a few inches to a foot and three-quarters. *Held*, that the evidence was insufficient to overcome the *prima facie* presumption that all proceedings were regular, including the proper grading of the block twenty years previously. [See also Ede v. Knight, 93 Cal. 159; Fanning v. Leviston, 93 Cal. 186; Himmelman v. Carpentier, 47 Cal. 43; Dorland v. McGlynn, 47 Cal. 47; Macadamizing Co. v. Williams, 70 Cal. 534; City of Stockton v. Creanor, 45 Cal. 643.]

Parol evidence is admissible to prove that the record made by the superintendent of streets of the completion of a contract was made after the assessment issued, although it is dated before the assessment issued. Such evidence does not contradict the record. It only goes to prove when the record was made. [Gately v. Irvine, 51 Cal. 172.]

The records of the council concerning the publication of notices of the award of the contract can not be contradicted by parol evidence. So that, if those records show that the council ordered the clerk to advertise the awards, they cannot be contradicted by parol. [Dorland v. McGlynn, 47 Cal. 47.]

Parol evidence is, however, admissible to show that a certain document, offered by the plaintiff as the record of the council ordering the work to be done, was not in fact a record of the council, and that the true record did not authorize the work. [Dyer v. Brogan, 70 Cal. 136.] Parol evidence is always admissible to prove which of two putative records is the true one, as such evidence does not contradict the record but establishes it. [*Id.*] The defendant must be proved to be the owner of the lot, if he denies it. [City of Santa Barbara v. Huse, 51 Cal. 217; Harney v. McLaren, 66 Cal. 34; Robinson v. Merrill, 87 Cal. 11.]

The affidavit of demand endorsed upon the contractor's
return is competent evidence to prove the demand. [Dyer
v. Brogan, 57 Cal. 234; Himmelmann v. Hoadley, 44 Cal. 214;
Deady v. Townsend, 57 Cal. 298; Ede v. Knight, 93 Cal.
160;] and it is also *prima facie* evidence of the agency of
the person making a demand on behalf of the contractor,
if the affiant in his affidavit states that he was such agent.
[Whiting v. Townsend, 57 Cal. 515; see Himmelmann v.
Woolrich, 45 Cal. 249.] In fact the statute [section 12]
expressly states that the affidavit of demand and non-payment, together with the warrant, assessment, etc., shall be
prima facie evidence "of the right of the plaintiff to recover
in the action."

If it be proved that a petition for grading has been filed
in the office of the clerk of the city council, and that it has
been lost and cannot be found, secondary evidence of its
contents is admissible. But while secondary evidence of
the contents of the petition is in such case admissible, a
writing copied by a short hand reporter from his notes of
the evidence taken in another case in which a certified copy
of such petition was read in evidence is not admissible, even
though the case be one in which secondary evidence of the
contents of the original petition is admissible. A copy of a
certified copy of an original instrument which has been lost,
is not competent evidence and is not admissible in any case,
to prove the contents of the original, unless shown to have
been compared with the original. [Dyer v. Hudson, 65 Cal.
372.]

As to what constitutes evidence of the grade of a street,
see Gafney v. San Francisco, 72 Cal. 146; Dorland v. Bergson, 78 Cal. 637; City of Napa v. Easterby, 61 Cal. 510;
Chambers v. Satterlee, 40 Cal. 497; Himmelmann v. Hoadley,
44 Cal. 213; Williams v. Savings & L. Soc., 97 Cal.
122. In Gafney v. San Francisco, *supra*, it was held
that a statute fixing the grades of certain streets in the city
and county of San Francisco at their points of intersection,
fixes the grade at all intermediate points by connecting the
named points by a straight line. But the points of intersection must not be more than one block apart. Thus in
Dorland v. Bergson, *supra*, it was held that the establishment of the official grade of two crossings of the same
street, which are two blocks apart, does not establish the
official grade of the intervening portion of the street.

VI. *Decree.* The statute [section 12] expressly provides
that "the court in which said suit shall be commenced shall
have power to adjudge and decree a lien against the premises assessed, and to order such premises to be sold on exe-

cution, as in other cases of the sale of real estate by the process of said courts." The statute does not provide for nor does it contemplate any personal judgment against the defendant. The expense of the improvement is a charge upon the property supposed to be benefited, *i. e.*, the property subject to assessment under the act, and is not a charge against the owner personally. It was held at an early day that a statute making the owner personally liable for a deficiency was, in this respect, unconstitutional and void. [Taylor *v.* Palmer, 31 Cal. 241; Baudry *v.* Valdez, 32 Cal. 270; Guerin *v.* Reese, 33 Cal. 292; Gafney *v.* Donohue, 36 Cal. 104; Coniff *v.* Hastings, 36 Cal. 292; Himmelmann *v.* Steiner, 38 Cal. 176; Randolph *v.* Bayue, 44 Cal. 366.] "In furtherance of this end [*i. e.*, that the expense of the improvement is a charge upon the property assessed, and not a charge upon the owner personally] the identity of the lot assessed, and not the person who may be the owner, is made the essential requirement of the statute,—the first must be specifically described, while the latter may be designated as 'unknown.'" [Gillis *v.* Cleveland, 87 Cal. 217.]

If a judgment provide for a personal judgment against the defendant for any deficiency that may remain after a sale of the lot assessed, it is unauthorized and erroneous. [Manning *v.* Den, 90 Cal. 610, decided under the present street improvement act—the Vrooman act of March 18, 1885.]

If a lot is assessed to one person, the contractor can not recover judgment against another. [Blatner *v.* Davis, 32 Cal. 328.]

A decree enforcing the lien cannot be entered until all the owners are made parties and served with process. [Hancock *v.* Bowman, 49 Cal. 413; Diggins *v.* Reay, 54 Cal. 525.]

When two or more lots are separately assessed each lot is chargeable only with the amount assessed upon it, and the judgment should state the amount for which each lot is liable, and should order a sale of each lot, or so much thereof as may be necessary to satisfy the amount assessed against it, and costs. [Brady *v.* Kelly, 52 Cal. 371.] The liability of each lot is independent of any other lot, and constitutes a separate demand, upon which a separate cause of action may be based. And, therefore, a recovery upon lot "A" in a former action, although between the same parties, is a different cause of action, and, consequently, not a good plea in bar of an action upon lot "B." [Gillis *v.* Cleveland, 87 Cal. 214, 218.]

When several defendants are owners of a lot, judgment

can not be ordered against only one of the defendants. [Clark *v.* Porter, 53 Cal. 409.]

When the court finds generally that the council had not acquired jurisdiction to order the work, but also finds particular facts sufficient to show that it did have jurisdiction, judgment should be rendered for plaintiff. [Dyer *v.* Chase, 57 Cal. 284.]

Judgment may be enforced against the property assessed even though it be defendant's homestead. [Perine *v.* Forbush, 97 Cal. 305.]

In Kreling *v.* Muller, 86 Cal. 465, it was held that under the Vrooman act of March 18, 1885,—prior to the amendment of sections 3 and 7 by the act of March 31, 1891,—a judgment charging upon a lot a sum greater than one-half the value of such lot, as borne upon the preceding assessment roll for municipal purposes, is erroneous, and that it makes no difference that the work called for by the resolution and order is split up into separate contracts and assessments. But this decision was based upon provisions of sections 3 and 7 of the act as it originally stood, by which it was provided that a lot could not be charged for work called for by one resolution of intention and order in a greater sum than one-half the value of such lot as it was last assessed for municipal taxation. These provisions of sections 3 and 7 were eliminated by the amendment of March 14, 1889. [Statutes 1889, pages 158–160, 163.] And in this respect the amendment of March 31, 1891, [statutes 1891, pages 196–199, 201,] follows the amendment of 1889; so that, as sections 3 and 7 now stand, *i. e.,* as amended by the act of March 31, 1891,—the last amendment of these sections—no part of the property assessed is exempt from the amount of the assessment, but the lot is chargeable with the whole amount assessed against it regardless of its value, even though the amount assessed may far exceed the value of the lot.

SECTION 12½. The city council, instead of waiting until the completion of the improvement, may, in its discretion, and not otherwise, upon the completion of two blocks or more of any improvement, order the street superintendent to make an assessment for the proportionate amount of the contract completed, and thereupon proceedings and rights of collection of such proportionate amount shall be had as in sections eight, nine, ten, eleven and twelve of the act of which this is amendatory is provided. [*Amendment approved March 14, 1889, statutes 1889, page 169.*]

[Section 12½ was added to the act in 1889 by the act of March 14, 1889, statutes 1889, page 169.]

SECTION 13. When any portion of any street, avenue, lane, alley, court or place in said city improved, or any sidewalk constructed thereon shall be out of repair, or needing reconstruction, and in condition to endanger persons or property passing thereon, or in condition to interfere with the public convenience in the use thereof, it shall be the duty of said superintendent of streets to require, by notice in writing, to be delivered to them or their agents personally, or left on the premises, the owners or occupants of lots or portions of lots fronting on said portion of said street, avenue, alley, lane, court, or place, or of said portion of said sidewalk so out of repair or needing reconstruction as aforesaid, to repair or reconstruct, or to do both, forthwith, said portion of said street, avenue, lane, alley, court, or place, to the center line of said street in front of the property of which he is the owner, or tenant, or occupant, and said superintendent of streets shall particularly specify in said notice what work is required to be done, and how the same is to be done, and what material shall be used in said repairs, or reconstructions, or both. If said repairs or reconstructions, or both, be not commenced within three days after notice given as aforesaid, and diligently and without interruption prosecuted to completion, the said superintendent of streets may, under authority from said city council, make such repairs, reconstruction, or both, or enter into a contract with any suitable person, at the expense of the owner, tenant or occupant, after the specification for the doing of said work shall have been conspicuously posted by him in his office for two days, inviting bids for the doing of said work, which bids shall be delivered to him at his office on or before the second day of said posting, and opened by him on the next day following the expiration of said two days of posting, and the contract by him be awarded to the lowest bidder, if such lowest bid, in the judgment of said street superintendent, shall be reasonable. All of said bids shall be preserved in his office and open at all times after the letting of the contract to the inspection of all persons, and such owner, tenant or occupant shall be liable to pay said contract price. Such work shall be commenced within twenty-four hours after the contract shall have been signed, and completed without delay to the satisfaction of said street superintendent. Upon the completion of said repairs, or reconstruction, or both, by said contractors as aforesaid to the satisfaction of said superintendent of streets, said superintendent of streets shall make and deliver to said contractor a certificate to the effect that said repairs, or reconstruction, or both, have been properly made by said contractor to the grade, and that the charges for the same are reasonable and just, and that he, said superintendent, has accepted the same. [*Amendment approved March 14, 1889, statutes 1889, p. 169.*]

[Section 13 was amended in 1889 by act of March 14, 1889, statutes 1889, p. 169.]

I. *Scope of Section Thirteen.* Sections 13, 14 and 15 are intimately correlated. Together they provide the machinery for repairing and reconstructing to the center line, at the expense of the owner of the abutting property, any portion of any unaccepted street, avenue, lane, alley, court or place improved, or any sidewalk out of repair and needing reconstruction. The superintendent of streets may himself do the repairing or reconstructing or may let a contract therefore to some suitable person, at the expense of the owner, tenant or occupant of the adjoining property, if the owner, tenant or occupant does not himself do the work of repairing or reconstructing after being notified so to do in writing, *provided*, that the street has not been "accepted" by the city council, by ordinance, as provided for by section 20 of the act, as by said section 20, after such acceptance, the street must thereafter be kept in repair and improved by the municipality, the expenses being paid out of a fund to be provided by the council for that purpose. And this provision of section 20 applies to the sidewalk as well as to the roadway. [Bonnet *v.* San Francisco, 65 Cal. 230; see also section 25 of the act.]

II. *Prerequisites to Imposition of Cost of Repair upon the Lot Owner.* There are several prerequisites to the imposition of this expense upon the abutting property owner, namely: (*1.*) The property owner can only be required to "*repair*" or "*reconstruct*" the street, alley, etc., or sidewalk. The term "repair" means to restore to a sound or good state, after decay, injury, delapidation or partial destruction. It does not mean to make a new thing, but to refit, make good or restore an existing thing. The repairs spoken of in street laws have been held to include the substitution of new curb-stones and gutters for old ones, [People *v.* Brooklyn, 21 Barb. (N. Y.) 484;] but does not include the substitution of a new and *different kind* of pavement from that already existing. [*In re* Fulton Street, 29 How. Pr. (N. Y.) 429; Blount *v.* Janesville, 31 Wis. 648.] "By the term 'repairs' is meant whatever is necessary to keep the road in a proper condition for the traffic, having regard for the character and original manufacture of the road, but nothing further; it does not include converting a macadamized road into a paved road." [Leek, etc., Commissioners *v.* Justices of Stafford, 20 Q. B. Div. 797.] It means, in short, restoration to orginal condition. (*2.*) The street, alley, etc., or sidewalk must not only be out of repair, or needing reconstruction, but it must be, *(a.)* "in condition to endanger persons or property passing thereon," or *(b.)* "in condition to interfere with the public convenience in the use thereof." (*3.*) The superintendent of streets, must, by notice in writing, notify the owners or occupants of lots or portions of lots fronting on the portions of the street, alley, etc., or sidewalk, so out of repair or needing reconstruction, to forthwith repair or reconstruct, or to both repair and reconstruct such portion of such street, alley, etc., to the center line thereof, in front of the property of which he is owner, or tenant or occupant. Said notice must be delivered to the owners or occupants personally or to their agents,-or must be left on the premises. [See Guerin v. Reese, 33 Cal. 292, for rules determining when service other than personal service is sufficient and justified by the statute.] The notice must specify what work is required to be done, how it is to be done, and what material shall be used. (*4.*) The superintendent must obtain from the council, by a resolution, order, or ordinance duly passed, authority to enter into a contract with some suitable person to do the work at the expense of the owner, tenant or occupant. (*5.*) The superintendent must post conspicuously in his office for two days specifications for doing said work inviting bids for doing the work. The specifications must remain posted in the office of the superintendent for two official days; *i, e.*, it must be posted before the commencement of the time on the first day when, by statute, the office is required to be opened, and must remain posted during the whole of the first and second day and until the end of the hour of the second day when by statute the office may be closed. [Himmelmann v. Cahn, 49 Cal. 285.] (*6.*) The bids must be delivered to him at his office on or before the second day of said posting. (*7.*) On the next day following the expiration of the said two days of posting, the bids must be opened by the superintendent. (*8.*) The superintendent must award the contract to the lowest bidder, if, in his judgment, the lowest bid shall be reasonable, and a contract in writing must be signed by him. (*9.*) The work must be commenced within twenty-four hours after the contract shall have been signed, and must be completed without delay to the satisfaction of the superintendent. (*10.*) The superintendent must make and deliver to the contractor, after the completion of the work, a certificate, which certificate must state, in effect, that the repairs or the reconstruction, or both, if both were done, have been properly made by the contractor, "*to the grade*," and that the charges for the same are reasonable and just, and that he, the superintendent, has accepted the same.

As the certificate must state that the repairs, etc., have been made "*to the grade*," it is evident that the section contemplates that owners shall only be required to repair or reconstruct streets that have been graded to the official grade. For a street cannot be graded except to the official grade. [Emery v. S. F. Gas Co., 28 Cal. 377; Sec. 2 of the act.] A street may be planked although it has not been graded to the official grade. [Knowles v. Seale, 64 Cal. 377.] But in such a case, a property owner could not be compelled to repair any portion of the planking if out of repair, as, until graded, it could not be repaired "to the grade."

The foregoing, ending with the certificate of the superintendent are ten essentials, required by section 13 of the act, as prerequisites to the right of the contractor to recover from the owner the expenses of the work. Two more essentials are required by section 14 as a prerequisite to the right of the contractor or his assigns to maintain a suit against the owner, namely, (*1.*) recordation of the certificate by the superintendent in a book kept by him in his office for that purpose, properly indexed, and (*2.*) demand upon the owner, tenant or occupant for the amount which is a lien upon the land. The section [section 14] does not state whether this "demand" may be other than personal, when the owner, etc., cannot conveniently be found, or how it shall be made; but, as the proceedings are *in invitum*, it is possible that in the absence of express statutory provision for any other demand, demand must be made personally upon the owner, tenant or occupant, unless the provision of section 14 that "the sum contracted to be paid shall be a lien, the same as provided in section 9 of the act, *and may be enforced in the same manner*," should be construed to mean that the demand should be made in the same manner. The demand may be construed as one of the steps necessary to the enforement of the lien.

III.   *No Primary Duty Resting upon the Owner to Repair or Reconstruct.* In Eustace *v.* Jahns, 38 Cal., 3, sections, 14, 15 and 16, of the San Francisco street work act of 1862 [statutes 1862, pages 399–400]—being the sections of that act which correspond to sections 13, 14 and 15 of the present general street improvement act, or Vrooman act of March 18, 1885,—came before the court for construction. In that case the question was: Do these sections of the act impose upon the owner of a lot fronting upon a public street the duty to repair a defect in that portion of that public street upon which his lot abuts or fronts? It was held that the duty imposed by these sections of the act upon the property owner was not a primary duty to repair, but only attached or became an existing obligation or duty after the superintendent had served the notice in writing required by section 14 of the act of 1862. [Section 13 of the present general street improvement act —the Vrooman act of March 18, 1885.] The present general street improvement act is, in the main, constructed upon the same lines as the said San Francisco street work act of 1862. [Statutes 1862, page 391, *et seq.*] Bearing this fact in mind, and, as tending to assist in correctly construing sections 13, 14 and 15 of the present act, the following is quoted from the opinion by Mr. Justice Sprague, in Eustace *v.* Jahns, *supra:* "Upon a careful examination of these several acts [San Francisco street work acts] and such portions thereof as were in force in May, 1866, we find that by those acts the entire supervision, control and management of the public streets, highways, lanes, alleys, places or courts within the corporate limits of the city and county of San Francisco was and still continues vested in the board of supervisors and superintendent of the public streets and highways of said city and county, and we find no authority delegated to, or duty imposed upon, the individual owner of lands or lots in said city to improve or repair any portions of such streets, lanes, alleys, highways, places or courts, or in any manner interfere or meddle with the same, in the way of improvement or repair thereof, of his own volition, or upon his individual responsibility. The only duty imposed upon the individual owner of such lots or lands in said city is the payment of such assessments as shall be lawfully made upon his lots or lands by the superintendent of public streets and highways, to defray the expenses of opening, constructing, improving or repairing the streets, highways, etc., after the same shall have been opened, constructed, improved or repaired by order of the board of supervisors and to the satisfaction of the superintendent of public streets and highways, except in the case of special local repairs required by written notice from the superintendent of public streets to be made or commenced by the owner, tenant or occupant of a lot within three days after the service of such notice, specifying what improvement is required, as provided in sections 14, 15 and 16 of an act approved April 25, 1862, amendatory of and supplementary to the act of 1856 heretofore referred to; [sections 13, 14 and 15 of the present street improvement act,—the Vrooman act of March 18, 1885,] and this, it will be observed by reference to the sections named, is not a primary duty imposed by the statute, but is left optional with the superintendent of public streets and highways to impose the duty or not, in his discretion, and does not attach to or become an existing obligation or duty until after the superintendent has exercised his discretion in the premises by service of the notice in writing, as required by section 14; [section 13 of the present act.] * * * And for special local repairs or improvements contemplated by the fourteenth section of the above act of 1862, and by the tenth subdivision of section 8 of the same act as amended April 25, 1863, (statutes 1863, page

528,) [subdivision 8 of section 7 of the present street
improvement act,] the lots fronting upon the street on the
side and at the point where such improvements or repairs
are required or made, are not even liable to assessment to
defray the expenses of such improvements or repairs,
without a notice, as required by section 14, [section 13 of
the present act] has been previously served upon the owner
or occupant of the lot, as is manifest by subdivision 2 of
the same section 8, [subdivision 2 of section 7 of the present street improvement act,—the Vrooman act of March
18, 1885,] when read in connection with subdivision ten,
same section, and sections 14 and 15 above referred to, and
sections 21 and 22, same act, as amended in 1863, (statutes
1863, pages 531–2,) [subdivision 8 of section 7 and sections
13, 14, 20 and 21 of the present act], and section 23, and
subdivision 2 of section 25, same act (statutes 1863, page
402;) [Sec. 22 and sub. 2 of sec. 34 of the present act].   By
the said sections 22 and 23 [of the act of 1863] it is
made the duty of the superintendent of public streets and
highways to devote his entire time and undivided attention
to the supervision and care of the public streets and highways, public buildings, parks, etc., of said city and county;
and for that purpose the board of supervisors is authorized
to allow him deputies, not exceeding six in number; and
for the faithful performance of his duties he is required
to give bonds to the city and county in such sum as
may be fixed by the board of supervisors.   And,
under said section 14, subdivisions 2 and 10 of said section 8, and said section 21, [section 13, subdivisions
2 and 8 of section 7 and section 20, of the present act] the
superintendent of streets is manifestly authorized to contract for simple repairs of street improvements already constructed and accepted by the proper authority, and cause
the same to be made, without reference to the adjoining
property, and the expense of such repairs would be properly
chargeable to the street department fund of the city and
county.   [See sections 25 and 26 of the Vrooman act of Mar.
18, 1885.]   *   *   *   From a most careful consideration of
all the statutes relating to the public streets and highways
of the city and county of San Francisco, we find no personal
duty primarily or inceptively cast upon the individual owners
of lots or lands therein, in respect to the care, management,
control, improvement or repair of the public streets or
highways;   *   *   *   and we are unable to comprehend by
what process of ratiocination the duty to repair a public
street or highway is devolved upon an individual, from the
fact that he is liable to be notified by the superintendent of

streets to make specific repairs, or owns or occupies a lot liable to be assessed to defray the expenses of repairs, when made by another at the instance of the superintendent." [Eustace v. Jahns, 38 Cal. pp. 15–17, 17 and 19.]

Section 23 of the present general street work act is the section which corresponds to section 24 of the act of 1862, referred to in Eustace v. Jahns, 38 Cal. p. 18. [See section 23 *infra*.]

IV. *Constitutionality of Section Thirteen*. Sections 13 and 14 provide that the expense of repairing or reconstructing any street, avenue, lane, etc., or any sidewalk, out of repair or needing reconstruction, shall be charged against the owners or occupants of the lots or portions of lots fronting such portion of said street, avenue, alley, etc., or sidewalk, as is out of repair or needing reconstruction, and shall be a lien, the same as provided in section 9 of the act, and may be enforced in the same manner.

In the case of Hart v. Gaven, 12 Cal. 477, work had been done by a contractor under sections 56, 57, 58 and 59 of the San Francisco consolidation act, passed April 19, 1856. These sections of the consolidation act correspond to sections 13, 14 and 15 of the present street work act, and it was held in this case of Hart v. Gaven that "the legislature had the right to provide, in the act known as the 'Consolidation act for the government of the city and county of San Francisco; that the owners of lots in said city should keep the streets in front of their lots in repair, and if an owner neglects to do so for three days, after notice from the superintendent of public streets, the superintendent has the right to make a contract for that purpose: and an action will lie in the name of the party performing the work against the owner of the lot adjacent for that amount." The court, per Baldwin, J., said: "Some provision being necessary for repairing the streets, the mode by which this is done, if it be uniform and equal in its operation, must be left to legislative discretion. This duty of repairing the streets is in the nature of a public burden or tax, and we do not see that the rule adopted applying to all the streets of a municipality is not as near an approximation to uniformity as could well be attained. Absolute justice in the operation of human laws is impossible; there is no rule, however just in its general working, which has not its exceptional instances of hardship; and especially in the results of the taxing power is this incurable infirmity of laws to secure exact and equal justice to all those upon whom they operate, apparent. No tax law could ever stand if subjected to a rigid test on the score of uniformity. All we can expect is a general equality of operation; and we think that this is secured by this act.''

As, however, sections 13 and 14 seem to provide for a personal judgment against the property owner in an action to recover the costs of repairs; and, in view of the fact that, as stated by Mr. Justice McKinstry in People *v.* Lynch, 51 Cal. 22, ''It has been repeatedly held that an attempt by the legislature to compel each lot upon a street to pay the whole expense of grading and paving along its front, cannot be maintained, because, while there is an apparent uniformity, the measure of equality required by the constitution is entirely wanting,'' it might be well, for these reasons, to further consider the constitutionality of this part of the act in respect to these two features, viz., *(1.)* the provision for a ''personal'' judgment, and *(2.)* as to the equality or inequality of the assessment.

(A.) In the first place, section 13 might be construed as imposing a personal liability upon the owner to pay the expense of the repairs or reconstruction. An act imposing a personal liability upon the owner for ''improving'' a street in the first instance is unconstitutional. [Taylor *v.* Palmer, 31 Cal. 241; Manning *v.* Den, 90 Cal. 611.] As to whether the same principle is applicable to the case of '' repairs'' or ''reconstruction'' provided for by section 13 of the act, is at least questionable in the absence of a decision by the Supreme Court directly upon the point. It is possible, however, that a personal liability, and the personal penalties provided by section 15 of the act, may, in the case of repairs or reconstructions, be justified as an exercise of the police powers of the state.

(B.) 1. Section 14 makes the expense of the work done under section 13, a lien upon the property, the same as provided in section 9 of the act. But there may be a question as to the constitutionality of such provision, even if there be no personal liability. This question arises out of the standard of apportionment of the expense, or rather it arises out of the want of a standard. Subdivisions 1 and 2 of section 7, make the expenses of all improvements, *"except such as are done by contractors under the provisions of section thirteen of this act,"* assessable upon the lots and lands fronting upon the work, "each lot or portion of a lot being separately assessed, *in proportion to the frontage, at a rate per front foot sufficient to cover the total expense of the work."* But, as to the expenses of the work done by contractors under the provisions of section 13, there is no such apportionment. Each lot is made liable for the whole cost of the work done in front of it upon the sidewalk, and to the center line of the street, avenue, alley, etc. While

the front-foot plan of assessment is constitutional, because, it in effect, makes an assessment district of the street, and apportions the expenses of the improvement upon the lots in proportion to their frontage, thus making some sort of a rough approximation to equality of apportionment, still, as is said by Judge Cooley in his work on Constitutional Limitations [page 508, 3rd edition], "A very different case is presented where the legislature undertakes to provide that each lot upon a street shall pay the whole expense of grading and paving the street along its front. For, while in such a case there would be something having the outward appearance of apportionment, it requires but slight examination to discover that it is a deceptive semblance only, and that the measure of equality which the constitution requires is entirely wanting." See also People v. Lynch, 51 Cal. 22–23, where Mr. Justice McKinstry says: "It has been repeatedly held, that an attempt by the legislature to compel each lot upon a street to pay the whole expense of grading and paving along its front cannot be maintained, because while there is an apparent uniformity, the measure of equality required by the constitution is entirely wanting."

On the other hand, Judge Dillon in his work on Municipal Corporations [Vol. 2, §753, 3rd Ed.], says: "It may be true that in some instances more hardships will be occasioned by requiring each owner to make or pay for the improvement in front of his own property than if the cost were assessed on the basis of frontage or of supposed benefits received; still, it seems to the author difficult to find satisfactory and solid grounds on which to discriminate the cases so as to hold that one is within the constitutional power of the legislature and the other is not."

2. Again it was stated by Mr. Justice Sharswood in Hammett v. Philadelphia, 65 Penn. St. 155–6; s. c. 3 Am. Rep. 615, that the legislature has not power in any case to require the owners to repair or reconstruct a street after it has once been improved. The learned justice says: "The original paving of a street brings the property bounding upon it into the market as building lots. Before that it is a road, not a street. It is therefore a local improvement, with benefits almost exclusively peculiar to the adjoining properties. Such a case is clearly within the principle of assessing the cost on the lots lying upon it. Perhaps no fairer rule can be adopted than the proportion of feet front, although there must be some inequalities if the lots differ in situation and depth. Appraising their market values and fixing the proportion according to these, is a plan open to favoritism or

corruption, and other objections. No system of taxation which the wit of man ever devised has been found perfectly equal. But where a street is once opened and paved, thus assimilated with the rest of the city and made a part of it, all the particular benefits to the locality derived from the improvements have been received and enjoyed. Repairing streets is as much a part of the ordinary duties of the municipality—for the general good—as cleaning, watching and lighting. *It would lead to monstrous injustice and inequality should such general expenses be provided for by local assessments.*" [See also Wistar *v.* Philadelphia, 80 Pa. St. 505; s. c. 21 Am. Rep. 112.] But these Pennsylvania cases seem to be contrary to the weight of authority. Judge Dillon [Dillon's Municipal Corporations, § 780, 3rd ed.] says: "Not only the power to tax, but the power to make local improvements at the expense of the property benefited, is, like all other legislative power of the municipality, a *continuing one,* unless there be something to indicate the contrary; and hence it is not exhausted by being once exercised. Therefore, the power to compel property owners to pave, ordinarily extends to compelling them to *repave* when required by the municipal authorities." [See McCormick *v.* Patchin, 53 Mo. 33, s. c. 14 Am. Rep. 440, where Hammett *v.* Philadelphia is commented upon.] And if property owners may be compelled to "repave," it would seem that they may likewise be compelled to "repair."

When the municipality itself takes up a pavement or disturbs the surface of a street, for the purpose of laying gas or water pipes, or for the purpose of constructing a sewer, the cost of repairing the street or replacing the pavement cannot be assessed against the property owners. [City of Bloomington *v.* Palmer, 67 Ia. 681.] But see section 20 of the act, where it is expressly provided that, after partial acceptance of a street, prior to the construction of a sewer, the lots liable to assessment for the cost of constructing a sewer shall remain liable to be assessed "for the cost of repairs and restoration of the street damaged in the said construction."

3. But, though it is possible that section 13 might be open to the above constitutional objections, still it is quite probable that the power to compel a property owner to repair or reconstruct that portion of a street which lies in front of his property, and to make his property chargeable with the whole cost thereof, is a part of the police powers of the state, and therefore constitutional.

In Reinken *v.* Fuehring, (Ind.) 30 N. E. Rep. 414, it was held that the city may, in the exercise of the police powers conferred upon it by the state, order its streets to be swept, and assess the abutting property owners to pay the expenses of the sweeping opposite their property. In this case the property owner was held liable for sweeping the street, *i. e.*, the roadway, as well as the sidewalk. [See also Village of Carthage *v.* Frederick, (N. Y.) 25 N. E. 480; *In re* Goddard, 16 Pick, 504; s. c. 28 Am. Dec. 259; Sands *v.* City of Richmond, 31 Gratt, 571; s. c. 31 Am. Rep. 742.] In this latter case, Sands *v.* City of Richmond, it was held that "a city ordinance, requiring the owners of lots on streets which have been graded, paved and guttered, to pave the sidewalks adjoining and in front of their lots, is valid, and if the owners do not comply, the city may do the work and collect the expenses from the owners." It was not decided whether the power to compel the property owner to improve the sidewalk in front of his property is referable to the police power, or whether it belongs to the taxing power. But, to sustain its position, the court cited the case of Goddard, Petitioner, 16 Pick. 504, in which it was held that the city might, in the exercise of its police powers, compel the property owner to sweep the snow off of that portion of the *sidewalk* which lies in front of his property, and in Reinken *v.* Fuehring, *supra*, 30 N. E. 414, it was held that, in the exercise of its police powers, the city might compel the property owner to pay the expense of sweeping the *street* in front of his property,—thus holding that the power extends over roadways as well as sidewalks. Therefore, if the decision in Goddard, Petitioner, 16 Pick. 504, supports the decision in Sands *v.* City of Richmond, 31 Gratt, 571, then, by a parity of reasoning, the decision in Reinken *v.* Fuehring supports the position that, in the exercise of its police powers, the city may compel a property owner to do any of the work mentioned in section 13 of the act, and may assess the expenses thereof against his property, as provided in said section 13 and section 14.

As, however, it is the purpose of this book, not to discuss general principles of street law, or questions of constitutional law, but to consider only the machinery provided by our street work acts for street improvements, and the decisions of our own Supreme Court expounding and construing those acts, the reader will be referred to other treatises for a further consideration of the questions of constitutional law arising under these sections of the act. The aim of this book will be accomplished if it succeeds in suggesting the questions of constitutionality that might possibly arise in this connection. The author's own opinion is, that the provisions of sections 13, 14 and 15 of the act are referable

174 STREET WORK LAW—STREET IMPROVEMENT ACT

to the police powers delegated to the municipalities by the state; and, as an exercise of police powers, they are constitutional, even to the extent of imposing a personal liability upon the property owner to improve the street in front of his property, after notice from the superintendent, or to pay the expense thereof, if done by some one else under a contract with the superintendent of streets.

SECTION 14. If the expenses of the work and material for such improvements, after the completion thereof, and the delivery to said contractor of said certificate, be not paid to the contractor so employed, or his agent or assignee, on demand, the said contractor, or his assignee, shall have the right to sue such owner, tenant, or occupant, for the amount contracted to be paid; and said certificate of the superintendent of streets shall be *prima facie* evidence of the amount claimed for said work and materials, and of the right of the contractor to recover for the same in such action. Said certificate shall be recorded by the said superintendent of streets in a book kept by him in his office for that purpose, properly indexed, and the sum contracted to be paid shall be a lien, the same as provided in section nine of this act, and may be enforced in the same manner. [*Statutes 1885, page 158.*]

[Section 14 never has been amended.]

SECTION 15. In addition, and as cumulative to the remedies above given, the city council shall have power, by resolution or ordinance, to prescribe the penalties that shall be incurred by any owner or person liable, or neglecting, or refusing to make repairs when required, as provided in section (13) thirteen of this act, which fines and penalties shall be recovered for the use of the city by prosecution in the name of the people of the state of California, in the court having jurisdiction thereof, and may be applied, if deemed expedient by the said council, in the payment of the expenses of any such repairs not otherwise provided for. [*Statutes 1885, page 158.*]

[Section 15 never has been amended.]

SECTION 16. The person owning the fee, or the person in whom, on the day the action is commenced, appears the legal title to the lots and lands, by deeds duly recorded in the county recorder's office of each county, or the person in possession of lands, lots or portions of lots or buildings under claim, or exercising acts of ownership over the same for himself, or as the executor, administrator or guardian of the owner, shall be regarded, treated and deemed to be the "owner" (for the purpose of this law), according to the intent and meaning of that word as used in this act. And in case of property leased, the possession of the tenant or lessee holding and occupying under such persons shall be deemed to be the possession of such owner. [*Statutes 1885, page 159.*]

[Section 16 never has been amended.]

Section 17 of the San Francisco street work act of 1872 [statutes 1872, page 818,] is similar to section 16 of the present general street improvement act. Section 17 of the act of 1872 came before the Supreme Court in Phelan *v.*

Dunne, 72 Cal. 229, and in Parker *v.* Bernal, 66 Cal. 113. In the latter case,—an action to recover on a street assessment, —it was held that this provision of the statute made an executrix an owner for all the purposes of the action, and that therefore the action might be brought against the executrix, even though the heirs of the deceased former owner should be in fact the owners. On the other hand, in Phelan *v.* Dunne, 72 Cal. 229, it was held that the heirs or devisees of a deceased person are in fact the owners of the property, subject to the liens of the creditors, etc., and that, since they are in fact such owners, they alone need be made parties defendant, even though under this section of the act the executors are, for the purposes of the act, to be deemed owners. It was held that while the executors might be *proper* parties they were not *necessary* parties, and therefore the plaintiff need not make them parties unless he so desires. Mr. Justice Patterson, delivering the opinion said: "It may be that under these provisions [*i. e.*, sections 13 and 17 of the act of April 1, 1872; sections 12 and 16 of the present street improvement act,—the Vrooman act of March 18, 1885,] persons other than the heirs and devisees are *proper* parties to the action, and that their rights cannot be foreclosed unless they are made defendants, but as to that we express no opinion. It is sufficient to say. that the defendant [the devisee under the will of the deceased former owner] is the owner in fee, that he is the only necessary party; and that plaintiff is entitled, under this act, to a decree of foreclosure, whatever may be the rights of other parties interested, who are not joined by defendants." [See *supra*, pages 146–8.] Of course the careful practitioner will not fail to make parties to the action those who are *proper* parties defendant, merely because they may not be *necessary* parties. The conclusion deducible from these decisions is that the executor or administrator of an estate might be made the sole party defendant, as was done in Parker *v.* Bernal, 66 Cal. 113, since the act makes him for all purposes of the act an "owner." By a fiction he is made the owner for the purposes of the act. Or the heirs or devisees, in whom the title is in fact vested, may alone be made parties defendant, as was the case in Phelan *v.* Dunne, 72 Cal. 229, since in such case the "owners" in fact are made defendants.

In the absence of provisions such as those contained in section 16 of the act, declaring that executors, administrators and others shall, for all the purposes of the act, be regarded, treated and deemed to be the "owner" according to the intent and meaning of that word, such persons could not be treated as owners for any of the purposes of the act. [Mulligan *v.* Smith, 59 Cal. 206, 225; Kahn *v.* Board of Supervisors, 79 Cal. 388.]

SECTION 17.   Any tenant or lessee of the lands or lots liable may pay the amount assessed against the property of which he is the tenant or lessee under the provisions of this act, or he may pay the price agreed on to be paid under the provision of section thirteen of this act, either before or after suit brought, together with costs, to the contractor, or his assigns, or he may redeem the property, if sold on execution or decree for the benefit of the owner, within the time prescribed by law, and deduct the amount so paid from the rents due and to become due from him, and for any sums so paid beyond the rents due from him, he shall have a lien upon and may retain possession of the said land and lots until the amount so paid and advanced be satisfied, with legal interest, from accruing rents, or by payment by the owner. [*Statutes 1885, page 159.*]

[Section 17 never has been amended.]

SECTION 18.   The records kept by the superintendent of streets of said city, in conformity with the provisions of this act, and signed by him, shall have the same force and effect as other public records, and copies therefrom, duly certified, may be used in evidence with the same effect as the originals.   The said records shall, during all office hours, be open to the inspection of any citizen wishing to examine them, free of charge [*Statutes 1885, page 159.*]

[Section 18 never has been amended.]

SECTION 19.   Notices in writing which are required to be given by the superintendent of streets under the provisions of this act, may be served by any person with the permission of the superintendent of streets, and the fact of such service shall be verified by the oath of the person making it, taken before the superintendent of streets, who for that purpose and for all other purposes, and in all cases where a verification is required under the provisions of this act is hereby authorized to administer oaths, or other person authorized to administer oaths, or such notices may be delivered to the superintendent of streets himself, who must also verify the service thereof, and who shall keep a record of the fact of giving such notices, when delivered by himself personally, and also of the notices and proof of service when delivered by any other person. [*Amendment approved March 14, 1889. Statutes 1889, p. 170.*]

[Section 19 was amended by the act of March 14, 1889. Statutes 1889, p. 170.]

SECTION 20.   Whenever any street, or portion of a street has been or shall hereafter be fully constructed to the satisfaction of the superintendent of streets and of the city council, and is in good condition throughout, and a sewer, gas pipes, and water pipes are laid therein, under such regulations as the city council shall adopt, the same shall be accepted by the city council, by ordinance, and thereafter shall be kept in repair and improved by the said municipality; the expense thereof, together with the assessment for street work done in front of city property, to be paid out of a fund to be provided by said council for that purpose; *provided,* that the city council shall not accept of any portion of the street less than the entire width of the roadway (including the curbing), and one block in length, or one entire crossing; and *provided further*, that the city council may partially or conditionally accept any street, or portion of a street, without a sewer, or gas pipes, or water pipes, therein, if the ordinance of acceptance expressly states that the council deems such sewer, or gas pipes, or water pipes, to be then unnecessary, but the lots of land previously or at any time assessable for the cost of constructing a sewer, shall remain and be assessable for such cost and for the cost of repairs and restoration of the street damaged in the said construction, whenever said council shall deem a sewer to be necessary, and shall order it to be constructed, the same as if no partial or conditional acceptance had ever been made. The superintendent of streets shall keep in his office a register of all streets accepted by the city council under this section, which register shall be indexed for easy reference thereto. [*Statutes 1885, p. 160.*]

[Section 20 never has been amended.]

When a street has been accepted by the city council, the expense of constructing and repairing the sidewalks must be paid by the municipality. The provisions of section 20 apply to "sidewalks" as well as to "roadways." [Bonnet *v.* San Francisco, 65 Cal. 230.]

SECTION 21. The superintendent of streets shall keep a public office in some convenient place within the municipality, and such records as may be required by the provisions of this act. He shall superintend and direct the cleaning of all sewers, and the expense of the same shall be paid out of the street or sewer fund of said city. [*Statutes 1885, p. 160.*]

[Section 21 never has been amended.]

SECTION 22. It shall be the duty of the superintendent of streets to see that the laws, ordinances, orders, and regulations relating to the public streets and highways be fully carried into execution, and that the penalties thereof are rigidly enforced. He shall keep himself informed of the condition of all the public streets and highways, and also of all public buildings, parks, lots, and grounds of said city, as may be prescribed by the city council. He shall, before entering upon the duties of his office, give bonds to the municipality, with such sureties and for such sums as may be required by the city council; and should he fail to see the laws, ordinances, orders and regulations relative to the public streets or highways carried into execution, after notice from any citizen of a violation thereof, he and his sureties shall be liable upon his official bond to any person injured in his person or property in consequence of said official neglect. [*Statutes 1885, p. 160.*]

[Section 22 never has been amended.]

SECTION 23. If, in consequence of any graded street or public highway improved under the provisions of this act, being out of repair and in condition to endanger persons or property passing thereon, any person while carefully using said street or public highway, and exercising ordinary care to avoid the danger, suffer damage to his person or property, through any such defect therein, no recourse for damages thus suffered shall be had against such city; but if such defect in the street or public highway shall have existed for the period of twenty-four hours or more after notice thereof to the said superintendent of streets, then the person or persons on

whom the law may have imposed the obligations to repair such defect in the
street or public highway, and also the officer or officers through whose official
negligence such defect remains unrepaired, shell be jointly and severally
liable to the party injured for the damage sustained; *pr .vided*, that said
superintendent has the authority to make said repairs, under the direction
of the city council, at the expense of the city. [*Statutes 1885, p. 161.*]

[Section 23 of the act never has been amended.]

Section 24 of the San Francisco street work act of 1862,
as amended in 1863 [statutes 1863, p. 532], is the section of
that act corresponding to section 23 of the present street
improvement act, and in Eustace *v.* Jahns, 38 Cal. pp. 18–19,
Mr. Justice Sprague spoke of this section of the act of 1862, as
follows: "This is the section containing the law which
seems to be especially relied upon by respondent as fixing
the liability·of defendant in this case. But we cannot discover that, with respect to private citizens or individuals,
it creates any new liability or imposes any duty. The
manifest design and only effect of the section is to exempt
the city and county, in its corporate capacity, from the
liability which, at common law, would otherwise attach,
by reason of the absolute and exclusive control of the streets
and public highways delegated to the corporation by the
provisions of its charter, and transfer such responsibility
to individual officers, agents and employés of the corporation whose personal neglect or malfeasance may have occasioned the injury. These streets and public highways are
public property, opened, constructed, controlled, improved
and repaired for public use and benefit, by the city and
county government, and no private individual possesses
any exclusive right to occupy, use or control any portion
thereof, by reason of his ownership or occupancy of adjacent lots and premises, by virtue of any statute of the state,
and we are unable to comprehend by what process of ratiocination the duty to repair a public street or highway is
devolved upon an individual from the fact that he is liable
to be notified by the superintendent of streets to make
specific repairs, or owns or occupies a lot liable to be
assessed to defray the expenses of repairs, when made by
another at the instance of the superintendent."

SECTION 24. The city council of such city shall have full power and
authority to construct sewers, gutters, and manholes, and provide for the
cleaning of the same, and culverts or cesspools, or crosswalks or sidewalks,
or any portion of any sidewalk, upon or in any street, avenue, lane, alley, court
or place in such city; and also for drainage purposes, over or through any
right of way obtained or granted for such purposes, with necessary and
proper outlet or outlets to the same, of such materials, in such a manner,
and upon such terms as it may be deemed proper. None of the work or
improvements described in this section shall be stayed or prevented by

any written or any other remonstrance or objection, unless such council deems proper. [*Amendment approved March 11, 1893, statutes 1893, p. 173.*]

[Section 24 was amended by the act of March 14, 1889, statutes 1889, p. 170; again by act of March 31, 1891, statutes 1891, p. 205; and again by the act of March 11, 1893, statutes 1893, p. 173.

SECTION 25. The city council may, in its discretion, repair and water streets that shall have been graded, curbed and planked, paved or macadamized, and may build, repair and clean sewers, and shall provide a street contingent fund at the same time and in the same manner as other funds are provided, out of which to pay the costs and expenses of making said repairs and watering said streets and building, repairing and cleaning said sewers; but whenever any unaccepted street or part of a street requires regrading, recurbing, repiling, repaving, replanking, regraveling or remacadamizing or requires new culverts or new crosswalks or new sidewalks or new sewers, the work shall be advertised and let out by contract, and the costs and expenses thereof shall be assessed upon the property affected or benefited thereby, the same as in the first instance. [*Statutes 1885, page 161.*]

[Section 25 of the act has never been amended. See notes to section 13 of this act, *supra*, page 162 *et seq.* See *supra*, pages 6 and 7, notes to section 2, of the act upon "regrading," "replanking," etc.

SECTION 26. The city council may, in its discretion, order, by resolution, that the whole or any part of the cost and expenses of any of the work mentioned in this act be paid out of the treasury of the municipality from such fund as the council may designate. Whenever a part of such cost and expenses is so ordered to be paid the superintendent of streets, in making up the assessment heretofore provided for such cost and expenses, shall first deduct from the whole cost and expenses such part thereof as has been so ordered to be paid out of the municipal treasury, and shall assess the remainder of said cost and expenses proportionately upon the lots, parts of lots and lands fronting on the streets where said work was done, or liable to be assessed for such work, and in the manner heretofore provided. [*Amendment approved March 31, 1891, statutes 1891, page 206.*]

[Section 26 was amended by act of March 14, 1889, statutes 1889, page 170, and again by the act of March 31, 1891, statutes 1891, page 206.]

PART II.

SECTION 27. Whenever the city council deem it necessary to construct a sewer, then the said council may, in its discretion, determine to construct said sewer, and assess the cost and expenses thereof upon the property to be affected or benefited thereby, in such manner and within such assessment district as it shall prescribe, and the lien therefor upon said property shall be the same as is provided in section nine of this act, or said council may determine to construct said sewer and pay therefor out of the street contingent fund. [*Statutes 1885, page 162.*]

[Section 27 of the act never has been amended.]

The sections embraced in Part II of the act,—sections 27 to 33, inclusive,—in addition to the ordinary method for paying the expenses of the work authorized by the act,— which ordinary method is by assessment according to the front-foot plan,—provide three extraordinary methods for paying the expenses of sewer construction, viz: (*1.*) By assessing the cost and expenses of sewer construction upon the property to be affected or benefited thereby, and in such manner and within such assessment district as the council shall prescribe; or (*2.*) by paying the cost of constructing the sewer out of the street contingent fund; or (*3.*) by incurring an indebtedness, created by the issuance of bonds, or by·such other mode as the council shall, by ordinance provide.

The first of said methods for paying the cost of sewer construction is provided for by section 27 of the act. The second is controlled by the provisions of sections 27 and 33. And the third method of paying the cost of sewer construction—namely, by the incurring of an indebtedness—is controlled by sections 28 to 33, inclusive.

The practical utility of these provisions of Part II of the act does not seem to be very apparent. It would seem at first blush to be a specially enabling provision applicable to sewers only. But all three modes provided by Part II for meeting the expenses of sewer construction seem to be provided either by other parts of the act or by an independent act. Thus, as to the two modes provided for by section 27,—assessing the cost and expenses upon the property lying within an assessment district, or paying out of the street contingent fund,—the first mode (district assessment plan) is amply provided for by section 3 of the act, where it is provided that, for the work of constructing sewers, specifications shall always be furnished to the council by the city engineer, and whenever the contemplated work or improvement is, in the opinion of the city council, of more than local or ordinary public benefit, etc., the city council may make the expense of such work or improvement chargeable upon a district, which the council shall, in its resolution of intention, declare to be the district benefited by said work or improvement, and to be assessed to pay the costs and expenses thereof. As to the second mode provided for by section 27,—paying the costs and expenses of sewer construction out of the street contingent fund—section 26 expressly empowers the city council to order the whole or any part of the cost and expenses of *any* of the work mentioned in the act to be paid out of the treasury of the municipality from such fund as the council may designate.

So that the two modes of meeting the expenses which are provided for by section 27 of the act, and made specially applicable to sewer construction, seem to be amply provided for by other parts of the act, unless it be held that it was the

intention of the legislature that the modes provided by Part
I of the act, for meeting the expense of any work, do not
include the cost of sewer construction, and that, as to sewer
construction, the modes provided by Part II of the act for
paying the expenses of the work are exclusive of all others;
that is to say, that by Part II of the act the legislature
intended to limit the modes for paying the costs and expenses
of sewer construction to the three modes provided for by
Part II, and that therefore, as to sewer construction, the
ordinary, or front-foot mode of assessment, is not applicable. But, this cannot have been the intention of the legislature, for the following reasons:

First: Subdivision one of section 7 provides that the
expenses incurred for any work authorized by this act
(except the cost of any work which shall have been declared
in the resolution of intention to be assessed on a district
benefited) shall be assessed upon the lots and lands according to the front-foot plan of assessment, except as thereinafter specifically provided; and subdivision 2 of said section
7 provides that the expense of all improvements (except
such as are done by contractors under the provisions of section 13 of this act, *i. e.*, "repairing" or "reconstructing"
streets out of repair or needing reconstruction) "shall be
assessed upon the lots and lands, *as provided in this section,*
[Sec. 7] according to the nature and character of the work."
But, aside from the work done by contractors under the
provisions of section 13 of the act, the only exception to the
front-foot plan of assessment recognized by section 7 is that
provided for by subdivision 12 of the section, where, carrying out the provisions of section 3, which authorize the
council to declare an assessment district wherever the contemplated work or improvement is, in the opinion of the
council, of more than local or ordinary public benefit, it is
provided that "whenever the resolution of intention declares
that the costs and expenses of the work and improvement
are to be assessed upon a district, the city council shall
direct the city engineer to make a diagram of the property
affected or benefited," etc. But, while subdivision 12 of
section 7 recognizes the fact that there might be a case
where the expenses shall be raised by assessing the property
within an assessment district, and supplies the appropriate
machinery for levying the assessment, when that mode is
adopted, still it does not state when or in what cases the
district assessment plan shall be adopted, while subdivision
2 of section 7 provides that, with the exception of such work
as is done by contractors under the provisions of section 13,
"the expense of all improvements shall be assessed upon the

lots and lands, as provided in this section, according to the nature and character of the work," and subdivision 1 provides that "the expenses incurred for any work authorized by this act * * * shall be assessed *upon the lots and lands fronting thereon*, except as hereinafter specifically provided; each lot or portion of a lot being separately assessed, in proportion to the frontage, at a rate per front foot sufficient to cover the total expense of the work."

The only exceptions recognized by subdivision one, section seven, to the ordinary, or front-foot mode of assessment, are: (*1.*) Where the work is done in such portion of any street as is required by law to be kept in order or repair by any person or company having railroad tracks thereon; (see *supra* pp. 67–69); (*2.*) where the cost of the work has been declared in the resolution of intention to be assessed on a district benefited—as provided for by section 3 of the act: and (*3.*) where any exception to the front-foot mode of assessment is elsewhere in section seven "*specifically provided.*" The phrase "except as hereinafter specifically provided," as used in subdivision 1 of section 7, must mean "except as hereinafter *in this section (section 7)* specifically provided," since subdivision 2 of section 7 provides that "the expense of *all* improvements, except such as are done by contractors under the provisions of section 13 of this act * * * shall be assessed upon the lots and lands *as provided in this section*, according to the nature and character of the work."

Second: Section 3 and subdivision 8 of section 7, at least countenance the adoption of the front-foot mode of assessment in connection with sewer construction, and thus show that the act contemplates that the expenses of sewer construction may be provided for according to the front-foot, or ordinary and usual plan provided by the act for all street work, as well as by either of the extraordinary modes provided by Part II of the act. Section 3 provides that the owners of a majority of the frontage of the property fronting on any proposed work or improvement, where the same is for one block or more, may make a written objection to the same within ten days after the expiration of the time of the publication and posting of the notice of the passage of the resolution of intention, and that such objections—except as to *sewers* and other expressly excepted work—shall be a bar for six months to any further proceedings in relation to the doing of said work or making such improvements. But as to sewers it is provided that "when the work or improvement proposed to be done is the constructions of sewers * * * and the objection thereto is signed by the owners of a majority of the *frontage* liable to be assessed for the expense of said work, as aforesaid, the city council shall at its next meeting, fix a time for hearing said objections, etc., and its decision shall be final and conclusive, and the said bar for six months to any further proceedings shall not be applicable thereto." [See also section 24.] And, by subdivision 8 of section 7, it is provided that when sewering or resewering is ordered to be done under the sidewalk on only one side of a street for any length thereof, the assessment for its expenses shall be made only upon the lots and lands *fronting nearest upon that side*," etc.

As to the third mode provided by Part II for raising the money necessary to pay the cost of sewer construction—incurring an indebtedness by the issuance of bonds or otherwise as provided by the council—this mode seems to be fully covered by the municipal indebtedness act of March 19, 1889 (statutes 1889, p. 399) entitled "An act authorizing the incurring of indebtedness by cities, towns and municipal corporations, incorporated under the laws of this state, for the construction of waterworks, sewers and all necessary public improvements, or for any purpose whatever, and to repeal an act approved March 9, 1885," etc., and the several acts amendatory thereof. See *infra* for the provisions of this act of March 19, 1889, as amended by subsequent amendatory acts. This municipal indebtedness act provides that whenever the cost of any sewers will be too great to be paid out of the ordinary annual income and revenue of the municipality, the city council may, after an election authorizing the same, issue bonds to pay the cost of such work, etc.

In view of the foregoing, and especially in view of the fact that section 27 of the act empowers the city council to adopt the district assessment plan in all cases of sewer construction, notwithstanding the fact that section 3 also confers upon the council the option to adopt the district assessment plan if it deems the contemplated work or improvement to be of more than local or ordinary public benefit,—the question might very pertinently be asked: If the three extraordinary modes especially provided by Part II of the Vrooman act for defraying the cost and expenses of sewer construction, are likewise provided by other parts of the act—in conjunction with the said municipal indebtedness act of March 19, 1889,—and if, therefore, Part II of the Vrooman act is of no practical utility, what object did the legislature have in view when it enacted this part of the statute? This question may be answered as follows:

1st. As to the provision of section 27 to the effect that the council may pay for the sewer out of the street contingent fund, it is difficult to perceive what object the legislature had in mind when enacting this provision, since it seems to be amply covered by section 26 of the act.

2nd. As to the provision of section 27 empowering the city council to assess the cost and expense of constructing a sewer upon an assessment district, notwithstanding the fact that section 3 empowers the council to do the same thing whenever, "in its opinion, the contemplated work or improvement is of more than local or ordinary public benefit." If this provision of section 27 be not regarded as affording an exclusive mode of assessment for the payment of the costs of sewer construction—a mode exclusive of the ordinary or front-foot mode of assessment—it might appear that there is no reason for this provision of section 27, and this apparent absence of all reason for this provision of section 27 might lead to the conclusion that it was the intention of the legislature that the modes provided by section 27 for paying the expenses of sewer construction should exclude all other modes, as held by the Superior Court of Los Angeles county in White *v.* Harris. [See *supra,* page 35, *et seq.*] But the reason for this conclusion disappears, and the apparent absence of a reason for the provisions of section 27 relative to assessment districts for sewer work, in view of the provisions of section 3 for assessment districts for all kinds of work, "whenever the contemplated work or improvement, in the opinion of the city council, is of more than local or ordinary public benefit," is easily explained, when we trace the history of the amendments to the act as it originally stood when approved March 18, 1885. As the act originally stood there was no provision empowering the city council to adopt the district assessment plan whenever, in its opinion, the contemplated work or improvement was of more than local or ordinary public benefit. [See statutes of 1885, page 147, *et seq.*] And, as a sewer is very frequently a work or improvement of more than local or ordinary public benefit, it was advisable to insert in the act as it originally stood before the amendments of 1889 and 1891 some provision, such as that contained in Part II, enabling the council to adopt the district assessment plan in the case of sewer construction, if, in its discretion, it deemed it best to do so. Hence the necessity for some such provision as that contained in section 27, although that necessity has been removed by the amendments to section 3 made by the amendatory acts of March 14, 1889 [statutes 1889, page 158,] and March 31,

1891, [statutes 1891, page 196,] which amendments expressly
empower the council to impose the burdens upon an assessment district, whenever, in its opinion, the contemplated
work or improvement is of more than local or ordinary public
benefit. In short, since the Vrooman act of March 18, 1885,
was originally enacted, section 3 has been so amended that
not only has the council become invested with all the
powers originally conferred upon it by Part II of the act,
relative to sewer construction, but these powers have
been extended to the kinds of work, and, as the whole is
greater than a part, so may the provisions of section 27,
relative to sewer construction assessment districts, be said to
have been included in and superseded by the provisions
of other parts of the act, notably by section 3, by which
larger powers have been vested in the council relative to
assessment districts.

3rd. As to the provisions of Part II relative to incurring
an indebtedness for the construction of sewers. These provisions were inserted in the act when it was first passed, and
have remained there ever since. At that time there was no
general act authorizing municipalities to incur an indebtedness to pay the cost of any municipal improvement when
such improvements required a greater expenditure than the
amount allowed therefor by the annual tax levy. And as
it is but just to pay the cost of sewer construction out of the
funds of the city, with money raised by a general tax levy
upon all the property within the city, whenever the sewer
to be constructed is a whole system directly benefiting all
parts of the city, it is obvious that the provisions of Part II
of the Vrooman act, in this respect, were necessary to the
attainment of justice at the time when the act became a
law,—March 18, 1885. But this necessity for these provisions of Part II has been removed by the adoption of said
general municipal indebtedness act of March 19, 1889,
authorizing cities and towns to incur indebtedness to pay
the cost of any municipal improvement requiring an expenditure greater than the amount allowed for such improvement by the annual tax levy. [Statutes 1889, p. 399.]
This act of March 19, 1889, expressly repeals all general
acts or special acts, or parts of acts, conflicting with it.

SECTION 28. If, at any time, the city council shall deem it necessary to
incur any indebtedness for the construction of sewers, in excess of the
money in the street contingent fund applicable to the construction of such
sewers, they shall give notice of a special election by the qualified electors
of the city, to be held to determine whether such indebtedness shall be
incurred. Such notice shall specify the amount of indebtedness proposed
to be incurred, the route and general character of the sewer or sewers to

be constructed, and the amount of money necessary to be raised annually by taxation for an interest and sinking fund as hereinafter provided. Such notice shall be published for at least three weeks in some newspaper published in such city, and no other question or matter shall be submitted to the electors at such election. If, upon a canvass of the votes cast at such election, it appear that not less than two-thirds of all the qualified electors voting at such election shall have voted in favor of incurring such indebtedness, it shall be the duty of the city council to pass an ordinance providing for the mode of creating such indebtedness, and of paying the same; and in such ordinance provision shall be made for the levy and collection of an annual tax upon all the real and personal property subject to taxation, within such city, sufficient to pay the interest on such indebtedness as it falls due, and also to constitute a sinking fund for the payment of the principal thereof, within a period of not more than twenty years from the time of contracting the same. It shall be the duty of the city council in each year thereafter, at the time when other taxes are levied, to levy a tax sufficient for such purpose, in addition to the taxes authorized to be levied for city purposes. Such tax, when collected, shall be kept in the treasury as a separate fund, to be inviolably appropriated to the payment of the principal and interest of such indebtedness. [*Statutes 1885, page 162.*]

[Section 28 has never been amended.]

See notes to act of March 19, 1889, [statutes 1889, p. 399] as amended, *infra.*

SECTION 29. If bonds are issued under the provisions of the last section, said bonds shall be in sums of not less than one hundred dollars nor more than one thousand dollars, shall be signed by the mayor and treasurer of the city, and the seal of the city shall be affixed thereto. Coupons for the interest shall be attached to each bond, signed by the mayor and treasurer. Said bonds shall bear interest, to be fixed by the city council, at the rate of not to exceed five per cent. per annum. [*Statutes 1885, page 163.*]

[Section 29 has never been amended.]

See notes to section 27, *supra.* See also *infra* act of March 19, 1889, [statutes 1889, p. 399] as amended. This act of March 19, 1889, expressly repeals all general acts or special acts, or parts of acts conflicting with it.

SECTION 30. Before the sale of said bonds, the council shall, at a regular meeting by resolution, declare its intention to sell a specified amount of said bonds, and the day and hour of such sale, and shall cause such resolution to be entered in the minutes, and shall cause notice of such sale to be published for fifteen days in at least one newspaper published in the city in which the bonds are issued and one published in the city and county of San Francisco, and in any other newspaper in the state, at their discretion. The notice shall state that sealed proposals will be received by the council for the purchase of the bonds on the day and hour named in the resolution. The council, at the time appointed, shall open the proposals and award the purchase of the bonds to the highest bidder, but may reject all bids. [*Statutes 1885, page 163.*]

[Section 30 has never been amended.]

See notes to section 27, *supra*. See also *infra* act of March 19, 1889, [statutes 1889, p. 399] as amended. This act of March 19, 1889, expressly repeals all general acts or special acts, or parts of acts, conflicting with it.

SECTION 31. The council may sell said bonds, at not less than par value, without the notice provided for in the preceding section. [*Statutes 1885, page 163.*]

[Section 31 has never been amended.]

See notes to section 27, *supra*. See also *infra* act of March 19, 1889, [statutes 1889, p. 399] as amended. This act of March 19, 1889, expressly repeals all general acts or special acts, or parts of acts, conflicting with it.

SECTION 32. The proceeds of the sale of the bonds shall be deposited in the city treasury, to the account of the sewer fund, but no payment therefrom shall be made, except to pay for the construction of the sewer or sewers for the construction of which the bonds were issued, and upon the certificate of the superintendent of streets and the city engineer, that the work has been done according to the contract; *provided*, that after the completion of the sewers, for the construction of which said bonds were issued, if there be any money of said fund left in the treasury, the same may be transferred to the general fund, for general purposes. [*Statutes 1887, page 148.*]

[Section 32 was amended by act of March 15, 1887, statutes 1887, p. 148.]

See notes to section 27, *supra*. See also *infra* act of March 19, 1889, [statutes 1889, p. 399] as amended. This act of March 19, 1889, expressly repeals all general acts or special acts, or parts of acts, conflicting with it.

SECTION 33. Whenever said council shall determine to construct any sewer, and pay therefor out of the street contingent fund, or by the issuance of bonds, as above provided, then said council shall cause to be prepared plans and specifications of said work in sections, and shall advertise for twenty days in at least one newspaper published in the city in which the sewer is to be constructed, and one in the city and county of San Francisco, for sealed proposals for constructing said sewer. The work may be let in sections, and must be awarded to the lowest responsible bidder, the council having the right to reject any and all bids. The work shall be done and the materials furnished under the supervision and to the satisfaction of the superintendent of streets and the city engineer. [*Statutes 1885, page 163.*]

[Section 33 has never been amended.]

See notes to section 27, *surpa*. See also *infra* act of March 19, 1889, [statutes 1889, p. 399] as amended. This act of March 19, 1889, expressly repeals all general acts or special acts, or parts of acts, conflicting with it.

PART III.

Section 34. *First*—The city engineer, or where there is no city engineer, the county, or city and county surveyor, shall be the proper officer to do the surveying and other engineering work necessary to be done under this act, and to survey and measure the work to be done under contracts for grading and macadamizing streets, and to estimate the costs and expenses thereof; and every certificate signed by him in his official character shall be prima facie evidence in all courts in this state of the truth of its contents. He shall also keep a record of all surveys made under the provisions of this act, as in other cases. In all those cities where there is no city engineer, the city council thereof is hereby authorized and empowered to appoint a suitable person to discharge the duties herein laid down as those of city engineer, and all the provisions hereof applicable to the city engineer shall apply to such person so appointed. Said city council is hereby empowered to fix his compensation for such services.

Second—The words "work," "improve," "improved," and "improvement," as used in this act, shall include all work mentioned in this act, and also the construction, reconstruction, and repairs of all or any portion of said work.

Third—The term "incidental expenses," as used in this act, shall include the compensation of the city engineer for work done by him; also, the cost of printing and advertising as provided in this act, and not otherwise; also, the compensation of the person appointed by the superintendent of streets to take charge of and superintend any of the work mentioned in section thirty-five of this act. All demands for incidental expenses mentioned in this sub-division shall be presented to the street superintendent by itemized bill, duly verified by oath of the demandant.

Fourth—The notices, resolutions, orders, or other matter, required to be published by the provisions of this act, and of the act of which this is amendatory, shall be published in a daily newspaper, in cities where such there is, and where there is no daily newspaper, in a semi-weekly or weekly newspaper, to be designated by the council of such city, as often as the same is issued, and no other statute shall govern or be applicable to the publications herein provided for; *provided, however*, that only in case there is no daily, semi-weekly or weekly newspaper printed or circulated in any such city, then such notices, resolutions, orders, or other matters, as are herein required to be published in a newspaper, shall be posted and kept posted for the same length of time as required herein for the publication of the same in a daily, semi-weekly, or weekly newspaper, in three of the most public places in such city. Proof of the publication or posting of any notice provided for herein shall be made by affidavit of the owner, publisher, or clerk of the newspaper, or of the poster of the notice. No publication or notice, other than that provided for in this act, shall be necessary to give validity to any of the proceedings provided for therein.

Fifth—The word "municipality," and the word "city," as used in this act, shall be understood and so construed as to include, and is hereby declared to include, all corporations heretofore organized and now existing, and those hereafter organized, for municipal purposes.

Sixth—The words "paved," or "repaved," as used in this act, shall be held to mean and include pavement of stone, whether paving blocks or macadamizing, or of bituminous rock or asphalt, or of iron, wood, or other material, whether patented or not, which the city council shall by ordinance adopt.

Seventh—The word "street," as used in this act, shall be deemed to, and is hereby declared to include avenues, highways, lanes, alley, crossings, or intersections, courts, and places, and the term "main street" means such actually opened street or streets as bound a block; the word "blocks," whether regular or irregular, shall mean such blocks as are bounded by main streets, or partially by a boundary line of the city.

Eighth—The terms "street superintendent," and "superintendent of streets," as used in this act, shall be understood, and so construed as to include, and are hereby declared to include any person or officer whose duty it is, under the law, to have the care or charge of the streets, or the improvement thereof in any city. In all those cities where there is no street superintendent or superintendent of streets, the city council thereof is hereby authorized and empowered to appoint a suitable person to discharge the duties herein laid down, as those of street superintendent or superintendent of streets; and all provisions hereof applicable to the street superintendent or superintendent of streets, shall apply to such person so appointed.

Ninth—The term "city council" is hereby declared to include any body or board which, under the law, is the legislative department of the government of any city.

Tenth—In municipalities in which there is no mayor, then the duties imposed upon said officer by the provisions of this act shall be performed by the president of the board of trustees, or other chief executive officer of the municipality.

Eleventh—The term "clerk" and "city clerk," as used in this act, is hereby declared to include any person or officer who shall be clerk of the said city council.

Twelfth—The term "quarter block," as used in this act as to irregular blocks, shall be deemed to include all lots or portions of lots having any frontage on either intersecting street half way from such intersection to the next main street, or when no main street intervenes, all the way to a boundary line of the city.

Thirteenth—The term "one year," as used in this act, shall be deemed to include the time beginning with January first and ending with the thirty-first day of December of the same year.

Fourteenth—References in certain sections, by number, to certain other sections of "this act" refer to the number of the sections of the original act as heretofore amended, unless it appears from the context that the reference is to the section of this amendatory act, when it shall be construed according to the context. [*Amendment approved March 31, 1891. Statutes 1891, page 206.*]

[Section 34 was amended by act of March 14, 1889, statutes 1889, page 157 also by the act of March 31, 1891, statutes 1891, page 206.]

SECTION 35. The superintendent of streets shall, when in his judgment it is necessary, appoint a suitable person to take charge of and superintend the construction and improvement of each and every sewer constructed or improved under the provisions of this act, and of piling and capping, sidewalking, or of the paving of whatever character heretofore mentioned, in whole or in part, of one block or more, whose duty it shall be to see that the contract made for the doing of said work is strictly fulfilled in every respect, and in case of any departure therefrom to report the same to the superintendent of streets. Such person shall be allowed for his time actually employed in the discharge of his duties such compensation as shall be just, but not to exceed four dollars per day. The sum to which the party so employed shall be entitled shall be deemed to be incidental expenses, within the meaning of those words as defined by this act. [*Amendment approved March 31, 1891, statutes 1891, page 208.*]

[The act of March 14, 1889, statutes '89, p. 157, attempted to amend section 35. and section 35 as amended is embraced in the body of the act, [statutes '89, p. 173,] but the title of the act does not mention this section. The section was amended in 1891 by the act of March 31, 1891, statutes '91, p. 208.]

SECTION 36. The act entitled "An act to provide for the improvement of streets, lanes, alleys, courts, places, and sidewalks, and the construction of sewers within municipalities," approved March sixth, eighteen hundred and eighty-three, is hereby repealed; *provided*, that any work or proceedings commenced thereunder prior to the passage of this act shall in nowise be affected hereby, but shall in all respects be finished and completed under said act of March sixth, eighteen hundred and eighty-three, and said repeal shall in nowise affect said work or proceedings. [*Statutes '85, p. 165.*]

[Section 36 has never been amended.]

SECTION 37. That said act shall take effect and be in force immediately upon its passage, and all acts and parts of acts in conflict with this act are hereby repealed; *and provided, however*, that any work or proceeding of the city council commenced under the act of which this is amendatory shall in nowise be affected thereby, but shall in all respects be finished and completed thereunder. [*Amendment approved March 11, 1893, statutes 1893, page 173.*]

[Section 37 was amended in 1889 by the act of March 14, 1889, statutes '89, p. 173; again in 1891 by the act of March 31, 1891, statutes '91, p. 209; and again in 1893 by the act of March 11, 1893, statutes '93, p 173.]

These three amendments to section 37 are all substantially the same. Section 3 of the said act of March 11, 1893, [statutes '93, p. 173] is as follows:

"SEC. 3. That section thirty-seven of *said* act [*i. e.*, the act of March 18, 1885] is hereby amended to read as follows:

"SECTION 37. That *said* act, [*i. e.*, the act of March 18, 1885, entitled "An act to provide for work upon streets, lanes, alleys, courts, places and sidewalks, and for the construction of sewers within municipalities"] shall take effect and be in force immediately upon its passage, and all acts and parts of acts in conflict with this act are hereby repealed; *and provided, however*, that any work or proceeding of the city council commenced under the act of which this is amendatory shall in nowise be affected thereby, but shall in all respects be finished and completed thereunder."

This is a palpable absurdity. It is evident that it was the intention of the legislature to provide by section 3 of the said amendatory act of March 11, 1893, amending certain sections of the act of March 18, 1885, that it—the amendatory act of March 11, 1893—should take effect and be in force from and after its passage, etc., and not that the original act of March 18, 1885, should take effect and be in force from and after its passage, since the original section 37 of the act of March 18, 1885, [statutes '85, p. 165] already provided that said act of March 18, 1885, should take effect and be in force from and after its passage. Furthermore, the original act—the act of March 18, 1885—was not amendatory of any act. It expressly repealed the first Vrooman act—the Vrooman act of March 6, 1883—and provided that any work or proceedings commenced under said act of March 6, 1883, prior to its own passage, shall in nowise be affected, etc. [See section 36 of the act of March 18, 1885—section 36, *supra*.] Section 3 of the act of March 11, 1893, should have read, "This act shall take effect," etc., instead of incorporating these provisions into section 37 of the act of March 18, 1885. But this is only one of the many stupid blunders that have been made in amending this street improvement act of March 18, 1885. The amendatory acts, next to be considered, by which certain sections were added to the act of March 18, 1885, are still more pregnant with blunders; and, while it is possible that the courts, by a process of construction, will so construe the act, with its amendments, as to give effect to what was obviously the legislative intent, yet in doing so they will have to give to the language of these amendatory acts a meaning that they do not bear when read literally. [See the notes to next section—section 38.]

SECTION 38. The city council is hereby empowered to change or modify the grade of any public street, lane, alley, place, or court, and to regrade or repave the same, so as to conform to such modified grade, in the manner as hereinafter provided. Before any change of grade is ordered the city council shall pass an ordinance or resolution of intention to make such change or modification of grade, and it shall have power at the same time and in the same ordinance or resolution to provide for the actual cost of performing the work of regrading, repaving, sewering, sidewalking, or curbing of said street or portion of street, with the same or other material with which it was formerly graded, paved, sewered, sidewalked or curbed; and that the cost of the same shall also be assessed upon the same district which is declared to be benefited by such changed or modified grade. One or more streets or blocks of streets may be embraced in the same ordinance or resolution. Such ordinance or resolution shall be published in the newspaper in which the official notices of the city council are usually printed and published; and such newspaper is to be designated in such ordinance or resolution. Such publication shall be made in every regular issue of such paper for not less than ten days, and shall describe the proposed change or modification of grade or regrading, and shall designate and establish the district to be benefited by such change or modification of grade or regrading, and to be assessed for the cost of the same. Within five days after the first publication of the ordinance or resolution of intention, the superintendent of streets shall cause to be conspicuously posted within the district designated in the ordinance or resolution, notice of the passage of said resolution. Said notices shall be the same in all requirements of contents and posting as the "notices of street work" provided for in section three of the original act to which this is amendatory. If no objection to said proposed change or changes, or modifications of grade, shall be filed with the clerk of the council within thirty days from the first publication of the ordinance or resolution of intention hereinbefore mentioned, the city council shall have power to declare such grades to be changed and established in conformity to said ordinance or resolution, *provided*, that no change of an established grade shall be ordered except on petition of the owners of a majority of the property affected by the proposed change of grade. [*Amendment approved March 9, 1893, statutes '93, p. 89.*]

The remaining sections of the act, sixteen in number—sections 38 to 53 inclusive—were added by the act of March 31, 1891. [Statutes '91, p. 461.] In 1893, by an act approved March 9, 1893, the legislature amended each of these sixteen new sections [statutes '93, p. 89] by an act entitled, "An act to amend sections thirty-eight to fifty three, inclusive, of an act approved March 31, 1891, adding those sections to 'An act to provide for work upon streets, alleys, lanes, courts, places, and sidewalks, and for the construction of sewers within municipalities,' approved March 18, 1885."

These sixteen new sections, thus added to the original act, the act of March 18, 1885, are intended to provide the machinery for changing the grades of streets in all cases where the official grade has once been established. They also make provision for performing the work of grading to the newly established grade in the same proceedings in which the grade is changed or newly established. The first sentence of section 38 proclaims the scope and object of the act. It is: "The city council is hereby empowered to change or modify the grade of any public street, lane, alley, place or court, and to regrade or repave the same, so as to conform to such modified grade, in the manner as hereinafter provided."

The act of March 31, 1891, by which these sections were first added to the original act of March 18, 1885, did not make provision for performing the work of grading or regrading to the grade as established by the proceedings to change the grade, but simply made provision for changing or modifying the grade of any street, leaving the subsequent proceedings to grade to the newly established grade to be regulated by the prior sections of the act.

By section 2 of the Vrooman act of March 18, 1885, as amended in 1893 [statutes '93 p. 172,] it is provided that "whenever the grade of a street, avenue, lane, alley, court, or place shall hereafter be changed, the petition of the owners of a majority of the feet *fronting thereon*, asking for grading the same to the new grade, shall be a condition precedent to the ordering of such grading to be done," [*supra* p. 6] and by sections 38 *et seq.*, as amended in 1893, provision is made for thus changing a grade and establishing a new one, and it is provided,—section 38—that "no change of an established grade shall be ordered except on petition of the owners of a majority of the property *affected* by the proposed change of grade." Section 2 provides for a petition to grade a street after a new grade has been established. Section 38 provides for a petition to establish a new grade changing or modifying the old one. In Kepple v. City of Keokuk, 2 Am. Eng. Corp. Cases 446, it is said: "The establishment of a grade means the passing of an ordinance or other legislative action of the council of the city, prescribing and fixing grade lines to which the surface shall be brought when the streets shall be improved." Section 38 of the act provides that where a grade, once established, is to be changed or modified, by refixing the grade lines, there shall first be filed or presented "the petition of the owners of a majority of the property *affected* by the proposed change of grade." Section 2 provides that where the surface is to be brought to the grade lines, as the same have been changed and established under the provisions of sections 38 *et seq.*,—unless in the proceedings to change the grade, proceedings to grade the surface to the new grade lines have also been included—there shall first be filed or presented "the petition of the owners of a majority of the feet *fronting* thereon." In the former case, *i. e.*, in proceedings under section 38 to change an old grade and establish new grade lines, the petition is required to be by "the owners of a majority of the property *affected* by the proposed change of grade." In the latter case, *i. e.*, in proceedings to grade a street after the official grade has been changed or altered, the petition required by section 2 in such case is required to be by "the owners of a majority of the feet *fronting*" on the street to be graded. The reason for this difference is, that, in proceedings to change the grade of a street,—*i. e.*, in proceedings under sections 38, *et seq.*, to establish new grade lines, to which the surface shall be brought when the streets shall be graded to the new grade, or otherwise improved—the costs and expenses are to be charged upon and assessed against the lands lying within a district declared by the resolution of intention to be the lands benefited by such changed or modified grade. Whereas, in proceedings under prior sections of the act,— sections 3 to 10—to grade a street to a new grade line, changed and established after the same has once been established, the costs and expenses are ordinarily to be charged against and assessed upon the lots and lands fronting thereon as provided by section 7 of the act.

Section 38 provides that, in proceedings thereunder, to change or modify a grade, "no change of an established grade shall be ordered, except on petition of the owners of a majority of the property *affected* by the proposed change of grade." This provision, if construed to mean that such petition shall precede all action by the council,—shall precede, for example, the passage of the resolution or ordinance of intention declaring the district to be benefited by the changed or modified grade—might defeat the whole of this part of the act. For, until the ordinance or resolution of intention is passed, declaring the district to be benefited, it can not be known what lands will be affected by the proposed change of grade,—assuming that the word "affected" applies to the lots which will be benefited by the proposed change of grade, and therefore liable to be assessed to pay the damages resulting from the change or modification of the grade—further than that all lots in the city, by being liable to be included in the district, are, in this sense, affected by any proposed change of the grade. Therefore, if the petition required by section 38, be a condition prerequisite to jurisdiction in the council to pass an ordinance or resolution of intention to change the grade, or to take any steps to change the grade of a street, there would seem to be such an element of uncertainty as to defeat any proceeding under these new and added sections of the act. [See Montgomery Avenue case, 54 Cal. 579.]

Section 38 provides that "before any change of grade is ordered the city council shall pass an ordinance or resolution of intention to make such change or modification of grade, * * * and that the cost of the same shall also be assessed upon the same district which is declared to be benefited by such changed or modified grade." This language does not expressly empower the council to *establish* or *define* the assessment district. However, it is followed by a provision that the ordinance or resolution shall be published and that "such publication shall * * * designate and establish the district to be benefited by such change or modification of grade or regrading, and to be assessed for the cost of the same." Since it is the resolution or ordinance of intention that is to be published, and since it is the publication that is to "establish" the district, these provisions, taken together, may possibly be construed as tantamount to a provision that the council, by and through its resolution of intention and the publication thereof, shall establish the district to be assessed. Nor does there seem to be any provision in this or the succeeding sections of the act directly providing for an opportunity to property owners to object to the extent of the district, after a notice, or for a hearing thereon. However, it seems to have been the intention of the legislature to provide by section 52 of the act that all the provisions contained in the first thirty-seven sections of the act, as amended since their original passage and approval, March 18, 1885, should apply to all matters contained in sections 38 to 52, inclusive, so far as they are not in conflict. If this be so, it is probable that the provisions of section 3 of the act, providing for an opportunity for filing objections to the extent of the district, etc., might be applicable. [See *infra*, section 52; also see section 3, *supra*, page 10.] And it is possible that section 38 might be construed as providing that the council shall, in the first instance, establish the district to be benefited and assessed, and that the petition from the owners of a majority of the property affected shall be filed after the establishment of the district and before the change of grade is ordered. If the section be capable of this construction, it is possible that sections 38, *et seq.*, may be constitutional—even though by the expression, "property affected," is meant the property *benefited* by the proposed change of grade, and, therefore, liable to be assessed to pay the expenses of the change, as well as the property fronting upon the street, and, therefore, directly affected by the proposed change of grade. But, if the phrase, "petition of the owners of a majority of the property *affected* by the proposed change of grade," be construed to mean a "petition of the owners of a majority of the property *benefited* by the proposed change of grade, and, therefore, liable to be assessed therefor, as well as the property *fronting* on the proposed change of grade"—and the property benefited, and, therefore, liable to be assessed, is "*affected*" by the proposed change of grade, as well as that fronting thereon,—then, if such petition must be filed

before the council acquires jurisdiction to pass the ordinance or resolution of intention, and if the council must
declare to be benefited the lands in the district described in
such petition, these sections of the act [sections 38 to 52,
inclusive,] would seem to be unconstitutional for the reason
stated in Moulton v. Parks, 64 Cal. 182–4.   It was held in
this case of Moulton v. Parks that the act of March 25,
1868, [statutes 1867–8, page 316,]—an act to provide for the
protection of certain lands in the county of Sutter from
overflow by the erection of levee districts,—was unconstitutional.   Section 21 of the act [statutes 1867–8, page 321,]
provided that "whenever a petition shall be received by
said board of supervisors from persons in possession of
more than one-half of the acres of any specified portion of
said county asking to be set apart and erected into a levee
district, said board *shall at once erect* such territory into a
levee district, and place it under the provisions of this act,
to be called Levee District No. 1, 2, 3, and so on, as the case
may be; *provided,* that it shall not be required to submit the
question of tax to a vote of the people of any district so
erected."   It was held that this was an attempt to transfer
to persons in possession of more than one-half of the acres
of any portion of the county of Sutter which *they* may
specify, the power to declare that such portion of the county
will be benefited by works erected at the expense of all the
property, real and personal, within it, and to set in motion
machinery for the enforcement of a tax and assessment
against the owners of a minority of the acreage, and that
therefore the act was unconstitutional.   The court, in this
connection, quoted from Mr. Justice Cooley on Taxation,
449, as follows: "The district within which the tax shall
be laid may be determined in either of two modes; (*1.*) the
legislative authority either of the state or, when properly
organized, of the municipality, may determine over what
territory the benefits are so far diffused as to render it
proper to make all lands contribute to the cost, or (*2.*) the
assessors or commissioners who, under the law, are to make
the assessment, may have the whole matter submitted to
their judgment, to assess such lands as in their opinion are
specially benefited, and ought therefore to contribute
to the cost of the work."   It was held that as
the act in question did not provide for the creation of an assessment district, in either of the said
two modes pointed out by Mr. Justice Cooley, but imposed
upon the board of supervisors the duty to erect the territory
described in the petition into a levee district, without conferring upon them any discretion to reject the petition, or

to modify or change the boundaries of the district, or otherwise to exercise any judgment with reference to the expediency of fixing the limits of the assessment district where the petition fixes them, the act was, therefore, unconstitutional and void.

It is stated *supra* that said sections 38 to 52, inclusive, of the Vrooman act, providing the machinery for changing grades that have been once established, might be unconstitutional for the reasons given in the case of Moulton v. Parks, but to bring the sections in question within the reasons given in Moulton v. Parks, two postulates must be assumed, viz: *(1.)* It must be assumed that it was the intention of the legislature to provide by the last clause of section 38, that the petition there referred to should precede any step taken by the council,—should precede the resolution of intention; and *(2.)* It must be assumed that the phrase "petition of the owners of a majority of the property affected by the proposed change of grade," means a "petition of the owners of a majority of the property liable to be assessed to pay the expenses of changing the grade, as well as the property fronting upon the proposed new or modified grade." As to the first assumption, it would seem by analogy to similar provisions in other acts, that it was the intention of the legislation that the petition should be a condition precedent to the passage of the ordinance or resolution of intention. [See Turrill v. Grattan, 52 Cal. 97; Dyer v. Miller, 58 Cal. 585; Gately v. Leviston, 63 Cal. 365.] As to the second assumption, there can be no question but that the property which will be *benefited* by the proposed change of grade, and which will therefore become chargeable with the expenses thereof, will be *"affected"* by the proposed change of grade. It is affected in two respects, viz: *(1.)* Because it will be benefited by the proposed change; and *(2.)* Because it will have to bear a portion of the burden of the expenses attending the change of grade. The property owners whose property fronts on streets, the grade of which it is proposed to change, are entitled to recover damages resulting therefrom. These damages constitute a part of the cost of the change, and lands not fronting upon such streets may be benefited by the proposed change, and therefore liable to be assessed to pay a portion of the costs, even though the owners thereof are not entitled to any damages. Therefore property may be "affected" by the proposed change of grade in at least two ways: (1.) It may be *directly* "affected" thereby because fronting on the streets, the grade of which it is proposed to change, or (2.) It may be benefited by the proposed change of grade, and therefore liable to be assessed to pay a portion of the expenses, and therefore, *indirectly* affected by the proposed change of grade, even though it does not front upon the street in question. It is possible therefore, that, in order to uphold the constitutionality of these sections of the act, the courts may hold that the last clause of section 38 only requires a petition from a majority of the owners of property *fronting* upon the street or streets the grade or grades of which it is proposed to change—property which may be said to be *directly* affected by the proposed change of grade, in the sense that the change in the grade lines, and the subsequent grading of the street to the new lines, will directly affect ingress and egress to and from the property fronting upon the street, the grade of which it is proposed to change. Such a construction would make it certain who the owners are by whom the petition should be filed and thus avoid the defect which existed in the act held to be unconstitutional in Montgomery Avenue Case, 54 Cal. 579, and would likewise leave the matter of fixing the extent of the assessment district wholly to the council, and thus avoid the defect which the Supreme Court in Moulton v. Parks held rendered the act there in question unconstitutional and void. Furthermore, in response to the objection which existed in Moulton v. Parks, it may be said, that while in that case the board of supervisors had no discretion to reject the petition, it does not appear but that the council may reject the petition required by section 38 of the Vrooman act, and it is possible therefore that by proceeding in accordance with the request of·the petitioners, this may be tantamount to an exercise by the council of its judgment upon the question as to whether or not the lands will be affected which the petitioners in effect declare will be affected by the change of grade, and thus in this indirect manner, it is possible that the council may determine over what territory the benefits are so far diffused as to render it proper to make all lands therein contribute to the cost. However, as has been stated before, it is not the purpose of this book to attempt to determine the questions of constitutional law which may arise under the provisions of these street improvement acts, nor even to go into an extended discussion of such question, but rather to suggest to the reader such possible questions of the constitutionality of these provisions as have suggested themselves to the author. Until finally settled by the Supreme Court, it would be idle to venture any postive opinions upon the constitutionality of provisions which are so susceptible of construction as those in question, especially where the constitutionality of the provisions may depend upon the scope of the meaning which should be given to one word; and the foregoing will suffice to point out some of the possible constructions of which these provisions of the act might be deemed capable.

Purpose of the Sections 38–52. The object of sections 38 *et seq.* is not only to provide means for changing the grade of a street, but also to provide suitable machinery for raising the money necessary to pay the damages suffered by those whose property is damaged by the change of grade. Two kinds of proceedings are contemplated by these sections of the act,—one against the property to be condemned for the use of the street, property that will be damaged by reason of the change in the grade,—the other to assess the property benefited by the change of grade.

Prior to the adoption of the constitution of 1879, adjoining property owners were not entitled, of legal right, in the absence of a statute allowing the same, to any compensation for damages which might result from a change of grade. [Secs. 989–990 Dillon's Municipal Corporations, 3rd ed. Shaw *v.* Crocker, 42 Cal. 435; Matter of Beal Street, 39 Cal. 495.] But this rule is altered by the new constitution which provides [Art. I, sec. 14] that "private property shall not be taken *or damaged* for public use without just compensation having been first made," etc. The old constitution [Art. I, sec. 8,] simply provided that no "private property shall *be taken* for public use without just compensation." As a result of this change in the provisions of the constitution, it is held that a municipal corporation is liable for such special consequential damages as the adjoining property receives over and above the common injury to the other abutters on the street, or the general public. [Reardon *v.* City and County of San Francisco, 66 Cal. 492.]

In Kepple *v.* City of Keokuk, 2 Am. & Eng. Corp. Cases 443, the statute in question provided that "when any grade of any street or alley shall have been established, and any person shall have built or made improvements on such streets or alleys according to the established grade thereof, and such city shall alter such established grade in such a manner as to injure or diminish the value of said property, said city shall pay to the owner or owners of said property so injured the amount of such damage or injury." Held, that, under this statute, the property owner could not recover for any changes in the surface of a street if he had erected buildings or otherwise improved his lots *before* the establishment of *any* official grade lines by the city. But in this case the right of recovery rested wholly upon the statute. The rule has been held to be otherwise in states where, as in California, the constitution expressly provides that no property shall be "damaged" without just compensation therefor. Thus in Nebraska, where the constitutional provision is similar to our own, it was held that a city is liable to a lot owner for damages sustained by him by raising the grade of the street even though he has erected improvements before any grade was established. [Harmon *v.* Omaha, 17 Neb. 548; s. c. 52 Am. Rep. 420.]

"The change of grade is a permament matter, and all resulting injury must be recovered in one action, for the property owner cannot maintain successive actions as each fresh annoyance or injury occurs. The reason for the rule is not far to seek. What is done under color of legislative authority and is of a permanent nature, works an injury as soon as it is done, if not done as the statute requires, and the injury which then accrues is, in legal contemplation, all that can accrue, for the complainant is not confined to a recovery for past or present damages but may, also, recover prospective damages resulting from the wrong. It is evident that a different rule would lead to a multiplicity of actions, and produce injustice and confusion." [Elliott on Roads and Streets, p. 345.]

In McCarthy *v.* City of St. Paul, 22 Minn. 527, the action was brought pursuant to a provision of the charter of the defendant corporation to the effect that if a grade established pursuant to the order of the common council, should be at any time thereafter altered, all damages, costs and charges arising therefrom shall be paid by the city to the owner of any lot, or parcel of land, or tenement, which may be affected or injured in consequence of the alteration of such grade. It was held *(1.)* that, under such provision of the charter, the city became liable to the plaintiff for all damage necessarily resulting to him, in respect to his property, from the change in the established grade of the street; *(2.)* that an action for the recovery of such damages accrued to plaintiff, and might be maintained by him, whenever and as soon as the alteration in the grade of the street became legally and finally determined and fixed. [By the "grade" is meant the grade line to which the surface of the street shall be brought whenever the street shall be graded or improved.] *(3.)* That, though neither the street nor the lots affected by the alteration of the grade have been actually graded to correspond therewith, the necessary cost of conforming the latter thereto is a proper element of the damages, and is not objectionable on the ground of its being contingent or prospective—so also as to the cost of building a retaining wall to protect the property from encroachments certain to occur by reason of the change of the grade. Upon this branch of the case the court said: "This statute clearly imposes upon the city, whenever it alters an established grade, a liability in favor of the owner of any lot, parcel of land, or tenement, affected or injured thereby, for all such damages, costs and charges as may be occasioned by reason of such alteration. *The alteration here referred to is not the change wrought in the surface of the street by bringing it to the altered grade, but the legal change in the grade line of the street affected by the final decision of the tribunal which is charged with the power and duty of acting in such matters.* Whenever such decision takes effect as to any street, the adjoining property is necessarily affected by it. Its value thereafter for purposes of sale or occupancy, is determined, in part, with reference to the new grade, which it must be presumed the city, in the discharge of its duty in the premises, will cause to be carried into effect as soon as may be. The right to damages arising from any such alteration accrues, therefore, to the property owner injured by it, whenever and as soon as the same becomes legally fixed and operative."

The same language is applicable to the added sections of the Vrooman act—sections 38–53. Their purpose is to enable the owner to recover from the city, whenever it alters an established grade, all such damages, costs and charges as may be occasioned by reason of such alteration. These damages are such as affect the value of the property for purposes of sale or occupancy, and are incurred as soon as the decision of the council is made changing the grade line. If the direct and necessary consequence of the act of alteration is to depreciate the value of the lots by reason of such change in the grade of the street, the expenses which must necessarily be incurred, in order to re-adjust the grade of the lots to conform to the changed condition of the street,— whenever the surface of the street shall be changed to conform to the new grade,—are as proper elements of damage as though the surface of the street had already been so changed, and such expenses had been actually incurred. The statute does not, however, contemplate a suit by the owner to recover such damages, but that the city shall itself assess the damages and offer the same, less the value of the benefits, etc., to the owner, and, if the owner refuses to accept the damages, as assessed by the city's commissioners, the city shall bring a condemnation suit, and in this suit, the property owner, as a defendant, may recover a judgment for the amount of his actual damages.

In Elliott on Roads and Streets, pages 353-4 it is said: "It is quite clear that the mere fact that a change has been made [in the grade] will not authorize the inference that private property is injured; on the contrary, the burden of showing a substantial injury rests upon the property owner, for the presumption is that the public officers, having no private interests to subserve, have not done a wrongful act to the injury of the citizen."

In their general features, the provisions of sections 38-53, as amended by the act of March 9, 1893, are quite similar to the provisions of an act approved March 28, 1868, entitled "An act to authorize the board of supervisors of the city and county of San Francisco to modify and change the grade of streets in said city and county." [Statutes 1867-8, page 463.] In fact it is not improbable that the person who drafted the act adding sections 38-53 to the Vrooman act, either copied from said act of March 28, 1868, or from some later act which had been modeled upon said act of 1868. Subdivision 2 of section 2 of said act of March 28, 1868, [statutes 1867-8, page 464] and section 39 of the Vrooman act, are substantially similar in all respects, with the exception of such differences as are necessitated by reason of the fact that in the act of 1868 the interposition of the county court is provided for, whereas no such provision is found in the Vrooman act. Both acts, in substance, require that, within a certain time after the first publication of the ordinance or resolution of intention to change the grade, any person entitled to recover damages, under the act, shall file a petition showing the fact of his or her ownership, the description and situation of the property claimed to be damaged, its market value, and the estimated amount of damages, over and above all benefits which the property would sustain by reason of the proposed change of grade if completed, etc. This provision of the said act of March 28, 1868, came before the Supreme Court in a case entitled In the Matter of Beal Street, etc., 39 Cal. 495, where it was held that under this provision of the act of March 28, 1868, it was the purpose of the legislature to confine the award of damages to those who should file the petition provided for in said subdivision 2 of section 2 of the act. The court, per Wallace J., page 499, said: "We think that a careful examination of the various provisions of the act will show that it was not its purpose to provide for the payment of damages to those who, not claiming them, might fairly be supposed to intentionally waive them; or who could not, upon their consciences, state [under oath] that they thought themselves entitled to receive them. Upon the filing of the required petition by a party supposing himself about to be damaged, all other property owners within the designated limits [*i. e.* limits of the assessment district] who possibly might thereafter be assessed as beneficiaries, must be considered as defendants denying the statements of the petitioner, interested, of course, in reducing the amount of damages claimed by him, and they should be afforded an opportunity to produce witnesses to disprove his allegations. But if no claim for damages be placed on file by the owner of a particular lot, the defendants are without the notice to enable them to prepare to resist it; and for much the same reason, we think that the commissioners, in their award of damages to any petitioner should not exceed the amount claimed by him in the petition itself, since those adversely interested may fairly be supposed to have acquiesced in the correctness of the amount claimed in the petition itself." This language seems to be just as applicable to the provisions of sections 38–53 of the present street work act, as to said act of March 28, 1868. The most important difference seems to be that at the time when the said act of 1868 was passed the property owners were not, in the absence of statutory provisions therefor, entitled, of right, to recover any damages suffered by reason of a change of grade, since such damages did not constitute a "taking of private property for public use," within the meaning of that phrase as used in the constitution. Whereas, under the provision of the present constitution, " private property shall not be taken *or damaged* for public use without just compensation," etc. So that now every property owner is, under the express provision of the constitution, entitled to recover such special consequential damages as he receives over and above the common injury to the other abutters on the street, or the general public by reason of the decision of the council changing the grade of a street. [Reardon *v.* S. F., 66 Cal. 492; Harmon *v.* Omaha, 17 Neb. 548; s. c. 52 Am. Rep. 420.] But while under the constitution the property owner has the legal right to recover such damages in such cases, and could do so in the absence of any statute giving such right, still the legislature may prescribe all reasonable regulations for the enforcement of the right, and may, therefore, provide that, to entitle a property owner to recover damages he must first file the petition provided for by section 39 of the act; and therefore, if under a similar provision of said act of March 28, 1868, it be held that the property owner cannot recover damages unless he files a petition therefor, the same reasoning should lead to a similar construction of the provisions of section 38 *et seq.* of the Vrooman act. The fact that the present constitution gives the right to recover such damages, without any special statutory provision therefor, cannot have any stronger bearing upon the question than the argument presented by the learned counsel for the respondents in said proceeding in the Matter of Beale Street, 39 Cal. 497. Public policy seems to demand that in this respect, the same construction be placed upon the provisions of sections 38–53 of the present act, as was placed upon said act of 1868, since those whose property is liable to be assessed to pay the expenses of the change of grade should be enabled to know how much will have to be paid in damages, before they can intelligently determine whether or not they will file objections to the proposed change of grade.

In Elliott on Roads and Streets, page 353, it is said: "Where the statute requires the municipality to pay or tender the damages caused by a change of grade, it has no right to proceed until this is done, and if it does an action will lie. The authority delegated is to proceed with the work in accordance with law, and if the municipal officers attempt to proceed in any other mode, they act, in legal contemplation, without authority and subject their principal to an action as a wrong-doer who has invaded private rights. The property owner who sustains and shows injury may, if he elects, enjoin the prosecution of the work until the damages are assessed and tendered."

Constitutionality of the Act adding Sections 38–53, and of the Act amending the same. The manner in which the Vrooman act of March 18, 1885, was amended by the addition of sections 38–53, demands a few words in respect to the constitutionality of the act adding these sections to the original act. But before proceeding with this question of constitutionality, it might be well to consider some of the legislative absurdities in the enactment of these amendatory acts. As stated, *supra*, these sections—sections 38–53—were first added by the act of March 31, 1891 (statutes '91, p. 461), and in 1893, by the act approved March 9, 1893, the legislature amended each of these sixteen new sections. [Statutes '93, p. 89.]

On March 17, 1891, by an act approved on that date [statutes '91, p. 116], there went into effect—if constitutionally enacted—an act entitled "An act to amend an act entitled 'An act to provide for work upon streets, lanes, alleys, courts, places, and sidewalks, and for construction of sewers within municipalities,' approved March 18, 1885, by adding thereto an additional part numbered four, consisting of sections thirty-eight, thirty-nine, forty, forty-one, forty-two, forty-three, and forty-four, relative to a system of street bonds." This act provided for a system of street bonds to cover the cost of street improvements, and added eight new sections, to the act of March 18, 1885, sections 38 to 45 inclusive. It was repealed in 1893 by the act of February 27, 1893. [Statutes '93, p. 33].

On March 31, 1891, by an act approved on that date [statutes '91 p. 461], there went into effect—if constitutionally enacted—an act entitled "An act to amend an act entitled 'An act to provide for work upon streets, lanes, alleys, courts, places, and sidewalks, and for the construction of sewers within municipalities,' approved March 18, 1885, by adding thereto certain new and additional sections, to provide for the mode of carrying into effect certain provisions of said act relative to changing grades." This act purported to amend said act of March 18, 1885, by adding thereto sixteen new sections numbered repectively 38 to 53, inclusive. But it will be observed that the said act approved March 17, 1891,—the bond act—likewise added sections numbered 38 to 45 inclusive, so that there was a conflict in the numbering of the sections. But, if there be no more serious absurdity than this, it is altogether likely that the courts will disregard this conflict in the numbers of the sections added by these two amendatory acts. Both acts have been repealed; the said act of March 17, 1891, by the act of Feb. 27, 1893 [statutes '93, p. 38], and the said act of March 31, 1891, has been superseded by the act of March 9, 1893. [Statutes '93, p. 89].

But the said act of March 9, 1893 [statutes, '93, p. 89], introduces another absurdity. It is entitled "An act to amend sections thirty-eight to fifty-three, inclusive, of an act approved March 31, 1891, adding these sections to 'An act to provide for work upon streets, alleys, lanes, courts, places, and sidewalks, and for the construction of sewers within municipalities,' approved March 18, 1885." This act, it will be noticed, purports to amend sections 38 to 53, inclusive, of the act approved March 31, 1891. But, while the act approved March 31, 1891, added sections 38 to 53, inclusive, to the act of March 18, 1885, it, itself, contained but one section, and that section was numbered number 1. By section number 1 of the act of March 31, 1891, sections 38 to 53, inclusive, were added to the act of March 18, 1885.

The act of March 9, 1893, should have amended sections 38 to 53 of the act of March 18, 1885, as those sections were added to the said act by the act of March 31, 1891, or it should have amended section 1 of the act of March 31, 1891 by providing that "Section 1 of the act of March 31, 1891, is hereby amended so as to read as follows:" etc.

But it is likely that a benignant court, merciful of such legislative stupidities as must ever be unavoidable so long as the people shall continue to compel their legislative servants to complete their bi-annual labors in a session of sixty days, or continue work as "a labor of love" only, will so far as possible, endeavor to reconcile with common sense these apparent blunders in the enactment of these statutes. But it is beyond comprehension that the draughtsman who drew these acts should not see the anomalies above pointed out. But aside from these absurdities in the enactment of these amendatory acts, there is a more serious question in connection with their enactment,—one that affects their constitutionality. Sections 38–53 were amended by the act of March 9, 1893. They were first added to the original act—the Vrooman act of March 18, 1885, by the act approved March 31, 1891. The act of March 9, 1893, is amendatory of the act of March 31, 1891. If this latter act was unconstitutional for any reason, sections 38–53 were never added to the original act, and the act of March 9, 1893, had no such sections to amend. It is possible that the act of March 31, 1891, is invalid and void, since it purports to amend the act of March 18, 1885, by adding new sections thereto, but does not re-enact and publish at length the act as amended. The constitution [Sec. 24, Art. IV,] provides: "No law shall be revised or amended by reference to its title; but in such case the act revised or section amended shall be re-enacted and published as revised or amended."

The *act revised* or *section amended* must be re-enacted and published as revised or amended.. If a *section* is amended it must be re-enacted and published as amended. Must every *act* which is *amended* be re-enacted and published as amended? Or does the constitution mean that the whole act is only to be re-enacted and published when it is *revised?* And what does the word "revised" mean? These are questions which can only be authoritatively answered by the Supreme Court. There can be no question but that an act is *"amended"* when new sections are added to it, provided they are not so far in conflict with the provisions of the original act as to operate as a repeal of portions of the old act. In such case the provisions of the latter act, which operate as a repeal of a portion of the older statute, are not, properly speaking, *amendments* of the old law. But, is the act in that case *"revised?"* An act is amended when it is revised. But, is it necessarily revised when it is amended? The only decision by our Supreme Court

which throws any light upon this question is the case of
Earl *v.* S. F. Board of Education, 55 Cal. 489. The question
in that case was as to the constitutionality of an act known
as the Traylor act, and entitled " An act to add a new section to the Political Code, to be known as section 1618,
relating to salaries of school teachers in cities having 100,-
000 inhabitants or more." Judge Ross seems to think that
this act was not an amendment to the Political Code,
because in this case it was so far in conflict with portions
of the Political Code as to operate a repeal of those portions
of the code, and in such case the provisions of the new law
are not, properly speaking, *amendments* of the old law. [See
the concurring opinion of Mr. Justice McKinstry, page 493.]

But Mr. Justice Ross says, page 492, "If treated as an
amendment at all, it is in direct conflict with section 24 of
Art. IV, of the constitution, which declares that   *   *   *
'no law shall be revised or amended by reference to its
title; but in such case, the act revised or section amended
shall be re-enacted, and published at length as revised or
amended.' There is no pretense here that the law, whatever it is, supposed to have been amended by the Traylor
act was re-enacted and published at length *as amended*, as is
expressly required by the constitution. If this law is to be
upheld as an amendment, it seems to us it would be opening the doors to the accomplishment by indirection of many
of the evils it was manifestly intended by the framers of
the constitution to prevent, and thus wipe out some of its
most salutary provisions." [But see Baum *v.* Raphael, 57
Cal. 361; see also, Mok *v.* Detroit Ass'n, 30 Mich. 511.]
The Missouri courts hold that under the constitution of
Missouri if an act is amended merely by the addition of
new sections thereto, the whole act as thus amended need
not be re-enacted and published. It is held that the provision of the Missouri constitution corresponding to the
provisions of section 24 of Art. IV of the California constitution, does not apply to such a case. [State *v.* Thurston,
(Mo.) 4 S. W. Rep. 930.]

In the absence of a direct decision by our Supreme Court
upon this question, in a case in which the question is fairly
and squarely presented, the question must remain, more or
less, in the realm of doubt, and the possible unconstitution-
ality of the act by which these new sections are added can
only be suggested, without venturing an unqualified opinion
thereon. It will be noticed that the Traylor act,—under consideration in the case of Earl *v.* S. F. Board of Education,—
did not in terms purport to amend the Political Code, but
merely stated in its title that it was "An act to add a new

section to the Political Code," etc. On the other hand, the act of March 31, 1891, by which the new sections—sections 38–53—were added to the act of March 18, 1885, expressly states in its title that it is "An act to *amend* an act entitled," etc., and section 1 expressly states that the act of March 18, 1885, "is hereby *amended* by adding thereto sections, as follows:"

SECTION 39. Within thirty days after the first publication of said notice, any person owning property fronting upon said portions of the street or streets where such change of grade is made, may file a petition with the clerk of the city council showing the fact of such ownership, the description and situation of the property claimed to be damaged, its market value, and the estimated amount of damages over and above all benefits which the property would sustain by the proposed change if completed. Such petition shall be verified by the oath of the petitioners or their agents. [*Amendment approved March 9, 1893, statutes 1893, page 90.*

Compare section 39 with subdivision 2 of section 2 of an act approved March 28, 1868 [statutes 1867–8, p. 464], and see *In re* Beale Street, 39 Cal. 495. See notes under preceding section, page   *et seq.,—supra.*

SECTION 40. Whenever such petition or petitions have been filed, the mayor, surveyor, and superintendent of streets, of the city, or city and county, acting as a board of commissioners, shall assess the benefits, damages, and costs of the proposed change of grade upon each separate lot of land situated within such assessment dsstrict, as said lot appears of record upon the last city, or city and county assessment roll. [*Amendment approved March 9, 1893, statutes 1893, p. 90.*]

SECTION 41. The commissioners shall be sworn to make the assessments of benefits and damages to the best of their judgment and ability, without fear or favor. [*Amendment approved March 9, 1893, statutes 1893, p. 90.*]

SECTION 42. The commissioners shall have power to subpœna witnesses to appear before them to be examined under oath, which any one of said commissioners is authorized to administer. [*Amendment approved March 9, 1893, statutes 1893, p. 90.*]

SECTION 43. The commissioners having determined the damage which would be sustained by each petitioner, in excess of all benefits, shall proceed to assess the total amount thereof, together with the costs, charges, and expenses of the proceedings, upon the several lots of land benefited within the district of assessment; so that each of the lots shall be assessed in accordance with its benefits caused by such work or improvement; and during the progress of their work shall make a report to such city council as often as it may be required. [*Amendment approved March 9, 1893, statutes 1893, p. 90.*]

SECTION 44. The commissioners shall make their report, in writing, and shall subscribe to the same and file with the city council. In their said report they shall describe separately each piece of property which will sustain damage, stating the amount of damages each will sustain over and above all benefits. They shall also gfve a brief description of each lot benefited within said assessment district, the name of the owner, if known, and the amount of benefits in excess of damages assessed against the same.

In case the three commissioners do not agree, the award agreed upon by any two of them shall be sufficient. In designating the lots to be assessed, reference may be had to a diagram of the property in the district affected; such diagram to be attached to and made a part of the report of the commissioners. [*Amendment approved March 9, 1893, statutes 1893, p. 91.*]

SECTION 45. If in any case the commissioners find that conflicting claims of title exist, or shall be in ignorance or doubt of the ownership of any lot or land, or any improvement thereon, or any interest therein, it shall be set down as belonging to unknown owners. Error in the designation of the owner or owners of any land or improvements, or particulars of their interest, shall not affect the validity of the assessment. On the filing of said report, the clerk of said city council shall give notice of such filing by the publication of at least ten days in one or more daily newspapers published and circulated in said city; or if there be no daily newspaper, by three successive issues in a weekly or semi-weekly newspaper so published and circulated; and said notice shall require all persons interested to show cause, if any, why such report should not be confirmed, before the city council, on a day to be fixed by the city council and stated in said notice, which day shall not be less than twenty days from the first publication thereof. [*Amendment approved March 9, 1893, statutes 1893, page 91.*]

SECTION 46. All objections shall be in writing and filed with the clerk of the city council, who shall at the next meeting after the date fixed in the notice to show cause, lay the said objections, if any, before the council, which shall fix a time for hearing the same; of which time the clerk shall notify the objectors in the same manner as are notified objectors to the original resolution of intention. At the time set, or at such other time as the hearing may be adjourned, the city council shall hear such objections and pass upon the same, and at such time shall proceed to pass upon such report, and may confirm, correct, or modify the same, or may order the commissioners to make a new assessment, report, and plat, which shall be filed, notice given and had, as in the case of an original report. In case the ordinance or resolution of intention also provides for the assessing upon the district the cost of regrading or repaving such street or streets to such changed or modified grade, after the report of the commissioners as to the damages caused by such change of grade has been passed upon by the city council, it shall then advertise for bids to perform the work of regrading, repaving, sewering, sidewalking, or curbing such street or streets with the same or other material with which the same had been formerly graded, paved, sewered, sidewalked, or curbed; first causing a notice, with specifications, to be posted conspicuously for five days on or near the council chamber door, inviting sealed proposals for bids for doing such work, and shall also cause notices of said work, inviting said proposals and referring to the specifications posted or on file, to be published two days in a daily, semi-weekly, or weekly newspaper published and circulated in said city, and designated by the city council for that purpose, and in case there is no newspaper published in the city, then it shall be posted as provided in section three of the original act to which this is amendatory. All proposals or bids offered shall be accompanied by a check, payable to the order of the mayor of the city, and certified by a responsible bank for that amount, which shall not be less than ten per cent. of the aggregate of the proposals; or by a bond for said amount, signed by the bidder and two sureties, who shall justify under oath in double said amount over and above all statutory exemptions. Said proposals or bids shall be delivered to the clerk of the said city council, and said council shall, in open session, examine and publicly declare the same; *provided, however*, that no proposal or bid shall be considered unless accompanied by a check or a bond satisfactory to the council. The city council may reject any and all bids, and may award the contract to the lowest responsible bidder, which award shall be approved by the mayor or the three-fourths vote of the city council. If not approved by the mayor or the three-fourths vote of the city council, the city council may re-advertise for proposals or bids for the performance of the work, as in the first instance, and thereafter proceed in the manner in this section provided. All checks accompanying bids 'shall be held by the clerk until the bearer has entered into a contract as herein provided; and in case he refuses so to do, then the amount of his certified check shall be declared forfeited to the city, and shall be collected and paid into its general fund, and all bonds so forfeited shall be prosecuted and the amount thereon collected paid into such fund. Notice of the awards of the contracts shall be published and posted in the same manner as hereinbefore provided for the posting of proposals for said work. [*Amendment approved March 9, 1893, statutes 1893, p. 91.*]

SECTION 47. After such contract has been awarded and entered into, the clerk of the city council shall certify to the city council that fact, together with the total amount of the cost of the same, whereupon the city council shall cause to be forwarded to the commissioners a copy of such certificate; whereupon such commissioners shall proceed to assess the cost of doing such work upon all the lots and land lying within the district to be assessed, distributing the same so that each lot will be assessed for its proportion of the same, according to the benefits it receives from the work, and in the same manner in which the damages caused by the change of grade were assessed upon the same. Such commissioners, in making such assessment, shall show the total amount for which each lot or tract is assessed, in excess of all benefits, for the total cost of changing and modifying the grade of the street, as well as the regrading, repaving, sewering, sidewalking, and curbing of the same, and costs or damages connected therewith. The provisions of the act to which this is amendatory in regard to the mode or manner of the assessment of the cost of such work shall not apply to the work herein contemplated; neither shall the provisions of the same in regard to the issuing of bonds to represent the cost of the same, nor the provisions in regard to the right of protest against the work. [*Amendment approved March 9, 1893, statutes 1893, p. 92.*]

Section 47 provides that "the provisions of the act to which this is amendatory in regard to the mode or manner of the assessment of the cost of such work shall not apply to the work herein contemplated," etc. There is an ambiguity here. If this language means that "the provisions of the act to which this *act* is amendatory * * * shall not apply," etc.—then the act referred to is the act of March 31, 1891, by which these new sections were first added to the old and original act. If the language means that "the provisions of the act to which this *section* is amendatory *

* * shall not apply," etc.—then the act referred to is, in all probability, the original act itself—the act of March 18, 1885. This latter construction is undoubtedly the true meaning of the section, as it is apparent that the intention of the legislature was to declare that the front-foot principle of assessment provided for by section 7 of the original act—the act of March 18, 1885,—should not apply in these original proceedings to change the grade, but that the district assessment plan should prevail. Neither section 47 nor section 46 provides who shall execute the written contract on behalf of the city. But section 52 provides that "all other provisions contained in the act to which this is amendatory, and which provisions are not in conflict herewith, shall apply to all matters contained herein," and as it was undoubtedly the intention of the legislature to declare by this language that the provisions of sections 1 to 37, inclusive, of the original act —the act of March 18, 1885—as the same have been amended from time to time since,—shall apply to all matters contained in the new sections—sections 38–53—when not in conflict, it seems reasonably certain that the contract is to be executed by the superintendent of streets in the same manner as the contracts for the work provided for in the prior sections of the act. [See subdivision 14 of section 34, *supra*, page 189.]

SECTION 48. The clerk of said city council shall forward to the street superintendent of the city a certified copy of the report, assessment, and plat, as finally confirmed and adopted by the city council. Such certified copy shall thereupon be the assessment roll, the cost of which shall be provided for by the commissioners, as a portion of the cost of the proceedings therein. Immediately upon receipt thereof by the street superintendent, the assessment therein contained shall become due and payable, and shall be a lien upon all the property contained or described therein. [*Amendment approved March 9, 1893, statutes 1893, p. 93.*]

SECTION 49. The superintendent of streets shall therupon give notice, by publication for ten days in one or more daily newspapers published and circulated in said city, or city and county, or two successive insertions in a weekly or semi-weekly newspaper so published and circulated, that he has received said assessment roll, and that all sums levied and assessed in said assessment roll are due and payable immediately, and that the payment of said sums is to be made to him within thirty days from the date of the first publication of said notice. Said notice shall also contain a statement that all assessments not paid before the expiration of said thirty days will be declared to be delinquent, and that thereafter the sum of five per cent. upon the amount of such delinquent assessment, together with the cost of advertising each delinquent assessment, will be added thereto. When payment of any assessment is made to said superintendent of streets, he shall write the word "paid" and the date of payment opposite the respective assessment so paid, and the name of the persons by or for whom said

assessment is paid, and shall give a receipt therefor. On the expiration of
said thirty days, all assessments then unpaid shall be and become delinquent, and said superintendent of streets shall certify such fact at the foot
of said assessment roll, and shall add five per cent. to the amount of each
assessment so delinquent. The said superintendent of streets shall, within
five days from the date of such delinquency, proceed to advertise the
various sums delinquent, and the whole thereof, including the cost of
advertising. which last shall not exceed the sum of fifty cents for each lot,
piece, or parcel of land separately assessed, by the sale of the assessed
property in the same manner as is or may be provided for the collection of
state and county taxes; and after the date of said delinquency, and before
the time of such sale herein provided for, no assessment shall be received,
unless at the same time the five per cent. added to as aforesaid, together
with the costs of advertising then already incurred, shall be paid therewith. Said list of delinquent assessments, with a notice of the time and
place of sale of the property affected thereby, shall be published daily for
five days, in one or more daily newspapers published and circulated in
such city, or by at least two insertions in a weekly newspaper so published
and circulated before the day of sale for such delinquent assessment. Said
time of sale must not be less than seven days from the date of the first
publication of said delinquent assessment list, and the place must be in or
in front of the office of said superintendent of streets. All property sold
shall be subject to redemption for one year, and in the same manner as in
sales for delinquent state and county taxes; and the superintendent of
streets shall, if there is no redemption, make and deliver to the purchaser
at such sale a deed conveying the property sold, and may collect for each
certificate fifty cents, and for each deed one dollar. All provisions of the
law in reference to the sale and redemption of property, for delinquent
state and county taxes, in force at any given time, shall also then, as far as
the same are not in conflict with the provisions of this act, be applicable
to the sale and redemption of property for delinquent assessments hereunder, including the issuance of certificates and execution of deeds. The
deed of the street superintendent, made after such sale, in case of failure
to redeem, shall be prima facie evidence of the regularity of all proceedings hereunder, and of title in the grantee. The superintendent of streets
shall from time to time pay over to the city treasurer all moneys collected
by him on account of any such assessments. The city treasurer shall,
upon receipt thereof, place the same in a separate fund, designating each
fund by the name of the street, square, lane, alley, court, or place for the
change of grade for which the assessment was made. Payments shall be
made from said fund to the parties entitled thereto, upon warrants signed
by the commissioners or a majority of them. [*Amendment approved March
9, 1893, statutes 1893, p. 93.*]

When a street work act merely provides that the assessment shall be collected in the manner prescribed by law
for the collection of general state and county taxes, the law
for the collection of taxes is referred to for the *manner* of
collecting, and not for what shall be collected, and in such
case the person collecting the assessment can not collect a
penalty for non-payment, as 5 per cent. for example, merely

because the revenue law referred to for the manner of making the collection, authorizes such a penalty. [Bucknall v. Story, 36 Cal. 67.] It is otherwise, however, when the street work act itself authorizes the collection of such penalty.

It will be noticed that section 49 provides that "all provisions of law in reference to the sale and redemption of property for delinquent state and county taxes, in force at any given time, shall also then, as far as the same are not in conflict with this act, be applicable to the sale and redemption of property for delinquent assessments hereunder."

SECTION 50. When sufficient money is in the hands of the city treasurer, in the fund voted for the proposed work or improvement, to pay the total cost for damages, as well as for the cost of doing the work, and all other expenses connected therewith, it shall be the duty of the commissioners to notify the owner, possessor or occupant of the premises damaged, and to whom damages have been awarded, that a warrant has been drawn for the payment of the same, which can be received at the office of such commissioners. Such notification may be made by depositing a notice, postage paid, in the post office, addressed to his last known place of residence. If, after the expiration of three days after the service or deposit of the notice in the post office, he shall not have applied for such warrant, the same shall be drawn and deposited with the city treasurer, to be delivered to him upon demand. [*Amendment approved March 9, 1893, statutes '93, p. 94.*]

SECTION 51. If the owner of any premises damaged neglects or refuses, for ten days after the warrant has been placed in the hands of the city treasurer, subject to his demand, to accept the same, the city council may cause proceedings to be commenced, in the name of the city, to condemn said premises, as provided by law under the right of eminent domain. The ordinance or resolution of intention shall be conclusive evidence of the necessity of the same. Such proceedings shall have precedence, so far as the business of the court will permit, and any judgment for damages therein rendered shall be payable out of the special fund in the treasury for that purpose. At any time after the trial and judgment entered, or pending appeal, the court may order the city treasurer to set apart in the city treasury a sufficient sum from said fund to answer the judgment, and thereupon may authorize or order the municipality to proceed with the proposed work or improvements. In case of a deficiency in said fund to pay the whole assessed judgment and damages, the city council may, in its discretion, order the balance thereof to be paid out of the general fund of the treasury, or to be distributed by the commissioners over the property assessed by a supplementary assessment; but in the last named case, in order to avoid delay, the city council may advance such balance out of any available fund in the treasury, and reimburse the same from the collection of assessments. The treasurer shall pay such warrants in the order of their presentation; *provided*, that warrants for damages and for costs of performing the work shall have priority over warrants for charges and expenses, and the treasurer shall see that sufficient money remains in the fund to pay all warrants of the first class before paying any of the second. The provisions of section one thousand two hundred and fifty-one of the Code of Civil Procedure, requiring the payment of damages within thirty days after the entry of judgment, shall not apply to damages rendered in proceedings under this act. [*Amendment approved March 9, 1893, statutes '93, p. 95.*]

Compensation must be made in advance, or a fund must be provided, out of which compensation must be made so soon as the amount can be determined. [Colton *v.* Rossi, 9 Cal. 595.]

SECTION 52. All other provisions contained in the act to which this is amendatory, and which provisions are not in conflict herewith, shall apply to all matters herein contained. All proceedings in any work or improvement, such as is provided for in this act, already commenced and now in progress under another act now in force, or by virtue of an ordinance or resolution of intention heretofore passed, may, from any stage of such proceedings already commenced and now in progress, be continued under this act by resolution of the city council. The said work or improvement may then be conducted under the provisions of this act, with full force and effect in all respects from the stage of such proceedings at and from which such resolution or ordinance shall declare the intention to have such work done or improvement cease under such other acts or ordinances and continued under this act; and from such election so made all proceedings theretofore had are hereby ratified, confirmed and made valid, and it shall be unnecessary to renew or conduct over again any proceedings prior to the passage of this act. [*Amendment approved March 9, 1893, statutes '93, p. 95.*]

Section 52, like section 47, *supra*, is ambiguous in this, that it does not clearly appear which act is referred to when it is declared that "all other provisions contained in the act to which this is amendatory * * * shall apply to all matters herein contained." By the act of March 31, 1891, (statutes '91, page 461,) section 52 was added to and made a part of the act of March 18, 1885, and by the act of March 9, 1893, section 52 was amended, but it still remains a part of the act of March 18, 1885, having been first imbedded therein by the said act of March 31, 1891; and, from and after the 31st day of March, 1891, the act of March 18, 1885, is to be read as though section 52—as it stood prior to the amendment of 1893—had always been a part thereof; and from and after March 9, 1893, the said act of March 18, 1885, is to be read as though section 52—as amended by the act of March 9, 1893—had always been a part thereof. "A statute which is amended is *thereafter, and as to all acts subsequently done,* to be construed as if the amendments had always been there, and the amendment itself so thoroughly becomes a part of the original statute that it must be construed in view of the original statute as it stands after the amendments are introduced, and the matters superseded by the amendments eliminated." [Endlich on the Interpretation of Statutes, § 294.] This is undoubtedly the correct rule of interpretation, but, by regarding section 52 as it now stands as being a part of the act of March 18, 1885, from and after the 9th day of March, 1893, the section speaks from out of the said act of March 18, 1885—as the same has been amended from time to time since—and according to the logical result of the application of the above rule of interpretation, the act spoken of in section 52, and whose provisions are continued in force by this section, must be some act of which the act of March 18, 1885, is amendatory. But, as the act of March 18, 1885, is not amendatory of any act, the logical consequence of the application of said rule of interpretation does not express the legislative intent, and the act referred to, the provisions of which are, by section 52, made applicable to all matters contained therein, must be either the act of March 18, 1885, itself, as it reads without the added sections—sections 38 to 53, inclusive—or else it must be the act of March 31, 1891, by which these new sections were first added. The act of March 9, 1893, by which sections 38–53 were amended, purports to be amendatory of the said act of March 31, 1891. But it cannot be that the legislature intended by section 52 to declare that "all provisions of the act of March 31, 1891, which are not in conflict herewith, shall apply to all matters herein contained," because the act of March 31, 1891, purports to add to the act of March 18, 1885, sections 38–53, and the act of March 9, 1893, purports to amend these added sections, and does so in such a complete manner that the act of March 9, 1893, must be regarded as superseding and, by implication, repealing all of the act of March 31, 1891. It seems to the author, therefore, that when section 52 declares that "all other provisions contained in the act to which this is amendatory * * * shall apply to all matters herein contained," the legislature intended thereby to declare that "all other provisions contained in the act of March 18th, 1885—to which act this is amendatory—and which provisions are not in conflict with sections 38 to 53, inclusive, shall apply to all matters in sections 38 to 53 contained."

There is another ambiguity in this part of section 52. The section declares that all other provisions contained in the act to which this is amendatory, etc., shall apply to all matters *"herein contained."* What does the phrase, "herein contained," refer to? Does it refer to the matters contained in this section, i. e., section 52; or to the matters contained in the act of March 18, 1885, as amended up to March 9, 1893; or does it refer to the matters contained in sections 38 to 53 only of the act of March 18, 1885—as these sections were

added to the said act of March 18, 1885, and subsequently
amended?

It would seem too narrow a construction to limit the
phrase "all matters herein contained," to "all matters contained in this section—section 52." And, it is obviously
too broad a construction to construe the phrase as meaning
all matters contained in the act in which section 52 is
imbedded as a part thereof, because this act, according to
the cannon of interpretation, quoted *supra*, from Endilich on
the Interpretation of Statutes, is the act of March 18, 1885,
itself, and it was obviously not the intent of the legislature
to declare that "all provisions contained in the act of March
18, 1885, * * * * shall apply to all matters contained
in the act of March 18, 1885." It is most probable therefore
that the legislature intended by this phrase to include all
matters contained in that portion of the act of March 18,
1885, which was added by the act of March 31, 1891, which
was amended by the act of March 9, 1893. So that the first
sentence of section 52 should be construed as reading as
follows: "All other provisions contained in the act of
March 18, 1885, and which are not in conflict with the
provisions of sections 38 to 53, inclusive, shall apply to all
matters contained in said sections 38 to 53, inclusive."
However, the section is so ambiguous and uncertain as to
almost defy interpretation. It is apparent that the
draughtsman who drew the act must have been deficient in
imagination. He could not have had clearly presented to
his mind the duality of the act which he was drafting,—he
could not clearly have separated in his mental vision those
portions of the act which, when the act took effect, became
a part of the original act—the act of March 18, 1885,—and
spoke out from that act as parts thereof,—from those portions of the act which did not thus become imbedded in
the act of March 18, 1885,—the last section, for example,—
section 17 of the act of March 9, 1893, which declares that
"This act (the act of March 9, 1893) shall take effect and
be in force immediately after its passage."

SECTION 53. The provisions of this act shall be liberally construed to
permit the objects thereof. [*Statutes 1893, page 96.*]

[Section 53 was amended by the act of March 9, 1893, statutes 1893, p. 96.]

Street Improvement Bond Act of 1893.

An Act to provide a system of Street Improvement Bonds to represent certain assessments for the cost of street work and improvement within municipalities, and also for the payment of such bonds.

[Approved February 27, 1893.]

The people of the state of California, represented in senate and assembly, do enact as follows:

SECTION 1. Wherever in this act the phrase "Street Work Act" is used, it means and shall be taken to mean the act entitled "An act to provide for work upon streets, lanes, alleys, courts, places and sidewalks, and for construction of sewers within municipalities," approved March eighteen, eighteen hundred and eighty-five, and all acts amendatory thereof or supplementary thereto; and wherever in this act the name of any municipal body or officer is used, or any word or phrase is used which is not herein expressly defined, it means and shall be taken to mean such municipal body or officer, or word or phrase as the same is expressly defined in said street work act, and in all acts amendatory thereof or supplementary thereto. [Statutes 1893, page 33.]

The object of the act is clearly declared by the first sentence of section 2, namely: "Whenever the city council of any municipality in this state shall find, upon estimates of the city engineer, that the cost of any proposed work or improvement authorized by said street work act, [the act of March 18, 1885] will be greater than one dollar per front foot along each line of the street so proposed to be improved, including the cost of intersection work assessable upon said frontage, it shall have the power, in its discretion, to determine that serial bonds shall be issued to represent the cost of said work or improvement in the manner and form hereinafter provided." Or, as more pithily stated in its title, the object of the act is "to provide a system of street improvement bonds."

The act is, in effect, supplementary to the Vrooman act of March 18, 1885. The latter act provides what work may be done upon streets, and provides the machinery for letting contracts for doing the work and for meeting the expenses of the same. The machinery for meeting these expenses, as provided for by the said act of March 18, 1885, contemplates cash payments after the assessment roll is made up, and fiter the proper proceedings prerequisite to the right to cash payments, such as "demand," etc., have been had. The above act of Feb'y 27, 1893, supplements this part of the machinery of the act of March 18, 1885, and provides different machinery for meeting the expenses of the improvements,—machinery that contemplates the issuance of serial bonds to pay for the cost of the work.

Throughout the act, the provisions of the street improvement act of March 18, 1885, and of all acts amendatory thereof or supplemental thereto, are referred to, and, by reference made a part of the act. These acts are referred to under the general designation of the "Street Work Act," which phrase is, by section 1 of the act, defined to be the said act of March 18, 1885, and all acts amendatory thereof or supplemental thereto, and, by section 6 of the said act of Feb'y 27, 1893, it is provided that "all provisions of the 'Street Work Act,' not inconsistent with the provisions hereof, shall apply hereto." But whether said phrase "provisions hereof" means "provisions of this section—section six," or "provisions of this act" may be open to question.

In 1891, [statutes' 91, p. 116] by an act approved March 17, 1891, the legislature passed an act similar in its provisions to the above act of Feb'y 27, 1893; only, while the latter act, in a measure stands by itself, and only *by reference*, incorporates within itself the provisions of the general street improvement act of March 18, 1885, and the acts amendatory thereof or supplemental thereto, the said act of March 17, 1891, on the other hand, tacked its provisions on to the act of March 18, 1885, by adding thereto an additional part numbered Part IV, consisting of seven new sections numbered 38 to 44, inclusive. [Statutes 1891, p. 116.] Section 8 of the act of Feb'y 27, 1893, [statutes '93, p. 38] expressly repeals said act of March 17, 1891, except as to proceedings theretofore commenced thereunder.

It will be noticed from a perusal of the bond act—the act of February 27, 1893—that it does not provide for the issuance of municipal bonds, backed by the resources of the whole city, authorized by popular vote, and payable out of general taxation. Such municipal bonds are provided for by the municipal indebtedness act, the act of March 19, 1889 [statutes 1889, p. 399], entitled "An act authorizing the incurring of indebtedness by cities, towns, and municipal corporations, incorporated under the laws of this state, for the construction of water works, sewers, and all necessary public improvements, or for any purpose whatever," etc., and the acts amendatory thereof. [See this municipal indebtedness act, *infra*.] The street improvement bond act—the act of Feb'y 27, 1893—on the other hand provides that each bond issued under it shall be a lien upon a particular lot or parcel of land, each bond being issued to represent the assessment against each particular lot or parcel of land, which is upon the list of unpaid assessments, mentioned in section 4 of the act. Each bond stands by itself; and if default be made in any payment, the bond becomes wholly due at the option of the holder, who can immediately collect *without suit*. The provisions of the act enabling the bond holder to collect without suit are most important. Under the general street improvement act— the Vrooman act of March 18, 1885,—the contractor or his assignee, after the issuance of a warrant, etc., and after demand, etc., brings suit against the lot owner as provided for in section 12 of that act, and in this suit the lot owner may set up in defense any facts which show that the assessment is void. [See *supra* p. 141 *et seq.*] But, when bonds are issued under this street bond act, the bond holder does not sue the property owner. He serves a written demand upon the city treasurer, who then proceeds to collect the amount due on the bond by sale of the lot in the same manner that unpaid state and county taxes are collected, as provided for in section 5 of the act. Furthermore, the bonds are, by section 4 of the act, made *conclusive evidence* of the regularity of all proceedings previous to the making of the certified list of unpaid assessments. [See notes under section 4 *infra*.] It is vitally important therefore, that the owner who desires to contest the validity of the proceedings, should give written notice to the city treasurer, as provided for by section 4, that he desires no bond to be issued for the assessment upon his lot or parcel of land. This notice will stop the issuance of such bond, and the contractor or his assignee will be compelled to bring suit as provided for by section 12 of the general street improvement act, and in this suit the property owner may set up in defense any facts showing the assessment to be invalid. See *supra* Sec. 12 of the act of March 18, 1885, p. 141 *et seq.*] But, if bonds are issued representing the assessment against his lot, and if the act be constitutional, he is practically remediless, except that after sale of his lot, he might have an action at law to recover possession. For as the bond holder does not have to initiate proceedings in court, but may collect without suit, the property owner does not enjoy the advantages of a defendant resisting the collection of an illegal assessment, but must himself take the initiative. His only possible remedy is an injunction to enjoin the sale of his lot. But even this remedy is denied to him, if the act'be constitutional. His property having received the benefit of the work, he cannot go into a court of equity and ask equitable relief. He who seeks equity must do equity. And this he cannot do without at least paying the reasonable value of the improvement to his lot.

Courts of equity do not review the proceeding of officers entrusted with the assessment of property. If proceedings taken by them are void, no title will pass by a sale of the real estate, and the party claiming to be injured must litigate his rights in an action at law for the possession of the premises. So long as a moral obligation to pay any portion of the tax exists, a court of equity will not lend its aid to prevent a cloud upon the title, but will leave the party to his remedy at law. [Esterbrook v. O'Brien, decided July 13, 1893, 33 Pac. Rep. 765; Weber v. San Francisco, 1 Cal. 455; Bucknall v. Story, 36 Cal. 67; Lent v. Tillson, 72 Cal. 433; See supra p. 143.] And if after the sale of his lot by the city treasurer the property owner commences ejectment to recover possession of his lot, he is confronted with that provision of the act [section 4 of the bond act—the act of Feb'y 27, 1893,] which makes the issuance of the bonds conclusive evidence of the regularity of all proceedings previous to the making of the certified list of unpaid assessments provided for by section 4 of the act. So that the owner who thinks he ought not to pay the sum assessed against his lot, should see that no bond is issued, by presenting to the city treasurer the affidavit and certificate of title, and notice in writing, provided for by section 4 of the act.

Constitutionality of the Act. The constitutionality of the bond act of Feb'y 27, 1893, might be attackable upon, *(1.)* grounds peculiar to acts of a similar nature, or *(2.)* upon grounds to which any act might be subject, *e. g.*, that the title is not sufficient, etc., or other defects respecting the form of the act, or the manner of its passage. A brief consideration may be given to the question as to whether the act is open to objections embraced by either one of these classes of constitutional grounds of attack, taking up first the second or broader class, *i. e.*, that class of defects which appertain to the form of the act, or the manner of its passage or enactment.

(a.) It is possible that the act might be unconstitutional upon the ground that it is violative of that provision of section 24 of article IV of the constitution, which declares that "no law shall be revised or amended by reference to its title; but in such case the act revised or section amended shall

be re-enacted and published at length as revised or amended." This provision of the constitution, and its possible applicability to the act of March 31, 1891, statutes 1891, page 461, by which sections 38–53 were added to the general street improvement act of March 18, 1885, as well as to the act of March 9, 1893, statutes 1893, page 89, by which these added sections were amended, was considered in the notes to section 38 of said general street improvement act of March 18, 1885. [See *supra*, page 204 *et seq*.]And if the said act of March 31, 1891, by which said sections 38–53 were added to the act of March 18, 1885, be violative of this provision of the constitution, then, for the same reason, the said bond act of March 17, 1891, by which Part IV was added to the act of March 18, 1885, must be unconstitutional. But the act of March 17, 1891, has been expressly repealed by the bond act of Feb'y 27, 1893, and the question is: Is this latter act constitutional? It is true this act—the act of Feb'y 27, 1893—does not, in terms, purport to be amendatory of any other act, yet, *for its own purposes*, it does make very important amendments to certain parts of the general street improvement act, the Vrooman act of March 18, 1885. Thus, for the purpose of effecting the objects of this act—*i. e.*, the bond act of Feb'y 27, 1893—the act declares that "when the council shall determine that serial bonds shall be issued to represent the expenses of any proposed work or improvement under the street work act, [*i. e.*, the act of March 18, 1885] it shall so declare in the resolution of intention to do said work, and shall specify the rate of interest which they shall bear," etc. [Section 3 of act of Feb'y 27, 1893.] Therefore, for the purpose of effecting the object of the bond act—the act of Feb'y 27, 1893—section 3 of the Vrooman act of March 18, 1885, is, in effect, amended. For, section 3 of the act of March 18, 1885—the general street improvement act—provides what the resolution of intention shall contain. But, when serial bonds are to be issued to pay the expenses of the work, then section 3 of the act of Feb'y 27, 1893—the bond act—provides that the resolution of intention shall contain certain other things; and, therefore, for the purpose of effecting the purposes of this act of Feb'y 27, 1893, section 3 thereof, in effect, amends section 3 of the general street improvement act—the Vrooman act of March 18, 1885—and, according to a decision of the Supreme Court of Michigan, this seems to be in contravention of the said provision of section 24, article IV of our constitution. The constitution of Michigan contains a similar provision, and in the case Mok *v.* Detroit Ass'n, 30 Mich. 511, the Supreme Court of Michigan, per Cooley, J., held that an act to authorize proceedings under another act, which simply refers for its rule of action to a third, the provisions of the latter being left unchanged for their original purposes, but modified by the act in question for its own purpose, is unconstitutional and void.   The act held to be void in this case was one for the incorporation of buildings and savings associations, passed in 1869.   It provided that such corporations should be organized under the provisions of an act of 1855 for the incorporation of companies for building and leasing houses, and this latter act, in turn, provided that such latter corporations should be organized under the provisions of an act of 1853, for the incorporation of mining and manufacturing companies.   Thus, the act of 1869 undertook, for the purposes of such corporations as it itself attempted to provide for, to dispense with and change some of the provisions and requirements of the act of 1853. *Held*, that the act of 1853, thus indirectly referred to, became, by construction, incorporated into and a part of the act of 1869, but with several changes and modifications; that the act of 1869, therefore, for its own purposes, amended portions of the act of 1853; and as these amendments were not made by re-enactment of the sections changed or modified, but only by indicating the extent of the changes, leaving the parties concerned in the act to fit the new act to the old as best they may, that, therefore, it was contrary to the constitution and void.

If this be a correct application of the constitutional provision above quoted,—section 24, act IV—it is difficult to differentiate this Michigan case from the case presented by the bond act,—the act of Feb'y 27, 1893.   It is true, that in the Michigan case the act of 1869, held to be unconstitutional, referred to the act of 1853, mediately and indirectly, by referring to the act of 1855, which in turn, referred to the act of 1853.   But this is inconsequential.   The act of 1869 was held unconstitutional because, by reference, it made portions of the act of 1853 a part of itself, and, *for its own purposes*, amended portions of the act of 1853.   So with the bond act—the act of Feb'y 27, 1893—by reference it makes the act of March 18, 1885, and the acts amendatory thereof or supplementary thereto—designated under the general phrase of "Street Work Act"—a part of itself, and, at the same time, and for its own purposes, changes and modifies some of the sections of the said act of March 18, 1885,—section 3 thereof, for example, as above pointed out,—but none of these sections of the general street improvement act, thus changed and modified for the purposes of the bond act, are re-enacted or published. See also

in this connection the opinion of Mr. Justice McKinstry in
Earle *v.* S. F. Board of Education, 55 Cal. 493-4, where he
says: "But if * * * the Traylor act can, for any purpose, be treated as an intended amendment of any portion
of the Political Code, it is an amendment of the section
thereof with which it conflicts, to wit: § 1617. * * * *
Section 24 of article IV of the constitution declares that 'no
law shall be amended by reference to its title, but in such
case, the section amended shall be re-enacted and published
at length.' The Traylor act is not a re-enactment of § 1617
of the Political Code *as amended.*" In that case Mr. Justice
McKinstry held that the Traylor act was not an amendment
of any section of the Political Code, because it was so far in
conflict with portions of the Political Code, as to operate a
repeal of these portions, instead of an *amendment* thereof,
and added that if it could, *for any purpose,* be treated as an
intended amendment of any portion of the Political Code, it
is the section thereof with which it conflicts, viz., § 1617,
but if this be admitted, then it contravenes the said provision
of section 24 of acticle IV of the constitution. But it cannot be said that the bond act—the act of Feb'y 27, 1893—
repeals any portions of the act of March 18, 1885.

For all the purposes of the Vrooman act—the act of
March 18, 1885—all the provisions of the said Vrooman
act are left as they stood prior to the enactment of the bond
act; but, to effect its own purposes, the bond act changes or
modifies certain provisions of the said Vrooman act of
March 18, 1885, or adds certain requirements to them,
without repealing. However, it is the author's purpose to
merely suggest these possible constitutional objections, and
not to advance any opinion of his own, and such possible
constitutional objections as might be raised to an act of this
nature, regardless of its form or the manner of its enactment, will next be considered.

(b.) It might be admitted that the legislature has the
power,—in the exercise of its taxing power—to compel
property owners to pay assessments to defray the expenses
of public street improvements,—provided there is adopted
some principle of apportionment approximating equality
and uniformity, which can be referred to the general
sovereign right of taxation,—and, nevertheless, it might be
urged that the legislature has not the power to issue bonds
to defray these expenses, and, by making these bonds a lien
upon the land for any number of years, thus, in effect,
execute for the property owner, in proceedings *in invitum,*
that which might be tantamount to a mortgage upon his
property.

The act provides, (section 4,) that a separate bond shall be issued for each lot or parcel of land assessed, representing upon each lot or parcel of land upon the list of unpaid assessments, the total amount of the assessment for such lot or parcel of land, as shown on such list. The same section likewise provides that the assessment shall be a first lien upon the property affected thereby, until the bond issued for the payment of such assessment, and the accrued interest thereon, shall be fully paid.

In answer to the constitutional objection above suggested, the reply might be made that the act, (section 4) makes it optional with each property owner as to whether he shall elect to have a bond issued representing the assessment upon his lot or elect to allow the assessment to be collected in the ordinary mode as provided in the general street improvement act,—the act of March 18, 1885. By section 4, it is provided that "if any person * * * * notifies said treasurer, in writing, that he desires no bond to be issued for the assessment upon said lot or parcel of land, then no such bond shall be issued therefore, and the payee of the warrant, or his assignee, shall retain the right for enforcing collection, as if said lot or parcel of land had not been so listed by the street superintendent." On the other hand, in rebuttal to this reply, it might be urged that, if the council shall determine that serial bonds shall be issued to represent the cost of any proposed work or improvement authorized by the said act of March 18, 1885, the contractors might for that reason put in bids in larger amounts than they otherwise would, and that therefore, notwithstanding any property owner may elect not to have issued a bond representing the assessment upon his lot, his assessment might be greater than it would be if the proceedings were not had under this bond act.

On the other hand it might be said, in reply to this last objection, as was said in Doyle v. Austin, 47 Cal. 353, 359, "As they (the property owners) have the benefit of the credit, it is but just that they should pay the accruing interest, *and any discount which might be suffered in the sale of bonds.*" In this case of Doyle v. Austin, the act of April 1, 1872,—an act to open and establish a street in the city and county of San Francisco, to be called "Montgomery avenue," and to take private lands therefor, [statutes 1871–2, p. 911]—was assailed on the ground that it was unconstitutional. That act provided [Sec. 8] that "all the damages, costs and expenses arising from or incidental to the opening of said avenue being fixed and determined, * * * said board shall cause to be prepared and issued bonds in sums of not less than one thousand dollars each, for such an amount as shall be necessary to pay and discharge all said damages, costs and expenses." By section 11 of that act it was provided that "There shall be levied, assessed and collected, annually, at the same time and in the same manner as other taxes are levied, assessed and collected in said city and county, a tax upon lands described in section 4 of this act, sufficient to pay the interest upon said bonds as the same mature.   *   *   *   There shall be levied, assessed and collected annually, commencing with the year 1880, at the same time and in the same manner, and upon the same lands, and in accordance with the same rule of assessment upon enhanced values,   *   *   *   a tax of one per cent. upon each one hundred dollars valuation, which shall constitute a sinking fund for the redemption of said bonds." Section 4 of the act described a certain district; and by section 3, it was provided that the lands in this district should be assessed to pay the value of the land taken, the damages to the improvements, and all other expenses, in proportion to the benefits accruing to the several lots in said district.   By section 24 it was provided that "the city and county of San Francisco shall not in any event whatever be liable for the payment of the bonds, nor any part thereof."   After deciding that the act provided for an "assessment" to defray the expenses, and not for a "tax," in the strict sense, the court, per Crockett, J., page 358, continued: "It is next objected that it is not competent for the legislature to impose upon the property to be benefited, a greater burden than will be sufficient to defray the cost of improvement, and it is said that under this act the property is charged not only with the actual cost of improvement, but with an additional sum sufficient to cover the interest to accrue on the bonds, and such discount as may be suffered in converting them into cash.   But instead of requiring the cost of the improvement to be paid in cash during the progress or on the completion of the work, the act provides for raising the money by the sale of bonds, payable at a future day, the annual interest on which, and the ultimate redemption of the principal, are provided for by an assessment of the property it can be claimed that by this process the property is charged with anything more than the cost of the improvement.   *The interest on the bonds, and the discount, if any, on the sale of them, are incidental expenses incurred in providing a sufficient fund for the accomplishment of the work,* without exacting in cash from the property owners the

necessary sum.   It is a provision for their benefit, which
enables them to pay the cost of the improvement in easy
installments, instead of paying the whole sum on the completion of the work.   As they will have the benefit of the
credit, it is but just that they should pay the accruing interest, and any discount which may be suffered in the sale of
bonds.   As before stated, the interest and discount are but
incidental expenses of the enterprise, and, upon principle,
stand upon the same footing as the compensation of the
officers who superintend it."

SECTION 2.   Whenever the city council of any municipality in this state
shall find, upon estimates of the city engineer, that the cost of any proposed work or improvement authorized by said street work act will be
greater than one dollar per front foot along each line of the street so proposed to be improved, including the cost of intersection work assessable
upon said frontage, it shall have the power, in its discretion, to determine
that serial bonds shall be issued to represent the cost of said work or
improvement in the manner and form hereinafter provided.   Said serial
bonds shall extend over a period not to exceed ten years from their date,
and an even annual proportion of the principal sum thereof shall be payable, by coupon, on the second day of January every year after their date,
until the whole is paid, and the interest shall be payable semi-annually,
by coupon, on the second days of January and July, respectively, of each
year, at the rate of not to exceed ten per cent. per annum on all sums
unpaid, until the whole of said principal and interest are paid.   Said
bonds and interest thereon shall be paid at the office of the city treasurer
of said municipality, who shall keep a fund designated by the name of
said bonds, into which he shall receive all sums paid him for the principal
of said bonds and the interest thereon, and from which he shall disburse
such sums upon the presentation of said coupons; and under no circumstances shall said bonds or the interest thereon be paid out of any other fund.
Said city treasurer shall keep a register in his office, which shall show the
series, number, date, amount, rate of interest, payee and indorsees of each
bond, and the number and amount of each coupon of principal or interest
paid by him, and shall cancel and file each coupon so paid.   [*Statutes 1893,
p. 33.*]

SECTION 3.   When said city council shall determine that serial bonds
shall be issued to represent the expenses of any proposed work or improvement under said street work act, it shall so declare in the resolution of
intention to do said work, and shall specify the rate of interest which they
shall bear.   The like description of said bonds shall be inserted in the
resolution ordering the work, in the resolution of award, and in all notices
of said proceedings required by said street work act to be either posted or
published; and also a notice that a bond will issue to represent each
assessment of fifty dollars or more remaining unpaid for thirty days after
the date of the warrant, or five days after the decision of said council upon
an appeal, and describing the bonds, shall be included in the warrant provided for in section nine of said street work act.   [*Statutes 1893, p. 34.*]

SECTION 4. After the full expiration of thirty days from the date of the
warrant, or if an appeal be taken to the city counci¹, as provided in section
eleven of said street work act, then five days after the final decison of said
council, and after the street superintendent shall have recorded the return
as provided in section 10 of the same act, the street superintendent shall make
and certify to the city treasurer a complete list of all assessments unpaid,
which amount to fifty dollars or over upon any assessment or diagram number; and said treasurer shall thereupon make out, sign and issue to the conractor or his assigns, payee of the warrant and assessment, a separate bond,
representing upon each lot or parcel of land upon said list the total amount
of the assessments against the same, as thereon shown. And if said lot or
parcel of land is described upon said assessment and diagram by its number or block, or both, and is also designated by its number or block, or
both, upon the official map of said municipality, or upon any map on file
in the office of the county recorder of the county in which said municipality is situated, then it shall be in said bond a sufficient description of said
lot or parcel of land to designate it by said number or block, or both, as it
appears on said official or recorded map. Said bond shall be substantially
in the following form :

STREET IMPROVEMENT BOND.

Series (designating it), in the city (or other form of the municipality) of
(naming it).

$———— 100̄   No. ————.

Under and by virtue of an act of the legislature of the state of California
(title of this act), I, out of the fund for the above designated street
improvement bonds, series ————, will pay to ————, or order, the
sum of ———— ($————), with interest at the rate of ———— per cent,
per annum, all as is hereinafter specified, and at the office of the ————
treasurer of the ———— of ————, state of California. This bond is
issued to represent the cost of certain street work upon ——— ——, in the
———— of ————, as the same is more fully described in assessment
number ————, issued by the street superintendent of said ——————,
after his acceptance of said work, and recorded in his office. Its amount
is the amount assessed in said assessment against the lot or parcel of land
numbered therein, and in the diagram attached thereto, as number ————,
and which now remains unpaid, but until paid, with accrued interest, is a
first lien upon the property affected thereby, as the same is described herein,
and in said recorded assessment with its diagram, to wit: the lot or parcel
of land in said ———— of ————, county of ————, state of California,
————————.

This bond is payable exclusively from said fund, and neither the
municipality nor any officer thereof is to be holden for payment otherwise
of its principal or interest. The term of this bond is ————— years from
its date, and at the expiration of said time the whole sum then unpaid
shall be due and payable; but on the second day of January of each year
after its date an even annual proportion of its whole amount is due and
payable, upon presentation of the coupon therefor, until the whole is paid,
with all accrued interest at the rate of ———— per centum per annum.
The interest is payable semi-annually, to wit, on the second days of January and of July in each year hereafter, upon presentation of the coupons

therefor, the first of which is for the interest from date to the next second day of ———————, and thereafter the interest coupons are for semi-annual interest, except the last, which is for interest from the semi-annual payment next preceding and to the date of the final maturity of this bond. Should default be made in the annual payment upon the principal, or in any payment of interest, from the owner of said lot or parcel of land, or any one in his behalf, the holder of this bond is entitled to declare the whole unpaid amount to be due and payable, and to have said lot or parcel of land advertised and sold forthwith, in the manner provided by law for sale of land assessed for state and county taxes delinquent in the payment thereof.

At said ——————— of ———————, this ——————— day of ———————, in the year one thousand ——————— hundred and ———————.

——————— ———————,

City Treasurer of the ——————— of ———————.

Provided, that in case the amount of unpaid assessments upon any lot or parcel of land shall be less than fifty dollars, then the same shall be collected as is hereinbefore provided in part one of said street work act.

Provided, also, that if any person, or his authorized agent, shall at any time before the issuance of the bond for said assessment upon his lot or parcel of land, present to the city treasurer his affidavit, made before a competent officer, that he is the owner of a lot or parcel of land in said list, accompanied by the certificate of a searcher of records, that he is such owner of record, and with such affidavit and certificate, such person notifies said treasurer, in writing, that he desires no bond to be issued for the assessments upon said lot or parcel of land, then no such bond shall be issued therefor, and the payee of the warrant, or his assigns, shall retain his right for enforcing collection, as if said lot or parcel of land had not been so listed by the street superintendent. The bonds so issued by said treasurer shall be payable to the party to whom they issue, or order, and shall be serial bonds, as is hereinbefore described, and shall bear interest at the rate specified in the resolution of intention to do said work. They shall have annual coupons attached thereto, payable in annual order, on the second day of January in each year after the date of the bond, until all are paid, and each coupon shall be for an even annual proportion of the principal of the bond. They shall have semi-annual interest coupons thereto attached, the first of which shall be payable upon the second day of January or July, as the case may be, next after its date, and shall be for the interest accrued at that time, and the last of which shall be for the amount of interest accruing from the second day of January or July, as the case may be, next preceding the maturity of said bonds to the maturity thereof. The city treasurer shall, in addition to his other duties in the premises, report all coupon payments of principal upon said bonds to the street superintendent, who shall forthwith indorse the same upon the margin of the record of the assessment to the credit of which the same is paid, and said assessment shall be a first lien upon the property affected thereby, until the bond issued for the payment thereof, and the accrued interest thereon, shall be fully paid. Said bonds, by their issuance, shall be conclusive evidence of the regularity of all proceedings thereto under said street work act and this act, previous to the making of the certified list of all assessments unpaid to the amount of fifty dollars or over by the street superintendent, to the city treasurer, and of the validity of said lien, up to the date of said list. [*Statutes 1893, page 34.*]

This section purports to make the bonds, by their issuance, *conclusive* evidence of the regularity of all proceedings thereto previous to the making by the superintendent of streets of the certified list of unpaid assessments; and also *conclusive* evidence of the validity of the lien, up to the date of said list. How far the legislature has the constitutional power to make these bonds *conclusive* evidence of the regularity of such proceedings, and of said lien, is a question which lies outside the plan of this book, and therefore will not receive that attention here which its importance would otherwise demand in a work upon the general principles of municipal corporation law in relation to the improvement of streets. A correct statement of the rule upon this matter is, perhaps as follows: The legislature has the power to declare that a neglect to perform any act, which it has the power to dispense with in the outset, will not affect the validity of the lien, and, therefore, it has the power to declare that the bonds shall be conclusive evidence of the due performance of such acts as it may thus dispense with at the outset; but, as to those things which the legislature can not dispense with, *e. g.*, notice, actual or constructive, to the property owner that his property is liable to be become charged with an assessment,—the legislature cannot make the bonds conclusive evidence that such things were done. It may make the bonds conclusive evidence as to regularity in respect to the *manner* of doing these necessary things, but may not make the bonds conclusive evidence that these things were, in in fact, done. [See McCready *v.* Sexton, 29 Iowa, 356; Strode *v.* Washer, (Or.) 16 Pac. Rep. 926; Joslyn *v.* Rockwell, 128 N. Y. 334; Cooley on Taxation, (ed. 1886) 521; Marx *v.* Hawthorn, 13 Sup. Ct. Rep. 508; Cooley's Constitutional Limitations (3rd ed.) page 369; Desty on Taxation, Vol. II p. 953.]

SECTION 5   Whenever, through the default of the owner of any lot or parcel of land to represent the assessment upon which such bond has been issued, any payment, either upon the principal or of the interest, shall not be made when the same is due, and the holder of the bond thereupon demands, in writing, that the said city treasurer proceed to advertise and sell said lot or parcel of land, as herein provided, then the whole bond, or its unpaid remainder, with its accrued interest, shall become due and payable immediately, and on the day following shall become delinquent; and the city treasurer shall have, and shall act thereafter with, all the powers and duties of the tax collector in the collection of unpaid state and county taxes, and shall forthwith proceed to advertise and sell said lot or parcel of land by proceedings in all respects the same as are provided by law for the collection of delinquent state and county taxes. All such provisions and proceedings, after taxes have become delinquent, including the certificate of sale, the right of redemption, and the deed, with the respective costs thereof, are hereby made applicable to this case. [*Statutes 1893, p. 36.*]

Where a street improvement act refers to the law for the collection of delinquent state and county taxes for the *manner* in which the street assessment is to be collected, the law for the collection of taxes is referred to as providing simply the *manner* of collecting, and not what shall be collected; and, therefore, in such case, a percentage as a penalty for delinquencies can not be added, simply because the general revenue law thus referred to, allows the collection of such penalty where a tax has become delinquent. [Bucknall *v.* Story, 36 Cal. 67.]

SECTION 6. Whenever any railroad track or tracks of any description exists upon any street or streets on which the city council has ordered word to be done or improvements made, excepting therefrom such portions as is required by law to be kept in order or repair by any person or company having railroad tracks thereon, the said council may, at any time thereafter, order such person or company to perform upon said excepted portion the work or improvements, similar in all respects to that already ordered to be performed under the same specifications and superintendence, with the same materials, within the same time, and to the like satisfaction and acceptance. Thereupon it shall be the duty of the clerk of said council to deliver immediately a copy of such order, certified by him, to such person or company, and to make and preserve in his office a certificate of such delivery, its date, and upon whom made. Should such person or company, for thirty days, or within such extension of time as the city council may grant, thereafter refuse or neglect to make or have made such work or improvement in the manner or time ordered, it shall be the duty of the city council to have such work or improvement performed, and such refusal or neglect punished in the manner provided by law. Within fifteen days after receiving the certified copy of said order, such person or company may file with the clerk of said council a written assumption of the performance of said work or improvement, according to the order, or a request to the council to have such work or improvement performed, for and at the expense of such person or company, in the manner herein provided. The failure to file such instrument within said time shall be taken and deemed to be a refusal to comply with the order. Upon reception of said assumption of the direct performance of said work or improvement, the city council shall take no further proceedings in the matter, unless such person or company neglects or fails for thirty days, or such further time as the council may grant, to comply with the provisions of the order. But if such person or company files the said request that the said council have such work or improvement performed, or fails to perform said work within thirty days, or within such further time as the council may grant, then said city council may pass an ordinance of intention to perform said work, which ordinance shall specify the work to be performed, and a statement that unless within thirty days after the recording of the return of the warrant, or within five days after the final decision of the council on an appeal, the said person or company shall pay the cost of said work, or the street superintendent of said city shall issue bonds to represent the cost of said work, stating also that the cost of said work, in case bonds shall issue, shall be paid in ten yearly installments, and also the rate of interest (not to exceed ten per cent. per annum) that the same shall bear. The subsequent procedure shall be as provided by the "street work act." A similar statement shall also be incorporated in all notices required to be posted or published by the provisions of the "street work act;" also in the ordinance or resolution ordering the work, advertisement for proposals, and in the contract. Whenever the person or company owning any such railroad shall not have, within thirty days after the recording of the return of the warrant, or within five days after the final decision of the council on an appeal, paid the cost of such work, the street superintendent shall issue to the contractor, or his assigns, bonds for the amount of such cost, which shall describe the franchise, tracks, and roadbed along or between which said work has been performed, and describing the same as upon the assessment and diagram, giving its assessment number. Such bonds shall also describe the work performed, giving the total amount of the cost of such work, the name of the owner of said railroad, the number of installments in which the cost of the work is to be paid, and the rate of interest which the deferred payments shall bear. Said bonds shall be in sums of not less than one hundred dollars or more than one thousand dollars, and shall recite that the total amount of the cost of such work, together with the interest thereon, as represented in said bonds, is, except state, county and municipal taxes, a first lien upon all the track, roadbed, switches and franchises of said railroad lying within the corporate limits of the city or town, on any part of which said work has been performed. Said street superintendent shall also keep a record of such bonds, as required by section eighteen of the "street work act." Whenever bonds have been issued, as herein provided, the same, together with the cost of such work and the interest thereon, shall be, except state, county or municipal taxes, a first lien upon all the tracks, roadbed, switches and franchises of said railroad within the corporate limits of the city or town, on any part of which said work has been performed. Sections four and five of this act, regarding the form, issuance and foreclosure of street bonds and the sale of property described therein, shall apply hereto, except that the work required to be performed by the treasurer by said sections shall be performed by the street superintendent, in so far as the bonds for the paving of railroads are concerned. None of the provisions of the "street work act" in regard to a protest against the work shall apply to any work contemplated by this section. All provisions of the "street work act" not inconsistent with the provisions hereof, shall apply hereto. [*Statutes '93, p. 36.*]

Section 6 purports to provide the machinery whereby the city authorities may compel the persons or companies owning or having railroads tracks on any street, to perform upon the portions of such street which such persons or companies are by law required to keep in order or repair, any work or improvement similar to that which may have been already ordered to be performed on such street. The other sections of the act assume that other acts, designated collectively under the phrase "Street Work Act," provide the machinery enabling the city authorities to order the improvement of streets and to compel the property owners affected to pay the expenses thereof by assessments; and then, as supplementary to the provisions of said other acts, these other sections of the bond act of February 27, 1893, provide the machinery for the issuance of said bonds to pay such expenses, in those cases where the council elects to do so as provided in section 2 of the act. The provisions of these other sections seem to be fully covered by the title of the act, "An act to provide a system of street improvement bonds to represent certain assessments for the cost of street work and improvements within municipalities, and also for the payment of such bonds." But section 6 of the act, not only provides for the issuance of bonds to pay the cost of such work as is required to be done by the owners of street railways, but likewise purports to provide the machinery for compelling the owners of such railways to do such work or to have it done at their expense. In this respect section 6 of the act seems to contravene the requirement of section 24 of article IV of the constitution that "every act shall embrace but one subject which subject shall be expressed in its title." Since, in so far as section six attempts to provide the machinery for enabling the city authorities to order to be done any work which they are not enabled to order to be done under the acts embraced by the general phrase "Street Work Act," the act embraces a subject not expressed in its title, and as to this subject the act seems to be void. "If any subject shall be embraced in an act which shall not be expressed in its title, such act shall be void only as to so much thereof as shall not be expressed in its title." [Section 24 article IV of Constitution.] Section 497 of the Civil Code empowers the city council, etc., to grant a franchise to a street railroad upon "such terms" as it may provide.

Section 498 of the Civil Code provides that "the city or town authorities in granting the right of way to street railroad corporations * * * must require a strict compliance with the following conditions: * * * (2.) To plank, pave or macadamize the entire length of the street used by their track, between the rails, and for two feet on each side thereof, and between the tracks, if there be more than one, and to keep the same constantly in repair, flush with the street, and with good crossings."

Section 511 of the Civil Code makes the above provisions

applicable in like manner to a natural person when a street railroad is constructed, owned or operated by any such person.

These provisions of the Civil Code are the only provisions of law known to the author which require any work to be done by any person or company having railroad tracks on a street. These Civil Code provisions provide that the city authorities, in granting a right of way to a street railroad corporation, or to a person owning or operating a street railroad, shall impose said conditions to do said street work. But they do not provide any machinery for compelling such corporations or persons to do such work. There is no doubt but that the city authorities without any special statutory provision therefor have an appropriate remedy if these conditions are not complied with, e. g., *mandamus* to compel the performance of the conditions. [Elliott on Roads and Streets, page 592.] But the question is: Is there any statutory provision providing the machinery for compelling the owners of street railroads to pay the expense of doing the work which such owners are required to do by said sections of the Civil Code. Is there any statutory provision compelling the owners of street railroads to pay for such expenses by assessing the same upon the tracks, roadbed, switches and franchises of said railroad? Subdivision 1 of section 7 of the general street improvement act—the Vrooman act of March 18, 1885—provides that the expense incurred for any work authorized by said act, and which is to be assessed according to the front-foot principle of assessment, "shall not include the cost of any work done in such portion of any street as is required by law to be kept in order or repair by any person or company having railroad tracks thereon." [See *supra* p. 64.] But said act does not declare what street work is to be done by persons or companies having railroad tracks, nor does it provide how the expense of doing such work is to be met. It provides no machinery for assessing the property of persons or companies having railroad tracks. The only act, known to the author, which does attempt to furnish such machinery is said bond act—the act of February 27, 1893, section 6 thereof. [See in this connection McVerry *v.* Boyd, 89 Cal. 309.] In the case of Schmidt *v.* Market St., etc., R. R. Co., 90 Cal. 37, Mr. Justice Harrison, page 39, said: "No mode is provided in the act [act of March 18, 1885] for collecting from a street railroad corporation, whose road occupies a portion of the street, any portion of the expense of improving the street." And, if section 6 of the bond act of February 27, 1893, in so far as it attempts to provide a mode for collecting from a person or company having a street railroad any portion of the expense of improving the street, be unconstitutional and void—as it certainly seems to be, in view of the mandatory requirement of section 24 of article IV of the constitution that "every act shall embrace but one subject"—then it must follow that there is still no special mode provided by law for collecting from a person or company having a street railroad any portion of the expense of improving the street, and the only way in which the conditions imposed under the provisions of section 498 of the Civil Code can be enforced, is by *mandamus*, or some other appropriate remedy not dependent for its existence upon any special statutory provision providing a special remedy in such cases.

In said case of Schmidt *v.* Market St., etc., R. R. Co., 90 Cal. 37, it was held that when, under section 497 of the Civil Code, the city council, in granting to a street railroad company the right of way or franchise, imposes as one of the conditions that the company shall pay the cost of improving the part of the street occupied by its tracks, etc., and that such cost shall be "collected in the manner provided for the collection of other street assessments," the acceptance of the franchise, subject to such condition, is equivalent to a contract to pay such cost in such manner. *Held,* further, that as the manner provided for the collection of other street assessments under the Vrooman act of March 18, 1885, is by suit brought by the contractor, that the defendant was liable *on said contract* in an action by the contractor to recover the amount of the assessment. In that case the defendant's liability was founded upon its contract with the city made by its acceptance of its franchise with a condition imposed that it would not only pay the cost of the street work in question, but that the same should be "collected in the manner provided for the collection of other street assessments." Defendant's liability in that case was not founded upon any provision of any statute providing a manner for the collection of assessments from persons or companies having street railroads, but was founded solely upon its said contract, arising out of its acceptance of said franchise subject to said conditions. [See this subject considered in the notes to subdivision 1 of section 7 of the Vrooman act of March 18, 1885, *supra,* page 67 *et seq.*]

SECTION 7. The term "city treasurer," as used in this act, shall be held to mean and include any person who, under whatever name or title, is the custodian of the funds of the municipality. [*Statutes '93, p. 38.*]

SECTION 8. The act entitled "An act to amend an act entitled 'An act to provide for work upon streets, lanes, alleys, courts, places and sidewalks, and for construction of sewers within municipalities,' approved March eighteenth, eighteen hundred and eighty-five, by adding thereto an additional part, numbered four, consisting of sections thirty-eight, thirty-nine, forty, forty-one, forty-two, forty-three and forty-four, relative to a system of street improvement bonds," approved March seventeenth, eighteen hundred and ninety-one, is hereby repealed, except as to any and all proceedings hitherto commenced thereunder, which proceedings may be completed and have full force as is therein provided. [*Statutes '93, p. 38.*]

SECTION 9. This act shall take effect and become of force from and after its passage. [*Statutes '93, p. 38.*]

Tree Planting Act of March 11, 1893.

An Act to provide for the planting, maintenance, and care of shade trees upon streets, lanes, alleys, courts and places within municipalities, and of hedges upon the lines thereof; also, for the eradication of certain weeds within city limits.

[Approved March 11, 1893, statutes 1893, p. 153.]

The people of the state of California, represented in senate and assembly, do enact as follows:

SECTION 1. All streets, lanes, alleys, places or courts in the municipalities of this state, now open or dedicated, or which may hereafter be opened or dedicated to public use, whose grade has been officially established, and which have been actually graded in conformity therewith, may be planted with shade trees along the edges of the sidewalks thereof, by order of the city council, which shall have power also to provide for the maintenance and care of the same; and the city council shall have power to prescribe the height, thickness and manner of trimming of all hedges set out, or that shall be hereafter set out, along the line of any street, lane, alley, place or court dedicated to public use, whether graded or not, and to compel compliance with its ordinances in the premises by the owners or occupants of the lots fronting thereon. The powers hereby conferred upon city councils shall be exercised in the manner and under the proceedings hereinafter described.

Section 1 of this act declares what work the city council is authorized to order to be done under the act. The subsequent sections provide the machinery by which the council is to acquire jurisdiction to order the work done, and likewise the machinery by which the cost of the work is to be paid for by means of assessments levied upon the property owners. As the procedure provided for by the act is very similar to that provided by the general street improvement act of March 18, 1885, *supra*, pages 1–216, the reader is referred to the notes to the corresponding and analogous sections of that act.

SECTION 2. The city council of any municipality in the state may, at its discretion, pass a resolution of intention to plant, or cause to be planted, with shade trees, any graded street, lane, alley, place or court within the limits of such municipality. Such resolution of intention may embrace the entire length of any street, lane, alley, place or court, or any portion thereof, but must specify the kind of trees to be planted, their size, age, and their distance apart. The street superintendent shall thereupon cause to be conspicuously posted along both sides of the street mentioned in the resolution, at not more than three hundred feet in distance apart, notices of the passage of said resolution. Said notice shall be headed, "Notice to plant shade trees," in letters not less than one inch in length, and shall, in legible characters, set forth the language of the resolution, and the date of its passage. The city clerk shall also cause a copy of the resolution to be published for six days in one or more daily newspapers published and circulated in said city, and designated by said city council.

[See notes to section 2 of act of March 18, 1885, *supra*, page 6.]

SECTION 3. The owners of a majority of the frontage of the property on both sides of the street proposed to be planted as aforesaid, may, within ten days after the expiration of the time of publication of said resolution, file their written statement of objections to the proposed work, with the city clerk, which must be signed by the objectors, each one writing after his or her name the number of feet frontage owned by him or her. Such objection must show wherein the parties making them will be injured or aggrieved by the proposed work, and if the objection be to the kind of trees proposed to be planted, they must name some other kind of tree to be substituted therefor. The city council shall, at its next meeting after the filing of said objections, fix a time for hearing the same, not less than one week thereafter. The city clerk shall thereupon notify each objector, or his agent, who has signed his or her name to the statement, by depositing in the post office of said city a notice addressed to him or her, postage prepaid, notifying the objectors of the time and place of hearing. At the time specified, the council shall hear the objections urged, and pass upon the same, and its decision shall be final and conclusive, except that in the choice of trees to be planted, it shall be governed by the written request of the owners of a majority of the frontage on both sides of the street which it is proposed to plant. If the objections be sustained, no further proceedings shall be taken under the resolution of intention for six months after the date of its passage. If it be again proposed to plant the street, the council shall commence proceedings *de novo*, as if no action had been previously taken.

[See notes to section 3 of act of March 18, 1885, *supra*, page 10.]

SECTION 4. At the expiration of ten days after the expiration of the time of publication of said resolution of intention, if no written objections to the work therein described shall have been filed with the city clerk, as hereinbefore provided. otherwise immediately upon the overruling of the objections by the council, the council shall be deemed to have acquired jurisdiction to order to be done the work which is authorized by this act, which order shall be published for two days in the same papers and manner as provided for the publication of the resolution of intention.

[See notes to section 4 of act of March 18, 1885, *supra*, page 37.]

SECTION 5. Before passing any resolutions for the planting of any street, the city council shall cause notice, with specifications, to be posted conspicuously for five days near the door of the council chamber, and shall advertise the same for five days in the same manner and papers as heretofore provided for the publication of the resolution of intention, inviting sealed proposals for bids for furnishing the trees and doing the work ordered. All bids shall state the sum or price for which the bidder will undertake to furnish the trees, of the kind, age and size required, and will suitably prepare the ground, set out the trees, warrant every one of them to grow, or replace all that fail to grow or receive damage from whatever cause with others of the same kind, and of suitable age and size to preserve uniformity, and will for three years care for, cultivate, protect, irrigate and trim said trees. And no order for the planting of any street shade trees shall be made that does not likewise provide for the care and maintenance of the trees for three years by the contractor planting the trees. All proposals or bids shall be accompanied by a check payable to the order of the mayor, or president of the city council, certified by a responsible bank, for an amount which shall not be less than ten per cent. of the aggregate of the proposal. Said proposals or bids shall be delivered to the clerk of the city council, indorsed "Proposals to plant trees," and said council shall, in open session, examine and publicly declare the same; *provided*, that no proposal or bid shall be considered unless accompanied by said check. The council may reject all proposals, should it deem this for the public good, and shall reject the bid of any party who has been delinquent, or unfaithful in any former contract with the municipality, and may award the contract to the lowest responsible bidder, at the prices named in his bid, which award shall be approved by the mayor, or president of the council. Notice of such awards of contract shall be posted and advertised for five days, in the manner hereinbefore provided, and it shall be the duty of the superintendent of streets to enter into a contract with the bidder to whom the work shall have been awarded by the council, and at the prices specified in his bid; whereupon the certified checks of all the other bidders shall be returned to them, respectively. But if such lowest bidder neglects, fails or refuses, for fifteen days after the first posting and publication of the award, to enter into the contract, then the city council, without further proceedings, shall again advertise for proposals or bids as in the first instance, and shall award the contract for said work to the then lowest bidder. If the contractor who shall have taken any contract shall not complete the planting within the time limited in the contract, or within such further time as the council may give him, the superintendent of streets shall report such delinquency to the council, which may relet the unfinished portion of the planting, and the future care of the trees, after pursuing the formalities hereinbefore prescribed for the letting of the whole in the first instance.

[See notes to section 5 of act of March 18, 1885, *supra*, page 44.]

SECTION 6. All contractors shall, at the time of executing any contract for the planting and care of trees, execute a bond to the satisfaction of the mayor, or president of the city council, with two or more sureties, and payable to the city, in such sums as the mayor, or president of the council, shall deem adequate, conditioned for the faithful performance of the contract, and the sureties shall justify before the recorder, or a justice of the peace, in double the amount mentioned in such bond, over and above all statutory exemption. Before being entitled to any contract, the bidder to whom the award shall have been made must pay into the city treasury the cost of the publication of notices, resolutions and orders, and all other incidental expenses required under the proceedings prescribed by this act.

[See notes to section 6 of act of March 18, 1885, *supra*, page 62.]

SECTION 7. All work done under the provisions of this statute shall be executed under the direction of the superintendent of streets, whose duty it shall be, under the general control of the council, to see that all the obligations assumed by contractors towards the city are faithfully complied with, and that all trees furnished are sound, healthy, free from infection by insects, and of the kind, size and age called for by the contract. He shall certify to the completion of all work, or portion of work, which, by the terms of the contract, shall entitle the contractor to payment in whole or in part, and the presentation of his certificate by the contractor shall be a condition precedent to each payment that shall become due under the contract.

[See notes to section 7 of act of March 18, 1885, *supra*, page 67.]

SECTION 8. All sums due to contractors under the provisions of this act shall be payable by installments, as follows, to wit: Not more than one-half the entire consideration in the contract shall be payable on the completion of the planting, and out of this amount the superintendent of streets shall see that the trees are paid for, to the party furnishing the same; one half the balance at the end of eighteen months after the completion of the planting; *provided*, all conditions shall have been complied with; the remaining one-half to be paid at the end of three years after the completion of the planting; *provided*, all conditions shall have been complied with.

SECTION 9. Immediately upon the execution of any contract for the planting and care of street trees under the provisions of this act, it shall be the duty of the city assessor to make an assessment to cover the sum to become due for the work specified in such contract (including all incidental expenses) upon the lots and land fronting on the street, lane, alley, court or place to which such contract relates, each lot or portion of a lot being separately assessed, in proportion to the frontage, at a rate per foot front sufficient to cover the total expenses of the work. Said assessment shall briefly refer to the contract, the work contracted for, and shall show the amount to be paid therefor, together with any incidental expenses, the rate per front foot assessed, the amount of each assessment, the name of the owner of each lot, if known to the assessor (if unknown, the word "unknown" shall be written opposite the number or description of the lot with the amount assessed thereon). And the assessor shall attach to said assessment a diagram, exhibitiug the street, lane, alley, place or court on which the work is contracted to be done, and showing the relative location and frontage of such lot, numbered to correspond with the numbers in the assessment. To said assessment shall be attached a warrant, which shall be signed by the superintendent of streets, and countersigned by the mayor, or president of the council. The said assessments and warrants shall be separately issued for each payment that shall be due the contractor, as specified in section eight of this act, and shall be substantially in the following form:

FORM OF THE WARRANT.

By virtue hereof, I (name of the superintendent of streets), of the city of ———, county of ———, and state of California, by virtue of the authority vested in me as said superintendent of streets, do authorize and empower (name of contractor), his agents or assigns, to demand and receive the several assessments upon the assessment and diagram hereto attached, and this shall be his warrant for the same.

Date ———, ———.   (Name of superintendent of streets.)

(Countersigned by name of mayor or president of council.)

Recorded (date ———, ———).   (Name of superintendent of streets.)

Said warrant, assessment and diagram shall be recorded in the office of the superintendent of streets. When so recorded the several amounts assessed shall be a lien upon the lands, lots or portions of lots assessed, respectively, for the period of two years from the date of said recordin unless sooner discharged. From and after the date of said record, all persons interested in any manner in any or all of the lots assessed, shall be deemed to have notice of the contents of said record.

[See notes to sections 7, 8 and 9, act of March 18, 1885, *supra*, pp. 67 to 107.]

SECTION 10. After said warrant, assessment and diagram shall have been recorded,the same shall be delivered to the contractor,his agents or assigns, on demand, who shall thereby be authorized to demand and receive the the amounts of the several assessments. In default whereof, and as regards enforced collections, interest, cost and penalties, and the correction of errors, the same proceedings are to be had as are specified in sections nine, ten, eleven, twelve, sixteen and seventeen of an act entitled "An act to provide for work upon streets, lanes, alleys, courts, places and sidewalks, and for the construction of sewers within municipalities," approved March eighteenth, eighteen hundred and eighty-five, amended March fourteenth, eighteen hundred and eighty-nine.

[See notes to sections 10, 11, 12 and 16 of act of March 18, 1885, *supra*, p. 108, *et seq.*]

SECTION 11. The city council of every municipality in this state has jurisdiction of the hedges and fences placed by property owners along street lines, and may, by ordinance, prohibit the planting of thorn-bearing hedges, and the use of barbed wire along street lines, and may regulate the height, width, and the mode of trimming hedges, and enforce ordinances enacted for such purposes against absentees, or other negligent or recusant owners or occupants of lots or lands on which hedges are maintained. They may also condemn, as public nuisances, any or all weeds whose seeds are of a winged or downy nature, and are spread by the winds, and may compel the eradication of such weeds by the owners of the lots whereon they grow, or at their expense.

SECTION 12. The city council or trustees of every municipality shall provide for the replacement of missing trees, and for the trimming and care of all trees that have or shall have been planted for three or more years in the streets and highways, whether such planting shall have been done under this act or otherwise; the expense whereof must be defrayed out of the street fund, and the work be done by the superintendent of streets of such municipality.

SECTION 13. This act shall only apply to such municipalities as shall by vote of the electors residing therein determine to come within its provisions.

SECTION 14. This act shall take effect from and after its passage.

Street Opening Act of March 6, 1889.

An Act to provide for laying out, opening, extending, widening, straightening, or closing up in whole or in part any street, square, lane, alley, court, or place within municipalities, and to condemn and acquire any and all land and property necessary or convenient for that purpose.

[Approved March 6, 1889, statutes 1889, p. 70.]

The people of the state of California, represented in senate and assembly, do enact as follows:

SECTION 1. Whenever the public interest or convenience may require, the city council of any municipality shall have full power and authority to order the opening, extending, widening, straightening, or closing up in whole or in part of any street, square, lane, alley, court, or place within the bounds of such city, and to condemn and acquire any and all land and property necessary or convenient for that purpose. [*Statutes 1889, p. 70.*]

The above act of March 6, 1889, is the first general act upon the subject of street opening, passed since the adoption of the new constitution.

Section 1 provides what work the city council is authorized to do under the act, and the following sections provide the machinery for doing that work. Two proceedings are contemplated and provided for in the act, one against the property to be condemned for the use of the street, and the other to assess other property benefited by the improvement.

As recited in the title, it is an act "to condemn and acquire any and all land and property necessary or convenient" for the purposes of the act, namely for opening extending, widening, straightening or closing up any street etc., and therefore the act necessarily involves the exercise of two different and high prerogative or sovereign powers, namely, that of "*eminent domain*" and that of "*taxation.*" By the power of "*eminent domain,*" the property is taken to open, widen, extend or straighten the street. By the power of "*taxation*" (which includes assessments upon the property specially benefited, or perhaps upon such as is legislatively deemed to be thus benefited), compensation is made to those whose property has been taken under the exercise of the power of eminent domain.

After providing in section 1 what work the city council is authorized to do under the act, namely, the opening, extending, widening, straightening or closing up any street, etc., the act provides the machinery for accomplishing these objects, in substance as follows: The council passes its resolution declaring its intention to do the work, and specifying the extreme boundaries of the district to be assessed to pay the damages and the expense of doing the work. [Section 2.] Notice of the passage of such resolution is then posted and published by the superintendent of streets. [Section 3.] Persons interested may file objections to said work or to the extent of the assessment district. [Section 4.] These objections, if filed, are heard and passed upon by the council, and if none are filed, or if being filed, are overruled, the council is then deemed to have acquired jurisdiction to order any of the work to be done which is authorized by section 1. [Section 5.] The council then passes an ordinance or resolution ordering the work to be done, and, unless the proposed work is for closing up, appoints three commissioners to assess the benefits and damages. These commissioners have the power of general supervision of the proposed work or improvement until the completion thereof. [Section 6.] The commissioners then proceed to view the lands affected, and to determine (*1.*) the value of the land actually taken for the improvement; (*2.*) the damage to improvements taken; (*3.*) damages to the property not actually taken—damages which will accrue to the property not actually taken, by reason of its severance from the portion which is sought to be taken, and damages resulting thereto from the doing of the proposed work; (*4.*) the amount of expenses incident to the proposed work or improvement, *e. g.* expenses of removing obstructions where a street is to be opened, and likewise the expenses enumerated in sections 6 and 7. The commissioners then assess upon the assessment district described in the resolution of intention the total amount, namely the amount of said value of said land and property taken, together with the amount of said damages and the amount of said expenses incident to said work or improvement. Such assessment is made upon all the lands in said district in proportion to the benefits derived. [Section 9.] The commissioners then make a written report to the council, accompanying the same with a plat of the district, showing the land taken or to be taken, etc. [Section 10.] The city clerk then gives notice, by publication, of the filing of said report. [Section 13.] Written objections to said report may be filed, and if filed the council fixes a day for hearing the same. The clerk notifies the objectors, by depositing notice in the post office. At the time set, the council hears the objections, and passes upon the same, and likewise upon the commissioners' report, and may confirm, correct, or modify the same, or order a new assessment, report, and plat. [Section 14.] The city clerk then forwards to the street superintendent a certified copy of the report, assessment and plat, and such copy becomes the assessment roll. [Section 15.] Thereupon the superintendent of streets publishes notice that he has received said assessment roll, and that all sums levied and assessed therein are due and payable immediately, and that payment of said sums is to be made to him within thirty days from the date of the first publication. If not paid within said time, the superintendent of streets proceeds to advertise and collect the sums delinquent, by the sale of the property assessed, in the same manner as is provided for the collection of state and county taxes. [Section 16.] The money collected from payment of the assessments is paid into a fund devoted to the proposed work, and all payments for land and improvements taken or damaged, as well as for the expenses incident to doing the work, are paid by the city treasurer upon warrants drawn upon said fund from time to time. [Sections 8 and 19.] When sufficient money is in the fund, the commissioners notify the owner, possessor, or occupant of any land or improvements to whom damages have been awarded, that a warrant has been drawn for the payment of the same, and that he can receive such warrant at the office of the commissioners upon tendering a conveyance of any property to be taken. [Section 17.] If any owner of land or property to be taken, neglects or refuses to accept the warrant drawn in his favor, or objects to the report as to the necessity of taking his land, the commissioners, with the approval of the council, may cause proceedings to be taken for the condemnation of such land or property, as provided by law, under the right of eminent domain. [Section 18.] Supplementary assessments may be ordered to make up a deficiency, and if there be a surplus the same may be divided *pro rata* to the parties paying the same. [Section 20.] Proceedings may be taken by the council to settle defective titles. [Section 21.] The council may declare the boundaries of the assessment district to include the whole city. [Section 22.]

The foregoing constitutes a brief outline of the machinery provided by the act for accomplishing its purpose; *i. e.*, for doing the work authorized to be done by section 1 of the act.

The act is authority for the opening, extending, widening, straightening and closing of streets, and authorizes the

damages, which must be paid to those whose property is to
be taken or damaged for any of such purposes, as well as
the expenses incident to such work or improvement, to be
assessed upon the property in the assessment district, in
proportion to the benefits to be derived. But the act does
not give the power to assess for any work other than that
described in section 1. It does not include the power to
assess any property in the assessment district for the
improvement of the street by grading, culverting, and the
like. These things must be done under the street improvement act—the Vrooman act of March 18, 1885. Thus, if
the council, proceeding under the street opening act of
March 6, 1889, resolve to *open* a street, it can not in the
same proceeding provide for any *improvement* on the street,
such as grading, etc. The term "opening" does not include
the improving of a street by grading, paving, etc. It refers
to throwing open to the public what before was appropriated
to individual use, and the removing of such obstructions as
exist on the surface of the earth, rather than any artificial
improvement of the surface. When proceedings are had
under the said act of March 6, 1889, to open a street, the
assessment which the act authorizes to be levied upon all
the property in the assessment district declared to be benefited by the proposed improvement, is an assessment confined to raising a fund necessary to pay what the right of
way might cost, which includes the cost of the land and
property taken or damaged, the cost of removing such
obstructions as exist on the surface of the earth, and all
costs and expenses incident to the work or improvement,
such as the commissioners' compensation, office rent, etc.
[Reed *v.* City of Toledo, 18 Ohio, 161.]

In Reed *v.* City of Toledo, *supra*, a bill in chancery
was filed to enjoin the collection of a tax by the
city of Toledo upon real estate of the complainant. The city council had commenced proceedings
under section 17 of the city charter to extend a street.
Section 16 of the charter corresponded to our general street
improvement act—the Vrooman act of March 18, 1885—
and provided that the city might grade, gravel, level, pave,
repair, plank, flag, or macadamize a street, and assess the
costs and expenses thereof upon the lots fronting thereon.
Section 17 of the city's charter corresponded to our general
street opening act—the act of March 6, 1889—and provided
that the city council shall have power to lay out and pro-
long and open streets, lanes, etc., and assess the damages
due property owners whose property is taken therefor, to
the real estate situated within an assessment district whose

*

boundaries were defined by the charter to be 60 rods on each side of such improvements. The city council, under said section 17 of the city's charter, passed an ordinance to extend Adams street, one of the streets of the town, from its then termination, so as to intersect what was known by the name of the terminal road; and at the same time the ordinance also provided that the street should be graded, and that the total expense—for grading as well as for extending the street—should be assessed upon the property lying within the district benefited. The court said: "Now it will be seen that all that this section [section 17] provides for, that would require any outlay of money, is the opening of the street and paying for the right of way. By the term opening, we do not understand the improvement of a street or highway by grading, culverting, etc.; the term is generally (we think always) clearly distinguishable from such kind of improvement. The term opening refers to the throwing open to the public what before was appropriated to individual use, and the removing of such obstructions as exist on the surface of the earth, rather than any artificial improvement of the surface. * * * The assessment provided for in the 17th section on all the lots within 60 rods benefited by an improvement, we suppose relates merely to raising a fund to pay for what the right of way might cost." See also City and County of San Francisco v. Kiernan, 33 Pac. Rep. 721 where it is said, per Vanclief, C., "No work or improvement, in the sense of the act of 1883, [the Vrooman act of March 6, 1883, statutes 1883, page 32, entitled, 'An act to provide for the improvement of streets, lanes, alleys,' etc.] could be done or made on the addition to the street made by the widening, until after the widening. All the work and improvements authorized by the act of 1883 [the Vrooman act of 1883] are to be done upon *existing* streets. Work and improvements upon *existing* streets constitute the whole subject matter of the act, and therefore the prohibition in the first section ["no public work or improvement of any description shall be done or made within any municipality organized and existing for municipal purposes, or hereafter organized, in, upon or about the streets thereof, the cost and expense of which is made chargeable, or may be assessed upon, private property by special assessment, except as in this act provided"] cannot extend to the subject of creating or partially creating streets. In this connection it should be observed that heretofore it seems to have been the policy of the legislature to provide for improvements upon existing streets by acts entirely distinct from acts providing for opening, extending and widening streets."

This street opening act of March 6, 1889, not only provides for opening, widening, entending and straightening streets but also for *"closing"* streets. In Polack *v.* S. F. Orphan Asylum, 48 Cal. 490, it was held that the legislature has power to close or vacate a street in a city; and it may delegate such power to the municipal authorities of a city, and after such power has been delegated to the municipal authorities, the legislature may revoke it in part, as well as in whole, or without any express revocation, may itself exercise it; that the municipal authorities cannot close or vacate a street without the consent of the legislature. It was also held that the legislature may vacate a portion of a street, even if a person owns property fronting on another portion of the street which will incidentally be injured thereby. Under section 14 of article I of the present constitution it is altogether probable that if, by reason of the closing of any street, a property owner should suffer special consequential damages over and above the common injury to the other abutters on the street, or the general public, the municipal corporation would be liable therefor; [Reardon *v.* San Francisco, 66 Cal. 492] but owners of lands abutting upon neighboring streets, or upon other parts of the same street, are not entitled to damages, even though the value of their lands should be lessened by the closing or partial closing of the street. [See Elliott on Roads and Streets, pp. 662-3. See also Brook *v.* Horton, 68 Cal. 554, as to power of the legislature to vacate a street.]

Constitutionality of the Street Opening Act. The question of the constitutionality of this street opening act,—the act of March 6, 1889,—came before the Supreme Court in the case of Davies *v.* City of Los Angeles, 86 Cal. 37, where it was held that the act was constitutional. It was held in the prevailing opinion, by Mr. Justice Works,—Justices Thornton, McFarland and Paterson concurring,—that the act is a general law within the meaning of section 6 of article XI of the constitution; that it supersedes all city charters existing prior to the adoption of the new constitution, and likewise such as have been framed since under section 8 of article XI of the constitution. The action was brought by a property owner,—upon who property an assessment had been made for the payment of the expenses of opening and widening a certain street,—against the city of Los Angeles and the street superintendent, as defendants, to enjoin the enforcement of said assessment. The defendants demurred to the complaint and the trial court overruled the demurrer. The city appealed. Plaintiff, respondent on appeal, contended that the statute was unconstitutional. While the prevailing opinion of the Supreme Court held the act to be constitutional, it nevertheless decided that the trial court did not err in overruling the demurrer, since the complaint did, in fact state a cause of action, notwithstanding the constitutionality of the act, since it sufficiently appeared from the complaint that all the property within the assessment district was not assessed. It was held that this allegation showed the assessment to be void, under the decisions in People v. Lynch, 51 Cal. 15; Moulton v. Parks, 64 Cal. 181; Dyer v. Harrison, 63 Cal. 447; and Diggins v. Brown, 76 Cal. 318, and that therefore the complaint in an action to enjoin the enforcement of the assessment, was sufficient,—even if the statute were in all respects constitutional. Justices Fox and Beatty concurred in the judgment, but dissented from all that was said in the main opinion in support of the proposition that the act is in force in cities which, like Los Angeles, have adopted freeholders charters since the adoption of the new constitution.

It was contended by counsel in this case: (1.) That, even if the act be constitutional, it is not applicable to the city of Los Angeles, since that city has a charter containing ample provisions for the opening and widening of streets. (2.) That the statute is unconstitutional for the following reasons: (a.) That, while it gives authority to assess property within assessment districts, the subject of such assessment is not included in the title of the act. (b.) That it provides for taking property without due process of law, because the notice provided for may be given generally by posting, and no personal notice to each of the parties interested is required or authorized. (c.) That it "authorizes an assessment for benefits and a sale, and conveyance on delinquency, while the improvement supposed to confer the benefits is hypothetical, and may be incapable of materialization." (d.) That the "provisions of the act admit of an assessment for benefits largely in excess of the amount needed." (e.) That the statute is in violation of section 13 of article XI of the constitution because it delegates to a special commission the power to perform municipal functions. (3.) That so much of the statute as provides for the assessment of the value of the property to be taken or condemned in opening or widening the street, is invalid for various reasons.

The prevailing opinion of the court decided against all of these contentions of counsel. As to the last contention, namely, that so much of the statute as provides for the assessment of the value of the property to be taken or condemned, is invalid, the prevailing opinion says: "For the purposes of this case, this point may be conceded. * * * This does not concern the party where property has been assessed. It is a question affecting the rights of the city and the party whose property is sought to be taken." [NOTE: It may be well to state here that the word "assessment," as used in connection with these street opening and closing acts, is often used in two different connections, and with two different meanings. *(1.)* It is used in connection with property which is to be assessed to pay the expenses of the work—these expenses including the damages to be paid to those property owners whose property is taken or damaged. In this connection it means the rating or fixing of the proportion of the total expenses which the property owners have to pay, whose property lies within the assessment district declared to be benefited by the proposed improvement. It means, in this connection, a charge against the property lying within the assessment district, and liable to be assessed to pay the cost of the work. *(2.)* The word "assessment" is likewise often used in connection with the proceedings to take or condemn the land necessary to be taken or condemned for the purpose of opening the street, etc. In this connection it means. the fixing by the commissioners of the value of the land thus sought to be taken or condemned. In the one connection it is a charge against the land burdened with the expenses of the work. In the other it is a valuation of the land which is to be taken or condemned for the street opening purposes. In the first connection the word "assessment" is used in that sense which it has as a part of the sovereign power of taxation; in the second connection it is used in the sense that attaches to the word "appraisment." In the first sense, *i. e.*, as a part of the sovereign power of taxation, it is applicable to all the property in the assessment district; in the other sense, *i. e.*, appraisement, it is applicable only to the property taken or damaged to open or widen the street, and as thus used, it is used in connection with the exercise of the power of "eminent domain."]

Mr. Justice Fox, in the said case of Davies *v.* City of Los Angeles, dissented only from so much of the main opinion as supported the proposition that the act applied to municipalities acting under freeholders charters.

Mr. Chief Justice Beatty concurred, in the main, in the dissenting opinion of Justice Fox, and thought, moreover, that the statute was unconstitutional on two grounds: *(1.)* That it does not provide for any proper notice to the owners of the property affected; and *(2.)* that it permits assessments upon the property supposed to be benefited in excess of the benefits.

The act again came before the Supreme Court in the case of Dehail v. Morford, 95 Cal. 457. The action was brought by plaintiff, a property owner whose property had been assessed, to restrain the defendant, the superintendent of streets of the city of Los Angeles, from making a sale of plaintiff's property to satisfy the assessment against it. The proceedings to widen the street were had under this act of March 6, 1889, by the city of Los Angeles, a city having a freeholders charter adopted pursuant to the provisions of section 8 of article XI of the constitution. It was held that the plaintiff was entitled to a judgment perpetually restraining the defendant from making such sale, because the resolution of intention did not specify the exterior boundaries of the districts to be assessed to pay the cost of the improvement, as it was required to do by section 2 of the act. But, the constitutionality of the act itself, and its applicability to cities which, like Los Angeles, have freeholders charters, containing ample provisions for the opening of streets, seems to have been assumed. The act again came before the Supreme Court in the very recent case of city and county of San Francisco v. Kiernan, 33 Pac. Rep. 721. In that case, proceedings had been begun under the act of April 25th, 1863, [statutes 1863, p. 560] "an act to confer further powers upon the board of supervisors of the city and county of San Francisco," and in effect, an amendment to the consolidation act. Subsequently and pursuant to the provisions of section 24 of the street opening act now being considered,—the street opening act of March 6, 1889, [see infra, section 24] the proceedings were continued under said last named act. The constitutionality of the provisions of section 18 of the act, providing for the form of complaints, in an action to condemn, was expressly upheld, and the constitutionality of the act, in its general features, was at least assumed.

The statute again came before the Supreme Court in the still more recent case of City of Santa Ana v. Harlin, No. 19,030, decided September 13, 1893, an action by the city under this street opening act of March 6, 1889, to condemn a right of way over the property of the defendant for the opening of Second street in said city. The court assumed the act to be constitutional.

It would seem therefore, that all the propositions laid down by the four judges who concurred in the prevailing opinion in Davies v. City of Los Angeles, 86 Cal. 37, may be assumed to be settled, and that the act of March 6, 1889, is the act under which streets are to be opened, closed, etc., in all the cities of this state, unless it has been repealed or superseded by any other act.

In 1893, the legislature passed an act approved March 23, 1893, [statutes 1893 p. 220] entitled "An act to provide for laying out, opening, extending, widening, straightening, diverging, curving, contracting, or closing up, in whole or in part, any street, square, lane, alley, court, or place within municipalities, or cities and cities and counties of forty thousand inhabitants or over, and to condemn and acquire any and all land and property necessary or convenient for that purpose."

By section 23 of this act of March 23, 1893, it is provided that "the act approved March 6, 1889, entitled 'An act for opening, widening and extending streets,' etc., after the passage of this act, shall not apply to any city or city and county having a population of forty thousand inhabitants or over, but as to any city or city and county having a population of forty thousand inhabitants or over said act shall not apply; but said cities and cities and counties shall be subject only to the provisions of this act in all matters embraced within the purview of this act."

Whether this act of March 23, 1893, is constitutional or not, and whether it operates to confine the provisions of the act of March 6, 1889, to municipalities of less than forty thousand inhabitants, are questions that are considered in the notes to section 1 of the said act of March 23, 1893, *infra.*

Decisions under Street Opening Acts passed prior to the adoption of the new Constitution and prior to the passage of a General Street Opening Act. A town that has no corporate existence, *e. g.*, because its act of incorporation is unconstitutional, cannot exercise the power of eminent domain to open a street. [Colton *v.* Rossi, 9 Cal. 595.]

A street cannot be extended, so as to take in private property, without condemnation. [People *v.* Kruger, 19 Cal. 411.]

The legislature may determine how the expense of opening a street shall be borne. Whether the cost of such enterprises shall be borne by contiguous property to be benefited thereby, or by all the property of the city, or by a certain proportion of such, is a matter for legislative discretion. [Sinton *v.* Ashbury, 41 Cal. 525.]

The power to lay out or change streets is in its nature legislative and not judicial. The legislature may itself perform these acts, or it may select such agencies for that purpose as it deems proper. Usually the requisite powers are conferred upon the authorities of the municipal government; but these powers, or some of them, may be devolved upon a court. In the latter case the proceedings are "special proceedings," and the court possesses jurisdiction only by virtue of the authority of the legislature, and does not derive it from any other source. Therefore if several tenants in common agree to run a street through the *middle* of a block owned by them, and, in pursuance of such agreement, execute a covenant by which, through mistake, the street is located at a place not in the middle of the block, and subsequently the municipal authorities locate and establish the street, not in the middle of the block, but in the position described in the covenant, the courts, in an action by parties to the covenant, or their assigns, cannot adjudge that the street be located in the middle of the block, because, if the action be regarded as an action to change the location of the street as fixed by the municipal authorities, the reply is that, in the absence of a statute specially delegating to the court powers to lay out or change streets, it has no such jurisdiction, and, if the action be regarded as having for its purpose an adjudication that the space through the middle of the block was dedicated as a street by the parties to the covenant, the judgment cannot be sustained because the covenant as executed does not locate the street in that position, and until the covenant is reformed, so as to express the alleged intent of the parties, there is no basis for such adjudication. [De Witt *v.* Duncan, 46 Cal. 343.]

Commissioners appointed to assess damages and benefits, in a proceeding to condemn land for a street, have no jurisdiction to determine questions of title. [Wilcox *v.* City of Oakland, 49 Cal. 29.

The act of March 28, 1878, "to provide for the opening of streets in the city of Oakland," required the petition of five or more residents and freeholders to the city council to contain, *inter alia* "a statement that in the opinion of the petitioners the public interests require that the improvement asked for [describing it generally] should be made." In the Matter of Grove Street, 61 Cal. 438, it appeared that the petition of the residents and freeholders to the council contained a statement that " in the opinion of the petitioners the improvement asked for should be made." *Held:* That the statement contained in the petition is not the same in substance as that required by the statute, and for this reason the petition of the freeholders did not give power or jurisdiction to the council. It was urged by respondent in that case that the council had itself conclusively determined that it had jurisdiction, when it passed the resolution of intention, it being claimed that in doing so, the council adjudicated the existence of facts upon which its jurisdiction depended. On this point the court, per McKinstry, J., pages 453–4, said: "An inferior board may determine conclusively its own jurisdiction or power by adjudicating the existence of *facts*, upon the existence of which its jurisdiction or power depends. Where, however, the power depends, not upon the existence or non-existence of matters *in pais*, to be established by evidence, but upon allegations in a petition, a portion of the record, the question is not the same."

Where the council is empowered to open or improve a street upon the petition of the owners of a majority of the frontage upon the proposed improvement, the council cannot include more than one street in one proceeding. [Boorman *v.* Santa Barbara, 65 Cal. 313.]

The interest which a street railroad company has in a street upon which it is authorized to lay down tracks, is an easement in the land, and is real property. The interest or estate of the company in the street is capable of being enhanced in value by the widening of the street, and by such widening a substantial benefit may accrue to the company, and the company may be assessed for its share of the expenses in widening the street. [Appeal of N. B. & M. R. R. Co., 32 Cal. 500.]

Where commissioners are appointed to assess benefits, etc., upon the lands affected by the improvement, the statutes sometimes provide that the courts shall receive the reports of the commissioners and exercise supervisory powers thereover, although in such matters it is not usual to permit an appeal to the courts while the proceedings are *in fieri*, and the right to supervise the acts and reports of the commissioners usually falls to the city councils or other municipal legislative bodies. Where, however, the statute thus grants these supervisory powers to the courts, the courts on appeal will not set aside the commissioners' report unless it is based upon an erroneous principle of law, or unless it is demonstrable that the commissioners have erred in respect to the facts, in fixing the values which they have arrived at. These reports, in respect to values, are in the nature of a verdict of a jury upon a question of fact, which is never set aside as against evidence unless it appears affirmatively and clearly to have been unwarranted by the proofs. [Appeal of Piper, 32 Cal. 530; Appeal of Brooks *et al.*, 32 Cal. 560.]

The benefits accrue to the lands and not to the buildings. [Appeal of Piper, *supra*.]

The assessment is properly chargeable to the owner of the fee, and not in part to the lessee, if it does not appear that the lessee will be benefited. [Appeal of Reese, 32 Cal. 568.]

For a very able review of some of the most important questions of constitutional law in connection with these street opening statutes, see the opinion of Mr. Justice Temple in Lent *v.* Tillson, 72 Cal. 404, reviewing the act of March 23, 1876, providing for the widening of Dupont street in the city and county of San Francisco, and the proceedings had thereunder.

It is not within the scope or plan of this book to discuss general principles. Its sole aim is to give the general street laws of California, as the same exist to-day, with amendments up to date, and to cite, in the notes to the sections of said acts, such decisions of our own Supreme Court as will serve to illustrate the working of these statutes, and the points of law liable to arise in the course of proceedings thereunder. The decisions of our own courts upon the street *improvement* acts,—*i. e.*, acts for the improvement of streets already in existence, by grading, macadamizing, paving, or otherwise improving such streets—have been so numerous that they alone suffice to shed ample light upon these street *improvement acts*. But this is not so in respect to acts for opening, closing, or widening streets. As to these opening and closing acts, the decisions of our own courts are meager, and, alone, do not afford much help in construing these street opening and closing acts. But, it is not the intention of this book to cite the decisions of the courts of other states—save in a few particular instances,—and the reader is, therefore, referred to chapter XVI of Dillon's Municipal Corporations —chapter on eminent domain,—where the subject matter of street opening acts is considered.

In many respects, the proceedings necessary to a valid assessment upon the property liable to be charged with the expenses of opening, extending, straightening, or closing streets, under this act,—act of March 6, 1889,—are analogous or similar to the corresponding proceedings under the Vrooman act of March 18, 1885, for the improvement of streets, and therefore the decisions, cited in the notes to that act, [*supra* pp. 1–216] are not cited in the notes to this act, but the reader is referred to the notes to those sections of said act of March 18, 1885, which contain provisions analogous to the corresponding sections of this street opening act, whenever the proceedings are similar or analogous.

SECTION 2. Before ordering any work to be done or improvement made which is authorized by section one of this act, the city council shall pass a resolution declaring its intention to do so, describing the work or improvement, and the land deemed necessary to be taken therefor, and specifying the exterior boundaries of the district of lands to be affected or benefited by said work or improvement, and to be assessed to pay the damages, cost and expenses thereof. [*Statutes '89, p. 70.*]

Section two requires the resolution of intention to specify "the exterior boundaries" of the district to be assessed to pay the cost of the improvement, and if the resolution does not specify the exterior boundaries, the council will not acquire jurisdiction over the matter, and the proceedings will be void. The following is not a description or specification of the exterior boundaries of any district, viz: "All lots and parcels of land fronting on the east side of First street, from the west side of Los Angeles street to the west line of Alameda street." In this case, the only boundaries of the district which are "specified" are the lines of First street between Los Angeles and Alameda streets, and these, instead of being the "exterior boundaries" of the district to be assessed are only the boundaries of a tract within the district which is exempted from assessment. There is nothing in the description of the district from which its extent in either direction from First street can be ascertained, or by which any one can determine the quantity of land which is to be assessed. [Dehail *v.* Morford, 95 Cal. 457.]

[See notes to section 3 of the act of March 18, 1885, *supra*, page 8 *et seq.*]

SECTION 3. The street superintendent shall then cause to be conspicuously posted along the line of said contemplated work or improvement, at not more than three hundred feet in distance apart, but not less than three in all, notices of the passage of said resolution. Said notice shall be headed, "Notice of public work," in letters not less than one inch in length, shall be in legible characters, state the fact of passage of the resolution, its date, and, briefly, the work or improvement proposed, and refer to the resolution for further particulars. He shall also cause a notice, similar in substance, to be published for a period of ten days in one or more daily newspapers published and circulated in said city, and designated by said city council; or, if there is no daily newspaper so published and circulated in said city, then by four successive insertions in a weekly or semi-weekly newspaper so published, circulated and designated. [*Statutes '89, p. 70.*]

[See notes to section 3 of act of March 18, 1885, *supra*, page 8, *et seq.*]

SECTION 4. Any person interested objecting to said work or improvement, or to the extent of the district of lands to be affected or benefited by said work or improvement, and to be assessed to pay the cost and expenses

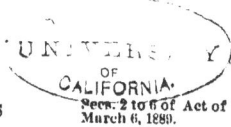

thereof, may make written objections to the same within ten days after the expiration of the time of the publication of said notice, which objection shall be delivered to the clerk of the city council, who shall indorse thereon the date of its reception by him, and at the next meeting of the city council after the expiration of said ten days, lay said objections before said city council, which shall fix a time for hearing said objections not less than one week thereafter. The city clerk shall thereupon notify the persons making such objections, by depositing a notice thereof in the post office of said city, postage prepaid, addressed to such objector. [*Statutes '89, p. 70.*]

If, by reason of some jurisdictional defect in the proceedings, *e. g.*, failure of the notice of intention to specify the exterior boundaries of the assessment district—the council fails to acquire jurisdiction, the property owner does not waive his right to object in court to this want of jurisdiction or to defeat an action upon the assessment, merely because he appeared before the city council and filed objections, as provided for in section 4. If the council failed to acquire jurisdiction of the subject matter of the improvement, it could not acquire jurisdiction by the consent of the property owner, much less by the fact that he objected to the improvement. [Dehail *v.* Morford, 95 Cal. 457.]

[See notes to sections 3 and 11 of act of March 18, 1885, *supra*, pages 8–37; 64–84.]

SECTION 5. At the time specified or to which the hearing may be adjourned, the said city council shall hear the objections urged and pass upon the same, and its decision shall be final and conclusive. If such objections are sustained, all proceedings shall be stopped, but proceedings may be again commenced at any time by giving notice of intention to do said work or make said improvement. If such objection is overruled by the city council, the proceedings shall continue the same as if such objection had not been made. At the expiration of the time prescribed during which objections to said work or improvement may be made, if no objections shall have been made, or if an objection shall have been, and said council, after hearing, shall have overruled the same, the city council shall be deemed to have acquired jurisdiction to order any of the work to be done, or improvements to be made, which is authorized by section one of this act. [*Statutes '89, p. 71.*]

[See notes to section 3 of act of March 18, 1885, *supra*, page 8 *et seq.*]

SECTION 6. Having acquired jurisdiction, as provided in the preceding section, the city council shall order said work to be done, and unless the proposed work is for closing up, and it appears that no assessment is necessary, shall appoint three commissioners to assess benefits and damages and have general supervision of the proposed work or improvement until the completion thereof in compliance with this statute. For their services they shall receive such compensation as the city council may determine from time to time; *provided*, that such compensation shall not exceed two hundred dollars per month each, nor continue more than six months, unless extended by order of the city council. Such compensation shall be added to and be chargeable as a part of the expenses of the work or improvement. Each of said commissioners shall file with the clerk of the city council an affidavit, and a bond to the state of California in the sum of five thousand dollars, to faithfully perform the duties of his office. The city council may at any time remove any or all of said commissioners for cause, upon reasonable notice and hearing, and may fill any vacancies occurring among them for any cause. [*Statutes '89, page 71.*]

[See notes to section 3 of act of March 18, 1885, *supra*, page 8 *et seq.*]

SECTION 7. Said commissioners shall have power to employ such assist-ance, legal or otherwise, as they may deem necessary and proper; also, to rent an office and provide such maps, diagrams, plans, books, stationery, fuel, lights, postage, expressage, and incur such incidental expenses as they may deem necessary. [*Statutes '89, p. 71.*]

SECTION 8. All such charges and expenses shall be deemed as expenses of said work or improvement, and be a charge only upon the funds devoted to the particular work or improvement as provided hereinafter. All pay-ments, as well for the land and improvements taken or damaged, as for the charges and expenses, shall be paid by the city treasurer, upon war-rants drawn upon said fund from time to time, signed by said commission-ers, or a majority of them. All such warrants shall state whether they are issued for land or improvements taken or damaged, or for charges and expenses, and that the demand is payable only out of the money in said fund, and in no event shall the city be liable for the failure to collect any assessment made by virtue hereof, nor shall said warrant be payable out of any other fund, nor a claim against the city. [*Statutes '89, p. 71.*]

SECTION 9. Said commissioners shall proceed to view the lands described in the resolution of intention, and may examine witnesses on oath, to be administered by any one of them. Having viewed the land to be taken, and the improvements affected, and considered the testimony presented, they shall proceed with all diligence to determine the value of the land and the damage to improvements and property affected, and also the amount of the expenses incident to said work or improvement, and having determined the same, shall proceed to assess the same upon the district of lands declared benefited, the exterior boundaries of which were fixed by the resolution of intention provided for by section 2 hereof. Such assess-ment shall be made upon the lands within said district in proportion to the benefit to be derived from said work or improvement, so far as the said commissioners can reasonably estimate the same, including in such esti-mate the property of any railroad company within said district, if such there be. [*Statutes '89, p. 72.*]

[See notes to sections 3, 8 and 11 of the Vrooman act of March 18, 1885, *supra*, pp. 34, 95 and 138. The street opening act of March 6, 1889, does not contain any provision for "appeal" similar to that contained in section 11 of the Vrooman act of March 18, 1885.]

If all property in the assessment district liable to assess-ment be not assessed, the assessment will be void, and there can be no recovery thereon. [Davies *v.* City of Los Angeles, 86 Cal. 37, 49; People *v.* Lynch, 51 Cal. 20; Moulton *v.*

Parks 64 Cal. 181; Dyer *v.* Harrison, 63 Cal. 447; Diggins *v.* Brown, 76 Cal. 318.] But property belonging to the United States, this state, or a municipal corporation, may be omitted from assessment. [Doyle *v.* Austin, 47 Cal. 353.]

The commissioners, under section 9, assess upon the lands lying within the assessment district, liable to assessment,—each lot being assessed in proportion to the benefits received by it—the total cost of the work or improvement. This total cost is made up of the value of the land and property taken, and the damages which accrue to the land and property not taken, plus the cost and expense incident to the work or improvement, which latter item includes the costs and expenses enumerated in sections 6 and 7 of the act, and, in the case of opening, widening or straightening a street, the cost of removing such obstructions as exist on the surface of the earth.

It is altogether probable that the act contemplates that the rules or principles by which the commissioners are to be guided in ascertaining the amount of damages which are to be paid or awarded to any property owner, whose property is to be taken or damaged for the opening of a street, or other improvement mentioned in section 1 of the act, are the rules or principles by which a jury is to be guided, under the provisions of section 1248 of the Code of Civil Procedure, relative to the exercise of the power of eminent domain. So that, where a street is to be opened, for example, the commissioners acting under section 9 of the act, should probably proceed about as follows: I. If the improvement takes *all* of the land and property of the owner, the commissioners determine the full and fair market value of the land and property at the time it is appropriated, but no more. [Section 624 Dillon's Municipal Corporations, 3rd ed.; Subdiv. 1 of section 1248 C. C. P.; Vol. 6, Am. and Eng. Enc. of Law, pp. 567–70.] II. If, however, as most commonly happens, *part* only of the property is to be taken, the commissioners should probably proceed as follows: (*1.*) Determine the full and fair market value of the land and property actually taken, at the time when it is appropriated. (*2.*) Determine the damages which will accrue to the portion not sought to be taken, by reason of its severance from the portion sought to be taken as well as by reason of the doing of the proposed improvement in the manner proposed by the city authorities. (*3.*) Determine how much the portion not sought to be taken, will be benefited, if at all, by the doing of the proposed improvement. (*4.*) Deduct from the damages which will accrue to the portion not sought to be taken, the said benefits thereto, if the benefits be less than the damages, and add the remainder to the value of the land and property which is actually taken, and the sum is the amount of damages to be awarded to the property owner. (*5.*) If the benefits which will accrue to the portion not sought to be taken, by reason of the proposed improvement, equal or exceed the damages which will accrue thereto, the owner will be entitled to the full and fair market value of the land and property actually taken, and no more. [Section 1248, C. C. P.; Sections 624–625 Dillon's Municipal Corporations, 3rd ed.; Vol. 6 Am. and Eng. Enc. of Law, pp. 571–584.] III. To the total amount of damages to be awarded to all the property owners whose property is sought to be taken,—ascertained according to the foregoing principles—the commissioners add the total amount of expenses incident to the work or improvement. These last mentioned incidental expenses include the cost of removing all obstructions upon the surface of the earth, —obstructions which must be removed before the street can be thrown open to public use to the width proposed,—also such incidental expenses as are mentioned in sections 6 and 7 of the act. IV. The commissioners then determine the amount of benefit which will accrue to each parcel of land in the assessment district, liable to be assessed to pay the expenses of the proposed work. V. The commissioners then assess upon all the lands within the assessment district, liable to be assessed, the total cost of the proposed work. Said total cost including (*1.*) the total amount to be awarded to property owners as damages to property taken or damaged, and (*2.*) the total amount of incidental expenses, incident to the doing of the work, as aforesaid. The said total cost of the proposed work is assessed upon the lands in the district in proportion to the benefits to be derived from said work or improvement, each lot or parcel of land being assessed with such a proportion of the total cost of the work, as the amount of benefit derived by it from the proposed work bears to the total amount of benefits which will accrue to all the lands in the assessment district, subject to assessment.

The commissioners having thus determined the amount of damages to be awarded to each property owner whose, property is to be taken or damaged for the proposed work and having thus determined the amount to be assessed against each lot or parcel of land to pay the total amount of damages to be awarded to the property owners, as well as the expenses incident to the work, make out a written report thereof and a plat of the assessment district, as provided for by sections 10 and 11 of the act.

Under section 14 of article I of the constitution, the benefits that will accrue to the portion of the land not sought to be taken may be deducted from the damages which will accrue to said portion, when the corporation for whose use the property is taken or damaged, is a "municipal corporation." [Pacific Coast R'y Co. *v.* Porter, 74 Cal. 261; Butte County *v.* Boydston, 64 Cal. 110; Tehama County *v.* Bryan, 68 Cal. 57.]

An assessment upon lands fronting on a street, to raise the amount to be paid the owner for land taken from him for a street, is not in violation of the provision of the constitution which declares that the compensation to be paid to a party for his land, taken for public use, shall be "without *deduction* for benefits." "Assessment" for benefits in the exercise of the sovereign power of taxation, is not the same as "deduction for benefits" in the exercise of the sovereign power of eminent domain. [Cleveland *v.* Wick, 18 Ohio St. 303.

For a discussion of some of the principles of assessment by street commissioners, in a proceeding to open or widen a street, see Appeal of Piper, 32 Cal. 530; Appeal of Brooks, 32 Cal. 559; Appeal of Reese, 32 Cal. 568.]

SECTION 10. Said commissioners having made their assessment of benefits and damage, shall, with all diligence, make a written report thereof to the city council, and shall accompany their report with a plat of the assessment district showing the land taken or to be taken for the work or improvement, and the lands assessed, showing the relative location of each district, block, lot, or portion of lot, and its dimensions, so far as the commissioners can reasonably ascertain the same. Each block and lot, or portion of lot, taken or assessed, shall be designated and described in said plat by an appropriate number, and a reference to it by such descriptive number shall be a sufficient description of it in any suit entered to condemn, and in all respects. When the report and plat are approved by the city council, a copy of said plat, appropriately designated, shall be filed by the clerk thereof in the office of the recorder of the county. [*Statutes 1889*, *page 72.*]

[See notes under section 8 of act of March 18, 1885, *supra*, page 85 *et seq.*]

SECTION 11. Said report shall specify each lot, subdivision, or piece of property taken or injured by the widening or other improvement, or assessed therefor, together with the name of the owner or claimants thereof, or of persons interested therein as lessees, incumbrancers, or otherwise, so far as the same are known to such commissioners, and the particulars of their interest, so far as the same can be ascertained, and the amount of value or damage, or the amount assessed, as the case may be. [*Statutes 1889, page 72.*]

[See notes under section 8 of act of March 18, 1885, *supra*, page 85, *et seq.*]

SECTION 12. If in any case the commissioners find that conflicting claims of title exist, or shall be in ignorance or doubt as to the ownership of any lot of land, or of any improvements thereon, or of any interest therein, it shall be set down as belonging to unknown owners. Error in the designation of the owner or owners of any land or improvements, or of the particulars of their interest, shall not affect the validity of the assessment or of the condemnation of the property to be taken. [*Statutes 1889, page 73.*]

[See notes under section 8 of act of March 18, 1885, *supra*, page 85, *et seq.*]

SECTION 13. Said report and plat shall be filed in the clerk's office of the city council, and thereupon the clerk of said city council shall give notice of such filing by publication for at least ten days in one or more daily newspapers published and circulated in said city; or if there be no daily paper, by three successive insertions in a weekly or semi-weekly newspaper so published and circulated. Said notice shall also require all persons interested to show cause, if any, why such report should not be confirmed, before the city council, on or before a day fixed by the clerk thereof, and stated in said notice, which day shall not be less than thirty days from the first publication thereof. [*Statutes 1889, page 73.*]

SECTION 14. All objections shall be in writing and filed with the clerk of the city council, who shall, at the next meeting after the day fixed in the notice to show cause, lay the said objections, if any, before the city council, which shall fix a time for hearing the same, of which the clerk shall notify the objectors in the same manner as objectors to the original resolution of intention at the time set, or at such other time as the hearing may be adjourned to, the city council shall hear such objections and pass upon the same; and at such time, or if there be no objections at the first meeting after the day set in such order to show cause, or such other time as may be fixed, shall proceed to pass upon such report, and may confirm, correct, or modify the same, or may order the commissioners to make a new assessment, report, and plat, which shall be filed, notice given, and hearing had as in the case of an original report. [*Statutes 1889, page 73.*]

SECTION 15. The clerk of said city council shall forward to the street superintendent of the city a certified copy of the report, assessment and plat, as finally confirmed and adopted by the city council. Such certified copy shall thereupon be the assessment roll. Immediately upon receipt thereof by the street superintendent the assessment therein contained shall become due and payable, and shall be a lien upon all the property contained or described therein. [*Statutes 1889, page 73.*]

SECTION 16. The superintendent of streets shall thereupon give notice by publication for ten days in one or more daily newspapers published and circulated in such city, or city and county, or by two successive insertions in a weekly or semi-weekly newspaper so published and circulated, that he has received said assessment roll, and that all sums levied and assessed in said assessment roll are due and payable immediately, and that the payment of said sums is to be made to him within thirty days from the date of the first publication of said notice. Said notice shall also contain a statement that all assessments not paid before the expiration of said thirty days will be declared to be delinquent, and that thereafter the sum of five per cent. upon the amount of each delinquent assessment, together with the cost of advertising each delinquent assessment, will be added thereto. When payment of any assessment is made to said superintendent

of streets he shall write the word "paid," and the date of payme nt, opposite the respective assessment so paid, and the names of persons by or for
whom said assessment is paid, and shall, if so required, give a receipt
therefor. On the expiration of said thirty days all assessments then
unpaid shall be and become delinquent, and said superintendent of streets
shall certify such fact at the foot of said assessment roll, and shall add five
per cent. to the amount of each assessment so delinquent. The said superintendent of streets shall, within five days from the date of said delinquency, proceed to advertise and collect the various sums delinquent, and
the whole thereof. including the cost of advertising, which last shall not
exceed the sum of fifty cents for each lot, piece, or parcel of land separately
assessed, by the sale of the assessed property in the same manner as is or
may be provided for the collection of state and county taxes; and after
the date of said delinquency, and before the time of such sale herein provided for, no assessment shall be received unless at the same time the five
per cent. added thereto, as aforesaid, together with the costs of advertising
then already incurred, shall be paid therewith. Said list of delinquent
assessments shall be published daily for five days in one or more daily
newspapers published and circulated in such city, or by at least one insertion in a weekly newspaper so published and circulated, before the day of
sale of such delinquent assessment. Said time of sale must not be less
than seven days from the date of the first publication of said delinquent
assessment list, and the place must be in or in front of the office of said
superintendent of streets. All property sold shall be subject to redemption in the same time and manner as in sales for delinquent state and
county taxes; and the superintendent of streets may collect for each certificate fifty cents, and for each deed one dollar. All provisions of the
law, in reference to the sale and redemption of property for delinquent
state and county taxes in force at any given time, shall also then, so far as
the same are not in conflict with the provisions of this act, be applicable
to the sale and redemption of property for delinquent assessments hereunder, including the issuance of certificates and execution of deeds. The
deed of the street superintendent made after such sale, in case of failure to
redeem, shall be prima facie evidence of the regularity of all proceedings
hereunder, and of title in the grantee. It shall be conclusive evidence of
the necessity of taking or damaging the lands taken or damaged, and of
the correctness of the compensation awarded therefor. The superintendent of streets shall, from time to time, pay over to the city treasurer all
moneys collected by him on account of any such assessments. The city
treasurer shall, upon receipt thereof, place the same in a separate fund,
designating such funds by the name of the street, square, lane, alley,
court, or place for the widening, opening, or other improvement of which
the assessment was made. Payments shall be made from said fund to the
parties entitled thereto upon warrants signed by the commissioners, or a
majority of them. [*Statutes 1889, page 73.*]

Where a street improvement act provides that the assessment shall be collected in the manner prescribed by law
for the collection of general state and county taxes, such
provision prescribes the *manner* of collecting, and not what
shall be collected, and therefore does not authorize the

addition of a per centage for delinquency, except such as the street improvement act, itself, may in terms provide for. [Bucknall v. Story, 36 Cal. 67.]

SECTION 17. When sufficient money is in the hands of the city treasurer, in the fund devoted to the proposed work or improvement, to pay for the land and improvements taken or damaged, and when in the discretion of the commissioners, or a majority of them, the time shall have come to make payments, it shall be the duty of the commissioners to notify the owner, possessor, or occupant of any land or improvements thereon to whom damages shall have been awarded, that a warrant has been drawn for the payment of the same, and that he can receive such warrant at the office of such commissioners upon tendering a conveyance of any property to be taken; such notification, except in the case of unknown owners, to be made by depositing a notice, postage paid, in the post office, addressed to his last known place of abode or residence. If at the expiration of thirty days after the deposit of such notice, he should not have applied for such warrant, and tendered a conveyance of the land to be taken, the warrant so drawn shall be deposited with the county treasurer, and shall be delivered to such owner, possessor, or occupant, upon tendering a conveyance as aforesaid, unless judgment of condemnation shall be had, when the same shall be canceled. [*Statutes 1889, page 75.*]

SECTION 18. If any owner of land to be taken neglects or refuses to accept the warrant drawn in his favor as aforesaid, or objects to the report as to the necessity of taking his land, the commissioners, with the approval of the city council, may cause proceedings to be taken for the condemnation thereof, as provided by law under the right of eminent domain. The complaint may aver that it is necessary for the city to take or damage and condemn the said lands, or an easement therein, as the case may be, without setting forth the proceedings herein provided for, and the resolution and ordinance ordering said work to be done shall be conclusive evidence of such necessity. Such proceeding shall be brought in the name of the municipality, and have precedence so far as the business of the court will permit; and any judgment for damages therein rendered shall be payable out of such portion of the special fund as may remain in the treasury, so far as the same can be applied. At any time after trial and judgment entered, or preceding an appeal, the court may order the city treasurer to set apart in the city treasury a sufficient sum from the fund appropriated to the particular improvement to answer the judgment and all damages, and thereupon may authorize and order the municipality to enter upon the land and proceed with the proposed work and improvement. In case of a deficiency in said fund to pay the whole of such judgment and damages, the city council may, in their discretion, order the balance thereof to be paid out of the general fund of the treasury or to be distributed by the commissioners over the property assessed by a supplementary assessment; but in the last named case, in order to avoid delay, the city council may advance such balance out of any appropriate fund in the treasury, and reimburse the same from the collections of the assessment. Pending the collection and payment of the amount of the judgment and damages, the court may order such stay of proceedings as may be necessary. [*Statutes 1889, page 75.*]

No condemnation proceedings can be inaugurated under the power of eminent domain, or by virtue of the provisions of section 18 of the act, until the municipality shall have acquired jurisdiction so to do, by the passage of a valid resolution of intention; and if the resolution of intention does not specify the exterior boundaries of an assessment district, it does not confer upon the city jurisdiction to take any steps toward making the improvement, and cannot be used as the basis of any action for condemnation of the land sought to be included in the improvement. [City of Los Angeles v. Dehail, 97 Cal. 13. See section 605, Dillon on Municipal Corporations, 3rd ed.] But see City and County of San Francisco v. Kiernan, 33 Pac. Rep. 724, where Mr. Commissioner Vanclief, said: "The court first rendered an interlocutory judgment, requiring the plaintiff, within thirty days, to pay to each defendant, or to the clerk of the court for his use, the sums of money awarded to him by the jury for the value of his land condemned, and for damages to his land not condemned. After plaintiff's compliance with the interlocutory order, by paying into court the money awarded to each defendant, the court rendered final judgment of condemnation. Whether the money thus tendered and paid into court for their use had been obtained by plaintiff through regular or irregular assessments on the property of others, did not concern the appellants, [defendants in the condemnation suit,] nor affect the right of the plaintiff to condemn their lands which had not been assessed. The proceedings to assess, and to enforce the payment of assessments are entirely distinct from actions to condemn land. There is no pretense that the money tendered was not the property of the plaintiff, nor that it did not amount to just compensation. Therefore the rights of the appellants in this action, [defendants in an action by the city to condemn] could not have been prejudiced by defects in proceedings to assess the property of others."

Even where lands are in terms taken, it may be questioned whether the title to the fee passes absolutely to the municipality. The prevailing doctrine in such cases is, that the title vests only to the extent necessary for the purpose for which the property is taken. No more of the title is divested from the former owner than what is necessary for the public use. [Heyneman v. Blake, 19 Cal. 579, 597.]

Compensation must be made in advance, or a fund must be provided, out of which compensation must be made so soon as the amount can be determined. The property of the citizen cannot be taken from him until ample means of remuneration are provided. [Colton v. Rossi, 9 Cal. 595; McCann v. Sierra Co., 7 Cal. 121.]

When the street is finally established, the party whose land has been taken is entitled to payment, although the street has not been opened. [Section 614 Dillon's Municipal Corporations, 3rd ed.]

When the purpose for which land is to be taken, to open a street for example, is as well met by construing the authority to warrant the taking of an easement only as of the fee, the grant, if doubtful, will be construed most favorably to the citizen. [Section 603 Dillon's Municipal Corporations,3rd ed.]

In an action to condemn a parcel of land for a public street, evidence tending to show a former dedication by the owner, for the purpose of establishing the amount of damage or compensation, is not admissible. As, if there had been a dedication, an action to condemn would not lie, and in an action to condemn the question of dedication is not involved for any purpose. Either the land has been dedicated, and is already a public street, or the defendant is the owner. [San Jose v. Reed, 65 Cal. 241.]

The provision of section 18 of the act that "the complaint [in an action to condemn] may aver that it is necessary for the city to take or damage and condemn the said lands, or an easement therein, as the case may be, without setting forth the proceedings herein provided for, and the resolution and ordinance ordering said work to be done shall be conclusive evidence of such necessity" is constitutional. City and County of San Francisco v. Kiernan, 33 Pac. Rep. 721, where Mr. Commissioner Vanclief said: "It is contended that this provision [of section 18] is unconstitutional, both as to the form of the complaint, and as to the conclusiveness of the evidence. As to the form of the complaint, in an action merely to condemn, I think the provisions is unobjectional, whether such a complaint in an action to enforce an assessment, would be subject to the objection here made, is a question not involved in this action."

When the several steps provided by the statute for acquiring jurisdiction have been regularly taken, and the resolution and ordinance ordering the work have been regularly adopted, the action of the council is final and conclusive of the necessity of the improvement, and the courts may not adjudicate the question of such necessity in an action or proceeding for condemnation of lands necessary to the improvement; and therefore, if the answer sets up that the proceedings were inaugurated, and the action to condemn was instituted upon the motion and at the request of a railroad corporation, for the purpose and benefit of such railroad company, the court may strike out such allegations in the answer; the question sought to be raised by such allegations is one going to the public character of the use and necessity for its establishment, and as such is properly solvable by the city council only. [City of Santa Ana *v.* Harlin, No. 19,030, decided September 13, 1893.] So also, the mere fact that individuals have subscribed money or given a bond to the city to contribute toward the expense of laying out a street will not vitiate the proceedings, or prove that the land was taken for the accommodation of private persons, and not for public use. [*Id.*]

In this case of City of Santa Ana *v.* Harlin, Mr. Commissioner Searls, said: "Under the act of March 6, 1889, statutes of 1889, page 70, the power to order the opening of streets in municipalities, and the method of its exercise, is conferred upon the city council or legislative department of the municipality. Provision is made whereby those interested and objecting to the improvement and to various of the measures for carrying it out may be heard and their objections passed upon by the council, and when the several steps provided by the statute have been taken and the resolution and ordinance ordering said work have been regularly adopted, the action of the council is final and conclusive of the necessity of the improvement, and the courts may not adjudicate the question of such necessity in an action or proceeding for condemnation of lands necessary to the improvement. [See section 18 of statutes of 1889, p. 75; Tehama Co. *v.* Bryan, 68 Cal. 57; Butte Co. *v.* Boydston (not reported), 11 Pac. Rep. 781; San Francisco *v.* Kiernan *et al.,* vol. 5, Cal., Dec., p. 207.] * * * * * * There is no doubt that in many instances of attempted taking of private property for public uses it devolves upon the courts to determine whether or not the use is a public use. [Con. Channel Co. *v.* C. P. R. R. Co., 61 Cal. 269; Varick *v.* Smith, 5 Paige Ch. 159; Loan Assn. *v.* City of Topeka, 20 Wall, 655.] These, however, are exceptions to a general rule which recognizes in the legislative department the source of the power to determine what shall be held to be a public use, and the action of the legislature on the question is not, except in extreme cases, open to review by the courts. [Napa Valley R. R. Co. *v.* Napa County, 30 Cal. 437.] That the use of land for public streets in an incorporated town is a public use is true beyond controversy. And, when, as under the statute of March 6, 1889, the duty of determining the *necessity* of opening such streets and where as under that statute the official declaration or order opening a street is made *conclusive evidence* of the *necessity* *therefor*, the field of inquiry, in proceedings for the condemnation of land for such purposes, is confined to comparatively narrow limits."

In this case of Santa Ana v. Harlin, it was, in effect, stated by the learned commissioner who wrote the opinion, that if the defendant, in an action under section 18 of the act to condemn, desires to defend upon the ground of any defect or irregularities in the proceedings, he must allege such defect or irregularities. In this connection the learned commissioner said:

"The answer contains no allegations of any defect or irregularity in the proceedings, and hence there was no issue under which such evidence was admissible. The case of Los Angeles County v. San Jose Land Co., 96 Cal. 93, involved a like principle with that urged by appellant here, although under a different statute."

In an action under section 18 of the act to condemn, the present market value of the land, is the measure of damages and not its use to the owner or to the parties seeking to condemn it. [City of Santa Ana v. Harlin, *supra*.] It cannot, for the purpose of proving the market value, be shown for what *general* purposes the land might be properly used, as it might be used for a great variety of purposes, but such fact would not enlighten the jury upon the question of its value. It may, however, be shown whether or not the land is adapted to and *peculiarly* suited for some *specific* purpose, as that, by reason of its location, or its characteristics or qualities, it is peculiarly suited for a court house, or for a college or school. The witnesses are not allowed to give their opinions as to the value of the property for a particular purpose, but they may state its market value in view of any purpose to which it is adapted. [*Id.*] As a general rule it is not competent for the owner to prove what he has been offered for his property, or what persons who have been looking for similar property were willing to give for it. Or, if such questions are allowed, the testimony as to such offers must be confined to a period near the time at which the value was to be ascertained. [*Id.*] Upon cross-examination, however, where great latitude is allowed for the purpose of testing witnesses, questions of this character are allowable. [*Id.*] In respect to these rules of evidence in such condemnation suits, Mr. Commissioner Searls, in said case of City of Santa Ana v. Harlin, said:

"The next error assigned relates to the exclusion of evidence offered by defendant to show the uses and purposes to which the land proposed to be taken could properly be applied. In proceedings for the condemnation of land, the present market value of the land is the measure of damages and not its value in use to the owner or to the parties seeking to condemn it. By the term 'present market value' is meant not what the owner could realize at a forced sale, but 'the price he could obtain after reasonable and ample time, such as would ordinarily be taken by an owner to make sale of like property.' [Little Rock J. Ry. v. Woodruff, 49 Ark. 390.]

"In the Boom Co. v. Patterson, 98 U. S. 403, it was said: 'The inquiry in such cases must be, what is the property worth in the market, viewed, not merely with reference to the uses to which it is at the time applied, but with reference to the uses to which it is plainly adapted—that is to say, what it is worth from its availability for valuable uses?' Again the court says: 'As a general thing we should say that the compensation to the owner is to be estimated by reference to the uses for which the property is suitable, having regard to the existing business or wants of the community, or such as may be reasonably expected in the immediate future.'

"The peculiar fitness of land for particular purposes is an element in estimating its value which may be shown, and when it appears, forms a factor in solving the problem of market value. [San Diego Land, etc. Co. v. Neale, 78 Cal. 63 and 88 Cal. 50; Drinkhouse v. S. V. W. W., 92 Cal. 528.]

"One of the questions ruled as inadmissible was the following: 'For what purpose could that property be used properly?' No doubt the land in question could be properly used for a great variety of purposes, but it is not perceived that such fact would enlighten a jury upon the question of its value. Whether or not it was adapted to and peculiarly suited for some specific purpose is quite a different proposition, and testimony was introduced in reference to its qualities, location, surroundings, etc., all of which was proper. The following question was asked by defendant: 'What are the characteristics or qualities of the land, Mr. Palmer, that renders it suitable for a court house?' Similar questions tending to draw out testimony showing the adaptation of the land for a college, and for the purpose of a school, etc., were put and ruled out on the objection of plaintiff, and the rulings are assigned as error.

"I am of opinion the court erred in some of these rulings. The rule as enunciated by Lewis on Eminent Domain, at section 479 is as follows: 'The conclusion from the authorities and reason of the matter seems to be that witnesses should not be allowed to give their opinions as to the value of property for a particular purpose, but should state its market value in view of any purpose to which it is adapted. The condition of the property and all its surroundings may be shown, and its availability for any particular use. If it has a peculiar adaption for certain uses, this may be shown; and if such peculiar adaptation adds to its value the owner is entitled to the benefit of it. But when all the facts and circumstances have been shown, the question at last is, what is it worth in the market?'

"It will be seen from the foregoing quotation, which is regarded as a correct exposition of the law on the subject, that as to some of the questions seeking to elicit the value of the property for a specific purpose, the rulings of the court below were correct. It should, however, it is thought, have permitted a full and free investigation as to the adaptbility of the land to the varied practical purpose to which it is naturally adapted. [Central Pacific R. R. Co. v. Pearson, 35 Cal. 247.] Such proof should be limited to showing the present condition of the property and the uses to which it is adapted, and may not be extended to speculative inquiries as to possible future uses under altered circumstances, which may or may not arise.

"There was no error in the ruling of the court excluding an answer to the following question propounded to defendant when testifying as a witness in his own behalf: 'Question. Have you ever received offers for this real estate property?' The witness had just testified that he owned the land described in the pleadings, and had resided there sixteen years. The question as to whether he had received offers for the property was in effect to ask him if he had received such offers at any time in sixteen years. The general rule in estimating the market value of property is that 'it is not competent for the owner to prove what he has been offered for his property [C. P. R. R. Co. v. Pearson, 35 Cal. 247], or what persons who have been looking for similar property were willing to give for it.' [Selma R. R. Co. v. Keith, 53 Ga. 178; Lewis on Eminent Domain, § 446; see, also, Drinkhouse v. S. V. W. Wks., 92 Cal. 528.] A case apparently at variance with the general line of decisions is to be found in Muller v. Railway Co., 83 Cal. 240, in which the court held a similar question admissible, saying: '*Bona fide* offers for property afford some test as to its value, and are, we think, admissible,' quoting Harrison v. Glover, 72 N. Y. 451. The case quoted was not in relation to the market price of land, but related to a subject so different as to lend no support to the case there under discussion. If the doctrine of Muller v. Railway Co. can be upheld, it must be only as an exception to a general rule applicable only in peculiar cases, of which the present is not one.

"Again, if the binding force of Muller *v.* Railway Co. be admitted, the question put to defendant was improper in not confining the witness to a period near the time at which the value was to be ascertained.

"Upon cross-examination, where great latitude is allowed for the purpose of testing witnesses, questions of this character are conceded on all hands to be allowable. The questions put upon cross-examination of defendant's witnesses and objected to were proper. Great liberality is properly extended in such cross-examinations, and for the purpose of testing the knowledge, judgment or bias of the witness, the liberality is wisely exercised. In such cases, and for such purposes, much must be left to the discretion of the trial court and it is only for an abuse of discretion that its action should be impugned. The witnesses, Pinther, Ames and Blee, should have been allowed to testify as to the market value of the property. They were not experts in the severe sense of the term but showed such knowledge and experience as to values of land in that neighborhood as entitled the defendant to their opinions. [Penn. & N. Y. R. R. Co. *v.* Bunnell, 81 Pa. St. 426; Robertson *v.* Knapp, 35 N. Y. 92; LeRoy & W. R. R. Co. *v.* Hawk, 39 Kan. 638; Shattuck *v.* Stoneham R. R. Co., 6 Allen, Mass. 117; People *v.* Sanford, 43 Cal. 32; San Diego Land, etc. *v.* Neale, 78 Cal. 77."]

SECTION 19. The treasurer shall pay such warrants out of the appropriate fund, and not otherwise, in the order of their presentation; *provided*, that warrants for land or improvements taken or damaged shall have priority over warrants for charges and expenses, and the treasurer shall see that sufficient money is and remains in the fund to pay all warrants of the first class before paying any of the second. [*Statutes 1889, page 76.*]

SECTION 20. If after the sale of the property for delinquent assessments there should be a deficiency, and there should be unreasonable delay in collecting the same, or if for the purpose of equalizing the assessments, supplying a deficiency, or for any cause it appears desirable, the commissioners may so report to the city council, who may order them to make a supplementary assessment and report the same in manner and form as the original, and subject to the same procedure. If by reason of such supplementary assessment, or for any cause, there should be at any time a surplus, the city council may appropriate the same and declare a dividend pro rata to the parties paying the same, and they, upon demand, shall have the right to have the amount of such pro rata dividends refunded to them, or credited upon any subsequent assessment for taxes made against said parties in favor of said city. [*Statutes 1889, page 76.*]

SECTION 21. If any title attempted to be acquired by virtue of this act shall be found to be defective from any cause, the city council may again institute proceedings to acquire the cause as in this act provided, or otherwise, or may authorize the commissioners to purchase the same and include the cost thereof in a supplementary assessment as provided in the last section. [*Statutes 1889, page 76.*]

SECTION 22. If the city council deem it proper that the boundaries of the districts of lands to be affected and assessed to pay the damages, cost, and expenses of any work or improvement under this act, shall include the whole city, then the commissioners appointed shall proceed in a summary manner to purchase the lands to be taken or condemned from the owners and claimants thereof. If said commissioners and the owners and claimants cannot agree upon the price to be paid for said lands, they shall proceed to view and value the same, and shall thereupon make a summary report to the city council. Upon final confirmation of the report, the city council, if there be not sufficient money available in the city treasury, shall cause the cost and expenses of the contemplated public improvement to be assessed upon the whole of the taxable property of said city, and to be included in and form part of the next general assessment roll of said city, and with like effect in all respects as if the same formed a part of the city, state and county taxes; and when the same shall have been collected the said city council shall cause the land required to be paid for or the value thereof tendered, and the said contemplated public improvement to be forthwith made and completed. All the provisions of the preceding sections not in conflict with this section shall be applicable thereto. [*Statutes 1889, page 76.*]

SECTION 23. *1.* The words "work" and "improvement," as used in this act, shall include all work mentioned in section one of this act.

2. In case there is no daily or weekly or semi-weekly newspapers printed and circulated in the city, then such notices as are herein required to be published in a newspaper shall be posted and kept posted for the length of time required herein for the publication of the same in a weekly newspaper, in three of the most public places in such city. Proof of the publication or posting of any notice provided for herein shall be made by affidavit of the owner, publisher or clerk of the newspaper, or of the poster of the notice.

3. The word "municipality" and the word "city" shall be understood and so construed as to include all corporations heretofore organized and now existing, or hereafter organized, for municipal purpose.

4. The term street superintendent and superintendent of streets, as used in this act, shall be understood and so construed as to include, and are hereby declared to include, any person or officer whose duty it is, under the law, to have the care or charge of the streets, or the improvement thereof, in any city. In all those cities where there is no street superintendent or superintendent of streets, the city council thereof is hereby authorized and empowered to appoint a suitable person to discharge the duties herein laid down as those of street superintendent or superintendent of streets; and all the provisions hereof applicable to the street superintendent or superintendent of streets shall apply to such persons so appointed.

5. The term "city council" is hereby declared to include any body or board which, under the law, is the legislative department of the government of any city.

6. The term "clerk" and "city clerk," as used in this act, is hereby declared to include any person or officer who shall be clerk of said city council.

7. The term "treasurer" or "city treasurer," as used in this act, shall include any person or officer who shall have charge and make payment of the city funds.

8. No publications or notice other than that provided for in this act shall be necessary to give validity to any proceedings had thereunder. [*Statutes 1889, page 77.*]

SECTION 24. The proceedings in any work or improvement, such as is provided for in this act, already commenced and now progressing under any other act now in force, or by virtue of any ordinance passed by any city council or board of supervisors of any city, county, or city and county, by virtue of any other act. now in force, may, from any stage of such proceedings already commenced and now progressing, be continued under this act by resolution of the city council. The said work or improvement may then be conducted under the provisions of this act with full force and effect in all respects, from the stage of such proceedings under such other acts or ordinances at and from which such resolution shall declare an election or intention to have said work or improvement cease under such other act or ordinance and continue under this act; and from such election so made, all proceeding theretofore had under such other act or ordinance are hereby ratified, confirmed, and made valid, and it shall be unnecessary to renew or conduct over again proceedings had under such other act or ordinance. This section shall not apply to any work or improvement proceedings in which were commenced more than eighteen months prior to the passage of this act. [*Statutes 1889, page 77.*]

The subject of section 24 providing that "the proceedings in any work or improvement, such as is provided for in this act, already commenced and now progressing under any other act * * * * may from any stage of such proceedings * * * * be continued under this act," is sufficiently expressed in the title of the act to render such provision of section 24 valid. [City and County of San Francisco v. Kiernan, 33 Pac. Rep. 721.] It was not necessary, immediately upon the passage of the act of March 6, 1889, to declare the intention of proceeding thereunder, but discretion might be used in determining the stage at which the change should be made. *(Id.)* See said case of City and County of Francisco v. Kiernan for what constitutes a commencement of proceedings, within the meaning of the above section of the act [section 24 of the act of March 6, 1889,] providing that any work or improvement commenced within eighteen months before its passage may be continued under this act.

SECTION 25. The provisions of this act shall be liberally construed to promote the objects thereof. This act shall take effect and be in force from and after its passage. [*Statutes 1889, page 78.*]

Street Opening Act of March 23, 1893.

An act to provide for laying out, opening, extending, widening, straightening, diverging, curving, contracting, or closing up, in whole or in part, any street, square, lane, alley, court or place, within municipalities, or cities, and cities and counties, of forty thousand inhabitants or over, and to condemn and acquire any and all land and property necessary or convenient for that purpose.

[Approved March 23, 1893. Statutes 1893, p. 220.]

The people of the state of California, represented in senate and assembly, do enact as follows:

SECTION 1. Be it enacted : Whenever the public interest or convenience may require, the city council of any municipality, or cities, and cities and counties, containing over forty thousand inhabitants, shall have full power to order, and upon the petition of the owners of a majority of the frontage to be taken for said purpose shall order, the opening, extending, widening straightening, diverging, curving, contracting, or closing up, in whole or in part, of any street, square, lane, alley, court or place within the bounds of such city, and shall condemn and acquire any and all lands necessary or convenient for that purpose. [*Statutes 1893, p. 220.*]

This street opening act of March 23, 1893, differs from the street opening act of March 6, 1889, principally in this: The act of March 6, 1889, applies to *all* municipalities, regardless of population, whereas, the provisions of the act of March 23, 1893, are confined to municipalities containing forty thousand inhabitants or over. Also the act of March 23, 1893—section 1 thereof—authorizes the city councils to order more and different kinds of work than the act of March 6, 1893. The machinery provided by the act of March 23, 1893, for doing the work or improvements authorized by that act, is substantially the same as the machinery provided by the act of March 6, 1889, for accomplishing its purposes. And therefore, the cases cited in the notes to the act of March 6, 1889, will not be repeated here, but, if the act of March 23, 1893, be constitutional for any purpose, and proceedings be had thereunder, the reader is referred to the notes to the act of March 6, 1889, [*supra* page 241, *et seq.*] since they are likewise applicable to this act of March 23, 1893.

Until the constitutionality of this act of March 23, 1893, is decided by our Supreme Court, no definite statement in respect thereto, can safely be made. But this much is certain: It is a very serious question whether or not the act of March 23, 1893, is not violative of subdivisions 7 and 33 of section 25 of article IV of the constitution, which are as follows: "The legislature shall not pass local or special laws in any of the following enumerated cases, that is to say: * * * *Seventh*: Authorizing the laying out, opening, altering, maintaining, or vacating roads, highways, streets, alleys, town plats, parks, cemeteries, graveyards, or public grounds not owned by the state. * * * *Thirty-third*: In all other cases where a general law can be made applicable." The question then is: Is the act of March 23, 1893, a local or special law? In view of the contrariety of opinion upon this subject, it would not be wise to attempt to define the meaning of the terms "local" and "special" laws. But it may be possible to determine whether or not the act of March 23, 1893, is a local or special law within the meaning of those terms as applied to analogous cases.

It is also a serious question as to whether the act is not violative of section 11 of article I of the constitution, which provides that "all laws of a general nature shall have a uniform operation."

In City of Pasadena *v.* Stimson, 91 Cal. 251, Mr. Chief Justice Beatty said: "Although a law is general and constitutional when it applies equally to all persons embraced in a class founded upon some *natural* or *intrinsic* or *constitutional* distinction, it is not general or constitutional if it confers particular privileges or imposes peculiar disabilities or burdensome conditions, in the exercise of a common right, upon a class of persons arbitrarily selected from the general body of those who stand in precisely the same relation to the subject of the law."

In Earl *v.* S. F. Board of Education, 55 Cal. 489, it was held that the Traylor act, "An act to add a new section to the Political Code, * * * relating to cities and counties having 100,000 inhabitants or more," was local and special, and unconstitutional.

Mr. Justice Myrick, in his concurring opinion in this case, page 495, said: "Subdivision 20, section 25, article IV, prohibits the passage of special or local laws, changing county seats. Could it be said not to be *special* legislation to pass a law changing county seats of all counties having more than one hundred thousand inhabitants, and prescribing another mode for counties having a less population?" Therefore, while the Traylor act might have been considered special and local legislation because made applicable

274 STREET WORK LAW—STREET OPENING ACT OF 1893

only to *cities and counties* having 100,000 inhabitants
or more, when there was but one *city and county* in the
state, (the city and county of San Francisco,) it will be seen
from the above quotation from the opinion of Mr. Justice
Myrick, that, in his opinion a law would be *special*, and
therefore unconstitutional, if made applicable only to all
counties having more than one hundred thousand inhabitants. If this be so, it is difficult to perceive why a law
would not be obnoxious as special legislation if made applicable only to all municipalities, or cities, or cities and
counties of forty thousand inhabitants or more.

In Desmond *v.* Dunn, 55 Cal. 242, it was held that the
" McClure Charter" was not a general law and was unconstitutional, because by the terms of the act, it was limited
in its operation to cities and counties of more than 100,000
inhabitants.

In Miller *v.* Kister, 68 Cal. 145, it was held that section 4
of the act of March 18, 1885, amending the act of March
14, 1883, (the county government act) was local or special
legislation, and unconstitutional. In that case the grounds
of the decision were: *(1.)* That the amendment in question
was a general law. *(2.)* That, as a general law, its operation was restricted so that as to certain salaries it did not
apply until the expiration of the terms of the incumbents
then in office, except as to the officers of counties coming
under three classes, and as to them it took effect at a date
named in the law. Mr. Justice McKee, delivering the opinion of the court, said: " The amendatory acts passed in 1885
must be regarded as general laws upon the subjects
embraced by them, *i. e.*, the classification of counties and
the compensation of officers within the classified counties.
But as general laws the legislature restricted their operation as follows: 'Section 3. The salaries herein provided
shall not take effect nor be in force until the expiration of
the terms of the present officers, except as hereinafter provided. Section 4. The salaries herein provided for the
officers of the tenth, thirty-fifth, and forty-sixth classes,
shall take effect and be in force from and after the first
day of the first month next succeeding its passage.'
By these sections the operation of the law upon the subject of the compensation of officers in the fifty-two counties
of the state, except the counties of three classes, is suspended until the expiration of the terms of the then incumbents in office, and is put in force almost immediately upon
officers of the three specified classes. Unquestionably, the
legislature has the power to suspend the operation of the
general laws of the state. But when it does so, the suspen-

sion must be general, and cannot be made in individual cases or for *particular localities*."

It was held in that case that the law was not uniform in its operation, because the act, itself, declared that it did not operate upon the large majority of the county officers in the counties of the state, but that it should operate upon the officers of three counties only. It was likewise held that a law which produced such an effect is special and local legislation.

If section 4 of the said act of March 18, 1885, amending the said county government act of March 14, 1883, suspended the operation of a general law, (the county government act of March 14, 1883) for *"particular localities"* viz., in counties of the tenth, thirty-fifth, and forty-sixth classes, and if for this reason, it was special legislation, and unconstitutional, it is difficult to perceive why the street opening act of March 23, 1893, does not in like manner suspend the operation of a general law (the street opening law of March 6, 1889,) for "particular localities," viz., in cities and cities and counties having a population of forty thousand or over. And if the said street opening act of March 23, 1893, does thus suspend the operation of a general law for particular localities, it is difficult to perceive why it is not obnoxious as special legislation for the same reason that the said act of March 18, 1885, amending the county government act of 1883, was held to be special legislation and unconstitutional in said case of Miller v. Kister.

In City of Pasadena v. Stimson, 91 Cal. 238, it was held that section 870 of the municipal incorporation act of 1883, requiring cities of the fifth and sixth classes to make an effort to agree with the owners of land sought to be condemned, before instituting condemnation proceedings, is a special law making a forbidden discrimination against two classes of municipal corporations, by imposing upon them alone, a burdensome condition to the exercise of a right common to all public and private corporations and to all natural persons *sui juris* in the state, from which condition all others are exempt by the general law, and that it was, therefore, unconstitutional and void. It being as special and local legislation, in conflict with section 25 of article IV of the constitution, and, as wanting in uniformity of operation, in conflict with section 11 of article I of the constitution. Under the general law of the state relative to the exercise of the power of eminent domain,—section 1001 of the Civil Code—it is provided that *"any person"* may exercise the power of eminent domain under the provisions of section 1238 of the Code of Civil Procedure. But section 870 of the said municipal incorporation act of 1883 [statutes 1883, page 93] sought to exempt cities of the fifth and sixth classes from the otherwise general application of said section 1001 of the Civil Code, by requiring cities of the fifth and sixth classes to make an effort to agree with the owner of the property, as a condition to the exercise of the right of eminent domain.

The court, per Beatty, C. J., page 249, said: "Can the legislature make such a discrimination? 'All laws of a general nature shall have a uniform operation.' [Constitution, art. I, section 11.] 'The legislature shall not pass local or special laws in cases where a general law can be made applicable.' [Constitution, art. IV, section 25.] It seem to us perfectly clear that the clause of the incorporation act requiring cities of the fifth and sixth classes to make an effort to agree, while all other persons are exempt from such condition, is in plain and direct conflict with both these constitutional inhibitions. It destroys the uniform operation of a general law, and is special in a case where a general law not only can be made applicable, but in which a general law has been enacted, and in which there is no conceivable reason for discrimination."

In Morrison v. Bachert, 112 Penn. St. 322; s. c. 5 At. Rep. 739, it was held that the Pennsylvania statute of 1878, entitled "An act to ascertain and appoint the fees to be received by sheriffs, etc., *except in counties containing more than 150,000 or less than 10,000 inhabitants,*" is an act "regulating the affairs of counties," within the meaning of article 3, section 7 of the constitution of Pennsylvania, which declares that "the general assembly shall not pass any local or special law regulating the affairs of counties, or prescribing the duties and powers of officers in counties;" and that, inasmuch as the act excludes counties of over and under a certain number of inhabitants, it is a local, or special law, and, as such, is unconstitutional, under said section of the constitution.

In State v. Trenton, 42 N. J. L. 486, it was held that a statute conferring upon all cities having a population of not less than 25,000 inhabitants the power of issuing bonds to fund their floating debt, is special and local legislation, and as such, is unconstitutional and void.

In State v. Herrmann, 75 Mo. 340, it was held that an act to regulate the appointment of notaries public in all cities having a population of 100,000 or more, and providing that the office of any notary in such city, holding a commission bearing date prior to the passage of the act, and whose term of office had not expired at the time the act became a law, should be abolished, was special legislation, and as such was unconstitutional and void.

In State v. Mitchell, 31 Ohio St. 592, a street improvement act providing for the improvement of streets in certain cities of the second class, to wit, cities having a population of 31,000 inhabitants, according to the last federal census, was held to be special legislation, and as such, unconstitutional and void.

In view of the above decisions, it seems to follow as a necessary conclusion that the said street opening act of March 23, 1893, providing for the opening, etc., of streets in municipalities having 40,000 inhabitants or over, is special and local legislation, and prevents the said street opening act of March 6, 1889, from having a uniform operation; and that, therefore, unless, the above decisions have been modified by some other and controlling decision by our Supreme Court, or unless there be some other provision of the constitution justifying such an act, the act in question—act of March 23, 1893—is unconstitutional and void.

The decision of our Supreme Court which seems to give the strongest support to the constitutionality of the act of March 23, 1893, is the decision in the case of People ex rel., S. F. Daniels v. Henshaw, 76 Cal. 442. The facts of the Henshaw case are as follows: The case came before the Supreme Court on an agreed statement of facts. It was stipulated that S. F. Daniels, the relator in the case, received the highest number of votes cast for police judge of the city of Oakland, at an election held March 8th, 1886. It was also stipulated that said relator, Daniels, was entitled to the office of police judge of the city of Oakland, if that office was not abolished by an act entitled "An act to provide for police courts in cities having thirty thousand and under one hundred thousand inhabitants, and to provide for officers thereof" approved March 18, 1885, and known as the Whitney act. It was also stipulated that, if the said act of March 18, 1885, did abolish the office of police judge of the city of Oakland as provided by an act of the legislature approved March 10, 1866, by which such office was established, the defendant, Henshaw, was, in that event, entitled to the office. As will be seen, the agreed statements of facts, by conceding the right of the relator, Daniels, to the office of police judge, if "such office now exists," and the right of respondent, Henshaw, to the office of judge of the police court if there is no such office as police judge, eliminated from the problem all questions except one viz: Was the office of police judge of the city of Oakland abolished by an act of the legislature, entitled "An act to provide for police courts in cities having thirty thousand and under one hundred thousand inhabitants, and to provide for officers thereof," approved March 18, 1885.

The question thus presented was divided into two heads, viz: *(1.)* Did the legislature seek by the act of 1885, to repeal the act of 1866? *(2.)* Had it the power so to do by the method pursued?

It was held that it was clearly the intention of the legislature that the act of 1885, should supersede the act of 1866 since the latter statute was so repugnant to the former, that the two could not stand together, and that therefore, the act of 1885 did repeal the act of 1866—provided the act of 1885 was constitutional.

The last section of the act of 1885, was as follows: "This act to go into effect upon the expiration of the term of office of the present police judge of said cities, or when a vacancy occurs therein." In connection with the second head into which the question was divided—had the legislature power to pass the act of 1885, by the method which it pursued, and thereby repeal the act of 1866—it was contended by counsel for the relator that the legislature had no such power, because: .*(1.)* It was contended that the act of 1885 conflicted with section 11 of article I of the constitution—which provides that "all laws of a general nature shall have a uniform operation"—in that, by its own terms, the act of 1885 must take effect in different cities at different times, that is to say when the term of the police judge expires, or when there shall be a vacancy in his office. *(2.)* It was contended that the act was local and special legislation, and therefore violative of section 25 of article IV of the constitution.

In answer to the first objection, that the law was not uniform in its operation because by its own terms it must take effect in different cities at different time—the court said: "If the law operates equally upon all the objects embraced within it, *when they come within the circle or scope of its authority,* the uniformity of operation contemplated by the constitution is attained. A general law to fill vacancies in office cannot be void for want of unformity of operation because such vacancies must occur at different periods. If it meets every contingency when it arises and treats all the contingencies of like character in like manner, it is uniform in its operation. * * * Under the same circumstances, existing at the same period of time, the law must apply equally at the same time, or uniformity of operation is not

attained. Beyond this, identity as to time of application is
not necessary."

In answer to the second contention of counsel,—that the
act of 1885 was local and special legislation—the court said
that under section 6 of article XI of the constitution, the
legislature had the power to classify municipal corporations according to population, and that "a law which applies
to one or more, but not to all, of these classes, is not *for
that reason* special legislation."

However, the reasons clearly pointed out by Mr. Justice
McKinstry, in his dissenting opinion page 452, seem to afford
most cogent reasons for holding that the said act of 1885
was special legislation, because it created a special class for a
special municipal purpose.

The learned justice who wrote the prevailing opinion in
the case seems to have demonstrated clearly that the act of
1885—the Whitney Act—was not obnoxious to the provisions of section 11 of article I of the constitution, requiring
that "all laws of a general nature shall have a uniform operation," merely because the act might take effect in different
cities at different times. Upon this branch of the question
there seems to be no doubt but that, as stated by the learned
writer of the prevailing opinion, "if the law operates equally
upon all the objects embraced within it, *when they come
within the circle or scope of its authority*, the uniformity of
operation contemplated by the constitution is attained."
But upon the other branch of the question, viz: Is the law local
or special legislation, and therefore unconstitutional because
made to apply only to cities having a population of thirty
thousand and under one hundred thousand inhabitants?—the
weight of reason seems to lie with the dissenting opinion of
Mr. Justice McKinstry, for, even admitting that, for the
incorporation, organization and government of cities and
towns, the legislature may by *general* laws classify them,
and by *general* laws provide for their incorporation, organization and government according to such classification,
giving to each class a complete system of municipal government, still, as pointed out by Mr. Justice McKinstry in his
dissenting opinion, the act in question, purporting to provide
for police courts in cities having thirty thousand and under
one hundred thousand inhabitants, attempted to create a
special class for a *special* and *particular* purpose. The class
of cities to which the provisions of the act were made applicable was not a class which had been created by any general law classifying all the cities and towns of the state
according to their population. It was a different class from
any provided for in any general law classifying cities and

towns.   And this special class wa° created not for *all* municipal purposes, but only for one *special* municipal purpose, namely for the purpose of creating and providing for police courts.

Under section 6 of article XI of the constitution, the legislature has the power by a general law to classify cities and towns according to population, and by general laws provide for the incorporation and organization of the cities thus classified, giving to each class a complete system of municipal government.

By the acts of March 2 and 13, 1883, [statutes 1883, pages 24, 93] the legislature had complied with the mandate contained in section 6 of article XI of the constitution. By the act of March 2, 1883, it provided "for the classification of municipal corporations," and by the act of March 13, 1883, provided "for the organization, incorporation and government of municipal corporations."

The first of these acts—act of March 2, 1883—provides that "all municipal corporations within this state are hereby classified as follows: Those having a population of *more* than one hundred thousand inhabitants shall constitute the first class; those having a population of *more* than thirty thousand and *not exceeding* one hundred thousand inhabitants shall constitute the second class," etc.   As said by Mr. Justice McKinstry in his dissenting opinion: "The act of March 18, 1885, [the Whitney act] which is claimed to be operative in the city of Oakland, attempts to create a *single* class for a particular purpose,—a *different class* from any provided for in the general law, passed in obedience to the behest of the constitution for the classification of municipal corporations. It attempts to provide for a police court in every city, '*having* thirty thousand and *under* one hundred thousand inhabitants.'   *   *   *   *   *   *   Will any one contend that after general laws have been passed for the incorporation, organization, and classification of cities in proportion to population, the legislature may create, not merely a new classification of *all* cities and towns for a special municipal purpose, but a single class, differing from any included in the general classification for a special municipal purpose?"

This position of Judge McKinstry that an act is obnoxious as special legislation, which for a special municipal purpose, creates a special class, differing from any included in the general classification, is fully sustained by the Supreme Court of New Jersey in the case of State *v.* Trenton, 42 N. J. L. 486.

But, as said by Beatty, C. J., in City of Pasadena v. Stimson, 91 Cal. 250, the author of the prevailing opinion in People v. Henshaw, "*assumed* that the class of cities to which the Whitney act—the act of 1885—was made applicable, was identical with the second class as defined in the general incorporation act, and *upon that assumption* concluded that as cities having a large population require different legislation from those containing few inhabitants, the Whitney act, though applying to only one class, was nevertheless constitutional." The class of cities to which the Whitney act was made applicable was not identical with the second or any class defined in the general incorporation act or in the municipal classification act of March 2, 1883. Because the second class of municipal corporations defined by the said municipal classification act are those having a population of *more* than thirty thousand and *not exceeding* one hundred thousand inhabitants; whereas the Whitney act was made applicable to cities *having* thirty thousand and *under* one hundred thousand inhabitants.

Now, if it be assumed that the class of cities to which the Whitney act was made applicable was identical with the second class as defined in the general municipal incorporation act of March 2, 1883, the decision in the Henshaw case may be upheld as good law, and still it would not afford any support to the street opening act of March 23, 1893, since the latter act clearly creates a special class of municipalities for one particular special municipal purpose, viz., for the purpose of opening streets, etc.

Again, as pointed out by Mr. Justice Thornton in his dissenting opinion in *Ex parte* Henshaw, 73 Cal. 507, under section 1 of article VI of the constitution, a police court, such as that established by the act of 1885, may be created by a special law for each city.

Again, it seems to have been assumed by the author of the prevailing opinion in People v. Henshaw, that, because under section 6 of article XI of the constitution, the legislature may by general laws provide for the incorporation, organization, and classification, in proportion to population, of cities and towns, that therefore, the legislature, by an act applying to all cities of any particular class created by the act of classification, might amend the charter of any city not incorporated under the general municipal incorporation act. [See dissenting opinion of Mr. Justice McKinstry.] Nevertheless, even if this assumption be admitted to be correct, it would not for that reason, follow that the street opening act of March 23, 1893, was constitutional. Because, it cannot well be said that an act dividing all the

municipalities of the state into municipalities having 40,000
inhabitants or over, and municipalities having less than
40,000 inhabitants, is an act providing "for the *classification*,
in proportion to population of cities and towns." It seems
rather to be an act applicable to "a class *arbitrarily* selected
from the general body of those who stand in precisely the
same relation to the subject of the law," and for this
reason,—as stated by Mr. Chief Justice Beatty, in City of
Pasadena *v.* Stimson, 91 Cal. 251-2, to be unconstitutional.

Furthermore, subdivision 7 of section 25, article IV of
the constitution, expressly prohibits all special or local
legislation "authorizing the laying out, opening, altering,
maintaining, or vacating roads, highways, streets, alleys,
town plats, parks, cemeteries, grave yards, or public grounds
not owned by the state." Therefore, while under section 6
of act XI, "the legislature, by general laws, shall provide
for the incorporation, organization, and classification, in
proportion to population, of cities and towns," still said
subdivision 7 of section 25, article IV might, perhaps, be
regarded as constituting an exception to the general rule contained in this part of section 6 of article XI. That is to say,
under section 6 of article XI, the legislature may pass a general law providing for a classification of all of the cities
and towns of the state, in proportion to population, and, by
the same, or another general law, may provide a complete
system of municipal government for each class thus created.
Now it is possible that this may be regarded as being
intrinsically special or local legislation, although expressly
allowed by the constitution for all general purposes of
municipal incorporation and organization, with the possible
exception of such municipal purposes as are described in
said subdivision 7 of section 25 of article IV, namely, laying
out, opening, altering, maintaining or vacating roads,
highways, streets, etc.

In Pasadena *v.* Stimson, 91 Cal. 251, Mr. Chief Justice
Beatty, said that a law is not special if it applies to all
members of a class, *provided* the class "be founded upon
some natural or intrinsic or constitutional distinction."
That is, the class must be founded upon some special
peculiarities or characteristics naturally inhering in
the class itself, thus differentiating it from all others
not members of that class. Sex, for example, affords
an illustration of such natural and intrinsic differentiating qualities. Or the class must be one defined by the
constitution itself. Thus, in his dissenting opinion in People *v.* Central Pac. R. R. Co., 83 Cal. 414, Mr. Chief Justice
Beatty gave it as his opinion that the legislation in ques-

tion there,—provisions of the Political Code relating to the assessment and collection of taxes levied upon railroads operated in two or more counties—was not special because it applied to all railroads of a class created and defined by the constitution itself. Now if the cases cited *supra*,— Earle *v.* S. F. Board of Education, 55 Cal. 489; Desmond *v.* Dunn, 55 Cal. 242; Miller *v.* Kister, 68 Cal. 145; Pasadena *v.* Stimson, 91 Cal. 230; Morrison *v.* Bachert, 112 Penn. St. 322; s. c. 5 At. Rep. 739; State *v.* Trenton, 42 N. J. L. 486; State *v.* Herrmann, 75 Mo. 340; and State *v.* Mitchell, 31 Ohio St. 592,—were correctly decided, it would seem to follow that the classes into which the said street opening act of March 23, 1893, divided the municipalities of the state, are not classes founded upon some "natural or intrinsic" distinction. And they are not classes defined or created by the constitution itself. While it is true that the constitution [article XI, section 6] allows the legislature to classify the cities and towns of the state, in proportion to population, so that they may be incorporated and organized by general laws, according to such classification, still the constitution itself nowhere classifies the cities or towns of the state. Consequently such a classification is not founded upon a constitutional distinction, *i. e.* cities classified according to their population do not form any class created or defined by the constitution itself, as was the case in said case of People *v.* Central Pac. R. R. Co., 83 Cal. 393. If, therefore, cities classified according to their population do not form a class founded upon any natural or intrinsic distinction, and do not form a class defined or created by the constitution itself, it is possible that, though section 6 of article XI of the constitution, from the necessities of the case, permits the legislature by general laws to classify cities and towns in proportion to population, and, for all general purposes of municipal incorporation, organization and government, permits the legislature by general laws to apply to each class of cities, thus legislatively created, a different system of municipal incorporation, organization and government, still the provisions of subdivision 7 of section 25 of article IV may possibly be regarded as constituting an exception to the general provisions of section 6 of article XI. That is to say, it is possible, and consistent with the provisions of section 6 of article XI, that, as to one of the purposes of municipal incorporation, organization and government, namely, the laying out, opening, widening and maintaining streets, etc., the provisions of section 6 of article XI do not apply, and that for this particular municipal function, the legislature must provide by a general law applicable alike to all the cities and towns of the state.

Resume. In view of the foregoing, it may, therefore, be said that there are good reasons for believing that the case of People *v.* Henshaw, does not establish that the said street opening act of March 23, 1893, is a general law, uniform in its operation, and does not sustain the constitutionality of that act, for the following reasons:

1. As stated by Mr. Chief Justice Beatty in Pasadena *v.* Stimson, 91 Cal. 250, the author of the prevailing opinion in the Henshaw case "*assumed* that the class of cities to which the Whitney act—the act of 1885—was made applicable was identical with the second class as defined in the general incorporation act, and, *upon that assumption*, concluded that as cities having a large population require different legislation from those containing few inhabitants, the Whitney act, though applying to only one class, was nevertheless constitutional." On the other hand, the said street opening act of March 23, 1893, is not made applicable to any class of cities created or defined by any general classification or municipal incorporation act. It creates and defines a special and particular class of cities for one special and particular municipal purpose.

2. In his dissenting opinion in the Henshaw case, Mr. Justice McKinstry says that an act which creates a special class of cities for a special and particular purpose is special legislation and is unconstitutional, notwithstanding the provisions of section 6 of article XI of the constitution.

3. It is possible that the decision in the Henshaw case, 76 Cal. 442, is correct, under the provisions of section 1 of article VI of the constitution, even if the law in question in that case was special legislation. It was partly upon this provision of the constitution that Mr. Justice Thornton based his concurring opinion, 76 Cal. 447. [See dissenting opinion of Mr. Justice Thornton in *Ex parte* Henshaw, 73 Cal. 507.]

4. Even if, under the provisions of section 6 of article XI of the constitution, the legislature might make a special classification of the cities and towns of the state for some particular and special municipal purpose—the creation of a police court, for example—still, it is quite possible that as to the opening of streets and the other municipal functions mentioned in subdivision 7 of section 25 of article IV of the constitution, an exception is created, and that as to these particular municipal functions, there must be some general law, such as that of March 6, 1889, operating alike in all the cities of the state.

Furthermore, it seems to have been assumed by the author of the prevailing opinion in People v. Henshaw, that, under the provisions of section 6 of article XI of the constitution, the legislature might enact a law which should apply to all the cities included in any class, classified in proportion to population, even though some of the cities of such class might never have been incorporated or organized under any general municipal incorporation act, such as that mentioned in and contemplated by said section 6 of article XI. Now, admitting the correctness of this view of said provision of the constitution, and admitting that the decision in People v. Henshaw was correct, for the reasons given therefor in the prevailing opinion, still that case seems to have reached the limits of liberality of construction in holding that the Whitney act was not an act of special or local legislation. Indeed, Mr. Justice Fox, in *Ex parte Ah You*, 82 Cal. 343, in a dissenting opinion, speaking of said case of People v. Henshaw, and the act under consideration in that case, says: "The act of the legislature then under consideration—' An act to provide for police courts in cities having thirty thousand and under one hundred thousand inhabitants, and to provide for officers thereof,' approved March 18, 1885, commonly called the ' Whitney act,' [statutes 1885, p. 213]—was, at the time of its passage, as clearly a special law as any ever passed by a legislative body, and under the constitution should have been declared void."

In view of this clear-cut, emphatic language, and in view of the opinions in the cases cited *supra*, page 283, holding laws similar to the said street opening act of March 23, 1893, to be special legislation, it does not seem probable that the constitutionality of said street opening act can find any material support from the decision in the Henshaw case.

In conclusion it may be said that there are grave reasons to believe the street opening act of March 23, 1893, to be unconstitutional. Those reasons are as follows:

1. A statute conferring upon all cities, having a population over a certain number, particular municipal powers, not given to other cities, is special and local legislation.

2. The constitution, subdivision 7 of section 25, article IV, expressly provides that the legislature shall not pass any special or local laws, authorizing the laying out, widening, opening of streets, etc.

3. The act prevents the act of March 6, 1889, from having a uniform operation.

4. The act does not confer upon any of the classes of

cities created by the general municipal classification act—
the act of March 2, 1883, "An act to provide for the classification of municipal corporations," any municipal powers
relative to streets. It does not follow that classification, but
creates a *special* class for a special or particular purpose,
and in this respect differs from the Whitney act, as that
act was assumed to be by the author of the prevailing opinion
in People *v.* Henshaw, which decision, by the way, might be
supported by the provisions of section 1 of articles VI of the
constitution, according to the concurring opinion of Mr.
Justice Thornton in People *v.* Henshaw, 76 Cal. 447 and
likewise the dissenting opinion of the same justice in *Ex
parte* Henshaw, 73 Cal. 507.
    5. For the purpose of opening and widening streets, etc.,
the act divides the municipalities of the state into those
having a population of 40,000 inhabitants or over, and
those having less. It is doubtful if this can be regarded as
a "classification, in proportion to population, of cities and
towns," within the meaning of that phrase as used in section 6 of article XI of the constitution. [See Morrison *v.*
Bachert, 112 Penn. St. 322; s. c. 5 At. Rep. 739.]

    If the street opening act of March 23, 1893, be unconsti-
tutional the question arises: Does it expressly or by
implication repeal the street opening act of March 6, 1889,
in so far as municipalities having a population of 40,000
inhabitants or over, are concerned?
    The act of March 23, 1893, does not in terms repeal the
street opening act of March 6, 1889, but in section 23 of the
former act it is provided that "The act approved
March sixth, eighteen hundred and eighty-nine, entitled
'An act for opening, widening and extending streets,'
etc., after the passage of this act, shall not apply to any
city or city and county having a population of forty thous-
and inhabitants or over."
    It is possible that if the act of March 23, 1893, in terms
repealed the act of March 6, 1889, the latter act would be
repealed, even though the repealing act—the act of March
23, 1893—should, in all other respects be unconstitutional.
It has been held that a repealing clause in a statute may
be valid, though every other portion of it be unconstitutional. [Ely *v.* Thompson, 3 A. R. Marsh (Ky.) 70.] But
the act of March 23, 1893, does not in terms repeal the
act of March 6, 1889. It merely provides that the latter
act—the act of March 6, 1889—shall not apply to cities
having a population of less than 40,000 inhabitants. But
if the act of March 23, 1893, be unconstitutional upon the

ground that it is special legislation then, for the same reason, this part of the act—the part which declares that the act of March 6, 1889, shall not apply to cities having a population of less than 40,000 inhabitants—must be unconstitutional, since, in that case, the act of March 23, 1893, in attempting to limit the application of the act of March 6, 1889, bases the limitation upon what is tantamount to special legislation. [See County of Orange v. Harris, 97 Cal. 600.]

If, therefore, the act of March 23, 1893, be unconstitutional and void, upon the ground that it is special legislation, the act of March 6, 1889, is still in full force and effect, and applicable to all the municipalities of the state.

SECTION 2. Before ordering any work to be done or improvement made, which is authorized by section one of this act, the city council shall then pass a resolution declaring the intention to do said work, describing the work or improvement, and the land deemed necessary to be taken therefor, and specifying the exterior boundaries of the district of land to be affected or benefited by said work or improvement, and be assessed to pay the damages, costs, and expense thereof.

SECTION 3. The street superintendent shall then cause to be conspicuously posted along the line of said contemplated work or improvement, and not more than three hundred feet in distance apart, but not less than three in all, notices of the passage of said resolution. Said notice shall be headed, "Notice of Public Work," in letters not less than one inch in length, shall be in legible characters, state the fact of passage of the resolution, its date, and, briefly, the work of improvement proposed, and refer to the resolution for further particulars. He shall also cause a notice similar in substance to be published for a period of ten days in one or more daily newspapers published and circulated in said city, and designated by said city council, or, if there is no daily newspaper so published and circulated in said city, then by four successive insertions in a weekly or semi-weekly newspaper so published, circulated, and designated.

SECTION 4. Any person through whose lands said proposed street extension runs, or who will be damaged or affected by said proposed work, may within ten days after the first publication of said notice, file with the clerk of the city council his written objections thereto, stating in what manner and to what extent he will be damaged, which objection shall be delivered to the clerk of the city council, who shall indorse thereon the date of its reception by him, and at the next meeting of the city council, after the expiration of said ten days, lay said objections before said city council, which shall fix a time for hearing said objections, not less than one week thereafter. The city clerk shall thereupon notify the persons making such objections by depositing a notice thereof in the postoffice of said city, postage prepaid, addressed to such objector.

SECTION 5. At the time specified, or to which the hearing may be adjourned, the city council shall hear the objections filed, and if the owners of a majority of the frontage of all lands to be assessed for benefits, as said owners appear on the last preceding annual assessment roll for state and county taxes, object, in writing, to said proposed opening, extending, and widening, straightening, diverging, curving, contracting, or closing up of said street, said city council shall sustain said objections, and all proceedings therefor shall be stopped for the period of twelve months. Proceedings may be again commenced by a new resolution of intention. If the owners of a majority of the frontage of all streets within the assessment district do not object, in writing, thereto, within the time specified in this act, the city council shall be deemed to have acquired jurisdiction to order any of the work to be done or improvements to be made which is authorized by section one of this act.

SECTION 6. Having acquired jurisdiction, as provided in the preceding section, the city council shall order said work to be done, and unless the proposed work is for closing up, and it appears that no assessment is necessary, shall appoint three disinterested persons, who shall constitute a board of commissioners in that regard, who shall have full supervision of the proposed work or improvement until the completion thereof in compliance with this statute. For their services they shall each receive, as compensation, not to exceed five dollars for every day of actual service; *provided*, that said compensation shall not be paid for a longer term than six months for each district, unless extended by the council. Such extension shall not exceed two months at one time, nor shall the term of office of said commissioners, for any district, continue for longer than one year. Such compensation shall be added to and be chargeable as a part of the expenses of the work or improvement. Each of said commissioners shall file with the clerk of the city council an affidavit and a bond to the state of California, in the sum of five thousand dollars to faithfully perform the duties of his office. The city council may at any time remove any or all of said commissioners for cause, upon reasonable notice and hearing, and may fill any vacancies occurring among them for any cause. At the end of the terms of said commissioners, they shall hand over all unfinished business to the city council, who shall complete the same. In all municipalities where there is a board of public works, such board shall constitute the board of commissioners in this section provided for, and shall perform the duties of such commissioners, and their salaries as members of the board of public works shall be in full compensation for such services. It shall be the official duty of the city attorney to render said commissioners all necessary legal services; *provided*, that the city surveyor shall, for any work or services which he may perform by the direction of the common council or other legislative department of the city government, receive, in addition to his salary allowed by law, all sums which he may lay out, pay out, or expend in the prosecution of said work, for materials or labor necessarily therein by him employed.

SECTION 7. Said commissioners shall have an office assigned to them by the city council, in the city hall, and shall have power to employ a secretary, at a salary not to exceed one hundred and fifty dollars per month, and such other clerical assistance as shall be provided them by the city council, the salaries and fees of whom shall be established and fixed by said city council.

SECTION 8. All such charges and expenses shall be deemed as expenses of said work of improvement, and be a charge only upon the funds devoted to the particular work or improvement as provided hereinafter. All payments, as well for the land and improvements taken or damaged, and for the charges and expenses, shall be paid by the city treasurer, upon warrants drawn upon said fund from time to time, signed by said commissioners, or a majority of them. All such warrants shall state whether they are issued for land or improvements taken or damaged, or for charges and expenses, and that the demand is only payable out of the money in said fund, and in no event shall the city be liable for the failure to collect any assessment made by virtue hereof, nor shall said warrant be payable out of any other fund, nor a claim against the city.

SECTION 9. Said commissioners shall proceed to view the lands described in the resolution of intention, and may examine witnesses on oath, to be administered by any of them. Having viewed the land to be taken, and the improvements affected, and considered the testimony presented, they shall proceed with all diligence to determine the value of the land, and the damage to improvement and property affected, and also the amount of the expenses incident to said work or improvement, and, having determined the same, shall proceed to assess the same upon the lands described in said district herein provided. The lands fronting on said extension or widening shall only be assessed to the depth of one hundred and twenty feet, or the full depth of the lots, not exceeding one hundred and fifty feet; and said lands shall be assessed with reference to the amount of grading to be done, and their location on the grades of said street or improvement; and the expenses of grading said lots or lands, whether filling or cutting shall be necessary to place them on the grade of said street or improvement, shall be estimated in determining the value of the land, and the damage to the improvement and property affected.

SECTION 10. Said commissioners having made their assessment of benefits and damage, shall, with all diligence, make a written report thereof to the city council, and shall accompany their report with a plat showing the land taken, or about to be taken, for the work or improvement, and the lands assessed, showing the relative location of each district, block, lot, or portion of lot, and its dimensions, so far as the commissioners can reasonably ascertain the same. Each block and lot, or portion of lot, taken or assessed, shall be designated and described in said plat by an appropriate number, and a reference to it by such descriptive number shall be a sufficient description of it in any suit entered to condemn and in all respects. When the report and plat are approved by the city council, a copy of said plat, appropriately designated, shall be filed by the clerk thereof in the office of the recorder of the county.

SECTION 11. Said report shall specify each lot, subdivision or piece of property taken or injured by the widening or other improvement, or assessed therefor, together with the name of the owner or claimant thereof, or of persons interested therein as lessees, incumbrancers, or otherwise, so far as the same are known to such commissioners, and the particulars of their interests, so far as the same can be ascertained, and the amount of value or damage, or the amount assessed, as the case may be.

SECTION 12. If in any case the commissioners find conflicting claims of title exist, or shall be in ignorance or doubt as to the ownership of any lot of land, or of any improvements thereon, or any interest therein, it shall be set down as belonging to unknown owners. Error in the designation of the owner or owners of any land or improvements, or of the particulars of their interest, shall not affect the validity of the assessment or the condemnation of the property to be taken.

SECTION 13. Said report and plat shall be filed in the clerk's office of the city council, and thereupon the clerk of said city council shall give notice of such filing by publication for at least ten days in one or more daily newspapers published and circulated in said city; or if there be no daily newspaper, by three successive insertions in a weekly or semi-weekly newspaper so published and circulated. Said notice shall also require all persons interested to show cause, if any, why such report should not be confirmed, before the city council, on or before a day fixed by the clerk thereof, and stated in said notice, which day shall be not less than thirty days from the first publication thereof.

SECTION 14. All objections shall be in writing, and filed with the clerk of the city council, who shall, at the next meeting after the day fixed in the notice to show cause, lay the said objections, if any, before the city council, which shall fix a time for hearing the same, of which the clerk shall notify the objectors in the same manner as objectors to the original resolution of intention. At the time set, or at such other time as the hearing may be adjourned to, the city council shall hear such objections and pass upon the same; and at such time, or if there be no objections at the first meeting after the day set in such order to show cause, or such other time as may be fixed, shall proceed to pass upon such report, and may confirm, correct, or modify, or may sustain the objections thereto, and order the commissioners to make a new report, assessment, and plat, which in either case shall be filed, and notice given and hearing had, as in the case of the original report; but no report, or plat, or assessment shall be filed by said commissioners after the expiration of ten months, after their appointment.

SECTION 15. The clerk of said city council shall forward to the street superintendent of the city a certified copy of the report, assessment, and plat as finally confirmed and adopted by the city council. Such certified copy shall thereupon be the assessment roll, and thirty days after such filing shall become a lien on the property assessed therein, for its proportion of the costs of said improvement, as hereinbefore provided.

SECTION 16. The superintendent of streets shall thereupon give notice by publication for ten days in two daily newspapers published and circulated in said city and county, or by two successive insertions in a weekly or semi-weekly newspaper so published and circulated, that he has received said assessment roll, and that all sums levied and assessed in said assessment roll are due and payable immediately, and that the payment of said sums is to be made to him within thirty days from the date of the first publication of said notice. Said notice shall also contain a statement that all assessments not paid before the expiration of said thirty days will be declared to be delinquent, and that thereafter the sum of five per cent. upon the amount of each delinquent assessment, together with the cost of advertising each delinquent assessment, will be added thereto. When payment of any assessment is made to said superintendent of streets he shall write the word "paid" and the date of said payment opposite the respective assessments so paid, and the names of persons by or for whom said assessment is paid, and shall, if so required, give a receipt therefor. On the expiration of said thirty days, all assessments then unpaid shall be and

addressed to his last known place of abode or residence. If, at the expiration of thirty days after the deposit of such notice, he should not have
applied for such warrant and tendered a conveyance of the land to be
taken, the warrant so drawn shall be deposited with the county treasurer,
and shall be delivered to such owner, possessor, or occupant upon tendering a conveyance as aforesaid, unless judgment of condemnation shall be
had, when the same shall be canceled.

SECTION 18. If any owner of land to be taken neglects or refuses to
accept the warrant drawn in his favor, as aforesaid, or objects to the
report as to the necessity of taking his land, the commissioners, with the
approval of the city council, may cause proceedings to be taken for the
condemnation thereof, as provided by law under the right of eminent
domain. The complaint may aver that it is necessary for the city to take
or damage and condemn the said lands, or an easement therein, as the
case may be, without setting forth the proceedings herein provided for,
and the resolution and ordinance ordering said work to be done shall be
conclusive evidence of such necessity. Such proceedings shall be brought
in the name of the municipality, and have precedence, so far as the business of the court will permit; and any judgment for damages therein rendered shall be payable out of such portion of the special fund as may
remain in the treasury, so far as the same can be applied. At any time
after trial and judgment entered, or preceding an appeal, the court may
order the city treasurer to set apart in the city treasury a sufficient sum
from the fund appropriated to the particular improvement, to answer the
judgment and all damages, and thereupon may authorize and order the
municipality to enter upon the land and proceed with the proposed work
and improvement. In case of a deficiency in said fund to pay the whole
of said judgment and damages, the city council shall order the balance
thereof to be paid out of the general fund of the treasury.

SECTION 19. The treasurer shall pay such warrants out of the appropriate
fund, and not otherwise, in the order of their presentation; *provided*, that
warrants for land or improvements taken or damaged shall have priority
over warrants for charges and expenses, and the treasurer shall see that
sufficient money is and remains in the fund to pay all warrants of the
first class before paying any of the second.

SECTION 20. If any title attempted to be acquired by virtue of this act
shall be found to be defective from any cause, the city council may again
institute proceedings to acquire the land as in this act provided, or otherwise, or may authorize the commissioners to purchase the same, and
include the cost thereof in a supplementary assessment, as provided in
the last section.

SECTION 21. 1. The words "work" and "improvement," as used in this
act, shall include all work mentioned in section one of this act.

2. In case there is no daily or weekly or semi-weekly newspaper printed
and circulated in the city, then such notices as are herein required to be
published in a newspaper shall be posted and kept posted for the length of
time required herein for the publication of the same in a weekly newspaper, in three of the most public places in such city. Proof of the publication of posting of any notice provided for herein shall be made by affidavit of the owner, publisher, or clerk of the newspaper, or of the poster of
the notice.

3. The word "municipality" and the word "city" shall be understood and so construed as to include all corporations heretofore organized and now existing, or hereafter organized, for municipal purposes.

4. The term "street superintendent" and "superintendent of streets," as used in this act, shall be understood and so construed as to include, and are hereby declared to include, any person or officer whose duty it is, under the law, to have the care or charge of the streets or the improvement thereof, in any city. In all those cities where there is no street superintendent or superintendent of streets, the city council thereof is hereby authorized and empowered to appoint a suitable person to discharge the duties herein laid down as those of street superintendent or superintendent of streets, and all the provisions hereof applicable to the street superintendent or superintendent of streets, shall apply to such persons so appointed.

5. The term "city council" is hereby declared to include any body or board which, under the law, is the legislative department of the government of any city.

6. The term "clerk" and "city clerk," as used in this act, is hereby declared to include any person or officer who shall be clerk of said city council.

7. The term "treasurer" or "city treasurer" as used in this act, shall include any person or officer who shall have charge, and make payment of the city funds.

SECTION 22. The mayor, tax collector, and city or city and county attorney, as the case may be, of all municipalities wherein there is existing at the passage of this act any commission appointed for the opening, extending, or widening of streets under the provision of said act of March sixth, eighteen hundred and and eighty-nine, and which commission is not within the proviso of section twenty-three of this act, are hereby constituted a board of audit, whose duty it shall be, upon petition of said commission, to carefully examine all the accounts, bills, and expenditures, made or contracted for by said commission, including the salaries of the said commissioners and said board of audit, or a majority of its members, is hereby authorized to audit and allow such amounts as it shall find to be just and reasonable, and report said amounts, with the items thereof and to whom payable, to the city council. Said report shall be final and conclusive as to said amounts. The city council is authorized to pass and allow, and order paid, to each of the persons entitled thereto, the amounts so found to be due, in the same manner as claims and demands against such municipality are passed, allowed, and ordered paid. The payment of said amounts shall be provided for in the tax levy next thereafter made by said city council, and when said taxes are collected the said amounts shall be paid out of the general fund of said municipality, in the same manner as other claims and demands are paid.

SECTION 23. The act approved March sixth, eighteen hundred and eighty-nine, entitled "An act for opening, widening, and extending streets," etc., after the passage of this act, shall not apply to any city or city and county having a population of forty thousand inhabitants or over; but as to any city or city and county having a population of forty thousand or over said act shall not apply; but said cities and cities and counties shall be subject only to the provisions of this act in all matters embraced within the purview of this act; *provided, however,* that the present city council, or other governing body of any municipality of forty thousand inhabitants or over, shall have power, by a three-fourths vote of its members, to extend the life of any existing commission until its work shall have been completed, as in said act provided; but in all other cases in cities or cities and counties of forty thousand inhabitants or over, the assessments, plats, and reports filed by said commissioners are declared to be null and void, and all moneys collected under the provisions of said act shall be refunded to the persons from whom the same were collected, in the same manner as taxes which have been twice collected, and the said commissioners are hereby removed from office; *provided, further, however,* that in case of the lands necessary to widen or open any street, there shall have been actually purchased and conveyed to the municipality, under the provisions of said act of March sixth, eighteen hundred and eighty-nine, more than one-half of the land necessary for said improvements, as shown by the report and plat on file, then said streets and the improvement thereof, shall not be affected by this act, but the same shall be completed as commenced.

SECTION 24. This act shall be liberally construed to promote the objects the reof.

This act shall take effect and be in force from the time of its passage. [*Statutes 1893, page 221.*]

Sanitary District Act.

It is a serious question as to whether this sanitary district act is constitutional or not. It provides, [section 1,] that twenty-five persons in any county, residents and freeholders within the proposed district, may present to the board of supervisors of such county a petition in writing, signed by them, stating the name of the proposed district, *and setting forth the boundaries thereof*, and praying that an election be held as provided by the act. Section 2 provides that "when such petition is presented * * the board of supervisors *must* within thirty days thereafter, order that an election be held as provided by this act. The order * * * must show the boundaries of the proposed district." Section 4 provides for an election at which every qualified voter, resident within the proposed district for the period requisite to enable him to vote at a general election, shall be entitled to vote, and that "if a majority of the votes cast at such election shall be in favor of a sanitary district, the board of supervisors shall make and cause to be entered in the minutes an order that a sanitary district of the same name *and with the boundaries stated in the petition* (setting forth such boundaries) has been duly established." It will thus be seen that the boundaries of the district may be fixed by the petition of twenty-five persons; that the board of supervisors, the legislative body of the county, have no discretion in the matter. They *must* call an election, upon the filing of the petition, and *must* declare to be established the very district described in the petition, if a majority of the electors, voting at the election, cast their votes in favor of the proposed district. Here is an attempt to transfer to a majority of the qualified electors of any proposed district, the power to declare that such portion of the county as is specified in said petition will be benefited by sewers and drains to be erected at the expense of all the property, real and personal, within the district, and to set in motion machinery for the enforcement of a tax and assessment against the minority of the qualified electors, even though such minority of the qualified electors may be the owners of a large majority of the property lying within the proposed district. Upon the principles laid down in Moulton v. Parks, 64 Cal. 166, there would seem to be room for grave doubts as to the constitutionality of the sanitary district act. In Moulton v. Parks, it was held that the act of March 25, 1868, [statutes 1867–8, page 316,]—an act to provide for the protection of certain lands in the county of Sutter from overflow, by the erection of levee districts—was unconstitutional. Section 21 of that act provided that "whenever a petition shall be received by said board of supervisors, from persons in possession of more than one-half of the acres of any specified portion of said county, asking to be set apart and erected into a levee district, said board *shall at once erect* such territory into a levee district, and place it under the provisions of this act, to be called Levee District, No. 1, 2, 3, and so on, as the case may be; *provided*, that it shall not be required to submit the question of tax to a vote of the people of any district so erected." It was held that this act was unconstitutional because the act did not provide for the creation of an assessment district by the legislative authority of the state, or by a properly organized municipality, or by assessors or commissioners authorized to ascertain what lands would be benefited by the proposed levees, as it should have done to be constitutional [Cooley on Taxation, 449], but provided, instead, that on the presentation of a petition the board of supervisors "shall at once proceed" to erect the territory described in the petition into a levee district, "and place it under the provisions of this act." The court per McKinstry, J., page 183, said: "Here is an attempt to transfer to persons in possession of more than one-half of the acres of any portion of the county of Sutter which *they* may specify, the power to declare that such portion of the county will be benefited by works erected at the expense of all the property, real and personal, within it, and to set in motion machinery for the enforcement of a tax and assessment against the owners of a majority of the acreage. The act provides for no judicial inquiry as to what lands will be benefited by a proposed work, nor does it contain any declaration by the state legislature that any specified lands will be benefited, nor provide that such declaration may be made by the supervisors, or by any officer or agent of the state or county. When those in possession of more than one-half of the land by them specified file a petition they assert that *they* will be benefited by the proposed work, and they also attempt to determine that the owners of other lands will be benefited. They determine that the work will benefit all, and attempt to levy a tax upon others as well as themselves, which shall be expended in work of *joint* as well as several benefit. No man can be a judge in his own cause, and no man's property can be taken without due process of law." And on page 184, the learned judge said: "The supervisors have no discretion to reject the petition, or to modify or change the boundaries of the district, or otherwise to exercise any judgment with reference to the expediency of fixing the limits of the assessment district where the petition fixes them. One man in possession of 3000 acres of land, which he believes will be protected by a levee, may thus decree that 5999 acres (of which 2999 are owned by one hundred other men), will be benefited by a levee, and arbitrarily adjudge the one hundred to pay almost half of the expense of building it. Under our constitution there never has been power in the legislature to delegate such legislative functions to interested individuals."

In like manner, it may be said of the sanitary district act: " The supervisors have no discretion to reject the petition, or to modify or change the boundaries of the district, or otherwise to exercise any judgment with reference to the expediency of fixing the limits of the assessment district where the petition fixes them." It is true that under this sanitary district act the board of supervisors are not compelled to at once proceed to erect the territory described in the petition into a sanitary district, as was the case in said levee district act of 1868, but if a majority of the qualified electors voting at the election vote for the district, the supervisors must then make an order that a sanitary district, of the name and with the boundaries stated in the petition, has been duly established. So that the whole matter is virtually taken out of their hands and left to the discretion of a majority of the electors, who may own a minority of the property affected and liable to be taxed or assessed. The supervisors exercise no judgment whatever with reference to fixing the boundaries of the district.

In Moulton v. Parks it was said that the owners of a bare majority of the acreage (3000 acres, for example) might arbitrarily decree that the owners of a minority of the acreage (2999 acres, for example) should contribute toward the expense of building a levee. But in the sanitary district act, the owners of a minority of the acreage might arbitrarily decree that the owner of a majority of the acreage should pay the greater part of the burdens. Thus, suppose a community of twenty-six persons. One of these owns twenty-five twenty-sixths of the land in the proposed district. The remaining twenty-five own one twenty-sixth of the land in the proposed district. These latter file a petition describing the proposed district. The supervisors, without any discretion in the matter, call an election. The twenty-five owners of one twenty-sixth vote for the establishment of the district. The owner of the twenty-five twenty-sixths of all the property in the district votes against it. Therefore, if there is any difference between this sanitary district act and the levee district act, considered in Moulton v. Parks, it is that the latter act empowered the owners of a *majority* of the lands, liable to be taxed for the proposed improvement, to declare that such portion of the county as *they* might specify would be benefited by the works to be erected at the expense of all the property in the district, and to set in motion machinery for the enforcement of a tax and assessment against the owners of a *minority* of the acreage. Whereas the sanitary district act gives the same powers to the owners of a *minority* of the lands liable to be taxed, to be exercised against the owner or owners of a *majority* of the lands.

Furthermore, the sanitary district act does not provide for the establishment of the district in either of the modes which, according to Mr. Justice Cooley, seem to be essential, namely *(1.)* by the legislative authority of the state, or, when properly organized, by a municipality; or, *(2.)* by assessors or commissioners, authorized by law to assess such lands as in their opinion are specially benefited, and ought, therefore, to contribute to the cost. [Cooley on Taxation, 449.]

Furthermore, the sanitary districts which the act provides for are public corporations for the exercise of a most important municipal function, viz., the building and maintaining of sewers and drains, in the exercise of which function the corporations are empowered to exercise the sovereign power of taxation, a power which may, perhaps, be justly regarded as the most important attribute of sovereignty. [See Dean v. Davis, 51 Cal. 406; People v. Williams, 56 Cal. 647; Reclamation District v. Hagar, 66 Cal. 54; Irrigation District v. Williams, 76 Cal. 360; In re Madera Irrigation District, 92 Cal. 296.] Under the act a sanitary district may be created wholly or partly within a city or town or other public corporation organized for municipal purposes and exercising municipal functions, or the boundaries of the sanitary district may coincide and be coterminous with the boundaries of such city, town, or other municipal corporation. It is possible, therefore, that the act may be considered as delegating to individuals, viz., the board of directors of the sanitary district, and the electors therein, powers over municipal improvement, and to exercise municipal functions that properly belong to the regular municipal authorities of a city or town; and, it is possible, that for this reason the act may be violative of section 13 of article XI of the constitution. This point was raised against the Wright Irrigation Act in Irrigation District *v.* Williams, 76 Cal. 360; Modesto Irrigation District *v.* Tregea, 88 Cal. 334, and *In re* Madera Irrigation District, 92 Cal. 296; and, while the point was decided in favor of the constitutionality of that act in those cases, still, as said by the court on rehearing in the latter case, [92 Cal. 344] "a system of irrigation contemplated by the act in question [the Wright act] cannot be considered as a 'municipal purpose,' within the scope of the organization of a city or town, and there can be no conflict between a corporation organized under the act to produce a system of irrigation within the district, and the municipal incorporation of the town of Madera;" whereas, the purpose of the sanitary district act—the construction of sewers, drains, etc. —is distinctively a municipal purpose, and this language of the court in *In re* Madera Irrigation District tends to cast doubt upon the constitutionality of the sanitary district act, rather than to clear up the question. However, it is not within the purview of this book to discuss these questions of constitutional law, but merely to briefly raise such questions of the constitutionality of these street work acts as have suggested themselves to the mind of the author.

An Act to provide for the formation, government, operation, and dissolution of sanitary districts in any part of the state, for the construction of sewers and other sanitary purposes; the acquisition of property thereby; the calling and conducting of elections in such districts; the assessment, levy, collection, custody, and disbursement of taxes therein: the issuance and disposal of the bonds thereof, and the determination of their validity, and making provision for the payment of such bonds, and the disposal of their proceeds.

[Approved March 31, 1891, statutes 1891, p 223.]

The people of the state of California, represented in senate and assembly, do enact as follows:

SECTION 1. Whenever twenty-five persons in any county of the state shall desire the formation of a sanitary district within the county, they may present to the board of supervisors of such county a petition, in writing, signed by them, stating the name of the proposed district, and setting forth the boundaries thereof, and praying that an election be held as provided by this act. Each of the petitioners must be a resident and freeholder within the proposed district.

SECTION 2. When such petition is presented as above provided, the board of supervisors must, within thirty days thereafter, order that an election be held as provided by this act. The order must fix the day of such election, which must be within sixty days from the date of the order, and must show the boundaries of the proposed district, and must state that at such election persons to fill the offices provided by this act, viz., a sanitary assessor, and five members of the sanitary board, will be voted for. This order shall be entered in the minutes of the board, and shall be conclusive evidence of the due presentation of a proper petition, and of the fact that each of the petitioners was at the time of the signature and presentation of such petition a resident and freeholder within the limits of the proposed district.

SECTION 3. A copy of such order shall be posted for four successive weeks prior to the election, in three public places within the proposed district, and shall be published for four successive weeks prior to the election, in some newspaper published in the proposed district, if there be one, and if not, in some newspaper published in the county. It shall be sufficient if the order be published once a week.

SECTION 4. The board of supervisors, at any time prior to the election, shall select one polling place within the proposed district, and make all suitable arrangements for the holding of such election. The tickets shall contain the words "For a Sanitary District," or "Against a Sanitary District," as the case may be, and the name of a person for sanitary assessor, and the names of five persons for members of the sanitary board. Such election shall be conducted in accordance with the general election laws of the state, so far as the same shall be applicable, except as herein otherwise provided. Every qualified elector, resident within the proposed district for the period requisite to enable him to vote at a general election, shall be entitled to vote at the election above provided for. If a majority of the votes cast at such election shall be in favor of a sanitary district, the board of supervisors shall make and cause to be entered in the minutes an order that a sanitary district of the name and with the boundaries stated in the petition (setting forth such boundaries) has been duly established, and said order shall be conclusive evidence of the fact and regularity of all prior proceedings of every kind and nature provided for by this act or by law, and of the existence and validity of the district. If a majority of the votes cast shall be against a sanitary district, the board shall, by order, so declare; no other proceedings shall be taken in relation thereto until the expiration of one year from the presentation of the petition.

SECTION 5. Every sanitary district formed under the provisions of this act shall have power to have and use a common seal, alterable at the pleasure of the sanitary board; to sue and be sued by its name; to construct and maintain and keep clean such sewers and drains as in the judgment of the sanitary board shall be necessary or proper, and for this purpose to acquire, by purchase, gift, devise, condemnation proceedings, or otherwise, such real and personal property and rights of way, either within or without the limits of the district, as in the judgment of the sanitary board shall be necessary or proper, and to pay for and hold the same; to make and accept any and all contracts, deeds, releases and documents of every kind which, in the judgment of the sanitary board, shall be necessary or proper to the exercise of any of the powers of the district, and to direct the payment of all lawful claims and demands against it; to issue bonds as hereinafter provided, and to assess, levy and collect taxes to pay the principal and interest of the same, and the cost of laying and the expense of maintaining any sewer or sewers that may be constructed subsequent to the issuance of said bonds, or any lawful claims against said district, and the running expenses of the district; to employ all necessary agents and assistants, and pay the same; to lay its sewers and drains in any public street or road of the county, and for this purpose to enter upon the same and make all necessary and proper excavations, restoring the same to proper condition, but in case such street or road shall be in an incorporated city or town, the consent of the lawful authorities thereof shall first be obtained; to make and enforce all necessary and proper regulations for the removal of garbage and the cleanliness of the roads and streets of the district, and for the purpose of guarding against the spread of contagious and infectious diseases, and for the isolation of persons and houses affected with such diseases, and for the notification of the other inhabitants of the existence thereof, and all other sanitary regulations not in conflict with the constitution and laws of the state; to impose fines, penalties and forfeitures for any and all violations of its regulations and orders, and to fix the penalty thereof by fine or imprisonment, or both; but no such fine shall exceed the sum of one hundred dollars, and no such imprisonment shall exceed one month; to call, hold, and conduct all elections necessary or proper after the formation of the district; to prescribe, by order, the time, mode and manner of assessing, levying, and collecting taxes for sanitary purposes, except as is otherwise provided herein; to compel all residents and property owners within the district to connect their houses and habitations with the street sewers and drains; and generally to do and perform any and all acts necessary or proper to the complete exercise and effect of any of its powers, or the purpose for which it was formed.

Section 6. The officers of the district shall be a sanitary assessor and five members of the sanitary board.

Section 7. There shall be an election for sanitary assessor on every even numbered year in which members of the sanitary board are elected, and at the same time, place and manner; and the person then elected shall hold office for two years next thereafter, and until the election and qualification of his successor. The person elected assessor at the election at which the district was formed shall hold office until the election and qualification of his successor; *provided,* that if at any time a vacancy occur in the office of assessor, the sanitary board shall appoint a suitable person to fill such vacancy until the next election at which an assessor may be elected under the provisions of this act.

Section 8. It shall be the duty of the sanitary assessor to make out, before the first Monday in July of each year, a list of all the tangible, real and personal property within the district. Such list shall contain a brief and general description of the property, an assessment of the value thereof, the name or names of the owner or owners, and such other matters as may be ordered by the sanitary board and such matters as shall be necessary to make such list conform to the provisions of the general laws of the state of California. The land shall be assessed separately from the improvements thereon. No mistake in the name of the owner of any of the real or personal property assessed, or any informality in the description, or in other parts of the assessment, shall invalidate the same

The sanitary assessor shall verify said list by his oath before some officer authorized to administer oaths, and shall deposit the same with the sanitary board on the first Monday of July of each year, or as soon thereafter as is practicable. He shall have power to administer all oaths and affirmations necessary or proper in the performance of his duty as assessor, and shall receive such compensation as shall be fixed by the order of the board. He shall also perform such further duties and do such further acts as may be ordered or required by the sanitary board.

SECTION 9. There shall be an election for two members of the sanitary board in every even numbered year, beginning with the second even numbered year after the election at which the district was organized, and the two members then to be elected shall hold office until the election and qualification of their successors in the next even numbered year; and there shall be an election for three members of the sanitary board in every odd numbered year, beginning with the second odd numbered year after the election at which the district was organized, and the three members then to be elected shall hold office until the election and qualification of their successors in the next odd numbered year. The five members elected at the election at which the district was organized shall, at their first meeting, or as soon thereafter as may be practicable, so classify themselves, by lot, that two of them shall go out of office in the second even numbered year after the election at which the district was organized, and upon the election and qualification of their successors, as provided by this act, and three of them in the second odd numbered year after the election at which the district was organized, and upon the election and qualification of their successors, as provided by this act. All elections for officers after the formation of the district shall be on the first Monday after the first Tuesday in the month of March. The members of the sanitary board shall receive no compensation whatever, either for general or special services.

SECTION 10. The sanitary board shall be the governing power of the district, and shall exercise all the powers thereof, except the making of an assessment list in the first instance, as herein provided. At its first meeting, or as soon thereafter as may be practicable, the board shall choose one of its members as president and another of its members as secretary. And all contracts, deeds, warrants, releases, receipts and documents of every kind shall be signed in the name of the district by its president, and shall be countersigned by its secretary. The board shall hold such meetings, either in the day or in the evening, as may be convenient. In case of the absence or inability to act, of the president or secretary, the board shall, by order entered upon the minutes, choose a president, *pro tem.*, or secretary, *pro tem.*, or both, as the case may be.

SECTION 11. The sanitary board shall sit as a board of equalization as soon as it receives the assessor's list, or as soon thereafter as practicable, and shall continue in session as such board, with convenient intermissions, until the entire list furnished by the assessor shall have been examined and rectified, if rectification be necessary. The board shall have power to hear complaints as to the proceedings of the assessor, and to adjudicate and determine the controversy thereon, and may of its own motion raise an assessment, after such reasonable notice to the party whose assessment is to be raised as may be ordered by the board. After the examination and rectification of the assessor's list shall have been completed, the board shall, by resolution, fix the rate of taxation for sanitary purposes, designating the number of cents on each one hundred dollars to be levied for each fund, and shall designate the fund into which the same shall be paid; but no more than fifteen cents on each one hundred dollars shall be levied for all the sanitary purposes of any one year, besides what shall be required for the payment of the principal and interest of such year upon outstanding bonds. After the entry in the minutes of the resolution fixing the rate of taxation, the sanitary board shall cause the assessor to compute the amount of the tax upon each piece of real and personal property and enter the same upon the assessment list in a suitable place. The list, when so completed, shall be verified by the assessor and signed by the president and secretary; and the amount of the tax shall thereupon become a lien upon the property upon which it is assessed, and shall have the effect of a judgment against the person of the owner thereof, and every such lien shall have the force and effect of an execution duly levied against all the property of the delinquent; and the judgment shall not be deemed satisfied or the lien extinguished until the taxes are paid or the property sold to satisfy the same, and no statute of limitation shall apply; but no more then seventy-five thousand dollars of bonds shall be voted for or issued at any one time, nor shall the bonded indebtedness of the district ever exceed the sum of seventy-five thousand dollars at any one period, whether it be made up of one issue of bonds or of several periods.

SECTION 12. On or before the first Monday in July of each year, the board shall transmit, or cause the assessor to transmit, a duplicate of the list so made to the tax collector of the county, who shall collect the taxes shown by said list to be due, in the same manner as he collects the county taxes, and all the provisions of the laws of the state as to the collection of taxes and delinquent taxes, and the enforcement of the payment thereof, so far as applicable, shall apply to the collection of taxes for sanitary purposes; and said tax collector, and the sureties on his official bond, shall be responsible for the due performance of the duties imposed upon him by this act; *provided*, that the sanitary board may, in its discretion, direct the district attorney of the county to commence and prosecute suits for the collection of the whole or any portion of the delinquent taxes; and it shall be the duty of the district attorney to carry out such directions of the sanitary board, and he, and the sureties upon his official bond, shall be responsible for the due performance of the duty imposed upon him by this act; *and provided further*, that the sanitary board may, at any time, by order entered in its minutes, provide a system for the collection of delinquent taxes, or make any change in the manner of their collection, which as to such taxes shall have the force of law. All money collected for sanitary purposes by the district attorney under this act shall be at once paid to the county treasurer.

SECTION 13. The tax collector shall pay over to the county treasurer all moneys collected by him for sanitary purposes, as fast as the same shall be collected, and the said treasurer shall keep the same in the county treasury as follows: In a fund called the bond fund for sanitary district (naming it) he shall place and keep the moneys levied by the sanitary board for such fund; and no part of the money in this fund shall be transferred to any other fund, or be used for any other purpose than the payment of the principal and interest of the bonds of the sanitary district, so long as any such bonds shall be unpaid; in a fund called the running expense of sanitary district (naming it) he shall place and keep the moneys levied by the sanitary board for such fund. The whole or any part of the money in the running expense fund may be transferred to the bond fund, or to the other fund hereinafter provided for, upon the order of the sanitary board, and it shall be the duty of the treasurer to comply with such order. The treasurer shall pay out moneys from either of said funds, or from the fund hereinafter mentioned, only upon the written order of the sanitary board, signed by the president and countersigned by the secretary, which order shall specify the name of the person to whom the money is to be paid and the fund from which it is to be paid, and shall state generally the purpose for which the payment is made, and such order shall be entered in the minutes of the sanitary board. The treasurer shall keep the order as his voucher, and shall keep a specific account of his receipts and disbursements of money for sanitary purposes. The treasurer and sureties upon his official bond shall be liable for the due performance of the duties imposed upon him by this act. The treasurer shall keep the money arising from the sale of bonds in the fund hereinafter mentioned.

Section 14. At any time after the district is organized, the sanitary board may, by order entered in the minutes, call an election for the purpose of determining whether bonds shall be issued for the construction of sewers. Such order shall fix the day of the election, and shall specify the amount of money to be raised, and shall state in general terms the purpose for which it is to be raised. A copy of such order shall be posted for four successive weeks prior to the election in at least three public places within the district, and shall be published for four successive weeks prior to the election, in some newspaper published within the district, if there be one, and if not, in some newspaper published in the county. It shall be sufficient if the order be published once a week.

*Section 15. At any time prior to the day fixed for the election, the board shall select one, and may select two, polling places within the district, appoint officers of election, and make all necessary and proper arrangements for holding the election. The tickets shall contain the words, "For the issuance of bonds as proposed by the sanitary board," or "Against the issuance of bonds as proposed by the sanitary board." The election shall be conducted in accordance with the general election laws of the state, so far as the same shall be applicable, except as herein otherwise provided. Every qualified elector, resident within the district for the length of time necessary to enable him to vote at a general election, shall be entitled to vote at the election above provided for. After the votes shall have been announced, the ballots shall be sealed up and delivered to the secretary or president of the sanitary board, which shall, as soon as practicable, proceed to canvass the same, and shall enter the result upon its minutes. Such entry shall be conclusive evidence of the fact and regularity of all prior proceedings of every kind and nature provided by this act or by law, and of the facts stated in such entry. If, at such election, two-thirds of the votes cast be in favor of the issuance of bonds as proposed by the sanitary board, the said board shall thenceforth have full power and authority to issue and dispose of bonds as proposed in the order calling the election.

SECTION 16. Such bonds shall be in sums of one thousand dollars each, payable in gold coin of the United States, and shall bear interest at the rate of five per cent. per annum, payable semi-annually, at dates to be fixed by the board, and specified, respectively, in the bonds and coupons, payable in like gold coin. The principal of each bond shall be payable in installments of one twentieth of the face of the bond, and one of such installments shall fall due at the end of each year, so that the whole principal shall be paid in twenty years from the issuance of the bond. Each bond shall refer to this act by its title and the date of its approval by the governor, and shall be payable to bearer; but every person into whose hands any bond or coupon shall come shall be deemed to have notice of any and all payments that have actually been made thereon. Each bond shall be signed by the president and countersigned by the secretary of the sanitary board. The bonds shall be numbered consecutively beginning with the number one. Each coupon shall refer to its bond by number, and shall be signed by the president and countersigned by the secretary. No bond shall be redeemed before it is due without the consent of the holder thereof, nor shall the rate of interest on any bond be reduced or the bonds be refunded without the consent of the holder thereof. When any payment of any installment of interest is made, the coupon therefor is directed to be surrendered to the county treasurer and to be canceled by him; and when any installment of principal is paid, such payment is directed to be indorsed upon the bond by such treasurer; and when the whole principal of any bond is paid, the bond is directed to be surrendered to the treasurer and to be by him canceled. The bonds must be disposed of by the sanitary board in such manner and in such quantities as may be determined by said board, in its discretion, but no bond must be disposed of for less than its face value. The proceeds of such sales shall be deposited with the county treasurer, and shall be by him placed in a fund to be called the sewer construction fund of —— sanitary district (naming it). The money in such fund shall be used for the purpose indicated in the order calling the election upon the question of the issuance of the bonds, and for no other purpose; *provided*, that if after such purposes are entirely fulfilled, any balance remain in such fund, such balance may, upon the order of the sanitary board, be transferred to either of the other funds provided by this act. If the result of the election be against the issuance of bonds, no other election upon the question shall be called or held for the period of one year.

SECTION 17. It is hereby made the duty of the sanitary board to levy, each year, upon the property within the district, a sufficient tax to pay off the interest accruing upon said bonds for the respective year, as it falls due, and also to pay one twentieth of the principal of said bonds, so that the entire amount of principal and interest of said bonds shall be paid within twenty years from the date of the issuance of said bonds; and it is hereby made the duty of the tax collector, or such other person as may be charged with the duty of collecting the sanitary taxes, to collect the said taxes so to be levied, and the duty of the sanitary board to order the same to be paid, in manner and form as provided by this act, and the duty of the county treasurer to pay the same. If, for any reason, any portion of the tax for any year remains unpaid, and in consequence thereof any portion of the interest or principal due for any year remains unpaid, the same shall be added to the levy for the next year, and be collected and paid accordingly. The payment of the whole amount of the principal and interest of all of said bonds, within twenty years from their issuance, is hereby made the imperative duty of the district; and, if necessary for that purpose, a special tax shall be levied; and it is hereby made the duty of every officer and board to do his respective part towards the levy, collection, and payment of such tax; and mandamus shall issue from the Superior Court of the county in which the district is situated, or from any other competent court, upon application of any party interested, for the purpose of compelling the performance of the duty imposed by this act upon any and all officers or boards.

SECTION 18. If the result of any election upon the question of the issuance of bonds be in favor of such issuance, the sanitary board may, in their discretion, before such issuance, commence in the Superior Court of the county, a special proceeding to determine their right to issue such bonds and the validity thereof, similar to the proceeding in relation to irrigation bonds, provided for by an act entitled "An act supplemental to an act entitled 'An act to provide for the organization and government of irrigation districts, and to provide for the acquisition of water and other property, and for the distribution of water thereby for irrigation purposes,' approved March seventh, eighteen hundred and eighty-seven, and to provide for the examination, approval and confirmation of proceedings for the issue and sale of bonds issued under the provisions of said act;" and all the provisions of said act shall apply to and govern the proceedings so to be commenced by the sanitary board, so far as the same are applicable; and said proceedings shall be in accordance with the provisions of said act, so far as the same are applicable, and the judgment in such proceedings shall have the same effect as a judgment in relation to irrigation bonds under the provisions of said act.

SECTION 19. Any general regulation of the sanitary board shall be by order entered in the minutes, but such order shall be published once a week for one week in some newspaper published within the district, if there be one, and if there be no such newspaper, then such order shall be posted for one week in three public places within the district. A subsequent order of the board that such publication or posting has been duly made shall be conclusive evidence that such publication or posting has been properly made. Orders not establishing a general regulation need not be published or posted (unless otherwise provided by this act), but shall be entered in the minutes, and the entry shall be signed by the secretary of the board. A general regulation shall take effect immediately upon the expiration of the week of publication or posting thereof. An ordinary order shall take effect upon the entry in the minutes.

SECTION 20. The board may instruct the district attorney of the county to commence and prosecute any and all actions and proceedings necessary or proper to enforce any of its regulations or orders, and may call upon said district attorney for advice as to any sanitary subject; and it shall be the duty of the district attorney to obey such instructions and to give advice when called on by the board therefor. The board may at any time employ special counsel for any purpose. All fines for the violation of any regulation or order of the sanitary board shall, after the expenses of the prosecution are paid therefrom, be paid to the secretary of the board, who shall forthwith deposit the same with the county treasurer, who shall place the same in the running expense fund of the district.

SECTION 21. The district may at any time be dissolved upon the vote of two-thirds of the qualified electors thereof, upon an election called by the sanitary board upon the question of dissolution. Such election shall be called and conducted in the same manner as other elections of the district. Upon such dissolution, the property of the district shall vest in any incorporated city or town that may at said time be in occupation of a considerable portion of the territory of the district, and if there be no such incorporated city or town, then the property shall be vested in the board of supervisors of the county until the formation of such a city or town; *provided, however,* that if at the time of such election to dissolve such district, there be any outstanding bonded indebtedness of such district, then, in such event, the vote to dissolve such district shall dissolve the same for all purposes excepting only the levy and collection of taxes for the payment of such indebtedness. And from the time such district is thus dissolved, until such bonded indebtedness, with the interest thereon, is fully paid, satisfied, and discharged, the legislative authority of said incorporated city or town, or the board of supervisors, if there be no such incorporated city or town, is hereby constituted ex-officio the sanitary board of such district. And it is hereby made obligatory upon such board to levy such taxes, and perform such other acts as may be necessary in order to raise money for the payment of such indebtedness, and the interest thereon, as herein provided.

SECTION 22. The sanitary board shall have power at any time after main sewers, or other sewers are laid, to order and contract for the construction of a sewer in any street of the district where a sewer is not already constructed, and to provide by such order that the cost thereof shall be borne by the property fronting along the line of the sewer so ordered; and in case such order is made, the said cost shall be assessed on the lots and lands fronting on such sewer, according to the provisions of the general law of the state in relation to street improvements in incorporated cities or towns, in force at the time such assessment is made, so far as the same shall be applicable; and the lien of the assessment so made shall be enforced by action to be brought by the district attorney of the county, in the name of the sanitary district; *provided,* that nothing in this section contained shall be construed to take away or impair the power of the board to provide that the expenses of the sewers above provided for shall be borne by the whole district, as in other cases.

SECTION 23. All acts and parts of acts in conflict with this act, or any portion thereof, are hereby repealed.

SECTION 24. This act shall take effect immediately.

*SECTION 15 was amended to read as above by an act approved March 9, 1893, statutes 1893, page 88.

Municipal Indebtedness Act.

An act authorizing the incurring of indebtedness by cities, towns, and municipal corporations, incorporated under the laws of this state; for the construction of water-works, sewers, and all necessary public improvements, or for any purpose whatever, and to repeal the act approved March 9, 1885, entitled an act to authorize municipal corporations of the fifth class, containing more than three thousand and less than ten thousand inhabitants, to obtain water-works: also to repeal an act approved March 15, 1887, entitled an act authorizing the incurring of indebtedness by cities, towns, and municipal corporations, incorporated under the laws of this state.

[Approved March 19, 1889. Statutes 1889, p. 399.]

The people of the state of California, represented in senate and assembly do enact as follows:

SECTION 1. Any city, town, or municipal corporation, incorporated under the laws of this state, may, as hereinafter provided, incur indebtedness to pay the cost of any municipal improvement, or for any purpose whatever requiring an expenditure greater than the amount allowed for such improvement by the annual tax levy. [*Statutes 1889, p. 399.*]

An act approved March 15, 1887, [statutes 1887, p. 120] seems to have been the first general act passed since the adoption of the new constitution, authorizing all municipal corporations, incorporated under the laws of this state, to incur indebtedness to pay the cost of any permanent municipal improvement requiring an expenditure greater than the amount allowed for such improvements by the ordinary annual tax levy, and to issue the bonds of the municipality therefor. This act of 1887 was repealed by section 12 of the above act of March 19, 1889, and the latter act, as amended in 1891 and 1893, is the act now in force authorizing the incurring of such indebtedness.

The legislature, by an act approved March 9, 1885, [statutes 1885, p. 42] authorized municipal corporations of the fifth class, to incur an indebtedness and issue bonds, to supply such city with public water-works. Then followed said general act of March 15, 1887. By an act approved February 16, 1889, section 4 of said act of March 15, 1887, was amended. [Statutes 1889, p. 14.] Then followed the act which, as amended is the act now in force,—the act of March 19, 1889,—section 12 of which expressly repeals the said act of March 9, 1885, entitled "An act to authorize municipal corporations of the fifth class, etc., to obtain public water-works;" likewise, repeals the said act approved March 15, 1887, entitled "An act authorizing the incurring of indebtedness by cities, towns, and municipal corporations, incorporated under the laws of this state;" and also repeals "all general acts, or special acts, or parts of acts," conflicting with said act of March 19, 1889. By an act approved March 11, 1891, [statutes 1891, p. 94] section 2 of the act of March 19, 1889, was amended. By another act approved March 11, 1891, [statutes 1891, p. 84] section 5 of the act of March 19, 1889, was amended. By an act approved March 19, 1891, [statutes 1891, p. 132] sections 9 and 10 of the act of March 19, 1889, were amended. By an act approved March 1, 1893, [statutes 1893, p. 61] sections 6 and 8 of the act of March 19, 1889, were amended.

This act of March 19, 1889, authorizes the incurring of such indebtedness by a municipality, exceeding in any year the income and revenue provided for it for such year, in the mode prescribed and required by section 18 of article XI of the constitution. The act authorizes the incurring of indebtedness by municipalities and the issuance of municipal bonds upon which the municipal corporation is directly liable. On the other hand the street improvement bond act,—the act of February 27, 1893, [statutes 1893, p. 33, *supra* p. 217 *et seq.*] provides, not for the issuance of municipal bonds, (the municipality is expressly excepted from all liability,) but for the issuance of bonds, secured by the property which has been assessed to pay the expenses of this work, each bond representing upon each lot or parcel of land upon the assessment list, the total amount of the assessment against such particular lot or parcel of land, as shown on such assessment list. The remedy of the bond holder, holding bonds issued under the municipal indebtedness act of March 19, 1889, authorizing the incurring of indebtedness by municipal corporations, is against the municipality itself, and its property. The remedy of the bond holder, holding a bond issued under the said street improvement bond act,—the act of February 27, 1893,—is against the particular lot or parcel of land upon which his bond is a lien. The assessment upon said lot or parcel of land is represented by his bond.

Section 18 of article XI of the constitution was amended at the general election held in 1892, so as to authorize a city or town, etc., to incur an indebtedness, the maturity of which shall not exceed forty years from the time of contracting the same. Prior to this amendment the section limited the maturity of the indebtedness to twenty years from the time of contracting the same. Accordingly, sections 6 and 8 of this act of March 19, 1889, were amended in 1893, [statutes 1893, p. 61] so as to make provision for the issuance of forty year bonds.

SECTION 2. Whenever the legislative branch of any city, town, or municipal corporation shall, by ordinance passed by a vote of two-thirds of all its members, and approved by the executive of said city, town, or municipal corporation, determine that the public interest or necessity demands the acquisition, construction, or completion of any municipal buildings, bridges, water-works, water rights, sewers, or other municipal improvements, the cost of which will be too great to be paid out of the ordinary annual income and revenue of the municipality, they may, after the publication of such ordinance for at least two weeks in some newspaper published in such municipality, and at their next regular meeting after such publication, or at an adjourned meeting, by ordinance passed by a vote of two-thirds of all its members, and also approved by the said executive, call a special election and submit to the qualified voters of said city, town, or municipal corporation, the proposition for the purpose set forth in the ordinance, and no question other than the incurring of indebtedness for said purpose shall be submitted. The ordinance calling such special election shall recite the objects and purposes for which the indebtedness is proposed to be incurred, the estimated cost of the proposed public improvement, the necessity for such improvement, and that the bonds of the municipality shall issue for the payment of the cost of such improvement, as in such ordinance set forth, if the proposition be accepted by the qualified voters, as hereinafter provided, and shall fix the day on which such special election shall be held, the manner of holding such election, and the voting for or against incurring such indebtedness; such election shall be held as provided by law for holding such election in such city, town, or municipal corporation; *provided, however*, that where by the terms or provisions of the charter of any city, town or municipal corporation, the cost of making the proposed improvements is to be or must be paid from a special fund created by such charter for that purpose, the proposition of incurring such an indebtedness may be submitted to the qualified voters at any general election for officers of the state of California or of such city, town, or municipal corporation. [*Statutes 1891, p. 94.*]

SECTION 3. Such ordinance shall be published once a day, for at least ten days, or once a week for two weeks before the publication of the notice of the special election, in some newspaper published in such municipality. After said publication said legislative body shall cause to be published, for not less than two weeks, in at least one of the newspapers published in such municipality, a notice of such special election, the purpose for which the indebtedness is to be incurred, the number and character of the bonds to be issued, the rate of interest to be paid, and the amount of tax levy to be made for the payment thereof. It shall require the votes of two-thirds of all the voters voting at such special election to authorize the issuance of the bonds herein provided. [*Statutes 1889, p. 400.*]

SECTION 4. It shall be the duty of the legislative branch of any municipality contemplating permanent public improvements, to first have plans and estimates of the costs of such improvements made by a competent engineer or architect, who has had successful experience in such work, before the question of incurring an indebtedness for such improvement is submitted to vote. [*Statutes 1889, p. 400.*]

SECTION 5. No city, town, or municipal corporation shall incur an indebtedness for public improvements which shall, in the aggregate, exceed fifteen per cent. of the assessed value of all the taxable real estate and personal property of such city, town, or municipal corporation. [*Statutes 1891, p. 84.*]

SECTION 6. All municipal bonds for public improvements issued under the provisions of this act shall be of the character of bonds known as serials, and shall be payable in gold coin or lawful money of the United States, in the manner following: One fortieth part of the whole amount of indebtedness shall be paid each and every year, on a day and at a place to be fixed by the legislative branch of the municipality issuing the bonds, together with the interest on all sums unpaid at such date. The bonds shall be issued in such denominations as the legislative branch of the municicality may determine, except that no bonds shall be of a less denomination than one hundred dollars, nor of a greater denomination than one thousand dollars each, payable on the day and at the place fixed in such bond, and with interest at the rate specified in the bond, which rate shall not be in excess of the legal rate of the state of California, and may be payable annually or semi-annually. Such bonds may be issued and sold by the legislative branch of the city, town, or municipal corporation, as they may determine, at not less than their face value, in gold coin of the United States, and the proceeds of such sale shall be placed in the municipal treasury to the credit of the proper improvement fund, and shall be applied exclusively to the purposes and objects mentioned in the ordinance, until such objects are fully accomplished, after which, if any surplus remains, such surplus shall be transferred to the general fund of such municipality. [*Statutes 1893, p. 61.*]

SECTION 7. The legislative branch of any city, town, or municipal corporation, issuing bonds under authority of this act, shall have the right to determine the rate of interest such bonds shall bear; *provided*, that in no case shall it exceed seven per cent. per annum, and to name the date and place where such bonds and interest shall be paid; *provided,* that the place of payment shall be either at the office of the treasurer of the municipality, or at some designated bank in San Francisco, Chicago, New York, or Boston. The said bonds shall be signed by the executive of the municipality, and also by the treasurer thereof, and shall be countersigned by the clerk. The coupons of said bonds shall be numbered consecutively and signed by the treasurer. [*Statutes 1889, p. 401.*]

SECTION 8. The legislative branch of said city, town, or municipal corporation shall, at the time of fixing the general tax levy, and in the manner for such general tax levy provided, levy and collect annually, each year, for the term of forty years, a tax sufficient to pay the annual interest on such bonds, and also one-fortieth part of the aggregate amount of such indebtedness so incurred. The taxes herein required to be levied and collected shall be in addition to all other taxes levied for municipal purposes, and shall be collected at the same time and in the same manner as other municipal taxes are collected. [*Statutes 1893, p. 61.*]

SECTION 9. It shall be the duty of the legislative branch of every city, town, or municipal corporation, wherein public improvements are being made under the provisions of this act, to make all needful rules and regulations for carrying out and maintaining such improvements; to appoint all needful agents, superintendents, and engineers to properly look after the construction and operation of such public works, and in all lawful ways to protect and preserve the rights and interests of the municipality; *provided, however*, that in cities, towns, or municipalities operating under a charter heretofore or hereafter framed under section eight of article eleven of the constitution, and having a board of public works, all the matters and things required in this section to be done and performed by the legislative branch of the municipality shall be done and performed by the board of public works of such city, town, or municipality. [*Statutes 1891, p. 132.*]

SECTION 10. All contracts for the construction or completion of any public works or improvements, or for furnishing labor or materials therefor, as herein provided, shall be let to the lowest responsible bidder. The legislative branch of the municipality shall advertise, for at least ten days, in one or more newspapers published in the municipality, inviting sealed proposals for furnishing the labor and materials for the proposed improvements, before any contract shall be made therefor. The said legislative branch shall have the right to require such bonds as they may deem best from the successful bidder, to insure the faithful performance of the contract work. They shall also have the right to reject any or all bids; *provided, however*, that in cities, towns, or municipalities operating under a charter heretofore or hereafter framed under section eight of article eleven of the constitution, and having a board of public works, all the matters and things required in this section to be done and performed by the legislative branch of the municipality shall be done and performed by the board of public works of such city, town, or municipality. [*Statutes 1891, p. 132.*]

SECTION 11. Whenever the legislative branch of any municipality shall by resolution deem it necessary, they may require the treasurer of such municipality to give additional bonds for the safe custody and care of the public funds. [*Statutes 1889, p. 402.*]

SECTION 12. The act approved March ninth, eighteen hundred and eighty-five, entitled an act to authorize municipal corporations of the fifth class, containing more than three thousand and less than ten thousand inhabitants, to obtain public water-works, and the act approved March fifteen, eighteen hundred and eighty-seven, entitled an act authorizing the incurring of indebtedness by cities, towns, and municipal corporations, incorporated under the laws of this state, and all general acts, or special acts, or parts of acts, conflicting with this act, are hereby repealed. [*Statutes 1889, p. 402.*]

SECTION 13. This act shall take effect and be in force from and after its passage.]*Statutes 1889, p. 402.*]

Street Work Act of March 18th, 1885

AS AMENDED BY

Subsequent Amendatory and Supplementary Acts up to and Including Acts of 1893.

An Act to provide for work upon streets, lanes, alleys, courts, places and sidewalks, and for the construction of sewers within municipalities.

[Approved March 18, 1885.]

PART I.

Section 1. All streets, lanes, alleys, places, or courts, in the municipalities of this state now open or dedicated, or which may hereafter be opened or dedicated to public use, shall be deemed and held to be open public streets, lanes, alleys, places, or courts, for the purposes of this act, and the city council of each municipality is hereby empowered to establish and change the grades of said streets, lanes, alleys, places, or courts, and fix the width thereof, and is hereby invested with jurisdiction to order to be done thereon any of the work mentioned in section two of this act, under the proceedings hereinafter described. [*Statutes 1885, page 147.*]

[Section 1 of the act of March 18, 1885, has never been altered or amended.]

Section 2. Whenever the public interest or convenience may require, the city council is hereby authorized and empowered to order the whole, or any portion, either in length or width, of the streets, avenues, lanes, alleys, courts, or places of any such city graded or re-graded to the official grade, planked or re-planked, paved or re-paved, macadamized or re-macadamized, graveled, or re-graveled, piled or re-piled, capped or re-capped, sewered or re-sewered, and to order sidewalks, manholes, culverts, cesspools, gutters, tunnels, curbing, and cross-walks to be constructed therein, or to order break-waters, levees, or walls of rock, or other material to protect the same from overflow or injury, and to order any other work to be done which shall be necessary to complete the whole or any portion of said streets, avenues, sidewalks, lanes, alleys, courts, or places, and it may order any of the said work to be improved; and also to order a sewer or sewers, with outlets, for drainage or sanitary purposes, in, over or through any right of way granted or obtained for such purpose; *provided*, that whenever the grade of a street, avenue, lane, alley, court, or place shall hereafter be changed, the petition of the owners of a majority of the feet fronting thereon, asking for grading the same to the new grade, shall be a condition precedent to the ordering of such grading to be done. [*Amendment, approved March 11, 1893, Statutes 1893, page 172.*]

[Section 2 was amended 1889, by act of March 14, 1889, statutes 1889, page 157; again in 1891, by act of March 31, 1891, statutes 1891, page 196; and again in 1893, by act of March 11, 1893, statutes 1893, page 172.]

SECTION 3. Before ordering any work done or improvement made, which is authorized by section two of this act, the city council shall pass a resolution of intention so to do, and describing the work, which shall be posted conspicuously for two days on or near the chamber door of said council, and published by two insertions in one or more daily, semi-weekly, or weekly newpapers published and circulated in said city, and designated by said council for that purpose. The street superintendent shall thereupon cause to be conspicuously posted along the line of said contemplated work or improvement, at not more than one hundred feet in distance apart, but not less than three in all, or when the work to be done is only upon an entire crossing or any part thereof, in front of each quarter block and irregular block liable to be assessed, notices of the passage of said resolution. Said notice shall be headed "Notice of Street Work," in letters of not less than one inch in length, and shall, in legible characters, state the fact of the passage of the resolution, its date, and briefly the work or improvement proposed, and refer to the resolution for further particulars. He shall also cause a notice, similar in substance, to be published for six days, in one or more daily newspapers published and circulated in said city, and designated by said city council, or in cities where there is no daily newspaper, by one insertion in a semi-weekly or weekly newspaper so published, circulated, and designated. In case there is no such paper published in said city, said notice shall be posted for six days on or near the chamber door of said council and in two other conspicuous places in said city, as hereinafter provided. The owners of a majority of the frontage of the property fronting on said proposed work or improvement, where the same is for one block, or more, may make a written objection to the same within ten days after the expiration of the time of the publication and posting of said notice, which objection shall be delivered to the clerk of the city council, who shall indorse thereon the date of its reception by him, and such objections so delivered and indorsed shall be a bar for six months to any further proceedings in relation to the doing of said work, or making said improvements unless the owners of the one-half or more of the frontage, as aforesaid, shall meanwhile petition for the same to be done. At any time before the issuance of the assessment roll, all owners of lots or lands liable to assessment therein, who, after the first publication of said resolution of intention, may feel aggrieved, or who may have objections to any of the subsequent proceedings of said council in relation to the performance of the work mentioned in said notice of intention, shall file with the clerk a petition of remonstrance, wherein they shall state in what respect they feel aggrieved, or the proceedings to which they object; such petition or remonstrance shall be passed upon by the said city council, and its decision therein shall be final and conclusive. But when the work or improvement proposed to be done is the construction of sewers, man holes, culverts, or cesspools, crosswalks or sidewalks, and curbs, and the objection thereto is signed by the owners of a majority of the frontage liable to be assessed for the expense of said work, as aforesaid, the said city council shall, at its next meeting, fix a time for hearing said objections, not less than one week thereafter. The city clerk shall *hereupon notify the persons making such objections, by depositing a notice thereof in the postoffice of said city, postage prepaid, addressed to each objector, or his agent, when he appears for such objector: At the time specified said city council shall hear the objections urged, and pass upon the same, and its decisions shall be final and conclusive, and the said bar for six months to any further proceedings shall not be applicable thereto. And when not more than two blocks, including street crossings, remain ungraded to the official grade, or otherwise unimproved, in whole or in part, and a block or more on each side upon said street has been so graded or otherwise improved, or when not more than two blocks at the end of a street remain so ungraded or otherwise unimproved, said city council may order any of the work mentioned in this act to be done upon said intervening, ungraded, or unimproved part of said street, or at the end of a street, and said work upon said intervening part, or at the end of a street, shall not be stayed or prevented by any written or other objection, unless such council shall deem proper. And if one-half or more in width or in length, or as to grading one-half or more of the grading work of any street lying and being between two successive main street crossings, or if a crossing has been already partially graded or improved, as aforesaid, said council may order the remainder improved, graded, or otherwise, notwithstanding such objections of property owners. At the expiration of twenty days after the expiration of the time of said publication by said street superintendent, and at the expiration of twenty-five days after the advertising and posting, as aforesaid, of any resolution of intention, if no written objection to the work therein described has been delivered, as aforesaid, by the owners of a major frontage of the property fronting on said proposed work or improvement, or if any written objection purporting to be signed by the owners of a major frontage is disallowed by said council, as not of itself barring said work for six months, because, in its judgment, said objection has not been legally signed by the owners of a majority of said frontage, the city council shall be deemed to have acquired jurisdiction to order any of the work to be done, or improvement to be made, which is authorized by this act; which order, when made, shall be published for two days, the same as provided for the publication of the resolution of intention. Before passing any resolution for the construction of said improvements, plans and specifications and careful estimates of the costs and expenses thereof shall be furnished to said city council, if required by it, by the city engineer of said city; and for the work of constructing sewers, specifications shall always be furnished by him. Whenever the contemplated work of improvement, in the opinion of the city council, is of more than local or ordinary public benefit, or whenever, according to estimate to be furnished by the city engineer, the total estimated costs and expenses thereof would exceed one-half the total assessed value of the lots and lands assessed, if assessed upon the lots or land fronting upon said proposed work or improvement, according to the valuation fixed by the last assessment roll whereon it was assessed for taxes for municipal purposes, and allowing a reasonable depth from such frontage for lots or lands assessed in bulk, the city council may make the expense of such work or improvement chargeable upon a district, which the said city council shall in its resolution of intention declare to be the district benefited by said work or improvement, and to be assessed to pay the costs and expenses thereof. Objections to the extent of the district of lands to be affected or benefited by said work or improvement, and to be assessed to pay the costs and expenses thereof, may be made by interested parties, in writing, within ten days after the expiration of the time of the publication of the notice of the passage of the resolution of intention. The city clerk shall lay said objections before the city council, which shall, at its next meeting, fix a time for hearing said objections, not less than one week thereafter. The city clerk shall thereupon notify the persons making such objections by depositing a notice thereof in the postoffice of said city, postage prepaid, addressed to each objector. At the time specified the city council shall hear the objections urged, and pass upon the same, and its decision shall be final and conclusive. If the objections are sustained, all proceedings shall be stopped; but proceedings may be immediately again commenced by giving the notice of intention to do the said work or make said improvements. If the objections are overruled by the city council, the proceedings shall continue the same as if such objections had not been made. [*Amendment approved March 31, 1891. Statutes 1891, page 192.*]

[Section 3 was amended in 1889 by act of March 14, 1889, Sta. '89, p. 158; and again in 1891, by act of March 31, 1891, Sta. '91, p. 196.]

Section 4. The owners of a majority in frontage of lots and lands fronting on any street, avenue, lane, alley, place or court, or of lots or lands liable to be assessed for the expense of the work petitioned to be done, or their duly authorized agents, may petition the city council to order any of the work mentioned in this act to be done, and the city council may order the work mentioned in said petition to be done, after notice of its intention so to do has been posted and published as provided in section 3 of this act. [*Amendment approved March 31, 1891, statutes 1891, page 199.*]

[Section 4 was amended in 1889 by act of March 14, 1889, statutes '89, p. 160; and again in 1891 by act of March 31, 1891, statutes '91, p. 199.]

SECTION 5. Before the awarding of any contract by the city council for doing any work authorized by this act, the city council shall cause notice, with specifications, to be posted conspicuously for five days on or near the council chamber door of said council, inviting sealed proposals or bids for doing the work ordered, and shall also cause notice of said work inviting said proposals, and referring to the specifications posted or on file, to be published for two days in a daily, semi-weekly ,or weekly newspaper published and circulated in said city, designated by the council for that purpose, and in case there is no newspaper published in said city, then it shall only be posted as hereinbefore provided. All proposals or bids offered shall be accompanied by a check payable to the order of the mayor of the city, certified by a responsible bank, for an amount which shall not be less than ten per cent. of the aggregate of the proposal, or by a bond for the said amount and so payable, signed by the bidder and by two sureties, who shall justify, before any officer competent to administer an oath, in double the said amount, and over and above all statutory exemptions. Said proposals or bids shall be delivered to the clerk of the said city council, and said council shall, in open session, examine and publicly declare the same; *provided, however*, that no proposal or bid shall be considered unless accompanied by said check or bond satisfactory to the council. The city council may reject any and all proposals or bids should it deem this for the public good, and also the bid of any party who has been delinquent and unfaithful in any former contract with the municipality, and shall reject all proposals or bids other than the lowest regular proposal or bid of any responsible bidder, and may award the contract for said work or improvement to the lowest responsible bidder at the prices named in his bid, which award shall be approved by the mayor, or a three-fourths vote of the city council. If not approved by him, or a three-fourths vote of the city council, without further proceedings, the city council may readvertise for proposals or bids for the performance of the work as in the first instance, and thereafter proceed in the manner in this section provided, and shall thereupon return to the proper parties the respective checks and bonds corresponding to the bid so rejected. But the checks accompanying such accepted proposals or bids shall be held by the city clerk of said city until the contract for doing said work, as hereinafter provided, has been entered into, either by said lowest bidder or by the owners of three-fourths part of the frontage, whereupon said certified check shall be returned to said bidder. But if said bidder fails, neglects, or refuses to enter into the contract to perform said work or improvement, as hereinafter provided, then the certified check accompanying his bid and the amount therein mentioned, shall be declared to be forfeited to said city, and shall be collected by it, and paid into its fund for repairs of streets; and any bond forfeited may be prosecuted, and the amount due thereon collected and paid into said fund. Notice of such awards of contract shall be posted for five days, in the same manner as hereinbefore provided for the posting of proposals for said work, and shall be published for two days in a daily newspaper published and circulated in said city, and designated by said city council, or in cities where there is no daily newspaper, by one insertion in a semi-weekly or weekly newspaper so published, circulated and designated; *provided, however*, that in case there is no newspaper printed or published in any such city, then such notice of award shall only be kept posted as hereinbefore provided. The owners of three-fourths of the frontage of lots and lands upon the street whereon said work is to be done, or their agents, and who shall make oath that they are such owners or agents, shall not be required to present sealed proposals or bids, but may, within ten days after the first posting and publication of said notice of said award, elect to take said work and enter into a written contract to do the whole work at the price at which the same has been awarded. Should the said owners fail to elect to take said work, and to enter into a written contract therefor within ten days, or to commence the work within fifteen days after the first posting and publication

of said award, and to prosecute the same with diligence to completion, it
shall be the duty of the superintendent of streets to enter into a contract
with the original bidder to whom the contract was awarded, and at the
prices specified in his bid. But if such original bidder neglects, fails or
refuses, for fifteen days after the first posting and publication of the notice
of award, to enter into the contract, then the city council, without further
proceedings, shall again advertise for proposals or bids as in the first
instance, and award the contract for the said work to the then lowest regular
bidder. The bids of all persons and the election of all owners as aforesaid,
who have failed to enter into the contract as herein provided, shall be
rejected in any bidding or election subsequent to the first for the same
work. If the owner or contractor who may have taken any contract, do
not complete the same within the time limited in the contract, or within
such further time as the city council may give them, the superintendent
of streets shall report such delinquency to the city council, which may
relet the unfinished portion of said work, after pursuing the formalities
prescribed hereinbefore for the letting of the whole in the first instance.
All contractors, contracting owners included, shall, at the time of executing any contract for street work, execute a bond to the satisfaction and
approval of the superintendent of streets of said city, with two or more
sureties and payable to such city, in such sums as the mayor shall deem
adequate, conditioned for the faithful performance of the contract; and
the sureties shall justify before any person competent to administer an
oath, in double the amount mentioned in said bond. over and above all
statutory exemptions. Before being entitled to a contract, the bidder to
whom the award was made, or the owners who have elected to take the
contract, must advance to the superintendent of streets, for payment by
him, the cost of publication of the notices, resolutions, orders, or other
incidental expenses and matters required under the proceedings prescribed
in this act, and such other notices as may be deemed requisite by the city
council. And in case the work is abandoned by the city before the letting
of the contract, the incidental expenses incurred previous to such abandonment shall be paid out of the city treasury. [*Amendment approved
March 31, 1891, statutes 1891, page 199.*]

[Section 5 was amended in 1889, by act of March 14, 1889, statutes 1889,
p. 160, and again in 1891 by act of March 31, 1891, statutes, 1891, p. 199.]

SECTION 6. The superintendent of streets is hereby authorized, in his
official capacity, to make all written contracts, and receive all bonds
authorized by this act, and to do any other act, either express or implied,
that pertains to the street department under this act; and he shall fix the
time for the commencement, which shall not be more than fifteen days
from the date of the contract, and for the completion of the work under
all contracts entered into by him, which work shall be prosecuted with
diligence from day to day thereafter to completion, and he may extend
the time so fixed from time to time, under the direction of the city council. The work provided for in section 2 of this act, must, in all cases, be
done under the direction and to the satisfaction of the superintendent of

streets, and the materials used shall comply with the specifications and be to the satisfaction of said superintendent of streets, and all contracts made therefor must contain a provision to that effect, and also express notice, that, in no case, except where it is otherwise provided in this act, will the city, or any officer thereof, be liable for any portion of the expense, nor for any delinquency of persons or property assessed. The city council may, by ordinance, prescribe general rules directing the superintendent of streets and the contractor as to the materials to be used, and the mode of executing the work, under all contracts thereafter made. The assessment and apportionment of the expenses of all such work or improvement shall be made by the superintendent of streets in the mode herein provided. [*Statutes 1885, p. 151.*]

[Section 6 of the act of March 18, 1885, never has been amended.]

SECTION 7. *Subdivision One*—The expenses incurred for any work authorized by this act (which expense shall not include the cost of any work done in such portion of any street as is required by law to be kept in order or repair by any person or company having railroad tracks thereon, nor include work which shall have been declared in the resolution of intention to be assessed on a district benefited) shall be assessed upon the lots and lands fronting thereon, except as hereinafter specifically provided; each lot or portion of a lot being separately assessed, in proportion to the frontage, at a rate per front foot sufficient to cover the total expense of the work.

Subdivision Two—The expense of all improvements, except such as are done by contractors under the provisions of section thirteen of this act, until the streets, avenues, street crossings, lanes, alleys, places, or courts are finally accepted, as provided in section twenty of this act, shall be assessed upon the lots and lands as provided in this section, according to the nature and character of the work; and after such acceptance the expense of all the work thereafter done thereon shall be paid by said city out of the street department fund.

Subdivision Three—The expense of the work done on main street crossings shall be assessed at a uniform rate per front foot of the quarter blocks and irregular blocks adjoining and cornering upon the crossings, and separately upon the whole of each lot or portion of a lot having any frontage in the said blocks fronting on said main streets, half way to the next main street crossing, and all the way on said blocks to a boundary line of the city where no such crossing intervenes, but only according to its frontage in said quarter blocks and irregular blocks.

Subdivision Four—Where a main street terminates in another main street, the expenses of the work done on one-half of the width of the street opposite the termination shall be assessed upon the lots in each of the two quarter blocks adjoining and cornering on the same, according to the frontage of such lots on said main streets, and the expense of the other half of the width of said street upon the lot or lots fronting on the latter half of the street at such termination.

Subdivision Five—Where any alley or subdivision street crosses a main street, the expense of all work done on said crossing shall be assessed on all lots or portions of lots half way on said alley or subdivision street to the next crossing or intersection, or to the end of such alley or subdivision street if it does not meet another.

Subdivision Six—The expense of work done on alley or subdivision street crossings shall be assessed upon the lots fronting upon such alley or subdivision streets on each side thereof, in all directions, half way to the next street, place, or court, on either side, respectively, or to the end of such alley or subdivision street, if it does not meet another.

Subdivision Seven—Where a subdivision street, avenue, lane, alley, place, or court terminates in another street, avenue, lane, alley, place, or court, the expense of the work done on one-half of the width of the sub-division street, avenue, lane, alley, place, or court opposite the termina-tion, shall be assessed upon the lot or lots fronting on such subdivision street, or avenue, lane, alley, place or court so terminating, according to its frontage thereon, half way on each side, respectively, to the next street, avenue, lane, alley, court or place, or to the end of such street, avenue, lane, alley, place or court, if it does not meet another, and the other one-half of the width upon the lots fronting such termination.

Subdivision Eight—Where any work mentioned in this act (man-holes, cesspools, culverts, crosswalks, piling and capping excepted) is done on either or both sides of the center line of any street for one block or less, and further work opposite to the work of the same class already done is ordered to be done to complete the unimproved portion of said street, the assessment to cover the total expenses of said work so ordered shall be made upon the lots or portions of the lots only fronting the portions of the work so ordered. And when sewering or resewering is ordered to be done under the sidewalk on only one side of a street for any length thereof, the assessment for its expenses shall be made only upon the lots and lands fronting nearest upon that side, and for intervening intersections only upon the two quarter blocks adjoining and cornering upon that side.

Subdivision Nine—Section one of chapter three hundred and twenty-five of the laws of this state entitled "An act amendatory of and supple-mentary to 'An act to provide revenue for the support of the government of this state,' approved April twenty-ninth, eighteen hundred and fifty-seven," approved April nineteenth, eighteen hundred and fifty-nine, shall not be applicable to the provisions of this section; but the property herein mentioned shall be subject to the provisions of this act, and be assessed for work done under the provisions of this section.

Subdivision Ten—It shall be lawful for the owner or owners of lots or lands fronting upon any street, the width and grade of which have been established by the city council, to perform at his or their own expense (after obtaining permission from the council so to do, but before said council has passed its resolution of intention to order grading inclusive of this) any grading upon said street, to its full width, or to the center line thereof, and to its grade as then established, and thereupon to procure, at his or their own expense, a certificate from the city engineer, setting forth the number of cubic yards of cutting and filling made by him or them in said grading, and the proportions performed by each owner, and that the same is done to the established width and grade of said street, or to the center line thereof, and thereafter to file said certificate with the superintendent of streets, which certificate the superintendent shall record in a book kept for that purpose in his office, properly indexed. Whenever thereafter the city council orders the grading of said street, or any portion thereof, on which any grading certified as aforesaid has been done, the bids and the contract must express the price by the cubic yard for cutting and filling in grading; and the said owner or owners, and his or their successors in interest, shall be entitled to credit on the assessment upon his or their lots and lands fronting on said street for the grading thereof, to the amount of the cubic yards of cutting and filling set forth in his or their said certificate, at the prices named in the contract for said cutting and filling; or, if the grade meanwhile has been duly altered, only for so much of said certified work as would be required for grading to the altered grade; *provided, however*, that such owner or owners shall not be entitled to such credit as may be in excess of the assessments for grading upon the lots and lands owned by him or them, and proportionately assessed for the whole of said grading; and the superintendent of streets shall include in the assessment for the whole of said grading upon the same grade the number of cubic yards of cutting and filling set forth in any and all certificates so recorded in his office, or for the whole of said grading to the duly altered grade so much of said certified work as would be required for grading thereto, and shall enter corresponding credits, deducting the same as payments upon the amounts assessed against the lots and lands owned, respectively, by said certified owners and their successors in interest; *provided, however*, that he shall not so include any grading quantities or credit any sums in excess of the proportionate assessments for the whole of the grading which are made upon any lots and lands fronting upon said street and belonging to any such certified owners or their successors in interest. Whenever any owner or owners of any lots and lands fronting on any street shall have heretofore done, or shall hereafter do, any work (except grading) on such street, in front of any block, at his or their own expense, and the city council shall subsequently order any work to be done of the same class in front of the same block, said work so done at the expense of such owner or owners shall be excepted from the order ordering work to be done, as provided in subdivision eleven of this section of this act; *provided*, that the work so done at the expense of such owner or owners shall be upon the official grade, and in condition satisfactory to the street superintendent at the time said order is passed.

Subdivision Eleven—The city council may include in one resolution of intention and order any of the different kinds of work mentioned in this act, and it may except therefrom any of said work already done upon the street to the official grade. The lots and portions of lots fronting upon said excepted work already done shall not be included in the frontage assessment for the class of work from which the exception is made; *pro-vided*, that this shall not be construed so as to affect the special provisions as to grading contained in subdivision ten of this section.

Subdivision Twelve—Whenever the resolution of intention declares that the costs and expenses of the work and improvement are to be assessed upon a district, the city council shall direct the city engineer to make a diagram of the property affected or benefited by the proposed work or improvement, as described in the resolution of intention, and to be assessed to pay the expenses thereof. Such diagram shall show each separate lot, piece, or parcel of land, the area in square feet of each of such lots, pieces, or parcels of land, and the relative location of the same to the work proposed to be done, all within the limits of the assessment district; and when said diagram shall have been approved by the city council, the clerk shall, at the time of such approval, certify the fact and date thereof. Immediately thereafter the said diagram shall be delivered to the superintendent of streets of said city, who shall, after the contractor of any street work has fulfilled his contract to the satisfaction of said superintendent of streets, or city council, on appeal, proceed to estimate upon the lands, lots or portions of lots within said assessment district, as shown by said diagram, the benefits arising from such work, and to be received by each such lot, portion of such lot, piece, or subdivision of land, and shall thereupon assess upon and against said lands in said assessment district the total amount of the costs and expenses of such proposed work, and in so doing shall assess said total sum upon the several pieces, parcels, lots, or portions of lots, and subdivisions of land in said district benefited thereby, to wit: Upon each, respectively, in proportion to the estimated benefits to be received by each of said several lots, portions of lots, or subdivisions of land. In other respects the assessment shall be as provided in the next section, and the provisions of subdivisions three, four five, six, seven, and eight of this section shall not be applicable to the work or improvement provided for in this subdivision. [*Amendment approved March 31, 1891, Statutes 1891, p. 201.*]

[Section 7 was amended in 1889, by act of March 14, 1889, statutes '89, p. 163; and again in 1891, by act of March 31, 1891, statutes '91, p. 201.]

SECTION 8. After the contractor of any street work has fulfilled his contract to the satisfaction of the street superintendent of said city, or city council on appeal, the street superintendent shall make an assessment to cover the sum due for the work performed and specified in said contract (including any incidental expenses,) in conformity with the provisions of the preceding section according to the character of the work done; or, if any direction and decision be given by said council on appeal, then in conformity with such direction and decision, wh.ch assessment shall briefly refer to the contract, the work contracted for and performed, and shall show the amount to be paid therefor, together with any incidental expenses, the rate per front foot assessed, if the assessment be made per front foot, the amount of each assessment, the name of the owner of each lot, or portion of a lot (if known to the street superintendent); if unknown the word "unknown" shall be written opposite the number of the lot, and the amount assessed thereon, the number of each lot or portion or portions of a lot assessed, and shall have attached thereto a diagram exhibiting each street or street crossing, lane, alley, place, or court, on which any work has been done, and showing the relative location of each district, lot or portion of lot to the work done, numbered to correspond with the numbers in the assessments, and showing the number of feet fronting, or number of lots assessed, for said work contracted for and performed. [*Amendment approved March 14, 1889. Statutes 1889, p. 166.*]

SECTION 9. To said assessment shall be attached a warrant, which shall be signed by the superintendent of streets, and countersigned by the mayor of said city. The said warrant shall be substantially in the following form:

FORM OF THE WARRANT.

By virtue hereof, I (name of the superintendent of streets), of the city of ——, county of —— (or city and county of ——), and state of California, by virtue of the authority vested in me as said superintendent of streets, do authorize and empower (name of contractor), (his or their) agents or assigns, to demand and receive the several assessments upon the assessment and diagram hereto attached, and this shall be (his or their) warrant for the same.

(Date.)   ——(name of superintendent of streets).

Countersigned by (name of mayor).

Said warrant, assessment and diagram, together with the certificate of the city engineer, shall be recorded in the office of said superintendent of streets. When so recorded the several amounts assessed shall be a lien upon the lands, lots, or portions of lots assessed, respectively, for the period of two years from the date of said recording, unless sooner discharged; and from and after the date of said recording of any warrant, assessment, diagram and certificate, all persons mentioned in section eleven of this act shall be deemed to have notice of the contents of the record thereof. After said warrant, assessment, diagram and certificate are recorded the same shall be delivered to the contractor, or his agent or assigns, on demand, but not until after the payment to the said superintendent of streets of the incidental expenses not previously paid by the contractor, or his assigns; and by virtue of said warrant said contractor, or his agent or assigns, shall be authorized to demand and receive the amount of the several assessments made to cover the sum due for the work specified in such contracts and assessments. Whenever it shall appear by any final judgment of any court of this state that any suit brought to foreclose the lien of any sum of money assessed to cover the expense of said street work done under the provisions of this act has been defeated by reason of any defect, error, informality, omission, irregularity or illegality in any assessment hereafter to be made and issued, or in the recording thereof, or in the return thereof made to or recorded by said superintendent of streets, any person interested therein may, at any time within three months after the entry of said final judgment, apply to said superintendent of streets who issued the same, or to any superintendent of streets in office at the time of said application, for another assessment to be issued in conformity to law; and said superintendent shall, within fifteen days after the date of said application, make and deliver to said applicant a new assessment, diagram and warrant in accordance with law; and the acting mayor shall countersign the same as now provided by law, which assessment shall be a lien for the period of two years from the date of said assessment, and be enforced as provided in section seven of this act. [*Amendment approved March 31, 1891, statutes 1891, page 205.*]

[Section 9 was amended in 1889, by act of March 14, 1889, statutes 1889, page 167; and again in 1891 by act of March 31, 1891, statutes 1891, page 205.]

SECTION 10. The contractor, or his assigns, or some person in his or their behalf, shall call upon the persons assessed, or their agents, if they can conveniently be found, and demand payment of the amount assessed to each. If any payment be made the contractor, his assigns, or some person in his or their behalf, shall receipt the same upon the assessment in presence of the person making such payment, and shall also give a separate receipt if demanded. Whenever the person so assessed or their agents, cannot conveniently be found, or whenever the name of the owner of the lot is stated as "unknown" on the assessment, then the said contractor, or his assigns, or some person in his or their behalf, shall publicly demand payment on the premises assessed. The warrant shall be returned to the superintendent of streets within thirty days after its date, with a return indorsed thereon signed by the contractor, or his assigns, or some person in his or their behalf, verified upon oath, stating the nature and character of the demand, and whether any of the assessments remain unpaid, in whole or in part, and the amount thereof. Thereupon the superintendent of streets shall record the return so made, in the margin of the record of the warrant and assessment, and also the original contract referred to therein, if it has not already been recorded at full length in a book to be kept for that purpose in his office, and shall sign the record. The said superintendent of streets is authorized at any time to receive the amount due upon any assessment list and warrant issued by him, and give a good and sufficient discharge therefor; *provided*, that no such payment so made after suit has been commenced, without the consent of the plaintiff in the action, shall operate as a complete discharge of the lien until the costs in the action shall be refunded to the plaintiff; and he may release any assessment upon the books of his office, on the payment to him of the amount of the assessment against any lot with interest, or on the production to him of the receipt of the party or his assigns to whom the assessment and warrant were issued; and if any contractor shall fail to return his warrant within the time and in the form provided in this section, he shall thenceforth have no lien upon the property assessed; *provided*, however, that in case any warrant is lost, upon proof of such loss a duplicate can be issued, upon which a return may be made, with the same effect as if the original had been so returned. After the return of the assessment and warrant as aforesaid, all amounts remaining due thereon shall draw interest at the rate of ten per cent. per annum until paid. [*Statutes 1885, p. 155*].

Section 10 of the act of March 18, 1885, never has been amended.

SECTION 11. The owners, whether named in the assessment or not, the contractor, or his assigns, and all other persons directly interested in any work provided for in this act, or in the assessment, feeling aggrieved by any act or determination of the superintendent of streets in relation thereto, or who claim that tne work has not been performed according to the contract in a good and substantial manner, or having or making any objection to the correctness or legality of the assessment or other act, determination, or proceedings of the superintendent of streets, shall, within thirty days after the date of the warrant, appeal to the city council, as provided in this section, by briefly stating their objections in writing, and filing the same with the clerk of said city council. Notice of the time and place of the hearing, briefly referring to the work contracted to be done, or other subject of appeal, and to the acts, determinations, or proceedings objected to or complained of, shall be published for five days. . Upon such appeal, the said city council may remedy and correct any error or informality in the proceedings, and revise and correct any of the acts or determinations of the superintendent of streets relative to said work; may confirm, amend, set aside, alter, modify, or correct the assessment in such manner as to them shall seem just, and require the work to be completed according to the directions of the city council; and may instruct and direct the superintendent of streets to correct the warrant, assessment, or diagram in any particular, or to make and issue a new warrant, assessment and diagram, to conform to the decisions of said city council in relation thereto, at their option. All the decisions and determinations of said city council, upon notice and hearing as aforesaid, shall be final and conclusive upon all persons entitled to appeal under the provisions of this section, as to all errors, informalities, and irregularities which said city council might have remedied and avoided; and no assessment shall be held invalid, except upon appeal to the city council, as provided in this section, for any error, informality, or other defect in any of the proceedings prior to the assessment, or in the assessment itself, where notice of the intention of the city council to order the work to be done, for which the assessment is made, has been actually published in any designated newspaper of said city for the length of time prescribed by law, before the passage of the resolution ordering the work to be done. [*Statutes 1885, p. 156.*]

[Section 11 of the act of March 18, 1885, never has been amended.]

SECTION 12. At any time after the period of thirty-five days from the day of the date of the warrants, as herein provided, or if an appeal is taken to the city council, as provided in section eleven of this act, at any time after five days from the decision of said council, or after the return of the warrant or assessment, after the same may have been corrected, altered or modified, as provided in said section eleven (but not less than thirty-five days from the date of the warrant), the contractor or his assignee may sue, in his own name, the owner of the land, lots or portions of lots, assessed on the day of the date of the recording of the warrant, assessment and diagram, or any day thereafter during the continuance of the lien of said assessment, and recover the amount of any assessment remaining unpaid, with interest thereon at the rate of ten per

cent. per annum until paid. And in all cases of recovery under the provisions of this act the plaintiff shall recover the sum of fifteen dollars in
addition to the taxable cost, as attorney's fees, but not any percentage
upon said recovery. And when suit has been brought, after a personal
demand has been made and a refusal to pay such assessment so demanded,
the plaintiff shall also be entitled to have and recover said sum of fifteen
dollars as attorney's fees in addition to all taxable costs, notwithstanding
that the suit may be settled or a tender may be made before a recovery in
said action, and he may have judgment therefor. Suit may be brought in
the Superior Court within whose jurisdiction the city is in which said
work has been done, and in case any of the assessments are made against
lots, portions of lots, or lands, the owners thereof cannot, with due diligence, be found, the service in each of such actions may be had in such
. manner as is prescribed in the codes and laws of this state. The said warrant, assessment, certificate and diagram, with the affidavit of demand
and non-payment, shall be held prima facie evidence of the regularity and
correctness of the assessment and of the prior proceedings and acts of the
superintendent of streets and city council upon which said warrant,
assessment and diagram are based, and like evidence of the right of the
plaintiff to recover in the action. The court in which said suit shall be
commenced shall have power to adjudge and decree a lien against the
premises assessed, and to order such premises to be sold on execution, as
in other cases of the sale of real estate by the process of said courts; and
on appeal the appellate courts shall be vested with the same power to
adjudge and decree a lien and to order such premises to be sold on execution or decree as is conferred on the court from which an appeal is taken.
Such premises, if sold, may be redeemed as in other cases. In all suits
now pending, or hereafter brought to recover street assessments, the proceedings therein shall be governed and regulated by the provisions of this
act, and also, when not in conflict herwith, by the codes of this state.
This act shall be liberally construed to effect the ends of justice. [*Amendment approved March 14, 1889, statutes 1889, page 168.*]

[Section 12 was amended in 1889 by act of March 14, 1889, statutes '89,
page 168.]

SECTION 12½. The city council, instead of waiting until the completion
of the improvement, may, in its discretion, and not otherwise, upon the
completion of two blocks or more of any improvement, order the street
superintendent to make an assessment for the proportionate amount of
the contract completed, and thereupon proceedings and rights of collection
of such proportionate amount shall be had as in sections eight, nine, ten,
eleven and twelve of the act of which this is amendatory is provided.
[*Amendment approved March 14, 1889, statutes 1889, page 169.*]

[Section 12½ was added to the act in 1889 by the act of March 14, 1889,
statutes 1889, page 169.]

SECTION 13. When any portion of any street, avenue, lane, alley, court
or place in said city improved, or any sidewalk constructed thereon shall
be out of repair, or needing reconstruction, and in condition to endanger
persons or property passing thereon, or in condition to interfere with the

public convenience in the use thereof, it shall be the duty of said superintendent of streets to require, by notice in writing, to be delivered to them or their agents personally, or left on the premises, the owners or occupants of lots or portions of lots fronting on said portion of said street, avenue, alley, lane, court, or place, or of said portion of said sidewalk so out of repair or needing reconstruction as aforesaid, to repair or reconstruct, or to do both, forthwith, said portion of said street, avenue, lane, alley, court, or place, to the center line of said street in front of the property of which he is the owner, or tenant, or occupant, and said superintendent of streets shall particularly specify in said notice what work is required to be done, and how the same is to be done, and what material shall be used in said repairs, or reconstructions, or both. If said repairs or reconstructions, or both, be not commenced within three days after notice given as aforesaid, and diligently and without interruption prosecuted to completion, the said superintendent of streets may, under authority from said city council, make such repairs, reconstruction, or both, or enter into a contract with any suitable person, at the expense of the owner, tenant or occupant, after the specification for the doing of said work shall have been conspicuously posted by him in his office for two days, inviting bids for the doing of said work, which bids shall be delivered to him at his office on or before the second day of said posting, and opened by him on the next day following the expiration of said two days of posting, and the contract by him be awarded to the lowest bidder, if such lowest bid, in the judgment of said street superintendent, shall be reasonable. All of said bids shall be preserved in his office and open at all times after the letting of the contract to the inspection of all persons, and such owner, tenant or occupant shall be liable to pay said contract price. Such work shall be commenced within twenty-four hours after the contract shall have been signed, and completed without delay to the satisfaction of said street superintendent. Upon the completion of said repairs, or reconstruction, or both, by said contractors as aforesaid to the satisfaction of said superintendent of streets, said superintendent of streets shall make and deliver to said contractor a certificate to the effect that said repairs, or reconstruction, or both, have been properly made by said contractor to the grade, and that the charges for the same are reasonable and just, and that he, said superintendent, has accepted the same. [*Amendment approved March 14, 1889, statutes 1889, p. 169.*]

[Section 13 was amended in 1889 by act of March 14, 1889, statutes 1889, p. 169.]

SECTION 14. If the expenses of the work and material for such improvements, after the completion thereof, and the delivery to said contractor of said certificate, be not paid to the contractor so employed, or his agent or assignee, on demand, the said contractor, or his assignee, shall have the right to sue such owner, tenant, or occupant, for the amount contracted to be paid; and said certificate of the superintendent of streets shall be *prima facie* evidence of the amount claimed for said work and materials, and of the right of the contractor to recover for the same in such action. Said certificate shall be recorded by the said superintendent of streets in a book kept by him in his office for that purpose, properly indexed, and the sum contracted to be paid shall be a lien, the same as provided in section nine of this act, and may be enforced in the same manner. [*Statutes 1885, page 158.*]

[Section 14 never has been amended.]

Section 15. In addition, and as cumulative to the remedies above given, the city council shall have power, by resolution or ordinance, to prescribe the penalties that shall be incurred by any owner or person liable, or neglecting, or refusing to make repairs when required, as provided in section (13) thirteen of this act, which fines and penalties shall be recovered for the use of the city by prosecution in the name of the people of the state of California, in the court having jurisdiction thereof, and may be applied, if deemed expedient by the said council, in the payment of the expenses of any such repairs not otherwise provided for. [*Statutes 1885, page 158.*]

[Section 15 never has been amended.]

Section 16. The person owning the fee, or the person in whom, on the day the action is commenced, appears the legal title to the lots and lands, by deeds duly recorded in the county recorder's office of each county, or the person in possession of lands, lots or portions of lots or buildings under claim, or exercising acts of ownership over the same for himself, or as the executor, administrator or guardian of the owner, shall be regarded, treated and deemed to be the "owner" (for the purpose of this law), according to the intent and meaning of that word as used in this act. And in case of property leased, the possession of the tenant or lessee holding and occupying under such persons shall be deemed to be the possession of such owner. [*Statutes 1885, page 159.*]

[Section 16 never has been amended.]

Section 17. Any tenant or lessee of the lands or lots liable may pay the amount assessed against the property of which he is the tenant or lessee under the provisions of this act, or he may pay the price agreed on to be paid under the provision of section thirteen of this act, either before or after suit brought, together with costs, to the contractor, or his assigns, or he may redeem the property, if sold on execution or decree for the benefit of the owner, within the time prescribed by law, and deduct the amount so paid from the rents due and to become due from him, and for any sums so paid beyond the rents due from him, he shall have a lien upon and may retain possession of the said land and lots until the amount so paid and advanced be satisfied, with legal interest, from accruing rents, or by payment by the owner. [*Statutes 1885, page 159.*]

[Section 17 never has been amended.]

Section 18. The records kept by the superintendent of streets of said city, in conformity with the provisions of this act, and signed by him, shall have the same force and effect as other public records, and copies therefrom, duly certified, may be used in evidence with the same effect as the originals. The said records shall, during all office hours, be open to the inspection of any citizen wishing to examine them, free of charge. [*Statutes 1885, page 159.*]

[Section 18 never has been amended.]

SECTION 19. Notices in writing which are required to be given by the superintendent of streets under the provisions of this act, may be served by any person with the permission of the superintendent of streets, and the fact of such service shall be verified by the oath of the person making it, taken before the superintendent of streets, who for that purpose and for all other purposes, and in all cases where a verification is required under the provisions of this act is hereby authorized to administer oaths, or other person authorized to administer oaths, or such notices may be delivered to the superintendent of streets himself, who must also verify the service thereof, and who shall keep a record of the fact of giving such notices, when delivered by himself personally, and also of the notices and proof of service when delivered by any other person. [*Amendment approved March 14, 1889. Statutes 1889, p. 170.*]

[Section 19 was amended by the act of March 14, 1889. Statutes 1889, p. 170.]

SECTION 20. Whenever any street, or portion of a street has been or shall hereafter be fully constructed to the satisfaction of the superintendent of streets and of the city council, and is in good condition throughout, and a sewer, gas pipes, and water pipes are laid therein, under such regulations as the city council shall adopt, the same shall be accepted by the city council, by ordinance, and thereafter shall be kept in repair and improved by the said municipality; the expense thereof, together with the assessment for street work done in front of city property, to be paid out of a fund to be provided by said council for that purpose; *provided*, that the city council shall not accept of any portion of the street less than the entire width of the roadway (including the curbing), and one block in length, or one entire crossing; and *provided further*, that the city council may partially or conditionally accept any street, or portion of a street, without a sewer, or gas pipes, or water pipes, therein, if the ordinance of acceptance expressly states that the council deems such sewer, or gas pipes, or water pipes, to be then unnecessary, but the lots of land previously or at any time assessable for the cost of constructing a sewer, shall remain and be assessable for such cost and for the cost of repairs and restoration of the street damaged in the said construction, whenever said council shall deem a sewer to be necessary, and shall order it to be constructed, the same as if no partial or conditional acceptance had ever been made. The superintendent of streets shall keep in his office a register of all streets accepted by the city council under this section, which register shall be indexed for easy reference thereto. [*Statutes 1885, p. 160.*]

[Section 20 never has been amended.]

SECTION 21. The superintendent of streets shall keep a public office in some convenient place within the municipality, and such records as may be required by the provisions of this act. He shall superintend and direct the cleaning of all sewers, and the expense of the same shall be paid out of the street or sewer fund of said city. [*Statutes 1885, p. 160.*]

[Section 21 never has been amended.]

SECTION 22. It shall be the duty of the superintendent of streets to see that the laws, ordinances, orders, and regulations relating to the public streets and highways be fully carried into execution, and that the penalties thereof are rigidly enforced. He shall keep himself informed of the condition of all the public streets and highways, and also of all public buildings, parks, lots, and grounds of said city, as may be prescribed by the city council. He shall, before entering upon the duties of his office, give bonds to the municipality, with such sureties and for such sums as may be required by the city council; and should he fail to see the laws, ordinances, orders and regulations relative to the public streets or highways carried into execution, after notice from any citizen of a violation thereof, he and his sureties shall be liable upon his official bond to any person injured in his person or property in consequence of said official neglect. [*Statutes 1885, p. 160.*]

[Section 22 never has been amended.]

SECTION 23. If, in consequence of any graded street or public highway improved under the provisions of this act, being out of repair and in condition to endanger persons or property passing thereon, any person while carefully using said street or public highway, and exercising ordinary care to avoid the danger, suffer damage to his person or property, through any such defect therein, no recourse for damages thus suffered shall be had against such city; but if such defect in the street or public highway shall have existed for the period of twenty-four hours or more after notice thereof to the said superintendent of streets, then the person or persons on whom the law may have imposed the obligations to repair such defect in the street or public highway, and also the officer or officers through whose official negligence such defect remains unrepaired, shall be jointly and severally liable to the party injured for the damage sustained; *provided*, that said superintendent has the authority to make said repairs, under the direction of the city council, at the expense of the city. [*Statutes 1885, p. 161.*]

[Section 23 of the act never has been amended.]

SECTION 24. The city council of such city shall have full power and authority to construct sewers, gutters, and manholes, and provide for the cleaning of the same, and culverts or cesspools, or crosswalks or sidewalks, or any portion of any sidewalk, upon or in any street, avenue, lane, alley, court or place in such city; and also for drainage purposes, over or through any right of way obtained or granted for such purposes, with necessary and proper outlet or outlets to the same, of such materials, in such a manner, and upon such terms as it may be deemed proper. None of the work or improvements described in this section shall be stayed or prevented by any written or any other remonstrance or objection, unless such council deems proper. [*Amendment approved March 11, 1893, statutes 1893, p. 173.*]

[Section 24 was amended by the act of March 14, 1889, statutes 1889, p. 170; again by act of March 31, 1891, statutes 1891, p. 206; and again by the act of March 11, 1893, statutes 1893, p. 173.]

SECTION 25. The city council may, in its discretion, repair and water streets that shall have been graded, curbed and planked, paved or macadamized, and may build, repair and clean sewers, and shall provide a street contingent fund at the same time and in the same manner as other funds are provided, out of which to pay the costs and expenses of making said repairs and watering said streets and building, repairing and cleaning said sewers; but whenever any unaccepted street or part of a street requires regrading, recurbing, repiling, repaving, replanking, regraveling or remacadamizing or requires new culverts or new crosswalks or new sidewalks or new sewers, the work shall be advertised and let out by contract, and the costs and expenses thereof shall be assessed upon the property affected or benefited thereby, the same as in the first instance. [*Statutes 1885, page 161.*]

[Section 25 of the act has never been amended.]

SECTION 26. The city council may, in its discretion, order, by resolution, that the whole or any part of the cost and expenses of any of the work mentioned in this act be paid out of the treasury of the municipality from such fund as the council may designate. Whenever a part of such cost and expenses is so ordered to be paid the superintendent of streets, in making up the assessment heretofore provided for such cost and expenses, shall first deduct from the whole cost and expenses such part thereof as has been so ordered to be paid out of the municipal treasury, and shall assess the remainder of said cost and expenses proportionately upon the lots, parts of lots and lands fronting on the streets where said work was done, or liable to be assessed for such work, and in the manner heretofore provided. [*Amendment approved March 31, 1891, statutes 1891, page 206.*]

[Section 26 was amended by act of March 14, 1889, statutes 1889, page 170, and again by the act of March 31, 1891, statutes 1891, page 206.]

PART II.

SECTION 27. Whenever the city council deem it necessary to construct a sewer, then the said council may, in its discretion, determine to construct said sewer, and assess the cost and expenses thereof upon the property to be affected or benefited thereby, in such manner and within such assessment district as it shall prescribe, and the lien therefor upon said property shall be the same as is provided in section nine of this act, or said council may determine to construct said sewer and pay therefor out of the street contingent fund. [*Statutes 1885, page 162.*]

[Section 27 of the act never has been amended.]

SECTION 28. If, at any time, the city council shall deem it necessary to incur any indebtedness for the construction of sewers, in excess of the money in the street contingent fund applicable to the construction of such sewers, they shall give notice of a special election by the qualified electors of the city, to be held to determine whether such indebtedness shall be incurred. Such notice shall specify the amount of indebtedness proposed to be incurred, the route and general character of the sewer or sewers to be constructed, and the amount of money necessary to be raised annually by taxation for an interest and sinking fund as hereinafter provided.

Such notice shall be published for at least three weeks in some newspaper published in such city, and no other question or matter shall be submitted to the electors at such election. If, upon a canvass of the votes cast at such election, it appear that not less than two-thirds of all the qualified electors voting at such election shall have voted in favor of incurring such indebtedness, it shall be the duty of the city council to pass an ordinance providing for the mode of creating such indebtedness, and of paying the same; and in such ordinance provision shall be made for the levy and collection of an annual tax upon all the real and personal property subject to taxation, within such city, sufficient to pay the interest on such indebt. edness as it falls due, and also to constitute a sinking fund for the payment of the principal thereof, within a period of not more than twenty years from the time of contracting the same. It shall be the duty of the city council in each year thereafter, at the time when other taxes are levied, to levy a tax sufficient for such purpose, in addition to the taxes authorized to be levied for city purposes. Such tax, when collected, shall be kept in the treasury as a separate fund, to be inviolably appropriated to the payment of the principal and interest of such indebtedness. [*Statutes 1885, page 162.*]

[Section 28 has never been amended.]

SECTION 29. If bonds are issued under the provisions of the last section, said bonds shall be in sums of not less than one hundred dollars nor more than one thousand dollars, shall be signed by the mayor and treasurer of the city, and the seal of the city shall be affixed thereto. Coupons for the interest shall be attached to each bond, signed by the mayor and treasurer. Said bonds shall bear interest, to be fixed by the city council, at the rate of not to exceed five per cent. per annum. [*Statutes 1885, page 163.*]

[Section 29 has never been amended.]

SECTION 30. Before the sale of said bonds, the council shall, at a regular meeting by resolution, declare its intention to sell a specified amount of said bonds, and the day and hour of such sale, and shall cause such resolution to be entered in the minutes, and shall cause notice of such sale to be published for fifteen days in at least one newspaper published in the city in which the bonds are issued and one published in the city and county of San Francisco, and in any other newspaper in the state, at their discretion. The notice shall state that sealed proposals will be received by the council for the purchase of the bonds on the day and hour named in the resolution. The council, at the time appointed, shall open the proposals and award the purchase of the bonds to the highest bidder, but may reject all bids. [*Statutes 1885, page 163.*]

[Section 30 has never been amended.]

SECTION 31. The council may sell said bonds, at not less than par value, without the notice provided for in the preceding section. [*Statutes 1885, page 163.*]

[Section 31 has never been amended.]

SECTION 32. The proceeds of the sale of the bonds shall be deposited in the city treasury, to the account of the sewer fund, but no payment therefrom shall be made, except to pay for the construction of the sewer or sewers for the construction of which the bonds were issued, and upon the certificate of the superintendent of streets and the city engineer, that the work has been done according to the contract; *provided*, that after the completion of the sewers, for the construction of which said bonds were issued, if there be any money of said fund left in the treasury, the same may be transferred to the general fund, for general purposes. [*Statutes 1887, page 148.*]

[Section 32 was amended by act of March 15, 1887, statutes 1887, p. 148.]

SECTION 33. Whenever said council shall determine to construct any sewer, and pay therefor out of the street contingent fund, or by the issuance of bonds, as above provided, then said council shall cause to be prepared plans and specifications of said work in sections, and shall advertise for twenty days in at least one newspaper published in the city in which the sewer is to be constructed, and one in the city and county of San Francisco, for sealed proposals for constructing said sewer. The work may be let in sections, and must be awarded to the lowest responsible bidder, the council having the right to reject any and all bids. The work shall be done and the materials furnished under the supervision and to the satisfaction of the superintendent of streets and the city engineer. [*Statutes 1885, page 163.*]

[Section 33 has never been amended.]

PART III.

SECTION 34. *First*—The city engineer, or where there is no city engineer, the county, or city and county surveyor, shall be the proper officer to do the surveying and other engineering work necessary to be done under this act, and to survey and measure the work to be done under contracts for grading and macadamizing streets, and to estimate the costs and expenses thereof; and every certificate signed by him in his official character shall be prima facie evidence in all courts in this state of the truth of its contents. He shall also keep a record of all surveys made under the provisions of this act, as in other cases. In all those cities where there is no city engineer, the city council thereof is hereby authorized and empowered to appoint a suitable person to discharge the duties herein laid down as those of city engineer, and all the provisions hereof applicable to the city engineer shall apply to such person so appointed. Said city council is hereby empowered to fix his compensation for such services.

Second—The words "work," "improve," "improved," and "improvement," as used in this act, shall include all work mentioned in this act, and also the construction, reconstruction, and repairs of all or any portion of said work.

Third—The term "incidental expenses," as used in this act, shall include the compensation of the city engineer for work done by him; also, the cost of printing and advertising as provided in this act, and not otherwise; also, the compensation of the person appointed by the superintendent of streets to take charge of and superintend any of the work mentioned in section thirty-five of this act. All demands for incidental expenses mentioned in this sub-division shall be presented to the street superintendent by itemized bill, duly verified by oath of the demandant.

Fourth—The notices, resolutions, orders, or other matter, required to be published by the provisions of this act, and of the act of which this is amendatory, shall be published in a daily newspaper, in cities where such there is, and where there is no daily newspaper, in a semi-weekly or weekly newspaper, to be designated by the council of such city, as often as the same is issued, and no other statute shall govern or be applicable to the publications herein provided for; *provided, however,* that only in case there is no daily, semi-weekly or weekly newspaper printed or circulated in any such city, then such notices, resolutions, orders, or other matters, as are herein required to be published in a newspaper, shall be posted and kept posted for the same length of time as required herein for the publication of the same in a daily, semi-weekly, or weekly newspaper, in three of the most public places in such city. Proof of the publication or posting of any notice provided for herein shall be made by affidavit of the owner, publisher, or clerk of the newspaper, or of the poster of the notice. No publication or notice, other than that provided for in this act, shall be necessary to give validity to any of the proceedings provided for therein.

Fifth—The word "municipality," and the word "city," as used in this act, shall be understood and so construed as to include, and is hereby declared to include, all corporations heretofore organized and now existing, and those hereafter organized, for municipal purposes.

Sixth—The words "paved," or "repaved," as used in this act, shall be held to mean and include pavement of stone, whether paving blocks or macadamizing, or of bituminous rock or asphalt, or of iron, wood, or other material. whether patented or not, which the city council shall by ordinance adopt.

Seventh—The word "street," as used in this act, shall be deemed to, and is hereby declared to include avenues, highways, lanes, alley, crossings, or intersections, courts, and places, and the term "main street" means such actually opened street or streets as bound a block; the word "blocks," whether regular or irregular, shall mean such blocks as are bounded by main streets, or partially by a boundary line of the city.

Eighth—The terms "street superintendent," and "superintendent of streets," as used in this act, shall be understood, and so construed as to include, and are hereby declared to include any person or officer whose duty it is, under the law, to have the care or charge of the streets, or the improvement thereof in any city. In all those cities where there is no street superintendent or superintendent of streets, the city council thereof is hereby authorized and empowered to appoint a suitable person to discharge the duties herein laid down, as those of street superintendent or superintendent of streets; and all provisions hereof applicable to the street superintendent or superintendent of streets, shall apply to such person so appointed.

Ninth—The term "city council" is hereby declared to include any body or board which, under the law, is the legislative department of the government of any city.

Tenth—In municipalities in which there is no mayor, then the duties imposed upon said officer by the provisions of this act shall be performed by the president of the board of trustees, or other chief executive officer of the municipality.

Eleventh—The term "clerk" and "city clerk," as used in this act, is hereby declared to include any person or officer who shall be clerk of the said city council.

Twelfth—The term "quarter block," as used in this act as to irregular blocks, shall be deemed to include all lots or portions of lots having any frontage on either intersecting street half way from such intersection to the next main street, or when no main street intervenes, all the way to a boundary line of the city.

Thirteenth—The term "one year," as used in this act, shall be deemed to include the time beginning with January first and ending with the thirty-first day of December of the same year.

Fourteenth—References in certain sections, by number, to certain other sections of "this act" refer to the number of the sections of the original act as heretofore amended, unless it appears from the context that the reference is to the section of this amendatory act, when it shall be construed according to the context. [*Amendment approved March 31, 1891. Statutes 1891, page 206.*]

[Section 34 was amended by act of March 14, 1889, statutes 1889, page 157 also by the act of March 31, 1891, statutes 1891, page 206.]

SECTION 35. The superintendent of streets shall, when in his judgment it is necessary, appoint a suitable person to take charge of and superintend the construction and improvement of each and every sewer constructed or improved under the provisions of this act, and of piling and capping, sidewalking, or of the paving of whatever character heretofore mentioned, in whole or in part, of one block or more, whose duty it shall be to see that the contract made for the doing of said work is strictly fulfilled in every respect, and in case of any departure therefrom to report the same to the superintendent of streets. Such person shall be allowed for his time actually employed in the discharge of his duties such compensation as shall be just, but not to exceed four dollars per day. The sum to which the party so employed shall be entitled shall be deemed to be incidental expenses, within the meaning of those words as defined by this act. [*Amendment approved March 31, 1891, statutes 1891, page 208.*]

[The act of March 14, 1889, statutes '89, p. 157, attempted to amend section 35. and section 35 as amended is embraced in the body of the act, [statutes '89, p. 173,] but the title of the act does not mention this section. The section was amended in 1891 by the act of March 31, 1891, statutes '91, p. 208.]

SECTION 36. The act entitled "An act to provide for the improvement of streets, lanes, alleys, courts, places, and sidewalks, and the construction of sewers within municipalities," approved March sixth, eighteen hundred

and eighty-three, is hereby repealed; *provided*, that any work or proceedings commenced thereunder prior to the passage of this act shall in nowise be affected hereby, but shall in all respects be finished and completed under said act of March sixth, eighteen hundred and eighty-three, and said repeal shall in nowise affect said work or proceedings. [*Statutes '85, p. 165.*]
[Section 36 has never been amended.]

SECTION 37. That said act shall take effect and be in force immediately upon its passage, and all acts and parts of acts in conflict with this act are hereby repealed; *and provided, however*, that any work or proceeding of the city council commenced under the act of which this is amendatory shall in nowise be affected thereby, but shall in all respects be finished and completed thereunder. [*Amendment approved March 11, 1893, statutes 1893, page 173.*]

[Section 37 was amended in 1889 by the act of March 14, 1889, statutes '89, p. 173; again in 1891 by the act of March 31, 1891, statutes '91, p. 209; and again in 1893 by the act of March 11, 1893, statutes '93, p 173.]

SECTION 38. The city council is hereby empowered to change or modify the grade of any public street, lane, alley, place, or court, and to regrade or repave the same, so as to conform to such modified grade, in the manner as hereinafter provided. Before any change of grade is ordered the city council shall pass an ordinance or resolution of intention to make such change or modification of grade, and it shall have power at the same time and in the same ordinance or resolution to provide for the actual cost of performing the work of regrading, repaving, sewering, sidewalking, or curbing of said street or portion of street, with the same or other material with which it was formerly graded, paved, sewered, sidewalked or curbed; and that the cost of the same shall also be assessed upon the same district which is declared to be benefited by such changed or modified grade. One or more streets or blocks of streets may be embraced in the same ordinance or resolution. Such ordinance or resolution shall be published in the newspaper in which the official notices of the city council are usually printed and published; and such newspaper is to be designated in such ordinance or resolution. Such publication shall be made in every regular issue of such paper for not less than ten days, and shall describe the proposed change or modification of grade or regrading, and shall designate and establish the district to be benefited by such change or modification of grade or regrading, and to be assessed for the cost of the same. Within five days after the first publication of the ordinance or resolution of intention, the superintendent of streets shall cause to be conspicuously posted within the district designated in the ordinance or resolution, notice of the passage of said resolution. Said notices shall be the same in all requirements of contents and posting as the "notices of street work" provided for in section three of the original act to which this is amendatory. If no objection to said proposed change or changes, or modifications of grade, shall be filed with the clerk of the council within thirty days from the first publication of the ordinance or resolution of intention hereinbefore mentioned, the city council shall have power to declare such grades to be changed and established in conformity

to said ordinance or resolution, *provided*, that no change of an established grade shall be ordered except on petition of the owners of a majority of the property affected by the proposed change of grade. [*Amendment approved March 9, 1893, statutes '93, p. 89.*]

SECTION 39. Within thirty days after the first publication of said notice, any person owning property fronting upon said portions of the street or streets where such change of grade is made, may file a petition with the clerk of the city council showing the fact of such ownership, the description and situation of the property claimed to be damaged, its market value, and the estimated amount of damages over and above all benefits which the property would sustain by the proposed change if completed. Such petition shall be verified by the oath of the petitioners or their agents. [*Amendment approved March 9, 1893, statutes 1893, page 90.*

SECTION 40. Whenever such petition or petitions have been filed, the mayor, surveyor, and superintendent of streets, of the city, or city and county, acting as a board of commissioners, shall assess the benefits, damages, and costs of the proposed change of grade upon each separate lot of land situated within such assessment district, as said lot appears of record upon the last city, or city and county assessment roll. [*Amendment approved March 9, 1893, statutes 1893, p. 90.*]

SECTION 41. The commissioners shall be sworn to make the assessments of benefits and damages to the best of their judgment and ability, without fear or favor. [*Amendment approved March 9, 1893, statutes 1893, p. 90.*]

SECTION 42. The commissioners shall have power to subpœna witnesses to appear before them to be examined under oath, which any one of said commissioners is authorized to administer. [*Amendment approved March 9, 1893, statutes 1893, p. 90.*]

SECTION 43. The commissioners having determined the damage which would be sustained by each petitioner, in excess of all benefits, shall proceed to assess the total amount thereof, together with the costs, charges, and expenses of the proceedings, upon the several lots of land benefited within the district of assessment; so that each of the lots shall be assessed in accordance with its benefits caused by such work or improvement; and during the progress of their work shall make a report to such city council as often as it may be required. [*Amendment approved March 9, 1893, statutes 1893, p. 90.*]

SECTION 44. The commissioners shall make their report, in writing, and shall subscribe to the same and file with the city council. In their said report they shall describe separately each piece of property which will sustain damage, stating the amount of damages each will sustain over and above all benefits. They shall also give a brief description of each lot benefited within said assessment district, the name of the owner, if known, and the amount of benefits in excess of damages assessed against the same. In case the three commissioners do not agree, the award agreed upon by any two of them shall be sufficient. In designating the lots to be assessed, reference may be had to a diagram of the property in the district affected;

such diagram to be attached to and made a part of the report of the commissioners.   [*Amendment approved March 9, 1893, statutes 1893, p. 91.*]

SECTION 45.   If in any case the commissioners find that conflicting
claims of title exist, or shall be in ignorance or doubt of the ownership of
any lot or land, or any improvement thereon, or any interest therein, it
shall be set down as belonging to unknown owners.   Error in the designation of the owner or owners of any land or improvements, or particulars of
their interest, shall not affect the validity of the assessment.   On the filing
of said report, the clerk of said city council shall give notice of such filing
by the publication of at least ten days in one or more daily newspapers
published and circulated in said city; or if there be no daily newspaper,
by three successive issues in a weekly or semi-weekly newspaper so published and circulated; and said notice shall require all persons interested
to show cause, if any, why such report should not be confirmed, before the
city council, on a day to be fixed by the city council and stated in said
notice, which day shall not be less than twenty days from the first publication thereof.   [*Amendment approved March 9, 1893, statutes 1893, page 91.*]

SECTION 46.   All objections shall be in writing and filed with the clerk
of the city council, who shall at the next meeting after the date fixed in
the notice to show cause, lay the said objections, if any, before the council,
which shall fix a time for hearing the same; of which time the clerk shall
notify the objectors in the same manner as are notified objectors to the
original resolution of intention.   At the time set, or at such other time as
the hearing may be adjourned, the city council shall hear such objections
and pass upon the same, and at such time shall proceed to pass upon such
report, and may confirm, correct, or modify the same, or may order the
commissioners to make a new assessment, report, and plat, which shall be
filed, notice given and had, as in the case of an original report.   In case
the ordinance or resolution of intention also provides for the assessing
upon the district the cost of regrading or repaving such street or streets to
such changed or modified grade, after the report of the commissioners as
to the damages caused by such change of grade has been passed upon by
the city council, it shall then advertise for bids to perform the work of
regrading, repaving, sewering, sidewalking, or curbing such street or
streets with the same or other material with which the same had been formerly graded, paved, sewered, sidewalked, or curbed; first causing a notice,
with specifications, to be posted conspicuously for five days on or near the
council chamber door, inviting sealed proposals for bids for doing such
work, and shall also cause notices of said work, inviting said proposals and
referring to the specifications posted or on file, to be published two days
in a daily, semi-weekly, or weekly newspaper published and circulated in
said city, and designated by the city council for that purpose, and in case
there is no newspaper published in the city, then it shall be posted as
provided in section three of the original act to which this is amendatory.
All proposals or bids offered shall be accompanied by a check, payable to
the order of the mayor of the city, and certified by a responsible bank for
that amount, which shall not be less than ten per cent. of the aggregate of
the proposals; or by a bond for said amount, signed by the bidder and two

sureties, who shall justify under oath in double said amount over and above all statutory exemptions. Said proposals or bids shall be delivered to the clerk of the said city council, and said council shall, in open session, examine and publicly declare the same; *provided, however*, that no proposal or bid shall be considered unless accompanied by a check or a bond satisfactory to the council. The city council may reject any and all bids, and may award the contract to the lowest responsible bidder, which award shall be approved by the mayor or the three-fourths vote of the city council. If not approved by the mayor or the three-fourths vote of the city council, the city council may re-advertise for proposals or bids for the performance of the work, as in the first instance, and thereafter proceed in the manner in this section provided. All checks accompanying bids shall be held by the clerk until the bearer has entered into a contract as herein provided; and in case he refuses so to do, then the amount of his certified check shall be declared forfeited to the city, and shall be collected and paid into its general fund, and all bonds so forfeited shall be prosecuted and the amount thereon collected paid into such fund. Notice of the awards of the contracts shall be published and posted in the same manner as hereinbefore provided for the posting of proposals for said work. [*Amendment approved March 9, 1893, statutes 1893, p. 91.*]

SECTION 47. After such contract has been awarded and entered into, the clerk of the city council shall certify to the city council that fact, together with the total amount of the cost of the same, whereupon the city council shall cause to be forwarded to the commissioners a copy of such certificate; whereupon such commissioners shall proceed to assess the cost of doing such work upon all the lots and land lying within the district to be assessed, distributing the same so that each lot will be assessed for its proportion of the same, according to the benefits it receives from the work, and in the same manner in which the damages caused by the change of grade were assessed upon the same. Such commissioners, in making such assessment, shall show the total amount for which each lot or tract is assessed, in excess of all benefits, for the total cost of changing and modifying the grade of the street, as well as the regrading, repaving, sewering, sidewalking, and curbing of the same, and costs or damages connected therewith. The provisions of the act to which this is amendatory in regard to the mode or manner of the assessment of the cost of such work shall not apply to the work herein contemplated; neither shall the provisions of the same in regard to the issuing of bonds to represent the cost of the same, nor the provisions in regard to the right of protest against the work. [*Amendment approved March 9, 1893, statutes 1893, p. 92.*]

SECTION 48. The clerk of said city council shall forward to the street superintendent of the city a certified copy of the report, assessment, and plat, as finally confirmed and adopted by the city council. Such certified copy shall thereupon be the assessment roll, the cost of which shall be provided for by the commissioners, as a portion of the cost of the proceedings therein. Immediately upon receipt thereof by the street superintendent, the assessment therein contained shall become due and payable, and shall be a lien upon all the property contained or described therein. [*Amendment approved March 9, 1893, statutes 1893, p. 93.*]

SECTION 49. The superintendent of streets shall thereupon give notice, by publication for ten days in one or more daily newspapers published and circulated in said city, or city and county, or two successive insertions in a weekly or semi-weekly newspaper so published and circulated, that he has received said assessment roll, and that all sums levied and assessed in said assessment roll are due and payable immediately, and that the payment of said sums is to be made to him within thirty days from the date of the first publication of said notice. Said notice shall also contain a statement that all assessments not paid before the expiration of said thirty days will be declared to be delinquent, and that thereafter the sum of five per cent. upon the amount of such delinquent assessment, together with the cost of advertising each delinquent assessment, will be added thereto. When payment of any assessment is made to said superintendent of streets, he shall write the word "paid" and the date of payment opposite the respective assessment so paid, and the name of the persons by or for whom said assessment is paid, and shall give a receipt therefor. On the expiration of said thirty days, all assessments then unpaid shall be and become delinquent, and said superintendent of streets shall certify such fact at the foot of said assessment roll, and shall add five per cent. to the amount of each assessment so delinquent. The said superintendent of streets shall, within five days from the date of such delinquency, proceed to advertise the various sums delinquent, and the whole thereof, including the cost of advertising which last shall not exceed the sum of fifty cents for each lot, piece, or parcel of land separately assessed, by the sale of the assessed property in the same manner as is or may be provided for the collection of state and county taxes; and after the date of said delinquency, and before the time of such sale herein provided for, no assessment shall be received unless at the same time the five per cent. added to as aforesaid, together with the costs of advertising then already incurred, shall be paid therewith. Said list of delinquent assessments, with a notice of the time and place of sale of the property affected thereby, shall be published daily for ·five days, in one or more daily news papers published and circulated in such city, or by at least two insertions in a weekly newspaper so published and circulated before the day of sale for such delinquent assessment. Said time of sale must not be less than seven days from the date of the first publication of said delinquent assessment list, and the place must be in or in front of the office of said superintendent of streets. All property sold shall be subject to redemption for one year, and in the same manner as in sales for delinquent state and county taxes; and the superintendent of streets shall, if there is no redemption, make and deliver to the purchaser at such sale a deed conveying the property sold, and may collect for each certificate fifty cents, and for each deed one dollar. All provisions of the law in reference to the sale and redemption of property, for delinquent state and county taxes, in force at any given time, shall also then, as far as the same are not in conflict with the provisions of this act, be applicable

to the sale and redemption of property for delinquent assessments hereunder, including the issuance of certificates and execution of deeds. The
deed of the street superintendent, made after such sale, in case of failure,
to redeem, shall be prima facie evidence of the regularity of all proceedings hereunder, and of title in the grantee. The superintendent of streets
shall from time to time pay over to the city treasurer all moneys collected
by him on account of any such assessments. The city treasurer shall,
upon receipt thereof, place the same in a separate fund, designating each
fund by the name of the street, square, lane, alley, court, or place for the
change of grade for which the assessment was made. Payments shall be
made from said fund to the parties entitled thereto, upon warrants signed
by the commissioners or a majority of them. [*Amendment approved March
9, 1893, statutes 1893, p. 93.*]

SECTION 50. When sufficient money is in the hands of the city treasurer, in
the fund voted for the proposed work or improvement, to pay the total cost
for damages, as well as for the cost of doing the work, and all other expenses connected therewith, it shall be the duty of the commissioners to notify
the owner, possessor or occupant of the premises damaged, and to whom
damages have been awarded, that a warrant has been drawn for the payment of the same, which can be received at the office of such commissioners. Such notification may be made by depositing a notice, postage paid
in the post office addressed to his last known place of residence. If, after
the expiration of three days after the service or deposit of the notice in the
post office he shall not have applied for such warrant, the same shall be
drawn and deposited with the city treasurer, to be delivered to him upon
demand. [*Amendment approved March 9, 1893, statutes '93, p. 94.*]

SECTION 51. If the owner of any premises damaged neglects or refuses,
for ten days after the warrant has been placed in the hands of the city
treasurer, subject to his demand, to accept the same, the city council may
cause proceedings to be commenced, in the name of the city, to condemn
said premises, as provided by law under the right of eminent domain. The
ordinance or resolution of intention shall be conclusive evidence of the
necessity of the same. Such proceedings shall have precedence, so far as
the business of the court will permit, and any judgment for damages therein
rendered shall be payable out of the special fund in the treasury for that
purpose. At any time after the trial and judgment entered, or pending
appeal, the court may order the city treasurer to set apart in the city treasury a sufficient sum from said fund to answer the judgment, and thereupon
may authorize or order the municipality to proceed with the proposed work
or improvements. In case of a deficiency in said fund to pay the whole
assessed judgment and damages, the city council may, in its discretion,
order the balance thereof to be paid out of the general fund of the treasury,
or to be distributed by the commissioners over the property assessed by a
supplementary assessment; but in the last named case, in order to avoid
delay, the city council may advance such balance out of any available fund
in the treasury, and reimburse the same from the collection of assessments.
The treasurer shall pay such warrants in the order of their presentation;

provided, that warrants for damages and for costs of performing the work shall have priority over warrants for charges and expenses, and the treasurer shall see that sufficient money remains in the fund to pay all warrants of the first class before paying any of the second. The provisions of section one thousand two hundred and fifty-one of the Code of Civil Procedure, requiring the payment of damages within thirty days after the entry of judgment, shall not apply to damages rendered in proceedings under this act. [*Amendment approved March 9, 1893, statutes '93, p. 95.*]

SECTION 52. All other provisions contained in the act to which this is amendatory, and which provisions are not in conflict herewith, shall apply to all matters herein contained. All proceedings in any work or improvement, such as is provided for in this act, already commenced and now in progress under another act now in force, or by virtue of an ordinance or resolution of intention heretofore passed, may, from any stage of such proceedings already commenced and now in progress, be continued under this act by resolution of the city council. The said work or improvement may then be conducted under the provisions of this act, with full force and effect in all respects from the stage of such proceedings at and from which such resolution or ordinance shall declare the intention to have such work done or improvement cease under such other acts or ordinances and continued under this act; and from such election so made all proceedings theretofore had are hereby ratified, confirmed and made valid, and it shall be unnecessary to renew or conduct over again any proceedings prior to the passage of this act. [*Amendment approved March 9, 1893, statutes '93, p. 95.*]

SECTION 53. The provisions of this act shall be liberally construed to permit the objects thereof. [*Statutes 1893, page 96.*]

[Section 53 was amended by the act of March 9, 1893, statutes 1893, p. 96.]

Street Improvement Bond Act of 1893.

An Act to provide a system of Street Improvement Bonds to represent certain assessments for the cost of street work and improvement within municipalities, and also for the payment of such bonds.

[Approved February 27, 1893.]

The people of the state of California, represented in senate and assembly, do enact as follows:

SECTION 1. Wherever in this act the phrase "Street Work Act" is used, it means and shall be taken to mean the act entitled "An act to provide for work upon streets, lanes, alleys, courts, places and sidewalks, and for construction of sewers within municipalities," approved March eighteenth, eighteen hundred and eighty-five, and all acts amendatory thereof or supplementary thereto; and wherever in this act the name of any municipal body or officer is used, or any word or phrase is used which is not herein expressly defined, it means and shall be taken to mean such municipal body or officer, or word or phrase as the same is expressly defined in said street work act, and in all acts amendatory thereof or supplementary thereto. [*Statutes 1893, page 33.*]

SECTION 2. Whenever the city council of any municipality in this state shall find, upon estimates of the city engineer, that the cost of any proposed work or improvement authorized by said street work act will be greater than one dollar per front foot along each line of the street so proposed to be improved, including the cost of intersection work assessable upon said frontage, it shall have the power, in its discretion, to determine that serial bonds shall be issued to represent the cost of said work or improvement in the manner and form hereinafter provided. Said serial bonds shall extend over a period not to exceed ten years from their date, and an even annual proportion of the principal sum thereof shall be payable, by coupon, on the second day of January every year after their date, until the whole is paid, and the interest shall be payable semi-annually, by coupon, on the second days of January and July, respectively, of each year, at the rate of not to exceed ten per cent. per annum on all sums unpaid, until the whole of said principal and interest are paid. Said bonds and interest thereon shall be paid at the office of the city treasurer of said municipality, who shall keep a fund designated by the name of said bonds, into which he shall receive all sums paid him for the principal of said bonds and the interest thereon, and from which he shall disburse such sums upon the presentation of said coupons; and under no circumstances shall said bonds or the interest thereon be paid out of any other fund. Said city treasurer shall keep a register in his office, which shall show the series, number, date, amount, rate of interest, payee and indorsees of each bond, and the number and amount of each coupon of principal or interest paid by him, and shall cancel and file each coupon so paid. [*Statutes 1893, p. 33.*]

SECTION 3. When said city council shall determine that serial bonds shall be issued to represent the expenses of any proposed work or improvement under said street work act, it shall so declare in the resolution of intention to do said work, and shall specify the rate of interest which they shall bear. The like description of said bonds shall be inserted in the resolution ordering the work, in the resolution of award, and in all notices of said proceedings required by said street work act to be either posted or published; and also a notice that a bond will issue to represent each assessment of fifty dollars or more remaining unpaid for thirty days after the date of the warrant, or five days after the decision of said council upon an appeal, and describing the bonds, shall be included in the warrant provided for in section nine of said street work act. [*Statutes 1893, p. 34.*]

SECTION 4. After the full expiration of thirty days from the date of the warrant, or if an appeal be taken to the city council, as provided in section eleven of said street work act, then five days after the final decison of said council, and after the street superintendent shall have recorded the return as provided in section 10 of the same act, the street superintendent shall make and certify to the city treasurer a complete list of all assessments unpaid, which amount to fifty dollars or over upon any assessment or diagram number; and said treasurer shall thereupon make out, sign and issue to the conractor or his assigns, payee of the warrant and assessment, a separate bond, representing upon each lot or parcel of land upon said list the total amount of the assessments against the same, as thereon shown. And if said lot or parcel of land is described upon said assessment and diagram by its number or block, or both, and is also designated by its number or block, or both, upon the official map of said municipality, or upon any map on file in the office of the county recorder of the county in which said municipality is situated, then it shall be in said bond a sufficient description of said lot or parcel of land to designate it by said number or block, or both, as it appears on said official or recorded map. Said bond shall be substantially in the following form:

STREET IMPROVEMENT BOND.

Series (designating it), in the city (or other form of the municipality) of (naming it).

$——— $\frac{}{100}$ No. ———.

Under and by virtue of an act of the legislature of the state of California (title of this act), I, out of the fund for the above designated street improvement bonds, series ———, will pay to ———, or order, the sum of ——— ($———), with interest at the rate of ——— per cent. per annum, all as is hereinafter specified, and at the office of the ——— treasurer of the ——— of ———, state of California. This bond is issued to represent the cost of certain street work upon ———, in the ——— of ———, as the same is more fully described in assessment number ———, issued by the street superintendent of said ———, after his acceptance of said work, and recorded in his office. Its amount is the amount assessed in said assessment against the lot or parcel of land numbered therein, and in the diagram attached thereto, as number ———, and which now remains unpaid, but until paid, with accrued interest, is a first lien upon the property affected thereby, as the same is described herein, and in said recorded assessment with its diagram, to wit: the lot or parcel of land in said ——— of ———, county of ———, state of California, ———.

This bond is payable exclusively from said fund, and neither the municipality nor any officer thereof is to be holden for payment otherwise of its principal or interest. The term of this bond is ——— years from its date, and at the expiration of said time the whole sum then unpaid shall be due and payable; but on the second day of January of each year after its date an even annual proportion of its whole amount is due and payable, upon presentation of the coupon therefor, until the whole is paid, with all accrued interest at the rate of ——— per centum per annum. The interest is payable semi-annually, to wit, on the second days of January and of July in each year hereafter, upon presentation of the coupons therefor, the first of which is for the interest from date to the next second day of ———, and thereafter the interest coupons are for semi-annual interest, except the last, which is for interest from the semi-annual payment next preceding and to the date of the final maturity of this bond. Should default be made in the annual payment upon the principal, or in any payment of interest, from the owner of said lot or parcel of land, or any one in his behalf, the holder of this bond is entitled to declare the whole unpaid amount to be due and payable, and to have said lot or parcel of land advertised and sold forthwith, in the manner provided by law for sale of land assessed for state and county taxes delinquent in the payment thereof.

At said ——— of ———, this ——— day of ———, in the year one thousand ——— hundred and ———.

———— ————,
City Treasurer of the ——— of ———.

Provided, that in case the amount of unpaid assessments upon any lot or parcel of land shall be less than fifty dollars, then the same shall be collected as is hereinbefore provided in part one of said street work act.

Provided, also, that if any person, or his authorized agent, shall at any time before the issuance of the bond for said assessments upon his lot or parcel of land, present to the city treasurer his affidavit, made before a competent officer, that he is the owner of a lot or parcel of land in said list, accompanied by the certificate of a searcher of records, that he is such owner of record, and with such affidavit and certificate, such person notifies said treasurer, in writing, that he desires no bond to be issued for the assessments upon said lot or parcel of land, then no such bond shall be issued therefor, and the payee of the warrant, or his assigns, shall retain his right for enforcing collection, as if said lot or parcel of land had not been so listed by the street superintendent. The bonds so issued by said treasurer shall be payable to the party to whom they issue, or order, and shall be serial bonds, as is hereinbefore described, and shall bear interest at the rate specified in the resolution of intention to do said work. They shall have annual coupons attached thereto, payable in annual order, on the second day of January in each year after the date of the bond, until all are paid, and each coupon shall be for an even annual proportion of the principal of the bond. They shall have semi-annual interest coupons thereto attached, the first of which shall be payable upon the second day of January or July, as the case may be, next after its date, and shall be for the interest accrued at that time, and the last of which shall be for the amount of interest accruing from the second day of January or July, as the case may be, next preceding the maturity of said bonds to the maturity thereof. The city treasurer shall, in addition to his other duties in the premises, report all coupon payments of principal upon said bonds to the street superintendent, who shall forthwith indorse the same upon the margin of the record of the assessment to the credit of which the same is paid, and said assessment shall be a first lien upon the property affected thereby, until the bond issued for the payment thereof, and the accrued interest thereon, shall be fully paid. Said bonds, by their issuance, shall be conclusive evidence of the regularity of all proceedings thereto under said street work act and this act, previous to the making of the certified list of all assessments unpaid to the amount of fifty dollars or over by the street superintendent, to the city treasurer, and of the validity of said lien, up to the date of said list. [*Statutes 1893, page 34.*]

SECTION 5   Whenever, through the default of the owner of any lot or parcel of land to represent the assessment upon which such bond has been issued, any payment, either upon the principal or of the interest, shall not be made when the same is due, and the holder of the bond thereupon demands, in writing, that the said city treasurer proceed to advertise and sell said lot or parcel of land, as herein provided, then the whole bond, or its unpaid remainder, with its accrued interest, shall become due and payable immediately, and on the day following shall become delinquent; and the city treasurer shall have, and shall act thereafter with, all the powers and duties of the tax collector in the collection of unpaid state and county taxes, and shall forthwith proceed to advertise and sell said lot or parcel of land by proceedings in all respects the same as are provided by law for the collection of delinquent state and county taxes. All such provisions and proceedings, after taxes have become delinquent, including the certificate of sale, the right of redemption, and the deed, with the respective costs thereof, are hereby made applicable to this case. [*Statutes 1893, p. 36.*]

SECTION 6.   Whenever any railroad track or tracks of any description exists upon any street or streets on which the city council has ordered word to be done or improvements made, excepting therefrom such portions as is required by law to be kept in order or repair by any person or company having railroad tracks thereon, the said council may, at any time thereafter, order such person or company to perform upon said excepted portion the work or improvements, similar in all respects to that already ordered to be performed under the same specifications and superintendence, with the same materials, within the same time, and to the like satisfaction and acceptance. Thereupon it shall be the duty of the clerk of said council to deliver immediately a copy of such order, certified by him, to such person or company, and to make and preserve in his office a certificate of such delivery, its date, and upon whom made. Should such person or company, for thirty days, or within such extension of time as the city council may grant, thereafter refuse or neglect to make or have made such work or improvement in the manner or time ordered, it shall be the duty of the city council to have such work or improvement performed, and such refusal or neglect punished in the manner provided by law. Within fifteen days after receiving the certified copy of said order, such person or company may file with the clerk of said council a written assumption of the performance of said work or improvement, according to the order, or a request to the council to have such work or improvement performed, for and at the expense of such person or company, in the manner herein provided. The failure to file such instrument within said time shall be taken and deemed to be a refusal to comply with the order. Upon reception of said assumption of the direct performance of said work or improvement, the city council shall take no further proceedings in the matter, unless such person or company neglects or fails for thirty days, or such further time as the council may grant, to comply with the provisions of the order. But if such person or company files the said request that the said council have such work or improvement performed, or fails to perform said work within thirty days, or within such further time as the council may grant, then said city council may pass an ordinance of intention to perform said work, which ordinance shall specify the work to be performed, and a statement that unless within thirty days after the recording of the return of the warrant, or within five days after the final decision of the council on an appeal, the said person or company shall pay the cost of said work, or the street superintendent of said city shall issue bonds to represent the cost of said work, stating also that the cost of said work, in case bonds shall issue, shall be paid in ten yearly installments, and also the rate of interest (not to exceed ten per cent. per annum) that the same shall bear. The subsequent procedure shall be as provided by the "street work act." A similar statement shall also be incorporated in all notices required to be posted or published by the provisions of the "street work act;" also in the ordinance or resolution ordering the work, advertisement for proposals, and in the contract. Whenever the person or company owning any such railroad shall not have, within thirty days after the recording of the return of the warrant, or within five days after the final decision of the council on an appeal, paid the cost of such work, the street superintendent shall issue to the contractor, or his assigns, bonds for the amount of such cost, which shall describe the franchise, tracks, and roadbed along or between which said work has been performed, and describing the same as upon the assessment and diagram, giving its assessment number. Such bonds shall also describe the work performed, giving the total amount of the cost of such work, the name of the owner of said railroad, the number of installments in which the cost of the work is to be paid, and the rate of interest which the deferred payments shall bear. Said bonds shall be in sums of not less than one hundred dollars or more than one thousand dollars, and shall recite that the total amount of the cost of such work, together with the interest thereon, as represented in said bonds, is, except state, county and municipal taxes, a first lien upon all the track, roadbed, switches and franchises of said railroad lying within the corporate limits of the city or town, on any part of which said work has been performed. Said street superintendent shall also keep a record of such bonds, as required by section eighteen of the "street work act." Whenever bonds have been issued, as herein provided, the same, together with the cost of such work and the interest thereon, shall be, except state, county or municipal taxes, a first lien upon all the tracks, roadbed, switches and franchises of said railroad within the corporate limits of the city or town, on any part of which said work has been performed. Sections four and five of this act, regarding the form, issuance and foreclosure of street bonds and the sale of property described therein, shall apply hereto, except that the work required to be performed by the treasurer by said sections shall be performed by the street superintendent, in so far as the bonds for the paving of railroads are concerned. None of the provisions of the "street work act" in regard to a protest against the work shall apply to any work contemplated by this section. All provisions of the "street work act" not inconsistent with the provisions hereof, shall apply hereto. [*Statutes '93, p. 36.*]

SECTION 7. The term "city treasurer," as used in this act, shall be held to mean and include any person who, under whatever name or title, is the custodian of the funds of the municipality. [*Statutes '93, p. 38.*]

SECTION 8. The act entitled "An act to amend an act entitled 'An act to provide for work upon streets, lanes, alleys, courts, places and sidewalks, and for construction of sewers within municipalities,' approved March eighteenth, eighteen hundred and eighty-five, by adding thereto an additional part, numbered four, consisting of sections thirty-eight, thirty-nine, forty, forty-one, forty-two, forty-three and forty-four, relative to a system of street improvement bonds," approved March seventeenth, eighteen hundred and ninety-one, is hereby repealed, except as to any and all proceedings hitherto commenced thereunder, which proceedings may be completed and have full force as is therein provided. [*Statutes '93, p. 38.*]

SECTION 9. This act shall take effect and become of force from and after its passage. [*Statutes '93, p. 38.*]

Street Opening Act of March 6, 1889.

An Act to provide for laying out, opening, extending, widening, straightening, or closing up in whole or in part any street, square, lane, alley, court, or place within municipalities, and to condemn and acquire any and all land and property necessary or convenient for that purpose.

[Approved March 6, 1889, statutes 1889, p. 70.]

The people of the state of California, represented in senate and assembly, do enact as follows:

SECTION 1. Whenever the public interest or convenience may require, the city council of any municipality shall have full power and authority to order the opening, extending, widening, straightening, or closing up in whole or in part of any street, square, lane, alley, court, or place within the bounds of such city, and to condemn and acquire any and all land and property necessary or convenient for that purpose. [*Statutes 1889, p. 70.*]

SECTION 2. Before ordering any work to be done or improvement made which is authorized by section one of this act, the city council shall pass a resolution declaring its intention to do so, describing the work or improvement, and the land deemed necessary to be taken therefor, and specifying the exterior boundaries of the district of lands to be affected or benefited by said work or improvement, and to be assessed to pay the damages, cost and expenses thereof. [*Statutes '89, p. 70.*]

SECTION 3. The street superintendent shall then cause to be conspicuously posted along the line of said contemplated work or improvement, at not more than three hundred feet in distance apart, but not less than three in all, notices of the passage of said resolution. Said notice shall be headed, "Notice of public work," in letters not less than one inch in length, shall be in legible characters, state the fact of passage of the resolution, its date, and, briefly, the work or improvement proposed, and refer to the resolution for further particulars. He shall also cause a notice, similar in substance, to be published for a period of ten days in one or more daily newspapers published and circulated in said city, and designated by said city council; or, if there is no daily newspaper so published and circulated in said city, then by four successive insertions in a weekly or semi-weekly newspaper so published, circulated and designated. [*Statutes '89, p. 70.*]

SECTION 4. Any person interested objecting to said work or improvement, or to the extent of the district of lands to be affected or benefited by said work or improvement, and to be assessed to pay the cost and expenses thereof, may make written objections to the same within ten days after the expiration of the time of the publication of said notice, which objection shall be delivered to the clerk of the city council, who shall indorse thereon the date of its reception by him, and at the next meeting of the city council after the expiration of said ten days, lay said objections before said city council, which shall fix a time for hearing said objections not less than one week thereafter. The city clerk shall thereupon notify the persons making such objections, by depositing a notice thereof in the post office of said city, postage prepaid, addressed to such objector. [*Statutes '89, p. 70.*]

SECTION 5. At the time specified or to which the hearing may be adjourned, the said city council shall hear the objections urged and pass upon the same, and its decision shall be final and conclusive. If such objections are sustained, all proceedings shall be stopped, but proceedings may be again commenced at any time by giving notice of intention to do said work or make said improvement. If such objection is overruled by the city council, the proceedings shall continue the same as if such objection had not been made. At the expiration of the time prescribed during which objections to said work or improvement may be made, if no objections shall have been made, or if an objection shall have been, and said council, after hearing, shall have overruled the same, the city council shall be deemed to have acquired jurisdiction to order any of the work to be done, or improvements to be made, which is authorized by section one of this act. [*Statutes '89, p. 71.*]

SECTION 6. Having acquired jurisdiction, as provided in the preceding section, the city council shall order said work to be done, and unless the proposed work is for closing up, and it appears that no assessment is necessary, shall appoint three commissioners to assess benefits and damages and have general supervision of the proposed work or improvement until the completion thereof in compliance with this statute. For their services they shall receive such compensation as the city council may determine from time to time; *provided,* that such compensation shall not exceed two hundred dollars per month each, nor continue more than six months, unless extended by order of the city council. Such compensation shall be added to and be chargeable as a part of the expenses of the work or improvement. Each of said commissioners shall file with the clerk of the city council an affidavit, and a bond to the state of California in the sum of five thousand dollars, to faithfully perform the duties of his office. The city council may at any time remove any or all of said commissioners for cause, upon reasonable notice and hearing, and may fill any vacancies occurring among them for any cause. [*Statutes '89, page 71.*]

SECTION 7. Said commissioners shall have power to employ such assistance, legal or otherwise, as they may deem necessary and proper; also, to rent an office and provide such maps, diagrams, plans, books, stationery, fuel, lights, postage, expressage, and incur such incidental expenses as they may deem necessary. [*Statutes '89, p. 71.*]

SECTION 8. All such charges and expenses shall be deemed as expenses of said work or improvement, and be a charge only upon the funds devoted to the particular work or improvement as provided hereinafter. All payments, as well for the land and improvements taken or damaged, as for the charges and expenses, shall be paid by the city treasurer, upon warrants drawn upon said fund from time to time, signed by said commissioners, or a majority of them. All such warrants shall state whether they are issued for land or improvements taken or damaged, or for charges and expenses, and that the demand is payable only out of the money in said fund, and in no event shall the city be liable for the failure to collect any assessment made by virtue hereof, nor shall said warrant be payable out o any other fund, nor a claim against the city. [*Statutes '89, p. 71.*]

SECTION 9. Said commissioners shall proceed to view the lands described in the resolution of intention, and may examine witnesses on oath, to be administered by any one of them. Having viewed the land to be taken, and the improvements affected, and considered the testimony presented, they shall proceed with all diligence to determine the value of the land and the damage to improvements and property affected, and also the amount of the expenses incident to said work or improvement, and having determined the same, shall proceed to assess the same upon the district of lands declared benefited, the exterior boundaries of which were fixed by the resolution of intention provided for by section 2 hereof. Such assessment shall be made upon the lands within said district in proportion to the benefit to be derived from said work or improvement, so far as the said commissioners can reasonably estimate the same, including in such estimate the property of any railroad company within said district, if such there be. [*Statutes '89, p. 72.*]

SECTION 10. Said commissioners having made their assessment of bene¯fits and damage, shall, with all diligence, make a written report thereof to the city council, and shall accompany their report with a plat of the assessment district showing the land taken or to be taken for the work or improvement, and the lands assessed, showing the relative location of each district, block, lot, or portion of lot, and its dimensions, so far as the commissioners can reasonably ascertain the same. Each block and lot, or portion of lot, taken or assessed, shall be designated and described in said plat by an appropriate number, and a reference to it by such descriptive number shall be a sufficient description of it in any suit entered to condemn, and in all respects. When the report and plat are approved by the city council, a copy of said plat, appropriately designated, shall be filed by the clerk thereof in the office of the recorder of the county. [*Statutes 1889, page 72.*]

SECTION 11. Said report shall specify each lot, subdivision, or piece of property taken or injured by the widening or other improvement, or assessed therefor, together with the name of the owner or claimants thereof, or of persons interested therein as lessees, incumbrancers, or otherwise, so far as the same are known to such commissioners, and the particulars of their interest, so far as the same can be ascertained, and the amount of value or damage, or the amount assessed, as the case may be. [*Statutes 1889, page 72.*]

SECTION 12.   If in any case the commissioners find that conflicting claims of title exist, or shall be in ignorance or doubt as to the ownership of any lot of land, or of any improvements thereon, or of any interest therein, it shall be set down as belonging to unknown owners.   Error in the designation of the owner or owners of any land or improvements, or of the particulars of their interest, shall not affect the validity of the assessment or of the condemnation of the property to be taken. [*Statutes 1889, page 73.*]

SECTION 13.   Said report and plat shall be filed in the clerk's office of the city council, and thereupon the clerk of said city council shall give notice of such filing by publication for at least ten days in one or more daily newspapers published and circulated in said city; or if there be no daily paper, by three successive insertions in a weekly or semi-weekly newspaper so published and circulated.   Said notice shall also require all persons interested to show cause, if any, why such report should not be confirmed, before the city council, on or before a day fixed by the clerk thereof, and stated in said notice, which day shall not be less than thirty days from the first publication thereof. [*Statutes 1889, page 73.*]

SECTION 14.   All objections shall be in writing and filed with the clerk of the city council, who shall, at the next meeting after the day fixed in the notice to show cause, lay the said objections, if any, before the city council, which shall fix a time for hearing the same, of which the clerk shall notify the objectors in the same manner as objectors to the original resolution of intention at the time set, or at such other time as the hearing may be adjourned to, the city council shall hear such objections and pass upon the same; and at such time, or if there be no objections at the first meeting after the day set in such order to show cause, or such other time as may be fixed, shall proceed to pass upon such report, and may confirm, correct, or modify the same, or may order the commissioners to make a new assessment, report, and plat, which shall be filed, notice given, and hearing had as in the case of an original report. [*Statutes 1889, page 73.*]

SECTION 15.   The clerk of said city council shall forward to the street superintendent of the city a certified copy of the report, assessment and plat, as finally confirmed and adopted by the city council.   Such certified copy shall thereupon be the assessment roll.   Immediately upon receipt thereof by the street superintendent the assessment therein contained shall become due and payable, and shall be a lien upon all the property contained or described therein. [*Statutes 1889, page 73.*]

SECTION 16.   The superintendent of streets shall thereupon give notice by publication for ten days in one or more daily newspapers published and circulated in such city, or city and county, or by two successive insertions in a weekly or semi-weekly newspaper so published and circulated, that he has received said assessment roll, and that all sums levied and assessed in said assessment roll are due and payable immediately, and that the payment of said sums is to be made to him within thirty days from the date of the first publication of said notice. Said notice shall also contain a statement that all assessments not paid before the expiration of said thirty days will be declared to be delinquent, and that thereafter the sum of five per cent. upon the amount of each delinquent assessment, together with the cost of advertising each delinquent assessment, will be added thereto. When payment of any assessment is made to said superintendent of streets he shall write the word "paid," and the date of payment, opposite the respective assessment so paid, and the names of persons by or for whom said assessment is paid, and shall, if so required, give a receipt therefor. On the expiration of said thirty days all assessments then unpaid shall be and become delinquent, and said superintendent of streets shall certify such fact at the foot of said assessment roll, and shall add five per cent. to the amount of each assessment so delinquent. The said superintendent of streets shall, within five days from the date of said delinquency, proceed to advertise and collect the various sums delinquent, and the whole thereof, including the cost of advertising, which last shall not exceed the sum of fifty cents for each lot, piece, or parcel of land separately assessed, by the sale of the assessed property in the same manner as is or may be provided for the collection of state and county taxes; and after the date of said delinquency, and before the time of such sale herein provided for. no assessment shall be received unless at the same time the five per cent. added thereto, as aforesaid, together with the costs of advertising then already incurred, shall be paid therewith. Said list of delinquent assessments shall be published daily for five days in one or more daily newspapers published and circulated in such city, or by at least one insertion in a weekly newspaper so published and circulated, before the day of sale of such delinquent assessment. Said time of sale must not be less than seven days from the date of the first publication of said delinquent assessment list, and the place must be in or in front of the office of said superintendent of streets. All property sold shall be subject to redemption in the same time and manner as in sales for delinquent state and county taxes; and the superintendent of streets may collect for each certificate fifty cents, and for each deed one dollar. All provisions of the law, in reference to the sale and redemption of property for delinquent state and county taxes in force at any given time, shall also then, so far as the same are not in conflict with the provisions of this act, be applicable to the sale and redemption of property for delinquent assessments hereunder, including the issuance of certificates and execution of deeds. The deed of the street superintendent made after such sale, in case of failure to redeem, shall be prima facie evidence of the regularity of all proceedings hereunder, and of title in the grantee. It shall be conclusive evidence of the necessity of taking or damaging the lands taken or damaged, and of the correctness of the compensation awarded therefor. The superintendent of streets shall, from time to time, pay over to the city treasurer all moneys collected by him on account of any such assessments. The city treasurer shall, upon receipt thereof, place the same in a separate fund, designating such funds by the name of the street, square, lane, alley, court, or place for the widening, opening, or other improvement of which the assessment was made. Payments shall be made from said fund to the parties entitled thereto upon warrants signed by the commissioners, or a majority of them. [*Statutes 1889, page 73.*]

Section 17. When sufficient money is in the hands of the city treasurer, in the fund devoted to the proposed work or improvement, to pay for the land and improvements taken or damaged, and when in the discretion of the commissioners, or a majority of them, the time shall have come to make payments, it shall be the duty of the commissioners to notify the owner, possessor, or occupant of any land or improvements thereon to whom damages shall have been awarded, that a warrant has been drawn for the payment of the same, and that he can receive such warrant at the office of such commissioners upon tendering a conveyance of any property to be taken; such notification, except in the case of unknown owners, to be made by depositing a notice, postage paid, in the post office, addressed to his last known place of abode or residence. If at the expiration of thirty days after the deposit of such notice, he should not have applied for such warrant, and tendered a conveyance of the land to be taken, the warrant so drawn shall be deposited with the county treasurer, and shall be delivered to such owner, possessor, or occupant, upon tendering a conveyance as aforesaid, unless judgment of condemnation shall be had, when the same shall be canceled. [*Statutes 1889, page 75.*]

Section 18. If any owner of land to be taken neglects or refuses to accept the warrant drawn in his favor as aforesaid, or objects to the report as to the necessity of taking his land, the commissioners, with the approval of the city council, may cause proceedings to be taken for the condemnation thereof, as provided by law under the right of eminent domain. The complaint may aver that it is necessary for the city to take or damage and condemn the said lands, or an easement therein, as the case may be, without setting forth the proceedings herein provided for, and the resolution and ordinance ordering said work to be done shall be conclusive evidence of such necessity. Such proceeding shall be brought in the name of the municipality, and have precedence so far as the business of the court will permit; and any judgment for damages therein rendered shall be payable out of such portion of the special fund as may remain in the treasury, so far as the same can be applied. At any time after trial and judgment entered, or preceding an appeal, the court may order the city treasurer to set apart in the city treasury a sufficient sum from the fund appropriated to the particular improvement to answer the judgment and all damages, and thereupon may authorize and order the municipality to enter upon the land and proceed with the proposed work and improvement. In case of a deficiency in said fund to pay the whole of such judgment and damages, the city council may, in their discretion, order the balance thereof to be paid out of the general fund of the treasury or to be distributed by the commissioners over the property assessed by a supplementary assessment; but in the last named case, in order to avoid delay, the city council may advance such balance out of any appropriate fund in the treasury, and reimburse the same from the collections of the assessment. Pending the collection and payment of the amount of the judgment and damages, the court may order such stay of proceedings as may be necessary. [*Statutes 1889, page 75.*]

SECTION 19. The treasurer shall pay such warrants out of the appropriate fund, and not otherwise, in the order of their presentation; *provided,* that warrants for land or improvements taken or damaged shall have priority over warrants for charges and expenses, and the treasurer shall see that sufficient money is and remains in the fund to pay all warrants of the first class before paying any of the second. [*Statutes 1889, page 76.*]

SECTION 20. If after the sale of the property for delinquent assessments there should be a deficiency, and there should be unreasonable delay in collecting the same, or if for the purpose of equalizing the assessments, supplying a deficiency, or for any cause it appears desirable, the commissioners may so report to the city council, who may order them to make a supplementary assessment and report the same in manner and form as the original, and subject to the same procedure. If by reason of such supplementary assessment, or for any cause, there should be at any time a surplus, the city council may appropriate the same and declare a dividend pro rata to the parties paying the same, and they, upon demand, shall have the right to have the amount of such pro rata dividends refunded to them, or credited upon any subsequent assessment for taxes made against said parties in favor of said city. [*Statutes 1889, page 76.*]

SECTION 21. If any title attempted to be acquired by virtue of this act shall be found to be defective from any cause, the city council may again institute proceedings to acquire the cause as in this act provided, or otherwise, or may authorize the commissioners to purchase the same and include the cost thereof in a supplementary assessment as provided in the last section. [*Statutes 1889, page 76.*]

SECTION 22. If the city council deem it proper that the boundaries of the districts of lands to be affected and assessed to pay the damages, cost, and expenses of any work or improvement under this act, shall include the whole city, then the commissioners appointed shall proceed in a summary manner to purchase the lands to be taken or condemned from the owners and claimants thereof. If said commissioners and the owners and claimants cannot agree upon the price to be paid for said lands, they shall proceed to view and value the same, and shall thereupon make a summary report to the city council. Upon final confirmation of the report, the city council, if there be not sufficient money available in the city treasury, shall cause the cost and expenses of the contemplated public improvement to be assessed upon the whole of the taxable property of said city, and to be included in and form part of the next general assessment rol of said city, and with like effect in all respects as if the same formed a part of the city, state and county taxes; and when the same shall have been collected the said city council shall cause the land required to be paid for or the value thereof tendered, and the said contemplated public improvement to be forthwith made and completed. All the provisions of the preceding

sections not in conflict with this section shall be applicable thereto. [*Statutes 1889, page 76.*]

SECTION 23. *1.* The words "work" and "improvement," as used in this act, shall include all work mentioned in section one of this act.

2. In case there is no daily or weekly or semi-weekly newspapers printed and circulated in the city, then such notices as are herein required to be published in a newspaper shall be posted and kept posted for the length of time required herein for the publication of the same in a weekly newspaper, in three of the most public places in such city. Proof of the publication or posting of any notice provided for herein shall be made by affidavit of the owner, publisher or clerk of the newspaper, or of the poster of the notice.

3. The word "municipality" and the word "city" shall be understood and so construed as to include all corporations heretofore organized and now existing, or hereafter organized, for municipal purpose.

4. The term street superintendent and superintendent of streets, as used in this act, shall be understood and so construed as to include, and are hereby declared to include, any person or officer whose duty it is, under the law, to have the care or charge of the streets, or the improvement thereof, in any city. In all those cities where there is no street superintendent or superintendent of streets, the city council thereof is hereby authorized and empowered to appoint a suitable person to discharge the duties herein laid down as those of street superintendent or superintendent of streets; and all the provisions hereof applicable to the street superintendent or superintendent of streets shall apply to such persons so appointed.

5. The term "city council" is hereby declared to include any body or board which, under the law, is the legislative department of the government of any city.

6. The term "clerk" and "city clerk," as used in this act, is hereby declared to include any person or officer who shall be clerk of said city council.

7. The term "treasurer" or "city treasurer," as used in this act, shall include any person or officer who shall have charge and make payment of the city funds.

8. No publications or notice other than that provided for in this act shall be necessary to give validity to any proceedings had thereunder. [*Statutes 1889, page 77.*]

SECTION 24. The proceedings in any work or improvement, such as is provided for in this act, already commenced and now progressing under any other act now in force, or by virtue of any ordinance passed by any city council or board of supervisors of any city, county, or city and county, by virtue of any other act now in force, may, from any stage of such proceedings already commenced and now progressing, be continued under this act by resolution of the city council. The said work or improvement may then be conducted under the provisions of this act with full force and effect in all respects, from the stage of such proceedings under such other

acts or ordinances at and from which such resolution shall declare an
election or intention to have said work or improvement cease under such
other act or ordinance and continue under this act; and from such election so made, all proceeding theretofore had under such other act or ordinance are hereby ratified, confirmed, and made valid, and it shall be
unnecessary to renew or conduct over again proceedings had under such
other act or ordinance. This section shall not apply to any work or
improvement proceedings in which were commenced more than eighteen
months prior to the passage of this act. [*Statutes 1889, page 77.*]

SECTION 25. The provisions of this act shall be liberally construed to
promote the objects thereof. This act shall take effect and be in force
from and after its passage. [*Statutes 1889, page 78.*]

APPENDIX.

FORMS USED UNDER THE VROOMAN ACT.

NOTE—Those parts which are not permanent parts of any similar form, such as dates descriptions, etc., are in italics.

No. 1. RESOLUTION OF INTENTION.

Resolution of Intention, No. *735*; Resolved, That it is the intention of the city council of the city of *Los Angeles*, state of California, to order the following street work to be done, in the said city, to wit: That that portion of *Hoover* street in said city from the *south curb* line *of Sixteenth* street to the *north curb* line of *Washington* street, *which is east of the west city boundary*, including all intersections of streets, (excepting such portion of said street and intersections as are required by law to be kept in order or repair by any person or company having railroad tracks thereon, and also excepting such portions as have already been *graded, graveled*, and accepted,) *be graded and graveled* in accordance with the plans and profile on file in the office of the city engineer and specifications on file in the office of the city clerk of the city of *Los Angeles for graveled* streets, said specifications being numbered *5*.

The *Los Angeles Herald*, a daily newspaper published and circulated in said city, is hereby designated as the newspaper in which this resolution of intention and notice of the passage thereof shall be published in the manner and by the persons required by law.

The superintendent of streets of said city is hereby directed to post notices of the passage of this resolution in the manner and in the form required by law, and to cause a similar notice to be published for six days in said newspaper, in the manner required by law.

The city clerk of said city is hereby directed to post this resolution of intention conspicuously for two days on or near the chamber door of the council, and to cause the same to be published by two insertions in the manner required by law, in said daily newspaper.

I hereby certify that the foregoing resolution was passed by the city council of the city of *Los Angeles* on the *13th* day of *November, 1893*, by the following vote:

Ayes; Messrs. *Campbell, Innes, Munson, Nickell, Pessell, and president Teed.*

Noes: Messrs. *Rhodes and Strohm.*

C. A. LUCKENBACH,

City clerk and ex officio clerk of the city council of the city of *Los Angeles.*

No. 2.   NOTICE OF PASSAGE OF RESOLUTION OF INTENTION.

NOTICE OF STREET WORK.

Notice is hereby given that on *Monday* the *13th* day of *November, A. D.*
1893, the city council of the city of *Los Angeles* did, at its meeting on said
day, adopt a resolution of intention, numbered *1923* (*new* series,) to order
the following street work to be done, to wit:

That a *cement sidewalk six feet in width be constructed along the west side of*
Burlington avenue, in said city, from the southerly curb line of Seventh street
to the northerly curb line of Ninth street (excepting such portions of said
street between said points along which *a cement or asphalt sidewalk* has
been constructed and accepted,) said *sidewalk* to be constructed in accordance with specifications on file in the office of the city clerk, said specifications being numbered *twelve.*

Reference is hereby made to the said resolution of intention for further
particulars.

D. A. WATSON,

Street Superintendent.

No. 3.   RESOLUTION ORDERING WORK TO BE DONE.

Resolution ordering street work, No. *926,* (*third* series):   Resolved, That
the street work herein described is required by the public interest and
convenience, and the city council of the city of *Los Angeles,* state of California, hereby orders the same to be done according to the specifications
contained in its ordinance, No. *1847,* and under the direction and to
the satisfaction of the superintendent of streets of said city, to wit:

That a *cement sidewalk five feet in width be constructed along the south side*
of Eleventh street in said city from the easterly curb line of Vernon street to
the westerly curb line of Sentous street, (excepting such portions of said street
between said points along which a *cement or asphalt sidewalk* has been constructed and accepted), said *sidewalk* to be constructed in accordance with
specifications on file in the office of the city clerk, said specifications being
numbered *12.*

The *Daily Journal,* a daily newspaper publisher and circulated in said
city, is hereby designated as the newspaper in which this resolution and
notice of said work, inviting sealed proposals, shall be published in the
manner and form and by the persons required by law.

The city clerk of said city is hereby directed to post conspicuously for
five days, on or near the chamber door of the council, in the manner and
form required by law, a notice, with specifications, inviting sealed proposals or bids for doing said work; and said clerk is hereby directed to
publish for two days, in the manner and form required by law, a notice of
said work, inviting sealed proposals or bids for doing said work, and
referring to the specifications posted or on file, in the said newspaper
hereby designated for that purpose as aforesaid.   Said notice shall require
a certified check or bond, either, as prescribed by law, and for an amount
not less than 10 per cent. of the aggregate of the proposal.   Said clerk is

also hereby directed to publish this resolution for two days, in the manner required by law, in said newspaper designated for that purpose as aforesaid.

I hereby certify that the foregoing resolution was passed by the city council of the city of *Los Angeles*, on the *13th* day of *November*, 189*2*, by the following vote:

Ayes: Messrs. *Campbell, Innes, Munson, Nickell, Pessell and President Teed.*

Noes: Messrs. *Rhodes and Strohm.*

C. A. LUCKENBACH,

City clerk and ex officio clerk of the city council of the city of *Los Angeles.*

No. 4. NOTICE INVITING SEALED PROPOSALS.

NOTICE INVITING STREET WORK PROPOSALS.

Pursuant to statutes and to resolution No. *1930* of the council of the city of *Los Angeles*, adopted *November 20th*, 189*2*, directing this notice, the undersigned invites and will receive at his office in the city hall up to *11* o'clock *A. M.* of *Monday, December 11*, 189*2*, sealed proposals or bids, for the following street work to be done according to the specifications No. *5* for *graded and graveled* streets in the city of *Los Angeles*, posted and on file, therefor adopted, or herein mentioned, to wit: That portion of *Lyell* street in said city from the *southerly curb* line of *Mozart* street to the *northerly curb* line of *Kuhrts* street, *including all intersections of streets*, (excepting such portions of said street and intersections as are required by law to be kept in order or repair by any person or company having railroad tracks thereon, and also excepting such portions as have already been *graded and graveled* and accepted) be *graded and graveled* in accordance with the plans and profile on file in the office of the city engineer and specifications on file in the office of the city clerk of the city of *Los Angeles* for *graveled* streets, said specifications being numbered *five*.

Bidders must file with each proposal or bid a check payable to the order of the mayor of this city, certified by a responsible bank, for an amount which shall not be less than ten per cent. of the aggregate of the proposal, or a bond for the said amount and so payable, signed by the bidder and by two sureties, who shall justify, before any officer competent to administer an oath, in double the said amount, and over and above all statutory exemptions.

In bidding use blanks which will be furnished by the city clerk upon application.

Los Angeles, Cal., *November 20th*, 189*2*.

FREEMAN G. TEED,

City clerk and ex officio clerk of the council of the city of *Los Angeles.*

[NOTE: The specifications must be posted with the notice which is posted on or near the council chamber door.]

No. 5. CONTRACTOR'S PROPOSAL WITH BOND.

[Attach Advertisement here.]

City of *Los Angeles, December 10,* 189*2.*

To the Honorable City Council of the city of *Los Angeles:*

In compliance with the advertisement calling therefor, a copy of which is hereto annexed, *I* hereby propose and agree to perform the work mentioned, upon *Lyell* street, in the city of *Los Angeles* from the *southerly curb* line of *Mozart* street, to the *northerly curb* line of *Kuhrts* street, and furnish materials in accordance with the specifications and execute the contract therfor, to the satisfaction and under the supervision of the street superintendent of said city at the following prices, viz.

	DOLLARS.	CENTS.
Grading per lineal foot	*$3*	*.00*
Paving per square foot		
Macadamizing per square foot		
Curb per lineal foot		*.50*
Sidewalk per square foot		*.12*
Sewer complete per lineal foot		
Manholes complete each		
Flushtanks complete each		
Lamp holes complete each		

CHARLES F. MUNSON,

Contractor.

BOND.

Know all men by these presents: That we *Charles F. Munson,* (or if the bidder is a corporation, *a corporation having its office and principal place of business in said city of Los Angeles*) as principal, and *Conrad Scheerer* and *Martin C. Marsh* as sureties, are held and firmly bound unto the mayor of the city of *Los Angeles,* state of California, in the just and full sum of *five hundred* dollars, for the payment whereof we hereby bind ourselves, (if a corporation, *successors,*) heirs, executors and administrators, jointly and severally, firmly by these presents.

Given under our hands and sealed with our seals, on this *10th* day of *December,* A. D., one thousand eight hundred and ninety-*two* (if by a corporation—*said company subscribing and setting its corporate seal hereto by ——— its ——— thereto authorized.)*

The condition of the foregoing obligation is such that, whereas the above bounden *Charles F. Munson* is about to hand in and submit to the council of the city of *Los Angeles,* the foregoing bid or proposal, for the performance of the work therein mentioned, which includes the furnishing of all materials in compliance with the specifications therefor, under an invitation of said council contained in the notice or advertisement attached to said bid or proposal: Now if the bid or proposal of the said *Charles F. Munson* shall be accepted, and the said work awarded to *him* thereupon by said council, and if the said *Charles F. Munson* shall fail or neglect to enter into a contract therefor, and to execute an adequate bond to the satisfaction of the mayor and superintendent of streets of said city, with two or more good and sufficient sureties, conditioned for the faithful performance of such contract on *his* part, in such case required by statute, then in that case the above named obligors will pay to the mayor of said city of *Los Angeles* the full sum of *five hundred* dollars as liquidated damages for such failure and neglect.

*CHARLES*J. MUNSON,*   [SEAL.]

WITNESS: *CONRAD SCHEERER,*   [SEAL.]

FRED. HARKNESS.   *MARTIN C. MARSH.*   [SEAL.]

State of California,   ⎰ ss.
County of *Los Angeles*, ⎱

Conrad Scherer and *Martin C. Marsh*, being severally duly sworn each for himself and not one for the other, says that he is one of the sureties named in the foregoing bond, and that he executed the same, and is worth double the sum mentioned therein over and above all statutory exemptions.

CONRAD SCHEERER,

MARTIN C. MARSH.

Subscribed and sworn to before me this *10th* day of *December*, 189*2*.

[SEAL.]   *FRED. HARKNESS,*

Notary Public.   •

No. 6.   RESOLUTION OF AWARD.

Resolved, That the city council of the city of *Los Angeles*, having in open session on the *20th* day of ¦*December*, 189*2* opened, examined, and publicly declared all sealed proposals or bids offered for the following work, to wit: *The construction of a redwood curb along each line of the roadway of Lyell street, in said city, from the southerly curb line of Mozart street to the northerly curb line of Kuhrts street, (excepting along such portions of the line of said roadway upon which a redwood, granite or cement curb has already been constructed and accepted,) in accordance with specifications in the office of the city clerk of said city, for constructing redwood curbs,* hereby rejects all of said bids except that next herein mentioned and hereby awards the contract for said work to the lowest regular responsible bidder, to wit: to *Frick Bros.*, at the price specified in *their* proposal on file for said work, to wit: *$1.50 per lineal foot on each side.*

The city clerk is hereby directed to post notice of this award conspicuously for five days on or near the council chamber door of this council, and also publish said notice for two days in the *Los Angeles Herald*, a daily newspaper published and circulated in this city, and hereby designated for that purpose by this council.

Passed by the council of the city of *Los Angeles, December 27,* 189*2*, by the following vote:

Ayes, Messrs. *Rhodes, Strohm, Campbell, Innes, Munson, and President Teed.*

Noes, Messrs. *Gaffey, Nickell and Pessell.*

FREEMAN G. TEED, President.

C. A. LUCKENBACH, City Clerk.

Approved this *28th* day of *December,* 189*2*,

HENRY T. HAZARD, Mayor.

No. 7. NOTICE OF AWARD OF CONTRACT.

Pursuant to statutes and to the resolution of award of the city council of the city of *Los Angeles*, passed *December 27*, 1892, directing this notice, notice is hereby given that the said city council, in open session, on the *20th* day of *December*, 1892, opened, examined, and publicly declared all sealed proposals or bids offered for the following work, to wit: *The construction of a redwood curb, along each line of the roadway of Lyell street, in said city from the southerly curb line of Mozart street to the northerly curb line of Kuhrts street, (excepting along such portions of the line of said roadway upon which a redwood, granite, or cement curb has already been constructed and accepted, in accordance with specifications in the office of the city clerk of said city for constructing redwood curbs.* And thereafter to wit, on the *27th* day of *December*, 1892, awarded the contract for said work to the lowest regular responsible bidder, to wit, to *Frick Bros.*, at the prices named for said work in *their* proposal on file, to wit, *$1.50 per lineal foot on each side*; and that the said award has been approved by the mayor.

Clerk's office, *Los Angeles*, Cal., *January 3*, 1893.

C. A. LUCKENBACH,

City clerk of the city of *Los Angeles.*

No. 8. CONTRACT.

Street contract, No. *1000.*

This agreement, made and entered into this *1st* day of *November*, 1893, by and between *Conrad Scheerer*, of the city of *Los Angeles*, state of California, party of the first part, and *Drury A. Watson*, street superintendent of the city of *Los Angeles,* state of California, under and by virtue of the authority granted to him as such by an act entitled " An act to provide for the improvement of streets, lanes, alleys, courts, places and sidewalks, and the construction of sewers within municipalities," approved March 18th, 1885, and all acts amendatory thereto, party of the second part.

Whereas, the said party of the first part, (as will more fully appear by reference to the record of the proceedings of the city council of said city on the *18th* day of *October*, 1893,) has been awarded the contract for the work hereinafter mentioned;

Now, therefore, these presents witnesseth, that the said party of the first part, for the consideration hereinafter mentioned, promises and agrees with said *Drury A. Watson,* as said street superintendent, and not otherwise, that *he* will do and perform, or cause to be done and performed in a good and workmanlike manner, under the direction and to the satisfaction of the street superintendent of said city, and furnish the necessary materials required for the execution and completion thereof, all the following work in the said city of *Los Angeles* to wit: *Grading and graveling Cummings street in said city, from the south curb line of First street to a point 350 feet south of the south line of Fourth street, including all intersections of streets, (excepting such portions of said street and intersections as are required by law to be kept in order or repair by any person or company having railroad tracks thereon, also excepting such portions as have already been graded, graveled and accepted.)*

Said work shall be according to, and the materials used shall comply with the plans and profile on file in the office of the city engineer, and the specifications on file in the office of the city clerk of said city, for *graveled streets*, said specifications being known as specification No. *5*, and hereby made part of this contract; and all the materials used shall be to the satisfaction of the street superintendent of said city. Said *Drury A. Watson*, acting in his official capacity as such street superintendent, and not individually, hereby fixes the time for the commencement of said work to be within *ten* days from date hereof, and for its completion to be within *thirty* days from the date hereof, and promises and agrees that upon the performance of the covenants aforesaid, by the said party of the first part, he will duly make and issue an assessment and diagram, and attach a warrant thereto, as provided for in the aforementioned act, for the expenses of the work aforesaid, at the following prices, in lawful money of the United States, to wit: *For grading and graveling, three dollars per lineal foot.*

And it is agreed and expressly understood by the parties to this agreement, that in no case (except where it is otherwise provided in the act aforementioned and referred to) will the said city of *Los Angeles*, or any officer thereof, be liable for any portion of the expense of the work aforesaid, nor for any delinquency of persons or property assessed.

It is further understood and agreed that eight (8) hours labor shall constitute a day's work, and that the said party of the first part will not contract for, receive or require more than eight (8) hours labor for a day's work of any person employed upon said work.   *

In witness whereof, the parties to these presents have hereunto set their hands and seals the day and year first herein written.

CONRAD SCHEERER. [SEAL.]
Contractor.

DRURY A. WATSON,   [SEAL.]
Street Superintendent City of *Los Angeles.*

Signed, sealed and delivered in the presence of
FRANK C. HANNON.

STREET CONTRACTOR'S BOND.

Know all men by these presents, that we, *Conrad Scheerer*, as principal, and *Charles F. Munson* and *Martin C. Marsh*, as sureties, residents of the city of *Los Angeles*, county of *Los Angeles*, state of California, are jointly and severally bound unto the city of *Los Angeles* in the state of California, in the sum of *One Thousand* dollars, lawful money of the United States of America, to be paid to the city of *Los Angeles*, for which payment well and truly to be made, we bind ourselves, our, and each of our heirs, successors, executors, administrators, or assigns, jointly and severally by these presents.

Sealed with our seals, and dated this *1st* of *November*, A. D. 189*3*.

The condition of this obligation is such, that if the above bounden *Conrad Scheerer, his* heirs, successors, executors, administrators, or assigns, shall in all things stand to and abide by, and well and truly keep and faithfully perform the covenants, conditions and agreements in that certain contract made between said *Conrad Scheerer*, as contractor, and *Drury A. Watson*, as street superintendent of the city of *Los Angeles*, state of California, of even date herewith, for furnishing materials in compliance with specifications and performing the following work, to wit:

[Here insert the description of the work in the contract.]

or cause the same to be kept and performed in the manner and form therein specified, then the above obligation to be void, else to remain in full force and virtue.

Sealed and delivered in presence of

FRED. HARKNESS.   *CONRAD SCHEERER,*   [SEAL.]

CHARLES F. MUNSON,   [SEAL.]

MARTIN C. MARSH,   [SEAL.]

State of California,   } ss.
County of *Los Angeles.*

Charles F. Munson and *Martin C. Marsh*, whose names are subscribed as sureties to the above bond, being severally duly sworn, each for himself, deposes and says he is worth double the sum mentioned therein, to wit, is worth the sum of *$2000.00* in fixed property and real estate, situated in said state of California, over and above his just debts and liabilities, exclusive of property exempt from execution, and over and above all sums for which he is already liable or in any manner bound, whether as principal, indorser or security, and whether such prior obligation or liability be conditional or absolute, liquidated or unliquidated, certain or contingent, due or to become due.

CHARLES F. MUNSON, [SEAL.]

MARTIN C. MARSH,   [SEAL.]

Subscribed and sworn to before me, this *1st* day of *November*, A. D. 1893.

FRED. HARKNESS,

Notary Public in and for the county of *Los Angeles*, State of California.

Approved this *1st* day of *November*, 1893.

DRURY A. WATSON,

Street Superintendent of the city of *Los Angeles.*

The sum mentioned in the above bond is by me deemed to be adequate, is the sum fixed by me for that purpose, and said bond is hereby approved by me this *1st* day of *November*, 1893.   *

T. E. ROWAN,

Mayor of the city of *Los Angeles.*

* The above clause in the contract relative to eight hours constituting a day's labor is required by section 3245 of the Political Code.

No. 9. Resolution of Extension.

Resolved, by the city council of The city of *Los Angeles*, in open session on this *28th* day of *November*, 1893, that the superintendent of streets of said city be,and he hereby is authorized and directed to extend, by ten days, the time fixed by him in that certain contract numbered No. *1000*, entered into by him with *Conrad Scheerer*, to do certain street work, viz: *To grade and gravel certain portions of Cummings street.*

I hereby certify that the foregoing resolution was passed by the city council of the city of *Los Angeles*, on the *28th* day of *November*, 1893, by the following vote:

Ayes: Messrs. *Campbell, Innes, Gaffey, Munson, Nickell, Pessell, Rhodes, Strohm, and President Teed.*

Noes: *None.*

C. A. LUCKENBACH,

City clerk and ex officio clerk of the city council of the city of *Los Angeles*

No. 10. Extension of Time.

Under the direction of the city council of the city of *Los Angeles*, by its resolution, passed *November 28th*, 1893, and by virtue of the authority vested, by statute, in me as street superintendent of said city, I hereby extend by *ten* days the time fixed by me in the within contract, numbered *1000*, for the work therein specified.

Office of the street superintendent, city of *Los Angeles*, this *28th*, day of *November*, A. D., 1893.

DRURY A. WATSON,

Street Superintendent of the city of *Los Angeles*.

No. 11. ASSESSMENT.

In the matter of *Requena street from the east line of Los Angeles street to the west line of Alameda street.*

ASSESSMENT NUMBER *1.*

Pursuant to statute, I, *D. .1. Watson,* as superintendent of streets of the city of *Los Angeles,* in the county of *Los Angeles* and state of California, do hereby assess and apportion, as shown hereinafter and in the diagram attached hereto, upon certain lots, portions of lots, and parcels of land, fronting on *Requena* street in said city, from the *east* line of *Los Angeles* street to the *west* line of *Alameda* street and on streets intersecting it between said lines, the sum of *five thousand two hundred and seventy-one and 44–100 dollars,* (*$5271 44–100*) to be paid to *The Porphyry Paving Company its* agents or assigns, to cover the sum due (including incidental expenses) for the work of *macadamizing and curbing with cement* said *Requena* street between said lines, as said work is more particularly specified in my official contract therefor with said *Porphyry Paving Company,* dated the *21st* day of *July,* A. D. 1891.

All of said work has been performed and materials furnished complying with the specifications and under my direction and to my satisfaction and acceptance. And because the names of the owners of said assessed property are unknown to me, I herein write the word "unknown" opposite the number of the lot and the amount assessed thereon and the number of each lot, portion of a lot, or parcel of land assessed.

Total cost of the work is *$5271 44–100,* as follows:

33,668.5 square feet of macadam at 14 cents per square foot.....$4713.59
743.37 lineal feet of cement curb at 40 cents per foot.............$297.35

Total contract cost $5010.94

INCIDENTAL EXPENSES.

City engineer's official fees...............................$ 76.90
Printing and advertising ....$ 38.60
Special *paving,* superintendent's compensation @ *$2.50* per day $ 145.00

Incidental expenses.............................$ 260.50
Contract cost ....$ 5010.94
Total cost, including incidental expenses......$ 5271.44

DIVIDED AS FOLLOWS:

DESCRIPTION	Macadamizing in Square Feet	Cement Curbing in lineal feet	Macadamizing Cost Dollars	Cts.	Cement Curbing Cost Dollars	Cts.	Incidental Expenses Dollars	Cts.	Total Assessments Dollars	Cts.	Number of Front Feet Assessed Frontage	Term'n	Opp. Term	Cross'g	Rate per front foot Assessed Dollars	Cents
Frontage..............	31,128.5		4,357	99			296	56	4,584	55	1850.32				2	50.478
Cement Curbing.........	2,540	743.37	35.5	60	297	35	15 / 18	45 / 49	312 / 374	80 / 09	743.37					42.0786 / 22.311826
Crossing on Wilmington St...							260	50	5,271	44				1676.64		
Totals,	33,668.6	743.37	4,713	59	297	35	260	50	5,271	44						

ASSESSED UPON

OWNERS	Assessment No.	Block	Tract or Subdivision	Lot	Front Feet on General Termination Front'ge	Term'l	Feet on Opposite Term.	Crossing	Frontage Assessment Dollars	Cts.	Termination Assessment Dollars	Cts.	Opposite Termination Assessment Dollars	Cts.	Crossing Assessment Dollars	Cts.	Total Assessment Dollars	Cts.	PAYMENTS
Unknown	1	B	Requena Tract	2	126.8				317	61							317	61	
Unknown	2	B	Requena Tract	3	24				60	11							60	11	
Unknown	3	B	Requena Tract	4	25				62	62							62	62	

Done at said City of Los Angeles, this 28th day of October, 1891.

DRURY A. WATSON,

Street Superintendent of the City of Los Angeles

Recorded this 28th day of October, 1891.

DRURY A. WATSON,

Street Superintendent of the City of Los Angeles.

LEAVENWORTH STREET.

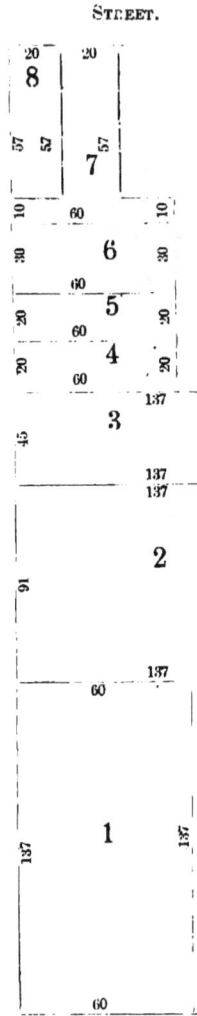

REED STREET. (14)

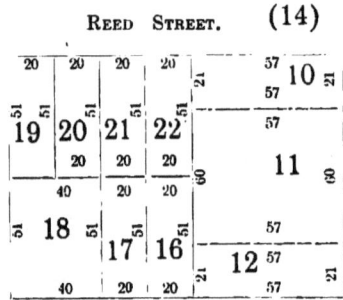

PRIEST STREET. (15)

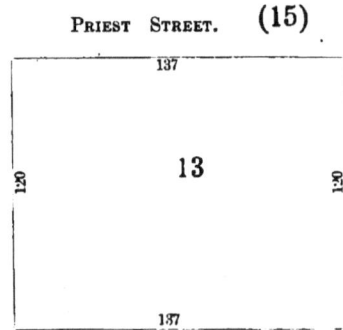

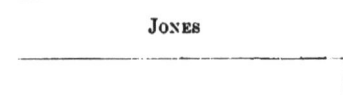

JONES STREET.

The above is a diagram exhibiting *Washington* street in the city *and county of San Francisco*, state of California, and its intersecting streets, from the *west curb* line of *Jones* street to the *east curb* line of *Leavenworth* street, on which work has been done under my official contract, dated the *27th* day of *October*, *1888*, and executed by me as superintendent of streets of said city *and county*, with *the Pacific Paving Company, a corporation*, for paving said *Washington* street from said line of *Jones* street to said line of *Leavenworth* street, as will more fully appear from said contract, to which reference is hereby made for further particulars. Said diagram shows the relative location of each district, lot, portion of lot and parcel of land assessed, to the work done; is numbered to correspond with the numbers in the assessment attached hereto,—said numbers being in red; and shows the number of feet fronting assessed for said work contracted for and performed. The figures in the diagram in black ink, represent feet and fractions of feet. Those next to property lines show, each, the length of said lines in feet. The figures in red ink show the numbers of the lots.

In witness whereof, I have hereto set my hand at said city *and county of San Francisco*, this *16th* day of *January*, 1889.

THOMAS ASHWORTH,

Superintendent of streets of the city and *county of San Francisco.*

Recorded this *16th* day of *January*, 1889. . •

THOMAS ASHWORTH,

Superintendent of streets of the city *and county of San Francisco.*

[NOTE: If any abbreviations are used, such as "No.," "ft.," "in.," etc., their meaning should be stated. Thus, it may be proper to insert something like the following: Herein, "No." is used for the word "number;" "ft." for the word "feet;" "in." for the word "inches." The marks ′ and ″ means respectively "feet" and "inches."]

No. 13. WARRANT.

By virtue hereof, I, *Drury A. Watson*, superintendent of streets, of the city of *Los Angeles*, county of *Los Angeles*, and state of California, by virtue of the authority vested in me as said superintendent of streets, do authorize and empower the *Porphyry Paving Company, its* agents or assigns, to demand and receive the several assessments upon the assessment and diagram hereto attached, and this shall be *its* warrant for the same.

Dated at *Los Angeles*, this *28th* day of *October*, 1891.

DRURY A. WATSON,

Superintendent of streets of the city of *Los Angeles.*

Countersigned by: *T. E. ROWAN,*

Mayor of the city of *Los Angeles.*

Recorded this *28th* day of *October*, 1891.

DRURY A. WATSON,

Superintendent of streets of the city of *Los Angeles.*

No. 14. CONTRACTOR'S RETURN.

STATE OF CALIFORNIA, ⎞
County of *Los Angeles,* ⎬ ss.
City of *Los Angeles.* ⎠

H. A. Palmer being duly sworn, says that he is the *secretary of the Porphyry Paving Co.,* contractor named in the annexed assessment, diagram and warrant; that said assessment for the total cost of certain street work upon *Requena street* between *Los Angeles and Alameda* streets in said city, as more fully described therein, and in the contract for said work with said *Porphyry Paving Company* made by the superintendent of streets of said city, dated the *21st* day of *July,* A. D. 1891, levied as therein described upon certain lots, portions of lots, or parcels of land, for the sum of *five thousand two hundred and seventy-one and 44-100* dollars, ($5271.44-100), payable to *Porphyry Paving Company, its* agents or assigns, was made, and with the city engineer's certificate of said work, was recorded and delivered by said superintendent of streets on the *28th* day of *October,* 1891, to affiant in behalf of said contractor; that there were attached to the same and delivered to the same in the same behalf at the same time by the said superintendent of streets, his diagram hereto attached, and a warrant in favor of *Porphyry Paving Company* for collecting said assessment, upon which warrant this return is endorsed; that in the case of all assessments therein described, but not included in the following table, affiant has, since the date last aforesaid, in the manner hereinafter described and in behalf of said contractor, made demand upon and received full payment from the owners of each and all such assessed lots and lands; and that besides all personal demands, affiant did, wherever the name of the owner of the lot is stated as "unknown" on the assessment, on the *27th* day of *November,* A. D. 1891, within thirty days from the date of said warrant, and between the hours of 9 A. M. and 5 P. M., in behalf of said contractor enter upon each of the corresponding lots, portion of lots, and parcels of land assessed, and with said certificate, assessment, diagram and warrant, and in a loud, audible voice, publicly make separate demands for the payment of each of said assessments from the unknown owners thereof, upon each lot, portion of lot, or parcel of land, for each of its own assessments as specified in said assessment; and that wherever he found a building, tenant or occupant upon any of said premises, besides the public demands as aforesaid, he, at the same time, in the same behalf, presenting and exhibiting said certificate, assessment, diagram and warrant in each instance, demanded from each tenant, or occupant, for the unknown owners, separately, the payment of each of said assessments upon said premises; and in the following table he states the name of such demandee, as "tenant" or "occupant," with the word "unknown;" but that, notwithstanding said demands, the following totals of said assessed sums, each separately demanded, and also the total, remain unpaid, to wit:

DEMAND MADE UPON AS OWNERS.	Assessment Number.	DATE OF DEMAND.	Assessment Due and Unpaid.		Subsequent Payments.
			Dollars.	Cents.	
Unknown.	*1*	*Nov. 27 '91*	*317*	*61*	
Unknown.	*2*	*Nov. 27 '91*	*60*	*11*	
Unknown.	*3*	*Nov. 27 '91*	*62*	*62*	

H. A. PALMER,

Subscribed and sworn to before me this *27th* day of *November*, 189*1*.

FRED. HARKNESS,

Notary Public.

Filed this *27th* day of *November*, 189*1*,

D. A. WATSON,

Superintendent of streets of the city of *Los Angeles.*

Recorded this *27th* day of *November*, 189*1*,

D. A. WATSON,

Superintendent of streets of the city of *Los Angeles.*

<hr/>

No. 15. CERTIFICATE OF RECORD.

I hereby complete and sign the foregoing record, from page *34* to page *44*, both inclusive, of the assessment, diagram, warrant, certificate of the city engineer, contractor's return; and also in the book of "contracts and bonds," the recorded contract and bond, each numbered No. *1000*, all for the work therein described upon *Requena* street, from the *east* line of *Los Angeles* street, to the *west* line of *Alameda* street, in the city of *Los Angeles*, state of California.

Office of the superintendent of streets of the city of *Los Angeles*, state of California, this *27th* day of *November*, 189*1*.

D. A. WATSON,

Superintendent of streets of the city of *Los Angeles.*

NOTE: The assessment, diagram, warrant and certificate of the city engineer must be recorded by the superintendent of streets before delivery to the contractor, and, to constitute a record, the record thereof must be authenticated by the signature of the street superintendent. See section 9 and the notes thereto.

<hr/>

No. 16. COMPLAINT TO FORECLOSE A STREET ASSESSMENT LIEN.

[TITLE OF COURT AND CAUSE.]

The plaintiff complains and alleges:

I.

That the defendant is, and at all the times herein mentioned was, the owner of the following described property, fronting on ——— street, in the city of *Los Angeles*, county of *Los Angeles*, state of California, between the ——— line of ——— street and the ——— line of ——— street, and more particularly described as follows, to wit:

[Here insert description of the property sought to be charged with the assessment lien.]

II.

That on the *13th* day of *January*, 1890, at the city of *Los Angeles*, state of California, the city council of said city duly passed and adopted a resolution in writing, wherein and whereby said city council duly resolved and determined that it was the intention of said city council to order the following described street work to be done, to wit:

[Here insert the description of the work contained in the resolution of intention.]

NOTE: It is not necessary to aver that the city by which the work was done, was a municipal corporation, nor is it necessary to aver that the street upon which the work was done was an open public street. The court will take judicial notice that the city in question was a municipal corporation, and the averment of the passage of a resolution of intention to do work upon a certain street is tantamount to an averment that it was an open public street in said city. Bituminous Lime Rock Paving and Imp. Co. v. Fulton, 33 Pac. Rep. 1117. Courts will take judicial notice of the streets of San Francisco, of their relation to each other and their location. Brady v. Page, 59 Cal. 52; Williams v. Savings and Loan Soc., 97 Cal. 122.

In common law pleading, in counting upon the judgment or determination of an inferior court or body, it was necessary to state the facts which conferred jurisdiction, both of the subject matter and over the person. Himmelman v. Danos, 35 Cal. 441. Under section 456 of the Code of Civil Procedure, it is sufficient, in pleading the judgment or determination of an office or board, to merely state that such judgment was duly made or given. This provision of the Code is applicable to the judgments and determinations of city councils in street work proceedings, and it is sufficient to aver that the judgment or determination of the council was duly made or given. Such an averment is a statement in legal effect that everything necessary to be done to give the order or resolution validity has been done. Pacific Paving Company v. Bolton, 97 Cal. 8; Bituminous Lime Rock Paving and Imp. Co. v. Fulton, 33 Pac. Rep. 1117. See notes to section 12 of the Vrooman Act, supra page 151, et. seq. An allegation that the resolution or order was "duly passed and adopted," is sufficient under the provisions of section 456 of the Code of Civil Procedure. Los Angeles v. Waldron, 65 Cal. 282.

"In pleading the existence of the resolution or order, the complaint, in stating that the council 'duly passed and adopted it,' is sufficient as stating in legal effect, that everything necessary to be done by the council, or under its direction, to give the order or resolution validity, had been done, without stating each particular thing or act." Los Angeles v. Waldron, 65 Cal. 282.

III.

That thereafter, to wit, on the *10th* day of *March*, 1890, at said city of *Los Angeles*, said city council, deeming that the public interest and convenience required it, duly passed and adopted a resolution in writing, wherein and whereby said city council duly gave and made its order and determination in writing ordering said street work to be done.

NOTE: This is a sufficient allegation under section 456 of the Code of Civil Procedure, that everything necessary to give validity to the order had been properly done. Pacific Paving Company v. Bolton, 97 Cal. 8; Bituminous Lime Rock Paving and Imp. Co. v. Fulton, 33 Pac. Rep. 1117; Los Angeles v. Waldron, 65 Cal. 282.

IV.

That thereupon, and before awarding the contract for doing said work, as hereinafter alleged, said city council, by order duly given and made, and contained in said resolution ordering said street work to be done, duly ordered and directed the city clerk of said city to publish, in the manner required by law, said resolution ordering said work to be done, for two days in the *Los Angeles Herald*, and to post and keep posted for five successive days, in the manner and form required by law, on [or near] the council chamber door of said city council, a written notice, with specifications, inviting sealed proposals or bids for doing said work; and also to publish, in the manner and form required by law, in the said *Los Angeles Herald*, for two days, consecutively, a notice of said work inviting said proposals, and referring to the specifications posted and on file.

V.

That said *Los Angeles Herald* is, and at all the times herein mentioned was, a daily newspaper, printed, published and circulated in said city of *Los Angeles*, and was the newspaper designated by said city council for the purpose of said publications, and of each of them.

VI.

That thereupon, and before the award of said contract, said city clerk, pursuant to the terms and directions of said order, and in his official capacity as such city clerk, duly caused said resolution, ordering said work to be done, to be published by two insertions for and on two consecutive days in said newspaper, and the same was duly published by two insertions for and on two consecutive days in said newspaper, as ordered and directed by said city council, to wit, on the *11th* and *12th* days of March, 1890.

VII.

That before passing said resolution ordering said work to be done, specifications were required by said city council for the construction of said work, and, pursuant to said requirement, were duly furnished to said city council by the city engineer of said city, acting in his official capacity.

VIII.

That thereafter, and before the awarding of said contract, and pursuant to the terms and directions of said order of said city council, ordering and directing him so to do as aforesaid, said city clerk, in his official capacity, on the *15th* day of *March*, 1890, posted, and for five successive days, to wit, the *15th, 16th, 17th, 18th* and *19th* days of *March*, 1890, kept posted, conspicuously on [*or near*] the council chamber door of said council, a *printed* notice, with the specifications, inviting sealed proposals or bids for doing said work.

IX.

That, pursuant to the said order and direction of said city council, duly given and made, and contained in said resolution ordering said work to be done, ordering and directing him so to do, said city clerk, in his official capacity as such, published in said *Los Angeles Herald* by two insertions for two days, consecutively, as often as said newspaper was issued, to wit, on the *15th and 16th* days of *March*, 1890, a printed notice of said work, describing the same, inviting sealed proposals or bids, and referring to the specifications so posted as aforesaid, and to the specifications on file.

X.

That thereafter, to wit, on the *20th* day of *March*, 1890, plaintiff delivered to the clerk of said city council a sealed proposal to do said work, signed by plaintiff, by which said proposal plaintiff proposed and offered to do said work fully in all respects as required by said specifications, and at the following prices, viz: [Here insert the prices for which each piece of work was proposed to be done.] Said proposal was then and there accompanied by a check payable to the order of the mayor of said city, certified by a responsible bank, to wit, the *Los Angeles National Bank*, a bank incorporated under the *national banking laws of the United States of America*, for an amount equal to ten per cent. of the aggregate amount of said proposal, [or by a bond, payable to the order of the mayor of said city, for an amount equal to ten per cent. of the aggregate amount of said proposal, signed by plaintiff and by two sufficient sureties, each of whom justified in said city of *Los Angeles* in double the said amount, and over and above all statutory exemptions, before *Fred. Harkness*, a notary public duly commissioned and appointed as such in and for the county of *Los Angeles*, in said state, and acting as such in said city of *Los Angeles*] and plaintiff then and there became and was and continued to be a responsible bidder for said work, until the award to him of the contract for said work, as hereinafter alleged.

XI.

That other sealed proposals to do said work were delivered to said clerk by other persons, and, on the *24th* day of *March*, 1890, said city council, in open session, in its council chamber in said city, opened all of said proposals, and then and there duly examined and publicly declared the same.

XII.

That thereafter, to wit, on the *31st* day of *March*, 1890, said city council, in open session, and at the same place aforesaid, considered all of said proposals, and then and there rejected each and all of said proposals or bids, other than plaintiff's said proposal, and that plaintiff's said proposal was the lowest regular proposal or bid of any responsible bidder, and plaintiff's said proposal was then and there found to be that of the lowest responsible bidder.

XIII.

That said city council at its said session on said *31st* day of *March*, 1890, at its said council chamber, duly passed and adopted a resolution in writing, wherein and whereby said city council duly awarded the contract for said work to the plaintiff, who was the lowest responsible bidder therefor, and at the said prices named in his said bid, and rejected all other proposals and bids. Said resolution was approved by the mayor of said city, acting in his official capacity as such [or, was passed and approved by a three-fourths vote of said city council.]

NOTE: If the order for the work to be done be the "judgment or determination" of a board, within the meaning of section 456 of the Code of Civil Procedure, and if, under that section, an allegation that such order was duly given or made, or an allegation that the resolution ordering the work to be done was "duly passed and adopted," be equivalent, in legal effect, to a specific allegation of each and everything necessary to be done to give such order or resolution validity—as was held in Pacific Paving Co. v. Bolton, 97 Cal. 8—then there does not seem to be any reason why an allegation that the resolution awarding the contract was duly passed and adopted, should not be held sufficient, and equivalent to a specific allegation of each and every thing preceding the resolution of award, and necessary to give it validity. For, if the resolution of construction, or order for the work to be done, be the "judgment or determination" of a board, within the meaning of said section of the code, then the resolution awarding the contract seems to be just as much a "judgment or determination" of a board. However, in the absence of an authority directly in point, it was deemed best, in the form of complaint given above, to allege specifically each of the necessary jurisdictional prerequisites intermediate between the resolution of construction, or order for the work to be done, and the resolution awarding the contract.

XIV.

That, at the same time and place, by order duly given and made, contained in said resolution awarding said contract, the said city council duly ordered and directed said city clerk to post notice of said award for five days in the manner and form required by law, and duly ordered and directed said city clerk to publish notice of said award for two days, in the manner and form required by law, in the *Evening Express*.

XV.

That said *Evening Express* was the newspaper designated by said city council for the purpose of said publication, and, at all the times herein mentioned was a daily newspaper printed, published and circulated in said city of *Los Angeles*.

XVI.

That thereafter, to wit, on the *2nd* day of *April*, 1890, the said city clerk, pursuant to the terms of said order and direction, ordering and directing him so to do, posted such notice of said award, conspicuously, on [or near] the council chamber door of said council, and kept the same posted for five successive days, to wit, the *2nd, 3rd, 4th, 5th and 6th* days of *April*, 1890, and at the same time, and pursuant to the terms of said order and direction, said city clerk caused a like notice of said award to be published for two successive days in said *Evening Express*, and, pursuant to said order, the same was published in said newspaper by two insertions for two successive days, as often as the same was issued, to wit, on the *2nd* and *3rd* days of *April*, 1890.

XVII.

That the owners of three-fourths of the frontage of the lots and lands upon said street, wherein said work was ordered to be done as aforesaid, to wit, —— street, between the —— line of —— street and the —— line of —— street, did not, either in themselves or in their own names, or by or through their agents, or otherwise, elect, at any time, to take said work, or any part thereof, or to enter into any contract to do the whole, or any part of said work, at the prices at which the same had been awarded as aforesaid, or at any other prices, but, said owners wholly failed, either themselves or by or through their agents, or otherwise, or at all, to elect to take said work or to enter into any contract therefor.

XVIII.

That thereafter, to wit, on the *14th* day of *April*, 1890, at said city, the superintendent of streets of said city, pursuant to said award, and in his official capacity as such superintendent of streets, duly entered into, made, and executed to and with plaintiff a contract for said work, at the prices specified in plaintiff's said bid. Said contract was then and there duly signed, entered into and executed by plaintiff.

XIX.

That the plaintiff, at the time of executing said contract, executed a bond to the satisfaction and approval of the said superintendent of streets, with two good and sufficient sureties, and payable to said city, in the sum of *three thousand* dollars, coin of the United States of America, conditioned for the faithful performance of said contract. Said sum of *three thousand* dollars, was the sum deemed adequate by the mayor of said city and fixed by him for that purpose. Said sureties, each for himself, justified in double the said amount mentioned in said bond, over and above all statutory exemptions, before *Fred Harkness*, a notary public, duly commissioned and appointed in and for the county of *Los Angeles*, in said state, and competent to administer oaths. Said bond was thereupon duly accepted by said superintendent of streets, and placed on file and recorded in his office.

That said contract and bond were in the words and figures of the copies thereof, which are hereto attached, marked exhibits "A" and "B", and made a part of this cause of action and complaint.

.NOTE: If the pleader does not choose to plead the contract in haec verba, but elects to plead it according to its legal effect, he must be careful to see that he alleges that the contract contained each of those provisions which, by section 6 of the act it is ·required to contain, i. e., for example, a clause that the work shall be done under the direction and to the satisfaction of the superintendent of streets, etc.

XX.

That, before the execution of said contract, and after said award, the plaintiff advanced to and deposited with the said superintendent of streets, for payment by him, the cost of the publication of all notices, resolutions, orders, and all other incidental expenses and matters required under the proceedings prescribed in an act of the legislature of the state of California, entitled "An act to provide for work upon streets, lanes, alleys, courts, places and sidewalks, and for the construction of sewers within municipalities," approved March 18, 1885, and likewise the cost of such other notices as might thereafter be deemed requisite by the said city council, viz, the sum of *fifty dollars*.

XXI.

That thereafter, and within the time fixed by said superintendent of streets, and by said contract for the completion of the same, the plaintiff did all the work in said contract and specifications mentioned, and duly performed all the conditions therein contained, on his part to be performed, under the direction and to the satisfaction of said superintendent of streets, and with the materials required by him and called for by said specifications, and duly fulfilled said contract to the satisfaction of said superintendent of streets.

XXII.

That, pursuant to the terms of said contract, the total contract cost of the work performed thereunder by plaintiff, at the prices stated in said contract, amounted to the sum of $———; that the incidental expenses incurred in connection therewith and paid by plaintiff, viz., the expenses of printing and publishing said resolutions and orders, special inspector's fees (and such other incidental expenses as may have been incurred,) amounted to the sum of $———, making a total of $———, assessable against the lots and lands liable to assessment.

XXIII.

That thereafter, to wit, on the *23rd* day of *August*, 1890, the said superintendent of streets duly made and issued an assessment to cover the sum due for the work performed and specified in said contract, including all incidental expenses, to wit, the said sum of ———dollars. Said assessment assessed said sum of ———dollars upon all the lots and lands fronting upon said ——— street, from said —— line of ——— street to said —— line of ——— street, and assessed each lot and portion of a lot separately, in proportion to the frontage of each such lot and portion of a lot, at a rate per front foot sufficient to cover the total expense of the work, to wit, at ———dollars and ——cents per front foot.

XXIV.

That said assessment briefly referred to said contract, the work contracted for and performed, and showed the amount to be paid for said work under said contract, together with all incidental expenses, likewise the rate per front foot assessed, and the amount of each assessment. The name of each and every owner of each lot and of each portion of a lot, so assessed as aforesaid, was unknown to the said superintendent of streets, and the word "unknown" was written opposite the number of each lot, portion and portions of a lot, assessed as aforesaid. Said assessment likewise showed the amount assessed upon each lot and portion of a lot assessed, also the number of each lot, portion and portions of a lot assessed. Said assessment was signed by said superintendent of streets, and had attached thereto a diagram exhibiting each street, street crossing, avenue, lane, alley, place and court on which any of said work was done, and showing the relative location of each district, lot and portion of lot assessed, to the work done, and numbered to correspond with the said numbers in said assessment, and showing, likewise, the number of lots assessed for said work contracted for and performed, and the number of feet fronting upon said ——— street, from said —— line of ——— street to said —— line of ——— street, to wit,   feet.

XXV.

That by said assessment and diagram the lot owned by defendant, and described in paragraph number I of this complaint, was separately assessed, in proportion to the frontage, and at a rate per front foot sufficient to cover the total expense of said work, viz: at $——— per front foot. That the frontage of said lot is —— feet, and the total amount so assessed against said lot and shown by said assessment to be assessed thereon, is the sum of $———. Said lot was assessed as the property of "unknown," the name of the owner of said lot being then and there unknown to said superintendent of streets. The word "unknown" was written opposite the number of said lot. The number of said lot is number ——, and said number —— was shown by said assessment to be the number of said lot.

XXVI.

That, to said assessment and diagram was attached a warrant, dated the *23rd* day of *August*, 1890, duly issued and signed by the superintendent of

streets of said city, in his official character as such, and duly countersigned by the mayor of said city, in his official character as such. Said warrant was in the words and figures following, to wit:
[Here insert warrant.]

XXVII.

That thereafter, to wit, on the *23rd* day of *August* 1890, said·warrant, assessment and diagram, together with the certificate of the city engineer of said city, relating to said work, were duly recorded by the said superintendent of streets in his office in a book kept by him for that purpose, viz., volume   page   of the assessment records, and said record was duly authenticated with his certificate of recordation signed and subscribed by the said superintendent of streets in his own name.

XXVIII.

That thereafter, to wit, on the *23rd* day of *August*, 1890, and after the payment to said superintendent of streets of all incidental expenses not previously paid by plaintiff or his assigns, said warrant, assessment, diagram, and certificate, after the recording of the same as aforesaid, were duly delivered by said superintendent of streets to plaintiff, contractor as aforesaid, on his demand therefor.

XXIX.

That thereafter, to wit, on the *21st* day of *September*, 1890, between the hours of *9* o'clock A. M. and *5* o'clock P. M. of that day, one *John J. O'Brien*, as the agent of this plaintiff, thereunto duly authorized by plaintiff, with the said warrant, assessment, diagram and certificate, did publicly, for and on behalf of this plaintiff, and as such agent, go upon the said premises owned by defendant and assessed as aforesaid, viz., the premises described in paragraph number I of the complaint, and did then and there, while upon said premises, between the hours aforesaid, and as such agent, publicly and in a loud and audible voice, demand payment of the said amount so assessed upon and against said premises as aforesaid, to wit, said sum ʼof ——— dollars.

XXX.

That thereafter, to wit, on the *21st* day of *September*, 1890, and within thirty days from the date of said warrant, the said warrant was duly returned to the said superintendent of streets, with a return endorsed thereon; said return was signed by said *John J. O'Brien* on behalf of this plaintiff, and was verified by him, in the said city of *Los Angeles* upon his oath taken and sworn to before *Fred. Harkness*, a notary public duly appointed and commissioned in and for the said county of *Los Angeles*. Said return stated whether any of the said assessments remained unpaid, in whole or in part, and the amount thereof, and stated the nature and character of the demand as set forth above, namely, that the same was made by said *John J. O'Brien*, as agent of this plaintiff, publicly, and on said above described premises, and for the amount so assessed upon said premises as aforesaid, and at the time aforesaid, and that said sum of money so assessed on the lot above described as aforesaid remained unpaid, though demand was made therefor as aforesaid.

XXXI.

That thereupon and thereafter, to wit, on said *21st* day of *September*, 18*90*, said superintendent of streets duly recorded the said return in the margin of the said record of said warrant and assessment, and authenticated said record with his certificate of recordation signed and subscribed in his name by himself. At the same time and place, said superintendent likewise duly recorded the original contract, referred to in said assessment, at full length in a book kept by him for that purpose in his office, and authenticated said record of said contract with his certificate of recordation signed and subscribed in his name by himself.

XXXII.

That more than thirty-five days have elapsed from the day of the date of said warrant, and no person whatever has appealed to said city council from or concerning any act of said contractor, or concerning said work, or from or concerning any act, proceeding or determination of said superintendent of streets in relation to said work, contract, diagram, assessment, or warrant, or either or any of them, or concerning any other act, proceeding or determination of said superintendent of streets whatever, or concerning any proceeding or proceedings prior to said assessment, or in the matter of or relating to said warrant, assessment, diagram or work, and that no written or other objection to said acts or proceedings, or to either or any of them, or to any part thereof, has ever at any time been filed with the clerk of said city council.

XXXIII.

That each and every act heretofore alleged to have been done or performed by the superintendent of streets, the mayor or the city clerk of said city, was duly done and performed by the duly elected, qualified and acting *street superintendent*, mayor and city clerk, respectively, of the city of *Los Angeles*, state of California, acting in his official capacity as such, and that each and every act, order, resolution or determination hereinbefore alleged to have been given, made, done or performed by the city council of said city, was duly given and made, done and performed by the duly elected, qualified and acting city council of the city of *Los Angeles*, **state** of California.

XXXIV.

That all the several acts and proceedings required to be done by said city council, said superintendent of streets, said mayor, said city clerk and this plaintiff, have been duly done, made and performed by it and them in the manner and at the times and in the form required by law, under the provisions of the act of the legislature of the state of California entitled "An act to provide for work upon streets, lanes, alleys, courts, places and sidewalks, and for the construction of sewers within municipalities," approved March 18, 1885, as the said act had been amended by all amendatory and supplementary acts thereto passed by said legislature and in force at the time when said acts and proceedings of said city council, superintendent of streets, mayor and plaintiff were made, done or performed.

NOTE: Paragraph XXXIV is taken from the complaint passed upon by the Supreme Court in the case of Bituminous Lime Rock Paving and Imp. Co. v. Fulton, 33 Pac. Rep. 1117, where it was held that certain defects in the allegations in regard to certain jurisdictional prerequisites, such as publication of notices, etc., were cured by the twelfth paragraph of the complaint in that case, which was in all respects substantially the same as paragraph XXXIV supra. And, although the general sweeping allegation in paragraph XXXIV may not be regarded as a model of neatness or of concise and scientific pleading, yet, as it seemed to rescue the complaint filed in the case just referred to, the practitioner who adopts it as a part of his pleading may not go very far amiss in doing so—especially in view of the many pitfalls which seem to lie in the path of those whose duties require them to proceed under the street improvement acts.

XXXV.

That the said sum of —— dollars, so assessed by said superintendent of streets upon said above described lot and parcel of land, as aforesaid, viz., the premises owned by defendant and described in paragraph number I of this complaint, has not been paid, nor any part thereof, but, although demand for the payment of said sum has been made as aforesaid, the whole thereof still remains and is due and unpaid, with interest thereon at the rate of ten per cent. per annum from the said *21st* day *September*, 1890, the date of the said return of said warrant and assessment.

XXXVI.

That before this suit was commenced, to wit, on the —— day of ——, 1890, at said city, the plaintiff made a personal demand upon the defendant, for the payment of said sum of ——dollars, assessed, upon the lots and lands described in paragraph I of this complaint, as aforesaid, but, notwithstanding such personal demand, said defendant then and there refused to pay said sum, or any part thereof, and still refuses to pay the same, or any part thereof.

NOTE: Where the property is assessed to "unknown," no personal demand is necessary; in fact, it is unavailing, in such case as a means of perfecting plaintiff's right of action upon the assessment. For that purpose, a demand made publicly upon the premises is indispensable, where the property has been assessed to "unknown." Macadamizing Co. v. Williams, 70 Cal. 534. But, by section 12 of the act, it is provided that "When a suit has been brought, after a personal demand has been made and a refusal to pay such assessment so demanded, the plaintiff shall also be entitled to have and receive said sum of fifteen dollars as attorney's fees, in addition to all taxable costs, notwithstanding that the suit may be settled or a tender be made before a recovery in said action, and he may have judgment therefor."

Wherefore plaintiff prays:

1. For a judgment for the sum of ——dollars, with interest thereon at the rate of ten per cent. per annum from the *21st* day of *September*, 1890, until entry of judgment.

2. That said sum with such interest to the date of entry of judgment, together with costs and $15.00 for attorney's fees, be adjudged to be a lien upon the lot of land described in paragraph number I of this complaint, and liable for the payment of the same.

3. That a decree in due form may be made for the sale of said lot by the sheriff of the county of *Los Angeles*, state of California, according to law and the practice of this court, and the proceeds of the sale be applied in payment of the amount found due to the plaintiff, with costs, and attorney's fees, and costs of sale.

4. That the defendant and all persons claiming under him, subsequent to the commencement of this action, either as purchasers, incumbrancers or otherwise, be barred and foreclosed of all right, claim or equity of redemption in the said premises, and every part thereof.

5. That any party of this suit may become a purchaser at such sale.

6. That plaintiff be allowed $15.00 in addition to the taxable costs, as attorney's fees.

7. That plaintiff may have such other and further relief as the case may require, and as to the court may seem just and equitable.

Attorney for Plaintiff.

No. 17. ORDINANCE OF INTENTION TO CHANGE GRADE.

ORDINANCE NO. *1921,* (new SERIES.)

An ordinance declaring the intention of the mayor and city council of the city of *Los Angeles* to change and establish the grade of *Grand Avenue* from *Fourth* street to *Fifth* street, and describing and establishing the district to be benefited by such change of grade, and to be assessed to pay the cost, damages and expenses thereof.

The mayor and council of the city of *Los Angeles* do ordain as follows:

SECTION 1. That it is the intention of the city council of the city of *Los Angeles* to change and establish the grade of *Grand Avenue* in said city from *Fourth* street to *Fifth* street, as follows:

At the intersection of *Fourth* street the grade shall be *115.50 on the southeast corner and 118.00 on the southwest corner; at a point 270 feet south from the southeast corner of Fourth street 93.80 on the east side and 94.00 on the west side; at a point 474 feet south from the southeast corner of Fourth street 53.00 on the east side;* at the intersection of *Fifth* street, *38.00 on the northeast corner and 45.00 on the northwest corner.*

And at all points between said designated points the grade shall be established so as to conform to a straight line drawn between said designated points.

The numbers used above, where their meaning is not shown to be otherwise by their immediate context, mean the number of feet which the points designated, in the proposed new grade, shall be above the city datum plane.

SEC. 2. The district to be benefited by said change of grade and to be assessed to pay the cost of the same, is hereby designated and established as follows:

Beginning at the northeast corner of Fifth street and Grand avenue, thence easterly along the northerly line of Fifth street to the southeast corner of lot 11, block 107, Bellevue Terrace tract; thence to the northeast corner of lot 7, block N, Mott tract; thence westerly along the southerly line of Fourth street to the northwest corner of lot 5, block M, of the Mott tract; thence to the present southwest corner of lot 2, block 108, of the Bellevue Terrace tract; thence easterly along the northerly line of Fifth street to the northwest corner of Fifth street and Grand avenue; thence across Grand Avenue to the point of beginning, excepting therefrom any public street or alley that may lie within the above described district.

SEC. 3. The city clerk shall certify to the passage of this ordinance, and shall cause the same to be published for ten days in the *Los Angeles Herald*, a daily newspaper published and circulated in said city, and hereby designated for said purpose, in the manner required by law, in every regular issue of said newspaper, during said period of ten days. Said *Los Angeles Herald* is the newspaper in which the official notices of this city council are usually printed and published.

SEC. 4. The superintendent of streets is hereby ordered and directed, within five days after the first publication of this ordinance, to cause to be conspicuously posted, in the manner and form required by law, within the said district, notices of the passage of this ordinance.

I hereby certify that the foregoing ordinance was adopted by the council of the city of *Los Angeles*, at its meeting of *November 13*, 1893, by the following vote:

Ayes: Messrs. *Gaffey, Innes, Munson, Nickell, Pessell and President Teed.*
Noes: Messrs. *Campbell, Rhodes and Strohm.*

C. A. LUCKENBACH,
City Clerk.

Approved this *17th* day of *November*, 1893.

T. E. ROWAN,
Mayor.

No. 18. NOTICE OF PASSAGE OF ORDINANCE OF INTENTION TO CHANGE GRADE.
NOTICE OF STREET WORK.

Notice is hereby given that on *Monday* the *13th* day of *November*, A. D. 1893, the city council of the city of *Los Angeles* did, at its meeting on said day, pass an ordinance of intention, numbered *1921* (*new* series,) to change and establish the grade of *Grand Avenue* in said city from *Fourth* street to *Fifth* street, as follows:

[Here insert the description in ordinance of intention, Form No. 17.]

The district declared by said ordinance to be benefited by said change of grade and to be assessed to pay the cost of the same, is described as follows, to wit:

[Here insert the description in ordinance of intention, Form No. 17.]

Reference is hereby made to said ordinance of intention for further particulars.

D. A. WATSON,
Superintendent of streets of the city of *Los Angeles.*

No. 19. ORDINANCE CHANGING AND ESTABLISHING GRADE.
ORDINANCE NO. *2000*, (*new* SERIES.)

An ordinance declaring the grade of *Grand Avenue* to be changed from *Fourth* street to *Fifth* street, and establishing the grade of the same.

The city council of the city of *Los Angeles*, having on the *13th* day of

November, 1893, duly passed an ordinance to change and establish the grade of said *Grand Avenue* from *Fourth* street to *Fifth* street, and describing and establishing the district to be benefited by such change of grade and to be assessed for the cost of the same, and the superintendent of streets having caused notices of the passage of said ordinance of intention to be conspicuously posted within said district, in the manner and form required by law, and no objection to said proposed change or changes or modifications of grade having been filed with the clerk of the council, and the petition of the owners of a majority of the property affected by said proposed change of grade having been duly filed with the clerk and presented to this city council,

The mayor and city council of said city of *Los Angeles* do now ordain as follows:

The grade of *Grand Avenue* from *Fourth* street to *Fifth* street is declared to be and the same hereby is changed and established, in conformity with said ordinance of intention, as follows:

At the intersection of *Fourth* street, etc. [Follow description in form 17.]

I hereby certify that the foregoing ordinance was passed by the city council of the city of *Los Angeles*, on the *20th* day of *December*, 1893, by the following vote:

Ayes: Messrs. *Gaffey, Innes, Munson, Nickell, Pessell, and President Teed.*

Noes: Messrs. *Campbell, Rhodes and Strohm.*

C. A. LUCKENBACH,

City clerk and ex officio clerk of the city council of the city of *Los Angeles*.

Approved this *20th* day of *December*, 1893.

T. E. ROWAN,

Mayor of the city of *Los Angeles*.

FORMS USED UNDER THE BOND ACT.

No. 1. Resolution Directing Engineer to Furnish Estimates.

RESOLUTION NO. *1938*, (*new* SERIES.)

Resolved, by the city council of the city of *Los Angeles*, state of California, that the city engineer of said city be, and he hereby is, directed to furnish to this city council estimates of the cost per front foot of the following street work along each line of *Omar avenue* in said city, from 'the *southerly,* line of *Third* street to the *northerly* line of *Fourth* street, including the cost of intersection work assessable upon said frontage, viz: Grading and graveling said *Omar avenue* from said *southerly* line of *Third* street to said *northerly* line of *Fourth* street, including all intersections of streets, (excepting such portions of said street and intersections as are required by law to be kept in order or repair by any person or company having railroad tracks thereon, and also excepting such portions as have been *graded, graveled* and accepted) in accordance with the plans and profile on file in the office of the city engineer and specifications on file in the office of the city clerk of said city for *graveled* streets, said specifications being numbered *five.*

Said estimates to be thus furnished in accordance with the provisions of an act of the legislature of the state of California, approved February 27, 1893, authorizing the issuance of serial bonds to represent the cost of certain street work or improvements, for the purpose of enabling this city council to determine whether bonds may be issued to represent the cost of the above described work or improvement.

I hereby certify that the foregoing resolution was passed by the city council of the city of *LosAngeles*, on the *13th* day of *November*, 1893, by the following vote:

Ayes: Messrs. *Campbell, Gaffey, Innes, Munson, Nickell, Pessell, Rhodes, Strohm, and President Teed.*

Noes: *None.*

C. A. LUCKENBACH,
City clerk and ex officio clerk of the city council of the city of *Los Angeles.*

No. 2. Resolution of Intention.

A resolution of the city council of the city of *Los Angeles*, declaring its intention to improve a portion of *Omar avenue*, and that bonds shall be issued to represent the cost thereof.

RESOLUTION NO. *737*. (*new* SERIES.)

Resolved, by the city council of the city of *Los Angeles*, state of California, that it is the intention of this city council to order the following street work to be done in said city, to wit: That *Omar avenue* in said city, from the *southerly* line of *Third* street to the *northerly* line of *Fourth* street, including all intersections of streets, (excepting such portions of said street and intersections as are required by law to be kept in order or repair by any person or company having railroad tracks thereon, and also excepting such portions as have been *graded, graveled*, and accepted,) be *graded and graveled* in accordance with the plans and profile on file in the office of the city engineer and specifications on file in the office of the city clerk of the city of *Los Angeles* for *graveled* streets, said specifications being numbered *five*.

The city engineer of said city having estimated that the total cost of said improvement will be greater than one dollar per front foot along each line of said portion of said street so proposed to be improved as aforesaid, including the cost of intersection work assessable upon said frontage, it is hereby determined and declared in pursuance of an act of the legislature of the state of California, approved February 27, 1893, that serial bonds shall be issued to represent the expenses of said proposed improvement. Said bonds shall be serial, extending over a period of *ten* years from their date; and shall be issued in the manner and form provided by said act approved February 27, 1893; an even annual proportion of the principal sum thereof shall be payable by coupons on the second day of January of each year after their date, until the whole is paid, and said bonds shall bear interest at the rate of 7 per cent. per annum on all sums unpaid, until the whole of said principal and interest are paid; said interest shall be payable semi-annually on the second days of January and July respectively, of each and every year.

The *Los Angeles Herald*, a daily newspaper published and circulated in said city, is hereby designated as the newspaper in which this resolution of intention and notice of the passage thereof shall be published in the manner and by the persons required by law.

The superintendent of streets of said city is hereby directed to post notices of the passage of this resolution in the manner and in the form required by law, and to cause a similar notice to be published for six days in said newspaper, in the manner required by law. Said notices, posted and published, shall describe said bonds and specify said rate of interest, in the manner required by law in such cases.

The city clerk of said city is hereby directed to post this resolution of intention conspicuously for two days on or near the council chamber door of this council, and to cause the same to be published by two insertions, in the manner required by law, in said daily newspaper.

I hereby certify that the foregoing resolution was passed by the council of the city of *Los Angeles*, at its meeting of *November 27*, A. D. 1893, by the following vote:

Ayes: Messrs. *Campbell, Gaffey, Innes, Munson, Pessell, Rhodes* and *Strohm*—7.

Noes: *None.*

                         C. A. LUCKENBACH,
City clerk and ex officio clerk of the city council of the city of *Los Angeles*.

No. 3. NOTICE OF PASSAGE OF RESOLUTION OF INTENTION.

NOTICE OF STREET WORK.

Notice is hereby given that on *Monday*, the *27th* day of *November*, A. D. 1893, the city council of the city of *Los Angeles* did, at its meeting on said day, pass a resolution of intention, numbered *1338*,(*new* series,) to order the following street work to be done, to wit:

That *Omar avenue* in said city, from the *southerly* line of, etc. [Here insert description of the work, as in preceding form.]

The city engineer of said city having estimated that the total cost of said improvement will be greater than one dollar per front foot along each line of said portion of said street, so proposed to be improved as aforesaid, including the cost of intersection work assessable upon said frontage, it was by said city council determined in and by its said resolution of intention, in pursuance of an act of the legislature of the state of California, approved February 27, 1893, that serial bonds shall be issued to represent the expenses of said proposed improvement. Said bonds will be serial, extending over a period of *ten* years from their date, and will be issued in the manner and form provided for by said act of the legislature; an even annual proportion of the principal sum thereof shall be payable, by coupon, on the second day of January of each year, after their date, until the whole is paid, and said bonds will bear interest at the rate of *seven* per cent. per annum on all sums unpaid, until the whole of said principal and interest are paid. Said interest will be payable semi-annually by coupon on the second days of January and July respectively of each and every year.

Reference is hereby made to said resolution of intention for further particulars.

D. A. WATSON,
Superintendent of Streets of the city of *Los Angeles.*

No. 4. RESOLUTION ORDERING THE WORK.

[Same as form No. 3, under the Vrooman act, except that the same description of the bonds and specification of the interest that is contained in the resolution of intention under the bond act is to be inserted in the resolution ordering the work.]

No. 5. NOTICE INVITING SEALED PROPOSALS.

[Same as form No. 4, under the Vrooman act, except that the same description of the bonds and specification of the interest that is contained in the notice of the passage of the resolution of intention under the bond act, is to be inserted in the notice inviting sealed proposals.]

No. 6. CONTRACTOR'S PROPOSAL WITH BOND.

[Same as form No. 5, under the Vrooman act.]

No. 7. Resolution of Award.

[Same as form No. 6, under the Vrooman act, except that the same description of the bonds and specification of the interest that is contained in the resolution of intention, under the bond act, is to be inserted in the resolution of award.]

No. 8. Notice of Award.

[Same as form No. 7, under the Vrooman act, except that the same description of the bonds and specification of the interest that is contained in the notice of the passage of the resolution of intention, under the bond act, is to be inserted in the notice of award.]

No. 9. Contract and Contractor's Bond.

[Same as form No. 8 under Vrooman act.]

No. 10. Assessment and Diagram.

[Same as forms Nos. 11 and 12, under the Vrooman act.]

In the margin of the assessment as recorded there should be appropriate headings to enable the street superintendent to endorse upon the margin of the record of the assessment, to the credit of which the same is paid, all coupon payments of principal upon the bonds reported to him by the city treasurer, as provided for by section 4 of the bond act.

No. 11. Warrant.

By virtue hereof, I, *Drury A. Watson*, superintendent of streets of the city of *Los Angeles*, county of *Los Angeles*, and state of California, by virtue of the authority vested in me as said superintendent of streets, do authorize and empower *Martin C. Marsh*, his agents or assigns, to demand and receive the several assessments upon the assessment and diagram hereto attached, and this shall be *his* warrant for the same. Serial bonds, bearing interest at the rate of *seven* per cent. per annum and extending over a period of *ten* years from their date, are to be issued to represent the cost and expenses of the work described in the assessment, and in the manner and form provided by an act of the legislature of the state of California, approved February 27, 1893; and notice is hereby given that a bond in such series will issue to represent each assessment of fifty dollars or more remaining unpaid for thirty days after the date of this warrant, or

five days after the decision of the city council of this city upon an appeal.
Dated *Los Angeles, November 1st,* A. D. 1893.

DRURY A. WATSON,

[SEAL.]   Superintendent of streets of the city of *Los Angeles.*
Countersigned by: *T. E. ROWAN,*

Mayor of the city of *Los Angeles.*

Recorded *November 1st,* A. D. 1893.

DRURY A. WATSON,

Superintendent of streets of the city of *Los Angeles.*

No. 12. CONTRACTOR'S RETURN.

[Same as form No. 14, under Vrooman act.]

No. 13. CERTIFICATE OF RECORD.

[Same as form No. 15, under the Vrooman act].

No. 14.   STREET SUPERINTENDENT'S CERTIFIED LIST OF UNPAID
ASSESSMENTS.

TREASURER'S LIST OF ASSESSMENTS.

H. J. Shoulters, City Treasurer of the City of *Los Angeles:*

I hereby certify to you that the following list of assessments, dated *October 30th, 1893,* "amounting to fifty dollars or over," each upon their respective assessment or diagram numbers, and being for the improvement of *Georgia Bell* street, between the *south* line of *Eighteenth* street and the *north* line of *Washington* street, are unpaid. You will therefore issue bonds therefor, as provided by law to *Conrad Scheerer,* contractor, extending over a period of *ten* years, and bearing interest at the rate of *seven* per cent per annum until paid.

ASSESSED UPON.					Total Assessm't on Assessment and Diagram Number		Date of Delinquency	REMARKS
Assessment No.	OWNERS	Lot	Block	Tract	Dollars	Cents		
1	Unknown	1	B	Bell Tract	159	70	Nov'r 30, 1893	
2	Unknown	2	B	Bell Tract	167	59	Nov'r 30, 1893	

Los Angeles, December 1st, 1893.

[Seal]

D. A. WATSON,

Street Superintendent of the City of *Los Angeles.*

FORMS USED UNDER THE STREET OPENING ACT.

No. 1. RESOLUTION DECLARING INTENTION.

RESOLUTION OF INTENTION, NO. 1896, (new SERIES.)

Resolved, by the city council of the city of *Los Angeles*, state of California:
1st. That it is the intention of the said city council to order the following street work to be done, in said city, to wit:

To *widen First* street in said city of *Los Angeles.*

2nd. That the land which is by this council deemed necessary to be taken therefor, and which this council intends to take therefor, is described as follows, to wit:

All that certain land situated, lying and being in said city of *Los Angeles*, and particularly described as follows:

Beginning at a point on the northerly line of First street, said point being the southwest corner of lot 4 of the subdivision of the garden of J. Murat, recorded in book 10, page 8, miscellaneous records of Los Angeles county, thence easterly along the northerly line of First street 50 feet and 6 inches to a point, thence northerly on a line parallel with and six inches easterly of the easterly line of said lot 4, 8.81 feet to a point on the new line of First street, thence westerly to a point on the westerly line of said lot 4, said point being 7.13 feet northerly from the southwest corner of said lot 4, thence southerly along the westerly line of said lot 4, to the point of beginning; being all of that portion of lot 4 and of the westerly six inches of lot 5 of said Murat garden subdivision, which lies between the old northerly line of First street and the new northerly line of First street, as shown by a map adopted by said city council at its meeting of December 16, 1889, and now on file in the office of the city clerk of said city.

3rd. That the exterior boundaries of the district hereby established, and the exterior boundaries of the district of lands hereby declared to be affected and benefited by said work or improvement, and to be assessed to pay the damages, cost and expenses thereof, are described as follows, to wit:

Beginning at a point on the east line of Los Angeles street, in the city of Los Angeles, said point being 10 feet northerly from the new northerly line of First street, as shown by said map adopted by the city council December 16, 1889, and now on file in the office of the city clerk, thence easterly on a line parallel with the new northerly line of First street as shown by said map to a point on the westerly line of Vine street, thence easterly on a line parallel with said new northerly line of First street to a point in the westerly line of Alameda street, thence southerly along said westerly line of Alameda street to a point 10 feet distant southerly from the new southerly line of First street, as shown by said map, thence westerly on a line parallel with the new southerly line of First street to a point in the easterly line of San Pedro street, thence northerly to the southwest corner of the Valla block, thence to the point of beginning; excepting therefrom the land in section 1 hereof, described as the land to be taken for widening said First street, and excepting also any land within said boundaries contained, which is now part of a public street or alley.

The *Los Angeles Herald*, a daily newspaper published and circulated in said city, is hereby designated as the newspaper in which the street superintendent of said city shall cause to be published, in the manner and form required by law, notice of the passage of this resolution, and the said street superintendent is hereby directed to cause notices of the passage of this resolution to be posted in the manner and form required by law, and to cause a notice, similar in substance, to be published in said newspaper for a period of ten days, in the manner required by law.

I hereby certify that the foregoing resolution was passed by the city council of the city of *Los Angeles*, on the *30th* day of *October*, 1893, by the following vote:

Ayes: Messrs. *Campbell, Innes, Munson, Nickell, Pessell,* and *President Teed.*

Noes: Messrs. *Gaffey, Rhodes* and *Strohm.*

C. A. LUCKENBACH,

City clerk and ex officio clerk of the city council of the city of *Los Angeles*.

No. 2. NOTICE OF PASSAGE OF RESOLUTION DECLARING INTENTION.

NOTICE OF PUBLIC WORK.

Notice is hereby given that on Monday, the *30th* day of *October*, A. D. 1893, the city council of the city of *Los Angeles*, state of California, did, at its meeting on said day, pass a resolution, number *1896,*(new series) declaring its intention to order the following street work to be done, to wit: To *widen First* street in said city of *Los Angeles.*

That the land which was by said city council deemed to be, and by its said resolution was declared to be necessary to be taken for said work or improvement, is described as follows, to wit:

[Here insert description as in preceding resolution, form No. 1.]

That the exterior boundaries of the district of lands established, and declared by said resolution to be affected and benefited by said work or improvement, and to be assessed to pay the damages, cost and expenses thereof, are described as follows:

[Here insert description of boundaries as in preceding resolution, form No.1.]*

Reference is hereby made to said resolution of intention for further particulars.   *D. A. WATSON,*
Superintendent of streets of the city of *Los Angeles.*

* The statute does not in terms expressly provide that the notice shall contain a description of the district of the lands deemed to be benefited by the work or improvement, and to be assessed to pay the damages, cost and expenses. Section 3 says "said notice shall * * * state (1) the fact of the passage of the resolution, (2) its date, and (3) briefly the work or improvement proposed, and (4) refer to the resolution for further particulars." A statement that First street, in the city of Los Angeles, for example, is to be widened, would doubtless be a compliance with the requirement of the statute that the notice shall state briefly the work or improvement proposed. But this, even though coupled with a reference to the resolution on file for further particulars, and a statement of the date thereof could hardly be construed as giving to the property owners, whose property is to be assessed to pay the cost of the improvement, that notice which is required by the requirement of the constitution that "no pers n shall be deprived of * * property without due process of law." And, if the act requires the notice

to contain no more than this, then there would seem to be great weight in the language of Chief Justice Beatty in his dissenting opinion in Davies v. City of Los Angeles, 86 Cal. 57, where he says that in his opinion the statute is unconstitutional upon the ground that "it does not, when tested by the liberal doctrine of Lent v. Tillson, 72 Cal. 414, provide for any proper notice to owners of property affected." But it is stated in Lent v. Tillson, 72 Cal. 421, that "the constitution is to be read in connection with laws of this character, and if no hearing is expressly provided by the statute, still, if the constitution guarantees it, the statute is to be properly construed so as to allow it, if possible, and not to deny it. The constitution and the statute will be construed together as one law." If, therefore, this statement, in effect, that the constitution is to be read into the statute be the correct doctrine, and if some description of the lands liable to be assessed must be contained in a notice posted or published, to satisfy the constitutional requirement that no person shall be deprived of property without due process of law, then, even though the statute may not in express terms require it, still it seems that the notice should contain a description of the district of lands deemed to be benefited by the work or improvement, and liable to be assessed to pay the damages, cost and expenses thereof. And for this reason a description of the district of lands to be assessed is inserted in the form of notice given above.

The statute, section 3, says that the street superintendent shall cause to be posted and published "notices of the passage of the resolution." To give notice of the passage of the resolution, the notice must describe the resolution. To describe it accurately, the notice should describe all of its material provisions and contents. One of those material parts of the resolution is the description of the district to be assessed. Therefore, the provision of the statute that the street superintendent shall cause to be posted and published "notices of the passage of the resolution," when read in connection with the requirements of the constitution, as, according to the opinion of Mr. Justice Temple, in Lent v. Tillson, should be done, may be construed as tantamount to a provision that the posted and published notices shall contain a description of the lands liable to be assessed to pay the damages, cost and expenses of the work or improvement.

No. 3.   RESOLUTION ORDERING WORK TO BE DONE.

Resolution No. *1367*, (*new* series) ordering the work of *opening* and *extending Primrose avenue* between *Pasadena avenue* and *Johnson* street, and appointing commissioners to assess the benefits and damages, and have general supervision of said work.

Resolved, by the city council of the city of *Los Angeles*, state of California that the public interest and convenience require, and that the said city council hereby order to be done the work of *opening* and *extending Primrose avenue*, in said city, between *Pasadena avenue* and *Johnson* street, in accordance with resolution of intention No. *1270*, (*new* series) declaring the intention of said city council to order said work to be done, and it is hereby ordered that said work be done in accordance with said resolution of intention.

Resolved that, subject to removal by said city council at any time for cause, *M.G. Willard*, *W. G. Scarborough* and *Geo. B. Griffin* be and they are hereby appointed commissioners to assess the benefits and damages, and have general supervision of said work until the completion thereof, in compliance with an act of the legislature of the state of California, approved March 6, 1889, and entitled "An act to provide for laying out, opening, extending, widening, straightening, or closing up, in whole or in part, any street, square, lane, alley, court or place within municipalities, and to con demn and acquire any and all land and property necessary or convenient for that purpose." For their services said commissioners shall receive as compensation the sum of $*4.00* per diem for the days upon which they are actually engaged in performing said services. Said commissioners shall, every *two weeks*, report their progress in said work to this council. Before proceeding with the performance of their duties, each of said commissioners shall file with the clerk of this city council an affidavit and a bond to the state of California in the sum of $5000.00 to faithfully perform the duties of his office, in the manner and form required by law.

I hereby certify that the foregoing resolution was passed by the city council of the city of *Los Angeles*, on the *20th* day of *June*, 1893, by the following vote:

Ayes: Messrs. *Campbell, Gaffey, Innes, Munson, Nickell, Pessell, Rhodes, Strohm and President Teed.*

Noes: *None.*

C. A. LUCKENBACH,
City clerk and ex officio clerk of the city council of the city of *Los Angeles.*

No. 4.   Report of Commissioners.

Los Angeles, Cal., *June 29*, 1892.

To the Honorable, the City Council of the City of *Los Angeles:*

We, the undersigned, commissioners appointed by your honorable body to *open* and *widen Third* street, in the city of *Los Angeles* from *Los Angeles* street to *San Pedro* street, do hereby make a written report as follows:

That we carefully viewed the lands described in that certain resolution of intention No. *1896,* (*new* series) passed by your honorable body on the *30th* day of *October*, 1892, declaring your intention to *open* and *widen* said street, and that we have carefully viewed the land to be taken for said work, and the improvements and property affected thereby; that, having done so, we proceeded with all diligence to determine, and did determine, the value of the land to be taken for said work or improvement, and the damage to the improvements and property affected thereby, and also the amount of expenses incident to said work or improvement; that, having determined the same, we proceeded to assess, and did assess, the same upon the district of lands declared benefited, the exterior boundaries of which were fixed by said resolution of intention.

We proceeded to determine, and did determine, the proportionate amount of benefit to be derived by each piece and parcel of land within said district from said proposed work or improvement, and said assessment was made upon the lands within said district in proportion to the benefit to be derived from said work or improvement, so far as we could reasonably estimate the same, including in such estimate the property of any railroad company within said district.

That the total amount of the value of the said land taken for said work or improvement, together with the damage to said improvements and property affected thereby, and the expenses incident to the same, as the said total amount has been assessed by us, is the sum of *$26,835.32*, as will more fully appear from the schedule hereunto attached and made a part of this report.

That we have assessed the said sum of *$26,835.32* upon the lands within said district in proportion to the benefit to be derived by said lands from said work or improvement, so far as we can reasonably estimate the same, including in such estimate the property of any railroad company within said district.

That we have made, and accompany this report with, a plat of the assessment district, showing the land taken or to be taken for said work or improvement, and the lands assessed, showing the relative location of each district, block, lot, or portion of lot, and its dimensions, so far as we can reasonably ascertain the same. Each block and lot, or portion of lot, taken or assessed, is designated and described in said plat by an appropriate number. Said plat is hereto attached and marked " Exhibit A."

That the amount of $97.11, mentioned as subsequent expenses, is intended to cover any subsequent expense after the filing of this report, to wit, for recording deeds, advertising, etc., which may hereafter be necessary in the course of the proceedings to complete said work or improvement.

Respectfully submitted,

JOHN McILMOILL,
N. E DAVIDSON, } Commissioners.
JOHN MORIARTY,

SCHEDULE ACCOMPANYING REPORT OF COMMISSIONERS.

No. on Plat	Description of property taken or injured by Improvement.	No. on Plat	Description of property assessed for improvement.	Frontage in feet.	Names of owners and claimants of property taken, and of persons interested therein as lessees, incumbrancers or otherwise.	Names of owners and claimants of property assessed and persons interested therein as lessees, incumbrancers or otherwise.	Particulars of Interest	Amt of Value of Land taken		Amt. of Damages to Improvements and Property effected by Improvement		Total Amount of Damages		Amount Assessed Against Property Assessed in Proportion to Benefit		Net Damages Allowed		Net Benefits		Date of Payment
								Dols.	Cts	Dols.	Cts	Dols.	Cts	Dols.	Cts	Dols.	Cts	Dols.	Cts	
a	A strip of land off southside of lot N. E. corner 3rd and Los Angeles streets, front ing 309.13 feet on N. side of 3rd street, and being 28.08 feet deep on W. side and 27.25 feet deep on E. side.	12	Lot on N. E. corner of Los An geles and 3d streets, as 3d street is pro posed to be widened, be ing 305.37 feet front on west side of Third street when o p e n e d, 112.57 feet deep on W. side and 114.50 feet deep on E. side.	305.37	Lena Sch- warz and Christian Henne and estate of C. Henne de- ceased.	Lena Sch- warz and Christian Henne and Henne de- ceased.	Owner	6248	65	450	00	6698	65	$771	71	2926	94			Paid by deed Au- gust 27, 1892.

NOTE: When abbreviations are used they s ould be accompanied by an explanatory note. Thus, if "No" is used, a note should accompany the schedule show- ing that, as used, it means "number," etc.

I hereby certify that all the assessments not marked "paid" in the foregoing assessment list are still unpaid and are now delinquent.

E. H. HUTCHINSON,
Street Superintendent of the City of Los Angeles.

No. 5. RESOLUTION DIRECTING CLERK TO PUBLISH NOTICE OF FILING REPORT
OF COMMISSIONERS.

RESOLUTION NO. 1400, (*new* SERIES.)

Resolved, by the city council of the city of *Los Angeles*, state of California,
that the clerk of this city council be, and he hereby is, authorized and
directed to give notice of the filing of the report of the commissioners heretofore appointed by this city council by resolution, No. *1367*,(*new* series) to
assess the benefits and damages and have general supervision of the work
of *opening* and *extending Primrose avenue* in said city from *Pasadena avenue*
to *Johnson* street, by publication of such notice, in the manner and form
required by law, for ten days in the *Los Angeles Times*, a daily newspaper
printed, published and circulated in said city, and hereby designated for
that purpose, requiring all persons interested to show cause, if any, on or
before *Saturday*, the *24th* day of *September*, 189*2*, why said report should not
be confirmed, before said city council.

I hereby certify that the foregoing resolution was passed by the city
council of the city of *Los Angeles*, on the *20th* day of *August*, 189*2*, by the
following vote:

Ayes: Messrs. *Campbell, Gaffey, Innes, Munson, Nickell, Pessell, Rhodes,
Strohm and President Teed.*

Noes: *None.*

C. A. LUCKENBACH,
City clerk and ex officio clerk of the city council of the city of *Los Angeles*.

———

No. 6. NOTICE OF FILING REPORT OF COMMISSIONERS WITH CITY CLERK.

Notice of filing report of commissioners appointed to *open* and *extend
Primrose avenue*, from *Pasadena avenue* to *Johnson* street.

Notice is hereby given that the commissioners appointed by the city
council of the city of *Los Angeles*, state of California, to assess the benefits
and damages and to have general supervision of the proposed work of *opening* and *extending Primrose avenue* in said city, from *Pasadena avenue* to
Johnson street, having made their assessment of benefits and damages,
have made and filed in the office of the undersigned, their written report,
together with a plat of the assessment district.

All persons interested are hereby notified and required to show cause, if
any they have, on or before *Saturday* the *24th* day of *September*, 1892, why
said report should not be confirmed by the said city council.

All objections must be in writing and filed with the clerk of said city
council.

Each person signing an objection will attach thereto his or her postoffice
address.

Office of city clerk,}
Aug. *24*, 189*2*. ⎰   FREEMAN G. TEED,
City clerk and ex officio clerk of the city of *Los Angeles*.

No. 7. CERTIFICATE OF CITY CLERK CERTIFYING TO COPY OF REPORT, ETC.

State of California, } ss.
City of *Los Angeles,* }

I, *Freeman G. Teed,* city clerk of the city of *Los Angeles,* do hereby certify the foregoing to be a full, true and correct copy of the report, assessment and plat made and filed by the commissioners appointed by the city council of the city of *Los Angeles,* state of California, to assess the benefits and damages, and to have general supervision of the proposed work of *opening* and *widening Third* street in said city, from *Los Angeles* street to *San Pedro* street, as finally confirmed and adopted by said city council.

In testimony whereof I have hereunto set my hand and affixed the corporate seal of said city, at my office, this *31st* day of *August,* A. D. 1892.
[SEAL.]   *FREEMAN G. TEED,*
City clerk and ex officio clerk of the city council of the city of *Los Angeles.*

No. 8. NOTICE BY SUPERINTENDENT OF STREETS THAT HE HAS RECEIVED THE ASSESSMENT ROLL.

Notice of receipt of assessment roll in the proceeding to *open* and *widen Third* street, from *Los Angeles* street to *San Pedro* street.

Notice is hereby given that the assessment roll in the proceeding to *open* and *widen Third* street in the city of *Los Angeles,* state of California, from *Los Angeles* street to *San Pedro* street, viz., a certified copy of the report, assessment and plat made and filed by the commissioners appointed by the city council of said city to assess the benefits and damages, and to have general supervision of the proposed work of *opening* and *widening* said *Third* street from *Los Angeles* street to *San Pedro* street, as finally confirmed and adopted by said city council, and certified by the city clerk and ex officio clerk of said city council, has been forwarded to, and filed in the office of the undersigned, the superintendent of streets of said city.

All sums levied and assessed in and by said assessment roll are due and payable immediately. The payment of said sums is to be made to me within thirty days from the date of the first publication of this notice. All assessments not paid before the expiration of said thirty days will be declared to be delinquent, and thereafter the sum of five per cent. upon the amount of each delinquent assessment, together with the cost of advertizing each delinquent assessment, will be added thereto.

Office of street superintendent, }
this *28th* day of *October,* 1892. }   *E. H. HUTCHINSON,*
Superintendent of streets of the city of *Los Angeles.*

No. 9. CERTIFICATE OF SUPERINTENDENT OF STREETS AT FOOT OF ASSESSMENT ROLL.

I hereby certify that all the assessments not marked "paid" in the foregoing assessment roll, are still unpaid, and have become and are now delinquent, and five per cent. is hereby added to the amount of each assessment so delinquent.
E. H. HUTCHINSON,
Superintendent of streets of the city of *Los Angeles.*

INDEX.

INTRODUCTION.

Vrooman Act of March 18, 1885.

INDEX TO BOND ACT.

INDEX TO SHADE TREE ACT.

INDEX TO STREET OPENING ACT OF 1889.

104*a*   STREET WORK LAW—INDEX

106a STREET WORK LAW—INDEX

Section twenty-one.. 270 43a
twenty-two... 270 43a
twenty-three.. 270 44a
twenty-four... 271 44a
twenty-five... 271 45a
Streets, including more than one in one proceeding, sec. 1..... 252
Street opening act of 1889, constitutionality of, sec. 1........... 246
Street opening act of 1889, outline of provisions of, sec. 1....... 241
Street opening acts do not provide for "improvements" upon
   existing streets, sec. 1................................ 244
Superintendent of streets must publish notice of receipt of assess-
   ment roll, sec. 16.................................... 260 40a
   who is, sec. 23....................................... 270 44a
Supplementary assessment, sec. 18......................... 262 42a
   when and how made, sec. 20....................... 269 43a
Surplus, how divided, sec. 20.............................. 269 43a
Title, commissioners to assess damages have no jurisdiction to
   determine, sec. 1.................................... 251
Treasurer, who is, sec. 23.................................. 271 44a
Value of land taken, evidence of, sec. 18.................... 266
Warrant drawn for payments for land or improvements taken
   or damaged, sec. 17.................................. 262 42a
Warrants for payments, contents of, sec. 8.................. 256 39a
               sec. 16.................. 261 41a
   order of payment of, sec. 19......................... 269 43a
   out of what fund payable, sec. 19.................... 269 43a
"Work," meaning of, sec. 23................................ 270 44a

INDEX TO STREET OPENING ACT OF 1893.

Act of March 6, 1889, limited to cities of less than forty thousand
   inhabitants, sec. 23.................................. 293
Act to be liberally construed, sec. 24...................... 294
Assessment for grading and filling lots, sec. 9.............. 289
   how collected, sec. 16............................... 291
   how made, sec. 9.................................... 289
   lien, when attaches, sec. 15.......................... 290
   supplementary, when authorized, sec. 20............. 292
   when new assessment ordered, sec. 14............... 290
Assessments, when delinquent, sec. 16...................... 290
Assessment, roll notice of receipt of by superintendent of streets
   to be published, sec. 16.............................. 290
   what is, sec. 15...................................... 290
Bar to proceedings, if objections sustained, sec. 5.......... 287
Board of audit, report of, final and conclusive as to amounts
   allowed, sec. 22..................................... 293
   who constitute and duties of, sec. 22................. 293
Board of public works, shall constitute the board of commissioners, sec. 6... 288
Boundaries of assessment district, sec. 2................... 287
Certificate of delinquency, sec. 16......................... 291
Certified copy of report, etc., forwarded to street superintendent,
   sec. 15.. 290
Cities of forty thousand inhabitants or over, subject to provisions
   of this act, sec. 1.................................... 272
               sec. 23.................................. 293
City, what is, sec. 21...................................... 293

INDEX TO SANITARY DISTRICT ACT.

INDEX TO MUNICIPAL INDEBTEDNESS ACT.

INDEX TO FORMS USED UNDER THE STREET OPENING
ACT OF 1889.

ERRATA.

(*1.*) Through an oversight, thirteen words were omitted from the first sentence of the notes to section 7 of the Vrooman act of March 18, 1885, page 67, thus changing the meaning completely. It should have read as follows:

Subdivision 1. Subdivision 1 of section 7 provides: (1) That the expense incurred for any work authorized by this act, *and which is to be paid for by the front-foot plan of assessment,* shall not include the cost of any work done in such portion of any street as is required by law to be kept in order or repair by any person or company having railroad tracks thereon, etc.

The words thus inadvertently omitted are in italics.

(*2.*) In the form of an assessment given on page 56a, certain words are abbreviated. In the manuscript these words were all written out in full, but the printer, for his own convenience in setting it up, not knowing how particular the courts have been where abbreviations have been used in assessments, used abbreviations in some places. Superintendents of streets who do not wish to encourage litigation will not follow the printer's example, or, if abbreviations are used, he will see that they are accompanied by an explanatory note.

www.ingramcontent.com/pod-product-compliance
Lightning Source LLC
Chambersburg PA
CBHW031813270326
41932CB00008B/402